COLLECTED REPORTS ON THE

Rheumatic Diseases

Published by
the Arthritis and Rheumatism Council for Research

Editors:
Dr Robin C Butler MD FRCP
Professor Malcolm I V Jayson MD FRCP

ARC Production Editor: Keir Windsor BA(Hons)

These reports are produced under the direction of the
Education Sub-Committee of the Council.
They were first published individually between 1985 and 1995

THE ARTHRITIS AND RHEUMATISM COUNCIL FOR RESEARCH
CHESTERFIELD, DERBYSHIRE

The Arthritis and Rheumatism Council for Research
Copeman House
St Mary's Court
St Mary's Gate
Chesterfield
Derbyshire
S41 7TD

A Registered Charity
No. 207711

This collection first published 1995

ISBN 0 950 1954 5 6

Original and additional typesetting by Greenleaf Communications Limited, Tunbridge Wells
Printed and bound by KSC Printers, High Brooms, Tunbridge Wells

TABLE OF CONTENTS

REGIONAL RHEUMATIC DISORDERS

INTRODUCTION

This volume consists of a series of articles which were published between 1985 and 1995 by the Arthritis and Rheumatism Council in its Reports on Rheumatic Diseases series. Subjects are chosen for review on the basis of advances in diagnostic criteria, investigation, management, or understanding of the causes of individual disorders. The volume should not therefore be regarded as a comprehensive textbook, although several articles have been written especially for this volume to rectify notable omissions.

Within the general series above, individual articles were published under the titles 'Practical Problems' or 'Topical Reviews' which were - and still are - produced three times each year. The former are intended as brief practical guides to common clinical problems whereas the latter are more comprehensive scientific reviews of a topic. This explains the difference in style between some of the reports. The articles have been reproduced as they appeared originally - with the exception of the headings which have been enlarged and the original series titles removed for the sake of consistency. Naturally, there are some variations in appearance between the reports produced over the 10-year period.

We are grateful to all the contributors, and also to Rachel Inglis and Keir Windsor at ARC for their editorial assistance.

Further copies of this volume can be obtained from the Arthritis and Rheumatism Council. We are always glad to receive comments on this volume, or suggestions of topics for future articles.

Robin Butler
Consultant Rheumatologist
Robert Jones and Agnes Hunt
Orthopaedic Hospital
Oswestry
Shropshire
SY10 7AG

Malcolm I V Jayson
Professor of Rheumatology
Rheumatic Diseases Centre
University of Manchester
Hope Hospital
Salford
M6 8HD

EDITORS

HISTORY & EXAMINATION TECHNIQUES

P T Dawes
Consultant Rheumatologist/Clinical Senior Lecturer
Staffordshire Rheumatology Centre/
University of Keele
The Haywood, High Lane, Burslem
Stoke on Trent
Staffordshire ST6 7AG

INTRODUCTION

Clinical medicine demands a knowledge and understanding of the link between the musculoskeletal system and all other body systems.

Patients can present with swollen, painful, stiff joints or in more subtle ways with non-specific pains, arthralgias or myalgias. Occasionally the diagnosis is made when an associated organ becomes involved, eg undiagnosed ankylosing spondylitis (AS) in a patient presenting with acute uveitis. All patients should have a standard musculoskeletal screen at initial presentation, akin to having their blood pressure checked. In patients with rheumatic disease the clinical history and examination should guide the clinician to a working differential diagnosis and allow him or her to assess disability, and plan investigations and therapy.

TAKING A HISTORY

Presenting complaint

Patients present with a combination of joint swelling, pain, loss of function, deformity and stiffness. There may be systemic involvement with fever, sweating, malaise, fatigue, weight loss and anorexia. Ask all patients with an acute rheumatic disease of any prodromal event such as an upper respiratory tract infection, diarrhoeal illness, genito-urinary infection, insect bite, or recent vaccination. Direct the patient to describe how their problems cause physical and functional disability.

Past medical history

Many diseases can present with or have early, late or coincidental musculoskeletal manifestations (Table 1). It is also recognised that an acute illness can precipitate an unassociated rheumatic disease like pseudogout.

Drug history

A detailed drug history both past and present is important eg diuretics/aspirin and gout, hydralazine/procainamide-induced systemic lupus erythematosis (SLE), steroids and avascular necrosis, betablockers and arthralgia.

Family history and ethnic origin

Polyarticular osteoarthritis (OA) and nodal generalised OA often have a familial predisposition. There is a genetic influence in rheumatoid arthritis (RA) and SLE. A history of neonatal heart block, rashes or thrombocytopenia in offspring should arouse suspicion of SLE in the mother. A family history of psoriasis, uveitis, or inflammatory bowel disease may point to a diagnosis of spondyloarthropathy. A familial metabolic arthropathy like primary gout (30% have a family history), pseudogout (rarely), ochronosis (autosomal recessive), haemochromatosis (autosomal recessive) and Wilson's disease (autosomal recessive) should be sought. Familial haemoglobinopathies and bleeding disorders present as joint disease. Ethnic origin should be considered, eg sickle cell disease and susceptibility to SLE in North American Negroids; osteomalacia or a tuberculous arthritis in patients from the Indian subcontinent; gout in Polynesians and Maoris; Behcet's disease and familial Mediterranean fever in Eastern Mediterranean races.

Social history

Lung cancer caused by smoking may present with hypertrophic pulmonary osteoarthropathy. A patient should know that smoking aggravates vasculitis in RA, impairs pulmonary function in the spondyloarthropathies and is detrimental in Raynaud's disease and osteoporosis. Excessive alcohol intake will influence the management of gout, may cause avascular necrosis, and is a contributory factor to osteoporosis and traumatic events like fractured ribs. A sexual history should be sought when appropriate particularly in patients with a reactive arthritis when a urethritis/cervicitis needs to be excluded. Be aware that HIV infection has numerous rheumatological manifestations. An early menopause raises the possibility of osteoporosis in the female patient with back pain. Osteomalacia and scurvy cause musculoskeletal symptoms. A careful nutritional assessment of chronically disabled patients may reveal a treatable cause of co-morbidity.

Occupational history

Chemical toxins such as vinyl chloride can induce a scleroderma syndrome and chronic lead exposure secondary gout. In addition there are numerous hobbies and work-related soft tissue syndromes resulting in specific pathological conditions such as carpal tunnel syndrome, tenosynovitis, bursitis, epicondylitis (golfer's and tennis elbow) and less well defined conditions often referred to under the term 'repetitive strain injuries'.

A history of previous trauma may be important in the pathogenesis of certain conditions like OA and neuroalgodystrophy, (reflex dystrophy syndrome), and is crucial when assessing those patients by whom financial compensation is being sought.

Travel history

Has the patient been abroad, even in the distant past? Brucellosis, leprosy, parasitic infections and other exotic tropical diseases may manifest themselves as joint disease. Recent travel to areas with deer may point to a possible diagnosis of Lyme disease.

Functional history

Any patient with rheumatic disease should be asked how their illness affects daily activities:- can the patient climb stairs, get outside their home, go shopping? Have they become socially isolated? How many different people have they seen in the last week? Have they a telephone? Can they independently transfer from bed, chairs, toilet and cope with self hygiene. Are they able to cook independently, feed and dress themselves. Who is at home and what support do they provide? If working, is their job at risk and do they have financial problems? Essentially, enquiry should be made on what prevents the patient from having a totally independent life.

Referral to the occupational therapist, medical social worker and disablement resettlement officer may be needed.

Psychological assessment

Patients with chronic disease often have their symptoms and disability compounded by underlying anxiety or depression. An assessment of the mental attitude and motivation in some patients, particularly those with chronic pain, is important. There may be problems with sexual activity due to their disease or secondary to the patient's perception of body image. Rectifying contributory emotional and social problems can be just as important as drug therapy in the patient with complex chronic disabling disease.

KEY ARTICULAR SYMPTOMS

Three specific screening questions should be asked of all patients. Establish how a symptom started, whether the onset was sudden or gradual and if it is episodic, self-limiting or persistent and progressive. Precipitating or relieving factors such as over-use and exercise, rest, emotional stress, temperature, sunlight, and treatment should be identified as well as the pattern and extent of the musculoskeletal involvement. What was the first joint to be affected, do the symptoms migrate, how many joints are now affected? Is the joint involvement symmetrical or asymmetrical. What does the patient feel their major disability is due to: is it pain, weakness or stiffness?

Pain

In osteoarthritis the pain is often worse at the end of the day, and after activity, and is relieved by rest. In active inflammatory diseases it tends to be worse after rest, particularly in the morning, and improves with exercise. Arthritic joints often cause referred pain, ie cervical spine disease presenting with shoulder pain, shoulder disease with upper arm pain, lumbar spine disease with hip or thigh pain, hip disease with knee pain. Referred pain from internal organs is usually unrelated to activity, is usually diffuse and may, for example, be altered by coughing, eating, defecating, urinating or menstruating. Psychogenic pain is often diffuse, varies little in intensity with rest or activity, is unresponsive to analgesics and is often associated with other non-specific symptoms.

Stiffness

A stiff joint is either the result of mechanical deformity or its involvement by an active inflammatory process. In chronic arthritis, stiffness is often due to a combination of both factors. Early morning stiffness is a feature of all inflammatory synovial diseases and its duration is often recorded as a measurement of disease activity. Acute or subacute onset of severe bilateral shoulder and pelvic girdle early morning stiffness in an elderly patient should arouse suspicion of polymyalgia rheumatica. Transient joint stiffness after rest occurs in osteoarthritis. With increasing age patients complain of their joints becoming stiffer and do not forget Parkinson's disease as a treatable cause of joint stiffness.

Swelling

Swelling of joints may be due to bony hypertrophy, synovitis, intra-articular fluid or a swollen periarticular structure. Unlike tenderness, objective evidence of swelling indicates organic disease. Occasionally patients complain of swelling which is not confirmed by examination and the clinician must then question the patient closely to establish its presence. Subjective swelling of joints can be a feature of psychosomatic conditions. In general, synovial swelling is most pronounced on the extensor surface of joints where the capsule is more distensible.

Loss of function

Impaired function is often due to a combination of pain, stiffness, tendon and joint damage, neurological impairment and muscle weakness. Patients with chronic rheumatic disease often under-report their problems so recent loss of function should be taken seriously, eg ruptured wrist extensor tendons or cervical myelopathy in RA. Loss of function from a joint does not always relate to deformity. Joint locking from damaged cartilage or intra-articular loose bodies is associated with acute episodes of pain. Some patients complain of their joint 'giving way'. This occurs commonly with the knee and may indicate intra-articular pathology or muscle weakness. If a patient complains primarily of weakness, observe the patient's gait and ask the patient to sit up from a supine position with their arms folded across their chest to exclude a primary muscle disease. Suspect patients who describe a loss of function out of proportion to the physical findings as having compounding psychological factors.

KEY EXTRA-ARTICULAR SYMPTOMS

There are many extra-articular associations with rheumatic disease (Table 1); some deserve specific consideration.

TABLE I
Systemic conditions and abnormalities with musculoskeletal relevance.

a) General	PUO, weight loss, lymphadenopathy.
b) Cutaneous	Psoriasis, onycholysis and nail pitting, vasculitis, erythema nodosum, erythema marginatum, photosensitivity, Raynaud's, butterfly rash, acne, purpura, alopecia, cutaneous calcinosis, livedo reticularis, sclerodactyly, heliotrope discoloration, collodion patches, pigmentation, keratoderma blenorrhagica, telangiectasia, periungal erythema, xanthoma, extensible skin, leg ulcers, palmar erythema, subcutaneous nodules.
c) Endocrine	Parathyroid and thyroid disease, diabetes, acromegaly.
d) Gastrointestinal	Oral ulcers, xerostomia, inflammatory bowel disease, malabsorption, blind loops, irritable bowel syndrome, hepato-splenomegaly.
e) Respiratory	Nasal ulceration, sinusitis, pleurisy, pleural effusion, asthma, pulmonary fibrosis, pulmonary TB, atypical pneumonia, pneumonitis, atelectasis, limited chest expansion.
f) Renal	Glomerulonephritis, renal tubular acidosis, renal stones, dialysis.
g) Metabolic	Haemochromatosis, amyloid, Paget's.
h) Neurological	Monoeuritis multiplex, sensory neuropathy, entrapment neuropathies, depression, psychosis, cerebrovascular accidents.
i) Cardiovascular	Pericarditis, valvular disease, myocarditis, conduction defects, absent or tender pulses.
j) Eye	Conjunctivitis, uveitis, scleritis, episcleritis, scleromalacia, keratoconjuctivitis sicca, optic atrophy.
k) Haematological	Anaemia, haemolysis, neutropenia, lymphopenia, eosinophilia, idiopathic thrombocytopenia, thrombocytosis, thrombotic episodes, coagulopathies.
l) Malignancy	Leukaemia, myeloma, secondary deposits, non-metastatic manifestations eg HPOA.
m) Genito-urinary	Ulceration, urethral syndromes, mid-trimester abortions, cervicitis.

Raynaud's phenomenon
Symptoms are usually bilateral and affect fingers more than toes. There is cold sensitivity. Symptoms are of numbness, tingling and burning with three sequential colour phases of pallor, cyanosis and finally erythema on recovery. Raynaud's is often idiopathic in young women but is associated with many of the connective tissue (CT) diseases, particularly progressive systemic sclerosis in which it is the initial complaint in over 70% of patients.

Skin and mucous membranes
Rashes that fluctuate with symptoms occur with rheumatic fever, erythema nodosum, adult and juvenile Still's disease and connective tissue diseases, particularly SLE when the rash may be photosensitive. Enquire about psoriasis which may be quiescent or hidden, eg natal cleft and scalp. Circinate balanitis in Reiter's disease may be asymptomatic and specific examination should be made when appropriate. Oral ulceration may be a feature of Reiter's, Behcet's and connective tissue diseases. Sjögren's syndrome causes a dry mouth (xerostomia) and results in poor oral hygiene and dental caries.

Eyes
Ask patients whether they have had red, gritty or painful eyes. Conjunctivitis occurs in Reiter's disease, uveitis in other spondyloarthropathies, episcleritis (painless), scleritis (painful) and keratoconjunctivitis sicca in RA and related diseases. Disturbance of vision and blindness occur in giant cell arteritis (GCA). Rarely, tenosynovitis affecting the ocular muscles can cause diplopia in RA.

Gastrointestinal
Transient diarrhoea precipitating a reactive arthritis may have been relatively mild. Chronic bowel symptoms including diarrhoea, blood loss and malabsorption should arouse suspicion of an enteropathic arthritis secondary to ulcerative colitis, Crohn's, Whipple's or coeliac disease. Oesophageal reflux and dysphagia is a common symptom of systemic sclerosis, dysphagia may also be prominent in polymyositis and can rarely occur in Sjögren's syndrome secondary to a dry mouth or even an oesophageal web. Acute abdominal pain from mesenteric ischaemia or even cholecystitis occur in the vasculitic syndromes particularly polyarteritis nodosa (PAN).

Cardiorespiratory
Episodes of pericardial and/or pleuritic chest pain may indicate the presence of a connective tissue disease. Record absent peripheral pulses which may occur in vasculitis. Asthma occurs in PAN and Churg-Strauss syndrome. Musculoskeletal chest pain is a common feature of the spondyloarthropathies. Breathlessness may indicate an associated pulmonary fibrosis or cardiac defect such as aortic regugitation in the spondyloarthropathies. Chronic nasal, sinus or middle ear disease occur in Wegener's granulomatosis and may complicate relapsing polychondritis.

Genito-urinary
Symptomatic urethritis or asymptomatic urethral discharge may point to a diagnosis of Reiter's disease. Testicular pain is a feature of PAN.

Dyspareunia occurs in Sjögren's syndrome. Miscarriages, particularly in the second trimester, occur in patients with the anti-phospholipid antibody syndrome.

Neurological
Peripheral neuropathies, particularly entrapment neuropathy (eg carpal tunnel syndrome), may be an early feature of inflammatory synovitis. A history of migraine, depression, psychosis, dementia or cerebro-vascular accident may point to a diagnosis of SLE, vasculitis or the anti-phospholipid syndrome. Headaches, scalp tenderness and jaw claudication are recognised features of giant cell arteritis.

EXAMINATION
All patients with rheumatic disease should routinely have their urine checked for protein, blood and sugar, be weighed and have their height recorded. A full and effective examination requires the patient to be in their underclothes in a warm environment with access to an examination couch. The muscu-

TABLE 2
Key screen questions to detect rheumatological disease.

(1) 'Have you any pain or stiffness in your muscles, joints or back?'

(2) 'Can you dress yourself completely without any difficulty?'

(3) 'Can you walk up and down stairs without any difficulty?'

loskeletal examination has the advantage of comparison between both sides of the body to assess for asymmetry in colour, deformity, swelling, function and muscle wasting. The following musculoskeletal screen of Gait, Arms, Legs, Spine (GALS) is a useful routine to be used and taught. It is aided by the examiner undertaking the movements and asking the patient to copy. This regional assessment will identify the site of the problem and enables a fuller more detailed examination. The following examination may be summarised in notes with a simple template (Table 3).

(1) GAIT. Observe the patient walking, turning and walking back, looking for smoothness and symmetry of leg, pelvis and arm movements, normal stride length and the ability to turn quickly.

(2) ARMS. Inspection from the front allows assessment of normal girdle muscle bulk and symmetry. After placing both hands down by the side with elbows straight in full extension (Figure 1), the patient should attempt to place both hands behind their head and then push the elbows back, which tests

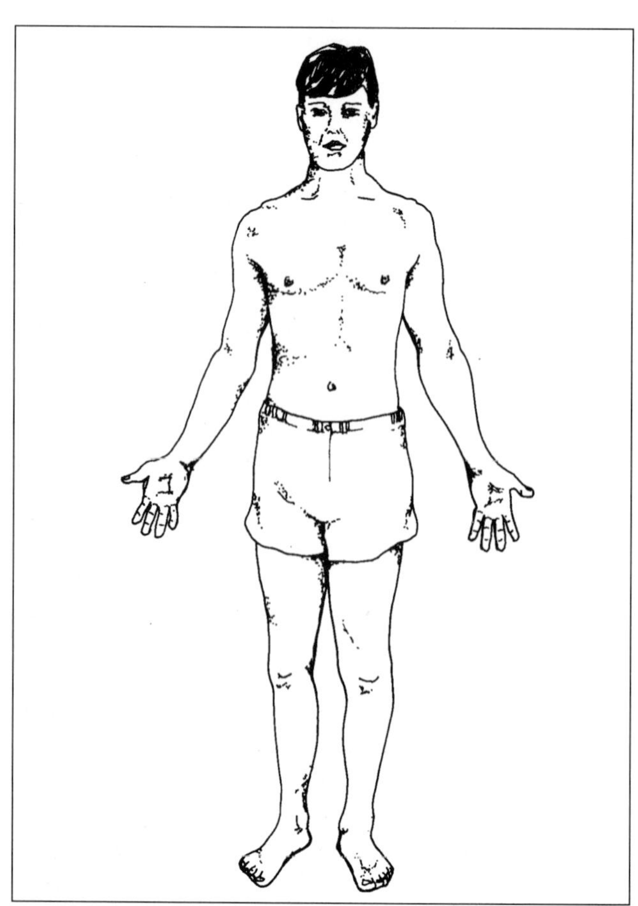

Figure 1.

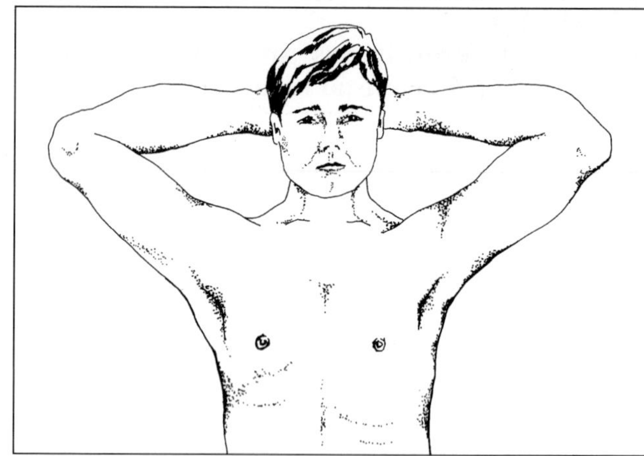

Figure 2.

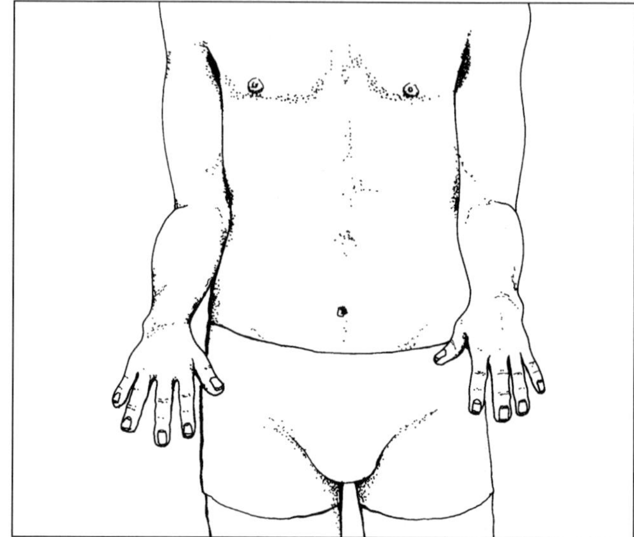

Figure 3.

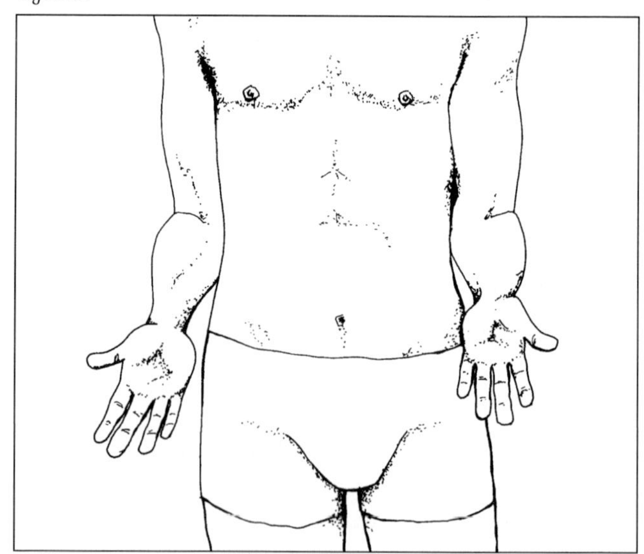

Figure 4.

glenohumeral, acromioclavicular, and sternoclavicular joints (Figure 2). Hands should be examined palms down with fingers straight to detect any swelling or deformity. It is important to observe normal supination/pronation (Figures 3 & 4) and grip (Figure 5). Place the tip of each finger onto the tip of the thumb in turn to assess normal dexterity and fine precision pinch (Figure 6). Discomfort in response to squeezing across the 2nd to the 5th metacarpals suggests synovitis (Figure 7).

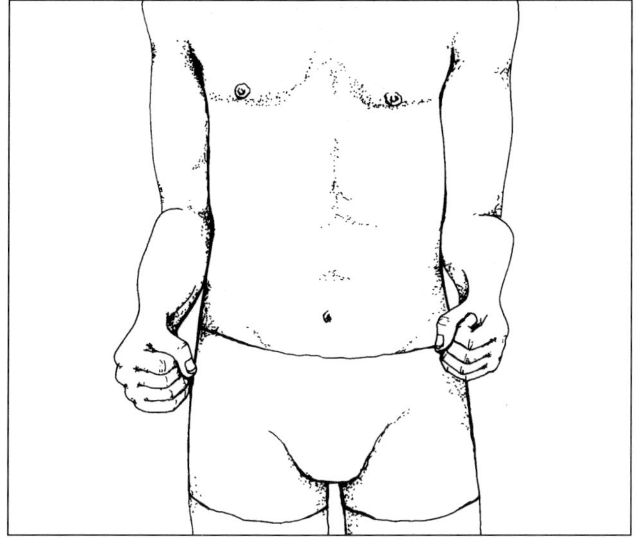

Figure 5.

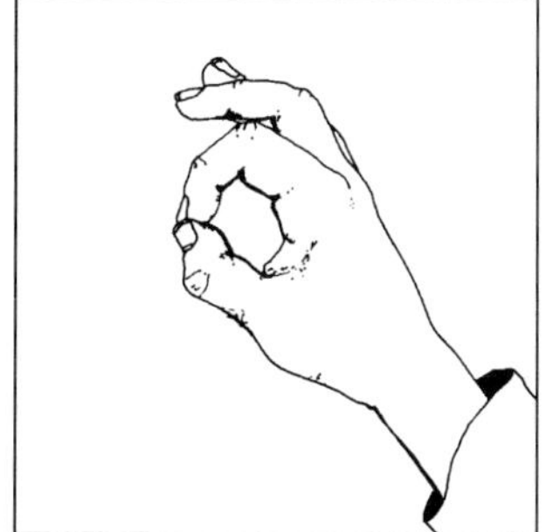

Figure 6.

Figure 7.

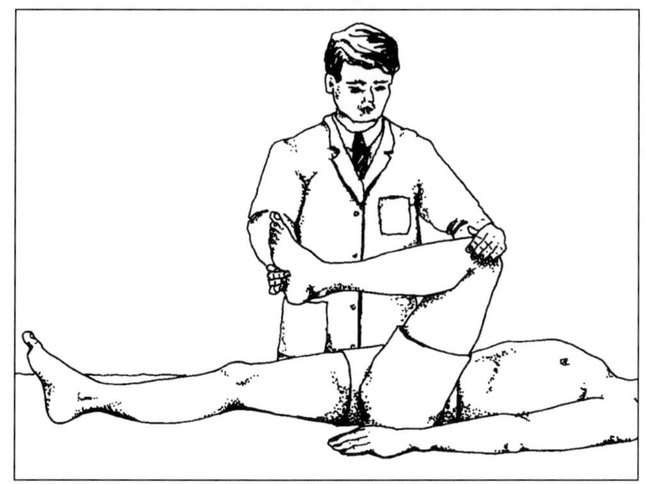

Figure 8.

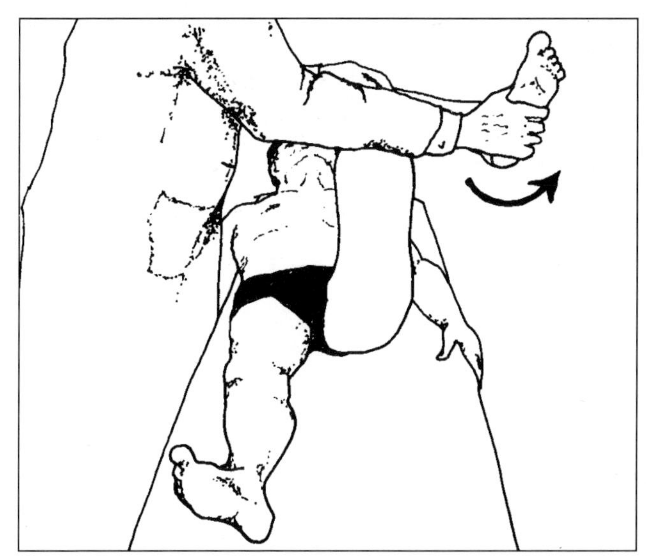

Figure 9.

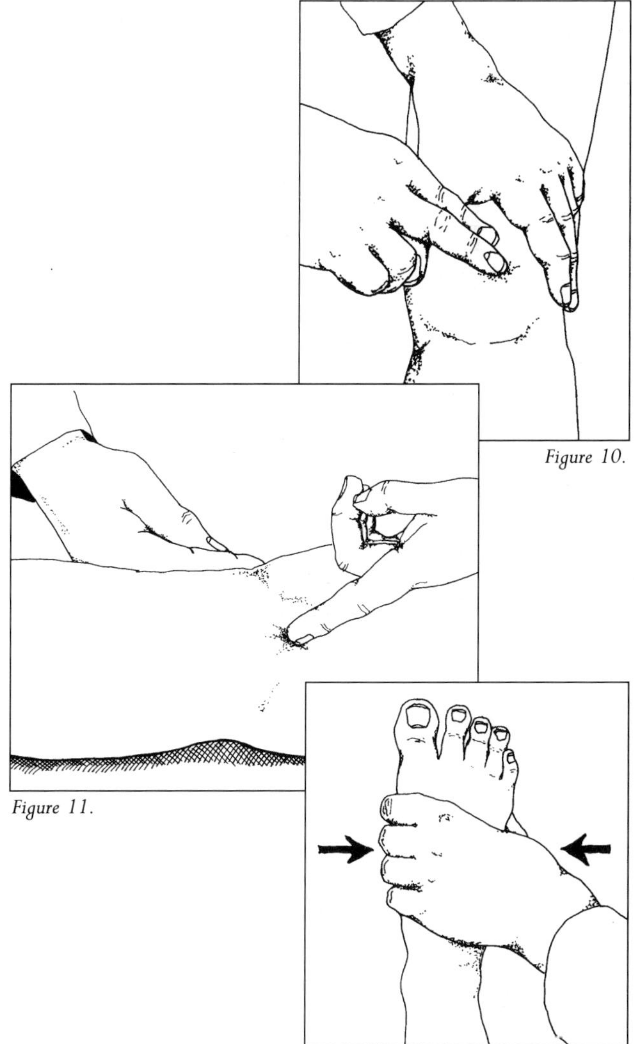

Figure 10.

Figure 11.

Figure 12.

(3) LEGS. Inspect the patient standing and observe any knee, hindfoot, midfoot or forefoot deformity. Later examination on the couch should include flexion of each hip and knee while supporting the knee to test normal hip and knee flexion and help detect crepitus (Figure 8).

Each hip should be passively internally rotated in flexion (Figure 9) and the knee carefully examined for the presence of fluid by pressing on each patella and palpated for the balloon sign and bulge sign (Figures 10 & 11). Squeeze across the metatarsals to detect synovitis (Figure 12). Inspect the soles of the feet for callosities or rashes such as keratoderma blenorrhagica in Reiter's syndrome (Figure 12b).

(4) SPINE. This is best inspected by the patient standing.

(a) From behind (Figure 13); Is the spine straight, are there level iliac crests, normal paraspinal and girdle muscle bulk symmetry? 'Try to place you ear on your shoulder each side' - this tests lateral cervical flexion (Figure 14). Press over the mid point of each supraspinatus - tenderness suggests fibromyalgia (Figure 15).

(b) From the side, note spinal curvatures (Figure 16). Ask the patient to bend forward and touch their toes with their knees straight which will give an impression of lumbar spine and hip flexion (Figure 17).

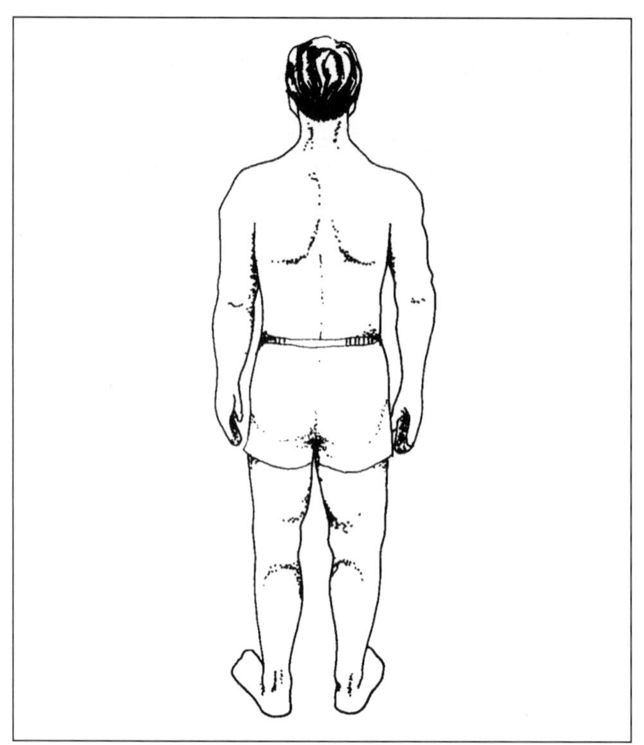

Figure 13.

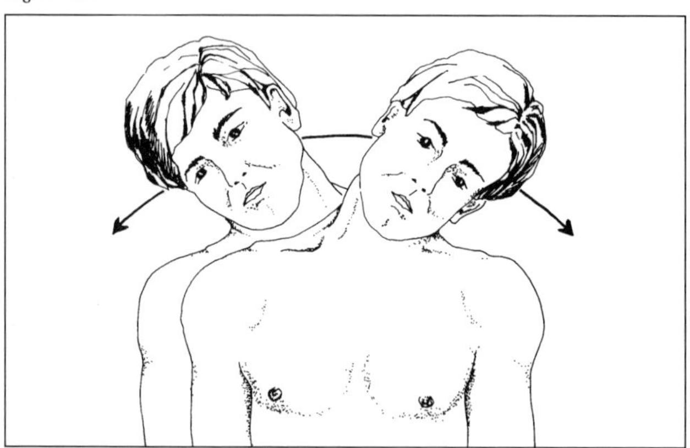

Figure 14.

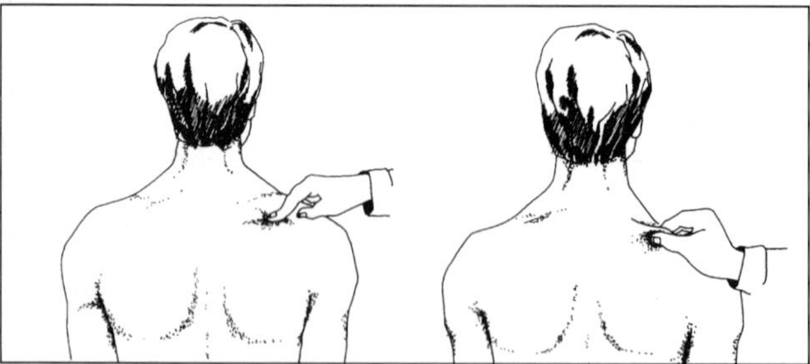

Figure 15.

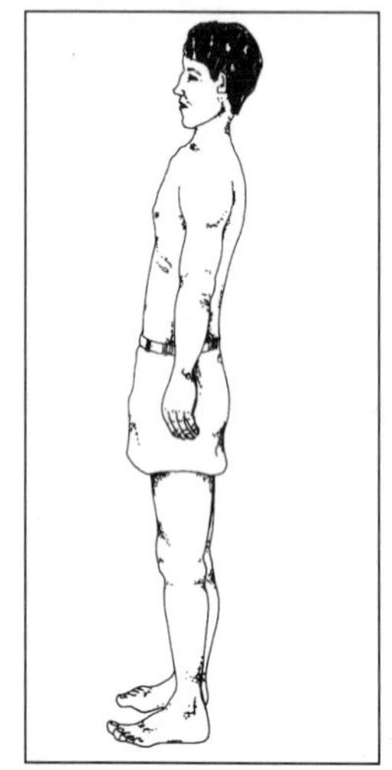

Figure 16.

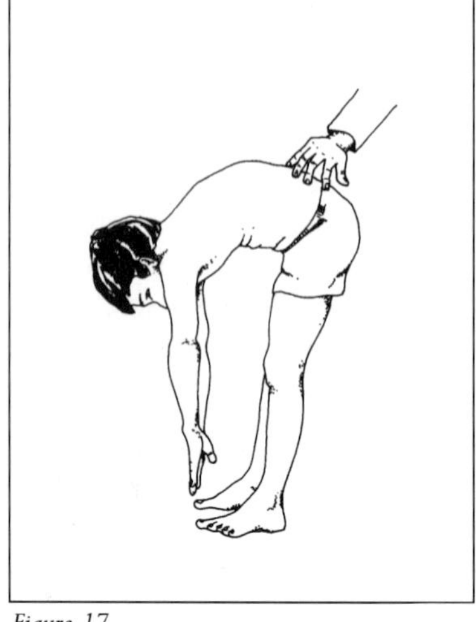

Figure 17.

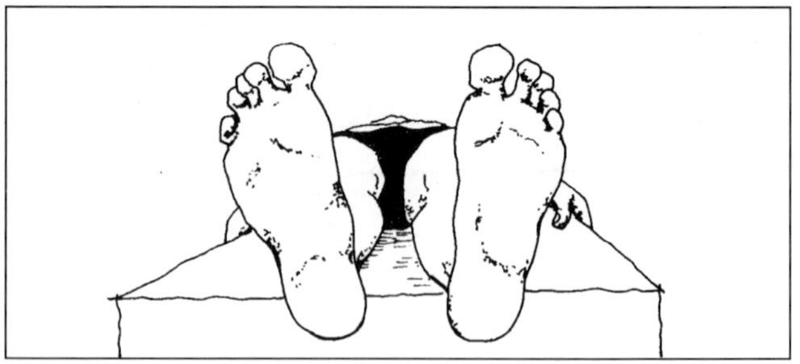

Figure 12b.

Peripheral joints

Peripheral arthritis may present as a monoarthritis or polyarthritis which may either be acute (Table 5) or chronic. Often there is overlap. Monoarthritis may have an acute exacerbation and may, with time, become polyarticular. Many types of chronic polyarthritis often start with an acute onset.

Monoarthritis

Certain causes of acute monoarthritis (Table 4) show a preference for particular joints:- for instance gout in the 1st MTP joint; pseudogout in the knee; calcific periarthritis in the shoulder; haemarthroses in the knees; foreign body synovitis in the feet (plant thorn synovitis). Distribution is often lower limb in Reiter's disease and the spondyloarthropathies and upper limb in gonococcal arthritis. Palindromic rheumatism (self-limiting attacks lasting 1-2 days) often starts in the knees, shoulders or small joints of the hand. It is important that synovial fluid is examined appropriately for infectious agents and crystals in all cases of acute monoarthritis. Septic arthritis should be excluded as a cause of monoarticular flare in a patient with established joint damage, particularly in those who are immunosuppressed, although avascular necrosis, stress fractures, cartilage tears and haemarthrosis should all be considered along with an exacerbation of the underlying disease. A less acute, evolving monoarthritis may be due to any of the above, OA or rarities such as pigmented villo-nodular synovitis.

Polyarthritis

Detection of early synovitis (Table 5) is paramount in the management of certain diseases, such as early RA, where there is mounting evidence that treatment is most efficacious if instituted early.

Spine

Clinically, spinal disease can be broadly categorised into inflammatory and non-inflammatory problems, although the differentiation is not always clear-cut.

Inflammatory spinal pain

Sleep disturbance due to back pain should arouse suspicion of ankylosing spondylitis, infection, Paget's disease or malignancy. Consider vertebral collapse in the patient with acute unremitting, progressive severe pain associated with localised tenderness. Spinal stiffness worse in the morning and relieved by exercise suggests ankylosing spondylitis; test for tender sacroiliac joints with the patient lying on the couch and applying pressure down and outwards onto the iliac crests or by placing the flexed knee onto the opposite shoulder. A reduced modified Schober's test is measured by the patient standing erect; a mark is made on the middle of the back at the level of the posterior iliac crest (approximately L5) and a point 10cm above. If the increase in the distance between these two points on maximum forward flexion is less than 3cm, spondyloarthritis is the likely cause of symptoms.

Non-inflammatory spinal pain

Pain due to degenerative spinal disease is worse with over-use and weight-bearing and improved by rest. The symptoms are often episodic with periods of acute exacerbations followed by improvement. Spinal movements are impaired and during the acute episodes there may be an acute scoliosis and associated paraspinal muscle spasm. Degenerative spinal disease is often associated with neurogenic symptoms. The pain, weakness, paraesthesia or numbness radiating into the arm or leg are caused by nerve compression and have a dermatome distribution often aggravated by movements which irritate the nerve root such as straight leg raising, sciatic and femoral stretch test. Wasting of muscles, loss of power, impaired reflexes and sensation may be present. Spinal cord claudication from a localised or diffuse spinal stenosis classically presents with weakness in the legs on walking with the patient having to sit down for relief of symptoms. This contrasts with the patient with peripheral vascular claudication who gets relief at rest by standing. Patients with spinal claudication often walk with a flexed spine and adopt a 'Simian' posture as this increases the spinal canal diameter.

Soft tissue

Soft tissue symptoms may be due to a localised anatomical problem associated with systemic disease or be a specific soft tissue syndrome like fibrositis. Localised peri-articular tenderness from epicondylitis such as tennis elbow (lateral epicondyle) or golfer's elbow (medial epicondyle) can be confirmed by an appropriate stress test such as forced extension of the wrist which exacerbates tennis elbow pain. Enthesitis is an area of pain arising from inflammation at a bony interface with a joint capsule, ligament or tendon and can be a feature of the spondyloarthropathies, eg plantar fasciitis. Localised ligamentous problems around a joint can be aggravated by an appropriate stress test, for example tenderness around the medial aspect of the knee due to ligamentous strain will be aggravated by stressing the joint into valgus. Diffuse tenderness around a joint line is more likely to occur with intra-articular disease. Tendons may become diffusely painful and swollen from repetitive trauma, infection, or as a result of synovial diseases such as RA and pigmented villondoular synovitis. Pain from inflamed tendons may be elicited by specific stress tests such as Finkelstein's test for deQuervain's tenosynovitis (extensor tendon of the thumb). Tendons should be palpated during movement to detect crepitus, nodules and triggering. Tenderness around joints may be due to a superficial bursitis with obvious swelling, eg pre-patellar bursitis,

TABLE 3
GALS template

If the patient's gait (G) is normal and there is no abnormal appearance (A) or movement (M) of their arms (A), legs (L), or spine (S), the following shorthand template may usefully be used in the notes:

G	√	A	M
A		√	√
L		√	√
S		√	√

If abnormality is detected at one or more of these regions the tick is replaced by an X and a further note of the abnormality is made. For instance a patient with ankylosing spondylitis with a knee synovitis would be recorded by the following:-

G	X	A	M
A		√	√
L		X	X
S		X	X

Kyphosis and loss of lumbar lordosis, with reduced Schober's test and chest expansion. Limps because of a painful, swollen left knee.

TABLE 4
Common causes of acute arthritis

Monoarticular (occasionally polyarticular)

1. Crystal arthritis - gout, pseudogout, calcific periarthritis
2. Septic arthritis
3. Haemarthrosis
4. Traumatic synovitis
5. Foreign body synovitis - plant thorn

Oligo & polyarticular arthritis (occasionally monoarticular)

1. Rheumatoid arthritis
2. Palindromic rheumatism
3. Reactive arthritis - Reiter's disease, rheumatic fever
4. Gonococcal arthritis
5. Post viral arthropathies - Rubella, Parvovirus, Hepatitis B
6. Adult and childhood Still's disease
7. Psoriatic arthritis and associated spondyloarthropathies
8. Systemic lupus erythematosis
9. Paraneoplastic syndromes
10. Polymyalgia rheumatica

TABLE 5
Detection of early synovitis in the absence of major joint deformity

(1) Evidence of vasospasm in the fingers which can be detected by stroking the dorsum of the examiner's hand across the patient's palm and fingers to detect sweating and a distal temperature drop.

(2) Observe each PIP joint for skin discolouration and firmly palpate each joint for tenderness.

(3) Ask the patient to clench their fist. The knuckles should be white and stand out clearly with no infilling between them.

(4) MCP squeeze test performed by squeezing across all 4 MCPs together to elicit tenderness.

(5) Inferior radio-ulnar stress test - if pain is elicited by forcibly stressing this joint at the extremes of pronation/supination it often indicates early wrist involvement.

(6) The bulge sign at the elbow - when the elbow is held in full extension a bulge of synovium is detected just above the radial head.

(7) The bulge sign at the knee is to detect small effusions that are too small to be detected by the patellar tap. The examiner applies pressure on the lateral side of the knee and observes the medial side for evidence of movement of fluid producing a bulge.

(8) The MTP squeeze test - by applying pressure across the heads of the metatarsals for evidence of tenderness.

or be in the deeper tissues and be less obvious, eg sub-trochanteric bursitis of the hip. Diffuse swelling around a joint may be due to oedema (hypostatic, fluid retention, lymphatic involvement) or be part of an inflammatory process such as leakage of synovial fluid from a ruptured popliteal cyst causing a pseudo-thrombophlebitis syndrome. Peri-articular soft tissue hypertrophy may be from a lipoma or be a more diffuse fatty swelling as seen in the tender medial fat pad syndrome of obese middle-aged ladies' knees, or the benign fibro-fatty pads seen over the proximal interphalangeal joints of the fingers (Garrod's pads). Peri-articular swellings also occur with arthritis and may be due to gouty tophi, RA and rheumatic fever nodules, xanthoma, calcific deposits associated with connective tissue diseases and rarities such as multi-centric reticulohistiocytosis. If fibromyalgia is suspected then trigger points and specific sites of tenderness should be sought: - lateral neck strap muscles, belly of trapezius, epicondylar area, medial aspect of the knee and over the hip greater trochanter. Hypermobility can cause arthralgia and is detected by passive apposition of thumb to forearm, hyperextension of fingers, elbows, knees, and subluxation of patella; the patient can also place their palms on the floor with their knees fully extended.

March 1995

ACUTE MONARTHRITIS - DIFFERENTIAL DIAGNOSIS & MANAGEMENT

H L F Currey
Emeritus Professor of Rheumatology
The London Hospital Medical College

Acute arthritis appearing in a single joint is a situation which demands prompt and effective action. At worst it may represent a bacterial infection which, if neglected, may destroy the joint and even kill the patient. Less seriously, effective treatment is available to terminate a painful attack of acute gout – if the correct diagnosis is made. Except in the case of a haemophilic bleed (see below) diagnosis comes before treatment, and the first question is often "Is it arthritis?".

IS IT ARTHRITIS?

Before diagnosing acute monarthritis it is necessary to consider whether the inflammation may actually lie outside the joint rather than within it. One trap is acute pre- or infra-patellar bursitis mimicking acute arthritis of the knee. Awareness is the main defence against this mistake, but eliciting conventional physical signs is equally important. First, tenderness is limited to the site of the bursa in question *(Figure 1)* and is not present over other exposed parts of the joint. Second, some pain-free range of movement of the knee should be possible. Extremes of movement (by distorting the inflamed bursa) may be painful, but the middle range is likely to be painless – unlike the situation in acute septic arthritis or crystal synovitis, in which any movement is likely to be painful. In small peripheral joints the important differential diagnosis is usually between acute arthritis (particularly gout) and infections such as cellulitis. Awareness is important but, again, careful physical examination should give the answer. The clue to an infection may be red streaks of lymphangitis (identification requiring a good light), regional lymphadenopathy, or a point of entry of infection such as a crack between the toes due to athletes foot. Rarely systemic disease in childhood, such as leukaemia or sickle cell disease, may mimic acute arthritis, but this is usually polyarticular.

Having decided that one is dealing with acute monarthritis, management strategy is determined by the likely diagnostic possibilities. The following are the more important conditions which have to be considered:

ACUTE SEPTIC (BACTERIAL) ARTHRITIS

Isolated acute monarthritis has always to be regarded as

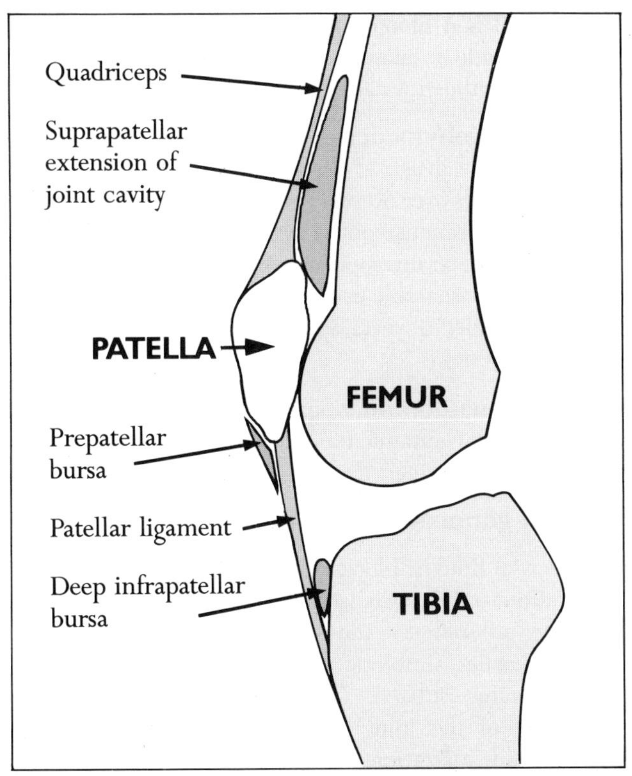

Figure 1. Diagram of the knee joint showing the position of the prepatellar and infrapatellar bursae.

possibly bacterial – and therefore treated as a medical emergency – until proved otherwise. This involves immediate referral to hospital for joint aspiration (using gloves! *[1]*) *(Figure 2)* and blood culture. Antibiotic treatment must be withheld until these specimens have been obtained. Detailed general investigation of the patient is required. A source of pyaemia, such as bacterial endocarditis or intravenous drug abuse, may be identified, while (usually in a young adult female) tell-tale necrotic skin lesions may point to disseminated gonococcal infection *[2]*. Any joint abnormality can predispose to bacterial infection, including prosthetic implants, and rheumatoid arthritis. An isolated flare in a rheumatoid joint is an indication to aspirate synovial fluid to exclude infection. It must be remembered that bacterial joint infections do not always present a very acute picture. In the elderly or debilitated and – above all – in those on corticosteroid treatment, the signs and symptoms may be much less dramatic. It is important also to appreciate the limitations of information which the laboratory can provide. While examination of synovial fluid may give absolutely reliable identification of organisms or crystals, cell counts and biochemical findings are less informative: rheumatoid and gouty joints may occasionally yield fluids which appear frankly "purulent", while in early septic arthritis the effusion may be serous. Nevertheless, high neutrophil counts (> 90%) are always an indication to perform a Gram stain and culture.

The effective management of a bacterial joint infection requires early collaboration with the clinical microbiologist. The laboratory should be warned in advance if there are reasons to suspect that an unusual organism may be involved, for example when the patient is immunosuppressed or is an intravenous drug abuser, or if antibiotics have already been given. The synovial fluid should be examined also by polarised light to exclude the presence of crystals. Treatment cannot await the result of synovial fluid and blood cultures, and a decision about antibiotics should be taken on the result of the initial Gram stain. Typical guidelines are:

Presumed staphylococcal. There is a choice of anti-staphylococcal drugs: flucloxacillin, clindamycin (caution: patients over 60 years of age are at increased risk of pseudomembranous colitis) or fucidin. Avoid fucidin alone as resistant strains soon appear; it is often combined with a ß-lactamase stable penicillin such as flucloxacillin. In children under 3 years add ampicillin in case of H *influenzae* infection.

Presumed Pseudomonas species or other Gram negative rods. Gentamicin combined with azlocillin or ticarcillin.

Presumed gonococcal. Penicillin G.

Once synovial fluid or blood cultures provide more exact identification and drug sensitivity the treatment can be accurately tailored to the organism. Unfortunately, misguided earlier antibiotic treatment may prevent the organism being isolated. Other aspects of treatment include rest of the joint by splinting, analgesics, and synovial fluid aspiration or drainage to prevent re-accumulation.

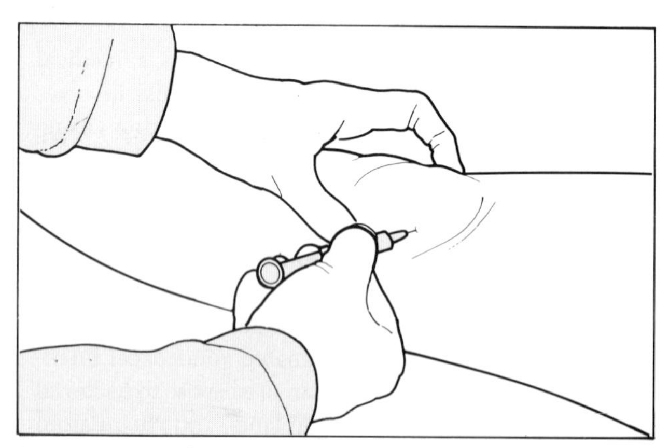

Figure 2. In any undiagnosed case of acute monarthritis the joint must be needled and synovial fluid obtained for examination before treatment is started.

GOUT

Various clues may point to the diagnosis of acute gouty arthritis, including previous similar attacks, involvement of small peripheral joints (particularly the metatarso-phalangeal joint of the great toe – podagra), or a positive family history. A raised level of plasma uric acid (> 430 μmol/1) does not in itself establish the diagnosis (a common error). Unless the clinical features are absolutely characteristic, the diagnosis requires identification of uric acid crystals within synovial fluid by polarised light microscopy. Tophaceous deposits should be sought on the helix of the ear, but seldom occur in the early stages when diagnosis is a problem. The same is true of radiological changes.

The management of gout has been described fully in a recent Report *[3]* and will not be discussed again here, except to reiterate that terminating an individual acute attack and controlling the disease in the longer term require quite different drug tactics, and that urate-lowering drugs are never started during an acute attack.

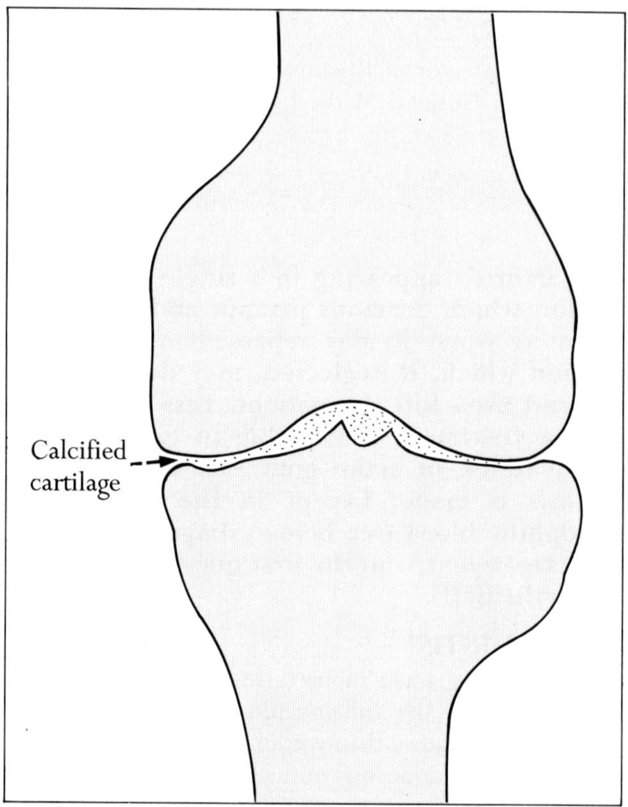

Figure 3. Radiological calcification of joint cartilage (chondrocalcinosis) may be a useful pointer to acute pyrophosphate arthropathy (pseudogout). It is best sought in the knee joint.

PYROPHOSPHATE ARTHROPATHY *[4]*

Acute attacks of crystal synovitis due to pyrophosphate deposition (pseudogout) differ from uric acid gout in that they usually affect larger joints, particularly the knee; the sexes are involved equally, and first attacks are common in the elderly, sometimes apparently triggered by trauma, acute illness or a surgical operation. When the attack is severe there may be mild fever and leucocytosis, misleadingly suggesting septic arthritis. However the answer is clear when the synovial fluid (easily obtained from the knee) is examined for the characteristic crystals by polarised light microscopy. In this condition radiology is useful, for the deposited material (calcium pyrophosphate dihydrate) is radio-opaque and may be visible as chondrocalcinosis, particularly in the cartilage of the knee *(Figure 3)* or wrist. However, such deposits may be asymptomatic and proof of diagnosis is by examination of synovial fluid.

Treatment of acute pseudogout attacks consists of draining the synovial fluid by aspiration (if accessible) and injecting a corticosteroid preparation. In addition a non-steroidal anti-inflammatory drug should be given in initially large, but decreasing, dosage, as for gout *[3]*.

PALINDROMIC RHEUMATISM *[5]*

This condition manifests as episodic attacks of acute arthritis lasting a few hours to a day or two, the joint returning completely to normal after each attack. Affected joints are acutely inflamed, often with erythema of the overlying skin, and very painful. Either large or small joints may be affected, and sometimes the inflammation is beside, rather than in, the joint. The pathogenesis of the condition is not understood. Attacks may occur at intervals of days, weeks or months and may continue for many years. Long-term follow up has shown that about half the cases of apparently typical palindromic rheumatism eventually turn into rheumatoid arthritis. Diagnosis in the early stages can be difficult. The patient is likely to be seen between attacks and will then have to be asked to return for examination during an acute episode. Treatment of an acute attack consists of giving a short course of a non-steroidal anti-inflammatory drug in relatively large doses. Claims have been made that the "second line" drugs used to treat rheumatoid arthritis, such as penicillamine, may reduce the number and severity of acute attacks.

HAEMOPHILIA *[6]*

Haemarthroses due to haemophilia or Christmas disease are usually acutely painful. Almost invariably the diagnosis will be known from previous bleeds and the family history. Effective treatment of a joint bleed requires intravenous replacement of the missing factor – as soon as possible. This is one medical situation in which treatment need not wait on diagnosis. If the patient or the family think that a bleed is starting, then replacement should be given at once. This may abort the bleed. Major bleeds require admission to hospital for aspiration (under full replacement cover), splinting, and subsequently graded mobilisation under further replacement cover. Strong analgesia may be required, but tissue injections must be avoided lest they start local bleeding.

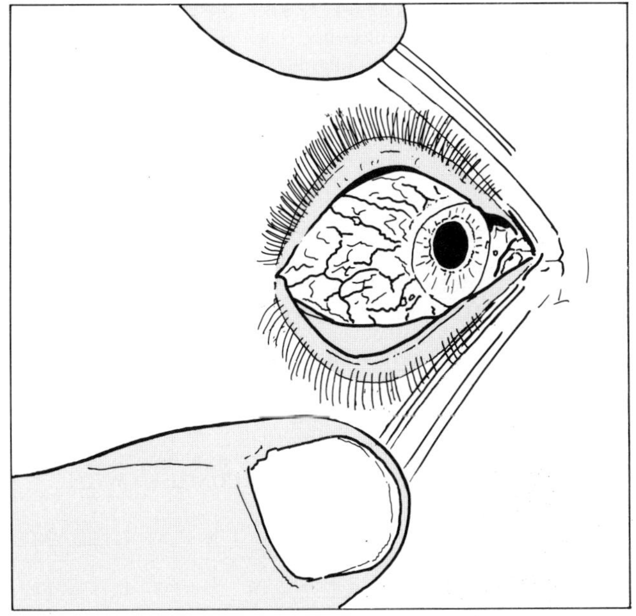

Figure 4. An extra-articular clinical feature may provide the clue to the cause of acute monarthritis. Iritis suggests a seronegative spondarthropathy such as Reiter's syndrome.

THE ACUTELY PAINFUL SHOULDER

In most isolated painful/stiff conditions of the shoulder the pain is referred to the point of insertion of the deltoid muscle and the pathology lies outside the synovial cavity. Usually the physical signs point to the pain arising in one or more of the tendons passing across the joint: pain is provoked by resisted movement in particular directions, but not in others. Occasionally, however, conditions such as acute calcific supraspinatus tendonitis may produce such acute pain that little movement is possible in any direction. In these circumstances it is necessary to consider whether the joint may be infected. Any clinical evidence of an effusion (usually bulging anteriorly) is an indication to aspirate the joint. X-rays may be useful by showing either calcification in the region or the supraspinatus tendon, or chondrocalcinosis (suggesting pseudogout). Systemic features such as fever may point to infection. The safe rule is to aspirate if in doubt.

ASEPTIC NECROSIS *[7]*

A rare cause of the sudden onset of acute pain, usually in one hip joint, is acute aseptic ("avascular") necrosis. Many general causes may predispose to this, including corticosteroid treatment, haemoglobinopathy, and alcoholism. Initial X-rays may be normal, but a radioisotope scan will reveal increased uptake beside the infarcted area.

OTHER CAUSES

Inflammatory joint diseases which are normally polyarticular may occasionally present initially in a single joint, and it may then be necessary to aspirate synovial fluid in order to exclude infection. This is most likely in seronegative arthritis, for example an ankle joint in Reiter's disease *(Figure 4)* or a finger joint in psoriatic arthritis.

AND FINALLY – THE MAIN MESSAGE AGAIN:

IN ANY UNDIAGNOSED CASE OF ACUTE MONARTHRITIS THE JOINT MUST BE NEEDLED AND SYNOVIAL FLUID EXAMINED BEFORE TREATMENT IS COMMENCED.

REFERENCES

1. Withrington, R.H., Cornes, P., Willie Harris, J.R., et al, Isolation of human immunodeficiency virus from the synovial fluid of a patient with reactive arthritis. *Brit. Med. J.* 1987; **294:** 484.
2. Masi, A.T. & Eisenstein, B.I., Disseminated gonococcal infection (DGI) and gonococcal arthritis (GCA): II. Clinical manifestations, diagnosis, complications, treatment and prevention. *Semin. Arth. Rheum.* 1981; **10:** 173-97.
3. Gibson, T., The treatment of gout: a personal view. *Reports on Rheumatic Diseases* (Series 2). 1988. Practical Problems No 8.
4. McCarty, D.J., Crystals, joints and consternation. *Ann. Rheum Dis.* 1983; **42:** 243-53.
5. Wajed, M.A., Brown, D.L., & Currey, H.L.F., Palindromic rheumatism. Clinical and serum complement studies. *Ann. Rheum. Dis.* 1977; **35:** 56-61.
6. Steven, M.M., Yogarajah, S., Madhok, R., et al, Haemophilic arthritis. *Quart. J. Med.* 1986; **58:** 181-97.
7. Glimcher, M.J., & Kenzora, J.E., The biology of osteonecrosis of the human femoral head and its clinical implications. *Clin. Orthop.* 1979; **138:** 284-309; **139:** 293-312; **140:** 273-312.

POLYARTHRITIS - DIFFERENTIAL DIAGNOSIS & EARLY MANAGEMENT

M E Shipley
Clinical Director
Trauma, Orthopaedics and Rheumatology
Arthur Stanley House
Tottenham Street
London W1P 9PG

Polyarthritis is symmetrical or asymmetrical and may affect large or small joints or both. It generally reflects an inflammatory process although nodal or generalised osteoarthritis may mimic it.

INTRODUCTION

Polyarthritis may be the manifestation of an unpleasant but transient post-viral arthritis, a reaction to some other infective process, the sign of early and potentially disabling rheumatoid arthritis or psoriatic arthritis, or rarely a life threatening infective polyarthritis due to septicaemia. Some of the rarer autoimmune connective tissue diseases may present as a polyarthritis or their manifestations may superficially resemble it, although the joints are painful but not inflamed (SLE) or the main problem may lie in the muscles (polymyalgia rheumatica or polyarteritis nodosa). Fibromyalgia is a generalised pain syndrome which may cause the patient to fear that they have arthritis; it is recognised by the finding of normal joints but multiple soft tissue tender trigger points and is often associated with a poor sleep pattern.

Acute polyarthritis may develop over a few hours, several days or many weeks or months. The time scale, the pattern of the joints affected and a variety of associated clinical features in the patient's present or past medical history or in his or her family history are all pointers which help to make a diagnosis. A careful clinical history is essential. The examination tests the differential diagnosis based on the history and checks for additional clues.

Blood tests and other investigations are often non-specific and rarely diagnostic in cases of polyarthritis. Exceptions include finding crystals in synovial fluid; diagnostic of gout or pseudo-gout, and a positive microbiological culture from joint fluid; diagnostic of septic arthritis. X-rays are often normal in early disease apart from soft tissue swelling but may show OA, chondrocalcinosis (pseudo-gout) or erosions (RA).

With the exception of the septicaemic patient, the exact diagnosis is not therapeutically urgent. Indeed, it may be possible to make a diagnosis only after a few weeks or months have elapsed. In the mean-time the majority of cases can and should be managed with non-steroidal anti-inflammatory drugs and/or analgesic agents, whatever the underlying cause. Most individuals with polyarthritis can live more or less normal lives with the help of drugs. Rest is necessary during acute flares. Making the diagnosis helps to provide a prognosis and it is this which the patient is anxious to receive. They hope the problem will be transient but are often unduly fearful of the worst.

WHAT QUESTIONS TO ASK AND WHAT TO LOOK FOR

The age and sex of the patient. Viral arthritis occurs in young women; rheumatoid and other

THE DIFFERENTIAL DIAGNOSIS OF POLYARTHRITIS

- Post viral arthritis.
- Rheumatoid arthritis (palindromic, transient, episodic, chronic/progressive or rapidly progressive forms can be differentiated).
- 'Seronegative' pattern of arthritis associated with psoriasis, ankylosing spondylitis, ulcerative colitis or Crohn's disease (enteropathic arthritis) or following dysentery or urethritis (Reiter's disease/reactive arthritis).
- Generalised osteoarthritis (nodal OA).
- Post Streptococcal arthritis (rheumatic fever, usually in teenagers).
- Systemic lupus erythematosus.
- Juvenile chronic arthritis (onset before 16 years)

PROBLEMS WHICH ARE MORE COMMONLY MONARTICULAR BUT WHICH MAY PRESENT AS POLYARTHRITIS

- Polyarticular gout (urate arthritis)
- Pseudo gout (pyrophosphate arthritis/chondrocalcinosis on X-ray)
- Septicaemic arthritis.

SYSTEMIC DISEASES WHICH MAY BE CONFUSED WITH POLYARTHRITIS

- Polymyalgia rheumatica.
- Polyarteritis nodosa.
- Hypertrophic pulmonary osteoarthropathy.
- Para-neoplastic syndromes.

SOFT TISSUE RHEUMATISM - FIBROMYALGIA

- No joint swelling but generalised muscular pain and multiple tender trigger points.

inflammatory arthritides are commoner in women. Gout rarely occurs in women unless they are post-menopausal and on diuretics. Nodal osteoarthritis is uncommon before the age of forty five. Juvenile chronic arthritis is rare but needs urgent specialist referral.

What is the pattern of the pain and stiffness? Is it there all the time or episodic? Is it worse with activity or after rest? Prolonged inactivity or early morning stiffness suggest an inflammatory arthritis. Post-inactivity pain and stiffness in generalised OA is more transient.

Is there associated joint swelling? Is this due to synovitis and/or an effusion suggesting inflammation or is it bony as in OA? Is the joint warm, again suggesting inflammation, or cool?

Which joints are affected and which were first affected? RA is generally a peripheral symmetrical polyarthritis. Seronegative arthritis more commonly starts as a monarthritis of the finger (psoriasis) or of the ankle or knee (Reiter's disease or enteropathic arthritis). Generalised OA is usually associated with nodal OA of the hands.

What was the time scale of the onset? Very acute onset RA generally has a good prognosis, especially in the older patient, and viral arthritis is usually sudden in onset.

Has there been a recent viral illness or contact with children who have had rubella or 'slap-cheek' disease (Parvovirus infection)?

Does the patient have or have they had any spinal problems (ankylosing spondylitis), **skin problems** (psoriasis or SLE), **colitis or Crohn's disease** (enteropathic arthritis) or any **recent diarrhoea** (Shigella spp., Salmonella spp. or Yersinia) or **urethritis** (Chlamydia is the commonest), suggesting Reiter's disease?

Does the patient have any other health problems? If they are systemically ill it is likely to be RA or seronegative arthritis, but SLE should be thought of. If there is a fever or weight loss think of septic polyarthritis due to septicaemia and other infections, including Gonococcus or HIV or, rarely, of neoplasia. Acute polyarticular gout or pseudogout may produce a fever and leucocytosis and mimic infection.

Has the patient been taking any medications or drugs? Polyarticular gout after starting diuretics (especially just after surgery) may be extremely severe.

Is there a family history of polyarthritis or of associated problems? Many of these conditions are familial to some extent.

Is the patient at risk of being HIV positive? Rarely such patients present with polyarthritis due to septicaemia or to an acute arthritis associated with psoriasis and/or spondylitis.

Examination of the patient should include all of the joints, the spine and a general medical examination. The aim is to ascertain the pattern of the arthritis, the number of joints affected, the degree of swelling and inflammation and the presence of any other associated clinical finding which may help to establish the diagnosis.

Screening tests for patients with polyarthritis may include:

1) Full blood count and ESR or C-reactive protein to look for an inflammatory reaction, a reactive anaemia or leucocytosis.

2) Serum urate level, if gout is suspected.

3) Aspiration of joint fluid. Clear yellow fluid suggests OA or trauma (rarely polyarticular). Cloudy fluid is consistent with RA or psoriatic arthritis. Very cloudy or purulent fluid suggests septic arthritis but also occurs in Reiter's disease, gout and pseudo-gout. If in doubt examine the fluid by emergency Gram stain and culture and arrange polarised light microscopy for urate or pyrophosphate crystals. Culture blood, urine, stool, urethral discharge and any skin lesions if septic arthritis is suspected.

4) Autoantibody screen to check for a positive ANA (SLE is unlikely if the test is negative). A positive ANA is non-specific - more specific tests include anti-DNA and anti-ENA antibodies. A positive rheumatoid factor test supports a clinical diagnosis of RA but is not of itself diagnostic - a persistently high titre suggests a poor prognosis.

5) X-rays give evidence of OA (joint space narrowing, subarticular sclerosis and osteophytes), RA (erosions rarely occur during the first 3-6 months), pseudo-gout (chondrocalcinosis) or sacroiliitis (if ankylosing spondylitis or seronegative arthritis is suspected and the patient has back pain and stiffness, worse in the morning).

COMMON MISTAKES MADE IN DIAGNOSING POLYARTHRITIS

It is important not to mistake generalised OA, which can cause episodic inflammation, with an inflammatory arthritis such as RA. A mixture of Heberden's (distal interphalangeal) and Bouchard's (proximal interphalangeal) joint nodes and painful osteoarthritic knees may cause confusion. This said, the two are common diseases and may coexist.

A positive rheumatoid factor is never diagnostic of RA, especially in the older patient, unless the clinical picture is correct for RA. Misunderstanding this causes the patient much unnecessary anxiety. If in doubt refer to a rheumatologist.

Patients with RA are caused undue anxiety if given insufficient counselling and support. It is not an inevitably disabling disease and one in four patients have no long term problems. With the help of drugs, RA is compatible with a more or less normal life for the majority. A small proportion become very severely disabled but this is difficult to predict. Severe systemic manifestations and a high and persistent titre of rheumatoid factor are poor prognostic indicators.

Patients with acute arthritis are sometimes treated with both an NSAID and antibiotics. This is a serious error of management. If septic arthritis (monarticular or polyarticular) is suspected, the patient must be referred for specialist care as a medical emergency. At the very least, joint fluid, blood, urine and swabs from any skin ulcers should be taken and only NSAIDs used until a positive culture has been obtained. If the patient is ill and needs antibiotics, they can be started once the culture specimens have been obtained, but specialist advice should be sought.

Polyarticular gout can be precipitated by treating acute gout with allopurinol or by starting allopurinol too soon after an acute attack or with inadequate cover of NSAIDs or colchicine during the first few weeks of treatment.

Young children with polyarthritis may not complain of pain. They often present with a limp or by not using the affected limbs. Specialist referral is mandatory.

POST SCRIPT

Polyarthritis is an important cause of distress. Correct diagnosis and early and appropriate drug management will help relieve symptoms and prevent irreversible joint damage. It is never the case that nothing can be done. In all but the most transient polyarthritis it is the duty of the doctor to establish a relationship of honesty and trust with the patient in order to support them through what may be a lifetime of pain and poor health. Patients value and benefit from care which is provided by a team of people. The ideal team is headed by the GP, working with a rheumatologist. The rheumatology team will then be able to draw on the help of a physiotherapist, a specialist nurse, a psychologist, an occupational therapist and a social worker as necessary. The patient's family and friends should always be involved in the development of a management plan.

January 1995

BAKER'S CYST OR DEEP VEIN THROMBOSIS?

J T Scott
Consultant Physician
Charing Cross Hospital and
Hon Physician
The Kennedy Institute of Rheumatology
London

Popliteal cysts, described during the last century by Adams of Dublin and Mourant Baker of London, are either abnormal distensions of the gastrocnemius-semimembranosus bursa, which usually connects with the synovial cavity of the knee joint, or protrusions from the knee joint itself. Many of the early cases were associated with tuberculosis involving the knee (still an occasional cause) but today the condition is seen characteristically in rheumatoid arthritis, although it can also occur with synovial effusions from other causes: degenerative arthritis, gout, meniscal tears, psoriatic arthritis, Reiter's syndrome, gonococcal arthritis and pyrophosphate arthropathy.

Baker's cysts can remain localised to the popliteal fossa where, depending on their size, they may be symptomless and clinically undetectable or perceptible as a lump behind the knee, sometimes painful and tender. On extension of the knee the cyst may occasionally disappear as fluid is forced back into the knee joint and suprapatellar pouch, but the connection between knee joint and cyst is often a rather tortuous channel which acts as a valve, allowing fluid to pass into the cyst as pressure in the knee rises but not permitting its passage in the opposite direction. Such a situation predisposes to persistence and enlargement of the cyst, extension downwards into the calf between muscle planes, or acute rupture with extravasation of synovial fluid into the tissues of the calf. It should be remembered that pressure within the knee joint, normally between 6 and 33 mmHg at rest, can rise ten times as high with muscular contraction, and up to 1000 mmHg during exercise.

Calf swelling

There are, therefore, three possible causes of calf pain and/or swelling in patients with arthritis of the knee (1).

(1) An intact synovial cyst in the calf.

(2) Acute rupture of the knee joint or of a synovial cyst with extravasation of fluid.

(3) Deep venous thrombosis, which is sometimes seen in the legs of patients with rheumatoid arthritis. It is probably no more common in this condition than in other chronic diseases in which the patient may spend some time in bed.

TABLE

DIFFERENTIAL DIAGNOSIS OF CALF SWELLINGS

Diagnostic Features	Calf Cysts	Synovial Rupture of the Knee Joint	Deep Vein Thrombosis
Pyrexia	–	–	±
Onset of swelling	Variable	Sudden	Several hours (if any swelling)
Pain	+	++	+
Calf swelling	Well-defined	Ill-defined	Ill-defined
Oedema	±	++	+
Knee effusion	+	+	–
Homans' sign	–	+	+
Fluid on aspiration of calf swelling	+	±	–
Intra-articular contrast	Well-defined	Irregular	No extra-articular contrast
Natural course	Persistence	Resolution	Resolution

However, relative immobility and pressure upon the popliteal vein by a tense knee effusion (or popliteal cyst itself) may contribute to venous stasis and thrombosis.

Practice Point:
CAUSES OF PAIN AND/OR CALF SWELLING IN ASSOCIATION WITH KNEE ARTHRITIS

SYNOVIAL CYST
ACUTE SYNOVIAL RUPTURE
DEEP VEIN THROMBOSIS

Precise diagnosis is important since inappropriate anticoagulation in a patient with a ruptured cyst is unnecessary and may cause bleeding into the calf with muscle contracture causing a delayed recovery. Diagnosis of a cyst which is confined to the popliteal fossa is a matter of simple palpation in that area, a routine part of examination of the knee joint, but differentiation between the three causes of calf swelling listed above may be a more difficult matter. Awareness of the problem is the first step.

Practice Point:
PALPATE THE POPLITEAL FOSSA FOR CYSTIC SWELLINGS AS PART OF THE ROUTINE EXAMINATION OF THE KNEE JOINT

Differential diagnosis of calf swelling

Points in the differential diagnosis are summarised in the Table. Diagnosis can be reached on clinical grounds, but confirmation by arthrography, ultra-sonography, venography, isotopic platelet studies or Döppler techniques may be required.

Constitutional symptoms are not a feature of calf cysts, intact or ruptured, apart from the presence of generalised arthritis, whereas deep venous thrombosis is often accompanied by some degree of malaise and pyrexia. Thrombosis was formerly regarded as a condition of the elderly, after pelvic surgery or immobilisation, for example. However, (perhaps associated with the use of oral contraception) it is increasingly seen in young adults with no evident localising cause.

Practice Point:
DEEP VENOUS THROMBOSIS IN THE LEG IS NOT LIMITED TO OLDER PATIENTS

Taking a history

A **careful** history should be elicited with regard to the onset of the pain or swelling. With an intact cyst in the calf this is variable, being sometimes gradual, sometimes more acute. Rupture of a popliteal cyst characteristically occurs on exercise,

Figure 1 Contrast injected into the knee entering a calf cyst through a channel.

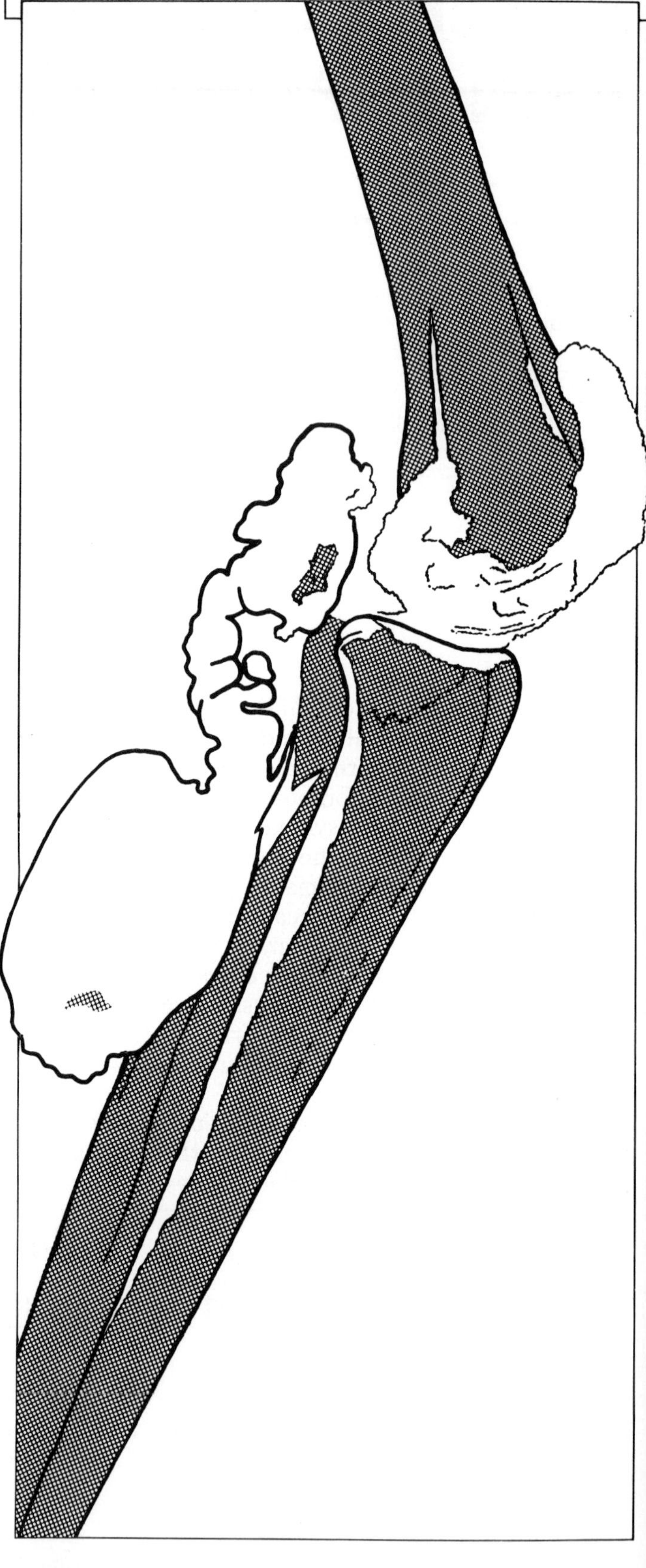

such as climbing stairs, with sudden onset of pain, often with swelling. Swelling consequent upon deep venous thrombosis is variable and usually follows local calf pain over a matter of hours. Pain with an intact cyst or venous thrombosis is also variable, but rupture is an acutely painful affair. Sometimes the patient may notice a reduction in size of knee swelling at the same time as the pain moves down into the calf. Later there may be bruising round the ankle.

Examination

Examination of the swelling will sometimes solve the problem because an intact calf cyst may be palpable as a well-defined mass extending downwards from the popliteal fossa, which is not the case with the other two conditions. However, if it is deep beneath thick musculature, an intact cyst can be difficult to define. The extent of ankle oedema can also be a useful sign, being more prominent and early following a sizeable rupture than in the other two conditions. Homans' sign, whereby pain in the calf is elicited by passive dorsiflexion of the foot with the knee held straight, is a characteristic feature of venous thrombosis, but it also occurs when fluid from a ruptured popliteal cyst tracks down into the calf muscles, so is of little help.

Figure 2 Arthrogram after acute synovial rupture, showing extravasation of fluid into the calf.

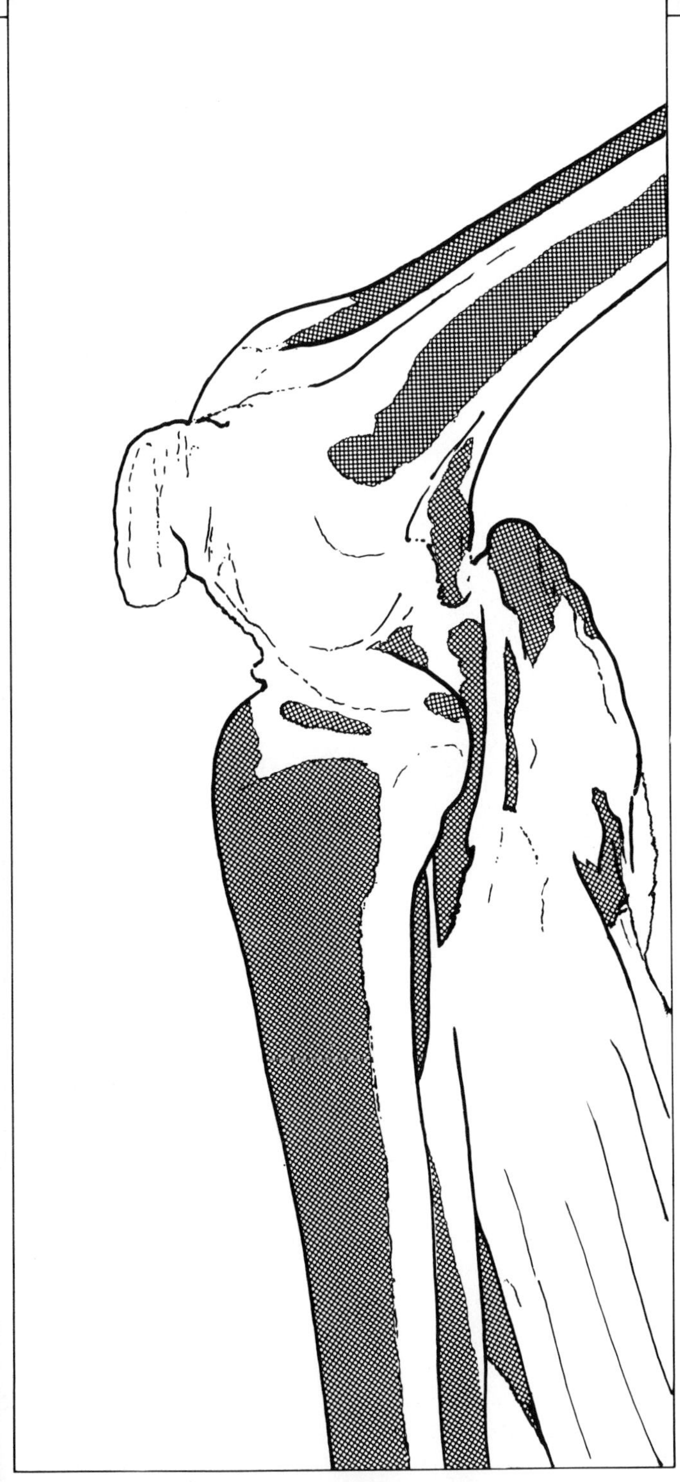

Effusion in the knee is usually detectable when a popliteal cyst has formed, with or without calf extension or rupture. Knee effusion is not *per se* associated with thrombophlebitis but may be a contributing factor to its development. It has been noted by several observers that synovial rupture tends to occur relatively early in the history of knee involvement in any patient with rheumatoid arthritis – two years or earlier – while the total disease duration in patients with intact cysts can be considerably longer.

Special techniques

(1) **Aspiration.** Fluid may be aspirated directly from an intact calf cyst. This is rarely possible with synovial rupture and cannot be achieved with deep venous thrombosis.

(2) **Arthrography** (2). This remains the definitive method of identifying a calf cyst. After aspiration of joint fluid from the knee, 10-15 ml of 45 per cent "Hypaque" is injected into the knee joint. Sometimes the contrast medium is injected with air ("air-arthrogram") but there appears to be little to choose between the two methods. Passage of contrast medium from the knee into a popliteal cyst or into the calf is facilitated by getting the patient to walk, squat or exercise the leg. An intact calf cyst can thus be identified with its channel from the knee joint (Fig. 1). Later the communication with the knee joint may seal off and the cyst does not fill with contrast. With acute synovial rupture the appearance is much less well-defined, sometimes showing extravasation of contrast medium into the calf (Fig. 2). In the deeper tissues of the calf the fluid may be seen coursing downwards presenting an appearance of linear streaking imparted by the muscle fibres with which it is in close contact. Superficial to this the fluid may form irregular clumps. Upward extravasation from the suprapatellar pouch may sometimes be seen.

(3) **Ultrasonography** (2). Ultrasonic scanning has been used to demonstrate popliteal and calf cysts; ultrasound can sometimes demonstrate cysts which do not fill on arthrography. It is a non-invasive technique complementary to arthrography.

(4) **Techniques demonstrating deep venous thrombosis** (3). Venography provides a useful method of diagnosis and localising venous thrombosis. The hazards of extension of thrombosis and embolisation may have been over-emphasised. The Döppler technique has turned out to be of little practical value, but methods using the injection of isotope-labelled platelets, detectable at the site of thrombosis, may be useful.

It is of course rarely, if ever, necessary to employ all these special techniques, their selection being made according to the clinical history and signs. When the diagnosis is in doubt, the first priority is usually to establish whether or not there is a deep vein thrombosis, and venography is the most direct technique for this.

Practice Point:

WHEN THE DIAGNOSIS IS IN DOUBT, THE FIRST PRIORITY IS TO ESTABLISH WHETHER OR NOT THERE IS A VENOUS THROMBOSIS

Management

Localised popliteal cysts are often painless and rarely require specific treatment. Intact calf cysts and synovial rupture may be treated conservatively in the same manner. Because popliteal cysts are caused by the presence of synovial fluid under pressure within the knee joint, it is rational to direct treatment at reducing this. Aspiration of any knee joint effusion followed by injection of 75 mg of hydrocortisone acetate (or equivalent quantities of more potent preparations) may be tried. A period of rest with splinting of the knee may be needed. The result is often very satisfactory. Synovectomy of the knee is sometimes indicated with persistent chronic effusion: removal of the calf cyst itself is rarely necessary and may be rather difficult technically.

For details of the assessment and management of deep venous thrombosis, which lie outside the scope of this short review, the reader may consult references 3 and 4.

REFERENCES

1. Hall AP, Scott JT. Synovial cysts and rupture of the knee joint in rheumatoid arthritis, *Ann Rheum Dis* 1966; **25:** 32-41.
2. Gompels BM, Darlington LG. Grey scale ultrasonography and arthrography in elevation of popliteal cysts. *Clin Radiol* 1979; **30:** 539-545.
3. Fenech A, Hussey JK, Smith FW et al. Diagnosis of deep vein thrombosis. *Br Med J* 1981; **282:** 1020.
4. Madden JL, Hume M, eds. *Venous thromboembolism. Prevention and treatment.* New York: Apple-Century-Crofts, 1976.

January 1987

ASSESSING DISEASE ACTIVITY & DISABILITY

M A Chamberlain
Consultant Rheumatologist
University of Leeds

Background

Eight million working days are lost each year in Britain because of rheumatism. This figure gives some indication of the disruption caused by rheumatic diseases. Behind this figure lies a vast, unmeasured burden of domestic and social difficulties.

Few of us are in the position to cure disease with any frequency: general practitioners particularly will hardly need to be reminded that we are mainly available "to comfort always". Nowhere is this more true than in the rheumatic diseases.

But a distinction needs to be made between sympathy and actual help. Most patients should remain in better health and keep more independent than, say, 30 years ago. It is the function of this report to discuss the first steps in this process: assessment of disease activity and disability in the patient with a rheumatic disease. Without accurate assessment comprehensive and appropriate help may be denied to a patient and increasing dependency will go unrecognised, even if the accompanying despair is witnessed.

Assessment of disease activity in inflammatory conditions

The aim of all treatment in inflammatory joint disease must be to decrease disease activity and prevent further joint damage. Sadly, analgesics and anti-inflammatory drugs have no effect on this and even the so-called disease-modifying agents for rheumatoid arthritis (eg gold, d-penicillamine etc) are the subject of debate as to how much benefit they bring.

The degree of joint inflammation

The physician should be aware of the level of disease activity, and the number of inflamed joints gives some indication of this. The **Ritchie Articular Index** (1) is an established method of recording this and is widely used to assess rheumatoid arthritis. The index is the sum of all joints scored on a scale of 0-3 (as judged by pain, wincing or withdrawal of the joint). The index is reproducible using a single observer over the course of time. A simpler, quick method for routine clinical use is to record the total number of limb joints which are *both swollen and tender to firm pressure* (2).

> **Practice Point:**
> **ASSESSMENT OF INFLAMMATION**
>
> NUMBER OF SWOLLEN AND TENDER JOINTS
> DURATION OF EARLY MORNING STIFFNESS
> RING SIZE (CLINICAL TRIALS)

Early morning stiffness

Early morning stiffness (EMS), which is another index of inflammation, causes great distress: some exhausted patients get up at 5-6 am to give themselves time to dress for work. Non-steroidal anti-inflammatory drugs, particularly if taken last thing at night, as well as disease-modifying agents will shorten this time to an acceptable level (under half an hour – the time taken to have a hot bath before starting the day). Although the end point of stiffness (or slowness in children) is inexact it remains a useful index of disease activity. One should consider the patient inadequately treated if stiffness is a major, as opposed to an isolated, unimportant, complaint.

Jeweller's rings and a plastic proprietary ring have been used to assess joint size and various other indices are used to assess inflammation. They have no relevance to general practice except for those undertaking drug trials.

Laboratory measures of disease activity

The erythrocyte sedimentation rate (ESR) remains the most commonly-used indication of disease activity. In rheumatoid arthritis the elevated values result mainly from three factors: raised levels of fibrinogen (an acute-phase reactant), raised levels of immunoglobulin, and anaemia. Anaemia itself often reflects disease activity ("anaemia of chronic disease"), although it may also result from iron deficiency due to gastrointestinal blood loss caused by drugs.

Other valid indicators of rheumatoid disease activity include plasma viscosity and C-reactive protein.

Functional assessment and classification

Steinbrocker in 1949 (3) divided patients with rheumatoid arthritis into four functional categories, those who functioned normally (I), those who managed work normally, even though with pain or difficulty (II), those whose ability to do paid work or housework was diminished (III), and those who were chair or bedridden (IV). This classification can be applied to any form of joint disease and, though crude, the grading is still used because it is quick to apply. Any change in the grade should alert the doctor to pursue the matter further. However, the steps between grades I and II are not of the same size as between grades III and IV and so the classification is of limited value. (The grading is an ordinal grading, but not interval). Furthermore, the ability to do paid work depends also on external factors: those with modern household appliances may manage better than those with similar disease severity, but living in poorer circumstances.

All the *"activities of daily living"* surveyed by occupational therapists are important to patients with rheumatic diseases. Although diseases of joints hardly ever cause any interference with breathing, and rarely interfere with vision or hearing, limited movement in the joints of the arms can cause difficulties in feeding, in selfcare and grooming, toileting, hygiene and sexual function. Stiff hips, knees and feet impair mobility, whether on foot or by powered transport though the car ameliorates many difficulties. Pain and limited joint function in both arms and legs affect the person's ability to find and keep a sexual partner, and may threaten to impair the lengthy process of childrearing.

How then can we best assess the functional impact of the disease ? For the planning of resources we may wish to use the methods of the Office of Population Census (4) or the Amelia Harris Classification (5) which has been validated and can be administered by relatively untrained interviewers. Clinical research workers may decide to use the Barthel Index (6) which, again, is validated; its gradings are clearly defined, are unambiguous and the index has been widely used for a number of years.

The use of questionnaires to assess the patient's limitations

The individual doctor seeking a method which is reproducible, quick to administer and relevant to the patient's needs, may find the **Stanford Health Assessment Questionnaire** (HAQ) (7) in its shortened, modified form acceptable (8). The patient can easily complete this form unaided in the waiting room. It may tell a busy doctor more than he wants to know but he is free to concentrate on those areas of greatest relevance at the time; this means, not the areas which interest or concern the doctor, or even the therapist, but those of most importance to the patient. Perhaps the best questions one can ask in a short interview are "what bothers you most" or "what do you want me to deal with today". This approach gains the patient's confidence so that later those factors which threaten long-term independence may be tackled. Valuable though the assessments of disease activity and joint involvement (discussed above) are, on their own they provide less important information than these functional assessments.

> **Practice Point:**
>
> **QUICK, USEFUL QUESTIONS**
>
> "WHAT BOTHERS YOU MOST?"
> "WHAT DO YOU WANT ME TO DEAL WITH TODAY?"

A spate of new health assessment questionnaires has recently appeared. Unlike earlier ones, these tend to be more reproducible, their results are less dependent on the interviewer (interobserver variability is lower), they are better validated and consist of linear scales which can be numbered. Often, unlike the Steinbrocker classification, the distance between one group or class and the next is the same.

These newer methods, eg AIMS (9), take account of the variety of effects of disease including disease activity, functional status, general well-being, and psychological factors such as anxiety or depression. The full standard HAQ also has sections which allow individual and health service costs to be computed. Such assessments are probably less useful to the GP than to the community physician or health economist.

Individual functional tests

Tests of particular functions or of function at individual joints may, however, be of use. Thus, the older person with osteoarthrosis of the hip is rarely ill and yet his ability to live alone may be compromised by worsening of this one joint. One needs to know how far the physiotherapist can be, or has been, able to help and whether the time has come for surgery. After surgery, further physiotherapy may be needed and again the question becomes: is the patient now fit – for what?

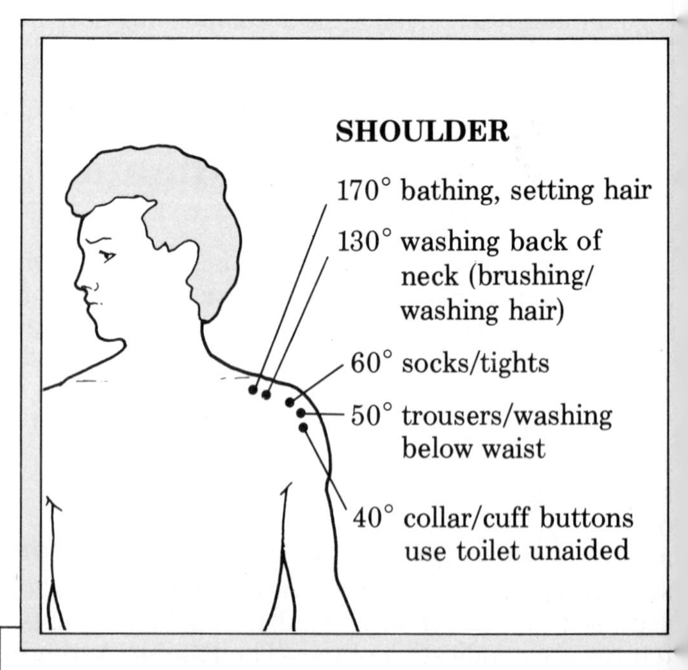

Figure 1 The range of shoulder movement needed to perform various functions.

Individual joint assessment

Joint range of movement remains a useful measure; the goniometer (protractor with long arms) is a simple clinical tool, adequate for routine work. Goniometers which record and retain maximum ranges have their value (Ellis (10)); similarly assessment of pinch grip by a pinch grip meter is preferable to the inflatable Davis bag in, for example, a drug trial. For practical purposes one has to remember that the patient rarely needs to make use of the full range of joint function. For instance, a painfree arthrodesis of the wrist is usually preferable to any range where pain is significant; but the midrange of flexion at the elbow is critical, and combined movement at elbow and shoulder is needed to allow a patient to feed himself. In practice, if range has to be restricted, it should be conserved in the midrange at the elbow, although activities such as donning a heavy coat may be difficult and, if the pronation range is reduced, the patient may not be able to operate a typewriter or computer keyboard. The range of movement at the shoulder necessary for a variety of functions is illustrated (Fig 1). Angulated equipment such as a comb may allow better function. (Fig2)

Any fixed flexion deformity at hip or knee must, if possible, be avoided; if present, it should be recorded before and after any corrective measures such as physiotherapy, or use of walking aids. No loss of extension at the hip is acceptable. Loss of abduction in a woman may lead to difficulty with sexual intercourse and with labour. Intermalleolar separation is easy to measure (from medial malleolus to medial malleolus). When less than the average kerb or step height (about 20 cm) one can anticipate that the patient will be unable to climb these, and physiotherapy, and later surgical intervention will be necessary. Climbing steps and stairs is necessary, for, even if patients live on the ground floor, their friends do not and their houses frequently have steps at the threshold. At least 90° of flexion (0° – 90°) at the knee is required to achieve stair climbing and good quadriceps function is an often neglected asset; for example, how many 1kg bags of sugar placed on the ankle can a sitting patient lift once by extending the knee fully? This gives a measure of weight lift.
The endurance of the patient, the ability to lift, repeatedly say one quarter of this weight, is of more practical importance.

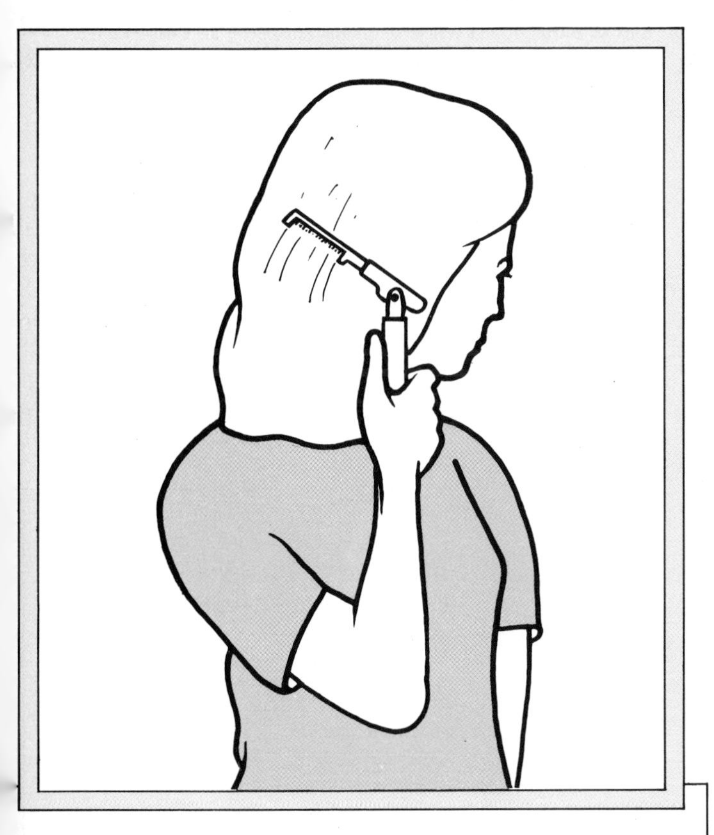

Figure 2 Angulated equipment can improve function

Practice Point:

CRITICAL JOINT RESTRICTIONS

ANY FIXED FLEXION AT KNEE OR HIP
LOSS OF HIP EXTENSION
LOSS OF INTERMALLEOLAR SEPARATION (HIP ABDUCTION)
LESS THAN 90° KNEE FLEXION

It is worth checking the line of weight bearing through the legs, because pain in the joints may result from varus or valgus deformity, be it at forefoot, hindfoot or knee level. Whilst certain activities such as driving demand some plantar/dorsiflexion at the ankle, its loss does not otherwise significantly reduce function. Loss of mobility in the midtarsal area quickly leads to local pain, and inability to transfer the body weight to the great toe will lead to abnormal and painful stresses on the smaller metatarsal heads lateral to it. These joints should be tested and the results recorded.

Functional tests of mobility

The physiotherapist may be concerned with walking or climbing stairs, and the time taken to do each of these over a fixed course makes a useful record. Patients who cannot walk 100 metres can rarely reach shops, post offices (for pension) and chemists (for prescription) and may be considered "virtually unable to walk" and thus eligible for the Mobility Allowance.

Many patients with advanced rheumatic disease are more or less housebound. The distances to be walked within most houses are small. But within this area, the patient's independence, fragile as it is, will be further threatened unless he is able to *transfer*, that is to move from horizontal to vertical or to the sitting position (Fig. 3).

One should note whether these transfers can be done and classify them into 5 grades: without help and without the use of aids (I), without personal help but with aids (II), with supervision or minimal help (III), or with the help of one person (IV) or two people (V).

If these abilities are about to be lost, the help of a physiotherapist to preserve or increase mobility and supply necessary walking aids should be sought. An occupational therapist's help may also be needed because seating will have an influence on these functions, as will the type of bed. A high chair with

Important transfers for the house-bound patient:

TRANSFER FROM BED TO CHAIR (OR WHEELCHAIR)
TRANSFER FROM BED TO STANDING (WALKING AID)
TRANSFER FROM WHEELCHAIR TO LAVATORY/COMMODE
TRANSFER TO WALKING FROM LAVATORY/COMMODE

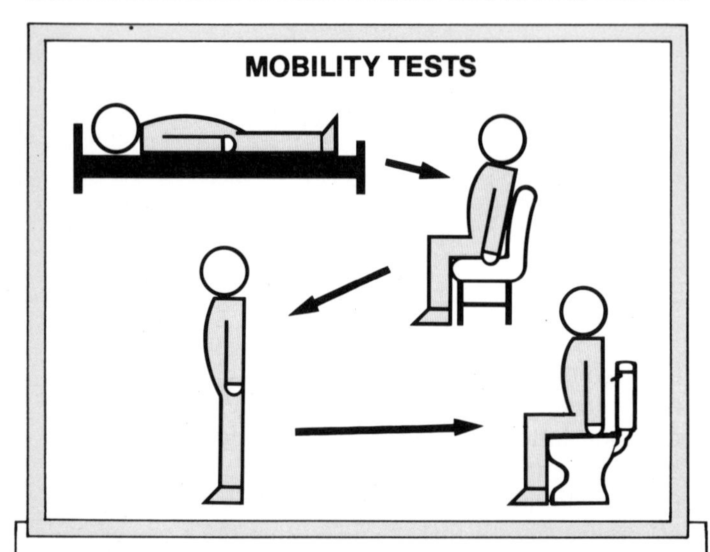

Figure 3 The patient's independence is threatened if he is unable to transfer from lying down to sitting or standing.

appropriate padded arms will facilitate transfer (11). A bed with a back that rises or has a monkey pole, or a solid piece of furniture beside it, or a commode attached to it, or even with adjustable height may be necessary.

It is not possible to consider all functions or all functional tests in this report. One has constantly to return to the patient asking the question: "functional ability – for what?" Progressive disability must not be accepted as inevitable. It is not. And in the UK much help – from therapists, from technical aids and from a variety of other sources – is available to be called on. One needs to know what to ask for, and when.

REFERENCES

(1) Ritchie DM, Boyle JA, McInnes JM, Jasani MK, Dalakos TG, Grieveson P and Watson Buchanan W. Clinical studies with an articular index for the assessment of joint tenderness in patients with rheumatoid arthritis. *Quarterly Journal of Medicine* 1968; **37:** 393-406.

(2) Thompson PW and Kirwan JR (1986). A comparison of articular indices in rheumatoid arthritis (Abstract) *British Journal of Rheumatology,* **25:** 98-9.

(3) Steinbrocker O, Traeger CH and Batterman RC. Therapeutic criteria in rheumatoid arthritis. *J Am Med Assoc* 1949; **140:** 659-62.

(4) Office of Population Census (Functional Assessment Scheme).

(5) Harris Amelia. *Handicapped and Impaired in Great Britain,* HMSO, London 1971.

(6) Barthel DW and Mahoney FI. Functional Evaluation. The Barthel Index, *Maryland State Medical Journal,* 6-165, Feb. 1965.

(7) Fries JF, Spitz PW, Kraines RG and Holman HR. Measurement of patient outcome in arthritis. *Arthritis and Rheum* 1980; **23:** 137-45.

(8) Kirwan JR and Reeback JS. Stanford Health Assessment Questionnaire modified to assess disability in British patients with rheumatoid arthritis. *British Journal of Rheumatology* 1986; **25:** 206-209.

(9) Meenan RF (1982). The AIMS approach to health status measurement: conceptual background and measurement properties. *Journal of Rheumatology,* **9,** 785-788.

(10) Ellis M, Burton K and Wright V. Simple goniometer for measuring hip function. *Rheum. and Rehab.* **Vol18,** 85-90, 1979.

(11) *Are You Sitting Comfortably?* A guide to choosing easy chairs. The Arthritis & Rheumatism Council. London 1985.

September 1986

QUANTIFYING PROGRESS IN ARTHRITIS

D Symmons
Consultant Senior Lecturer
ARC Epidemiology Research Unit
Manchester
and Manchester Royal Infirmary

INTRODUCTION

Many forms of joint disease have a chronic disabling course which may extend over several decades. Sometimes the resultant deformity and disability advance with such stealth that neither the patient nor the physician notices them. In order to avoid this situation it is important to try and quantify the progress in each individual patient. Monitoring progress means assessing the patient's status today (the absolute or cross-sectional view) and comparing the result with that at some point in the past (the relative or longitudinal view). In fact it is useful to make at least two comparisons - one with a fixed point in the past (for example the time of presentation) in order to assess the cumulative damage caused by the disease - and the other with a moving time point (for example the last visit) in order to assess the current rate of change.

These points can be illustrated graphically (Figure 1). Point 'a' represents the patient's current status, $\triangle_o$ represents the change since the last visit and $\triangle_o/\triangle_t$ represents the rate of deterioration. Also of importance is the area under the curve: $\int \frac{\triangle_o}{\triangle_t}$

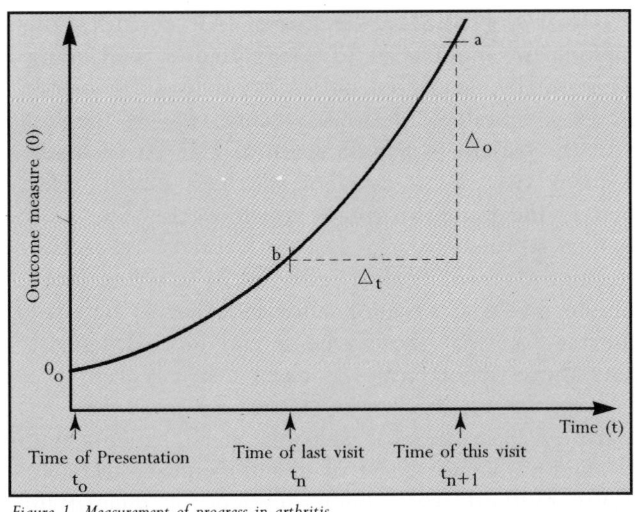

Figure 1. Measurement of progress in arthritis.

If, as seems possible, we cannot influence the long-term outcome of arthritis (1), we may still be able to improve the course of the disease by ensuring that the patient arrives via route 1 rather than by route 2 (Figure 2).

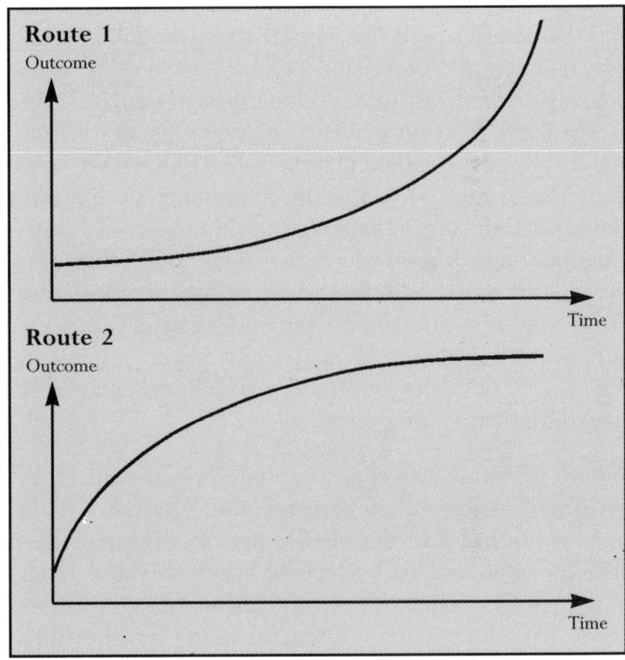

Figure 2. Different routes to the same outcome.

This report is not, however, about the mathematics of quantifying progress but about the best measures to use in particular circumstances in the two major classes of joint disease - inflammatory arthritis and joint failure. The primary considerations when selecting any quantitative measure in clinical medicine are that it should be (i) valid - ie it should be measuring what is intended (ii) reliable - ie it should be reproducible and (iii) feasible - ie it should be possible to carry out in the proposed setting (2). In the context of assessing progress it is also important to choose measures which are sensitive to change - ie responsive. In order to be responsive a measure should be capable of change and should have a small standard deviation (SD). If a measure changes by 10 units but has an SD of 20 units then the change observed cannot be distinguished from random error (ie it will not be statistically significant). Functional class (3) is not sensitive to change because patients often score the same over long periods. Duration of stiffness and grip strength are not responsive because they usually have large SDs.

Confusion can easily arise from the varying use of the word 'outcome' in the study of joint disease. The term 'outcome measure' is used to describe all methods of patient assessment (clinical, laboratory and radiological) regardless of the stage of the disease at which they are applied. The term 'disease outcome' is used to mean the cumulative damage caused by the disease.

MEASURING PROGRESS IN INFLAMMATORY ARTHRITIS

Rheumatoid arthritis (RA) has been chosen to illustrate the principles of measuring progress in inflammatory arthritis because it is the most common and the most studied of these diseases. There are two major components to the rheumatoid process in the joint - inflammation (which is potentially reversible) and erosive damage of the articular cartilage and underlying bone (which is essentially irreversible). It is generally believed that the cumulative amount of inflammation and the cumulative amount of erosive damage are correlated (4). However the relationship is far from perfect and every rheumatologist has patients with no evidence of synovitis and a normal erythrocyte sedimentation rate (ESR) who continue to erode. Most drug treatments in RA are aimed at reducing inflammation. Non-steroidal anti-inflammatory drugs reduce the signs and symptoms associated with inflammation, while second-line drugs suppress the underlying inflammatory process (and so reduce the ESR and acute phase response). There are no drug treatments which are primarily directed at preventing erosions.

When it comes to choosing outcome measures in RA there is a conflict between the clinician's main area of interest and that of the patient. The patient's primary goals are to be free of symptoms and functioning well. Thus the most relevant outcome measures for the patient are well-being (sometimes called the patient global assessment), pain, stiffness and a functional assessment. The clinician, however, is aware that many of these are hybrid measures of inflammation and joint damage. Even if the inflammatory process is completely controlled in a patient with long-standing RA, it is unusual for the patient not to experience pain. The clinician, therefore, tends to favour 'pure' measures of inflammation (such as laboratory tests or an articular index) and 'pure' measures of damage (such as X-rays). In fact even these 'pure' measures of inflammation may be contaminated by the effect of past damage.

Table 1.
THE GOALS OF TREATMENT IN RHEUMATOID ARTHRITIS

- Control synovitis
- Relieve pain
- Maintain function
- Improve quality of life
- Minimise drug side-effects
- Be cost effective

Since the goals of treatment in RA are multiple (Table 1) it is necessary to sample several outcome domains in order to assess progress. The various measures then have to be combined in order to decide whether, overall, the patient is better or worse. An international group called OMERACT (Outcome Measures in RA Clinical Trials) has been using the principles outlined above to identify a core set of outcome measures for use in all RA clinical trials (Table 2) (5). This core set has been endorsed by the International League Against Rheumatism (ILAR) and the American College of Rheumatology (ACR). Since it is likely that all future published trials will include these measures it makes sense for the individual clinician to use the same ones in order to facilitate comparisons. The OMERACT set represents a consensus on the generic outcome domains (eg pain, joint swelling) rather than the actual technique to be used (eg visual analogue scale (VAS) or categorical pain scales). The following section reviews the methods available for assessing these selected endpoints.

Table 2.
CORE SET OF OUTCOME MEASURES FOR RHEUMATOID ARTHRITIS AS RECOMMENDED BY OMERACT FOR USE IN CLINICAL TRIALS (5)

DOMAIN	VALUE IN ASSESSING: inflammation	cumulative damage
1. Patient global assessment	+(*)	+(*)
2. Physician global assessment	+(*)	+(*)
3. Pain	+	?
4. Disability	+	+
5. Swollen joint count	+	–
6. Tender joint count	+	–
7. Acute phase reactants	+	–
8. Radiographic studies in any trial of one year or more	–	+

(*) using a different question

Patient's global assessment All consultations include an inquiry as to the patient's well-being. This can be quantified either by using a 10cm VAS or by a modified McConkey score (6). At the first visit the patient is given a score of 100. At each subsequent visit she is asked if she feels much better, better, the same, worse or much worse. The score is then adjusted by -2, -1, 0, +1, or +2 respectively. Improvement is thus reflected by a falling score. In the non-trial situation allowance has to be made for the fact that those who attend more frequently have more opportunities to change their scores.

Pain A pain score is valuable in all patients with RA and in the assessment of all anti-rheumatic therapies. Many methods have been devised for quantifying pain but the most commonly used are a 10cm VAS and a 5 point descriptive (Likert) scale. The assessment of pain is a very sensitive measure in short term drug trials in RA. Its value in longitudinal studies has not been assessed. Preliminary work suggests that the pain score plateaus or even improves with time. This is a situation where the more relevant measure of disease outcome is the area under the curve.

Disability The oldest instrument which measures disability is the Steinbrocker functional index (3). This has recently been revised (7). It divides patients into 4 broad functional classes and is relatively insensitive to change in the short term. It is thus of more value in assessing damage than inflammation. An important advance over the last decade has been the development of validated self-administered questionnaires (for a review of questionnaires on function in RA see reference 8). They are more reproducible than non self-report questionnaires. The one in most widespread use is the Stanford Health Assessment Questionnaire (HAQ) (9) which has been modified and validated for use in the UK (10). The HAQ lists 20 everyday tasks and asks the patient to rate her difficulty in performing these tasks on a 4 point scale. The HAQ is sensitive to change and is able to discriminate between therapies in short-term studies (11). In addition current disability is the strongest predictor of a premature death in RA. It has been suggested that a self-report functional questionnaire is the single most useful tool in the quantitative assessment of the rheumatoid patient (12).

Swollen and tender joint counts A count of the number of swollen joints is the closest the clinician comes to quantifying the bulk of inflamed tissue. Joint tenderness is another way of assessing pain. The correlation between joint swelling and tenderness is not as high as might be expected, which is why both need to be assessed. There is no consensus on a single standardised method of assessing joint involvement. The methods available vary in the number of joints assessed, whether these joints are weighted according to size, and whether the joint abnormality is scored on a linear scale or simply as being normal or abnormal (12). A joint count is obtained when the number of abnormal joints is recorded. A joint score is obtained when the abnormality is graded. Joint counts are more reproducible than joint scores. The Ritchie articular index (13), which has been widely used in the UK, is an example of a tender joint score. Fifty-two peripheral joints or joint areas are graded on a 4 point scale for tenderness. There seems to be no advantage conferred by examining large numbers of joints. A 28-joint index (which includes 10 metacarpophalangeal, 10 proximal interphalangeal and 2 shoulder, elbow, wrist and knee joints) (14) performs as well as the 80 joint count recommended by the ACR.

Acute phase reactants Recent research suggests that circulating levels of cytokines may be a more direct indication of inflammatory activity. However no routine assays are available to detect these substances. The ESR and C-reactive protein (CRP) remain the two most widely used laboratory tests to assess inflammation in RA. They are closely correlated so there is no need to measure both when assessing progress. In patients with long-standing RA (more than 20 years) the ESR may be persistently elevated with no clinical evidence of inflammation and in this situation the CRP is the better measure. Both the ESR and the CRP are sensitive to change in the short term. Neither has any value in assessing the long-term damage caused by RA. Although initial rheumatoid factor titre is of prognostic significance, serial measurements are not useful in assessing progress.

Radiological assessment Unlike all the measures described above the radiograph records *only* what has happened in the past. There is only a modest correlation between the radiological score and self-reported function. So the X-ray tells us little about how the patient is doing, but has come to be regarded as the gold standard for judging how our treatment is doing! There is a variety of methods for quantifying radiological findings (for a review see reference 15). The first was a global score derived by Steinbrocker et al (6). Sharp was the first to introduce a separate numerical assessment of erosions and joint space narrowing (16). Twenty-seven areas in each hand are scored for both joint space narrowing (on a 5 point scale) and erosions (up to a maximum of 5). Sharp has since modified and simplified (17) his method but it remains very time consuming. It is the most widely used system in the USA. The preferred system in Europe is that proposed by Larsen (18). Larsen's method involves comparing the patient's films with a set of standard radiographs graded on a 0-5 scale. The MCP and PIP joints are scored individually and the wrist is scored as a whole and then weighted by multiplying by 5. Although Larsen's method is most commonly used to score hand and feet X-rays, standard films are also available for other joints. Amos proposed a method which is of particular value in serial studies (19). It involves counting the number of new discrete erosions which develop in the hands and wrists during a particular time period. All three of these methods are reproducible.

Radiological scores rise progressively with disease duration. A number of longitudinal studies have shown a plateauing of radiological score with time which has led to the suggestion that most radiological damage occurs early in disease. However this observation may be an artefact of a scoring system which has a built-in ceiling effect (ie it is possible to deteriorate within the highest grade). Also, once a certain amount of damage has occurred within a joint, further deterioration may be inevitable as a result of mechanical forces, regardless of whether there is persistent inflammation. For this reason the involvement of previously unaffected joints may be a more relevant outcome measure when it comes to judging the efficacy of treatment.

MEASURING PROGRESS IN JOINT FAILURE

Joint failure, or osteoarthritis (OA), is the final common pathway of a number of different insults including RA. It is characterised by focal destruction of articular cartilage, sclerosis of the underlying bone, and marginal hypertrophy of bone and soft tissue. Pathologically OA shows combined features of cartilage damage and a repair response. These processes are reflected on X-ray by joint space narrowing and new bone formation respectively. There is, however, not a good correlation between the pathological changes of OA (as shown on X-ray) and the clinical features. The principal symptoms of OA are use-related pain, 'gelling' on inactivity and disability. Abnormal examination findings include bony enlargement, crepitus and a reduced range of movement.

The goals of treatment in OA are to reduce the pain and disability. There are, as yet, no treatments which slow the progression of OA. The physician also tries to estimate the point at which surgery may be required. Both progressive and non progressive forms of OA exist and so assessing the speed of progression in the individual patient is essential. Unfortunately there is no standard way of assessing OA clinically. A review of OA clinical trials showed that 41 different outcome measures had been used (20). The European League Against Rheumatism (EULAR) proposed 5 measures for use in OA clinical trials (21) (Table 3) - but this did not follow the rigorous assessment behind the OMERACT list. It ignores a number of important aspects, while including walking time which is not sensitive to change.

Table 3. EULAR MEASURES OF EFFICACY FOR ASSESSING DRUGS IN OSTEOARTHRITIS

1 - Index of severity of hip and knee disease (Lequesne)
2 - Investigator's overall opinion
3 - Pain on VAS
4 - Patient's global assessment
5 - Walking time (or stair climbing time for knee)

The following list is a personal selection of outcome measures for OA. It does not include bony enlargement or crepitus as these are not capable of change in the short term. Range of movement has shown to be responsive in the trial setting (20) - however clinicians are advised to check their intraobserver error before adopting it as a routine assessment!

Patient global assessment As with RA this provides a valuable insight into how the patient rates her own progress.

Pain score Whereas in RA the pain score usually relates to the total amount of pain experienced by the patient, in OA it is useful to distinguish between use-related pain, pain at rest, and pain which disturbs sleep.

New joint score The Doyle index (21) is an adaptation of the Ritchie index for use in OA. It assesses joint tenderness on pressure or movement in 48 joints or joint groups. It provides a total score but it may be more useful to keep the result disaggregated. Dieppe has pointed out that the natural history of OA is the slow accumulation of new sites (23). Thus progress can by quantified by measuring new sites clinically and radiographically.

Severity score Lequesne has developed indices of severity for knee and hip OA (24). The Lequesne questionnaires consist of 10-12 doctor-administered questions which cover pain at rest, duration of morning and inactivity stiffness, walking distance and appropriate activities of daily living. The Lesquesne indices have not been fully validated. It is unlikely that they will prove sufficiently sensitive to change to be of use in the trial situation. However they are already being used in epidemiologically based needs assessment for joint replacement and are likely to be helpful in quantifying cumulative damage in the individual patient.

Disability The HAQ is useful in assessing disability in patients with OA in multiple joints. However patients with OA in a single joint often have almost normal HAQ scores. Bellamy and Buchanan have developed a 24 item self-administered questionnaire for use in the assessment of knee and hip OA, called the Western Ontario and McMaster Universities (WOMAC) Osteoarthritis index, which covers 3 domains: pain, stiffness and physical function (25). It has been validated but is not in widespread use.

Radiological assessment Progress in OA has traditionally been assessed radiologically despite the poor correlation between X-ray findings and symptoms. The method introduced by Kellgren and Lawrence in the 1950s remains the gold standard (26). This involves comparing the patient's films with a set of standardised X-rays graded from 0 (normal) to 4 (severe OA). The system has been shown to be reproducible but it is not sensitive to change and, as with some of the systems used to score RA, it has a ceiling effect. Standardised measures of joint space narrowing are more sensitive to change but less reproducible (27). The rate of progression in OA is highly variable and non-linear. Out of the research setting there is little to be gained by routinely re-X-raying patients with OA unless their symptoms are worsening.

THE ADVANTAGES AND DISADVANTAGES OF POOLED OUTCOME MEASURES (INDICES)

Disease outcome in arthritis is multi-dimensional and so progress must be assessed in a number of domains - some of which have been listed above. There are others which may be equally important.

They include ability to work and quality of life. The situation can appear very confused when some measures are getting better and others are getting worse. There is therefore something inherently appealing about an index which pools several outcome measures and comes up with a single answer. A pooled index is composed of a number of measures appropriately selected and weighted. Selection and weighting are based either on clinical judgement (28) or on mathematical criteria (29). Statistically derived indices have the added advantage of minimising the number of measures since they select items which are not closely correlated with one another. Because they have a smaller SD, pooled indices are more sensitive to change than a single measure. This in turn means that smaller sample sizes are needed in order to demonstrate clinically important differences in the trial situation. Thus a pooled index may be the best single outcome measure in a clinical trial. In routine clinical practice there are some disadvantages. One is that the index may be difficult to compute. Secondly there may be problems in comprehending and interpreting the result. As yet experience with pooled indices is limited and none is in routine use.

THE PRACTICALITY OF QUANTIFYING PROGRESS IN THE ROUTINE CLINICAL SETTING

Much of our understanding of the long term course of arthritis has come from units which have incorporated a standardised assessment into their routine clinical practice. This is usually achieved by having a single assessment sheet which includes a self-report functional questionnaire, mannequin for recording examination findings, and certain standard questions. Even if this system does not appeal there is much to be said for selecting some of the above measures and using them at regular intervals. A patient global assessment, pain score and articular index can be completed at each attendance. A measure of disability can be used once or twice a year in order to identify new areas of difficulty. X-rays need to be done less frequently.

REFERENCES

1. Scott DL, Symmons DPM, Coulton BL, Popert AJ. The long-term outcome of treating rheumatoid arthritis: results after 20 years. *Lancet* 1987; **i**: 1108-11

2. Tugwell P, Bombardier C. A methodologic framework for developing and selecting endpoints in clinical trials. *J Rheumatol* 1982; **9**: 758-62

3. Steinbrocker O, Traeger CH, Batterman RC. Therapeutic criteria in rheumatoid arthritis. *J Am Med Assoc* 1949; **140**: 659-62

4. Borg G, Allander E, Birger L et al. Auranofin improves outcome in early rheumatoid arthritis. Results from a 2 year double blind placebo controlled trial. *J Rheumatol* 1988; **15**: 1747-58

5. Tugwell P, Boers M. OMERACT conference on outcome measures in RA clinical trials: Conclusion. *J Rheumatol* 1993; **20**: 590

6. McConkey B, Crockson RA, Crockson P. The assessment of rheumatoid arthritis. A study based on measurements of the serum acute-phase reactants. *Quart J Med* 1972; **41**: 115-25

7. Hochberg MC, Chang RW, Dwosh I, Lindsey S, Pincus T, Wolfe F. The American College of Rheumatology 1991 revised criteria for the classification of global functional status in rheumatoid arthritis. *Arthritis Rheum* 1992; **35:** 498-502

8. Bell MJ, Bombardier C, Tugwell P. Measurement of functional status, quality of life, and utility in rheumatoid arthritis. *Arthritis Rheum* 1990; **33**: 591-601

9. Fries JF, Spitz P, Kraines RG, Holman HR. Measurement of patient outcome in arthritis. *Arthritis Rheum* 1980; **23**: 137-45

10. Kirwan JR, Reeback JS. Stanford Health Assessment questionnaire modified to assess disability in British patients with rheumatoid arthritis. *Br J Rheumatol* 1986; **25**: 206-9

11. van der Heijde DMFM, van Riel PLCM, van der Putte LBA. Sensitivity of a Dutch Health Assessment Questionnaire in a trial comparing hydroxychloroquine and sulphasalazine. *Scand J Rheumatology* 1990; **19**: 407-12

12. Pincus T, Callahan LF. Quantitative measures to assess, monitor and predict morbidity and mortality in rheumatoid arthritis. *Clinical Rheum* 1992; **6**: 161-191

13. Ritchie DM, Boyle JA, McInnes JM et al. Clinical studies with an articular index for the assessment of joint tenderness in patients with rheumatoid arthritis. *Quart J Med* 1968; **37**: 393-406

14. Fuchs HA, Brooks RH, Callahan LF, Pincus T. A simplified 28-point quantitative articular index in rheumatoid arthritis. *Arthritis Rheum* 1989; **32**: 531-7

15. Dawes PT. Radiological assessment of outcome in rheumatoid arthritis. *Br J Rheumatol* 1988; **27 (suppl 1)**: 21-36

16. Sharp JT, Lidsky MD, Collins LC, Moreland J. Methods of scoring the progression of radiologic changes in rheumatoid arthritis. Correlation of radiologic, clinical and laboratory abnormalities. *Arthritis Rheum* 1971; **14**: 706-20

17. Sharp JT, Young DY, Bluhm GB et al. How many joints in the hands and wrists should be included in a score of radiologic abnormalities used to assess rheumatoid arthritis? *Arthritis Rheum* 1985; **28**: 1326-35

18. Larsen A, Dale K, Eek M. Radiographic evaluation of rheumatoid arthritis and related conditions by standard reference films. *Acta Radiologica* (Diagnosis) 1977; **18**: 481-91

19. Amos RS, Constable TJ, Crockson RA, Crockson AP, McConkey B. Rheumatoid arthritis: relation of serum C-reactive protein and erythrocyte sedimentation rates to radiographic changes. *Br Med J* 1977; **i**: 1195-7

20. Bellamy N, Buchanan WW. Outcome measurement in osteoarthritis clinical trials: the case for standardisation. *Clin Rheumatol* 1984; **3**: 293-300

21. Guidelines for the clinical investigation of drugs used in rheumatic diseases. European drug guidelines, Series 5. EULAR 1985 21-4 WHO Regional Office for Europe, Copenhagen

22. Doyle DV, Dieppe PA, Scott J, Huskisson EC. An articular index for the assessment of osteoarthritis. *Ann Rheum Dis* 1981;**40**:75-8

23. Dieppe PA. Some recent clinical approaches to osteoarthritis research. *Semin Arthritis Rheum* 1990; **20**: 2-11

24. Lequesne MG, Samson M. Indices of severity in osteoarthritis for weight bearing joints. *J Rheumatol* 1991; **18 (suppl 27)**: 16-18

25. Bellamy N, Buchanan WW, Goldsmith CH, Campbell J, Stitt LW. Validation study of WOMAC: A health status instrument for measuring clinically important outcomes in anti rheumatic therapy in patients with osteoarthritis of the hip or knee. *J Rheumatol* 1988; **15**: 1833-40

26. Kellgren JH, Lawrence JS. Radiological assessment of osteoarthritis. *Ann Rheum Dis* 1957; **16**: 494-502

27. Altman RD, Fries JF, Bloch DA et al. Radiographic assessment of progression in osteoarthritis. *Arthritis Rheum* 1987; **30**: 1214-25

28. Scott DL, Dacre JE, Greenwood A, Treasure I, Huskisson EC. Can we develop simple response criteria for slow acting anti-rheumatic drugs? *Ann Rheum Dis* 1990; **49**: 196-8

29. van der Heijde DMFM, van't Hoff MA, van Riel PLCM, van der Putte LBA. Judging disease activity in clinical practice in rheumatoid arthritis: first step in the development of a disease activity score. *Ann Rheum Dis* 1990; **49:** 916-20

January 1994

REFERRAL GUIDELINES FOR GPs - WHICH PATIENTS WITH LIMB JOINT ARTHRITIS SHOULD BE SENT TO A RHEUMATOLOGIST?

P Dieppe
ARC Professor of Rheumatology
Bristol University Rheumatology Unit
Bristol Royal Infirmary
Bristol
BS2 8HW

T Paine
Principal
Whiteladies Family Practice
Western College
Bristol; and Hospital Practitioner in Rheumatology
Bristol Royal Infirmary

INTRODUCTION

It has been estimated that some 10% of the population in the UK suffer from a rheumatic disorder. As the population is about 55 million, served by some 45,000 GPs but fewer than 350 rheumatologists, it follows that the majority of those with a rheumatic disease will never see a specialist. Surveys of the work load of general practitioners have shown that between 15 and 20% of all consultations are for disorders of the musculoskeletal system. Rheumatologists only see a small minority of these people, but this is not inappropriate, as most rheumatological diagnosis and much management is well within the scope of general practice.

However, there is a huge number of different disorders of the musculoskeletal system including some complex, multisystem life-threatening diseases, as well as some uncommon but important conditions, which need to be recognised and treated urgently. Furthermore, the management of patients with established rheumatic diseases can be complex and difficult, and require considerable knowledge, skill and experience. Rheumatologists have experience of and access to special investigations, such as modern imaging techniques and immunological tests, as well as the multidisciplinary team necessary for effective management.

It is important that general practitioners are able to recognise which people with musculoskeletal problems should be referred to the specialist, and that they appreciate how to make best use of the resources available. This will clearly depend on the expertise of the practitioner, and on availability of specialist services such as physiotherapy. Ideally, GPs should be able to develop a rapport with the local rheumatologists. 'Shared care' of patients, as well as dialogue about problems is then possible.

This article relates to peripheral joint disease in adults. It contains some approaches that might be of value to GPs who are uncertain about the need for referral, or are concerned that they might be missing an important diagnosis or complication of a rheumatic disease. Some 'red flags' have been included, to signal presentations that should cause concern.

PAIN IN ONE JOINT

Diagnosis

Pain in or around a single joint, particularly the knee or shoulder, commonly presents to GPs. The decision tree that needs to be followed to achieve a working diagnosis is shown in Fig 1. Through a combination of the history and physical examination it should be possible to delineate periarticular from articular problems; to further define the anatomical origin of periarticular disease (eg bursa, tendon, ligament etc); and to differentiate articular problems into those with a prominent inflammatory component (such as acute gout) and those of a mainly mechanical nature (such as a torn meniscus).

Red flags

Features which should cause concern include an inflamed joint with associated fever or constitutional disturbance (beware infection), and any joint which is 'locked' or so painful that movement is impossible. Any new case of undiagnosed acute inflammatory arthritis may need specialist investigation such as synovial fluid analysis for organisms and crystals, and severe mechanical derangements may require interventions such as examination under anaesthesia or arthroscopy. Severe pain at rest or at night, or pain that gets relentlessly worse over a period of days or weeks are also features that suggest the possibility of serious underlying pathology, such as a bone tumour.

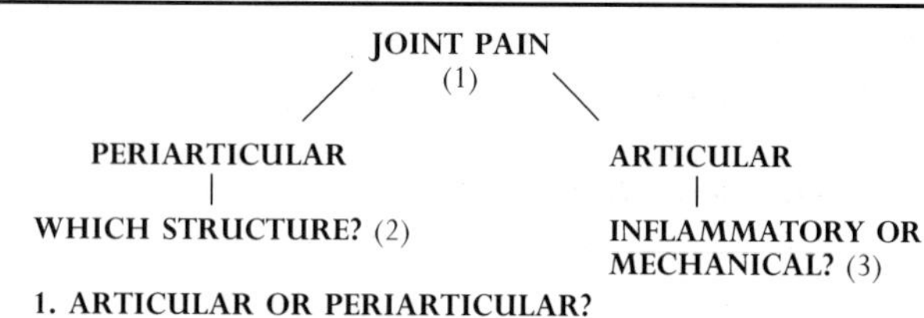

1. ARTICULAR OR PERIARTICULAR?

Is there any joint line tenderness?
Which movements cause pain?

Articular disease is usually characterised by joint line tenderness and pain at the end range of movement in any direction. Periarticular problems are characterised by point tenderness over the involved structure, and pain exacerbated by movements involving that structure.

2. WHICH PERIARTICULAR STRUCTURE?

Bursa?
Tendon?
Tendon sheath?
Ligament?
Other?

Careful examination can usually delineate the specific anatomical structure giving rise to periarticular pain.

3. INFLAMMATORY OR MECHANICAL?

Are there any signs of inflammation?
(warmth, redness, effusions etc)
Are there any features of a mechanical problem?
(locking, catching etc)

Figure 1. Sorting out the single painful joint.

PAIN IN MANY JOINTS

Diagnosis

The initial differentiation is similar to that for monoarticular disease - ie whether the patient has genuine articular disease or not. The next decision to be made is whether the problem is an inflammatory one such as rheumatoid disease or one of the many other inflammatory arthropathies, or whether the generalised joint pain is of a non-inflammatory nature (as in fibromyalgia, osteoarthritis, or arthralgia secondary to endocrine disorder, or other systemic disease). Examination is usually sufficient to establish this, although the signs of an early inflammatory arthropathy may be relatively subtle, and disorders such as fibromyalgia and polyarticular osteoarthritis can mimic an inflammatory disease. Screening with blood tests indicative of an inflammatory disorder, such as an ESR, blood viscosity or C-reactive protein, may help with the distinction. The next step in the differential diagnosis of polyarticular pain is to establish the pattern distribution and associated features; both the joint sites involved, and the presence or absence of disease in other systems provide key diagnostic clues (Table 1).

Red flags

Severe systemic symptoms should cause concern. High fevers, significant weight loss or a very ill patient should raise suspicion of underlying sepsis or malignancy; although these features can occur in active rheumatoid arthritis. Focal systemic signs, such as rashes, ocular inflammation, nodules or gastrointestinal disturbances can provide diagnostic clues, but also indicate systemic disease of significance. The other key 'red flags' of which the GP must be aware are the degree of pain and disability. There is some evidence that the severity of generalised rheumatic diseases and their impact on the individual, are often underestimated. Pain, particularly if it prevents sleep, and disability resulting in loss of ability to dress or toilet normally, for example, are issues that require urgent attention, and for which hospital based services may be required. Associated depression is a common complication of arthritis, making the burden of pain and disability much greater. Discussion of the significance of symptoms may reduce the need for analgesia.

Table 1.
POLYARTICULAR DISEASE - WHICH ARTHROPATHY IS IT ?

COMMON ARTHROPATHIES OF ADULTS IN THE UK - ANALYSIS BY AGE, SEX AND ASSOCIATED FEATURES

AGE	MALES	FEMALES
YOUNG	REACTIVE ARTHRITIS (conjunctivitis, urethritis rash)	SLE (rash, hair loss, Rayaud's, mouth ulcers, depression etc)
	ANKYLOSING SPONDYLITIS (iritis)	RHEUMATOID ARTHRITIS
	PSORIATIC ARTHRITIS (rash, nail pitting, scaly scalp)	
	ENTEROPATHIC ARTHROPATHY (Ulcerative Colitis; Crohn's)	
MIDDLE AGE	GOUT (obesity, alcohol, hypertension etc)	RHEUMATOID ARTHRITIS (nodules, anaemia etc)
		SICCA SYNDROME (dry eyes and mouth)
		GENERALISED OSTEOARTHRITIS
ELDERLY	POLYMYALGIA RHEUMATICA (malaise, weight loss, cranial arteritis)	
	PSEUDOGOUT (radiological chondrocalcinosis)	
	MALIGNANCY PRESENTING WITH JOINT PAIN	

Table 2.
COMMON REASONS FOR REFERRAL TO RHEUMATOLOGY CLINICS

- DIAGNOSTIC UNCERTAINTY
- MANAGEMENT UNCERTAINTY
- UNCONTROLLED SYMPTOMS
- INCREASING DISABILITY OR DEFORMITY
- DISEASE COMPLICATIONS
- PATIENT OR FAMILY ANXIETY
- PATIENT DEMAND FOR A SPECIALIST OPINION

IS REFERRAL ALWAYS NECESSARY ?

The main reasons for new referrals, as well as re-referral to the specialist clinic are shown in Table 2. Nobody would deny that patients with active progressive or disabling joint disease should be referred for specialist advice and help. Fortunately most patients with rheumatic disorders pose simpler diagnostic and management problems which do not require hospital referral.

Before referring a patient to a specialist clinic, it may be useful to consider the options available in general practice. Some of these options, and suggested actions, are outlined in Table 3. The GP should ask him/herself several questions before referring a patient. The first step is to consider whether, using the schemes outlined above, a clear diagnosis has been reached. If not, options prior to referral include seeking other opinions from within the practice, asking advice over the telephone, or looking at the literature. If a diagnosis is still not possible, and the condition is troublesome, referral is advisable. The degree of urgency will depend upon the presence or absence of any of the 'red flags'. If a confident diagnosis can be reached, the next decision concerns management options. These include the use of physical therapy, appliances, drug treatments, injections, counselling etc, and will depend on an assessment of the degree of pain, psychosocial problems and disability accompanying the problem, as well as the working diagnosis. Referral might be considered if the best options are not available to the GP, or when these prove inadequate.

WHICH PATIENTS DO RHEUMATOLOGISTS LIKE TO SEE?

Rheumatologists have much to offer patients with early inflammatory polyarthritis, particularly early rheumatoid disease. Such patients may benefit greatly from the counselling, education, joint protection techniques, physical therapy, specialist drug treatment and other interventions available to a rheumatology unit. A second category of disorders that might benefit particularly from specialist input are the systemic connective tissue diseases, including SLE, and vasculitis including giant cell arteritis; the range of treatments and benefits available to such patients has increased enormously in recent years. However, arguably the most important set of patients to be sent to a specialist are those with uncontrolled symptoms, or significant disability or psychosocial problems resulting from a rheumatic disorder or its complications, irrespective of the diagnosis. The prevention and treatment of the major consequences of musculoskeletal disorders are among the main aims of the rheumatologist.

Additionally, rheumatologists generally have a number of special investigative and treatment services available to them which can supplement those available to the GP, and improve patient care (Table 4).

SHARED CARE AND INTERACTION BETWEEN GPS AND SPECIALISTS

When a patient is referred from general practice, it may be helpful to have certain information made available to the hospital. Any blood tests done (particularly a full blood count, ESR or viscosity) and any radiographs (the films rather than the report!) can be of great value. If rheumatoid arthritis is suspected, for example, radiographs of the hands and feet, as well as the *titre* of rheumatoid factor (not just a 'positive' or 'negative' result) and degree of activity shown by the ESR can help with management decisions made in a hospital clinic.

The specialist should always come back to the GP with his/her impression of the diagnosis and prognosis

Table 3.
A 'PRE-REFERRAL' CHECK LIST

DIAGNOSTIC UNCERTAINTY?
Consider the schemes outlined above.

What is likely?
Am I likely to be missing anything urgent?

MANAGEMENT UNCERTAINTY?
Consider what modalities you have available:

Physiotherapy, OT, aids and appliances, soft tissue injections, local applications, counselling, education, self-care plans, psychological support, social support, drugs and surgery

STILL UNCERTAIN?

1. WHY NOT CONSULT THE LITERATURE?

There are many rheumatological textbooks available and the local postgraduate medical centre should be able to supply copies of relevant papers.

2. WHY NOT INVOLVE A PRACTICE COLLEAGUE?

An increasing number of GPs are becoming skilled in injection techniques and other types of rheumatological expertise.

3. WHY NOT USE THE TELEPHONE?

Many hospital services include a telephone 'hot line', or include access to a specialist nurse or other expert to advise patients and GPs, without having to wait for a hospital appointment.

Table 4.
WHAT HAS A RHEUMATOLOGIST GOT TO OFFER ?

DIAGNOSIS	– Skill with musculoskeletal examination
	– Synovial fluid analysis
	– Interpretation of immunological tests
	– Access to special imaging modalities
	– Tissue biopsy techniques
	– Experience of rare rheumatic disorders
TREATMENT	– Skills with counselling arthritis patients
	– Educational and self-help programmes
	– Therapeutic team of specialist paramedics
	– (ie specialised physio, OT, nurses etc)
	– Admission rights for ill patients (including those with active arthritis)
	– Ability to aspirate/inject any joint
	– Special knowledge of suppressive drugs (including optimum monitoring regimes)
	– Ability to assess arthritis (including activity and progression)
	– Access to combined orthopaedic clinics
	– Experience with rare disease complications
	– Special therapeutic interventions: eg radiocolloid injections, joint lavage, pulse therapy, experimental agents

Table 5.
A 'SHARED CARE' PLAN

Various models of 'shared care' exist. One of the simplest is to have a standard 'care card' for use by patient, GP and hospital rheumatology service.

Such a card might include the following information:

1. Identification (SS and hospital numbers etc)
2. Relevant diagnoses
3. Key investigation results (eg RF positive)
4. Current management plan:
   - Self-care
   - Physical therapy/exercises
   - ADL
   - Medication
5. Changes that require action, eg:
   - What to do if the condition 'flares'
   - What to watch for with medication
   - What to do if disability worsens
6. Contacts/enquiry service:
   - GP contact/telephone number
   - Hospital contact/telephone number (eg arthritis support nurse)

and a suggested care plan (Table 5), as well as the results of any tests done and a list of any interventions carried out. Many patients with disorders like rheumatoid arthritis will need continuing shared care, and a shared care card held by the patient may be of value in the interaction between hospital and the GP. Exploring other models of shared care, and other systems to help communication and decision making between community and hospital based departments for these very common disorders is becoming increasingly important in the new NHS. A variety of such models are being explored, and many rheumatologists have established special links with local GPs, thereby improving the quality of care available to their patients.

REFERRAL GUIDELINES

Referral guidelines are being considered by Hospital Trusts and GPs throughout the UK. There is clearly no single plan which can be used by everyone. The population demography, specialist time available, and nature and balance of the support teams in hospitals and the community, varies greatly in different parts of the country. Appropriate referral guidelines, and plans for shared care will therefore have to be developed locally. However, the clinical problems are similar everywhere, and the basis of good practice remains the ability to make the correct diagnosis, and to deliver the appropriate care. Some of the principles outlined in this report may be of value to clinicians struggling with the problem at a local level.

January 1994

OSTEOARTHRITIS - CLINICAL FEATURES & MANAGEMENT

C W Hutton
Consultant Rheumatologist
Mt Gould Hospital
Plymouth

THE NATURE OF OSTEOARTHRITIS

Osteoarthritis is a condition characterised by hyaline cartilage damage, changes in subchondral bone of sclerosis and osteophyte formation. There is considerable controversy about the mechanisms and significance of these changes. More understanding may, in future, enable interventions that reduce the destructive changes, slow or even reverse progression. However presently there are no interventions which are known to alter the long term outcome. There are however many possible approaches to ameliorate the clinical problems the disease causes.

Epidemiological and clinical observation emphasise the diversity of the condition and its natural history. Changes are common in the population but relatively few have symptoms. Even fewer have a painful disabling disease that presents to doctors.

GROUPS AND SUBGROUPS

Unlike most joint diseases there is no shortage of known conditions that can cause osteoarthritis. This has led to the concept of osteoarthritis being a final common pathway of many different joint problems. It is seen as the process that a joint undergoes as it responds to injury. Elements of this may be adaptive, others are maladaptive. The balance results in stable non-progressive and often asymptomatic disease or progression to joint destruction.

In many people the disease occurs spontaneously and no previous cause can be identified. In these people there are however associations and patterns in primary, idiopathic osteoarthritis. Its incidence increases with increasing age. Some joints are often involved whereas others are rarely affected. Different patterns suggest there may be subgroups within primary osteoarthritis. The presence of multiple joint involvement suggests some people have a generalised osteoarthritis. The commonest distribution is bilateral involvement of the thumb carpometacarpal joint, the interphalangeal joints, the knee and metatarsophalangeal joint of the great toe. This group in turn has been subdivided depending on the presence of bony swellings on the dorsum of the distal interphalangeal joints: Heberden's nodes.

Table I.
SECONDARY OSTEOARTHRITIS

Developmental abnormality	Congenital dislocation of the hip
Trauma	Intra-articular fracture
Previous arthritis	Rheumatoid, infection
Metabolic disease	Haemochromatosis

The subgroup, generalised nodal osteoarthritis, is particularly common in women. Its onset is in middle age often with painful inflamed Heberden's nodes. These may settle leaving a bony swelling. The onset around the menopause suggests an endocrine cause but there is no evidence of oestrogen-dependent effects. Whether hand osteoarthritis is associated with an increased risk of developing major joint disease is still unknown. An apparent association may be coincident involvement of common independent sites, and may be better termed a mono arthritis multiplex.

The concept of generalised disease is helpful clinically as an unusual pattern of joint involvement should suggest a possible secondary cause. Prominent metacarpophalangeal joint disease may be associated with haemochromatosis and pyrophosphate deposition. Shoulder involvement also suggests pyrophosphate deposition. It may also indicate that a second different inflammatory arthritis, such as rheumatoid, is developing in someone with pre-existing osteoarthritis.

RELATIONSHIP WITH JOINT USE

Confusion remains about how use influences the development of osteoarthritis. The classic study of Hadler suggests that use influences at least the pattern

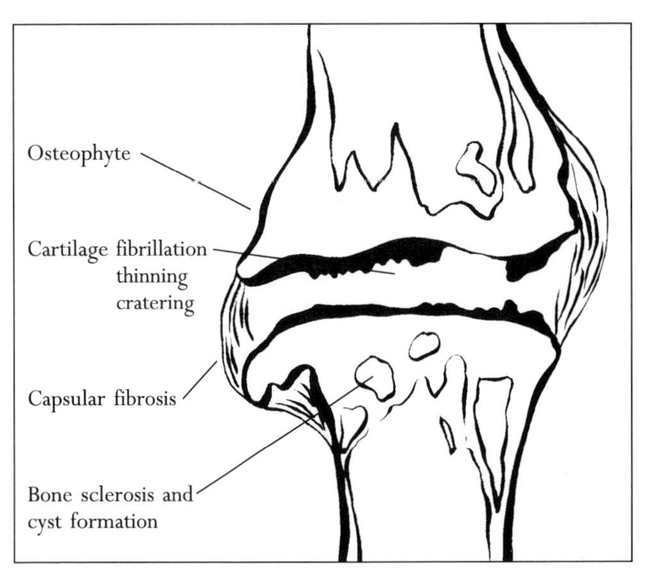

Figure 1. Pathological features of OA.

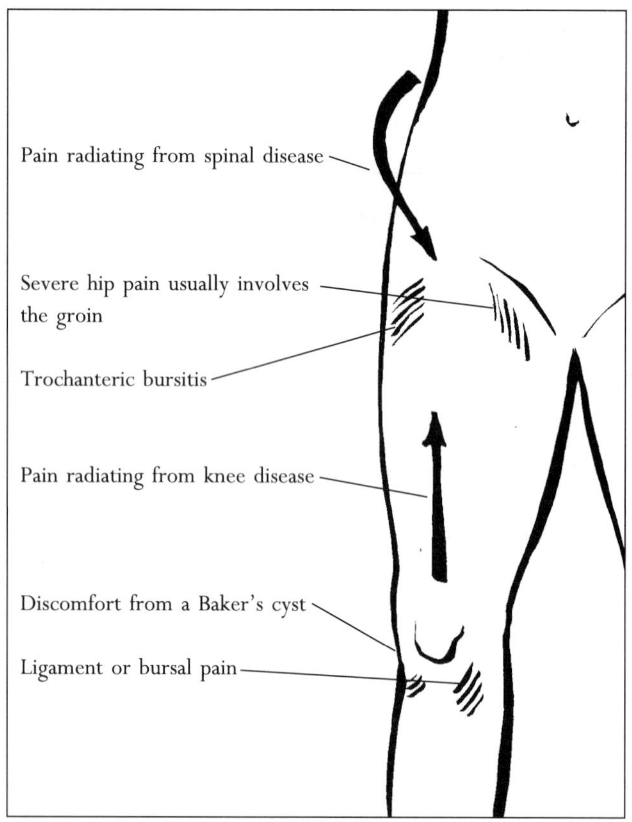

Figure 2. Pain around the hip and knee joints.

of involvement. Severe trauma with intra-articular fracture produces rapid onset disease. It is unclear what the tolerance of a normal joint to peak or repetitive loading is, what happens if the person is trained to high fitness and what happens if there is already joint damage. Nevertheless the importance of maintaining muscle means activity should be encouraged.

CLINICAL PROBLEMS

The two major clinical problems are pain and impaired function.

Pain

Hyaline cartilage has no nerve supply but many of the other structures in the joint are richly innervated although the mechanisms of pain are only partially understood. The pain is often described as worse with joint movement or weight bearing. There may be severe pain on initial movement that eases and then worsens with continuing activity. The pain may be localised or be more diffuse. It may be referred to an unaffected joint. Hip pain may present with knee pain or vice versa.

Initially pain may be variable, with periods that are symptom free. Sudden exacerbations that may be extremely severe may occur. This may be associated with joint swelling and a coincident episode of some other type of arthritis must be considered, such as acute pseudogout. Single joint presentation must initially be investigated as a subacute infection and diagnosed as osteoarthritis by exclusion.

Pain is associated with soft tissue structures like ligament and tendon insertions and bursae. This gives important treatable pain patterns different with each joint. Examples are the lateral pain of the trochanteric bursitis in the hip and the medial focal pain of an anserine bursitis of the knee *(Figure 2)*.

Table 2. MANAGEMENT PRINCIPLES
Educate
Correct contributing factors
Correct deformity
Control pain
Correct contributing lifestyle factors
Anticipate future problems

Later in disease pain becomes constant; it may be described as burning and may be associated with night pain. This should be distinguished from pain on movement at night. Both, however, produce sleep disturbance, sleep deprivation and amplify the pain problem.

Dysfunction and handicap

The loss of function produced by an osteoarthritic joint varies with the joint. The handicap that results will reflect a multitude of interacting factors. This means that apparently identical joint pathology may give a wide spectrum of clinical problems. In the leg instability, a sense of instability, and joint locking combine with pain to decrease mobility. In the arm weakened power of grip and problems with dexterous movement may make it difficult to continue to work.

Assessment

The diagnosis is by exclusion of other diseases and is confirmed by radiography. Three clinical questions need to be considered:
(1) Is there a contributing or complicating disease?
(2) In particular is there pyrophosphate or urate crystal deposition?
and (3) Is there a resultant or contributing mechanical factor?

Look for instability of the joint, leg length inequality, marked valgus or varus deformity. Simple corrective orthosis may reduce pain. Hallux rigidus may be made less symptomatic by a rocker sole.

Is there associated deformity and muscle wasting?

Much of the disability results from secondary weakness which if partially corrected may markedly reduce handicap. Effective motivation of the patient to improve muscle power is a major challenge to the clinician.

Management

As no treatment can influence the disease progression, treatment might seem pointless. There is a wide-spread sense of nihilism on one side and misplaced enthusiasm for fashions on the other. Most interventions are untested, reflecting the difficulty of doing long-term studies in a complex variable condition. Clinical management must be based on being logical and not doing harm.

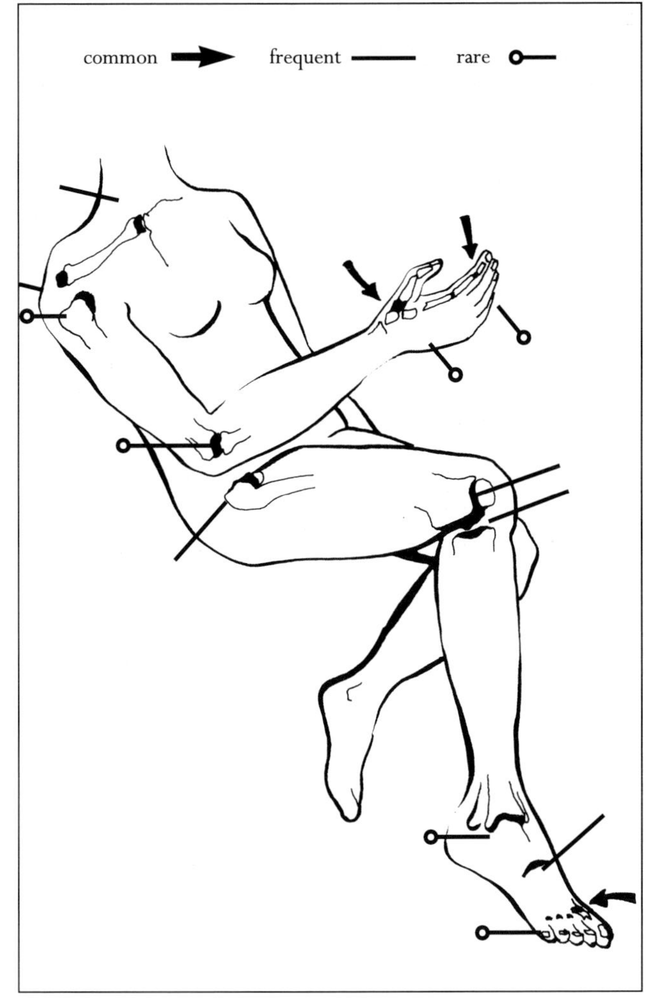

Figure 3. Distribution of joints involved in primary osteoarthritis.

The principles are the same as managing any chronic disease. Educate the patient to understand the problem. Identify realistic expectations for interventions. Simple understanding of the diagnosis and low probability of a crippling outcome will reassure many. It is important for the patient to create a sense of control over his or her disease.

Second is to correct any contributing factors which have been identified – the primary cause, the dysfunction with muscle strengthening exercises and orthotics. A walking stick of the correct height held in the contralateral hand and a non-worn ferrule will allow weight to be deflected on to the good leg. Correct flexion deformities; with exercise or possibly using hydrotherapy; a splinting system such as continuous passive movement that gradually works the joint straight, or flowtron splints that squeeze it straight. Unfortunately contractures recur readily as enthusiasm for maintenance exercise has a short half life! Emphasise the importance of muscle strengthening. The third objective is to control pain. The doctor or therapist should work with the patient to analyse their pain and work towards a 'pain strategy'. There is a set of modalities to try. Simple low toxicity analgesia, possibly in combination, should be tried first. Anti-inflammatory drugs are then added even though it is often regarded as a non-inflammatory condition. If the drugs have a poor effect they should be discontinued. Different strategies suit different individuals. The dilemma of giving long-term non-steroidals to patients with a history of peptic ulcer with or without use of gastro-protection remains. Evidence is beginning to support using misoprostol, H2 blockers or proton pump blockers with non steroidals in the elderly. However this needs continuous review as new trial evidence becomes available.

Joint effusions are common, particularly in the knee. They may cause discomfort, be associated with pain and are associated with reflex quadriceps wasting. This sets up a cycle of weakness and instability. The effusion may be inflammatory but often has a low cell count and probably results from changes in the fluid flows in the synovium. They often respond to intra-articular injection of crystalline steroids such as triamcinolone, but they often recur. Repeated injection in the joint must be done with caution as concern about promoting collapse of the subchondral bone remains. Intra-articular injection is commonly used in joints to reduce pain, with widespread anecdotal evidence of transient effectiveness. Great care must be taken not to damage periarticular structures as the joint may be very disorganised and fibrosed making location of the needle difficult.

Correct other contributing lifestyle factors... encourage exercise and control of weight.

Anticipate future problems particularly in relation to potential major joint surgery. One common difficulty with lower limb surgery is leg ulceration, so care is necessary to prevent ulcers.

Surgery

The outlook for patients with severe hip and knee osteoarthritis has been transformed by arthroplasty. At other large joints surgery is possible but not so well established. Elbow and shoulder replacement are increasingly routine. In the foot and hand arthroplasty is less well established.

The indication is uncontrolled pain. In the hip this is often clear, but knee pain is more difficult. It seems to phase more gradually from tolerable to intolerable. Milder disease is extremely common. With monoarticular joint disease and a considerable expectation of activity after surgery, loosening may occur early. So even though the procedures are technically feasible there is concern that early surgery may increase the risk of difficult later revision. Procedures such as osteotomy may buy time in a younger patient. In elderly patients with multiple pathology the risks of the procedure, particularly perioperative vascular events, need to be weighed carefully against potential benefits. Despite anti-thrombotic prophylaxis young people can die from pulmonary embolism.

In the smaller joints interventions are more difficult. The various operations available for hallux rigidus underline the varied results. Controlled studies are needed. Various procedures including arthroplasty, tendon reorientation, fusion or scaphoid exision have been proposed for thumb base arthritis, but should

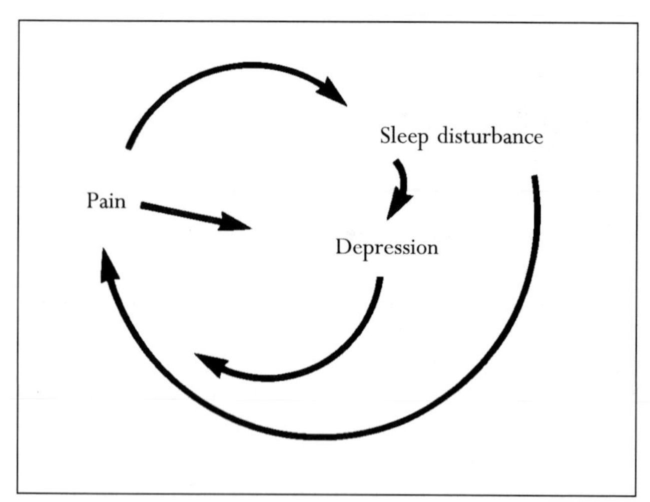

Figure 4. Pain amplification in osteoarthritis

be considered only in persistent severe, painful disease not responding to intra-articular injection.

The future

The outlook for osteoarthritic patients is changing. At last the conceptual challenge of influencing the natural history of the process has been accepted and research is gearing up to understand the biology in a way that should lead to therapeutic advances. However, even with more effective intervention, the principles of care will be similar to those we should follow today.

FURTHER READING

Hadler NM, Gillings DB, Imbus HR, Levitin PM, Makuc D, Utsinger PD, Yount WJ, Slusser D, Moskovitz N. Hand structure and function in an industrial setting. Influence of three patterns of stereotyped repetitive usage. *Arthritis & Rheumatism* 1978; **21(2)**: 1019-1025.

Bland JH, Cooper SM. Osteoarthritis. A review of the cell biology involved and evidence for reversibility. Management rationally related to known genesis and pathophysiology. *Seminars in Arthritis & Rheumatism* 1984; **14(2)**: 106-133.

Peyron JG. Epidemiologic and etiologic approach of osteoarthritis. *Seminars in Arthritis & Rheumatism* 1979; **8(4)**: 288-306.

Sokoloff L. *The pathology of degenerative joint disease.* Chicago University Press, (1969).

January 1995

RHEUMATOID ARTHRITIS

D J Walker
Consultant Rheumatologist
Musculoskeletal Unit
Freeman Hospital
High Heaton
Newcastle upon Tyne NE7 7DN

The term rheumatoid arthritis (RA) is used to describe an inflammatory polyarthritis that is both enormously variable in every clinical and investigational facet yet at the same time presents a striking clinical pattern which is easily recognizable. It is therefore not surprising that historically the first good evidence for rheumatoid arthritis comes from paintings, particularly those of Peter Paul Rubens, where the classical hand changes can be seen. Rheumatoid arthritis can vary from a temporary problem causing pain and stiffness in the joints for a few months and resolving completely, through to the severe disabling destructive arthritis that confines sufferers to wheelchairs. Both of the extremes are rare and most patients will follow a relapsing and remitting course over many years.

This variation in the severity of the disease causes major problems in defining the disease. The definitions largely depend on the summation of different features that add up to a confident diagnosis. The threshold at which a diagnosis will be accepted may vary according to the opinion of the clinician. The more features demanded for diagnosis will give more homogeneous disease, but will also tend to include only the more severe end of the spectrum. Similarly inclusion of mild cases with few features will diminish the diagnostic certainty. The most widely used diagnostic criteria are those of the American Rheumatism Association 1987 (Table 1). With these criteria most estimates suggest that approximately 1% of the population are affected (prevalence). It affects females more than males in a proportion of approximately 3:1, and it has a peak onset in the 40's and 50's with onset being rare below the age of twenty and above the age of eighty.

TABLE I
The revised ARA criteria of 1987*

Criterion	Definition
1. Morning Stiffness	Duration > 1 h lasting > 6 weeks
2. Arthritis of at least 3 areas	Soft tissue swelling or exudation > 6 weeks
3. Arthritis of hand joints	Wrist, metacarpophalangeal joints or proximal interphalangeal joints lasting > 6 weeks
4. Symmetrical arthritis	At least one area, lasting > 6 weeks
5. Rheumatoid nodules	As observed by physician
6. Serum rheumatoid factor	As assessed by a method positive in less than 5% of control subjects
7. Radiographic changes	As seen on anteroposterior films of wrists and hands

* Presence of 4 criteria = Diagnosis of Rheumatoid Arthritis

The clustering of rheumatoid arthritis within families shows that genetic factors are important. The best estimates of identical twin concordance rates are around 16% with diazygotic twin concordance rates of around 5%, being similar to that between siblings. A substantial proportion of the genetic risk of RA seems to lie in the HLA region with the association with HLA-DR4. Indeed, added to the risk of being female it may account for the entire risk. There are clearly environmental factors in the onset and continuation of rheumatoid arthritis but despite extensive research to implicate infective agents none has been consistent.

PATHOGENESIS

The main pathology that occurs in rheumatoid arthritis is thickening and inflammation of the synovial membrane which becomes infiltrated with lymphocytes in the deeper layers (Figure 1). Puzzlingly it is polymorphs that are the predominant cells found in the synovial fluid. The synovial lining layer becomes continuous with vascular tissue, termed pannus, that grows over the cartilage and causes erosion into the bone. This results in degeneration of the cartilage and ultimately of the joint.

CLINICAL FEATURES

Rheumatoid arthritis in its full blown form typically shows the pattern of symmetrical peripheral polyarthritis with very frequent involvement of MCP's, PIP's and wrists, as shown in Figure 2, and it is this pattern of arthritis that helps differentiate it from other forms of arthritis, in particular the other inflammatory conditions such as the sero-negative spondarthritides. Mode of onset can be very variable and so in early arthritic disease it is a difficult diagnosis to exclude.

The degree of non-articular involvement will also vary. It may, rarely, for instance, precede the onset of

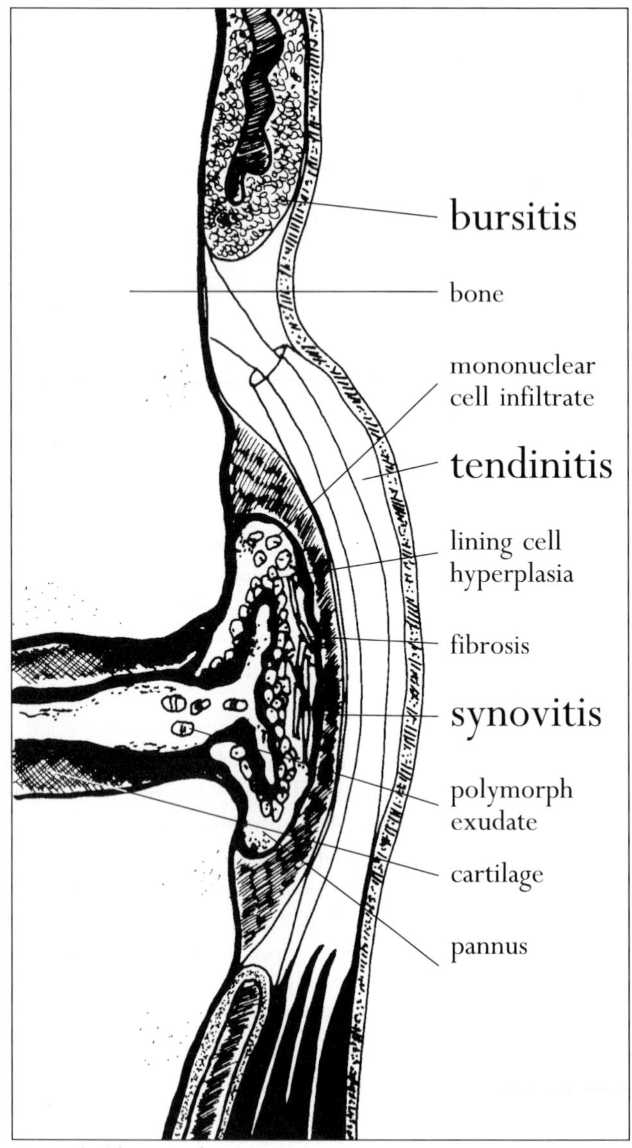

Figure 1. Rheumatoid synovitis.

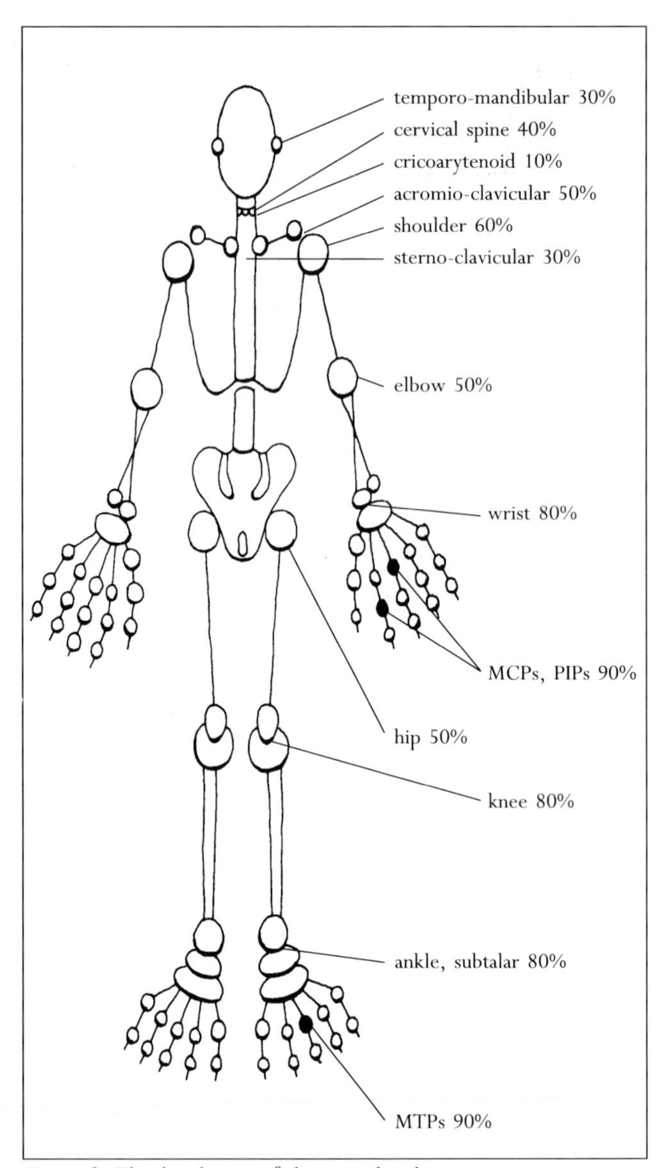

Figure 2. The distribution of rheumatoid arthritis.

articular disease. In some cases there may be some confusion between the diagnosis of rheumatoid arthritis and systemic lupus erythematosus because of multisystem involvement (Figure 3).

Certain subgroups are also recognizable from within RA (eg disease that remains substantially confined to hands and feet and has a good prognosis) and proximal onset in the elderly that can be confused with polymyalgia rheumatica.

Other features, as well as distribution, are helpful in differentiating RA from degenerative arthritis. Of particular importance is the duration of morning stiffness which will tend to be prolonged (greater than half an hour) in rheumatoid and brief in degenerative arthritis, although the quality of the stiffness may be worse in the OA group. This is very difficult to measure. Typically a patient with degenerative arthritis will stiffen up during the day after any period of rest, whereas that patient with an inflammatory condition, once the morning stiffness has worn off, will tend to be free of stiffness though it often recurs later in the evening. A good discriminating question relates to stiffness after sitting down for lunch, when the RA patient will be going into the best part of the day and the OA patient will have stiffened up because of the immobility.

Once RA is established, secondary degenerative symptoms start, so that stiffening on rest will become a feature. In late disease if the inflammatory component dies down then the patient will have OA-type symptoms in an RA distribution. Joints then have entered a final common pathway of degeneration.

The relationship between symptoms and use of the joint will tend to be more marked in the degenerative group and this arthritis will therefore be more predictable to the patient. By contrast in rheumatoid arthritis the description of having "good days and bad days" is more pronounced than the relationship to use, although joints will tend to be painful when stressed.

EXAMINATION

Examination of the joints will reveal the soft boggy swelling of synovitis, as opposed to the hard knobbly bony outgrowths of osteoarthritis. The exception to

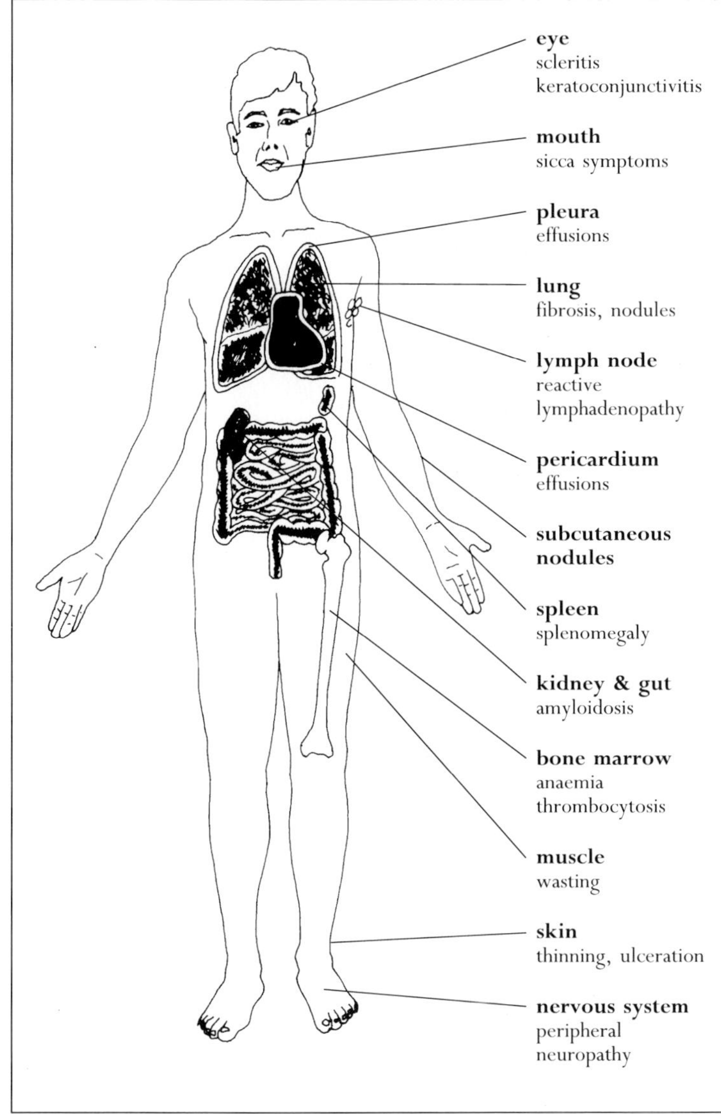

Figure 3. Multisystem involvement in rheumatoid arthritis.

this is the knee where effusions are common, although there is a subtly different feel between the thin wall effusion of OA and the thick synovitis of rheumatoid. Crepitus will also be more marked in the degenerative joint, especially in early disease.

Synovitis may be found at sites other than the joints, for instance the flexor tendon sheaths of the forearm and hand (Figure 1). Other extra-articular features of rheumatoid occur, for example, rheumatoid nodules which tend to occur at sites of pressure particularly over the extensor aspects of the forearm.

INVESTIGATION

A confident diagnosis may be arrived at without the use of any investigation and there are no pathognomic tests. Investigations, therefore, add to the overall picture, like brush strokes to a painting and give some ideas as to the prognosis.

Rheumatoid factor

This is immunoglobulin directed against human IgG and the class of immunoglobulin usually tested for is IgM. There are various different commercial rheumatoid factor tests, all with slightly varied sensitivity and specificity but rheumatoid factor of sufficient concentration to be considered positive will be found in roughly 70% to 80% of RA patients seen in hospital. This percentage will decrease if milder forms are recruited, as for instance would be the case in general practice and would be higher in more severe cases such as patients requiring joint replacement surgery. High titre rheumatoid factor positivity broadly correlates with more severe disease but by no means without exception, and false positive rheumatoid factors will occur in many conditions including acute infections (eg infectious mononucleosis). False positive rheumatoid factor tests like other auto-antibodies will tend to increase with age.

Other blood tests

Acute phase reactants are increased in acute phases of the disease and broadly correlate with disease activity. The most frequently measured are ESR, plasma viscosity and C-reactive protein. Patients with persistently elevated acute phase reactants tend to have a worse prognosis. The blood count itself may also show abnormalities, in particular the platelet count will tend to be elevated in proportion to disease activity and the haemoglobin will be depressed often to around the 10g mark in females. Anaemia is very common but at the same time patients with rheumatoid arthritis taking anti-inflammatories and particularly menstruating women who are more border-line for iron reserves, are at risk of developing an iron deficiency anaemia on top of the anaemia of chronic disease. Most tests for iron status are unreliable in rheumatoid arthritis and currently serum ferritin is the best way of assessing iron deficiency, with a value under 60mg/l indicating iron deficiency and over 60mg/l indicating active disease. Ferritin acts as an acute phase reactant and so will tend to be high when the anaemia of chronic disease is worse, but is also a measure of iron stores although the normal range quoted for ferritin is too low to be useful in RA.

Radiology

X-rays of joints are helpful both diagnostically and in monitoring progression. Conventionally hand and feet radiographs are used as these joints are affected early in the disease, many joints are observed for few x-rays and the patterns of arthritis can be observed. Diagnostically x-rays are helpful in that the first change in rheumatoid arthritis is periarticular osteopenia, perhaps with some soft tissue swelling, whereas the first change in degenerative arthritis will tend to be subchondral sclerosis. Radiologically, rheumatoid arthritis progresses with marginal erosion, loss of joint space and ultimately secondary degenerative change. The cervical spine is of particular importance because of the risk of atlanto-axial subluxation and thereby risk of spinal cord compression. Any RA patient who is going to endoscopy or surgery should have cervical spine x-rays available.

PERCEPTION OF POTENTIAL BENEFIT	PATIENT	PERCEPTION OF RISKS
Kg		Kg
Increased by:- worse disease - - erosion - sero +ve - symptoms worse handicap Perception of effectiveness of drug (expectation)	How do they want to play it? "I'm still coping" "This isn't right - do something" Their perceptions of risks/benefits "I don't like taking drugs" Special needs (eg keep job for 2 years etc)	Perception of risks of drugs:- Figures available but to them it is 0% or 100% Inconvenience of monitoring

COMMENTS

(1) Perception affected by experience. Not hard and fast.
(2) You never know what they would have been like if you hadn't used drugs.
(3) Solution requires discussion - but information given affects CHOICE.
(4) Keep treatment in proportion to problem
(5) There is a spectrum of opinion.
(6) Don't leave it too late.

Figure 4. Intervention in RA

While neck problems tend to occur in patients with severe peripheral arthritis, any RA patient could have subluxation.

Histology

Histology is rarely necessary and not diagnostically specific in rheumatoid arthritis. Biopsy is mainly useful in excluding tuberculosis in monoarticular onset of disease. Histology of a rheumatoid nodule is characteristic and as near to pathognomic as one can get.

TREATMENT

It is most important that a patient should gain a realistic prognosis and expectation of treatment, otherwise they will be disappointed. The treatment of rheumatoid arthritis demands a multidisciplinary team approach. Education has been shown to be beneficial in outcome, understanding going a long way towards having control. The balance between exercise and rest is also important. Acutely inflamed joints require rest but strong muscles protect joints and maintaining a good range of movement is important. Rest is recommended during the acute phase but as soon as this has settled down, exercise of the joint using maximum range and minimum weight bearing should be undertaken. Swimming is the classical low weight-bearing exercise recommended for people with arthritis. Similarly, splinting of painful joints either to maintain them in the position of function, such as straightening the knee, or to support them during activity, eg fabric wrist splint, can be helpful.

DRUG TREATMENT

This is conventionally divided into first-line and second-line drugs. First line treatment is purely for symptomatic control. Nearly all patients with significant inflammatory arthritis will take non-steroidal anti-inflammatories (NSAIDs). There are very many NSAIDs on the market and they show great variation both in terms of therapeutic effect (efficacy) and side-effects (toxicity). The variation in patients far outweighs any variations in the drugs and therefore finding the best drug is an individual exercise. Patients should find an anti-inflammatory that they can tolerate and which does most for their arthritis. They should then take this in the minimum dose required to control their arthritis. In mild cases, or in patients in a very good phase of the disease, it may be possible to stop the anti-inflammatory medication. Even patients who are reluctant to take tablets should be encouraged to explore anti-inflammatories, partly so that they know what therapy they are choosing not to take and partly so they will know which drug to take should they have worse trouble later on.

Patients whose symptoms are not adequately controlled by anti-inflammatories should be given straightforward analgesics to take as well, starting with the simplest and safest (ie paracetamol) and increasing to codeine and paracetamol combinations. It is rarely necessary to go above this but occasionally stronger analgesics may be required at night to facilitate sleep. Under these circumstances anti-inflammatories should be taken regularly as prescribed and the analgesics as required. As with all interventions in medicine, the perceived benefits of the treatment should outweigh the perceived risks of treatment. This is not always an easy balance (Figure 4).

Second-line drugs

For patients not adequately controlled on first-line medication, second-line medication can be justified. Satisfactory control will of course vary from patient to patient, as will the patient's willingness to accept the risk of side-effects. The use of second-line drugs will usually be the patient's decision, based on the information they have received both from the doctor primarily involved in their treatment and from other sources. Signs that the patient is doing badly (eg progression of x-ray changes, persistently high acute phase response) would also be an indication for second-line therapy. The individual second-line drugs are covered in detail elsewhere in this book. Perceptions amongst rheumatologists vary considerably over the perceived toxicity and effectiveness of these drugs. Indeed the conventional medical assessment of double-blind placebo controlled trials is better at defining the side-effect profile of the drugs than their effectiveness.

Cortico-steroids

Steroids can be used in different ways in rheumatoid arthritis. Intra-articular injections can give good but temporary symptomatic relief within the joint injected, lasting usually about six weeks. This can be useful if one or two joints are troublesome and the patient can be tided over into a better phase of the disease. It can also be useful if the patient wishes to be better for a specific reason, such as a family wedding. A particular joint would not normally be reinjected within three months. There is legitimate argument as to whether injection of joints may result in progression of the disease and they should only therefore be used for specific reasons.

Intra-muscular injections of depo steroid can similarly be used to give temporary relief from symptoms, usually lasting for approximately two weeks. They may be used either as a trial to assess the responsiveness of the arthritis to steroids; to tide the patient over a particularly bad phase that is affecting many joints; or when a patient wishes to be better for a particular reason. An intra-muscular injection is to be preferred to a short course of oral steroids as there is less danger of the patient ending up on long-term treatment and the onset is quick and the tail off gradual, not resulting in rebound flare.

The use of a short course of steroid, as is used for asthma, going from 40mg to zero over a week, is inappropriate. Its use in asthma is justified by the threat to life and the expectation that a week later the acute exacerbation will no longer be there. The arthritis will almost certainly be present a week later and all that has been achieved is to remind the patient what it would be like not to have the arthritis.

The use of long-term low dose steroid (less than 10mg a day of prednisolone) can be justified when it is the next least toxic drug available for treatment. The decision should be made according to the patient's response that the benefit gained outweighs the risks of long-term use of steroids. Under these circumstances the steroids should be used in the minimum dose that produces sufficient benefit.

Intra-venous steroid boluses have also been used in arthritis and can be very effective. They do however occasionally result in catastrophies such as silent perforation of the gut, avascular necrosis of bone or cardiogenic complications which have restricted their usefulness.

Other therapies

A combination of cytotoxic drugs, as used in the treatment of lymphoma, has been tried in resistant cases of arthritis and they may be effective in treatment of the extra-articular manifestations but are usually ineffective against articular disease. Other novel treatments are under investigation. These may be aimed at the immune system, as with anti-CD4 monoclonal antibodies, aimed at the inflammatory mediator cascade such as anti-TNF alpha and may in future be directed against adhesion molecules and the migration of inflammatory cells to the sites of inflammation.

Alternative/complementary therapy

In a condition such as rheumatoid arthritis where conventional therapy is not offering a cure, it is very common for patients to try alternative/complementary therapy and one can imagine how difficult it would be to ignore the possibility that they might help even if one were sceptical. In general it is not worth dissuading patients from taking such therapy and many do get significant benefit for whatever reason. I think that patients should be encouraged to be logical in trying non-prescribed medicines, making sure they change only one thing at a time and being critical about what the treatment has done for them. Exclusion diets are an example of patient driven interventions which don't have major financial consequences and for patients who express an interest can have very positive benefits. The patient is doing something about their own arthritis rather than being in the hands of 'doctors'.

JOINT REPLACEMENT SURGERY

Joint replacement surgery is a very effective way of relieving pain and improving function in a joint that has been damaged beyond repair (ie failed medical management). Replacement of multiple joints has been effective at keeping patients ambulant even at long-term follow up. The threshold for operation will vary from surgeon to surgeon and will be performed when the surgeon perceives that the risks of surgery are outweighed by the potential benefit. The potential benefit is increased the more severe the symptoms are. Thresholds for well tried joints such as hips and knees will be lower than for less well tried replacements such as elbows and shoulders.

PROGNOSIS

To be able to predict the prognosis of rheumatoid arthritis would be immensely useful in justifying more aggressive treatment. Unfortunately despite many different factors that tend to be associated with a particular prognosis (Table 2), none are sufficiently reliable to be useful in justifying such treatment. Table 2 shows the features associated with a bad outcome. It is however possible to identify patients who have most of these features and end up with a good outcome, and vice versa.

TABLE 2 Features suggesting a bad prognosis
Persistently high acute phase response
High titre rheumatoid factor
Erosion during first year
Family history of RA
Possession of HLA-DR4
Extra-articular disease
Insidious onset
Being female
Low educational attainment
(Doing badly)!

FURTHER READING

Maddison P J, Isenberg D A, Woo P and Glass D N. *Oxford Text Book of Rheumatology*, Oxford Medical Publications.

January 1995

THE MORTALITY OF RHEUMATOID ARTHRITIS

D L Scott
St Bartholomew's Hospital
West Smithfield
London EC1A 7BE

D P M Symmons
The Medical School
University of Birmingham
Birmingham B15 2TJ

NO-ONE THINKS THAT RHEUMATOID ARTHRITIS IS A FATAL ILLNESS. NONETHELESS IT SHORTENS LIFE. THE FACTORS INFLUENCING ITS INCREASED MORTALITY ARE COMPLEX; THEY INCLUDE THE DISEASE ITSELF, ITS TREATMENT, AND PROBLEMS RESULTING FROM CHRONIC ILL HEALTH. THE METHODS USED TO CALCULATE MORTALITY VARY AND THERE IS DEBATE ABOUT ITS CAUSES AND SIGNIFICANCE. THIS REVIEW SUMMARISES THE MAJOR STUDIES, AND ATTEMPTS TO PLACE THEM IN A RELEVANT CONTEXT WITHOUT HIDING THEIR PROBLEMS AND AREAS OF DISAGREEMENT.

METHODS OF MEASURING MORTALITY

There have been 13 major studies of mortality in rheumatoid arthritis in the last 30 years, and the results are summarised in *Table 1*. They differ in selection of patients, diagnostic criteria, methods used to establish the cause of death, length and completeness of follow-up, and the choice of control groups. Two major factors affecting these studies are the relative duration of rheumatoid disease and the method of statistical analysis. Most studies look at cohorts of patients with rheumatoid arthritis of varying and unstated duration. They assume mortality is similar whether it occurs early or late in the course of the disease. Only Rasker and Cosh (12) followed patients from within a few months of the onset of rheumatoid arthritis; early deaths were due to infection and vasculitis, whereas fatal amyloidosis did not occur until 7 years after onset. Prior and her colleagues (17) also showed that causes of death and mortality rates differ in early and late disease. In calculations of altered mortality patterns the observed numbers and causes of death in rheumatoid patients are compared with the "expected" experience in people without the disease. Expected figures may be derived from age and sex matched controls (5, 6, 7, 8) or from age and sex specific rates in the general population, allowing for person-years at risk. The selection of suitable controls is difficult (16). Official mortality statistics for the general population may produce problems if the rheumatoid patients are not a representative sample in terms of occupation and social class.

There are three main statistical methods for comparing observed and expected numbers of death.

(i) PROPORTIONAL MORTALITY

Deaths from a particular cause are expressed as a percentage of the total number of deaths. This method, which was used in all the early studies (1, 3, 4, 18), causes problems because the figures must add up to 100%. For example, if 1,000 rheumatoid patients and 1,000 controls are studied for 10 years there may be 200 deaths in rheumatoid patients and 100 deaths in the controls. Examining deaths due to one cause, such as malignant

Table 1 **Methodological differences in the mortality studies of rheumatoid arthritis**

Ref	First Author	Size of Series	No of deaths	(%)	Category	Diagnostic Criteria	Follow-up Mean	(rge) yrs	Control Group	Completeness of follow-up	Cause of death	ICD
1	Cobb (1953)	583	137	(23)	IP	NS	10	(-)	GP	NS	DO PM	NO
2	Reah (1963)	185	80	(43)	IP	ARA	12	(11-14)	None	100%	DC	NO
3	Duthie (1964)	307	72	(24)	IP	NS	9	(-)	GP	90%	NS	NO
4	Uddin (1970)	475	94	(20)	OP	ARA	NS	(4-10)	GP	93%	DC & PM	NO
5	Isomaki (1975)		122	(12)			3					NO
6	Koota (1977)	1000	176	(18)	OP	ARA	5		CC	100%	DC	NO
7	Mutru (1985)		256	(27)			10					8th revision
8	Monson (1976)	1035	670	(67)	IP	NS	NS	(12-42)	CC.GP	73%	DC	7th revision
9	Linos (1980)	521	143	(27)	GP	ARA	NS	(1-25)	LP	NS	DC	NO
10	Lewis (1980)	311	46	(15)	OP	ARA	NS		GP	100%	DC & PM	7th revision
11	Allebeck (1981)	293	84	(29)	GP	NY	11		GP	100%	DC & PM	7th revision
12	Rasker (1981)	100	43	(43)	OP	ARA	18	(NS)	None	100%	DC & PM	NO
13	Allebeck (1982)	1165	473	(43)	IP	DO	6		GP	100%	DC & PM	7th revision
14	Vandenbroucke (1984)	209	165	(79)	OP	ARA	25	(NS)	GP	NS	DO	7th revision
15	Prior (1984)	448	199	(44)	OP	ARA	11	(3-18)	GP	97%	DC	8th revision

Abbreviations: ARA – American Rheumatism Association; DO – doctor's opinion; IP – in-patient; NY – New York; CC – case control; GP – general population; LP – local population; OP – out-patient; DC – death certificate; ICD – International Classification of Disease; NS – not stated; PM – post-mortem neoplasms, may show 30 deaths (15%) in rheumatoid cases and 20 deaths (20%) in controls. The proportional figures (percent) suggest malignancy is less common in rheumatoid disease, whereas the absolute numbers show that more rheumatoid patients died of malignancy than controls.

(ii) COHORT ANALYSIS

Most studies published in the last ten years have analysed the absolute number of deaths (7-11, 13, 15). The results are most easily compared if standardised mortality ratios are used (8, 11, 13, 15); then the number of patients under observation is multiplied by the death rate for the corresponding age-sex category in the general population for each year under observation to obtain the expected number of deaths:

$$\text{Standardised mortality ratio} = \frac{\text{observed number of deaths}}{\text{expected number of deaths}} \times 100$$

Monson and Hall (8) analysed their data using standardised mortality ratios and proportional analysis. Proportional mortality showed a deficit of deaths in rheumatoid arthritis due to malignancy and cerebrovascular disease and a small excess of cardiovascular deaths. The standardised mortality ratio showed significant excesses for all three categories.

(iii) SURVIVAL CURVES

A number of studies have shown survival curves with (1, 11, 13, 14) and without (3, 4) comparative curves from the general population. Two (7, 17) have used conventional life table methods.

SURVEY OF MORTALITY STUDIES

LENGTH OF LIFE IN RHEUMATOID ARTHRITIS

Despite the differences in methodology, all studies except one show that rheumatoid patients have a reduced life expectancy. The one exception (9) was based on all the cases of rheumatoid disease identified within a community, and many were mildly involved. The only other population-based survey (11) found a significant increase in mortality confined to patients seen in hospital before the investigation began. Thus shortened survival is not due to rheumatoid disease *per se*, but is restricted to patients with more severe disease requiring hospital referral. This should be remembered when assessing patients with mild rheumatoid arthritis for life insurance (19). A number of investigations suggest that men fare worse than women (1, 4, 8, 9), especially when there is a young onset (under 50 years). Over 50 years the prognosis is worse for women than for men (5, 6, 7, 17), perhaps due to menopausal hormonal changes. Severe disease is a poor prognostic sign (14). Rasker and Cosh (12) found that the highest mortality was in patients who already satisfied the criteria for classical rheumatoid arthritis within one year of onset.

Estimates of the exact loss of life expectancy vary from 3 (14) to 18 years (2). Overall, severe rheumatoid arthritis reduces life expectancy to the same extent as cigarette smoking and diabetes mellitus (20).

CAUSES OF DEATH

Patients may die from the same causes as the general population (11, 21), though at an earlier age. However, the situation is complex: about 20% of deaths (12) may be directly related to rheumatoid arthritis and a further 25% to therapy (22). Figures 1-3 illustrate the causes of death found in different studies.

DEATH FROM INFECTION

All studies have shown an increased death rate from infection (1-15, 18, 23). The exact figures vary, depending on whether the authors have devised their own groupings of causes of death or have adopted the WHO International Classification of Disease (ICD) (24). The ICD classifies all infection, except septicaemia and epidemic infections, under the systems in which they occur. Pneumonia is therefore classified under respiratory disease and accounts for the excess of respiratory deaths in studies using the ICD (7, 8, 13-15).

Rheumatoid patients have an increased susceptibility to all bacterial infections (1). Sepsis predominantly affects the lungs, urinary tract and joints, and diagnosis may be masked by steroids, so that infections reach an advanced stage before being recognised. Steroids may perhaps also increase susceptibility to infection, but this is manifest in patients who never had them. Infection is more common in patients with longstanding disease (17, 25).

CARDIOVASCULAR DEATHS

Cardiovascular disease is the commonest cause of death both in rheumatoid disease and the general population. However, due to the numerous deaths from infection, proportional analyses have sometimes indicated a reduction in cardiovascular deaths in RA (4); but when absolute numbers are used cardiovascular deaths are found to be the same (9, 14) or higher (6, 11, 15) than in the general population. The differences may be explained by variations in steroid usage and smoking habits.

There is controversy over the incidence of myocardial infarction in rheumatoid arthritis. Two autopsy studies (23, 26) found fewer fatal and non-fatal infarctions in rheumatoid patients than controls. It has been suggested that rheumatoid patients are protected against coronary artery thrombosis by regular aspirin ingestion (27). However, Monson and Hall (8) showed that aspirin offered no protection. The dose of aspirin used in rheumatoid disease far exceeds the low doses needed to reduce platelet adhesiveness.

DEATHS FROM MALIGNANCY

Overall patients with established rheumatoid arthritis seem to have the same incidence of malignancy as the general population. Mortality studies (4, 28) and an autopsy series (18) which used proportional analysis found a deficit in deaths from malignancy but most other reports (7, 10, 13, 14) found no significant difference between total numbers of deaths from malignancy in arthritis and in control populations. In many studies no indication is given of the site of origin of the tumours reported (7, 9, 11, 14). Only two series (8, 15) have shown an excess of deaths from malignancy. In one (8) the tumours occurred predominantly in the kidney, and lymphatic and haemopoietic systems; in the other (15) the excess malignancies were confined to the lymphatic and haemopoietic systems.

LYMPHOPROLIFERATIVE MALIGNANCIES

Although the overall incidence of malignancy is not elevated there is some evidence that rheumatoid patients do have an excess risk of developing lymphoproliferative malignancies. Lea (29) first raised this question when he reviewed a large number of men in the Armed Forces who developed reticuloses; they had more rheumatic disorders than controls, but unfortunately the nature of the rheumatic disorders was not specified. Subsequently Oleinick (30) and Miller (31) failed to show an incidence of lymphoproliferative malignancy in rheumatoid arthritis. However, both were series of patients without controls. Interest in an association between rheumatoid arthritis and lymphoproliferative malignancy was rekindled by reports of an increased incidence in other autoimmune diseases, such as Sjøgren's syndrome (32, 33), diabetes mellitus (34) and thyroid disease (35). The widespread use of cytotoxic and immunosuppressive drugs in rheumatoid disease is another factor, for these may also be associated with development of malignancy of lymphoid tissues (36-38).

The clearest evidence of an association between rheumatoid arthritis and lymphoproliferative malignancy comes from a large Finnish study first published in 1978 (39) and updated in 1985 (40). It used two computerised nationwide data registers, and the resulting very large series of rheumatoid patients had an increased incidence of Hodgkin's disease, non-Hodgkin's lymphoma, multiple myeloma and leukaemia compared with the general population. There are criticisms about the "purity" of a diagnosis of rheumatoid arthritis in these patients. Nevertheless it is an impressive study with a very large number of patients and would be difficult to emulate. Smaller studies with clearer diagnostic criteria have confirmed an increased incidence of Hodgkin's disease, non-Hodgkin's disease, leukaemia (41) and multiple myeloma (42) in rheumatoid arthritis. These malignancies are most likely a result of chronic rather than severe rheumatoid disease (43). The increased risk of developing lymphoproliferative malignancy is independent of treatment with immuno-suppressive drugs.

DEATHS DUE TO DISEASES OF THE GENITO-URINARY SYSTEM

Renal problems are common. Lawson and McLean (44) found that nearly three-quarters of 61 rheumatoid patients examined at autopsy had significant renal disease. These patients were alive when Phenacetin was still being used, which may account for the large number who had renal papillary necrosis. Most renal complications seen today are related to amyloidosis (see below) or therapy. Both gold and penicillamine can cause renal side-effects, but deaths directly attributable to these agents are rare (45). The risk of renal disease due to non-steroidal anti-inflammatory drugs is not known, but a tide of opinion blames them for causing considerable renal problems. Monson and Hall (8) showed that aspirin is related to increased deaths from renal disease. The standardised mortality ratio for genito-urinary disease was 120 in patients not taking aspirin, 230 in occasional users, and 280 in patients regularly taking aspirin.

AMYLOIDOSIS

Amyloid consists of protein fibrils with a unique beta-pleated sheet structure deposited in tissues (46). In rheumatoid arthritis amyloid fibrils are of the AA type. Estimates of the frequency of amyloidosis in rheumatoid disease vary. Some autopsy studies have found it in 14-26% of cases (47). Another careful post-mortem study found deposits typical of AA amyloid in only one rheumatoid patient, with senile amyloid deposits present in 13 of 17 arthritic subjects and 19 of 47 controls (48). Estimates of amyloidosis from biopsy series suggest an incidence ranging from 5-11% (49).

Amyloid appears several years after the onset of rheumatoid arthritis, with insidious proteinuria followed by nephrosis and hepatosplenomegaly. It is usually fatal, though occasional reports suggest that it can be reversed with intensive therapy. Death is usually due to renal disease. A Scandinavian post-mortem study showed that 17% of 41 rheumatoid patients died from amyloid (18) and a similar number was found in a Scottish post-mortem series (44). Mortality studies without post-mortems give more conflicting results and a lower incidence. Mutru and colleagues (7) found 6% of deaths were due to amyloid. A British study (15) showed only 1.5% of deaths had amyloidosis on the death certificate, and in none was it the underlying cause of death. AA amyloid is also uncommon in the USA and there may be a geographical component in its aetiology.

THE EFFECT OF DRUGS

Some patients have undoubtedly died as a result of treatment, although the precise number is unknown, because it is hard to dissociate deaths due to drugs from those due to the disease itself.

NON-STEROIDAL ANTI-INFLAMMATORY DRUGS (NSAIDs) have received considerable attention in recent years with their disadvantages being brought to the fore. Phenylbutazone, benoxaprofen, fenclofenac and others have been withdrawn as a result of their unfavourable adverse reactions and probable associated risk of death, especially in the elderly. NSAIDs cause gastro-intestinal ulceration which contributes to increased mortality in some studies (1, 3, 15), but not all (4, 7, 11). As already mentioned, they are also implicated in renal deaths, although the evidence is weak.

Figure 1 Proportional mortality in a hospital series (7)

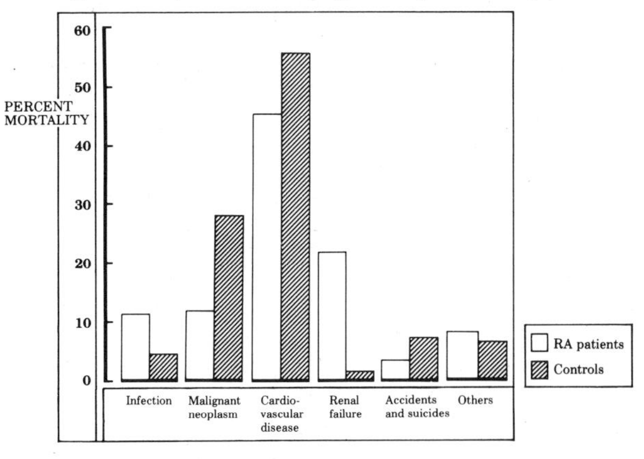

Figure 2 Proportional mortality in a population survey (11)

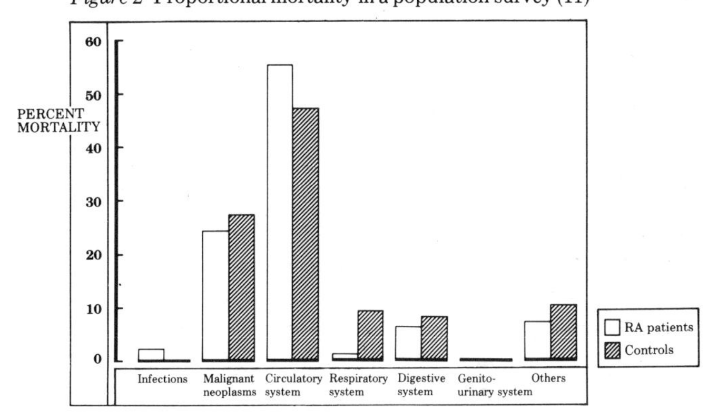

Figure 3 Observed and expected deaths in a hospital series (15)

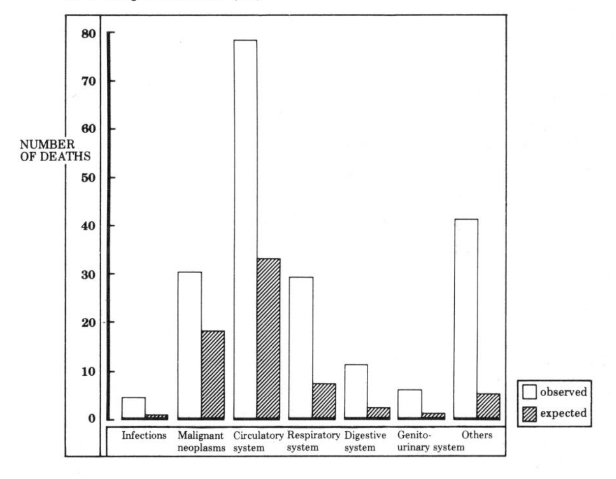

SUPPRESSIVE DRUGS such as gold and penicillamine often cause adverse reactions which lead to their withdrawal. There is a substantial mortality associated with gold. Girdwood (50) found 16 deaths due to gold in a seven-year period and estimated a death rate of 1.6 per 6000 prescriptions for gold; five times higher than that of any other drug. Bone marrow aplasia is a dreaded though uncommon complication of chrysotherapy; 12 of 20 patients described by McCarty *et al* died (51) as did 15 of 20 described by Kay (52). Thrombocytopaenia is more common, but all 32 patients described by Kay recovered, though in some it was more than a year before the platelet count returned to normal. Agranulocytosis and leukopaenia are also seen due to gold and may be symptomatic, but usually resolve when treatment is stopped. Penicillamine is similar. Kay (53) found that 14 of 18 deaths due to penicillamine between 1964 and 1977 were ascribed to blood dyscrasias. Fatal toxic reactions also involve the kidneys, lungs and other systems.

CORTICOSTEROIDS are used in many severe cases and it is difficult to dissociate their deleterious effects from that of the disease. On balance, the evidence is strongly in favour of steroids increasing the risk of infections and associated deaths (54) and this is borne out by analysis of treatment effects on mortality (12, 17). Hypertension and cardiovascular disease may also be influenced by steroids but the evidence is more difficult to evaluate. Many of the significant adverse reactions of steroids, such as osteoporosis, cause morbidity without directly affecting mortality.

HOW MANY DEATHS ARE PREVENTABLE?

To improve survival we must try and identify those patients particularly at risk. This question was examined in detail in an analysis of 489 hospitalised patients in the West Midlands (17). No simple answer emerged. Women may have initially milder disease and hormonal status may affect prognosis. The time that patients are seen at the hospital is also important. For some obscure reason the excess mortality is high initially, falls at 5-9 years after first attendance, and rises to a higher level after 10 years of attending the clinic. This is true whether patients are first seen early or late in the course of their disease. This implies that the way we manage rheumatoid disease influences mortality, but does not identify the precise factors. This study together with other analyses of cohorts of rheumatoid patients followed for 9-18 years (12, 55-57) suggests that preventable deaths due to infection and similar problems occur in patients with severe disease given corticosteroids.

In an 18 year follow-up of 100 rheumatoid patients from Bath (12) there were 43 deaths: 9 were directly attributable to the disease itself; in 7 rheumatoid arthritis or its treatment were contributory factors; and 27 were considered unrelated to rheumatoid arthritis. Examples of deaths directly due to the disease were vasculitis, amyloidosis, and rheumatic heart disease. The mean age of "unrelated" deaths was 72 years; the other two groups had mean ages of death in the sixties. Improved management of severe cases could thus reduce mortality, though the path leading to better management remains poorly signposted.

CONCLUSIONS

* The method of calculating mortality is important. Studies using proportional mortality or standardised mortality ratios give different results and are not directly comparable.
* Most causes of death are increased in rheumatoid disease.
* Cardiovascular, renal, and deaths related to infection are especially important and may be preventable.
* Anti-rheumatic drugs increase the risk of death in some patients.
* There is a definite increased risk of death due to lymphoproliferative malignancy in rheumatoid disease, but the number of cases involved is small. Other neoplasms do not cause an increased mortality.
* To improve life expectancy in rheumatoid arthritis we must concentrate upon reducing mortality in severely disabled cases attending rheumatology clinics.

January 1986

1. Cobb S, Anderson F, Bauer W. Length of life and cause of death in rheumatoid arthritis. *NEJM* (1953) **249:** 553-556.
2. Reah TG. The prognosis of rheumatoid arthritis. *Proc.R.Soc.Med.* (1963) **56:** 813-7.
3. Duthie JJR, Brown PE, Truelove LH et al. Course and prognosis of rheumatoid arthritis. *Ann Rheum Dis* (1964) **23:** 193-202
4. Uddin J, Kraus AS, Kelly HG. Survivorship and death in rheumatoid arthritis. *Arth Rheum* (1970) **13:** 125-130.
5. Isomaki HA, Mutru O, Koota K. Death rate and cause of death in patients with rheumatoid arthritis. *Scand J. Rheum* (1975) **4:** 205-8.
6. Koota K, Isomaki H, Mutru O. Death rate and causes of death in RA patients during a period of 5 years. *Scand J. Rheum* (1977) **6:** 241-4.
7. Mutru O, Laakso M, Isomaki H, Koota K. Ten year mortality and causes of death in patients with rheumatoid arthritis. *Br. Med. J.* (1985) **290:** 1797-9.
8. Monson RR, Hall AP. Mortality among arthritis. *J.Chron.Dis* (1976) **29:** 459-467.
9. Linos A, Worthington JW, O'Fallon WM, Kurland LT. The epidemiology of rheumatoid arthritis in Rochester, Minnesota: A study of incidence, prevalence and mortality. *Am.J. Epidemiol* (1980) **111:** 87-98.
10. Lewis P, Hazleman BL, Hanna R, Roberts S. Causes of death in patients with rheumatoid arthritis with particular reference to azathioprine. *Ann. Rheum. Dis* (1980) **39:** 457-461.
11. Allebeck P, Ahlbom A, Allander E. Increased mortality among persons with rheumatoid arthritis, but where RA does not appear on the death certificate. *J.Rheum* (1981) **10:** 301-6.
12. Rasker JJ, Cosh JA. Cause and age at death in a prospective study of 100 patients with rheumatoid arthritis. *Ann Rheum Dis* (1981) **40:** 115-20.
13. Allebeck P. Increased mortality in rheumatoid arthritis *Scand J. Rheum* (1982) **11:** 81-6.
14. Vandenbroucke JP, Hazevoet HM, Cats A. Survival and cause of death in rheumatoid arthritis: A 25 year prospective follow-up. *J.Rheum* (1984) **11:** 158-61.
15. Prior P, Symmons DPM, Scott DL et al. Cause of death in rheumatoid arthritis. *Br.J.Rheum* (1984) **23:** 92-9.
16. Cosh JA. Survival and death in rheumatoid arthritis. *J.Rheum* (1984) **11:** 117-8.
17. Symmons DPM, Prior P, Scott DL et al. Factors influencing mortality in rheumatoid arthritis. *J.Chron.Dis* (In press).
18. Mutru O, Koota K, Isomaki H. Causes of death in autopsied RA patients. *Scand J Rheum* (1976) **5:** 239-40.
19. Abruzzo JL. Rheumatoid arthritis and mortality. *Arth Rheum* (1982) **25:** 1020-3.
20. Fries JF. Epidemiology of cancer in rheumatoid arthritis: methodologic pitfalls. *Am J Med* (1985) **78(1A):** 12-14.
21. Bywaters EGL, Curwen M, Dresner E, Dixon A St.J. 10 year follow-up study of rheumatoid arthritis. *Ann Rheum Dis* (1961) **20:** 198.
22. Constable TJ, McConkey B, Paton A. The cause of death in rheumatoid arthritis. *Ann Rheum Dis* (1978) **37:** 569.
23. Ball J. *Post-mortem findings and articular pathology in rheumatoid arthritis.* In Rheumatic Diseases: Pfizer Medical Monograph No. Ed Duthie JJR, Alexander WRM. Univ. Press Edinburgh (1968) p.124-130.
24. *The International Classification of Disease and causes of death* (8th revision). World Health Organisation 1967 (WHO) Geneva.
25. Rimoin DL, Wennberg JE. Acute septic arthritis complicating chronic rheumatoid arthritis. *JAMA* (1966) **196:** 617-621.
26. Davis RF, Engleman EG. Incidence of myocardial infarction in patients with rheumatoid arthritis. *Arth Rheum* (1974) **17:** 527-33.
27. Czaplicki S, Gietka J, Sulek K. The frequency of coronary heart disease and myocardial infarction in rheumatoid arthritis patients. *Cor Vasa* (1978) **20:** 249-54.
28. Fries JF, Block D, Spuitz P, Mitchell DM. Cancer in rheumatoid arthritis: A prospective long-term study of mortality. *Am J Med* (1985) **78(1A):** 56-59.
29. Lea AJ. An association between the rheumatic disease and the reticuloses. *Ann Rheum Dis* (1964) **23:** 480-484.
30. Oleinick A. Leukaemia or lymphoma occurring subsequent to autoimmune disease. *Blood* (1967) **29:** 144-153.
31. Miller DG. The association of immune disease and malignant lymphoma. *Ann Intern Med* (1967) **66:** 507-521.
32. Kassan SS, Thomas TL, Moutsopoulos HM et al. Increased risk of lymphoma in sicca syndrome. *Ann Intern Med* (1978) **89:** 888-892.
33. Anderson LG, Talal N. The spectrum of benign to malignant lymphoproliferation in Sjøgren's Syndrome. *Clin Exp Immunol* (1972) **10:** 199-221.
34. Ragozzino M, Melton LJ, Chu C-P, Palumbo PJ. Subsequent cancer risk in the incidence cohort of Rochester, Minnesota residents with diabetes mellitus. *J. Chron Dis* (1982) **35:** 13-19.
35. Holm L-E, Blomgren H, Lowhagen T. Cancer risks in patients with chronic lymphocytic thyroiditis. *NEJM* (1985) **312:**601-604.
36. Renier J-C, Bregeon Ch, Bonnette Ch et al. Le devenir des sujets atteints de polyarthrite rhumatoide et traites par les immunodepresseurs entre 1965 et 1973 inclus. *Revue de Rhumatisme* (1978) **45:** 453-461.
37. Kahn MF, Arlet J, Bloch-Michel H et al. Leucemies aigues après traitement par agents cytotoxiques en rhumatologie. *Nouv Press Med* (1979) **8:** 1393-7.
38. Kinlen LS, Sheil AGR, Peto J, Doll R. Collaborative United Kingdom – Australian study of cancer in patients treated with immunosuppressive drugs. *Br Med J* (1979) **2:** 1461-6.
39. Isomaki HA, Hakulinen T, Joutsenlahti U. Excess risk of lymphomas, leukaemias and myeloma in patients with rheumatoid arthritis. *J Chron Dis* (1978) **31:** 691-696.
40. Hakulinen T, Isomaki H, Knekt P. Rheumatoid arthritis and cancer studies based on linking nationwide registries in Finland. *Am J Med* (1985) **78(1A):** 29-32.
41. Prior P, Symmons DPM, Hawkins CF, Scott DL. Cancer morbidity in rheumatoid arthritis. *Ann Rheum Dis* (1984) **43:** 128-131.
42. Katusic S, Beard CM, Kurland LT et al. Occurrence of malignant neoplasms in the Rochester, Minnesota rheumatoid arthritis cohort. *Am J Med* (1965) **78(1A):** 50-55.
43. Symmons DPM, Ahern M, Bacon PA et al. Lymphoproliferative malignancy in rheumatoid arthritis: a study of 20 cases. *Ann Rheum Dis* (1984) **43:** 132-5.
44. Lawson AAH, McClean N. Renal disease and drug therapy in rheumatoid arthritis. *Ann Rheum Dis* (1966) **25:** 441-449.
45. Vaamonde CA, Hunt FR. The nephrotic syndrome as a complication of gold therapy. *Arthritis Rheum* (1970) **13:** 826-834.
46. Glenner GG. Amyloid deposits and amyloidosis. *NEJM* (1980) **302:** 1283-1292 and 1333-1343.
47. Calkins E, Cohen AS. Diagnosis of amyloidosis. *Bull Rheum Dis* (1960) **10:** 215-218.
48. Ozdemir AI, Wright JR, Calkins E. Influence of rheumatoid arthritis on amyloidosis of ageing: comparison of 47 rheumatoid patients with 47 controls matched for age and sex. *NEJM* (1971) **285:** 534-538.
49. Arapakis G, Tribe CR. Amyloidosis in rheumatoid arthritis investigated by means of rectal biopsy. *Ann Rheum Dis* (1963) **22:** 256-262.
50. Girdwood RH. Death after taking medicaments. *Br Med J* (1974) **1:** 501-505.
51. McCarthy DJ, Brill JM, Harrop D. Aplastic anaemia secondary to gold salt therapy.*JAMA* (1962) **179:** 655-657.
52. Kay AGL. Myelotoxicity of gold. *Br Med J* (1976) **1:** 1266-1268.
53. Kay AGL. Myelotoxicity of D-penicillamine. *Ann Rheum Dis* (1979) **38:** 232-236.
54. Goddard D, Butler R. *Rheumatoid arthritis: the treatment controversy.* Macmillan Press Ltd., London; 1984.
55. Scott DL, Coulton BL, Chapman JH et al. The long-term effects of treating rheumatoid arthritis. *J R Coll Physicians Lond* (1983) **17:** 79-85.
56. Pincus T, Callahan LF, Sale WG et al. Severe functional declines, work disability, and increased mortality in seventy-five rheumatoid arthritis patients studied over nine years. *Arthritis Rheum* (1984) **27:** 864-872.
57. Million R, Kellgren JH, Poole P, Jayson MIV. Long-term management of rheumatoid arthritis. *Lancet* (1984) **1:** 812-816.

ANAEMIA IN RHEUMATOID ARTHRITIS - DOES IT MATTER?

A Turnbull
Consulting Physician
The London Hospital
London E1 1BB

Anaemia is a common feature of rheumatoid arthritis (RA), its severity paralleling that of the disease and seldom being more than moderate in degree. Other causes include lack of haematinic factors – iron, folic acid or vitamin B12 – and such deficiency is usually found if the haemoglobin is less than 9 g/dl. Rarely haemolysis or bone marrow depression may be the cause.

Possible causes of anaemia in patients with RA

1. The Anaemia of Rheumatoid Arthritis. Essentially the "anaemia of RA" is a particular example of the anaemia of chronic disorders. Haemoglobin levels of about 10 g/dl are common and tend to vary inversely with the ESR and other markers of disease activity. The mechanism is complex but includes failure of incorporation of iron into red cell precursors. For this reason the morphology of the red cells may to some extent mimic the anaemia of true iron deficiency with microcytosis and reduction in the corpuscular concentration of haemoglobin (MCHC). However, in contrast to the findings in true iron deficiency anaemia (lack of total body iron), the mean corpuscular volume (MCV) is rarely below 70 fl, total iron-binding capacity of the plasma (TIBC) is low, and serum ferritin is more than 60 ng/ml. Finally, bone marrow smears contain stainable iron stores.

Practice Point

THE ANAEMIA OF CHRONIC DISORDERS IS USUALLY NORMOCYTIC AND NORMOCHROMIC BUT CAN BE CONFUSED WITH THAT OF TRUE IRON DEFICIENCY

2. Iron Deficiency is common in RA, and is usually due to gastro-intestinal bleeding related to consumption of aspirin or other NSAIDs. This may be aggravated by menstrual loss, occasionally by poor dietary intake or absorption. In true iron deficiency the red cells are usually obviously hypochromic and microcytic, but only if these changes are very marked can the appearance of the blood film reliably distinguish between true iron deficiency and the anaemia of chronic disorders. The distinction is important. Iron deficient patients require iron therapy. In contrast, the anaemia of chronic disorders will not respond to iron, and iron treatment may actually be harmful. Biochemical findings have to be interpreted with care, for RA itself may affect the levels of iron binding capacity (TIBC) and serum ferritin (an "acute phase reactant"). As a general rule, an anaemic rheumatoid patient will respond to iron if the TIBC is greater than 55 umol/1 and the serum ferritin less than 60 ng/ml (1). The final proof of true iron deficiency is lack of stainable iron in a marrow smear.

Practice Point

IN ACTIVE RA TRUE IRON DEFICIENCY IS INDICATED BY A TIBC GREATER THAN 55 umol/1 AND SERUM FERRITIN LESS THAN 60 ng/ml

3. Folic Acid Deficiency is less common than iron deficiency as a cause of anaemia in RA. When it does occur it is usually due to a combination of reduced intake and increased requirement, for example pregnancy in a patient on a restricted diet. It is important to remember that the typical markers of folate deficiency (peripheral blood macrocytosis and megaloblastic marrow changes) may not be obvious because of the additional anaemia of chronic disorders. The diagnosis is established by a reduction in serum and red cell folate levels.

Practice Point

IN ACTIVE RA THE CHARACTERISTIC MORPHOLOGICAL CHANGES OF FOLATE DEFICIENCY MAY BE MASKED BY THE ADDITIONAL ANAEMIA OF CHRONIC DISORDERS

4. Vitamin B12 Deficiency in rheumatoid patients is generally due to the coincidence of Addisonian pernicious anaemia (autoimmune lack of gastric intrinsic factor) and RA. Rarely other gastro-intestinal abnormalities may be responsible. The prevalence of pernicious anaemia is increased amongst rheumatoid patients and their relatives, probably due to a shared genetic tendency to autoimmunity.

5. Autoimmune Haemolytic Anaemia is occasionally seen in RA patients, particularly those with Felty's syndrome (RA plus splenomegaly and neutropenia). The Coombs' direct antiglobulin test is positive.

6. Bone Marrow Hypoplasia is a rare but serious form of anaemia which may complicate Felty's syndrome or drug treatment, particularly with gold, penicillamine, immunosuppressive drugs (azathioprine, cyclophosphamide etc) or renal failure. Azathioprine may also produce anaemia with megaloblastic changes but without haematinic deficiency.

The Significance of Anaemia in RA

Anaemia in RA is important in providing an indicator of activity of the disease, and also as a pointer to complications which may add to the patient's disability. Any severe anaemia can be responsible for general deterioration in health, but true iron deficiency causes more subtle effects even when anaemia itself is mild. These include functional and metabolic changes in muscles, brain, and both neutrophils and lymphocytes, as well as depression of immunity, particularly to monilial infection. Iron deficiency may also be the clue to the presence of occult disease, particularly gastro-intestinal cancer, which may be of greater importance to the patient than the arthritis. Correction of anaemia is particularly important as part of the preparation for surgical procedures. Blood transfusion may be required.

Practice Point

IRON DEFICIENCY MAY BE A CLUE TO THE PRESENCE OF OCCULT DISEASE SUCH AS GASTRO-INTESTINAL CANCER

The Diagnosis of Anaemia in RA

Identifying the cause of anaemia in a rheumatoid patient begins with the history, particular attention being paid to diet, consumption of drugs known to cause bleeding (with or without peptic ulceration), haemolysis or bone marrow depression, as well as the presence of any digestive symptoms or bowel disturbance. Examination may reveal evidence of gastro-intestinal pathology or an enlarged spleen.

A full blood count will determine the severity of the anaemia and some indication of its cause may be given by the MCV and MCHC and the appearance of the bleed cells in the film. When the degree of anaemia is disproportionate to the disease activity, one should measure the blood urea, serum ferritin, and vitamin B12 and folate levels. A raised blood urea will indicate the need for investigation of the renal tract with particular reference to the possibility of renal damage by drugs or amyloid. Serum ferritin levels below 60 ng/ml indicate the presence of true iron deficiency in a patient with active RA; and while observing the effect of oral iron therapy the clinician must decide whether there is a likely simple cause such as menorrhagia or aspirin, or whether an occult bleeding lesion needs to be sought by appropriate radiological and/or endoscopic investigation. The patient's history will usually be the best guide.

A low serum folate suggests the possibility of folic acid deficiency, but may be due just to recent poor intake of the vitamin. The red cell folate should be measured as this is a more reliable guide. The possibility of the deficiency being a manifestation of general malabsorption should be considered, but is unlikely in the absence of a history suggesting steatorrhoea or of biochemical evidence of osteomalacia (raised serum alkaline phosphatase). Serum B12 is often low in folic acid deficiency, so the combination of low levels of both these vitamins does not necessarily mean deficiency of both. In a patient with a low serum B12 level, a normal serum gastrin should exclude pernicious anaemia. However, it is safer to assess absorption of vitamin B12 by the Schilling test rather than just treat with folic acid and follow the serum B12.

Practice Point

IN FOLATE DEFICIENCY SERUM B12 LEVELS MAY BE REDUCED. IN THIS CASE EXCLUDE PERNICIOUS ANAEMIA BY A SCHILLING TEST WHILE TREATING WITH FOLIC ACID

In vitamin B12 deficiency serum folate is normal or increased. Such patients should always have a barium meal to exclude gastric carcinoma, as well as the tests already mentioned. An autoantibody screen will usually reveal gastric parietal cell antibody and sometimes intrinsic factor antibody in patients with Addisonian pernicious anaemia, but these will be absent if deficiency is related to previous gastric surgery or to jejunal diverticulosis or stricture. When ordering the barium meal it is advisable to ask the radiologist to follow the barium through the small intestine if there is nothing abnormal in the stomach. Marrow biopsy should be performed if the anaemia is more severe than expected for the activity of the RA and cannot be explained by lack of a haematinic factor.

Practice Point

MARROW BIOPSY SHOULD BE PERFORMED IF ANAEMIA IS MORE SEVERE THAN EXPECTED FOR THE ACTIVITY OF RA AND CANNOT BE EXPLAINED BY LACK OF A HAEMATINIC FACTOR

Enlargement of the spleen not clearly due to liver disease, or conspicuous lymphadenopathy also indicates the need for marrow examination with trephine as rheumatoid patients are not immune to lymphoma, particularly if they have received immunosuppressive drugs. Depression of the white cells or platelets also points to the need for marrow examination.

Coombs' antiglobulin test should be performed if haemolysis is suspected from splenic enlargement, reticulocytosis or increased urinary urobilinogen. Rarely, measurement of red cell life span using radioactive chromium may be carried out if the anaemia is severe enough to warrant consideration of splenectomy.

Treatment

Correction of haematinic deficiency by administration of iron, folic acid or vitamin B12 as appropriate will improve the haemoglobin and the patient's well-being. Iron should not be given unless there is definite evidence that it is deficient. Corticosteroids will lessen autoimmune haemolysis, but are not justified as treatment of the anaemia of chronic disorders. Marrow depression by immuno-suppressive drugs requires their withdrawal or at any rate dose reduction and a review of the management of the arthritis.

Practice Point

DO NOT ADMINISTER IRON IN RA UNLESS THERE IS LABORATORY EVIDENCE OF A TRUE DEFICIENCY

Summary

Mild anaemia is a feature of active RA. Moderate or severe anaemia contributes to the patient's disability and may indicate some serious complication or coincident disease. The nature of the anaemia cannot be determined from the blood count alone. Appropriate investigation will elucidate the problem and often provide the basis for effective therapy.

REFERENCE:

(1) Rajapakse CNA, Holt PJL and Perera BS (1980). Diagnosis of true iron deficiency in rheumatoid arthritis (Abstract). *Annals of the Rheumatic Diseases*, **39**, 596.

Normal values of some laboratory tests mentioned in the text. There is some variation between different laboratories.

Investigation	Normal Values	Comments
Haemoglobin g/dl	12.0 – 16.0 (women) 13.5 – 18.0 (men)	
Mean corpuscular volume (MCV) fl	75 – 95	Above 70 fl in anaemia of chronic disease
Mean corpuscular haemoglobin concentration (MCHC) g/dl	32 – 36	Reduced in iron deficiency
Serum iron umol/l	13 – 32	Reduced in iron deficiency and anaemia of chronic disease
Total iron binding capacity umol/l	45 – 70	Reduced in active RA
Serum ferritin ug/l	25 – 400	An acute phase reactant therefore elevated in active RA
Serum folate ug/l	2 – 14	Dependant on recent dietary intake
Red cell folate ug/l	125 – 600	Reflects folate status better than serum folate
Serum vitamin B12 ng/l	210 – 925	May be reduced in folate deficiency
Serum gastrin	<100 pg/ml	Increased whenever intrinsic factor production fails due to gastric disease
Schilling test B12 alone B12 plus intrinsic factor	 11 – 28% 12 – 30%	Can elucidate the cause of vitamin B12 deficiency

May 1987

FELTY'S SYNDROME

G Campion
Lecturer in Rheumatology
Bristol Royal Infirmary
P J Maddison
Consultant Rheumatologist
Royal National Hospital for Rheumatic Diseases

HISTORY

When in 1924 Felty reported his observations in a paper entitled "Chronic arthritis in the adult associated with splenomegaly and leucopenia"[1] there was already a considerable European literature in existence. 1896 had seen the publication of articles by Still describing splenomegaly, lymphadenopathy and chronic arthritis in children, and by Chauffard reporting the association of lymphadenopathy and "le rheumatisme chronique infectieux" in adults[2]. Since this time, numerous reports including those of Von Jaksch (1908)[3] and Pollitzer (1914)[4] had been made of the association in both children and adults of chronic arthritis with splenomegaly, and the eponym "Still-Chauffard's disease" came to be used.

It was in 1924, however, that Felty's report of the association of arthritis with splenomegaly and leucopenia in five patients established these clinical features as a triad in the English literature. His patients were of middle age and gave a history of marked loss of weight against a background of chronic arthritis. Besides evidence of wasting, physical findings included splenomegaly, lymphadenopathy (in three of the five) and yellowish-brown pigmentation. Laboratory tests revealed a slight anaemia and a striking leucopenia. Felty contrasted the chronic course of the arthritis with surprisingly mild joint changes evident both clinically and radiologically. The eponym "Felty's Syndrome" was created by Hanrahan and Miller in October 1932. They described a similar patient although additional features of recurrent infections, fever and nodules were noted[5]. Their patient was the first reported to undergo splenectomy.

Felty felt the leucopenia was caused by a "noxa which simultaneously affects the joints, the spleen and the blood leucocytes". Singer and Levy in 1936 wrote a paper on "the relationship of Felty's and allied syndromes to sepsis lenta"[6]. Wiseman and Doan in 1942[7] considered that the leucopenia resulted from increased splenic sequestration and phagocytosis, whereas Dameshek[8] believed that an undefined hormone produced by the spleen exerted an inhibitory effect on neutrophil production by the marrow. Moeschlin in 1952[9] cited the importance of leucocyte agglutinins whilst in 1966 Faber and Elling[10] advocated the effect of leucocyte-specific antinuclear factors with destruction of antibody-coated neutrophils primarily by the spleen. Denko and Zumpft[11] concluded that the majority of cases represented a chance association of arthritis, usually rheumatoid arthritis, and hypersplenism of various causes, most often systemic lupus erythematosus. More recently, Logue[12] demonstrated granulocyte bound immunoglobulin G and used their proposed specificity of this for Felty's syndrome to describe a case of Felty's syndrome without splenomegaly.

Denko and Zumpft apart, most authors consider Felty's syndrome to be a rare variant of rheumatoid arthritis or "super rheumatoid disease" with a high incidence of extra-articular manifestations. Despite over 60 years of observations since Felty's report, the aetiology, pathogenetic mechanisms and treatment of this uncommon disease still remain obscure.

CLINICAL FEATURES OF FELTY'S SYNDROME

Figure 1

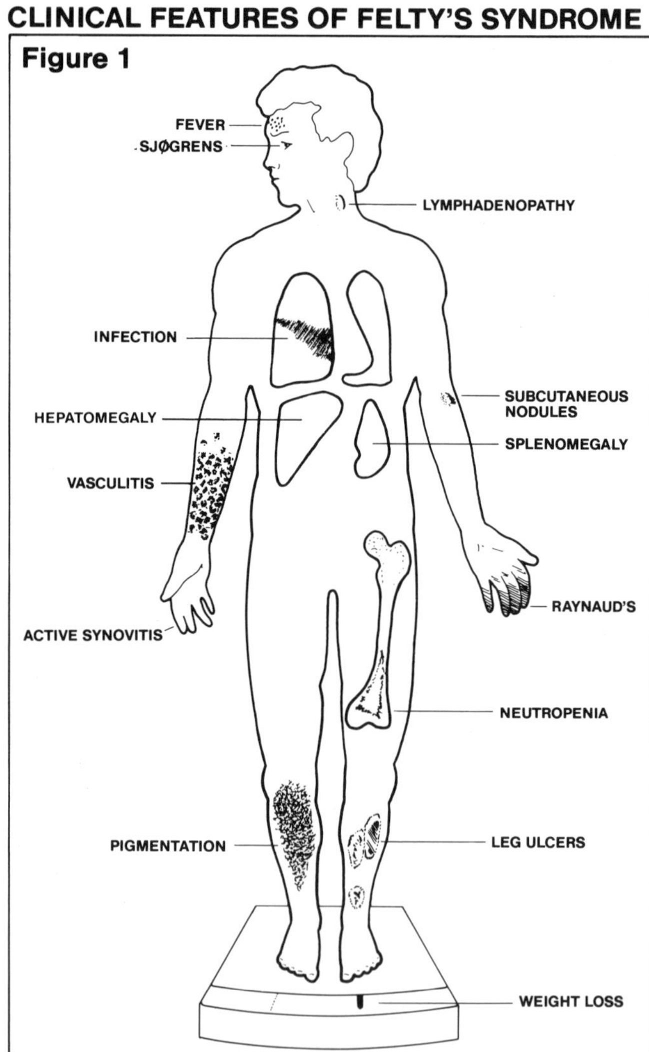

CLINICAL FEATURES

Felty's syndrome is uncommon representing approximately 1% of the rheumatoid population. Neutropenia is the hallmark of Felty's syndrome and as emphasized by Spivak (1977)[13] and Logue (1979)[12] splenomegaly is not necessarily present. Furthermore, patients with RA and splenomegaly alone are clinically similar to uncomplicated RA patients[14]. Our experience, summarized in table 1, is based on 33 patients who fulfil the accepted clinical criteria: RA with splenomegaly and neutropenia of less than 2 x 10^9 per litre. This, in keeping with other reports, shows that Felty's patients are part of the spectrum of rheumatoid disease where extra-articular features including systemic vasculitis are prominent. These features are illustrated in figure 1. Occasionally, Felty's syndrome develops within months of the onset of arthritis and, rarely, neutropenia may precede joint disease, but in the majority the arthritis is of long duration, severe and destructive. Only a fifth of our patients, however, had clinical evidence of joint inflammation at the time Felty's syndrome was diagnosed, though the proportion with active synovitis is higher in other series[18]. The female preponderance in these patients is not so marked as in uncomplicated RA and men seem to develop Felty's syndrome earlier in the course of their disease[23].

TABLE 1: FELTY'S SYNDROME

CLINICAL FEATURES

	Bath/Bristol series	Previous +	RA *
	%	%	%
lymphadenopathy	15	15	12
pigmentation	3	5	10
nodules	82	66	53
weight loss	30	38	
fibrosis	15	27	20
vasculitis	24	28	
neuropathy	15	10	
infections	60	47	
ulcers	15	25	
Raynaud's	20	10	10
Sjøgren's	36	38	
hepatomegaly	30	34	

\+ 166 patients in 8 reports (Thorn 1982[15], Goldberg 1980[16], Laszlo 1978[17], Sienknecht 1977[18], Ruderman 1968[19], O'Neil 1968[20], De Gruchy 1965[21])

* Gordon[22] 127 consecutive RA patients.

Infections, generally involving common organisms, occur in the majority of cases and are the dominant clinical feature in some, but there is no relationship between the risk of infection and the degree of neutropenia. Hyperpigmentation, emphasized by Felty, is a feature in some and affects exposed surfaces especially the shins. Chronic leg ulcers appear to be more common than in uncomplicated RA. Abnormalities of the liver in Felty's syndrome have recently received emphasis[24]. Although a mild degree of hepatomegaly and abnormal liver function tests are common in RA with or without Felty's syndrome, the histological picture of nodular regenerative hyperplasia has been reported in Felty's but not in uncomplicated RA. This may contribute significantly to the portal hypertension sometimes complicated by haemorrhage from oesophageal varices, which may rarely occur in Felty's syndrome.

The natural history of Felty's syndrome is variable, and there are a number of reports of spontaneous remission of the neutropenia and other clinical features[25]. However both morbidity and mortality are high, and in one study the 5 year mortality was 36%, infection being the leading cause of death[15].

HAEMATOLOGICAL AND SEROLOGICAL FEATURES OF FELTY'S SYNDROME

Leucopenia is due entirely to a neutropenia which may be profound. The degree of neutropenia bears no relationship to the spleen size and often varies during the course of the disease. Elevation of the neutrophil count often accompanies infection but may be spontaneous and occasionally returns to the normal range. A mild to moderate anaemia occurs in virtually all patients with the features of anaemia of chronic disease. This may be compounded in some by a shortened red cell half life and may be corrected by splenectomy. A moderate thrombocytopenia occurs in approximately 50% but is rarely profound enough to cause purpura or other clinical complications.

Figure 2: NEUTROPENIA IN FELTY'S SYNDROME – POSSIBLE MECHANISMS

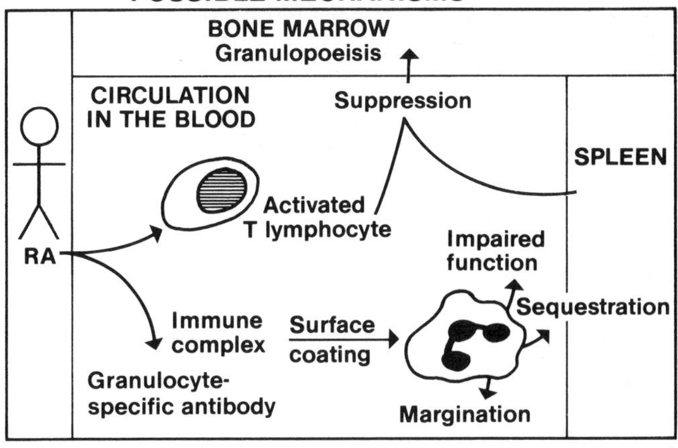

Bone marrow findings are variable. Cellularity is usually either normal or shows myeloid hyperplasia. Occasionally there is hypoplasia and rarely lymphocytic infiltration. The most common abnormality is a relative shift to the left with an excess of immature forms which has been termed "maturation arrest". There are rare cases where Felty's syndrome has been associated with lymphocytosis of marrow and peripheral blood involving large granular lymphocytes[26].

Serological abnormalities are very prominent in Felty's syndrome. In our series, all have high titres of IgM rheumatoid factor, and 81% have IgG rheumatoid factor mostly in high titre. ANA is present in 80%, and significant DNA-binding occurs in one-third, with antibodies directed predominantly to single-stranded DNA, although antibodies to native DNA have been detected by the Crithidia lucilliae technique in one patient. Hypocomplementaemia, usually manifested by a moderate reduction in C4 levels, has been observed in 32%, and circulating immune complexes, usually in high titre, have been detected by C1q binding in 90%, a feature which has been emphasized by others[27].

HLA ASSOCIATIONS IN FELTY'S SYNDROME

Dinant *et al* (1980)[28] demonstrated that the association of RA with HLA-DR4 is strongest in the Felty's population. We have confirmed this, and all but one of our patients with Felty's syndrome are DR4 positive, and in 50%, DR4 was the only DR antigen detected.

PATHOGENESIS OF FELTY'S SYNDROME

The mechanism for leucopenia in Felty's syndrome is controversial, and almost certainly more than one factor is involved. Suggested mechanisms (figure 2) include increased margination and sequestration of neutrophils, and bone marrow suppression.

Granulocyte kinetic studies mainly using ^{32}P-labelled diisopropylfluorophosphate have yielded conflicting results largely due to methodological problems with such neutropenic patients. In one large study[29], however, excessive margination was the major factor in the neutropenia and while neutrophil production was reduced in a minority, excessive neutrophil destruction was not a feature. Assessment of marrow reserve using i.v. hydrocortisone or aetiocholanolone shows that is reduced in a majority of Felty's patients.

Granulocyte-specific ANA and autoantibodies specifically interacting with the granulocyte surface have been reported but there is no evidence that they have a role in pathogenesis. On the other hand non-specific binding of immune complexes to the Fc receptor of neutrophils may have a role in the leucopenia[30].

Neutrophils from patients with Felty's syndrome differ from those of patients with uncomplicated RA with respect to the level of both surface bound and intracytoplasmic immunoglobulins, and this feature may be related to the higher circulating levels of immune complexes. This could lead to increased margination and sequestration of neutrophils possibly by activating complement particularly since intravenous injection of *in vitro*-formed immune complexes causes a transient neutropenia in experimental animals.

Not all patients with RA and high levels of circulating immune complexes develop neutropenia, and similarly neutrophil-bound immunoglobulin is not an invariable feature of Felty's syndrome. This suggests additional factors causing the leucopenia which may include cell mediated and humoral suppression of neutrophil production by the bone marrow. Peripheral blood leucocytes from certain Felty's patients, for example, have been shown to inhibit normal marrow granulocyte colony growth *in vitro*[31]. Conversely, a failure of blood monocytes to generate a haemopoietic stimulating factor has been demonstrated in a different population of patients with Felty's syndrome[32]. A serum factor capable of inhibiting *in vitro* colony formation by human bone marrow granulocyte precursors has also been demonstrated in a proportion of Felty's patients[33].

The increased susceptibility to infection is almost certainly related to other factors in addition to neutropenia and reduced granulocyte reserves. Abnormal neutrophil function has been demonstrated including, for example, defective chemotaxis[34] and phagocytosis[35]. Hypocomplementaemia may also play a role in this respect.

TREATMENT OF FELTY'S SYNDROME

Treatment aimed at suppressing rheumatoid disease quite frequently improves the leucopenia and reduces the susceptibility to infection. Good response, for example, has been reported with gold, cytotoxic drugs and penicillamine. In 1966[36] Pengelly described a patient who was successfully treated with corticosteroids but subsequent experience has been disappointing. High dose parenteral testosterone was reported to be successful in 3 male patients[37] but it would not be suitable for females. Lithium carbonate has been shown to cause neutrophilia in psychiatric patients and to attenuate neutropenia induced by cancer chemotherapy. Gupta (1975)[38] demonstrated that lithium improved the neutropenia in Felty's patients, but long-term effects in preventing infection are unknown, and side-effects frequently induced by chronic therapy are a major disadvantage. Plasmapheresis has been reported to be effective in Felty's but experience is very limited.

SPLENECTOMY

The role of splenectomy first suggested by Chevalier in 1930 remains controversial. Table 2 summarizes some of the experiences of the past 15 years. It is noteworthy that in the series reported by Thorn (1982)[15] which incorporated 5 years follow-up the white cell count became normal in 7/14 patients and the spleen size reduced to normal in 6 patients who had not undergone splenectomy. Post-splenectomy, 7 patients continued to have infections and 3 died from sepsis. Reporting the results of 27 patients undergoing splenectomy for Felty's syndrome Laszlo[17] records more favourable results. In 19 patients the white cell count returned to normal, 3 remained neutropenic but 9 had recurrent episodes of neutropenia following splenectomy. Two patients went into remission of their arthritis post-operatively whilst 17/22 patients were promptly cured of chronic infection and leg ulcers. Their series of patients lacks comparison with non-splenectomised Felty patients and the indications for splenectomy may well have been different in the two groups. Factors which are important in assessing the rationale for splenectomy include reports of spontaneous remission of Felty's syndrome, the morbidity of operation, the increased risk of infection particularly with pneumococcus in normals following splenectomy and the lack of correlation between the degree of neutropenia and incidence of infection. Splenectomy for uncomplicated neutropenia therefore is probably not indicated. However, it may still have a role in life-threatening disease unresponsive to gold or immunosuppressive treatments.

TABLE 2: SPLENECTOMY IN FELTY'S SYNDROME

DISEASE COURSE FOLLOWING SPLENECTOMY

Series	No.	Indications	Blood count	Arthritis	Infections/ Leg Ulcers	Length of follow up	Recommendations
Thorn 1982	11/25	1. infections (7) 2. leucopenia (severe) 3. skin ulceration (1) 4. portal hypertension (1) spleen size became N in 6 patients without splenectomy	9/11 had WCC > $5 \times 10^9/1$ 7/14 WCC → N *without* splenectomy 5 of patients whose WCC → N post splenectomy continued to have recurrent infections	12/21 improved ? no. with splenectomy	7 post-splenectomy 3 died from sepsis	5 years	splenectomy not protective for sepsis
Goldberg 1980	6/19	recurrent infection	1 haemological remission 2 transient remission of 2 months' duration 2 recurrent granulocytopenia		no infections for 5 years 2 recurrent infections 1 died postop from septicaemia		
Laszlo 1978	27	1. severe granulocytopenia 2. infections	19 → N 3 had ↓ WCC 9 of 27 (33%) had recurrent ↓ WCC after splenectomy	2 patients remission following surgery	21/27 had infections or leg ulcers prior to surgery 17/22 were promptly cured of chronic infection of ulcers postop	4-7 yrs	elective surgery if granulocyte count lower than $0.5 \times 10^9/6$ that persists over several months
Barnes 1971	10/21	infection 7 neutropenia 10 HA 2	0-28 days *short-term* WCC → N in 8 low in 2 HA stabilised in 2 *long-term* N 5 neutropenia 4	1 same 4 improved 3 bad	nil 3 improved 3 same or worsened 3 died ? from sepsis 1		splenectomy remains treatment of choice for patients with very severe infections
Moore 1971	15	infection 9 neutropenia 15 leg ulcers 3	66% N for least 1½ yrs follow-up 3 failed to rise 2 ? CLL or leukosarcoma		5/9 had reduced frequency 1 repeated infection 2 died from septicaemia postop 1 died febrile illness 8/12 postop	3.8 yrs (6 days – 11 yrs)	splenectomy in patients with Felty's + recurrent infections

N = normal WCC = white cell count CLL = chronic lymphatic leukaemia

1. Felty AR. *Chronic arthritis in the adult, associated with splenomegaly and leukopenia: A report of five cases of an unusual clinical syndrome.* Bull John Hopkins Hosp 1924, **35,** 16-20.
2. Chauffard A, Ramond F. *Des adenopathies dans le rheumatism chronique infectieux.* Rev de Med, Paris (May) 1896, **16,** 345-8.
3. Von Jaksch A. *Arthritis urica, Megalosplenie und Leukopenie.* Deutsche Med Wochenschr 1908, **34,** 634-8.
4. Pollitzer H. *Ueber chronischen Gelenkrheumatismus mit Drusenschwellung und Milztumor (Typus Still-Chauffard).* Med Klin 1914, (Sep 27) **10,** 1511-16.
5. Hanrahan EM Jr, Miller SR. *Effect of splenectomy in Felty's syndrome.* JAMA 1932, **99,** 1247-52.
6. Singer HA, Levy HA. *Relationship of Felty's and allied syndromes to sepsis lenta.* Arch Intern Med 1936.
7. Wideman BK, Doan CA. *Primary splenic neutropenia: A newly recognised syndrome, closely related to congenital hemolytic icterus and essential thrombocytopenia purpura.* Ann Intern Med 1942, **16,** 1097-1117.
8. Dameshek W. *Hypersplenism.* Bull NY Acad Sci 1955, **31,** 113-136.
9. Moeschlin S, Wagner K. *Agranulocytosis due to the occurrence of leukocyte agglutinins.* Acta Haematol 1952, **8,** 29-41.
10. Faber V, Elling P. *Leucocyte-specific antinuclear factors in patients with Felty's syndrome, rheumatoid arthritis, systemic lupus erythematosus and other diseases.* Acta Med Scand 1966, **179,** 257-267.
11. Denko CW, Zumpft CW. *Chronic arthritis with splenomegaly and leukopenia.* Arthritis Rheum 1962, **5,** 478-491.
12. Logue GL, Silberman HR. *Felty's syndrome without splenomegaly.* Am J Med 1979, **66,** 703-706.
13. Spivak JL. *Felty's syndrome: an analytical review.* John Hopkins Med J 1977, **141** 156-162.
14. Bucknall RC, Davis P, Bacon PA, Verrier Jones J. *Neutropenia in rheumatoid arthritis: studies on possible contributing factors.* Ann Rheum Dis 1982, **41,** 242-247.
15. Thorn C, Urowitz MB. *Long-term outcome in Felty's syndrome.* Ann Rheum Dis 1982, **41,** 486-489.
16. Goldberg J, Pinals RS. *Felty's Syndrome.* Seminars in Arthritis Rheum 1980, **10,** 52-65.
17. Laszlo J, Jones R, Silberman HR, Banks PM. *Splenectomy for Felty's syndrome. Clinicopathological study of 27 patients.* Arch Intern Med 1978, **138,** 597-602.
18. Sienknecht CW, Urowitz MB, Pruzanski W, Stein HB. *Felty's syndrome, clinical and serological analysis of 34 cases.* Ann Rheum Dis 1977, **36,** 500-507.
19. Ruderman M, Miller LW, Pinals RS. *Clinical and serological observations on 27 patients with Felty's syndrome.* Arthritis Rheum 1968, **11,** 377-384.
20. O'Neill JA Jr, Scott HW, Billings FT, Forster JH. *The role of splenectomy in Felty's syndrome.* Ann Surg 1968, **167,** 81-84.
21. De Gruchy GC. *Diagnosis and treatment of Felty's syndrome.* Geriatrics 1965, **20,** 219-226.
22. Gordon DA, Stein JL, Broder I. *The extra-articular features of rheumatoid arthritis: a systemic analysis of 127 cases.* Am J Med 1973, **54,** 445-452.
23. Barnes CG, Turnbull AL, Vernon-Roberts B. *A clinical and pathological survey of 21 patients and their response to treatment.* Ann Rheum Dis 1971, **30,** 359-374.
24. Thorn C, Urowitz MS, Wanless I, Roberts E, Blendis LM. *Liver disease in Felty's syndrome.* Am J Med 1982, **73,** 35-40.
25. Luthra MS, Munder CG. *Spontaneous remission of Felty's syndrome.* Arthritis Rheum 1975, **18,** 515-517.
26. Wallis WJ, Loughran TP, Kadin ME, Clark EA, Starkebaum GA. *Polyarthritis and neutropenia associated with circulating large granular lymphocytes.* Ann Int Med 1985, **103,** 357-362.
27. Hurd ER, Chubick A, Jasin HE, Ziff M. *Increased Clq binding immune complexes in Felty's syndrome.* Arthritis Rheum 1979, **22,** 697-702.
28. Dinant HJ, Hissink Muller W, van den Berg-Coonen EM, Nijenhuis LE, Engelfriet CP. *HLA-DRW4 in Felty's syndrome.* Arthritis Rheum 1980, **23,** 1336-1337.
29. Vincent, PC, Levi JA, MacQueen A. *The mechanism of neutropenia in Felty's syndrome.* Brit J Haematol 1974, **27,** 463-475.
30. Breedveld FC, Lafeber GJM, Docker G, Claas FMJ, Cats A. *Felty's syndrome: auto-immune neutropenia or immune-complex-mediated disease?* Rheumatol Int 1985, **5,** 253-258.
31. Starkebaum G, Singer JW, Arend WP. *Humoral and cellular immune mechanisms of neutropenia in patients with Felty's syndrome.* Clin Exp Immunol 1980, **39,** 307-314.
32. Abdou NI. *Heterogeneity of bone-marrow directed immune mechanisms in the pathogenesis of neutropenia of Felty's syndrome.* Arthritis Rheum 1983, **26,** 947-952.
33. Goldberg LS, Bacon PA, Bucknall RC, Fitchen J, Cline MJ. *Inhibition of human bone marrow-granulocyte precursors by serum from patients with Felty's syndrome.* J Rheumatol 1980, **7,** 275-278.
34. Howe GB Fordham JN, Brown KA, Currey HLF. *Polymorphonuclear cell function in rheumatoid arthritis and in Felty's syndrome.* Ann Rheum Dis 1981, **40,** 370-375.
35. Breedveld FC, van den Barselaar MT, Leigh PCJ, Cats A, van Furth R. *Phagocytosis and intracellular killing of polymorphonuclear cells from patients with rheumatoid arthritis and Felty's syndrome.* Arthritis Rheum 1985, **28,** 395-404.
36. Pengelly CDR. *Felty's syndrome: good response to adrenocorticosteroids; possible mechanism of the anaemia.* Br Med J 1966, **2,** 986-988.
37. Wimer BM, Sloan MM. *Remission in Felty's syndrome with long-term testosterone therapy.* JAMA 1982, **223,** 671-673.
38. Gupta RC, Robinson WA, Smyth CJ. *Efficacy of lithium in rheumatoid arthritis with granulocytopenia (Felty's syndrome).* Arthritis Rheum 1975, **18,** 179-184.

May 1986

PSORIATIC ARTHRITIS

V Wright
ARC Professor of Rheumatology
University Department of Clinical Medicine
General Infirmary at Leeds
P S Helliwell
Consultant Rheumatologist
Royal Infirmary
Huddersfield

HISTORY

In the 1850s an association between arthritis and psoriasis was made by Alibert, yet in the first half of this century such patients were still considered either variants of RA or coincidental psoriasis and RA. The discovery of rheumatoid factor in the serum of the majority of patients with RA proved an important tool in helping to separate forms of polyarthritis from rheumatoid disease, and was used in the extensive clinical studies which have distinguished psoriatic arthritis from RA (4,5). In 1964 the ARA recognised psoriatic arthritis as a distinct clinical entity in their classification of rheumatic diseases (3).

Further clinical and radiological family studies have supported the concept (4), although it is still thought by some authors that psoriasis merely modifies the clinical manifestations of pre-existing RA (5). Moreover, recent evidence from individuals infected with HIV who have developed AIDS supports the distinction between RA and psoriatic arthritis. It appears that the acquisition of HIV infection and subsequent depletion of T helper lymphocytes is usually beneficial to people who have RA, but may exacerbate existing psoriasis or psoriatic arthritis (6).

Further studies of the families of patients with psoriatic arthritis, inflammatory bowel disease, and ankylosing spondylitis, culminated in the concept of the seronegative spondarthritides (7). The members share common clinical features, including sacro-iliitis, a seronegative, anodular, asymmetrical, peripheral oligoarthritis, psoriasiform lesions and sometimes a pustular rash on the hands and soles (keratoderma blenorrhagica), ankylosing spondylitis, iridocyclitis, muco-cutaneous ulceration, and familial aggregation. The increased frequency of HLA B27 in this group of diseases provides confirmation of the concept (8).

CLASSIFICATION

Five groups have been identified (Table 1). These comprise an asymmetrical oligoarthritis involving scattered dip, pip, and mtp joints, a distal joint type of disease in which the distal joints are predominantly (although rarely exclusively) involved, a symmetrical polyarthritis like RA but with an absence of rheumatoid factor, arthritis mutilans, and ankylosing spondylitis with or without peripheral arthritis. Whereas our original work suggested that oligoarthritis was common, recent surveys suggest a symmetrical polyarthritis resembling RA is the most frequent (9,10) and our later studies using tighter definitions would support this (11). The frequency is largely a matter of selection of study groups.

Table I: CLASSIFICATION OF PSORIATIC ARTHRITIS

Classical psoriatic arthritis confined to dip's of hands and feet (5%).

Arthritis mutilans with sacro-iliitis (5%).

Symmetrical polyarthritis indistinguishable from rheumatoid arthritis but with negative serology (15%).

Asymmetrical, pauci-articular, small joint involvement, with 'sausage' digits (70%).

Ankylosing spondylitis with or without peripheral arthritis (5%).

Moll, J.M.H. and Wright, V. Psoriatic arthritis. *Sem. Arthr. Rheum.* 1973, **3:** 55-78.

EPIDEMIOLOGY

Precise prevalence figures are difficult to achieve because of the variable criteria used by different authors, and the presence of mild lesions often unnoticed by the patients. 39% of in-patients with severe psoriasis are said to have inflammatory arthritis (12). The generally accepted figure, however, is around 5-8% of patients with psoriasis (4,13). In general practice the annual incidence has been reported as 80 cases/100,000 from a small practice, using rather loose definitions of psoriatic arthritis (14). The sex ratio in psoriatic arthritis is close to unity, although in distal joint arthritis and spinal arthritis males predominate. Juvenile psoriatic arthritis is rare, and similar groupings occur to those seen in adults. The epidemiology of AIDS overlaps with that of psoriasis. Anyone presenting for the first time with widespread severe psoriasis and a rapidly progressive arthritis should be considered for HIV testing.

CLINICAL FEATURES

Psoriasis usually precedes joint disease (75%), but in 15% the onset is synchronous, and in 10% arthritis precedes psoriasis. In patients with seronegative polyarthritis careful search should be made for lesions of psoriasis in skin and nails, a careful history taken of previous skin lesions, and a detailed family history obtained.

Table 2: PSORIATIC ARTHRITIS - CLINICAL FEATURES
Any form of psoriasis or a history compatible with psoriasis.
Peripheral polyarthritis, frequently symmetrical.
Typical inflammatory involvement of dip's.
Asymmetrical spondylitis and sacro-iliitis.
Uncommon but characteristic mutilating arthritis associated with telescoping of fingers.
Dactylitis (sausage digits).
Absent rheumatoid nodules.

DIP involvement This type of psoriatic arthritis is nearly always associated with psoriatic nail changes.

Arthritis mutilans is rare but striking. Dissolution of the bones produces shortening of the digits with redundant folds of skin, the main-en-lorgnette deformity (opera glass hands), and a comparable phenomenon in the feet.

Symmetrical polyarthritis is indistinguishable from RA and involves small joints of the hands and feet, wrists, ankles, knees and elbows, but without subcutaneous nodules and with a negative sheep cell agglutination test.

Asymmetrical, pauciarticular arthropathy of small joints is most likely to be due to psoriatic arthritis. Sausage digits may occur due to tenosynovitis and involvement of the interphalangeal joints. Dactylitis may occur in a finger or toe (this may also be seen in reactive arthritis).

Spondylitis Enthesopathy is characteristic, particularly at the insertion of the tendo-achilles, the plantar fascia, and the musculo-tendonous insertions around the pelvis. Spondylitis may be regarded as an example of multiple enthesopathies.

Juvenile psoriatic arthritis is similar to the adult form, but the arthritis may precede the psoriasis. Its clinical manifestations are an asymmetrical polyarthritis often involving the digits, pauciarticular arthritis involving mainly the knee, and spondylitis (15, 16). Dactylitis occurs as well as eye involvement, although chronic iridocyclitis is associated with a positive anti-nuclear factor.

Skin lesions The clinical sub-types of psoriatic arthritis are not associated with any particular type of cutaneous psoriasis, but distal joint arthropathy is virtually never found unless there is associated psoriatic involvement of the nails.

Palmar-plantar pustulosis differs from classical psoriasis, and is associated with an inflammatory condition affecting the anterior chest wall (17, 18). The syndrome has been widened to include acne conglobata, acne fulminans, and hydroadenitis suppurativa. Sterno-clavicular hyperostosis, chronic sterile multifocal osteomyelitis, hyperostosis of the spine and a peripheral arthritis, have been grouped under the acronym, SAPHO (18). Our own recent studies, showing sterno-clavicular and manubrio-sternal inflammation in association with psoriasis vulgaris, suggest SAPHO should be included within the clinical spectrum of psoriatic arthritis (11).

Eye lesions Ocular inflammation may be found in a third of these patients, conjunctivitis in 20%, and iritis in 7% (19).

Oedema We have seen a number of cases of unilateral oedema associated with psoriasis (20). Although it has been suggested that this might be the 'whole limb' version of dactylitis, in our experience individual member joints are not particularly inflamed, and the mechanism may be similar to that observed in limb oedema in RA.

HIV infection An explosive and severe form of psoriasis may occur in association with HIV (21). This is often a poor prognostic factor and a rapidly progressive psoriatic arthritis may supervene. There is dispute about the first occurrence of psoriasis in association with HIV infection, reported prevalences ranging from 5% (22) to no more than the general population (23). The one prospective study undertaken by a dermatologist reported no increase in the prevalence of psoriasis, although a severe form of seborrheic dermatitis occurred in 12% (24). When HIV is acquired from intravenous drug abuse, the incidence of arthritis is 0.5%, much less than that associated with sexually acquired HIV (45).

COURSE

Some authors have suggested that the presenting oligoarthritis evolves into a symmetrical polyarthritis (9), although in our series only 6% changed pattern (11). Psoriatic arthritis usually follows a mild course in our experience (25), although in Toronto 10% of a series of 220 patients were in ARA functional class IV (9). This group finds there is inexorable gradual progression in terms of the number of joints affected, but not necessarily in functional status (26). Over several years similar increments in syndesmophyte frequency have been observed in the thoraco-lumbar spine (27).

Most patients with juvenile psoriatic arthritis do well, although a few progress into adult life, and some are confined to a wheelchair (15). No predictive factors have been identified yet; HLA DR4 does not appear to predict a more severe course and worse functional outcome (9). In our own study (25), employment was not adversely affected in most patients. In Canada, however, patients were twice as likely to be unemployed as a group with psoriasis and other joint complaints (28). This difference is likely to be due to selection, since the Canadian patients required PUVA treatment, and presumably, therefore, had more severe psoriasis.

In terms of mortality, 18 patients died of 168 followed for more than 10 years in the Leeds study (25). Two of these had pulmonary infection, probably related to immobility as a result of the arthritis. One other death was related to haemorrhage associated with immunosuppressive treatment for psoriasis. Amyloid has been reported in the juvenile disease, occurring in 2 out of 43 cases (15).

BLOOD TESTS

Rheumatoid factor is by definition absent. The biochemical response to active disease is similar to that of rheumatoid arthritis (29). In a recent study symmetrical polyarthritis produced the greatest changes in ESR, histidine and C-reactive protein. Overall, ESR was the best laboratory guide to clinical disease activity. Cytidine deaminase was not helpful in monitoring synovial inflammation in psoriatic arthritis, in contrast to RA where it is a useful marker (30). This is doubtless due to the fact that cytidine deaminase is derived from neutrophils, which are abundant in psoriatic skin. HLA B27 is positive in 71% of patients with psoriatic spondylitis (31), and in 32.5% of those in the distal joint group (8).

RADIOLOGY

Characteristic features include asymmetrical small joint involvement of the interphalangeal joints of the hands and feet, marginal erosions with adjacent proliferation of bone resulting in 'whiskering', a tendency to ankylosis of the joint, osteolysis involving phalangeal and metacarpal bones resulting in telescoping digits, characteristic pencil-in-cup deformity with arthritis mutilans, periostitis, whittling of the terminal phalanges (particularly of the hallux), and proliferative new bone formation at entheses, particularly around the pelvis and os calsis.

In spinal disease asymmetrical sacro-iliitis, and asymmetrical syndesmophytes of different shape from those found in idiopathic ankylosing spondylitis occur (32). Psoriatic spondylitic patients are also said to have less zygoapophyseal disease and fewer syndesmophytes than idiopathic AS. We have found it difficult to define the 'other-than-marginal' or 'chunky' syndesmophytes which have been described in psoriatic spondylitis; they are often indistinguishable from hyperostotic lesions associated with DISH. Resnik (33) has described hyperostosis of the anterior surface of the vertebral bodies, particularly in the cervical spine, severe cervical spine involvement and associated sacro-iliitis with relative sparing of the thoraco-lumbar spine, and parave tebral ossification - a fact previously noted by Bywaters and Dixon (34).

Imaging with bone-seeking radio-isotopes gives additional information on the distribution of joint involvement (11). We have noted an unexplained abnormal uptake at several sites of the long bone, which may represent sub-clinical 'sterile' focal osteomyelitis. Periarticular uptake in 12 patients in the absence of overt arthropathy has been described (35).

DIFFERENTIAL DIAGNOSIS

The absence of rheumatoid factor in the serum and of sub cutaneous nodules helps to distinguish psoriatic arthritis from RA. Moreover, cardiac, pleural, vasculitic, lymph node and renal involvement are rare in psoriatic arthritis. The positive features in favour of a diagnosis are the pattern of joint involvement - dip and anterior chest wall involvement commonly occurs, whereas temporo-mandibular joints are infrequently involved (11). Dactylitis, iritis, unilateral oedema, and enthesopathy (particularly around the heel) are very suggestive. Radiological features of proliferative new bone at the enthesis, whiskering around the joints, acro-osteolysis, periostitis and pencil-in-cup deformities are typical radiological features, as is spinal involvement. The presence or history of psoriatic skin lesions and/or a family history of psoriasis must immediately raise the possibility of psoriatic arthritis, although with two common diseases such as psoriasis and RA, there will be coincidental cases.

It is often impossible to distinguish psoriatic arthritis and reactive arthritis, particularly when keratoderma blennorrhagica occurs. A clear infective trigger, whether venereal or dysenteric, will help distinguish those cases.

Table 3:
MANAGEMENT OF SKIN AND JOINT LESIONS IN PSORIATIC ARTHRITIS.

Base decision to start second line therapy on severity of each particular system.

Skin and joint symptoms may fluctuate together so that specific dermatological therapies may help the joints indirectly.

A number of preparations may help both skin and joint problems, including methotrexate, azathioprine, cyclosporin A, and etretinate.

Selection of appropriate drug depends on several factors, including medical, social and severity of joint and skin lesions.

TREATMENT

NSAID's and analgesics for arthritis, and dithranol and/or coal tar for psoriasis, are all that are needed in most cases. If a second-line agent is required for the arthritis, then salazopyrine EN is the drug of choice (36), followed by intra-muscular gold (37). Anti-malarials have a beneficial effect, although the occasional development of exfoliative dermatitis makes one cautious in their use.

PUVA benefits moderately severe psoriasis and may improve peripheral arthritis, but not spinal disease (38). The traditional skin treatments do not benefit the arthropathy.

Methotrexate at a dose of 7.5-25 mg weekly, azathioprine 1-3 mg per kg daily, and cyclosporin A 3-5 mg per kg daily, benefit the skin and joint lesions (39). Retinoids, such as etretinate, dose 0.75mg/kg/day for 2-4 weeks (which may be titrated up to 1mg/kg with a maximum total dose of 75mg), are effective for the arthritis associated with psoriasis, as well as being beneficial to the skin, particularly in generalised pustular and erythrodermic psoriasis (40). This drug must be avoided in young females who are likely to become pregnant.

SURGERY

With adequate pre- and post-operative multi-disciplinary care, together with careful operative and peri-operative antisepsis there is no reason why patients with psoriatic arthritis should be denied potential benefits of arthroplasty or other orthopaedic procedures (41-44).

Table 4: SECOND-LINE DRUGS USED IN PSORIASIS AND PSORIATIC ARTHRITIS.

Arthropathy alone:	
Salazopyrine EN -	40 mg/kg/day (benefits axial and peripheral arthropathy).
Gold compounds -	intra-muscular sodium-auro thiomalate 50mg weekly to a total of 1G.
Anti-malarials -	chloroquine, hydroxychloroquine 5 mg/kg/day.
Arthropathy and skin:	
*Methotrexate -	oral or intra-muscular 7.5-25 mg weekly
Azathioprine -	1-3 mg/kg/day orally
Etretinate -	0.75 mg/kg/day orally for 2-4 weeks (see text)
Cyclosporin-A -	3-5 mg/kg/day orally

*Commonly used but not yet licensed.

Table 5: GUIDELINES FOR ORTHOPAEDIC PROCEDURES IN PSORIATIC ARTHRITIS

Criteria for operation as with any other severe arthropathy.
Liaison between medical, physiotherapy, and occupational therapy staff prior to and after operation.
Adequate cleaning of psoriatic plaques with alcohol based antiseptic.
Systemic antibiotics specifically against staphylococci and streptococci.
Early post-operative mobilisation.

REFERENCES

1. Wright, V. Psoriatic arthritis. *Ann. rheum Dis.* 1961; **20:** 123-132.

2. Baker, H., Golding, D.N. and Thompson, M. Psoriasis and arthritis. *Ann. Int. Med.* 1963; **58:** 909-925.

3. Blumberg, B.S., Bunim, J.J., Calkins, E., Pirani, C.L. and Zvafler, N.J. ARA nomenclature and classification of arthritis and rheumatism (tentative). *Arth Rheum.* 1964; **7:** 93-97.

4. Wright, V. and Moll, J.M.H. *Seronegative Polyarthritis.* 1976. North Holland Publishing Company, Amsterdam.

5. Cats, A. Is psoriatic arthritis an entity? In: *Rheumatology/85.* Brookes, P.M. and York, J.R. Eds., 1985: pp.295-301. Elsevier, Amsterdam.

6. Arnett, F.C., Reveille, J.D. and Duvic, M. Psoriasis and psoriatic arthritis associated with human immunodeficiency virus infection. In: *Rheumatic Disease Clinics of North America.* Winchester, R. Ed., 1991; **17:** 59-78. Saunders, Philadelphia.

7. Moll, J.M.H., Haslock, I., Macrae, I.F. and Wright V. Association between ankylosing spondylitis, psoriatic arthritis, Reiter's disease, the intestinal arthropathies and Behçet's syndrome. *Medicine* 1974; **53:** 343-364.

8. Eastmond, C.J. and Woodrow, J.C. The HLA system and the arthropathies associated with psoriasis. *Ann. rheum Dis.* 1977; **36:** 112-120.

9. Gladman, D.D., Shuckett, R., Russell, M.L., Thorne, J.C. and Schachter, R.K. Psoriatic arthritis: an analysis of 220 patients. *Quart. J. Med.* 1987; **62:** 127-141.

10. Oriente, C.B., Scarpa, R., Puccino, A. and Oriente, P. Psoriasis and psoriatic arthritis. Dermatological and Rheumatological Co-operative Clinical Report. *Acta Venereol.* (Stockholm) 1989: **Suppl.146:** 69-71.

11. Helliwell, P.S., Marchessoni, A., Peters, M., Barker, M. and Wright, V. A re-evaluation of the osteoarticular manifestations of psoriasis. *Brit J. Rheum.* 1991; **30:** 339-345.

12. Leonard, D.G., O'Duffy, J.D. and Rogers, R.S. Prospective analysis of psoriatic arthritis in patients hospitalised for psoriasis. *Mayo Clinic Proc.* 1978; **53:** 511-518.

13. Espinoza, L.R. Psoriatic arthritis: further epidemiologic and genetic considerations. In: *Psoriatic Arthritis.* Gerber, L.H. and Espinoza, L.R. Eds., 1985. Grune and Stratton, New York.

14. Hodgkin, K. *Towards Earlier Diagnosis in Primary Care.* 4th Edition, 1978. Churchill-Livingstone.

15. Lambert, J.R., Ansell, B.M., Stevenson, B.E. and Wright V. Psoriatic arthritis in childhood. In: *Clinics in Rheumatic Diseases.* Ansell, B.M. Ed., 1976; **2:** 339-352. Saunders, Eastbourne.

16. Hamilton, M.L., Gladman, D.D., Shore, A., Laxer, R.M. and Silverman, E.D. Juvenile psoriatic arthritis and HLA antigens. *Ann. rheum. Dis.* 1990; **49:** 694-697.

17. Matsuura, M., Azuma, A., Okai, K. and Kawashima, M. Clinical features of 53 cases with pustulotic arthro-osteitis. *Ann. rheum. Dis.* 1981; **40:** 547-553.

18. Benhamou, C.L., Shamot, A.M. and Kahn, M.F. Synovitis acne pustulosis hyperostosis osteomyelitis syndrome (SAPHO). A new syndrome among the spondylo-arthropathies? *Clin. Exp Rheum.* 1988; **6:** 109-112.

19. Lambert, J.R. and Wright, V. Eye inflammation in psoriatic arthritis. *Ann. rheum. Dis.* 1976; **35:** 354-356.

20. Vasey, F.B. and Espinoza, L.R. Psoriatic arthropathy. In: Spondyarthropathies. Calin, A. Ed., 1984: pp.151-185. Grune and Stratton, New York.

21. Johnson, T.M., Duvik, M., Rapini, R.P. and Rios, A. AIDS exacerbates psoriasis. *New Eng. J. Med.* 1985; **313:** 1415.

22. Espinoza, L.R., Berman, A., Vasez, F.B., Cahalin, C., Nelson, R. and Germain, B. Psoriatic arthritis and acquired immunodeficiency syndrome. *Arthr. Rheum.* 1988; **31:** 1034-1040.

23. Duvik, N., Johnson, T.M., Rapini, R.P., Freeze, T., Brewton, G. and Rios, A. Acquired immuno-deficiency syndrome, associated psoriasis and Reiter's syndrome. *Arch. Derm.* 1987; **123:** 1622-1632.

24. Valle, S.L. Dermatologic findings related to immuno-deficiency virus infection in high risk individuals. *J. Am. Acad. Derm.* 1987; **17:** 951-961.

25. Roberts, M.E.T., Wright, V., Hill, A.G.S. and Mehra, A.C. Psoriatic arthritis. A follow-up study. *Ann. rheum. Dis.* 1976; **35:** 206-212.

26. Gladman, D.D., Stafford-Brady, F., Chang, C.H., Lewandowski, K. and Russell, M.L. Longitudinal study of clinical and radiological progression in psoriatic arthritis. *J. Rheum.* 1990; **17:** 809-812.

27. Hanly, J.G., Russell, M.L., and Gladman, D.D. Psoriatic spondylo-arthropathy: a longterm prospective study. *Ann. rheum. Dis.* 1988; **47:** 386-393.

28. Stern, R.S. The epidemiology of joint complaints in patients with psoriasis. *J. Rheum.* 1985; **12:** 315-320.

29. Sitton, N.G., Dixon, J.S., Bird, H.A. and Wright, V. Serum biochemistry in rheumatoid arthritis, seronegative arthropathies, osteoarthritis, SLE and normal subjects. *J. Rheum.* 1987; **26:** 131-135.

30. Helliwell, P.S., Marchessoni, A., Peters, M., Platt, R. and Wright, V. Cytidine deaminase activity, C-reactive protein, histidine, and erythrocyte sedimentation rate as measures of disease activity in psoriatic arthritis. *Ann. rheum. Dis.* 1991; **50:** 362-365.

31. Lambert, J.R. and Wright, V. Psoriatic spondylitis; a clinical and radiological description of the spine in psoriatic arthritis. *Quart. J. Med.* 1977; **46:** 411-425.

32. McEwen, C., DiTata, D., Lingg, C., Porini, A., Good, A. and Rankin, T. Ankylosing spondylitis and spondylitis accompanying ulcerative colitis, regional enteritis, psoriasis and Reiter's disease. *Arthr. Rheum.* 1971; **14:** 291-318.

33. Resnik, D. and Niwayama, G. Psoriatic arthritis. In: *Diagnosis of Bone and Joint Disorders.* Vol. 2. Resnik, D. and Niwayama, G. Eds.,1981; chapter 30: 1103-1129. Saunders, Philadelphia.

34. Bywaters, E.G.L. and Dixon, A.St. J. Paravertebral ossification in psoriatic arthritis. *Ann. rheum. Dis.* 1965; **24:** 313-331.

35. Namey, T.C. and Rosenthal, L. Periarticular uptake of 99M Technetium Diphosphanate in psoriasis. *Arthr. Rheum.* 1976; **19:** 607-612.

36. Farr, M., Kitas, G.D., Waterhouse, L., Jubb, R., Felix-Davies, D. and Bacon, P.A. Sulphasalazine in psoriatic arthritis: a double-blind placebo controlled study. *Brit. J. Rheum.* 1990; **29:** 46-49.

37. Palit, J., Hill, J., Capell, H.A., Carey, J., Daunt, S.O'N., Cawley, M.I.D., Bird, H.A. and Nuki, G. A multicentre double-blind comparison of auranofin intramuscular gold thiomalate and placebo in patients with psoriatic arthritis. *Brit. J. Rheum.* 1990; **29:** 280-282.

38. Perlman, S.G., Gerber, L.H., Roberts, R.M., Nigra, T.P. and Barth, W.F. Photochemotherapy and psoriatic arthritis. *Ann. Int. Med.* 1979; **91:** 717-722.

39. Gupta, A.K., Matteson, E.L., Ellis, C.N., Ho, V.C., Tellner, D.C., Voorhees, J.J. and McCune, W.J. Cyclosporin in the treatment of psoriatic arthritis. *Arch. Derm.* 1989; **125:** 507-510.

40. Hopkins, R., Bird, H.A., Jones, H., Hill, J., Surrall, K., Astbury, C., Miller, A. and Wright, V. A double-blind controlled trial of etretinate (Tigason) and ibuprofen in psoriatic arthritis. *Ann. rheum. Dis.* 1985; **44:** 189-193.

41. Lambert, J.T., and Wright, V. Surgery in patients with psoriasis and arthritis. *Rheum. Rehab.* 1979; **18:** 35-37.

42. Menon, T.J. and Wroblewski, B.M. Charnley low friction arthroplasty in patients with psoriasis. *Clin. Orthop.* 1983; **176:** 127-128.

43. Stern, S.H., Insall, J.M., Windsor, R.E., Inglis, A.E. and Dines, D.M. Total knee arthroplasty in patients with psoriasis. *Clin. Orthop.* 1989; **248:** 108-111.

44. Beyer, C.A., Hanssen, A.D., Lewallen, D.G. and Pittelkow, M.R. Primary total knee arthroplasty in patients with psoriasis. *J. Bone Jt.Surg.* 1991; **73B:** 258-259.

45. Munoz-Fernandez, S., Cerdunal, A., Balsa, A., Quiralte, J., de Arco, A., Pera, J.M., Barbado, F.J., Vezquez, J.J. and Gijon, J. Rheumatic manifestations in 556 patients with human immuno-deficiency virus infection. *Sem. Arthr. Rheum.* 1991; **21:** 30-39.

May 1992

REITER'S SYNDROME & REACTIVE ARTHRITIS

A Keat
Senior Lecturer in Rheumatology
Charing Cross and Westminster Medical School
Westminster Hospital
London

Until the introduction of penicillin the distinction between septic and aseptic arthritis associated with sexually transmitted genital-tract infection (GTI) was blurred and of uncertain significance. The establishment of Reiter's syndrome (RS) as a readily recognisable clinical entity comprising the concurrence of aseptic arthritis, usually affecting a few lower limb joints, ocular inflammation and genital-tract inflammation was therefore a critical advance, identifying a common joint disease quite distinct from the septic complications of gonorrhoea. Since that time it has become clear that aseptic arthritis may be associated with either gonococcal or non-gonococcal GTI and the spectrum and diversity of the clinical picture is wide. Furthermore, rigid adherence to the triad of RS or to any clinically-defined set of criteria has become of limited value in either clinical practice or research.

Behind the clinical pigeon-hole of RS is the concept that a localised infection at one site may initiate a train of incompletely understood events which result in the development of synovitis at a distant site without viable micro-organisms travelling to the joint. Joint disease believed to result from infection in this way is referred to as "reactive". Hence reactive arthritis refers solely to an hypothetical relationship between infection and arthritis and is not tied down to any set of clinical criteria. It is a useful diagnostic group, avoiding the semantic problems of disease which does not tidily fit into a closely-defined syndrome, but the reactive arthritis concept remains an hypothesis which needs to be more extensively tested. Reactive arthritis is the commonest form of inflammatory arthritis in young men.

INFECTIOUS TRIGGER FACTORS

Reactive arthritis is well documented after both gastrointestinal and genital-tract infections. The clinical picture in the two instances is indistinguishable. A third group of patients exists in whom the clinical and genetic features are typical of reactive arthritis but in whom no infection is found. This group has been referred to as incomplete Reiter's syndrome[1] and reactive arthritis of unknown origin[2].

SEXUAL ACQUISITION

In the United Kingdom sexually-transmitted GTI is the commonest aetiological factor; when the history and clinical findings strongly suggest such a cause the term sexually-acquired reactive arthritis (SARA) has been applied[2]. There are no definitive criteria for deciding

CLINICAL FEATURES OF REACTIVE ARTHRITIS

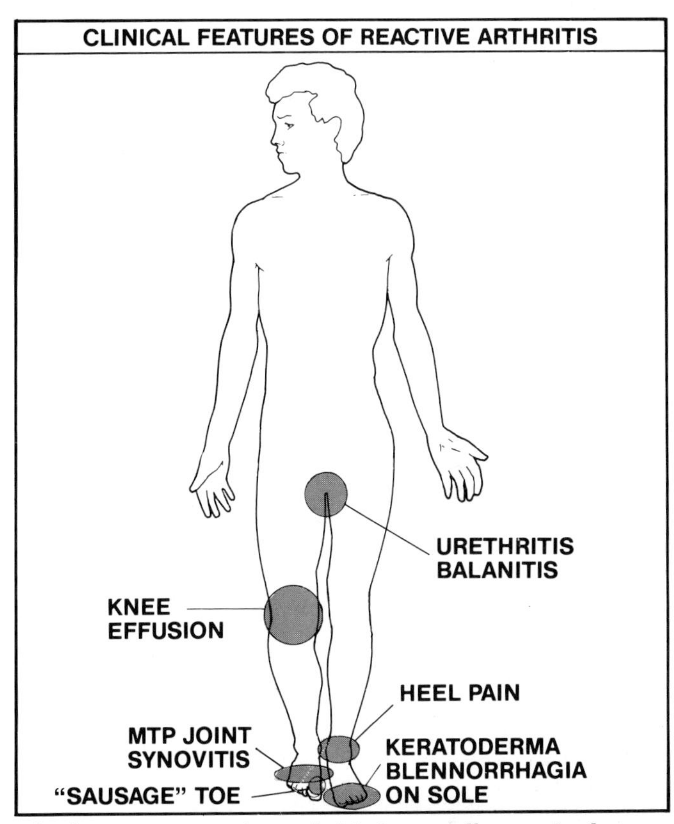

whether or not reactive arthritis is sexually acquired. In practice, a new sex partner within 3 months of the onset, clear evidence of GTI either gonococcal or non-gonococcal with rheumatic lesions developing within 4 weeks of symptoms of GTI makes the diagnosis likely. Finding GTI in the sex partner is strong corroborating evidence of a sexually-transmitted disease so that examination of the partner is important. It must be borne in mind that even marked urethritis or cervicitis may be symptomless especially in women, so that it is less often possible to reach a firm diagnosis of SARA in women, and that not all urethritis is sexually transmitted. Most patients give frank answers when asked direct, unprejudiced questions.

It remains uncertain whether the cause of the GTI is also the trigger for reactive arthritis but working on this assumption three micro-organisms have come under scrutiny as possible arthritogens.

CHLAMYDIA TRACHOMATIS

Approximately 50% of cases of uncomplicated non-gonococcal urethritis (NGU) and of SARA follow **Chlamydia trachomatis** infections. In those with arthritis, however, serum chlamydial antibody titres and specific cell-mediated immune responses are greater than in those without joint disease [3 4 5]. It is possible, therefore, that in these individuals **C. trachomatis** is specifically involved in the pathogenesis of the arthritis. Several reports document isolation of **C. trachomatis** from peripheral joints of patients with Reiter's syndrome [6 7 8] but the significance of those intriguing findings has yet to be resolved. There is a clear need for further culture studies.

NEISSERIA GONORRHOEAE

Approximately 10% of patients with SARA have gonorrhoea. Some, but not all, of these patients have simultaneous gonococcal and non-gonococcal infections. Joint disease in these individuals is quite distinct from septic gonococcal arthritis. As with **C. trachomatis** enhanced humoral and cellular immune responses to gonococcal antigens have been demonstrated in patients with arthritis compared with those with uncomplicated urogenital gonorrhoea[9].

MYCOPLASMAS

The place of **Ureaplasma urealyticum** has yet to be established. This micro-organism is commonly isolated from the genital tracts of healthy individuals though it is important as it has been demonstrated to be pathogenic in the human genital tract. It presently appears unlikely that other mycoplasmas play a part in reactive arthritis.

GASTROINTESTINAL INFECTION

Reactive arthritis is well documented in association with outbreaks and sporadic cases of bacterial diarrhoea. **Shigella flexneri,** though not **S. Sonnei, Salmonella enteritidis** and **Campylobacter jejuni** are the main offenders[10] though **Yersinia enterocolitica** is a major aetiological factor in some areas, especially Scandinavia[11]. Only a handful of cases of Yersinia arthritis have been diagnosed in the United Kingdom. **Campylobacter enteritis** is important as symptoms may be sufficiently trivial or short-lived to be overlooked by the patient. More recently reactive arthritis has been reported in association with antibiotic-induced colitis so that **Clostridium difficile** may also be important[12]. Arthritis has also been reported in outbreaks of diarrhoea in which no pathogens were identified and as a complication of cases with "traveller's diarrhoea" in which the common bacterial pathogens were excluded. Reports of aseptic arthritis complicating amoebic dysentry, brucellosis and giardiasis are of uncertain importance. It is relevant to note that both **Salmonella** and **Brucella** may cause septic lesions in the peripheral or spinal joints; these must be carefully distinguished from aseptic arthritis.

GENETIC SUSCEPTIBILITY

Peripheral arthritis, psoriasis and spondylitis occur with increased frequency in the family members of probands with reactive arthritis. The HLA-B27 antigen is present in 60-80% of patients[13] although to date no special susceptibility has been associated with any of the B27 variant antigens. An HLA-B27 positive man is approximately 20 times more likely to develop arthritis after developing urethritis or bacterial diarrhoea than a B27 negative one.

The role of the B27 antigen in the pathogenesis of reactive arthritis remains a hotly controversial topic. A major question is whether the B27 antigen itself is directly involved in the pathogenesis of arthritis or whether this determinant is only a marker of the real disease susceptibility genes which are genetically linked to it. Much work has been done in the context of ankylosing spondylitis but this may not be directly pertinent to reactive arthritis. Arguments in favour of each possibility are controversial and presently inconclusive. It appears that HLA-B27 positive individuals develop more severe disease[14] than those lacking the antigen and homozygosity for B27 may also enhance this effect[15].

EPIDEMIOLOGY

At least 1% of men presenting to Sexually-Transmitted Diseases (STD) clinics with NGU develop arthritis. [16]The incidence of arthritis in those presenting with gonorrhoea is unknown though is probably of a broadly similar order. The incidence of reactive arthritis in women with acute GTI is also unknown but as GTI in women may be asymptomatic reactive arthritis due to this cause is probably underdiagnosed. Present figures indicate a true male:female ratio for SARA of 9:1.

In reactive arthritis associated with bacterial diarrhoea males and females are affected equally. The prevalence of arthritis in outbreaks varies somewhat according to the genetic constitution of affected individuals. In Caucasian populations affected by Shigella, Salmonella or Campylobacter infections approximately 2-3% of individuals develop reactive arthritis[10]. Arthritis probably develops in a similar proportion of individuals with yersiniosis though reported figures are selective and suggest a much higher incidence.

PRESENTATION

Reactive arthritis should always be suspected in a young man presenting with joint symptoms. Rheumatic symptoms generally develop 0-30 days after the onset of urethritis, cervicitis or diarrhoea (mean 14 days). In many, however, the diagnosis is missed because this relationship is not clear cut. In some, urogenital or bowel symptoms predominate and joint symptoms are not volunteered because they are either trivial or assumed to

TABLE I

RHEUMATIC FEATURES

	Shigella	Salmonella	Campylobacter	Yersinia	Sexuall Acquir
Mean no joints affected	3.7	3.0	3.2	2.9	2.8
% mono-arthritis	3.6	18.2	19.0	14.7	8.9
% sacro-iliitis	–	6.5	9.5	7.3	9.8
% tendinitis/ enthesopathy	7.8	13.0	4.8	10.8	34.0
Mean episode duration (wk)	19.5	19.3	19.0	18.0	19.0
% patients with multiple episodes	–	16.7	33.3	15.3	48.2
% patients symptoms > 12/12	17.8	–	4.8	9.7	16.5

TABLE II

NON-RHEUMATIC FEATURES (expressed in percenta

	Shigella	Salmonella	Campylobacter	Yersinia	Sexua Acqui
Conjunctivitis)	)	26.5	19.0	9.2	35.0
Acute anterior uveitis)	) 88.7)	5.9	4.8	2.3	4.1
Circinate balinitis	23.7	–	–	–	23.2
Keratoderma blennorrhagia	–	–	–	–	11.6
Oral ulcers	2.4	–	9.5	–	9.8
Erythema nodosum	–	–	–	5.0	–
ECG carditis	7.5	–	9.5	14.1	6.3
Aortic valve disease	–	–	–	1.1	1.6
Nephritis	1.7	–	–	1.0	–
Myositis	–	–	–	2.7	–
Neurological lesions	0.7	–	–	–	0.7
Amyloidosis	–	–	–	–	0.2

be due to a minor injury. In others the converse is true so that presentation is with an apparently isolated episode of arthritis.

In 50% of patients synovitis with effusion at one or both knees is the presenting complaint. Less commonly the first symptoms arise at the metatarsophalangeal (MTP) or ankle joints or as a result of extensor tendinitis or enthesopathy. Joint symptoms may be absent or minimal in spite of substantial joint effusion. All men presenting to STD clinics should be asked about joint and heel symptoms and similarly all men presenting to other departments with acute arthritis should be questioned closely about genital-tract symptoms.

CLINICAL LESIONS

The principal clinical features of reactive arthritis are summarised in Tables I and II. **Synovitis** usually affects the knees, ankles and small joints of the feet. Upper limb involvement should raise the possibility of psoriatic arthritis. Scintiscan studies suggest that acute **sacroiliitis** occurs in up to 73% of patients[17] although X-ray changes at these joints are much less common (see Table II). **Spondylitis** develops in up to 20% of individuals with severe relapsing disease but in a much lower proportion of others. **Inflammatory enthesopathies** are highly characteristic of reactive arthritis, classically producing heel pain at the calcaneal attachments of the Achilles' tendon and plantar fascia[18]. Other sites such as the tendinous insertions at the feet and around the pelvis may also be affected. It is important to

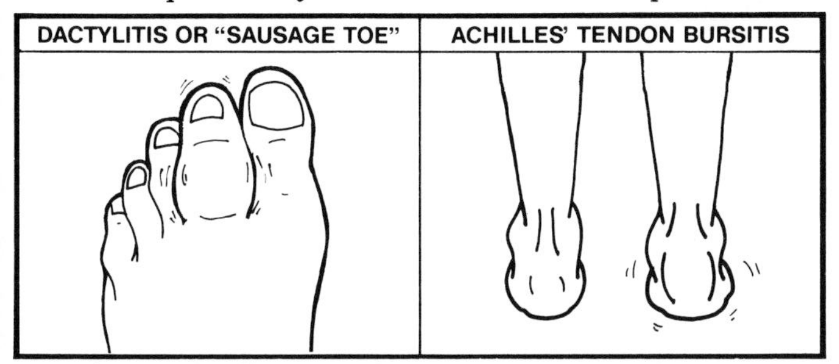

search specifically for such lesions, especially heel tenderness, as the significance of minor symptoms may escape the patient, while the presence of such lesions may be diagnostic.

Skin and mucous membrane lesions also provide important diagnostic clues although they are present in less than a third of patients. **Keratoderma blennorrhagia** appears to be associated only with sexually-acquired disease although **circinate balanitis** and **vulvitis** may occur in other forms of reactive arthritis or in isolation. It is essential, therefore, to inspect the external genitalia and the soles of the feet. In contrast **erythema nodosum** and other skin rashes have only been reported in yersinia arthritis.

Conjunctivitis is a valuable diagnostic sign when present but because of the possibility of more damaging eye lesions such as iritis, keratitis, corneal ulceration and posterior uveitis examination by an ophthalmologist should be mandatory.

Inflammatory aortitis identical to that seen in ankylosing spondylitis occurs in a small minority of patients. This results in clinical aortic regurgitation in around 1% although cardiac conduction defects occur in up to 10% of patients, some of whom require pacing.

It is clear that reactive arthritis whether initiated by genital-tract or gastrointestinal infection is essentially the same disease. It can be seen from the Tables, however, that these two groups differ in three important respects – sex ratio, likelihood of recurrence and nature of associated skin lesions.

CLINICAL OVERLAPS – SPONDARTHRITIS

Reactive arthritis may be indistinguishable from psoriatic arthritis with clinically and histologically identical psoriasiform skin, nail and mucous membrane lesions. Similarly the peripheral joint disease and enthesopathies associated with ankylosing spondylitis follow an identical pattern, and indeed sacroiliitis and spondylitis occur in a minority of patients with reactive arthritis. Peripheral arthritis, sacroiliitis and spondylitis are also significantly associated with inflammatory bowel disease – then referred to as enteropathic arthritis – and acute anterior uveitis may occur in association with each of these conditions. The term "seronegative spondarthritis" has been applied to this inter-related group of disorders[19]. HLA-B27 constitutes a common thread although psoriasis and inflammatory bowel disease appear to act as additional independent susceptibility factors.

DIFFERENTIAL DIAGNOSIS AND INVESTIGATION

It is important to distinguish reactive arthritis from acute gout, sarcoidosis and septic, including gonococcal and tuberculous, arthritis. Therefore, in addition to a clinical search for clues such as tophi, cutaneous granulomata and the characteristic pustular skin lesions of disseminated gonococcal infection it is essential to examine synovial fluid by culture and by polarised light microscopy for crystals and to X-ray the chest.

Examination of the genital tract must include at least microscopy of a gram stained smear of urethral and/or cervical exudate and culture for gonococci if pus cells are present. Where the possibility of gonococcal arthritis exists blood cultures should also be performed. It is essential that the term gonococcal arthritis is reserved for septic joint disease with bacteraemia with or without characteristic pustular skin lesions, and not confused with reactive arthritis associated with localised genital-tract gonococcal infection. The arthritis of Behçet's syndrome is also similar to that of reactive arthritis although the presence of painful genital and oral ulcers rather than painless psoriatic lesions and aphthi and aggressive anterior or posterior uveitis favours this diagnosis. If persistent diarrhoea is present in the absence of specific pathogens sigmoidoscopy, barium enema and small bowel meal may demonstrate the presence of ulcerative colitis or Crohn's disease indicating a diagnosis of enteropathic arthritis. In older men Whipple's disease may also be considered.

Other causes of knee or other joint effusions in young adults include traumatic meniscus injuries, villonodular synovitis, infiltration by lymphoma or leukaemia, viral infection including **Parvovirus, Mycoplasma pneumoniae** infection and mycoplasma infection in hypogammaglobulinaemic individuals. Investigation may, therefore, include arthroscopy and synovial biopsy in addition to further microbiological studies.

PROGNOSIS

In many patients reactive arthritis follows a brief and benign course. While a significant minority remains in whom chronic peripheral joint, spinal or eye disease leads on to persistent pain, deformity and disability, published reports vary widely in their estimates of the frequency of such serious sequelae. In 16-18% of cases active rheumatic disease persists for more than 12 months. In sexually-acquired reactive arthritis the acute episode lasts, on average, approximately 20 weeks, persisting for more than 6 months in 30% of patients. Fifty percent of patients with this form of disease subsequently suffer one or more recurrence although the recurrence rate is much lower following gastrointestinal infection. Recurrences of arthritis may or may not be associated with further episodes of infection and conversely re-infection may occur without recurrence of arthritis. The presence of HLA-B27 predisposes to a longer acute episode, greater likelihood of recurrence and the development of additional features, in particular sacroiliitis, spondylitis and iritis. Recurrent or chronic joint disease may lead to characteristic ("Launois") foot deformities and recurrent iritis may lead to scarring and cataract formation.

MANAGEMENT

Patients with short-lived and minor disease may need no more than an accurate diagnosis and observation. The presence of urethritis or cervicitis necessitates antibiotic treatment usually with a tetracycline for 1-3 weeks although there is currently no firm evidence that this influences the duration of arthritis or the likelihood of recurrence. It is also prudent to treat the sex partner(s) in addition. Bacterial diarrhoea is usually best managed without antibiotics.

If arthritis is restricted to one or a few joints local steroid injections after appropriate exclusion of joint infection may avoid the need for oral medication although, in the majority, treatment with a non-steroid anti-inflammatory drug such as naproxen or indomethacin is indicated. Systemic steroids are seldom indicated or useful and there is little evidence that gold or penicillamine are effective. When arthritis is severe, progressive and disabling cytotoxic drugs such as methotrexate and azathioprine may be helpful. Painful enthesopathies may also respond well to local steroid injections provided that meticulous care is taken to avoid injecting into weight-bearing tendon attachments. Radiotherapy may be valuable in the treatment of resistant heel pain. Inflammatory eye disease requires urgent ophthalmological examination as acute anterior uveitis requires immediate topical, subconjunctival or systemic corticosteroid treatment.

REFERENCES

1. Arnett FC, McClusky OE, Schacter BZ and Lordon RE. "Incomplete Reiter's syndrome; discriminating features and HLA-B27 in diagnosis." *Ann Intern Med* (1976) **84** 8-12.
2. Keat AC, Maini RN, Pegrum GD and Scott JT. "The clinical features and HLA associations of reactive arthritis associated with non-gonococcal urethritis." *Quart J Med* (1979) **48** 323-342.
3. Kousa M, Saikku P, Richmond S and Lassus A. "Frequent association of chlamydial infection with Reiter's syndrome." *Sex Transm Dis* (1978) 5 57-61.
4. Keat AC, Thomas BJ, Taylor-Robinson D, Pegrum GD, Maini RN and Scott JT. "Evidence of *Chlamydia trachomatis* infection in sexually acquired reactive arthritis." *Ann Rheum Dis* (1980) **39** 431-437.
5. Martin DH, Pollock S, Kuo CC, Wang SP, Brunham RC and Holmes KK. *"Chlamydia trachomatis* infections in men with Reiter's syndrome." *Ann Int Med* (1984) **100** 207-213.
6. Schachter J. *"Can chlamydial infections cause rheumatic disease?'* In: Ed Dumonde DC Infection and Immunology in the Rheumatic Diseases. Oxford. Blackwell (1976) 151-157.
7. Vilppula AH, Yli-Kerttula VI, Ahlroos ALC and Terho PE. "Chlamydial isolations and serology in Reiter's syndrome." *Scand. J. Rheum.* (1981) **10** 181-185.
8. Amor B. *"Chlamydia and Reiter's syndrome."* in Ziff M. and Cohen S.B. Eds. Advances in Inflammation Research **9.** The Spondylo-arthropathies. New York. Raven Press. (1985) 203-210.
9. Rosenthal L, Olhagen B and Ek S. "Aseptic arthritis after gonorrhoea." *Ann Rheum Dis* (1980) **39** 141-146.
10. Keat A. "Reiter's syndrome and reactive arthritis in perspective." *New Engl J Med* (1983) **309** 1606-1615.
11. Ahvonen P. "Human Yersinosis in Finland. II Clinical features." *Ann Clin Res* (1972) **4** 34-48.
12. McCluskey J, Reiley TV, Owen ET and Langlan DR. "Reactive arthritis associated with *Clostridium difficile." "Austr. NZ J Med* (1982) **12** 535-537.
13. Brewerton DA "HLA-B27 and the inheritance of susceptibility to rheumatic disease." *Arthr Rheum* (1976) **19** 656-668.
14. Laitinen O, Leirisalo M and Skylv G. "Relation between HLA-B27 and clinical features in patients with yersinia arthritis." *Arthr Rheum* (1977) **20** 1121-1124.
15. Arnett FC, Schacter BZ, Hochberg MC, Hsu SH and Bias WB. "Homozygosity for HLA-B27. Impact on rheumatic disease expression in two families." *Arthr Rheum* (1977) **20** 797-804.
16. Csonka GW. "The course of Reiter's syndrome." *Brit Med J* (1958) **i** 1088-1090.
17. Russell AS, Davis P, Percy JS and Lentle BC. "The sacroiliitis of acute Reiter's syndrome." *J Rheumatol* (1977) **4** 293-296.
18. Niepel GA and Sit'aj S. "Enthesopathy." *Clinics in Rheumatic Diseases* (1979) **5** 857-872.
19. Wright V. "Seronegative polyarthritis, a unified concept." *Arthr Rheum* (1978) **21** 619-633.

September 1986

ANKYLOSING SPONDYLITIS

A Rai
Senior Registrar
Walsgrave Hospitals NHS Trust
Coventry
West Midlands

G R Struthers
Consultant Rheumatologist
Walsgrave Hospitals NHS Trust
Coventry
West Midlands

SUMMARY

Ankylosing spondylitis (AS) is a chronic inflammatory disorder affecting the axial skeleton predominantly, although peripheral joint involvement may also be a significant feature. The disease affects synovial and cartilaginous articulations, and the sites of tendon and ligament attachment to bone (enthesopathy). In the primary care setting it is a clinical diagnosis supported by radiological evidence of sacro-iliitis.

AS AND THE SERONEGATIVE SPONDYLARTHRITIDES

The seronegative spondylarthritides (see Table 1) form a group of disorders which share a number of characteristic overlapping clinical features (Table 2) and an association with HLA B27. One therefore needs to be aware of these conditions as features of sacro-iliitis or spondylitis may occur later in, for example, patients with Reiter's syndrome or psoriatic arthritis.

The association with HLA B27 is greatest with AS (over 95%) and weaker with psoriatic and enteropathic arthritis. Interestingly certain populations have a predilection to develop AS (eg Pima Indians) whilst others develop Reiter's syndrome. An environmental trigger is also important as suggested by the observation that HLA B27 positive identical twins may be discordant for AS. Although HLA B27 may be important in antigen presentation the precise patho-aetiological role remains to be determined. One school of thought (Arthrogenic Peptide Theory) is that the B27 molecule acts as a receptor for an environmental (eg bacterial) peptide trigger. This leads to the generation of primed cytotoxic T lymphocytes which target sites where mimicking self-peptides are being presented by B27 on the surface of cells. Recent research with HLA B27 transgenic mice offers an animal model for AS. Further advances have been made in subtyping of HLA B27 using PCR (polymerase chain reaction) methods and in determining the three-dimensional structural analysis of the B27 molecule.

Table 1.

Seronegative spondyloarthropathy

Grouped together with following clinical characteristics:

1. Peripheral arthritis - lower limb, asymmetrical
2. Radiological sacro-iliitis
3. Negative for rheumatoid factor
4. Absence of nodules and other extra-articular features of rheumatoid arthritis
5. Overlapping extra-articular features characteristic of the group
6. Significant familial aggregation
7. Association with HLA B27

Table 2.

Seronegative spondyloarthropathy

- Ankylosing spondylitis (AS)
- Reiter's syndrome -
  a) sexually acquired reactive arthritis (SARA)
  b) post dysenteric
- Arthropathy of inflammatory bowel disease
- Psoriatic arthritis
- 'Forme fruste' and 'undifferentiated' presentations
- Certain forms juvenile chronic arthritis
- (? Whipple's disease and ?Behçet's disease)

DIAGNOSTIC FEATURES

It is important to assess from the history and examination the features of inflammatory back pain as detailed in Table 3. The significance of distinguishing the causes of 'low back pain' is discussed in a previous ARC report (1).

AS does affect women and, according to data from Bath, UK, the sex ratio prevalence becomes less marked in males as the age of onset increases from less than 16 years (M:F=6:1) to about 30 years (M:F=2:1).

The typical presentation of AS is a young adult with insidious onset of back-pain and stiffness. A misdiagnosis of mechanical pain with symptoms present for a few years is not unusual. The initial involvement of the sacro-iliac joint often produces pain that radiates to one or both buttocks, sometimes to the back of the knee or the thigh. Fatigue can also be a significant problem as a result of chronic discomfort which

Table 3.

Features of inflammatory back pain

	Mechanical	Inflammatory
Onset	acute	gradual
Age at onset (years)	any age	usually < 40
Effect of exercise	worse	better
Effect of rest	better	worse
Morning stiffness	+	+++
Pain radiation	nerve root irritation/ tension signs - L4, L5, S1	diffuse
Sleep disturbance	+/–	+++
Tenderness, spasm	local	diffuse
Scoliosis	+	–
Deficit in movement range	asymmetrical	symmetrical

frequently disturbs the normal sleep pattern. Lumbar spondylitis is debilitating and progression to the thoracic spine also reduces chest expansion which may impair lung function further if there is associated interstitial lung disease. Enthesopathy may present with pain in the back of the heels (achilles tendinitis), heel pain on weight bearing in the mornings (plantar fasciitis), or 'pleuritic' chest pains (intercostal muscle insertions).

In chronic progressive disease there is loss of lumbar lordosis with increased thoracic and cervical kyphosis which becomes fixed as a result of fibrosis and bony ankylosis at which stage pain is generally less prominent.

Examination of the patient should include assessment of:

1) Axial spine involvement.
The following measurements are helpful.

(a) Modified Schober's test of lumbar flexion *(Figure 1)*.
(b) Finger-floor distance on trying to touch the toes. This test by itself is unreliable as it is more of a test for hip flexion.
(c) Occiput-wall distance or tragus-wall distance *(Figure 2)*.
(d) Chest expansion.

The serial assessment of these measurements (eg by physiotherapists) is useful to assess progress but other aspects of disability are discussed later.

2) Sacro-iliac (SI) joint examination
eg springing of pelvis test.
Tenderness over other axial joints eg manubrio-sternal, costovertebral and symphysis pubis may also be present.

3) Peripheral joints, temporo-mandibular joints, shoulders and hips.
Assessment of flexion contractures of the hips and knees at an early stage is particularly important.

4) Enthesopathy eg achilles tendinitis, plantar fasciitis. The intermalleolar straddle (ie distance between medial malleoli with hips abducted wide apart) is reduced in enthesopathy of the pelvic attachments, and in hip joint disease.

5) General examination in relation to the extra-articular features of AS

Self-administered assessments can also be useful, for example the Bath Ankylosing Spondylitis Disease Activity Index (BASDAI) and the Bath Ankylosing Spondylitis Functional Index (BASFI). Enthesopathy can also be documented formally, eg using the Haywood Hospital Enthesitis Index. It is important to distinguish between disease activity/process measures, eg stiffness, and disease severity/outcome measures, eg assessment of deformity.

EXTRA-ARTICULAR FEATURES

General symptoms of fatigue, weight loss and low grade fever are common. Asymptomatic prostatitis is also evident in the majority of male patients. Recurrent acute uveitis (iritis) and conjunctivitis can occur early in the disease, particularly in those with peripheral arthritis, but unrelated to the severity of the spondylitis. Severe uveitis will require ophthalmological assessment and treatment with topical corticosteroids.

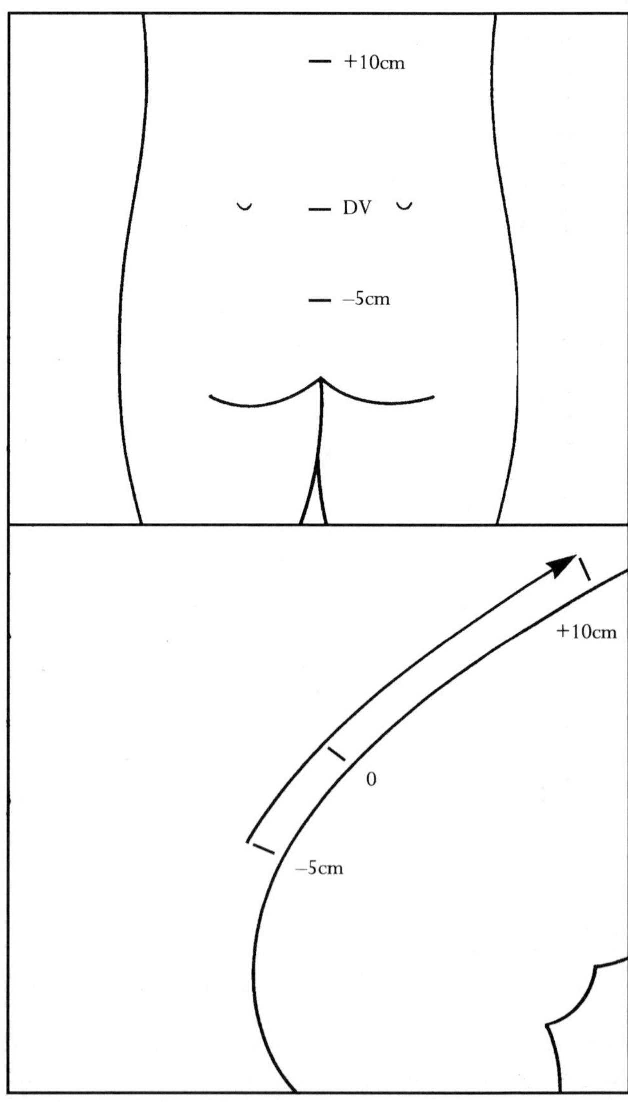

Figure 1. Flexion of lumbar spine measured as increase in distance between points 5cm below and 10cm above the level of the dimples of Venus (DV).

Chronic infiltrative and fibrotic changes in the upper lung fields associated with cough, sputum and dyspnoea are recognised in severe cases. Haemoptysis may occur following apical cavitation and infection with aspergillus producing a clinical picture mimicking tuberculosis, but this is rare.

Cardiac involvement may be clinically silent eg picked up on echocardiography, or cause significant problems. Post-inflammatory scarring may lead to aortic/mitral incompetence or conduction defects.

Other rare complications include an association with IgA nephropathy and the cauda equina syndrome secondary to spinal arachnoiditis.

INVESTIGATIONS

Routine blood tests may prove unhelpful. For example, a normal ESR does not exclude active disease. Non specific abnormalities include raised serum IgA levels. HLA B27 tissue typing is an expensive test which is not readily available in district general hospitals and is not recommended as part of the initial screening tests. In fact 8% of the normal population is HLA B27 positive and X-ray of the sacro-iliac joints is of equal diagnostic value. Occasionally (ie in about 20% of cases) patients present with an asymmetrical seronegative peripheral inflammatory arthropathy/enthesopathy - typically they are in the adolescent age group and may also be seen in the combined paediatric/rheumatology clinic. In such circumstances HLA B27 typing can be useful.

The X-ray changes affecting the sacro-iliac joints may develop some years after the onset of symptoms. Changes may be difficult to interpret in the teenage 'immature' pelvis or in the older patient with patchy 'degenerative' changes. One must not forget to distinguish the characteristic features of osteitis condensans ilii which may be seen incidentally in the multiparous female. Occasionally early changes affecting the SI can be seen on computerised tomography (CT) scanning with equivocal plain X-rays of the joints, but this investigation should not be over-used. In established cases with complications, however, CT scanning is useful in determining spinal fractures, spinal stenosis and thecal diverticulae.

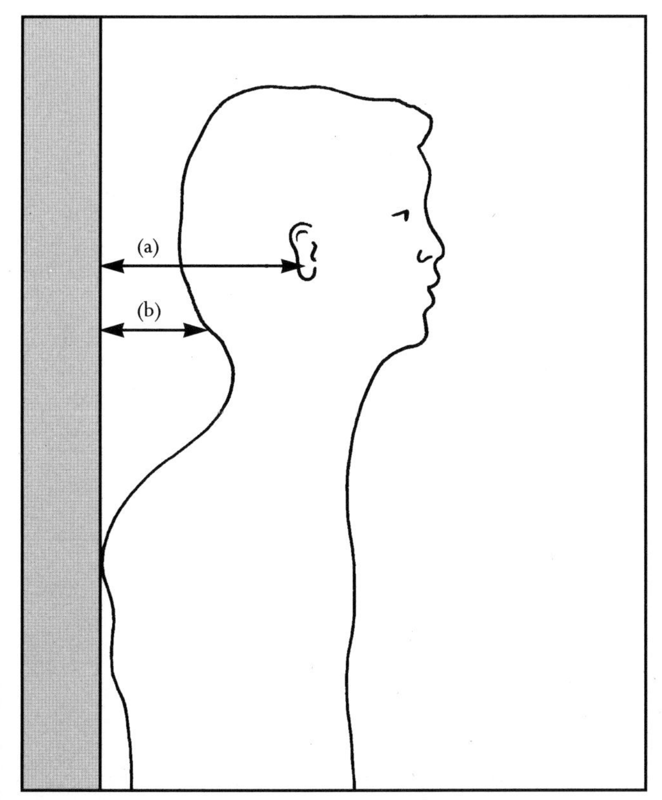

Figure 2. Wall-tragus (a) and wall-occiput (b) measurements.

MANAGEMENT

One cannot over-emphasize the importance of a number of general measures which, together with patient/ family education and awareness of the condition, can help to achieve a good prognosis in the majority of cases compared with the non-compliant, uninformed patients, some of whom may be from a poorer socio-economic background and require extra attention.

The objectives in early disease are to relieve pain and stiffness, and to maintain good posture and function. General exercises (eg swimming, extension exercises) are actively encouraged but specific measures are also necessary. Adverse conditions affecting posture at work and at home should be corrected. Occupational therapists can assess the need for any appliances, eg home aids, driving mirrors. Many hospital physiotherapy departments now run 'spondylitis classes', often in the evenings, on a regular basis.

Non-steroidal anti-inflammatory drugs provide symptomatic relief and slow release preparations taken in the evenings are helpful. Occasionally there is still a role for the use of phenylbutazone, with monitoring of the full blood count, on a named-patient prescription from a consultant rheumatologist. The use of sulphasalazine is mainly reserved for those with significant active peripheral joint involvement which has progressed despite other local measures including intra-articular joint injection. There is no convincing data or appropriate trials supporting the long term use of various drugs (eg methotrexate, pulse methylpredniolone, other second line agents) in the treatment of active spinal disease.

HLA B27 AND GENETIC COUNSELLING

The majority of patients with AS are HLA B27 positive. The risk of a patient transmitting the same HLA B27 antigen to the child is 1 in 2. The risk of an HLA B27 relative developing AS is about 1 in 3. Hence the overall risk for the children to develop AS is around 1 in 6. However, sporadic disease (the majority of cases) tends to be more severe than familial disease. There may be additional genetic factors for disease 'susceptibility' or 'severity' and other loci under current investigation include HLA B60 and other Class II MHC genes such as TAP (Transporters associated with Antigen Processing) and LMP (Large Multi-functional Protease) genes.

SPECIAL CONSIDERATIONS

1) Disability and psychological factors

Although much attention can be paid to the medical condition per se, the psychological aspects should not be forgotten. In patients with rheumatoid arthritis anxiety and depression have been shown not to be directly related to objective measurements of arthritis severity. Lack of social support and the experience of social stress are important factors for psychological adjustment.

Skeletal changes (eg kyphosis) make the impact of AS visible to others and may influence perception of self-worth. Problems of 'body image' (tending to be focused primarily on people with eating disorders) may also be relevant to psychological adjustment.

Work has shown that patients who perceived a sense of personal control over AS, despite the pain and debilitating effects of the disease, were less psychologically distressed than those who doubted their ability to exert control over various aspects of AS. 'Doctor' control belief was shown to play a generally weaker role in the process of psychological adjustment.

Instilling confidence in exercise regimes is also an important factor to ensure compliance.

2) Surgical intervention

About 20% of patients with juvenile onset AS develop significant hip problems requiring total hip replacement, within 20 years of disease onset. However this figure falls sharply with increasing age of onset and the risk of requiring joint replacement is quite small if onset occurs later on in the 30s. The outcome of hip replacement is good and should be considered as a practical option.

Vertebral wedge osteotomy is performed in specialist centres after careful consideration eg to correct marked flexion deformity where forward vision is severely impaired.

Acute painful exacerbation of back symptoms due to spondylodiscitis and/or spinal fracture should be recognised and treatment usually involves temporary restriction of spinal movements by using a corset if necessary.

REFERENCES

1. Haslock I. The management of low back pain - a personal view. ARC *Practical Problems* May 1988, No.9, in Reports on Rheumatic Diseases, Series 2.

2. Laurent, R. Are there any anti-rheumatic drugs that modify the course of Ankylosing Spondylitis? *Balliere's Clinical Rheumatology* 1990, Vol **4**, **2**, p387-400.

The National Ankylosing Spondylitis Society (NASS). Mr Fergus Rogers, 3 Grosvenor Crescent, London, SW1X 7ER. A self help society for people with AS and their families and friends.

September 1994

THE TREATMENT OF GOUT: A PERSONAL VIEW

T Gibson
Consultant Physician
Guy's Hospital
London

Amongst the rheumatic disorders, gout is uniquely satisfying to treat. The agony of acute attacks can be ameliorated within hours by any of several drugs and the underlying cause, hyperuricaemia, can be eradicated. Realisation that this is one of the few joint disorders which may be cured has prompted therapeutic complacency. Inattention to the circumstances of individual patients and to the details of treatment often lead to inadequate management.

Causes of Hyperuricaemia and Gout

The archetypal patient with gout is an obese man who drinks excessive quantities of alcohol. Males are more susceptible because of their naturally higher blood uric acid levels. The risk to females rises sharply after the menopause when blood urate levels increase to approximate those of males. In both sexes, blood uric acid levels correlate with body size. The influence of diet on uric acid is considerable but the precise nature of the relationship is not understood. In poor countries where diet is barely adequate, gout is rarely seen. Abundance of high energy foods and subsequent obesity together with alcoholic beverages which accentuate hepatic production of purines are major factors. Purine rich food and drink such as offal meat and beer contribute to the uric acid body pool but their impact is relatively small. High protein diets are not a cause of hyperuricaemia.

Not all individuals who are fat or over-indulgent develop sufficiently sustained hyperuricaemia to cause gout. Susceptibility resides in a relative impairment to excrete uric acid and this trait, in the context of dietary plenty, provides the mechanism for disease. The renal capacity to eliminate uric acid may be inherited and may thus account for familial aggregation of gout and its high prevalence in some ethnic groups. Exceptionally, this factor may be sufficient to cause gout in the most lean and abstemious of individuals. Endogenous over-production of uric acid is an uncommon explanation for hyperuricaemia. All diuretics impair uric acid excretion and thereby induce hyperuricaemia. This is a common explanation for the development of tophaceous deposits in the elderly, some of whom may not exhibit florid arthritis.

Diagnosis – not always simple

There is little difficulty in recognising podagra, an acute, red, painful swelling at the base of a big toe. Gout affecting one or more joints at other sites may be more perplexing but a clinical diagnosis may be suggested by the presence of the predisposing factors discussed above; a previous history of big toe pain or the presence of tophi. A consistently normal blood uric acid usually excludes gout but this is not necessarily the case. For example, a decline from previously hyperuricaemic levels by sudden alcohol withdrawal may precipitate gout, and acute gout is well known to occur during the early weeks of urate-lowering treatment. Demonstration of urate crystals in synovial fluid provides unequivocal confirmation of the diagnosis as well as excluding sepsis and pseudogout. Even in hospital practice this simple manoeuvre may be woefully neglected. Suggestive clinical features allied with hyperuricaemia allow a presumptive diagnosis but not all patients with arthritis and hyperuricaemia have gout. Too many patients receive hypo-uricaemic treatment unnecessarily.

Acute gout – old fashioned colchicine or NSAID?

It is essential to plan the management of gouty arthritis in two phases. It is only after the abolition of joint symptoms that attention should be directed toward persistent hyperuricaemia and other concomitant health problems.

Happily, the response to anti-inflammatory drugs, including systemic features of fever and malaise, is wholly gratifying to both patient and doctor. Oral colchicine is an ancient alternative to non-steroidal anti-inflammatory drugs (NSAID) and is conventionally prescribed in doses of 0.5 mg every hour until symptoms improve or gastrointestinal symptoms ensue. The maximum recommended total dose is 10 mg but nausea, vomiting and diarrhoea are the usual rule before one-third of this has been achieved. Such symptoms may preoccupy a patient who would otherwise be continuing to complain of joint pain but this hardly recommends its use unless there are contra-indications to NSAID use such as active peptic ulceration, previous drug intolerance or anticoagulation. Intravenous colchicine substantially reduces the risk of gastrointestinal symptoms but may occasionally cause bone marrow suppression which is more likely in renal impairment and the elderly. The risk does not justify this therapeutic approach.

It is preferable to employ an NSAID for acute gout. Indomethacin is conventionally recommended but this is probably by virtue of its long-term availability. Evidence that high doses (up to 600 mg daily) are better than modest doses (200-300 mg daily) in the first 24 hours of treatment are unconvincing. The risks of abdominal pain, vomiting and drowsiness are accentuated by high doses and an adequate schedule is indomethacin 50 mg every 4 hours for the first day and every 8 hours thereafter until the attack has resolved. Pain usually begins to relent within 2 hours of the first dose but complete resolution of inflammation may require as little as 48 hours or as long as 2 weeks of continuous treatment.

Conventional doses of azapropazone, diclofenac, naproxen, piroxicam, ketoprofen and fenoprofen have been compared with indomethacin or phenylbutazone and found to be equally efficacious. The choice of NSAID for acute gout is thus arbitrary and depends on patient acceptability and practitioners' custom. There is no reason why indomethacin should occupy an exclusive role in this disease.

Bolt from the blue?

Gout is frequently a forewarning, if not from high then from the inner man, that something is amiss with life's conduct. The clinician must explore the possibility of alcohol abuse and its physical and psychological sequelae. Associated hypertension may be attributable to alcohol or obesity and this may provide an additional reason for urging patients to modify their drink and food intake. These efforts really are worthwhile and may achieve normo-uricaemia as well as other health benefits. Such strictures are not relevant to every patient and some are not prepared to heed advice. Diuretics should be withdrawn if possible. Only after these measures have been considered should hypo-uricaemic drugs be contemplated.

Hypo-uricaemic drug treatment – whom and how?

Some patients experience isolated or sporadic attacks of gout. Beyond relevant weight reduction and dietary discretion it is not justifiable to commit such patients to indefinite treatment. Hypo-uricaemic drugs should be confined to those with more than two annual attacks, visible tophi, joint deformity, radiological joint damage or renal impairment. Asymptomatic hyperuricaemia never warrants treatment.

It is prudent to wait for all signs of joint inflammation to recede before embarking on treatment. Gouty inflammation may be perpetuated or precipitated by reductions of blood uric acid and this risk will persist until microtophi within the joints have been resorbed, a process which may require months. Concurrent colchicine 0.5 mg twice daily will lessen the risk of further gouty attacks with minimal risk of side-effects. This should be taken alongside hypo-uricaemic treatment for 6 months. NSAIDs may also be given prophylactically and should in any case be held in reserve by patients and taken at the first indication of an impending attack.

The choice of hypo-uricaemic agent in the UK rests between the uricosuric drugs probenecid and sulphinpyrazone or the xanthine oxidase inhibitor, allopurinol. There are several constraints on the use of uricosuric drugs: they should not be used when there is a history of kidney stones or renal impairment; the risk of uric acid crystal formation in the renal collecting ducts needs to be reduced by increased fluid intake during the first week of treatment; they are ineffective in the presence of renal failure. An adverse reaction to allopurinol is the principal indication for their use. The initial dose of probenecid is 500 mg daily, if necessary increasing to 2.0 g daily in two divided doses. It may reduce the excretion of anti-inflammatory drugs and indomethacin toxicity has been recorded in this context. The dose of sulphinpyrazone is also best increased gradually from 200 mg to 600 or 800 mg daily in divided doses. Azapropazone is a NSAID with modest uricosuric properties best used as an adjunct to other hypo-uricaemic treatment.

Allopurinol is more convenient and is relatively safe. It has a wide dose range but in the presence of renal dysfunction and in the elderly a dose of 50 mg daily must be tried initially. Skin rash and more severe toxicity may ensue if more than 100 mg daily is used in such patients since the active metabolite is dependent on the kidneys for disposal. The conventional dose of 300 mg daily is adequate for the majority, but occasionally up to 900 mg daily may be necessary to achieve normo-uricaemia, especially in patients continuing to take diuretics. Apparent resistance may also be overcome by concurrent prescription of standard doses of allopurinol and a uricosuric agent. The uricosuric NSAID, azapropazone, may be usefully employed in this situation since it may also obviate the need for concurrent colchicine or other NSAID prophylaxis. A commitment to hypo-uricaemic treatment demands a high degree of compliance. Hyperuricaemia recurs within days of stopping treatment and the tiresome cycle of re-introducing treatment and precipitating gout cannot be repeated often without exasperating patient or doctor.

The persistence of an allopurinol rash despite dose reduction very often occurs in those with renal impairment, the very patients who are unresponsive to uricosuric drugs. Desensitisation can be effective and involves dissolving 50 mg allopurinol powder in 500 ml water and increasing the dose from 0.5 ml to 250 ml daily by slow increments before reintroducing tablets.

Once established, hypo-uricaemic therapy should be continued indefinitely or until risk factors such as alcohol abuse have been eliminated. Large tophi may ulcerate and discharge for a variable period during the course of treatment and patients should be reassured that this is a good portent. Long-term compliance is such an important aspect of successful treatment that it is essential for patients to understand the different actions of NSAID and hypo-uricaemic drugs. Regrettably, they all too often receive uninformed prescriptions for these agents and are offered neither advice nor follow-up.

In summary; 1. Acute gout can be treated with any NSAID. 2. Colchicine should be reserved for patients with peptic ulcers, NSAID intolerance and those on anti-coagulants. 3. Once the acute arthritis has resolved attempts should be made to rectify any recognisable cause of hyperuricaemia. 4. Hypo-uricaemic drug treatment is indicated for recurrent gout, joint damage, tophi, renal dysfunction. 5. Allopurinol is the hypo-uricaemic drug of choice and should be given in low dose for the elderly and in renal dysfunction. 6. Concurrent colchicine twice daily for 6 months will reduce the risk of further gout. 7. Patient education and encouragement are essential components of treatment.

REFERENCES

1. Gibson, T., *Non steroidal anti-inflammatory drugs in crystal induced arthropathies,* In Non-steroidal Anti-inflammatory Drugs, Mechanisms and Clinical use. Ed. Lewis, A.J., Furst, D.E., Marcel Dekker, N. York, Basle, 1987; 57-69.
2. Gibson T., *Hypo-uricaemic drugs* In Copeman's Textbook of the Rheumatic Diseases, Ed. J. T. Scott, Churchill Livingstone, Edinburgh, London. 1986; 569-83.
3. Fam, A.G., Paton, T.W., Chaiton, A., Reinstitution of allopurinol therapy for gouty arthritis after cutaneous reactions. *Can. Med. Assoc. J.* 1980; **123:** 128-9.

January 1988

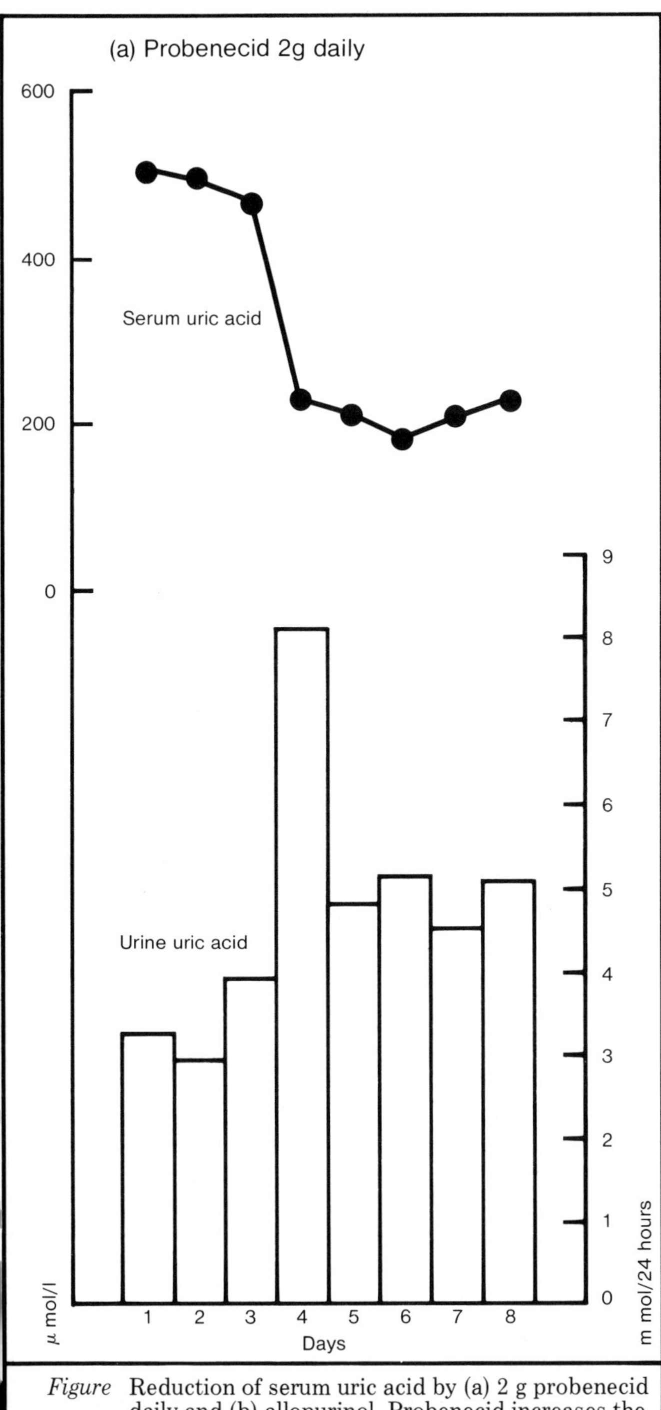

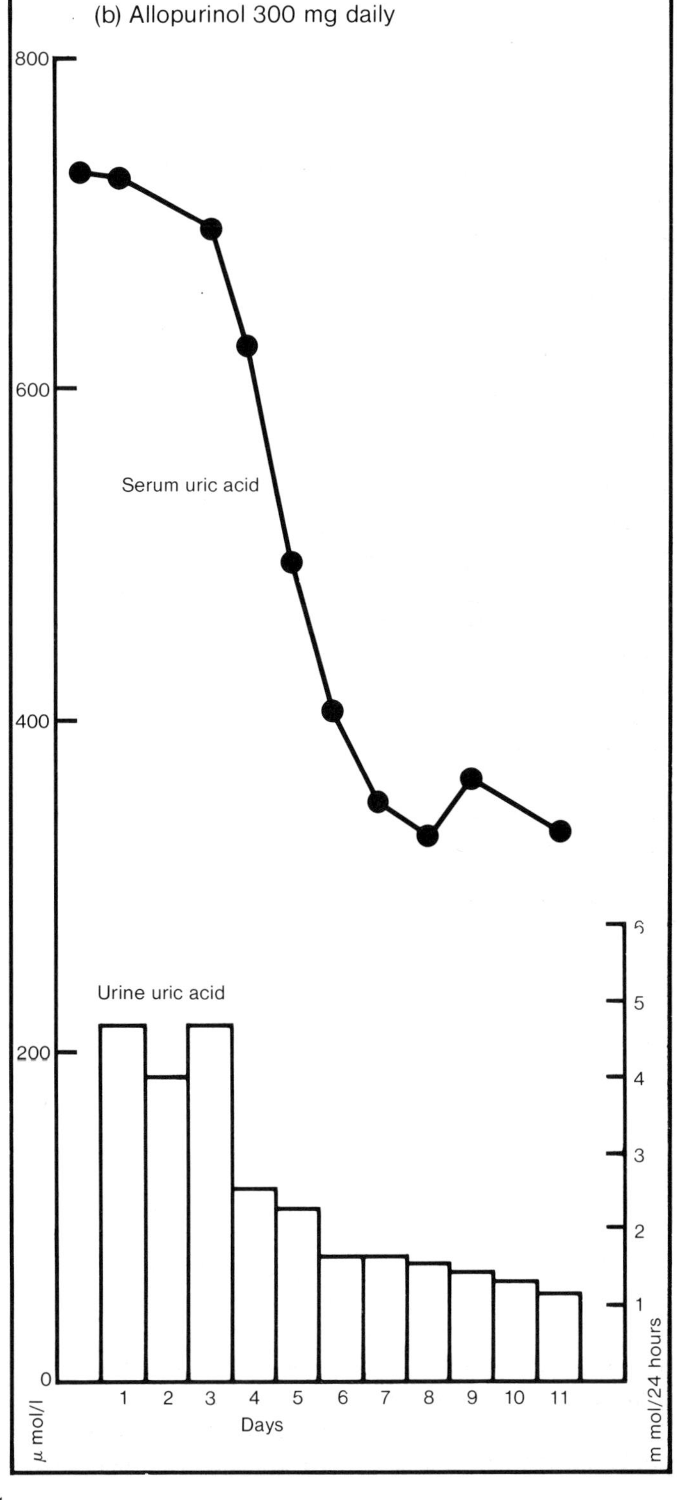

Figure Reduction of serum uric acid by (a) 2 g probenecid daily and (b) allopurinol. Probenecid increases the excretion of uric acid, shown by the columns. Allopurinol inhibits the formation of uric acid and urinary uric acid therefore falls.

JUVENILE CHRONIC ARTHRITIS

A M Leak
Consultant Rheumatologist
Royal Sea Bathing Hospital
Margate

INTRODUCTION

Juvenile chronic arthritis (JCA) is defined, in Europe, as an inflammatory arthritis beginning before the 16th birthday (1). George Frederic Still is credited with the first description of this condition in 1896, when he was working as a registrar at Great Ormond Street Hospital, and his original article has recently been reprinted (2). For many years the term Still's Disease was synonymous with childhood arthritis. However, delineation of the major subgroups of this condition has revealed a marked heterogeneity and Still's name now lives on only in relation to the evanescent 'Stills' rash seen in systemic onset arthritis and, interestingly, in adult onset 'Stills' disease which is again the systemic form. In fact only 15 - 20% of children exhibit systemic features and the majority have either a pauciarticular or polyarticular arthritis, which is seronegative for IgM Rh Factor.

In North America this same group of conditions is labelled juvenile rheumatoid arthritis (JRA) (3). Since juvenile arthritis rarely resembles adult rheumatoid arthritis this term is somewhat misleading, and in Europe the term JRA is reserved for the small number of patients with seropositive adult-type polyarthritis.

Lower limb pauciarticular arthritis in adolescents with or without enthesitis may be related to juvenile spondylitis. Children with this condition are thought of as a subgroup of JCA in Europe, but spondyloarthropathies are considered a separate condition in the USA. The clinical features of these children will be discussed in this review since differentiation from true JCA is difficult in the early stages.

A recent review of incidence and prevalence data concerning JCA noted that there are few UK studies (4). Amongst 6 from Europe or North America, similar conclusions have emerged despite different methodologies. Thus the annual incidence of new cases is 0.12 to 0.19 per 1,000 children, with prevalence estimated as up to 1.13 per 1,000. Current data from the British Paediatric Rheumatology Group database suggests that JCA is responsible for between 30% to 50% of new cases referred to a specialist paediatric rheumatology clinic.

CLASSIFICATION

The prime use of classification criteria is to define homogeneous groups of patients for studies of pathogenesis, prognosis and therapeutic outcome. They are of limited use in the diagnosis of individual cases (5). The criteria for classification of JCA are the presence of at least 2 of pain, swelling and limitation, in at least one joint for at least 3 months, in a child under 16 years of age. Pauciarticular JCA with 4 joints or less is the most common onset type while polyarticular onset is defined as 5 joints or more.

TABLE 1.
TYPICAL CLINICAL FEATURES OF SUBGROUPS OF JCA

PATTERN OF ONSET	AGE OF ONSET: 0 - 5 years	6 - 10 years	11 - 16 years
PAUCI-ARTICULAR	F>>M Knees, ankles, wrists especially. Often ANA positive. Chronic uveitis.	F = M ← Overlap either way →	M>>F Lower limb arthritis. Enthesitis. Acute uveitis, ± later sacroiliitis
POLY-ARTICULAR	F>M Small and large joints. Flexor tenosynovitis (spares MCP jts)	F>M Similar to under 5 yrs.	F>>M Symmetrical, often RhF positive with erosive arthritis
SYSTEMIC ONSET	ALL AGE GROUPS Fever, rash Variable arthritis Acute phase response ++		M = F Auto AB negative

Most children at onset of disease can be satisfactorily classified into one of the well recognised subgroups of JCA (Table 1). However, with the course of time some of the distinctions become less clear cut such that patients with either pauciarticular or systemic onset disease may develop a polyarthritis which is clinically indistinguishable from seronegative polyarticular onset JCA. By contrast some children who have more than 4 joints affected at onset nevertheless run a mild pauciarticular-type course.

Aetiology

Transient childhood arthritis is commonly related to viral infections, such as rubella, mumps or parvo virus, but evidence that chronic arthritis is caused by viruses is limited (6,7). Theoretical mechanisms exist whereby intercurrent infections may trigger abnormal immune responses in a genetically susceptible individual. Interaction of antigen-presenting cells and host genetic factors, causing the proliferation of immunoreactive T cells and cross-reactive antibodies may lead to autoimmune disease. Evidence of impaired T cell function in response to EBV infection is of interest in speculation regarding viruses as aetiopathogenic agents.

Factors which lead to the persistence of chronic arthritis in childhood may involve similar mechanisms to those in adults including abnormal neuroendocrine responses. The influence of hormones is less clear cut than in adult seropositive RA. The onset of adolescence does not usually affect established JCA although post-partum recrudescence of previously inactive juvenile onset arthritis may occur.

Pathology and Impaired Growth

The pathology of JCA is similar to adult rheumatoid arthritis but fibrosis and contracture of periarticular tissues are more common in seronegative disease, and fibrous or even bony ankylosis develops quickly. Diseases involving the growing skeleton offer potential for repair following remission, but depending on the age of onset and joints affected, normal growth may be affected.

Localised growth defects arise due to involvement of the epiphysis which initially causes overgrowth, but subsequently premature fusion may occur.

Thus for example, involvement of a proximal interphalangeal joint may result in a short finger and arthritis of a large joint such as an ankle or knee may cause shortening of the adjacent long bone.

Generalised growth retardation is limited to persistently active polyarticular or systemic disease and is particularly marked if corticosteroids are used.

CLINICAL FEATURES

Since juvenile chronic arthritis is essentially a clinical diagnosis, emphasis must be given to careful elucidation of symptoms and, more particularly, to abnormal signs in the assessment of a child with musculo-skeletal problems.

Symptoms

Symptoms may be difficult to evaluate in the very young child. Swelling of individual joints may, or may not, be noticed. Failure to use both hands in play, a limp or reluctance to walk are early pointers, although trauma is often perceived to be the precipitating factor. The child is characteristically stiff on waking but also may be tired later in the day.

Systemic symptoms including fever and rash should be sought specifically as well as evidence of preceding upper respiratory tract or gastrointestinal infection, suggesting a differential diagnosis of infective or reactive arthritis.

Signs

The cardinal signs of inflammatory arthritis are soft-tissue swelling of the joint, (usually with limitation of movement) and pain or tenderness. The latter two signs are frequently absent in children. Secondary signs include muscle wasting, flexion contractures and eventually growth defects.

Pattern of Arthritis

The number of joints involved, and their distribution, usually indicates the type of disease. Addition of 'new' sites should be monitored carefully, especially in the first 6 months. The majority of children will have pauciarticular disease, most commonly involving knees, ankles, wrists or elbows. Isolated interphalangeal joint involvement may be seen in pauciarthritis, psoriatic arthritis or in the late onset spondyloarthropathy group. Cervical spine involvement is occasionally a presenting feature, and the neck will eventually be affected in up to 60% of children with JCA.

The small joints of the hands and feet may become symmetrically involved in polyarthritis; typically interphalangeal joints with flexor tenosynovitis in seronegative arthritis, while metacarpophalangeal arthropathy suggests seropositive disease. Hip, shoulder and temperomandibular joint arthritis are also seen, being more common than involvement of acromioclavicular, sternoclavicular or manubriosternal joints.

The clinical features of juvenile onset psoriatic arthritis have recently been reviewed (8). Proposed criteria for definite diagnosis are either typical psoriasis with JCA, or 3 of the minor criteria selected from dactylitis, nail pitting, family history or psoriasis-like rash. Probable psoriatic arthritis has 2 minor criteria. Psoriatic arthritis in children is not associated with enthesitis or HLA B27 and resembles JCA rather than the spondyloarthropathies.

Extra Articular Features

Diagnosis of systemic onset disease requires the presence of intermittent fever up to 39°C once or twice daily, for at least 2 or 3 weeks plus the classic Still's rash, which is usually macular, erythematous, transient and often present with the pyrexia. Other typical features include lymphadenopathy, hepatosplenomegaly and pericarditis. A recent EULAR study attempting to refine diagnostic criteria for JCA (9) noted the decreasing frequency of all these systemic features over 6 months: for example fever, present in 25% of children in the first 3 months, decreased to 9% between 3 and 6 months, and rash from 16% to 6%.

Ocular symptoms are uncommon. Acute red eye may be seen in adolescents in association with seronegative spondyloarthropathies. Dry eye may be associated with seropositive disease, also usually in teenagers. Ocular symptoms in the **young** child suggest longstanding chronic anterior uveitis with complications. In the EULAR study chronic anterior uveitis increased in incidence from 2.5% in the first 3 months to 4.5% by 6 months, but will be seen in up to 18% of children by 5 years of disease. This form of uveitis occurs mainly in early onset pauciarthritis, and virtually never in systemic onset disease. The clinical features of chronic anterior uveitis including the association with antinuclear antibodies, have been well described (10,11). The important point is that in the early stages it is completely asymptomatic and can only be diagnosed and treatment initiated following slit-lamp biomicroscopy. Table 2 gives guidelines for screening. Uveitis occasionally presents in adults but at that time is more likely to be symptomatic.

Nodules and classical vasculitis are seen only in seropositive arthritis in which all manifestations found in adult rheumatoid arthritis, including ocular, cardiac and pulmonary involvement may be seen. Proteinuria is uncommon in any subgroup at onset, but may be related to drug therapy, intercurrent infection or secondary amyloidosis.

TABLE 2.
RISK OF UVEITIS IN SERO-NEGATIVE JCA ACCORDING TO ONSET TYPE

Degree of Risk	HIGH	MEDIUM	LOW
Clinical Group	Pauciarticular under 9 years ANA positive	Polyarticular under 9 years ANA positive **or** Pauciarticular under 9 years ANA negative	Polyarticular under 9 years ANA negative **or** Systemic onset **or** All over 9 years at onset
Screen	3 monthly for 2 years 6 monthly up to 5 years Yearly to 10 years	4-6 monthly for 2 years 9-12 monthly up to 5 years Yearly to 10 years	Annual check ups for 5 years

TABLE 3.
DIFFERENTIAL DIAGNOSIS OF JCA

1. **INFECTION RELATED:** SEPTIC arthritis
   VIRAL eg rubella, mumps, parvo
   BACTERIAL eg Lyme
   REACTIVE incl.POST-STREP (Rh Fever)
2. **CONNECTIVE TISSUE DISEASES:** eg SLE
   Sjögrens
   Scleroderma
   Dermatomyositis
   Systemic vasculitis
3. **MECHANICAL/ORTHOPAEDIC:** eg Slipped femoral-epiphysis
   Anterior knee pain
   Isolated enthesitis
4. **SYSTEMIC DISEASES:** eg Haemophilia
   Endocrine disorders
   Lipid storage diseases
   Malignancy

Differential Diagnosis

Since there are no specific tests for JCA the diagnosis is based on clinical features, supported by appropriate laboratory findings and implies the exclusion of other conditions which mimic juvenile arthritis (Table 3). Many of these are self-limiting, for example viral arthritis, but the most important condition to exclude is septic arthritis. In a young child with monoarthritis the findings of a positive ANA or anterior uveitis are very helpful diagnostically. Strict adherence to a 3-month period before diagnosing definite JCA is advisable.

Lyme disease, caused by the spirocete Borrelia Burgdorferi, frequently causes a pauciarticular arthritis early in the course of disease in children. Since the typical rash is also less common in this age group, differential diagnosis between JCA and Lyme disease in endemic areas requires Lyme serology (12).

INVESTIGATIONS

Laboratory Features

Indicators of an acute phase response (raised ESR, CRP, IgG and reduced haemoglobin) are frequently present in association with active synovitis in all types of JCA, but are most marked in systemic onset disease, when there is also a leucocytosis and thrombocytosis. Anaemia out of proportion to the degree of synovitis suggests gastro-intestinal blood loss either from non-steroidal anti-inflammatory drugs or from unsuspected inflammatory bowel disease. Poor intake of iron in the diet may also be a factor in sick children. Liver function tests may be abnormal in active systemic disease, or due to drugs.

Immunology

IgM Rheumatoid Factor detected by latex haemagglutination is found in less than 10% of cases, mainly teenage girls with adult-type erosive polyarthritis, and is regarded as a bad prognostic indicator, calling for early use of long-acting anti-rheumatic drugs. More sensitive tests for rheumatoid factor by ELISA (13) do not aid disease classification or assessment of prognosis, nor differentiate JCA from juvenile onset connective tissue diseases. Anti Nuclear Antibodies (ANA) are found in around 30% of children with JCA according to the type of assay, and the case mix studied. ANA are most common in early onset pauciarticular JCA. Highest titres are seen early in the disease in association with active synovitis, but in addition ANA, particularly if persistently positive, are a helpful marker for chronic anterior uveitis aiding the evaluation of risk and frequency of ophthalmological screening (Table 2).

Sensitive enzyme linked immunoassays have detected antibodies to several classes of histones, and current research implicates specific histone peptides as triggering factors for anti-nuclear antibody formation (14). Cross reactivity with ubiquitous microbial antigens, such as yeast histone, has led to speculation of an aetio-pathogenic role in chronic uveitis, but direct evidence is lacking.

Immunogenetic Markers

Study of HLA class I, II and III antigens has lent credence to the clinical subdivisions in JCA which have evolved over the last 20 to 30 years. The main findings are listed in Table 4. No clear data exists in systemic onset JCA (15), and prospective studies of the relationship between HLA antigens and clinical outcome are needed (16). Future research to delineate DNA sequence date of class II DR ß genes may establish the critical nucleotides which control disease susceptibility in specific groups such as early onset pauciarticular arthritis (17).

TABLE 4.
MAJOR HLA ASSOCIATIONS IN JCA

	EARLY ONSET	LATE ONSET
PAUCI-ARTICULAR	A2 DR5 DRW8	B27
POLY-ARTICULAR	DRW8	DR4 (seropositive)

Radiology

Early changes visible on plain radiographs include soft-tissue swelling, juxta-articular osteoporosis and also periosteal new bone formation, which may lead to permanent widening of the shafts of small bones, such as the phalanges. Erosions are much less frequently seen in juvenile than adult arthritis, whereas joint space narrowing, epiphyseal irregularity and bony ankylosis, particularly in the carpus and tarsus, are common. Magnetic resonance imaging (MRI) now reported in juvenile onset arthritis may reveal unsuspected bone erosion as well as providing imaging of soft tissue inflammation (18). Sacroiliitis associated with juvenile spondylitis is difficult to diagnose on plain radiographs but MRI or CT scanning can aid detection.

MANAGEMENT

The management of JCA is best undertaken by an experienced multi-disciplinary team. Joint clinics run by a paediatrician with a rheumatologist are increasingly being established. They require the support of a designated physiotherapist and occupational therapist. There must be access to an interested ophthalmologist for regular slit-lamp examinations to identify and treat anterior uveitis. Interaction is also needed with an orthopaedic surgeon, since up to 25% of children attending a specialist centre require an orthopaedic procedure during the course of disease (19). This is more common in children with seropositive polyarthritis.

General measures include attention to a healthy diet, ensuring protein and calories for growth and adequate calcium to prevent osteoporosis. Dental hygiene is important in children taking regular anti-inflammatory syrup and in those with limited neck movement or underdeveloped jaws. Participation of the child in as normal a family life and education as possible must always be encouraged, and independence should be promoted. It is important to evaluate how the child with chronic pain and disability is coping (20). Psychological problems are not uncommon and adequate support should be given.

Physiotherapy and Splinting

Physiotherapy and splinting are widely employed in JCA to maintain position and function of affected and unaffected joints. All children, even with monoarticular JCA, must be seen by a physiotherapist and taught an exercise programme to be done twice a day. Muscle spasm due to pain from arthritis is common, and disuse quickly leads to muscle atrophy, as well as to flexed joints.

Use of a tricycle is appropriate for children with lower limb arthropathy where restriction of weight bearing may be needed. As well as dry-land exercises, hydrotherapy is particularly helpful and small children can undertake their exercises in the bath at least once a day. Introduction of games or incentive devices into the programme are useful to maintain co-operation.

The parents must be made to feel part of the team treating the child, to encourage and assist exercises and help with methods of pain relief at home (ice or hotpacks) as well as to apply splints and administer medication. Regular reappraisal of joint ranges and function by both the physiotherapist and doctor aims to identify potential problems at an early stage. Simple measures such as a shoe raise to equalise leg lengths and prevent development of secondary deformities, or insistence on a period of prone lying each day to minimise flexion deformities of hips or knees, must be introduced early rather than late.

Bedrest is rarely indicated in JCA except in patients with active systemic disease with cardiac involvement. However, fatigue is common with polyarthritis, and short rest periods may be required, which preferably should be taken lying prone. Prolonged sitting should be avoided in children with hip or knee involvement, and here prone standers are useful in the classroom. Recent introduction of the continuous passive motion machine has improved management of flexion deformities of knees.

Rest splints are frequently needed at night time to hold affected joints in their optimum position, e.g. full extension of the knees, neutral position of the hind foot, dorsiflexion of the wrist. Lightweight material such as plastazote can be moulded individually and the fastening made of velcro. A collar may be needed for a torticollis, and night traction can be employed for painful hips.

Worksplints are helpful to maintain a good position at the wrist during the day's schooling and other activities.

Serial splinting can be used to gradually correct deformities.

TABLE 5.
NON-STEROIDAL ANTI-INFLAMMATORY DRUGS APPROVED FOR USE IN JCA (UK)

	mg/kg/day	dosage	liquid	smallest tablets	suppository
IBUPROFEN	20 - 40	tds	20 mg/ml	200 mg	-
NAPROXEN	10 - 20	bd	25 mg/ml	250 mg	500 mg
DICLOFENAC	2 - 3	bd	dispersible 50 mg	25 mg	12.5 mg
TOLMETIN	15 - 30	tds	-	200 mg	-
PIROXICAM	0.2-0.4	od	dispersible 10mg	10 mg	20 mg

Drug Treatment

Non-steroidal anti-inflammatory drugs (NSAID)

Most children with JCA benefit from treatment with NSAIDs. Whereas 10 years ago salicylates were still commonly prescribed, high-dose aspirin is now infrequently used except for control of fever. Several non-aspirin

NSAIDs, which are easier to administer, are approved for use in children (Table 5). Studies of the time to response suggest that a significant anti-inflammatory effect may take between 2 weeks and 3 months (21) and drugs should not be changed too frequently because of lack of response. These drugs are surprisingly well tolerated in children but all the usual side-effects have been seen.

Long-acting Anti-rheumatic Drugs

These have little place to play in the management of seronegative JCA and are not generally prescribed in pauciarticular onset disease, even when this extends to the polyarticular form, as experience suggests that these patients respond poorly to such drugs. However children with probable or definite juvenile spondylitis may respond to sulphasalazine. Long-acting drugs should be avoided in systemic onset disease even in the presence of active polyarthritis, as the incidence of drug side-effects seems to be particularly high in this subgroup.

In the seropositive polyarticular subset who are liable to develop early erosive change, long-acting drugs should be prescribed at an early stage and should also be considered in sero-negative polyarthritis. In these groups the same spectrum of drugs is available as in adult rheumatoid arthritis.

In a review of long-acting drugs in juvenile arthritis, Grondin et al concluded that 'improvement' was seen in 60% - 70% of children but remission was infrequent (22). However in controlled studies, auranofin, D-penicillamine and anti-malarials appear to offer little benefit compared to placebo. Intra-muscular myocrisin and oral methotrexate are perceived as more effective agents (23). Once weekly low-dose methotrexate may become the drug of choice due to its excellent tolerance and apparent efficacy (24).

However, in view of the natural remission expected in this disease, drugs with potentially serious side-effects should be avoided where possible. Vigorous reappraisal of physical measures is always required. Long-acting drugs should only be prescribed and monitored by the paediatric rheumatology clinic.

Corticosteroids

Intra-articular injection of corticosteroids (e.g. triamcinolone) is very helpful in the treatment of persistent active arthritis. In small children, intra-articular injections should be performed under a light general anaesthetic,to ensure accurate placement and should be followed by prolonged pressure to prevent leakage into subcutaneous tissue and reduce the risk of skin atrophy. Post injection rest in a splint for 24 - 48 hours may be advisable. Systemic corticosteroids are sometimes required in systemic onset disease, but should only be used after an adequate trial of full dose non-steroidal anti-inflammatory drugs has failed to control symptoms adequately. Myocarditis remains an absolute indication for the use of steroids, whereas arthritis, fever and rash are not. In children with active polyarthritis in association with a vigorous acute phase response, anaemia may impair the child's ability to co-operate with a full exercise programme. In this situation, low-dose steroids, for example 10 mg prednisolone on alternate days, are useful in alleviating the symptoms without undue side-effects. Wherever possible daily steroids should be avoided so as to prevent growth retardation.

This is generally only required in the most severely affected cases, but, at the same time, surgical procedures such as soft-tissue release of the knee or hip, should be considered at an early stage to improve position and function. Total hip replacements have been undertaken at a young age and, although their outcome is uncertain, getting a child out of a wheelchair is a powerful incentive. Current thinking on surgery in JCA has recently been reviewed (19).

PROGNOSIS

The overall prognosis in JCA is good (25). This is largely dependent on the number and size of affected joints. Sixty percent to 70% of children are probably in remission at 10 years from onset, but a mild degree of disability persists in 45% of patients assessed after the age of 18 years, and several will be more severely affected. However, most patients have a comparable social standing with their siblings in relation to school achievements, current salaries, marriages and children (26).

Blindness is still a potential complication of chronic anterior uveitis and emphasises the need for early detection, leading to a better visual prognosis (27).

Mortality is low in JCA, but may reach 14% after 15 years of disease in systemic onset JCA. The commonest causes of death are infection, myocarditis and renal failure due to secondary amyloidosis.

CONCLUSIONS

JCA is uncommon and many general practitioners will only see 1 or 2 cases in a lifetime of practice. Early referral for a comprehensive interdisciplinary approach to management will ensure excellent functional outcome in the long term for most children. Support for the family in this chronic disorder should not be overlooked.

ACKNOWLEDGEMENTS

The author wishes to thank Dr D P M Symmons for a critical reading of this review, and Mrs M H Hopker for expert secretarial assistance.

FURTHER READING

Paediatric Rheumatology Update. Edit Woo, White and Ansell 1990. Oxford University Press.

Textbook of Paediatric Rheumatology. 2nd Edition. Edit Cassidy, Petty 1990. Churchill Livingstone Inc.

REFERENCES

1. E. Munthe (Ed.) *The Care of Rheumatic Children. EULAR Bulletin, Basle 1977;* **47-50**

2. Still G F. On a Form of Chronic Joint Disease in Children. *Clin. Orthop. Related Res. 1990;* **259:** 4-10

3. Cassidy J T, Levinson J E, Bass J E et al. A Study of Classification Criteria for a Diagnosis of Juvenile Rheumatoid Arthritis. *Arth Rheum 1986;* **29:** 274-281

4. Benjamin C M. Review of UK Data on the Rheumatic Diseases - 1 Juvenile Chronic Arthritis. *Br J Rheumatol* 1990; **29:** 231-233

5. Holt PJL. The Classification of Juvenile Chronic Arthritis. *Clin Exp Rheumatol* 1990; **8:** 331-333

6. Petty RE, Tingle AJ. Arthritis and Viral Infection. *J Ped* 1988; **113:** 948-949

7. Phillips PE. Evidence implicating infectious agents in Rheumatoid Arthritis and Juvenile Rheumatoid Arthritis. *Clin Exp Rheumatol* 1988; **6:** 87-94

8. Southwood TR, Petty RE, Malleson PN et al. Psoriatic Arthritis in Children. *Arth Rheum* 1989; **32:** 1007-1013

9. Prieur AM, Ansell BM, Bardfield R et al. Is Onset Type Evaluated During the First 3 Months of Disease Satisfactory for Defining the Subgroups of Juvenile Chronic Arthritis? A EULAR Cooperative Study (1983-1986). *Clin Exp Rheumatol* 1990; **8:** 321-325

10. Petty RE. Current Knowledge of the Etiology and Pathogenesis of Chronic Uveitis Accompanying Juvenile Rheumatoid Arthritis. *Rheum Dis Clinics N Am* 1987; **13:**19-36

11. Rosenberg AM. Uveitis Associated with Juvenile Rheumatoid Arthritis *Semin Arth Rheum* 1987; **16:** 158-173

12. Steere AC. Lyme Disease. *N Eng J Med* 1989; **321:** 586-96

13. Walker SM, Shaham B, McKurdy DK et al. Prevalence and concentration of IgM rheumatoid factor in polyarticular onset disease as compared to systemic or pauciarticular onset disease in active juvenile rheumatoid arthritis as measured by ELISA. *J Rheumatol* 1990; **17:**936-940

14. Leak AM, Woo P. Juvenile Chronic Arthritis, Chronic Iridocyclitis and Reactivity to Histones. *Ann Rheum Dis* 1991; **50:** 653-657

15. Maksymowych WP, Glass DN. Population Genetics and Molecular Biology of the Childhood Chronic Arthropathies. *Ballieres Clin Rheumatol* 1988; **2:** 649-671

16. Woo P. Genetic Aspects of Juvenile Chronic Arthritis. *Clin Orthop Related Res* 1990; **259** 11-17

17. Fernandez-Vina MA, Fink CW, Stastney P. HLA Antigens in Juvenile Arthritis. Pauciarticular and Polyarticular Juvenile Arthritis are Immunogenetically Distinct. *Arth Rheum* 1990; **33:** 1787-1794

18. Verbruggen LA, Shahabpour M, Van Roy P, Osteaux M. Magnetic Resonance Imaging of Articular Destruction in Juvenile Rheumatoid Arthritis. *Arth Rheum* 1990; **33:** 1426-1430

19. Swann M. The Surgery of Juvenile Chronic Arthritis: An Overview. *Clin Orthop Related Res* 1990; **259:** 70-75

20. Vandvik LH, Eckblad G. Relationship Between Pain, Disease Severity and Psychosocial Function in Patients with Juvenile Chronic Arthritis. *Scand J Rheumatol* 1990; **19:** 295-302

21. Lovell DJ, Giannini EH, Brewer EJ Jnr. Time Course of Response to Nonsteroidal Anti-inflammatory Drugs in Juvenile Rheumatoid Arthritis *Arth Rheum* 1984; **27:** 1433-1437

22. Grondin C, Malleson P, Petty RE. Slow-acting Anti-Rheumatic Drugs in Chronic Arthritis of Childhood. *Semin Arth Rheum* 1988; **18:** 38-47

23. Gabriel CA, Levinson JE. Advanced Drug Therapy in Juvenile Rheumatoid Arthritis. *Arth Rheum* 1990; **33:** 587-590

24. Rose CD, Singsen BH, Eichenfield AH, et al. Safety and Efficacy of Methotrexate Therapy In Juvenile Rheumatoid Arthritis *J Ped* 1990; **117:** 653-659

25. Hull RG. Outcome in Juvenile Arthritis. Br *J Rheumatol 1988;* **27** (Suppl 1): 66-71

26. Miller JJ, Spitz PW, Simpson U, William GF. The Social Function of Young Adults who had Arthritis in Childhood. *J Ped* 1982; **100:** 378-382

27. Wolf MD, Lichter PR, Ragsdale CG. Prognostic Factors in the Uveitis of Juvenile Rheumatoid Arthritis. *J Ophthalmol* 1986; **94:**1242-1248

September 1991

NON-ARTHRITIC LOCOMOTOR DISORDERS IN CHILDHOOD

T R Southwood
Childhood Arthritis Unit
Department of Rheumatology
University of Birmingham
Birmingham B15 2TT
J A Sills
Department of Paediatrics
Alder Hey Children's Hospital
Liverpool

INTRODUCTION

As many as 15-20% of children experience idiopathic musculoskeletal pain; this represents the second most frequent form of pain (after headache) reported by apparently healthy school attenders (1). A proportion develop chronic pain which is not associated with an obvious cause, yet is associated with obvious disability. Several syndromes have been described which together encompass the majority of children and adolescents with idiopathic musculoskeletal pain. This report will describe four such syndromes: hypermobility syndrome, nocturnal idiopathic musculoskeletal pain syndrome ('growing pains'), localised idiopathic musculoskeletal pain syndrome, and diffuse ('whole body') idiopathic musculoskeletal pain syndrome. Because the features of the syndromes may be subtle and intermittent, a high degree of physician awareness is necessary to make a correct diagnosis. Unnecessary laboratory investigations, multiple referrals, and lack of a diagnosis may contribute to chronicity of the illness.

HYPERMOBILITY SYNDROME

Hypermobility of joints in children is a common clinical finding and in most cases is not symptomatic. It is more frequent in younger children (15% of 6-10 year olds) than in older children (8% of 11-14 year olds), and in girls. In total, 7-12% of school age children fulfil criteria for the definition of generalised joint hypermobility (Table 1). Recurrent episodes of joint pain occur in approximately 40% of children with hypermobility; this is significantly more frequent than that observed in non-hypermobile children (2). The pathogenesis of the pain is unclear, but four explanations have been put forward. Repetitive sub-clinical trauma resulting in mild synovitis may have a role. Increased muscle tension may also play a part; hypermobile children may have to work harder to maintain an upright posture because of their tendency to pes planus, ankle valgus, knee valgus, hip flexion and increased lumbar lordosis. The valgus knee may be predisposed to chondromalacia patellae. A strong association between joint hypermobility and diffuse idiopathic musculoskeletal pain has been reported; this will be discussed in a later section.

The typical patient complains of intermittent knee pain, and to a lesser extent, ankle, hip, back and upper limb pain. Exercise may precipitate a painful episode, and is rarely associated with mild, bland swelling of the knees, ankles and feet. Other clues which suggest a family predisposition to hypermobility include congenital hip dislocation, scoliosis, and rarely features of Marfan or Ehlers-Danlos syndromes.

TABLE 1. CRITERIA FOR THE DIAGNOSIS OF JOINT HYPERMOBILITY (ADAPTED FROM (2))

ABILITY TO PERFORM THREE OR MORE OF THE FOLLOWING:

1. Passive hyperextension of the fingers with extension of the wrist until the fingers are parallel to the forearm
2. Passive apposition of the thumb to touch the forearm with the wrist flexed
3. Hyperextension of the elbows > 10°
4. Hyperextension of the knees > 10°
5. Flexion of the trunk and hips with the knees extended until the palms of the hands touch the floor

Reassurance of the patient and parents is the most important aspect of treatment. Joint hypermobility is a relatively benign condition, although it may increase the risk of osteoarthritis. As the child matures, there is normally a progressive reduction of joint mobility, and any associated pain also tends to become less troublesome. Physiotherapists may aid this process by prescribing exercises aimed at increasing muscle bulk. Pes planus and ankle valgus deformities can be improved by using custom moulded foot orthotics made of polypropylene or similar material which fit inside the child's shoes; a combination heel cup-longitudinal foot arch support is often most effective in reducing knee, hip and back pain as well.

NOCTURNAL IDIOPATHIC MUSCULOSKELETAL PAIN SYNDROME ('GROWING PAINS')

Nocturnal idiopathic musculoskeletal pain ('growing pain') is very common. These pains are most frequent in children of primary school age, when the rate of skeletal growth is comparatively slow, so the term 'growing pain' is probably a misnomer! However, this syndrome does cover a characteristic constellation of symptoms. The pain is nocturnal and wakes the child from sleep, although it may occasionally prevent the child from getting to sleep. It is commonly confined to the lower limbs, especially around the knees. The child will often appear in great distress, but usually the pain settles with local massage or heat, simple analgesia, and general comfort. Episodes of pain often last for 15-30 minutes, and are usually irregular, with a frequency of attacks ranging from once every few months to virtually every night. They occasionally appear to be precipitated by vigorous physical activity during the preceding day. Most importantly, the child should not have persistent symptoms the day after the pain; any child who limps on awakening in the mornings is likely to have organic disease.

Physical examination of the child with nocturnal idiopathic pain will almost invariably be normal, and there are few other conditions which mimic its characteristic symptoms. Osteoid osteoma may cause primarily nocturnal pain, which can resolve rapidly on administration of aspirin or other non-steroidal anti-inflammatory drugs (NSAIDs).

The treatment is primarily reassurance and explanation that the child will improve spontaneously with time (although it may take years for the attacks to disappear completely). If the child has particularly frequent or severe attacks, the routine administration of nocturnal analgesics or NSAIDs may be beneficial.

LOCALISED IDIOPATHIC PAIN SYNDROMES

Localised idiopathic musculoskeletal pain syndromes are frequently stress-related. Criteria for their diagnosis are presented in Table 2. Within the paediatric age group, they are more frequently seen in girls and during the pre-adolescent years. There may be a past history of recurrent headaches or abdominal pain, and occasionally there is an identifiable illness or event which precedes the onset of limb pain. The lower limbs are more often affected than the upper, and a bizarre gait may be a presenting feature. The key physical sign is allodynia (a painful response to a non-noxious stimulus), manifesting as a 'grimace and gasp' or 'wince and withdrawal' to even light touch of the affected area. The syndrome may persist for many months, and approximately half of the patients will have recurrent episodes.

TABLE 2. CRITERIA FOR THE DIAGNOSIS OF LOCALISED MUSCULOSKELETAL PAIN SYNDROMES IN CHILDREN (ADAPTED FROM MALLESON ET AL (4))

LOCALISED IDIOPATHIC PAIN SYNDROME - Both of:

1. Pain localised to all or part of one limb persisting for more than one week despite medically directed treatment, or more than one month without treatment.
2. Absence of recent trauma or other aetiologic factors that could reasonably explain the finding (eg bone tumour, sepsis, chronic arthritis, etc)

REFLEX SYMPATHETIC DYSTROPHY - Both of the above, and all of:

1. Localised tenderness
2. Altered skin colour and/or temperature
3. Soft tissue swelling or atrophy

Reflex sympathetic dystrophy (RSD)

Reflex sympathetic dystrophy (also known as algodystrophy, Sudeck's atrophy, or reflex neurovascular dystrophy) is a defined form of severe localised pain syndrome associated with abnormal autonomic function (3). An affected limb will often have a pallid or purple mottled appearance which can be accentuated by placing the limb in a dependent position. Reduced skin temperature, slow capillary filling, and soft tissue swelling are sometimes prominent. 'Tache cerebrale', the appearance of an erythematous line 15-30 seconds after the skin of an affected area has been stroked by a blunt object, has been reported. Peripheral pulses and perspiration of the affected limb are variably affected. In its most severe form, the affected limb is held in a bizarre posture, and can become virtually fixed in that position with muscle wasting and soft tissue atrophy. Sometimes, despite extraordinary deformity, the patient can have a 'smiling indifference' to the problem ('la belle indifference').

TABLE 3. DIFFERENTIAL DIAGNOSIS OF CHRONIC LOCALISED MUSCULOSKELETAL PAIN IN CHILDREN

1. Infection: Osteomyelitis
2. Tumour: Osteoid osteoma (rarely malignant tumours)
3. Trauma: including non-accidental injury
4. Chronic inflammation: arthritis, connective tissue diseases
5. Hypermobility
6. Local osteonecrosis: Osgood Schlatter disease etc
7. Localised idiopathic pain syndromes

Laboratory investigations

Although many differential diagnoses (Table 3) of localised pain can be ruled out clinically, laboratory investigations have an important role. The full blood count and measurement of acute phase proteins (ESR, CRP, or serum viscosity), should be normal. Blood chemistry is unlikely to provide diagnostic clues, with the possible exception of muscle enzyme estimation (CPK, AST, LDH) to exclude myositis. Plain radiographs of the affected limb (and contralateral limb for comparison) may show patchy or diffuse osteopaenia, although this is less commonly seen in children than in adults with RSD. A bone scan will help to rule out localised bone tumours such as osteoid osteoma, and may also support the diagnosis of a localised pain syndrome with findings of either diffusely decreased or increased isotope uptake in the affected limb. Thermography can quantify differences in skin temperature, but this remains a research tool. Further investigations are unlikely to help make the diagnosis or exclude differential diagnoses, and should be avoided if possible.

DIFFUSE IDIOPATHIC PAIN SYNDROMES

Diffuse or 'whole-body' idiopathic musculoskeletal pain syndromes have a number of features in common with local syndromes. They are both stress-related, and 10-15% of patients with one syndrome will also have distinct episodes of the other (4). They may represent different aspects of the same continuum of disease, and appear to respond to similar treatment.

Criteria have been proposed for the diagnosis of diffuse pain syndromes (Table 4). Most paediatric patients are girls in their pre-adolescent years with complaints of generalised, often symmetrical, musculoskeletal aches and pains, fatiguability, anxiety and lethargy.

Fibromyalgia

Fibromyalgia is the best defined diffuse pain syndrome, but again it probably represents only the severe end of a spectrum of disease. Most patients complain of pain and stiffness at several sites, including knees, ankles, elbows, lower back, upper/mid back, and less frequently wrists, cervical spine, trapezius, fingers, thighs and feet (5). Early morning stiffness of several hours' duration, usually regarded as an important feature of inflammatory arthropathy, is also found in 75% of children and adolescents with fibromyalgia. Abnormalities of sleep are almost universal, and in particular waking in the morning feeling tired (non-restorative sleep) is commonly reported.

Despite complaints of joint swelling, there is characteristically no evidence on physical examination of arthritis or other definite organic disease. One exception is hypermobility; in a recent study of 338 school children, 21 had fibromyalgia of whom 80% were hypermobile, compared with only about 11% of the children without fibromyalgia. Conversely, 1.4% of non-hypermobile children had fibromyalgia compared with 40% of those with hypermobility (6). The most characteristic findings are the presence of multiple, symmetrical hyperalgesic tender sites, elicited by firm digital pressure on soft tissues around the upper and lower limb girdles, the medial aspect of the knee and lateral aspect of the elbow (see the previous 'Practical Problems' issue, Jan 1993: Fibromyalgia syndrome, Dr M Doherty). The multiplicity of the tender points is an important feature; one or two tender points are not uncommonly found in normal patients.

TABLE 4. CRITERIA FOR THE DIAGNOSIS OF DIFFUSE IDIOPATHIC MUSCULOSKELETAL PAIN SYNDROMES IN CHILDREN (ADAPTED FROM MALLESON ET AL (4))

DIFFUSE IDIOPATHIC PAIN SYNDROME - Both of:

1. Diffuse/widespread pain affecting at least 3 areas of the body persisting for more than 3 months.
2. Absence of other aetiologic factors that could reasonably explain the finding (eg bone tumour, sepsis, chronic arthritis, etc). Normal laboratory results.

FIBROMYALGIA (5) - Both of the above and:

1. At least 5 tender points, defined as areas of exaggerated tenderness elicited on moderately firm fingertip palpation of pairs of specific anatomic sites:

   Upper border of trapezius; lower part of sterno-cleido mastoid; lateral part of pectoralis major; mid-supraspinatus; lateral epicondyle of elbow; upper outer quadrant of gluteal region; greater trochanter of hip; medial fat pad of knee.

2. At least 3 of the following ten features:

   Chronic anxiety or tension; fatigue; poor sleep; chronic headaches; irritable bowel syndrome; subjective soft tissue swelling; numbness; pain modulation by physical activities, weather, or stress.

Laboratory investigations

In most cases, the diagnosis of fibromyalgia can be made on the basis of the clinical symptoms and signs. Occasionally, patients with an underlying inflammatory disease may also have fibromyalgia, so investigations to rule out the differential diagnoses (Table 5) may need to be performed. A minimum set of investigations might include a full blood count and differential, an ESR, a biochemical profile including bone, thyroid, and muscle studies, antinuclear antibodies, and perhaps plain radiographs of the worst affected areas. Previous studies have shown that bone scans are negative in this condition.

TABLE 5. DIFFERENTIAL DIAGNOSIS OF CHRONIC DIFFUSE MUSCULOSKELETAL PAIN IN CHILDREN

1. Infection: reactive arthritis
2. Tumour: leukaemia/lymphoma/other malignancy
3. Trauma: including non-accidental injury
4. Chronic inflammation: arthritis, dermatomyositis, SLE, inflammatory bowel disease
5. Hypermobility
6. Scheuermann's disease and osteochondritis
7. Hypertrophic osteoarthropathy (secondary to pulmonary disease, malignancy, or chronic inflammation)
8. Metabolic, endocrine and dietary deficiencies: rickets, hypothyroidism, scurvy
9. Diffuse idiopathic pain syndromes

TREATMENT OF IDIOPATHIC PAIN SYNDROMES

The treatment of idiopathic musculoskeletal pain is usually most successful using a team approach, involving a physician, physiotherapist, occupational therapist, psychologist and/or psychiatrist, and others as appropriate. It is most important that the team should have empathy with the patient's condition. It is not helpful for anyone to be judgmental or imply that the pains are imaginary; failing to accept or give credence to the symptoms is likely to be counterproductive. Sometimes admission to hospital is warranted for both close observation and initiation of treatment.

Stress is associated with both local and diffuse idiopathic pain syndromes. In some cases, the source of the stress is readily perceived; for example, a 12 year old national level swimmer whose incapacitating hand pain prevented him competing. In others, covert stress may be important, as illustrated by a 10 year old girl from a very disturbed family background who presented with chronically painful feet, hips, back and shoulders. The family were so outwardly cohesive that it was only discovered to be severely disrupted a year after she came to medical attention. The most commonly recorded categories of stress include scholastic or sporting high- or over-achievement, learning difficulties, single parent families and sexual abuse.

(1) Patient and parent disease education

The aims of disease education include restoration of patient confidence, enhanced feelings of self-control over the illness, and understanding of any specific stressors which may be contributing to the problems.

One educative approach to reflex sympathetic dystrophy is to illustrate the potentially vicious cycle of pain → immobility → more pain. The patient (or parent, or even the physician!) clenches one hand in an unusual posture for a few minutes, and then tries to move it again. Movement after even short periods of rigid immobility can be uncomfortable, emphasising the importance of maintaining mobility. Pamphlets which help to explain the illness have been developed in the USA (Dr D D Sherry, Reflex Neurovascular Dystrophy: Answers to commonly asked questions. Children's Hospital and Medical Center, Seattle, Washington).

An approach to patient education about fibromyalgia is to emphasise that insufficient deep sleep has an important role. Another useful and often reassuring explanation is that fibromyalgia is a disease associated with hard working, high-achieving children, who as a consequence may be more exposed to, and aware of, stress.

(2) Physical therapy

Physiotherapy and occupational therapy are invaluable in the management of both local and diffuse idiopathic pain syndromes. In some cases, this is best initiated in hospital, as it is very labour intensive and may continue for many hours each day.

There are three aspects to the physical treatment of local pain: joint range of movement exercises, muscle power exercises, and limb splinting in a position of function. The patient should actively participate in a graduated exercise programme, virtually regardless of pain. Hydrotherapy is often useful initially. Rarely, external appliances may be required: transcutaneous nerve stimulation to reduce the pain and/or a continuous passive motion machine to maintain movement, although the implicit lack of self control is one obvious disadvantage. Limb splints also have disadvantages, but may help to maintain the limb in a position of function when the patient is not actively involved in the physiotherapy programme.

Diffuse idiopathic pain is often associated with reduced physical fitness ('physical deconditioning'), which may be corrected with a graduated aerobic exercise programme. Swimming and cycling (particularly on an exercise bike) may be useful. Compliance in the longer term can be improved if the whole family undertakes the programme. In addition, specific muscle groups can be targeted for strengthening/stretching exercises depending on the sites of most pain. The use of local ice and heat, ultrasound, and transcutaneous nerve stimulation has been found to modulate the pain, and aid the physical therapy programme.

(3) Psychological support and intervention

There are two main objectives to psychological intervention: to facilitate coping with the pain, and to clarify (and possibly treat) any stress-related or psychological factors which initiated or exacerbated the illness. Various coping mechanisms have been taught to children; successful outcomes have been reported using progressive muscular relaxation followed by guided imagery. Hypnotherapy has been used successfully in adult patients, but its benefit in children is not documented.

(4) Pharmacotherapy

Virtually all patients will have used analgesics, and many will have also tried NSAIDs by the time they seek medical attention. One of the aims of the treatment programme should be to reduce the patient's 'dependence' on these drugs. In the treatment of refractory reflex sympathetic dystrophy there have been anecdotal reports of improvement with guanethidine infusions. Low dose tricyclic antidepressant medication such as amitriptyline (25-50mg at night for an adolescent) may improve the sleep patterns and decrease the morning fatigue associated with fibromyalgia.

In the longer term, one role of the physician in the management of all children with non-arthritic locomotor disorders is to remain alert for new symptoms or changes in disease pattern. Very rarely, a long time interval may separate the onset of symptoms from the appearance of recognisable organic pathology including malignancy.

REFERENCES & FURTHER READING

1. Goodman JE and McGrath PJ. The epidemiology of pain in children and adolescents: a review. *Pain* 1991; **46:** 247-264.
2. Gedalia A and Press J. Articular symptoms in hypermobile schoolchildren: A prospective study. *J Pediatr* 1991; **119:** 944-946.
3. Sherry DD, McGuire T, Mellins E, Salmonson K, Wallace CA and Nepom B. Psychosomatic musculoskeletal pain in childhood: Clinical and psychological analyses of one hundred children. *Pediatrics* 1991; **88:** 1093-1099.
4. Malleson PN, Al-Matar M, and Petty RE. Idiopathic musculoskeletal pain syndromes in children. *J Rheumatol* 1992; **19:** 1786-1789.
5. Yunus MB, and Masi AT. Juvenile primary fibromyalgia syndrome. *Arthritis Rheum* 1985; **28:** 138-144.
6. Gedalia A, Press J, Klein M, Buskila D. Joint hypermobility and fibromyalgia in children. *Ann Rheum Dis.* In press 1993.

May 1993

FIBROMYALGIA SYNDROME

M Doherty
Consultant Senior Lecturer
Rheumatology Unit
City Hospital
Nottingham NG5 1PB

SUMMARY

Fibromyalgia syndrome is a common but often overlooked condition that occurs predominantly in women and is associated with marked disability and handicap. It presents a variable symptom complex of widespread musculoskeletal pain, severe fatiguability and multisystem 'functional' disturbance. Diagnosis is based on typical symptoms, the presence of multiple hyperalgesic tender sites (with negative control sites), and exclusion of inflammatory or endocrine disease. There is no specific treatment and the prognosis is poor. Nevertheless, individual patients may be considerably helped by an adequate explanation of the condition, limited tricyclic treatment, an increase in aerobic exercise, and various coping strategies that shift the locus of control (responsibility) back to the patient.

THE NATURE OF THE FIBROMYALGIA SYNDROME

The patient problem that results from 'fibromyalgia' has probably been recognised for many years and categorised within various diagnostic terms depending on the principal presenting symptom (Table 1). All such labels encompass patients with marked symptoms and functional impairment in the absence of demonstrable inflammatory, metabolic or structural abnormality. Medicine has a bias towards a pathological explanation of 'disease' and these conditions have often been considered expressions of psychological disturbance of little medical interest. Such symptoms and disability, however, are real, not fabricated or imagined, and reflect 'functional' rather than 'pathological' abnormality.

TABLE I. DIAGNOSTIC TERMS THAT MAY COMMONLY INCLUDE PATIENTS WITH FIBROMYALGIA SYNDROME

PRINCIPAL PRESENTING SYMPTOM	DIAGNOSTIC LABEL
Locomotor pain	Psychogenic rheumatism Fibrositis Pain amplification syndrome
Fatigue	Myalgoencephalitis ('ME') Chronic fatigue syndrome
Headache	Tension headache
Abdominal pain, bowel disturbance	Irritable bowel syndrome

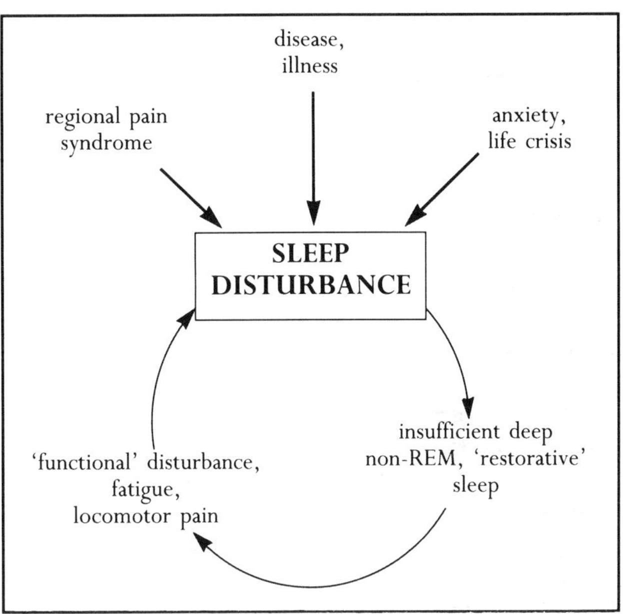

Fig 1. A possible mechanism of induction and perpetuation of fibromyalgia syndrome.

Two important advances in the last twenty years have given respectability to 'fibromyalgia' and led to an explosion of research interest, particularly in Canada and America. Firstly, the recognition of multiple hyperalgesic tender sites as a characteristic feature, permitting delineation of diagnostic criteria. Secondly, an association with sleep disturbance, as evidenced by:

(1) universal presence of symptoms of non-restorative sleep in fibromyalgia patients

(2) EEG evidence of reduced deep, non-dreaming, non Rapid-Eye-Movement (non-REM) sleep with interruption by alpha waves ('alpha-delta intrusion') in fibromyalgic patients,

(3) reproduction of fibromyalgia symptoms and hyperalgesic tender sites in normal subjects (especially if aerobically unfit) by selective deprivation of non-REM (but not REM) sleep.

TABLE 2. COMMON SYMPTOMS OF FIBROMYALGIA

pain -	predominantly axial (neck, back) often aggravated by stress, cold; activity often associated with generalised morning stiffness; pain may be "all over;" unresponsive to analgesics/NSAIDs
fatiguability -	often extreme, following minimal exertion

both may severely limit daily activities

subjective swelling of extremities;
paraesthesiae, dysaesthesiae of hands, feet;
waking unrefreshed;
poor concentration, forgetful;
low affect, irritable, weepy;
headache - occipital, bifrontal;
diffuse abdominal pain, variable bowel habit;
urinary frequency, urgency (day and night).

Although the mechanism of fibromyalgia remains unclear, one possible explanation based on chronic non-restorative sleep is outlined in Fig. 1. Various factors (eg regional pain syndromes, anxiety relating to a life crisis such as bereavement) may cause reduction in deep sleep with resultant somatic symptoms and fatigue. Once established, poor daily functioning, declining aerobic fitness and pain could encourage perpetuation of this aberrant sleep pattern. Fibromyalgia may be superimposed upon pre-existing painful conditions such as osteoarthritis or cancer ('secondary fibromyalgia'). Usually, however, it affects subjects with no other discernible diagnosis ('primary' fibromyalgia). There is obvious overlap in symptoms and impaired function between fibromyalgia, anxiety and depression, and patients with fibromyalgia score highly on anxiety and depression questionnaires.

Although the term 'fibromyalgia syndrome' is not ideal, it does not imply causation and describes the commonest symptom. Many 'chronic fatigue syndrome' patients fulfil criteria for fibromyalgia, and represent one end of a spectrum of presentations rather than a separate entity. Evidence for triggering viral infections in the vast majority of patients is lacking, and unlike fibromyalgia most 'post-viral' myalgia/fatigue syndromes are self-limiting and are not associated with hyperalgesic tender sites. For the present, therefore, 'fibromyalgia syndrome' is an appropriate compromise term.

RECOGNITION AND DIAGNOSIS

Common presenting symptoms are listed in Table 2. The condition is rare in children and most patients are women in their forties and fifties. Pain and fatigue are often associated with severe disability. Although able to dress and wash the patient often cannot cope with their job or with ordinary household activities (eg shopping, cleaning). Pain is predominantly axial and diffuse, but may affect any region and at different times be felt "all over". Characteristically the pain is not helped by analgesics or NSAIDs. The patient often admits to a poor sleep pattern, awaking unrefreshed and feeling more tired in the morning than later in the day. Quality of sleep is more important than quantity, and a good duration of sleep is not incompatible with the diagnosis.

A full medical (multisystem) history and examination is important since fibromyalgia may complicate disease in other systems. Clinical findings, however, are usually unremarkable with no objective weakness, synovitis or neurological abnormality.

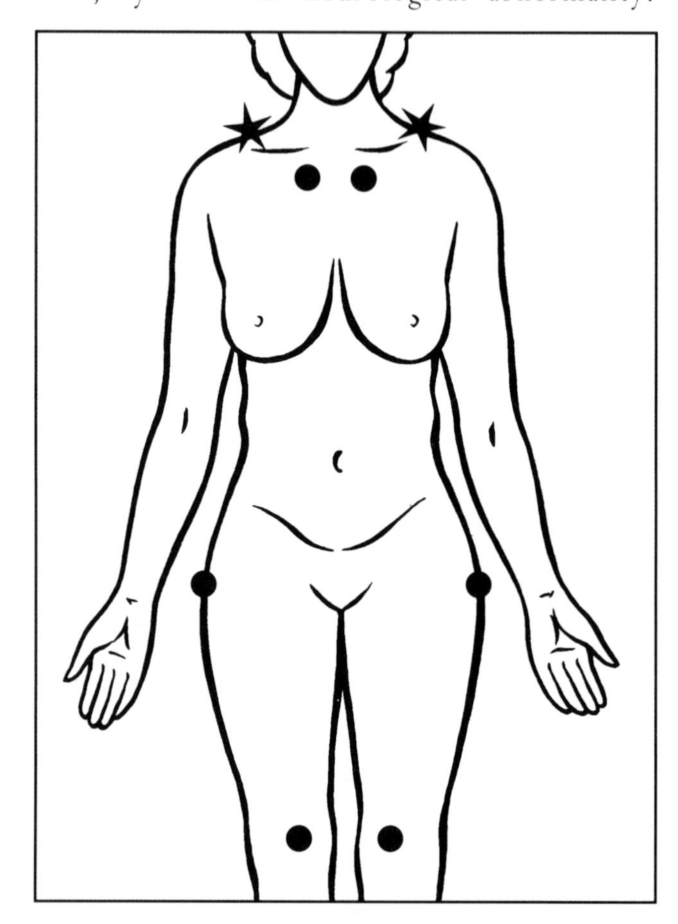

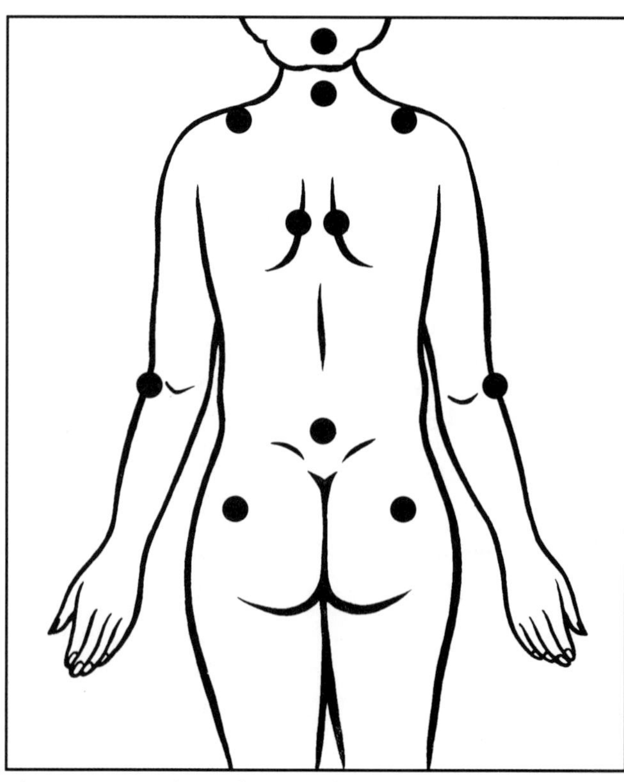

Fig 2. Common hyperalgesic tender sites

TABLE 3. COMMON HYPERALGESIC TENDER SITES IN FIBROMYALGIA

- low cervical spine (C4-6 interspinous ligaments)
- low lumbar spine (L4-S1 interspinous ligaments)
- suboccipital muscle (posterior base of skull)
- supraspinatus
- mid-point of upper trapezius
- skin roll tenderness of skin overlying mid-trapezius
- pectoralis insertion, maximal lateral to 2nd costo-chondral junction
- lateral epicondyle, 'tennis elbow' site, 1-2 cm distal to epicondyle
- gluteus medius - upper, outer quadrant of buttock
- greater trochanter
- medial fat pad of knee

Osteoarthritis and regional periarticular lesions are common and may be present as an incidental or triggering abnormality. From the physicians's perspective however, the symptoms and disability of fibromyalgia appear totally disproportionate to any examination (or investigational) findings, and such discordance alone suggests the diagnosis. The important, sometimes only, positive examination finding is the presence of multiple hyperalgesic tender sites (Table 3, Fig. 2). These naturally occurring sites are uncomfortable to firm digital pressure in normal individuals, but in fibromyalgia similar pressure elicits marked tenderness and a wince/withdrawal response. The degree of pressure is obviously relevant - for trial purposes a standardised pressure is sometimes delivered via a spring device (dolorimeter), but for clinical purposes reasonable firm unmetered digital pressure suffices. It is not uncommon to find a hyperalgesic response at just one or two sites in the same quadrant, reflecting a local periarticular lesion or referred tenderness from an axial structure. For diagnosis of fibromyalgia, however, this response should be obtained at tender sites

TABLE 4. DIFFERENTIAL DIAGNOSIS AND INVESTIGATIONS

differential diagnosis:
- hypothyroidism
- systemic lupus erythematosus
- inflammatory myopathy
- hyperparathyroidism
- osteomalacia
- (Parkinsonism)
- (polymyalgia rheumatica)
- (myeloma, carcinomatosis)

investigations:
- full blood count , ESR/viscosity
- calcium, creatine kinase
- thyroid function
- antinuclear factor

TABLE 5. ASPECTS OF MANAGEMENT

- patient (and family) education
- limited trial of amitriptyline (25-75mg) at night
- stop other ineffective drugs
- graded aerobic exercise regime
- coping strategies (eg yoga)

axially, in upper and lower limbs, and on both sides (ie widespread, symmetrical). The number of tender sites required for diagnosis varies with different criteria sets, but 10 or more are usually necessary. In addition, hyperalgesia should be absent at 'non-tender' (negative control) sites such as the forehead, distal forearm, and lateral fibular head. If tenderness is present wherever the patient is touched fabrication of symptoms or psychiatric disturbance is most likely.

INVESTIGATIONS

The only tests required to exclude alternative diagnoses that may present with widespread pain, weakness or fatigue are listed in Table 4. Additional investigations may be warranted if the history and examination findings suggest a predisposing or coexistent condition. Undertaking all investigations together reinforces the patient's confidence in the accuracy of the diagnosis and is preferable to a drawn-out sequence of tests.

MANAGEMENT

Approaches to management are listed in Table 5. The single most important intervention is a full, comprehensible explanation to the patient. This should convey:

(1) sympathy for the fact that the patient has real symptoms and disability.

(2) reassurance that the pain does not indicate cancer, inflammation, arthritis or damage to muscles and joints. Most patients understandably are expecting a pessimistic explanation for the cause of their devastating symptoms.

(3) a clear understanding of the nature of the prob lem. An explanation based on insufficient deep sleep is a useful, acceptable construct that helps patients rationalise their symptoms and disability.

It is helpful to give such explanation in the presence of a close family member. Further enquiry concerning life events that could have initiated disturbed sleep may reveal suppressed problems that deserve open discussion and counselling. Patients in whom a specific sublimated anxiety is identified and then successfully addressed are most likely to do well.

The only two interventions shown in clinical trials to be useful in some patients with fibromyalgia are (1) low dose amitriptyline at night, and (2) a graded exercise programme to increase aerobic fitness. The dose of amitriptyline (25-75mg) is less than that used for depression but similar to that used to good effect in other chronic pain syndromes. The rationale for its use, which should be explained to the patient, is twofold: firstly, its effects on the sleep centre to normalise deep sleep; and secondly, its influence on 'gating' of pain at the spinal cord level. If a limited trial of 4-6 weeks is ineffective further drug therapy should be avoided.

An increasing aerobic exercise regime, individualised to the patient, aims to improve sleep via a non-drug approach. The patient should be warned that such exercise may initially exacerbate symptoms (because they are unfit), but that they should push themselves despite pain (the opposite advice to someone with synovitis/joint damage). An important element of exercise is that the locus of control for the patient's problem is now with the patient - it is up to them, rather than the doctor or drugs, to improve their situation.

If these interventions fail, coping strategies (eg meditational yoga) may permit the patient to control the extent to which pain and fatigue intervene in their life. The prognosis of fibromyalgia is poor: in a Nottingham study less than one in ten hospital-diagnosed patients lost their symptoms over a five year period. Nevertheless with suitable advice most patients, though not 'cured', can learn to live better with their condition and importantly avoid further unnecessary investigations and drug treatments

FURTHER READING

The Fibromyalgia Syndrome. *Rheumatic Disease Clinics of North America*, 1989, **15(1)**: 1-191.

January 1993

SYSTEMIC LUPUS ERYTHEMATOSUS (SLE)

P Emery
Senior Lecturer
Department of Rheumatology
University of Birmingham
Consultant Rheumatologist
Queen Elizabeth and Selly Oak Hospitals
Birmingham

SUMMARY

Systemic lupus erythematosus (SLE) is a chronic autoimmune disease which produces symptoms varying from very mild to life-threatening. It characteristically affects young women but all ages can be affected. The most distinct immunological abnormality is the presence of autoantibodies, with anti-nuclear antibodies directed against native double-stranded DNA being diagnostic. The course of the disease is characterised by periods of remission and relapse. The skill of management is to predict and hence prevent flares of disease activity. A continued awareness of the possibility of the disease and the necessity of prompt referral for expert management are two important aspects of care.

Epidemiology

The prevalence of SLE is 4-280 cases per 100,000 (based on ARA criteria, Table 1), the highest prevalence being in Afro-Caribbeans, followed by Asians. The sex ratio is 13:1 in favour of females, which is reduced in both children (ratio 1.4:1) and the elderly in whom it is rarer and milder. Disease onset is usually between the ages of 16 and 55. Blacks have a worse prognosis associated with increased prevalence of renal disease and certain autoantibodies (anti-Sm, anti-RNP). The concordance rate for monozygotic twins is up to 50%, and 10% of relatives of patients with SLE may be affected. Multiple genes have been implicated (eg HLA B8, DR2, DR3 and complement deficiency genes). There are clear associations between certain genetic markers, autoantibodies and clinical disease.

Clinical features

See Table 2. SLE can produce pathology in any organ. Key clinical features produced as a consequence are noted below.

Systemic features

Fatigue or lethargy is present in virtually all patients and is strongly associated with reduced exercise tolerance. Attribution of fatigue is often very difficult, but when due to disease it may correlate with the serum immunoglobulin level and other measures of disease activity. Fever may suggest the diagnosis: characteristically it is episodic.

Table 1.

REVISED CRITERIA OF THE AMERICAN RHEUMATISM ASSOCIATION FOR THE CLASSIFICATION OF SYSTEMIC LUPUS ERYTHEMATOSUS (SLE)

1.	Malar rash
2.	Discoid rash
3.	Photosensitivity
4.	Oral ulcers
5.	Arthritis
6.	Serositis: (a) pleuritis, or (b) pericarditis
7.	Renal disorder: (a) proteinuria > 0.5g/24 h or 3+, persistently, or (b) cellular casts
8.	Neurological disorder: (a) seizures or (b) psychosis (having excluded other causes, eg drugs)
9.	Haematologic disorder: (a) haemolytic anaemia or (b) leucopenia of < 4.0 x 10^9/1 on two or more occasions (c) lymphopenia of < 1.5 x 10^9/1 on two or more occasions (d) thrombocytopenia < 100 x 10^9/1
10.	Immunologic disorders: (a) positive LE cell or (b) raised anti-native DNA antibody binding or (c) anti-Sm[a] antibody or (d) false positive serologic test for syphilis, present for at least 6 months
11.	Antinuclear antibody in raised titre

"... A person shall be said to have SLE if four or more of the 11 criteria are present, serially or simultaneously, during any interval of observation."

[a]Sm, Smith antigen after Tan et al (1982)

Musculoskeletal manifestations

The arthritis of SLE is migratory with little synovial thickening or effusion. It is generally non-destructive and non-deforming contrasting with that of rheumatoid disease, probably because of a difference in the cytokines produced. This also explains the difference in acute phase response in these two diseases (see later). The most commonly affected joints are the knees, wrists and the proximal interphalangeal joints.

Avascular necrosis of bone, especially of the femoral head, can occur during therapy with high dose steroids but hip disease can result from the disease itself. Osteoporosis is a frequent complication of the disease and its therapy: spinal osteoporosis may be attributable to glucocorticoids. Myalgia is frequent

Table 2.

FREQUENCY OF CLINICAL SYMPTOMS IN SLE

Symptoms	Approx %	Comment
Fatigue	80-100	Treatable when due to disease.
Fever	80	
Weight loss	60	Usually before diagnosis.
Arthritis, arthralgia	95	Symptomatic but usually non-deforming.
Skin	80	
Butterfly rash	50	
Photosensitivity	60	
Mucous membrane lesion	40	
Alopecia	70	
Raynaud's phenomenon	25	
Purpura	15	
Urticaria	8	
Renal	50	
Nephrosis	18	
Gastrointestinal	38	Mild
Pulmonary		
Pleurisy	45	Frequently symptomatic but only rarely severe.
Effusion	24	
Pneumonia	29	
Cardiac		
Pericarditis	30	Common but rarely of haemodynamic importance.
Murmurs	23	Libman Sachs endocarditis has increased risk of bacterial endocarditis and stenosis.
ECG changes	35	
Lymphadenopathy	50	
Splenomegaly	10	
Hepatomegaly	25	
Central nervous system		
Mood disturbance	50	
Psychosis	20	
Convulsions	15	

although myositis is relatively uncommon; weakness may be due to medication (eg steroid myopathy, anti-malarial therapy).

Mucocutaneous

UVB light can induce a rash in about 60% of patients. Furthermore it can also cause a generalised disease exacerbation. The mechanism is multi-factorial and includes UV damage to DNA. Patients also react to UVA or even the visible light spectrum with blue eyed, fair skinned individuals and those possessing anti-Ro being most susceptible. The classical butterfly rash often occurs after UV exposure and tends to be short-lived. There may be a longer lasting maculopapular eruption. Discoid lesions are discrete and annular with slightly infiltrated plaques which extend at the inflammatory periphery leaving depressed central scarring with telangiectasia and de-pigmentation. These may occur in the absence of systemic manifestations (cutaneous discoid), and 10% of these latter patients will develop systemic lupus. Subacute cutaneous lupus erythematosus is a mild overlap form associated with HLA DR3 and anti-Ro antibodies. Panniculitis is a rare severe complication affecting the mid/deep-dermal or subcutaneous layer leaving a depressed scar on resolution. When associated with a cutaneous nodule it is called lupus profundus. Epidermal bullous lesions may also be seen occasionally in SLE.

70% of patients suffer from alopecia which is usually non-scarring except when due to discoid lesions. Painful mucous membrane involvement, livedo reticularis, periungual erythema, Raynaud's phenomenon, telangiectasia and lupus pernio (chilblain-like lesions) are also seen. Immune complex deposition in post-capillary venules produces urticaria and vasculitis of the small arteries and micro-infarcts of the fingertips and toes. Infarction is best treated conservatively (non-surgically).

Pulmonary manifestations

Pleuritic chest pain is an extremely common manifestation of lupus. When accompanied by a pleural rub or effusion the diagnosis of serositis is facilitated, but alternative sources for chest pain need to be excluded, especially in view of the increased risk of pulmonary infarction/embolism.

Acute lupus pneumonitis is uncommon and may coincide with infection in immunosuppressed individuals. Progressive interstitial fibrosis and pulmonary hypertension are less common than in systemic sclerosis and have a poor prognosis. A characteristic but rare clinical picture is the "shrinking lung syndrome", probably due to a mixture of myositis affecting the diaphragm, pleural adhesions with atelectasis and perhaps phrenic nerve dysfunction.

Cardiovascular manifestations

Innocent systolic murmurs and mild pericarditis are frequent. Diastolic murmurs are indicative of Libman Sachs endocarditis (often associated with anti-cardiolipin antibodies). These are due to accumulations of inflammatory material and thrombus. Coronary artery disease is increased, possibly due to an association with hyperlipidaemia and long term corticosteroid therapy. Conduction defects and congenital heart block are part of the rare neonatal lupus syndrome occurring in some babies of mothers possessing anti-Ro or anti-La antibodies. Hypertension is a serious problem, often causing deterioration in renal function.

Haematological abnormalities

Normochromic/normocytic anaemia is frequent and reflects inflammation. Haemolytic anaemia may be present in 25% of patients and is associated with a positive direct Coombs' test. Leucopaenia is common with reductions in both granulocytes and lymphocytes. Lymphocytopaenia has a particular association with

Table 3. Patients with high probability of SLE

THINK OF SLE IN PATIENTS (ESPECIALLY YOUNG FEMALES) WITH ANY OF THE FOLLOWING*:

- Photosensitivity
- Arthralgia and rash
- Raynaud's or mouth ulcers
- Pleurisy
- Proteinuria
- Haematological abnormalities (especially low white cell count or thrombocytopaenia)
- Abortion (recurrent, midtrimester)
- Any neurological abnormality (including seizures)
- Fatigue/depression

* When one of the above features present enquire about others

active disease due to anti-lymphocyte antibodies but may also be a consequence of therapy. Thrombocytopaenia is common in SLE and is usually due to anti-platelet antibodies with a hypercellular marrow, the spleen being the major site of platelet destruction. The risk of bleeding increases significantly when the platelet count is less than 20,000. Lymphadenopathy occurs especially during disease exacerbation, and when persistent may require a biopsy to exclude the development of lymphoma.

Lupus anti-coagulant and anti-phospholipid syndrome

Antibodies to a number of clotting factors occur in SLE. Lupus anti-coagulant due to an antiphospholipid antibody is found in up to 25% of patients (and overlaps with anti-cardiolipin antibody). It produces a prolongation of clotting time and will prolong the PTT of normal plasma. Anticardiolipin antibodies of IgG class are associated with thrombocytopaenia, arterial and venous thrombosis including cerebral vascular accidents, pulmonary hypertension and recurrent foetal loss. These antibodies account for the false positive Wasserman reaction for syphilis. The syndrome can occur in patients without clinical lupus: the anti-phospholipid syndrome.

Acute phase response

The ESR is elevated in virtually all patients with SLE, particularly during active disease and immunoglobulin and lipid abnormalities contribute to this. By contrast C reactive protein (CRP) tends to be normal or only slightly raised unless there is infection (when the CRP is invariably raised) or tissue damage.

Renal lupus

About 50% of SLE patients develop urinary or functional renal abnormalities, but virtually all patients have histological abnormalities. Proteinuria is the most common manifestation and usually presents within the first five years after diagnosis. A renal biopsy is useful in differentiating lupus nephritis from other causes of renal abnormalities such as infection, but more importantly it determines the precise histology and therefore likely response to therapy. It is generally performed on patients with haematuria/proteinuria or a fall in creatinine clearance.

The major abnormalities observed are proliferative glomerulonephritis, either focal (less than 50% glomeruli involved) or diffuse (greater than 50%), membranous glomerulonephritis and mild mesangial nephritis. For prognosis the assessment of the degree of active inflammation, scarring and of tubulo-interstitial involvement is critical. The correlation between pathological findings, clinical features, and ultimately prognosis, has been controversial. Patients with mild **mesangial** proliferation may have proteinuria and abnormal sediments, plus decreases in total complement and C3 level. Patients with **focal** proliferative nephritis usually have greater, more severe abnormalities of urinalysis and greater impairment in renal function and immune function. Those with **diffuse** proliferative nephritis are even more abnormal with considerable complement and immune complex abnormalities. **Membranous** nephritis, by contrast, typically presents with a nephrotic syndrome.

Neuropsychiatric abnormalities

There is a spectrum of disease which varies from the purely functional to the completely organic. Functional abnormalities, including depression and anxiety are common and can often be helped by counselling. Psychosis may respond to steroids but the latter can also induce psychosis. Headaches are frequent in SLE, and organic cause is suggested by their sudden development, an association with double vision, minor seizures or a change in personality. Metabolic abnormalities and other secondary causes need to be excluded when seizures occur. Often no specific abnormality is found and it is assumed that the seizures are secondary to the disease process. Peripheral neuropathy occurs in around 10% of

Table 4. Investigations

DIAGNOSIS		
1. Initial Screening	**2. If ANA Positive**	**MONITORING**
FBC and WC differential	ds DNA*	Blood pressure
ESR/CRP	ENA (for anti-Ro and anti-La)	Urinalysis
ANA	Clotting screen	FBC and WC differential
	Complement (C3, C4)	ESR
	Anticardiolipin antibody (Coombs test)	ds DNA**
	Chest x-ray	Complement (C3d)
	Urinalysis	Serum creatinine
	Creatinine clearance	
	Renal biopsy where indicated	

* Specific assay for diagnosis (Crithidia)
**Quantitative assay for monitoring

Note
1. ANA is best screening test but non-specific
2. Antibodies to native ds DNA (Crithidia) or high levels in quantitative assay are specific
3. A negative test for ds DNA antibodies does not exclude SLE

patients, and can involve the cranial nerves and multiple individual nerves. Cerebro-vascular accidents and transverse myelitis occur secondary to vasculitis or thrombosis/embolism. Rarely, movement disorders including choreoathetosis and hemiballismus are seen. SLE can affect the eye with characteristic cotton wool exudates (cytoid bodies) reflecting microangiopathy of the retinal capillaries. Diagnosis of CNS lupus is difficult because **there may be little correlation with disease activity elsewhere.** CSF usually needs to be examined to exclude infection, and to provide indirect evidence of active disease. An EEG is often helpful in patients with active CNS lupus while MRI has increased sensitivity for vasculitis. Positron emission tomography using radiolabelled oxygen may have particular virtues in this disorder. Distinguishing active inflammation from past damage can be difficult.

Hormones, drugs and lupus

Some patients notice a flare of their disease after starting oral contraceptives containing oestrogen and standard advice is to avoid these where possible. Likewise pregnancy is often advised against, although it is now clear that with well controlled non-renal lupus there is very little increased risk to the patient. Patients with recurrent miscarriage should be monitored in a specialised unit. There is a case for prescribing aspirin to all SLE patients during pregnancy to prevent foetal growth retardation.

A number of drugs (hydralazine, procainamide, isoniazid, chlorpromazine, D-penicillamine and methyldopa) can result in **drug-induced lupus** in predisposed individuals. This can be differentiated from the idiopathic disease on genetic and immunologic grounds. Furthermore, it is mild and reversible on stopping the drug, renal disease and double stranded anti-DNA are rare (although antibodies specific for histones may be present) and the sex ratio is equal.

Differential diagnosis

Entertaining the diagnosis of lupus is the necessary first step. Specific clinical situations in which there is a high risk of lupus are shown in Table 3, and should raise a physician's awareness. Joint disease is often confused with rheumatoid arthritis when first seen and SLE should be considered in any case of inflammatory arthritis which is non-destructive and negative for rheumatoid factor. It should be noted that patients with other autoimmune diseases may overlap and evolve into SLE. Furthermore, therapy for these diseases can sometimes induce the disease, eg penicillamine inducing drug-induced lupus in rheumatoid patients. The ARA revised criteria are for classification rather than diagnosis of SLE, but in practice it is usually less important to make a precise diagnosis of SLE than to realise that the pathological process is immunological, rather than an alternative such as infection. For features helpful in distinguishing lupus from other diseases see under headings above.

Suggested **screening tests** are shown in Table 4. The screening test of choice is a sensitive anti-nuclear antibody test. Using a substrate such a HEp2 the test is positive in virtually all cases of SLE. The finding of a positive ANA, especially in low titre however, is non-specific, being positive in other conditions, and additional confirmation is required. The pattern of immunofluorescence can be of help, for example homogeneous or rim staining immunofluorescence is specific for SLE. The usual method used to confirm the diagnosis is testing for double-stranded DNA antibodies. But a significant proportion of patients with SLE do not have these antibodies (but will have a positive ANA usually with a speckled pattern due to antiRo, anti-La, anti-RNP or anti-Sm) and in these patients the diagnosis is a clinical one. Of the confirmatory tests the most specific are those testing for antibodies directed against native DNA; the Crithidia test is a convenient version of this. Other quantitative assays allow measurement and change in DNA antibody titre and are helpful in monitoring. These tests are less specific but high titres in such assays are found in few conditions other than SLE. Antibodies of the IgG isotype, as in other conditions, suggest pathogenicity.

MANAGEMENT OF SLE

General considerations

Because of the variety of organs affected, the management of SLE patients in the past involved many different consultants. Awareness of this problem has led centres with a special interest in this disease to set up specific Lupus clinics with ready access to all the relevant specialties on one site. The overall prognosis has improved considerably with a greater than 80% 10-year survival. The initial few months after diagnosis are often the most dangerous for the patient as a rapid deterioration in disease activity can occur before the disease has stabilised. Once a flare has occurred, disease management is considerably complicated and the outcome worse. For this reason an urgent referral to a specialist centre for accurate assessment of disease activity is advised as soon as diagnosis is made. Whenever a flare occurs rigorous screening for infection is required. This is especially relevant when patients are immunosuppressed or on high doses of steroids since unusual infections, particularly fungal, need to be excluded.

The importance of good blood pressure monitoring and control cannot be stressed too strongly. Poor control of blood pressure aggravates and maintains renal pathology and for this reason measurement of blood pressure and urinalysis are mandatory at every visit.

The disease is a chronic one and a crucial aspect of care is the doctor/patient relationship. Helping the patient understand the disease is the first step, and this can require lengthy education and support. Furthermore the frequency of neuropsychiatric problems means that the patient/doctor relationship is often tested and support from the family particularly is important. Many patients gain a great deal of valuable support from the self-help organisation Lupus UK (1).

Table 5.

STEROID USE AND SERIOUS DISEASE	
Steroid responsive	Steroid non-responsive
Dermatitis (local)	Thrombosis
Polyarthritis	Renal damage
Serositis	Hypertension
Vasculitis	Steroid-induced psychosis
Haematological	Infection
Glomerulonephritis (most)	
Myelopathies	

Non-steroidal anti-inflammatory drugs and anti-malarials

Arthritis, arthralgia and myalgia are the most common manifestations of SLE and are treated by non-steroidal anti-inflammatory drugs. Side-effects of these drugs include a reduction in glomerular filtration rate (less with sulindac and nabumetone), interstitial nephritis (rare), gastrointestinal toxicity and hepatotoxicity (which is increased in patients with SLE).

Some SLE patients will find their symptoms are not well controlled by a NSAID. **Anti-malarials** (see later) are often effective in these patients but are slow to act. Local therapy including steroid injections can be useful adjuncts. Failure of this approach may lead to institution of low dose glucocorticoids, occasionally higher dose glucocorticoids, or cytotoxic drugs including methotrexate.

The majority of patients with SLE are photosensitive. Not only can UV light cause flares of skin disease but also flares of systemic disease. Photosensitive patients should minimise their exposure by wearing protective clothing and using sun screens effective against UVA and UVB. A sun protection factor of 15 or higher should be used. Topical steroids are helpful for most lupus dermatitis but scarring discoid or extensive lesions usually require management by a dermatologist. All types of lupus skin disease have been shown to respond to anti-malarials. The mechanism of action is unclear although **anti-malarials** have sun blocking, anti-inflammatory and immunosuppressive effects. Furthermore they result in a reduction in cholesterol. Recommended doses for hydroxychloroquine are 200-400mg/daily with reduction to 5 days/week in the maintenance phase. Anti-malarials may produce retinal damage at a cumulative dose greater then 200g, or if a daily dose of 4mg/kg for chloroquine phosphate, or 6.5mg/kg for hydroxychloroquine is exceeded. Other rare problems include peripheral neuropathies and myopathies. Dapsone can be used as an alternative in severe skin disease. Recently it has been demonstrated that anti-malarials have a significant role in suppressing systemic disease flares.

Systemic complaints and immunosuppressive therapy

Weight loss and fatigue rarely respond to therapy other than **corticosteroids.** Fatigue in particular is underestimated by physicians and often a small dose of steroids can be effective in relieving it. It is important to decide the balance between effective disease suppression and the side-effects of therapy. While much has been written about the side-effects of steroids and cytotoxic agents, rather less has been written about the side-effects of active disease and its effect on the quality of life. Steroids are the mainstay of therapy. Small doses may be very effective in suppressing disease. Often it may be necessary for a trial of steroids to assess the benefits before a proper cost/benefit analysis can be made. Increasingly, when higher doses of steroids are prescribed they are accompanied by a 'bone-sparing' agent, eg calcium. Steroid responsive aspects of the disease are shown in Table 5. Immunosuppressive therapy is required for life-threatening complications. Therapy of renal disease is a specialist area. There are now randomised studies assessing the benefit of various immunosuppressive regimens with outcome measures including toxicity and quality of life as well as renal function. In order to improve further the outcome of patients with this complex disease it is important that all patients are formally assessed in a suitable protocol.

Azathioprine is, in general, used for maintenance regimens when steroids have induced a remission. The addition of azathioprine in doses up to 2.5mg/kg can allow a reduction of prednisolone below 10mg/day with disease stability. The evidence for efficacy in severe renal disease is debatable. Regular blood monitoring is required.

Cyclophosphamide is used in life-threatening conditions (vasculitis, renal disease and severe thrombocytopaenia and disease-induced cytopaenias). There has been a trend toward intermittent pulse regimens, mainly because this mode of administration allows effective use of Mesna, an antidote to acrolein, the metabolite responsible for hemorrhagic cystitis (and consequent risk of bladder carcinoma). Other serious potential side-effects are bone marrow and gonadal toxicity, infertility and teratogenesis. However toxicity (including alopecia) is less than might be expected and in combination with pulse steroids cyclophosphamide is often well tolerated.

Other therapies (see Table 6)

Patients with thrombosis require **anticoagulants**. The recent evidence suggests that therapy should be life-long if thrombosis is associated with evidence of risk factors for clotting. Abortion and foetal loss are treated with **aspirin** in the first instance. Many other therapies including immunosuppression have been used for resistant cases. There is a case for treatment of all SLE pregnancies with aspirin to prevent foetal growth retardation. Cytopaenias usually respond to steroids. **Intravenous gamma globulin** has been shown to be effective short term therapy for thrombocytopaenia. Cytotoxics are often used when knowledge of bone marrow status is available. Glomerulonephritis is now usually treated with pulse cytotoxics and steroids. CNS disease is treated with anti-coagulants when the pathogenesis is thrombosis, and steroids and cytotoxics when there is a vasculitic element.

Table 6.

Treatment of Specific Problems (see text)

Thrombosis	Aspirin/anticoagulants
Abortion/foetal loss	Aspirin± other therapies
Cytopaenias	Steroids, danazol, ivIg, cytotoxics
Glomerulonephritis	Steroids, cytotoxics
CNS - thrombosis	Anticoagulants
- vasculitis	Steroids, cytotoxics
Infarction (secondary to vasculitis)	Steroids, cytotoxics, prostacyclin

ivIg = intravenous gamma globulin

Laboratory monitoring of disease activity

The crucial aspect of care of patients is treating patients prior to flare of their disease. During a disease flare many laboratory disease parameters become abnormal but usually by this time the flare is clinically obvious. For example, during exacerbation of renal disease the ESR, ANA and double-stranded DNA antibody titre and C3d levels all rise, whilst levels of C3 and C4 usually fall. Screening for infection should always be performed whenever there is a major flare. A normal CRP is very helpful in indicating that infection is unlikely. Increasing use is being made of markers which may allow **prediction** of disease activity in advance of clinical disease flare. These include certain of the standard markers mentioned above (especially C3d), and more recently others such as soluble IL-2 receptor and adhesion molecules. This is an area of importance in that it is likely to lead to the greatest improvement in quality of care. There are several disease assessment scores which have been recently reviewed, including that of the British Isles Lupus Assessment Group (2).

POINTS ABOUT LUPUS

- Overall the outlook is now good
- The period prior to stabilisation is one of the most dangerous for disease flares
- Avoid delay in referring for expert management
- Monitor blood pressure obsessionally and test urine at each visit
- Illness in lupus patients needs to be taken seriously
- Always think of infection as initiating/accompanying flares of disease
- Keep in mind overall quality of life

REFERENCES

1. Lupus UK, 51 North Street, Romford, Essex RM1 1BA. Telephone: 01708 731251

2. E Hay, C Gordon and P Emery. Assessment of lupus: where are we now? *Annals of the Rheumatic Diseases.* 1993; 52: 169-172

May 1994

SJÖGREN'S SYNDROME

P Venables
Senior Lecturer & Hon Consultant in Immunology of the Rheumatic Diseases
The Kennedy Institute & Charing Cross Hospital
London

DEFINITION AND DIAGNOSTIC CRITERIA

Sjögren's syndrome represents a group of diseases characterised by a common pathological feature: namely inflammation and destruction of exocrine glands. The salivary and lachrymal glands are principally involved giving rise to dry eyes and mouth, though other exocrine glands including those of the pancreas, sweat glands and mucus-secreting glands of the bowel, bronchial tree and vagina may be affected. It was originally described as the triad of dry eyes, dry mouth and rheumatoid arthritis *(1)* though it is now classified as (i) primary Sjögren's syndrome, where the disease exists on its own and (ii) secondary Sjögren's syndrome where it is associated with another autoimmune rheumatic disease such as rheumatoid arthritis (RA), systemic lupus erythematosus (SLE) or more rarely, polymyositis, scleroderma, primary biliary cirrhosis and chronic active hepatitis.

Sjögren's syndrome is the second commonest autoimmune rheumatic disease *(2)*. The exact prevalence is not known as there are thought to be many sufferers whose symptoms are so mild that they do not seek medical advice. It is nine times commoner in women than men and its onset is any age from 15-65. The patients rarely complain of dry eyes, but rather a gritty sensation, soreness, photosensitivity or intolerance of contact lenses. The dry mouth is often manifest as the "cream cracker" sign, inability to swallow dry food without fluid, or the need to wake up in the night to take sips of water.

Keratoconjunctivitis sicca can be detected by Schirmer's test, tear break-up time, and Rose Bengal staining *(3)* and xerostomia, by observing a diminished salivary pool, by a reduced parotid salivary flow rate and by reduced uptake and clearance on isotope scans *(4)*. The majority of patients have a raised ESR, often associated with a mild normocytic anaemia, hypergammaglobulinaemia and rheumatoid factors. Antibodies to Ro (SS-A) are found in about 85% of patients and La (SS-B) in 60%.

Based on these clinical features the criteria of Bloch et al (1965) *(5)* became the first for the diagnosis of Sjögren's: namely a triad of keratoconjunctivitis sicca, xerostomia and RA or other connective tissue disease. Whaley et al *(6)* made some minor modifications to Bloch's criteria in 1973 to include the results of objective measurements such as Shirmer's test. Daniels et al *(7)* added salivary gland biopsy findings to the list, which subsequently reached a peak of complexity and objectivity with the criteria of Manthorpe et al in 1981 *(8)* which required no less than 6 tests, including lip biopsy and salivary gland scintigraphy. The heavy reliance on the demonstration of dry eyes and dry mouth in all of these criteria can be criticised on two counts: firstly dryness only occurs after significant exocrine damage and may therefore not be a feature of early disease; secondly dry eyes and dry mouth can occur with age, presumably due to glandular atrophy *(9)*, and with a variety of drugs and other medical conditions.

Keratoconjunctivitis sicca, without any evidence of immunopathology, is sometimes termed "primary sicca syndrome" or "non-systemic sicca syndrome". These terms suggest a similarity or a relationship to Sjögren's syndrome and are therefore best avoided.

Because of the importance of immunopathology in the definition of Sjögren's syndrome, the recent criteria of Fox et al *(10)* are probably the most practical but may miss early disease. Four were proposed: (i) dry eyes (by Schirmer's and by Rose Bengal or fluorescein staining); (ii) dry mouth (symptoms and decreased salivary flow rate); (iii) lymphocytic infiltrates on lip biopsy (iv) demonstration of serum autoantibodies (rheumatoid factors, antinuclear antibodies, Ro or La antibodies). Four criteria represent "definite" and three "possible" SS.

EXTRA GLANDULAR MANIFESTATIONS AND CLASSIFICATION OF SJÖGREN'S SYNDROME

The relationship of Sjögren's syndrome to other rheumatic diseases has been clarified by associations between clinical subsets, tissue types and autoantibody specificities. These findings, tentatively classified by Maini *(11)*, suggest that three subsets of the disease are now distinguishable. *(Table 1)*

1. Primary Sjögren's syndrome.
2. Sjögren's-associated overlap syndromes.
3. Secondary Sjögren's syndrome with rheumatoid arthritis.

1. PRIMARY SJÖGREN'S SYNDROME

Primary Sjögren's syndrome occurs when the disease predominantly affects exocrine glands. Most of the patients have systemic or extraglandular features which, by definition are not numerous enough to fulfil criteria for other connective tissue diseases. Prominent amongst these are non-erosive arthritis, Raynaud's phenomenon and a purpuric vasculitis on the lower legs. A high incidence of pulmonary function abnormalities has been described though these are rarely clinically significant. Alexander *(12)* has also noted a wide range of neurological diseases including central nervous system disorders resembling multiple sclerosis. However, some selection bias may account for the unusually high frequency of such complications in her patients. Characteristic but rare complications of Sjögren's syndrome include renal tubular acidosis and the development of lymphomas.

Table 1

CLINICAL, SEROLOGICAL AND IMMUNOGENETIC FEATURES OF PRIMARY SJÖGRENS SYNDROME, SS/SLE OVERLAP AND SECONDARY SS WITH RA

	PRIMARY SS	SS/SLE	SS/RA
Arthritis	non-erosive	non-erosive	erosive
Raynaud's	++	+++	±
Purpura	++	++	±
Digital infarcts	–	±	++
Subcutaneous ulcers	–	±	++
Leukopaenia	++	+++	– (except Felty's)
Rheumatoid factors	++	+	++
Anti-Ro*	85%	90%	1%
Anti-La*	60%	75%	0
DR3*	63%	60%	30%
DR4*	24%	20%	68%

*Data from our unit

Primary Sjögren's syndrome is strongly associated with HLA DR3, and the linked genes B8, and DQ2, and C4A null gene *(13)* and with two major antibody systems, anti-Ro (SS-A) and anti-La (SS-B). Anti-La (SS-B) is found in about 60% of SS patients *(14, 15)* and shows a striking association with HLA DR3, with up to 90% of patients with this antibody being HLA-DR3 positive. Anti-Ro occurs in 85% of SS patients. It is almost invariably present in sera containing anti-La *(15)* though it can occur on its own (without anti-La) in patients with SS and in patients with other diseases, particularly SLE, and occasionally polymyositis, rheumatoid arthritis and apparently healthy subjects. It is associated with DR2 and the linked DQ1 gene, as well as DR3 *(13)*.

2. SJÖGREN'S-ASSOCIATED OVERLAP SYNDROMES

For an overlap syndrome to occur between two diseases they must share clinical, serological and immunogenetic features. This is certainly the case with primary Sjögren's syndrome where the extra glandular features resemble the clinical features of SLE and often become sufficiently numerous to fulfil criteria for SLE *(15, 16)*. Conversely, in SLE, anti-La occurs in about 15% of patients and most of them have Sjögren's syndrome *(14, 16)* and may be diagnosed as SS-SLE overlap syndromes. Anti-Ro (without anti-La) occurs in about 30% of SLE patients without dry eyes or mouth; though a study by Moutsopoulos et al *(17)*, in which the majority of anti-Ro positive SLE patients had inflammatory changes on labial gland biopsies, would suggest that they may have subclinical Sjögren's syndrome. In other connective tissue diseases in which anti-Ro is occasionally found, such as polymyositis, scleroderma and primary biliary cirrhosis the antibody is almost invariably associated with Sjögren's syndrome *(16)*. In the context of SLE, anti-La, and to a lesser extent anti-Ro, is (as it is in primary Sjögren's syndrome) associated with HLA DR3 suggesting that the overlap is not only justified serologically but also immunogenetically.

3. SECONDARY SJÖGREN'S SYNDROME WITH RHEUMATOID ARTHRITIS

The ocular and oral symptoms of Sjögren's syndrome with rheumatoid arthritis are similar to those of primary SS and SS/SLE though they are said to be relatively mild. However, the systemic manifestations, autoantibodies and immunogenetics are quite distinctive and justify the separation of RA/SS from other forms of Sjögren's syndrome.Predominant among the systemic features occurring in RA/SS are rheumatoid nodules, and a distinct pattern of vasculitis comprising nailfold infarcts and ulcers, rather than the purpuric rashes of primary SS. Conversely the SLE-like extraglandular features of primary Sjögren's, particularly Raynaud's phenomenon, lymphadenopathy and leukopaenia are, with the exception of Felty's syndrome, rare in SS/RA.

The serological and immunogenetic features of SS/RA are even more distinctive. Over 20 years ago, Bloch et al *(5)* described precipitating antibodies termed SjT and SjD, now thought to be La and Ro *(14)*, that were found in primary sicca syndrome but not in SS/RA. Similar observations were made by Alspaugh et al *(18)* with anti-SS-A (Ro) and anti-SS-B (La), again absent in SS/RA, though they described a third antibody, anti-SS-C, later to be termed anti-RANA *(19)* which occurred in RA but not in other forms of Sjögren's syndrome. However, anti-RANA, now known to react with a specific epitope on Epstein-Barr nuclear antigen *(20)* occurs commonly in sera from healthy people *(21)*. It has not proved to be of diagnostic value in Sjögren's syndrome, though we did find a trend towards higher titres of anti-RANA in RA patients with a positive Schirmer's test. Rheumatoid factors, as measured by routine assays, do not distinguish SS/RA from other forms of Sjögren's syndrome, and their detection in primary SS is a common reason for misdiagnosing patients with primary Sjögren's syndrome as RA.

The absence of any serological overlap between SS/RA and primary SS is also reflected in the absence of any immunogenetic similarities. Rheumatoid arthritis is associated with HLA DR4, and we found that SS/RA patients were also DR4 positive, rather than DR3 *(22)*. There have been reports of anti-Ro positive patients with SS-RA *(23)* though these seem to be unusual, not associated with DR3, and rare compared to the SS/SLE overlaps.

AETIOPATHOGENESIS OF SJÖGREN'S SYNDROME

The main pathology of Sjögren's syndrome accessible to investigation is in the salivary gland. Sialotropic viruses such as Epstein-Barr virus (EBV) and cytomegalovirus have therefore been examined without any serological evidence of an abnormal response to infection *(24)*. However, using DNA hybridisation techniques, EBV has been detected in parotid gland *(25)* and in labial biopsies *(26, 27)*, and we have shown that salivary epithelium can contain up to 50 copies of EBV DNA per cell in healthy people without inducing an immune response, suggesting that the gland is an important site of persistence *(27)*. In infected glands, viral antigen expression was limited to the luminal side of duct epithelium, away from immune surveillance (figure), perhaps explaining the striking lack of immunological reactivity to a heavy virus load. It is possible that in Sjögren's syndrome there is an abnormal inflammatory response to the virus. These findings, combined with case reports of patients with infectious mononucleosis developing Sjögren's syndrome *(28)*, have led to EBV being considered a major candidate for involvement in the pathogenesis of SS.

The pathology consists of focal infiltrates of mononuclear cells around salivary ducts, which show epithelial class II (and to a lesser extent class I) antigen expression *(9, 29)*. The majority of the lymphocytes are of the CD4 helper/inducer *(30)* phenotype with a relative paucity of CD8 (suppressor/cytotoxic) cells. The recent descriptions of class II restricted, CD4 positive cytotoxic T cells raises the possibility that many of the lymphocytes are directly involved in the destruction of the salivary epithelium. About 10% of the lymphocytes are B cells. There are also plentiful plasma cells whose cytoplasm contains IgA. Horsfall et al *(31)* have demonstrated anti-La idiotypes within these plasma cells as well as specific concentration of IgA anti-La and IgA rheumatoid factors in saliva *(32)* suggesting local production of autoantibody within the gland.

All these findings suggest that the disease starts with a persistent virus infection of salivary epithelium which, mediated by interferon γ *(33)* induces class II together with the expression of viral and/or host antigens. The cellular response, predominantly of the helper/inducer phenotype and unchecked by the deficient suppressor cells, leads to the production of autoantibodies and an immune attack on salivary epithelium.

As in RA *(34)*, patients with primary Sjögren's syndrome have an increased number of CD5 positive B cells in their

PERSISTENT EPSTEIN-BARR VIRUS IN SALIVARY GLAND

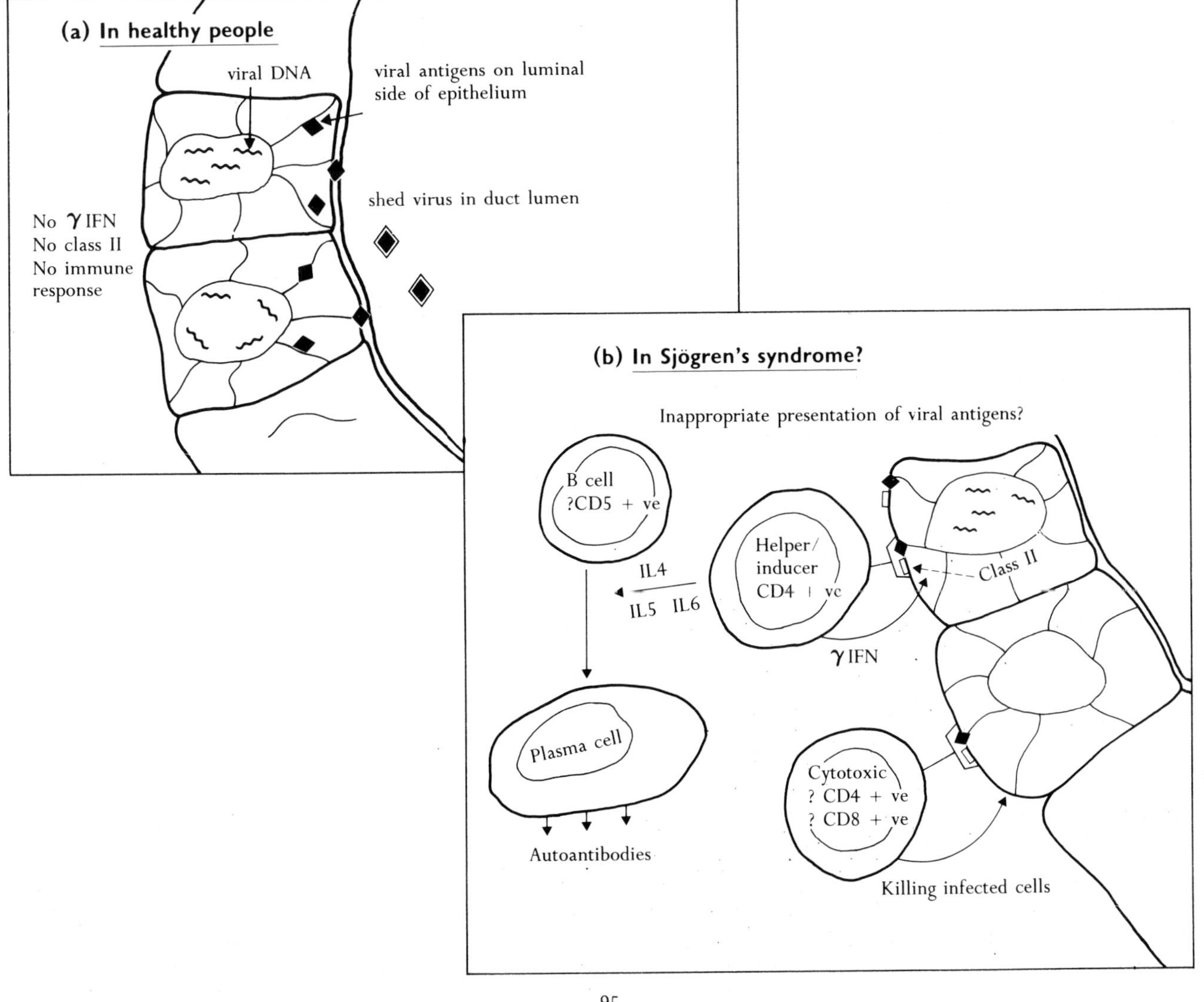

peripheral blood. The CD5 marker, normally present on T cells, is also found on B cells from patients with chronic lymphocytic leukaemia and in foetal blood suggesting that the cells are of primitive ontogeny and showing an intriguing link with B cell malignancy. In mice the equivalent cell secretes autoantibodies. If a similar function is defined in man, it is possible that the CD5 positive B cell may play a role, not only in the autoimmunity of SS, but also in the lymphomas that occasionally complicate it.

REFERENCES

1. Sjögren H (1933) Zur Kenntnis der Keratoconjunctivitis Sicca (Keratitis Filiformis bei Hypofunktion der Tränendrusen). *Acta Ophthal* **11** : 1–15

2. Schearn MA (1977) Sjögren's syndrome. *Med clin No Am* **61** : 271-282

3. Daniels TE **(1987)** *Oral manifestations of Sjögren's syndrome.* In: Sjögren's syndrome: clinical and immunological aspects, Eds Talal N, Moutsopoulos HM, Kassan SS. Springer-Verlag. p15–24.

4. Kincaid MC **(1987).** *The eye in Sjögren's syndrome.* In: Sjögren's syndrome: clinical and immunological aspects, Eds Talal N, Moutsopoulos HM, Kassan SS. Springer-Verlag. p25–33.

5. Bloch KH, Buchanan WW, Wohl MJ, Bunim JJ (1965) Sjögren's syndrome: a clinical, pathological and serological study of sixty-two cases. *Medicine (Balt)* **44** : 187–231

6. Whaley K, Williamson J, Chisholm DM, Webb J, Mason DK, Buchanan WW (1973). Sjögren's syndrome: 1. Sicca components. *QJ Med* **42** : 297–304

7. Daniels TE, Silverman S, Michalski JP, Greenspan JS, Sylvester RA, Talal N (1975). The oral component of Sjögren's syndrome. *Oral Surg* **39** : 875–885.

8. Manthorpe R, Frost-Larsen K, Isager H, Prause JU. (1981)Sjögren's syndrome: a review with emphasis on immunological features. *Allergy* **36** : 139–153

9. Morrow J, Isenberg D **(1987).** *Sjögren's syndrome.* In: Autoimmune rheumatic diseases, by Morrow J, Isenberg D. Blackwell scientific publications.

10. Fox RI, Robinson C, Kozin F, Howell FV (1986). Sjögren's syndrome: proposed criteria for classification. *Arthr Rheum* **29** : 577–585

11. Maini RN **(1987).** *The relationship of Sjögren's syndrome to rheumatoid arthritis.* In: Sjögren's syndrome: clinical and immunological aspects, Eds Talal N, Moutsopoulos HM, Kassan SS. Springer-Verlag. p165-176.

12. Alexander EL, Malinow K, Lijewski JE, Jerdan MS, Provost TT, Alexander GE (1986). Primary Sjögren's syndrome with central nervous system dysfunction mimicking multiple sclerosis. *An Intern Med* **104** : 323–330.

13. Harley JB, Reichlin M, Arnett FC, Alexander EL, Bias WB, Provost TT (1986). Gene interaction at HLA-DQ enhances autoantibody production in primary Sjögren's syndrome. *Science* **232** : 1145–1147.

14. Tan EM (1982) Autoantibodies to nuclear antigens (ANA): their immunobiology and medicine. *Adv Immunol* **33** : 167–240

15. Venables PJW, Charles PJ, Buchanan RC, Tung Yi, Mumford PA, Schriber L, Room GRW, Maini RN (1983) Quantitation and detection of isotopes of anti-SS-B antibodies by ELISA and Farr assays using affinity purified antigens. *Arthr Rheum* **26** : 146–155

16. Venables PJW **(1986)** *Antibodies to nucleic acid binding proteins: their clinical and aetiological significance.* MD Thesis, University of Cambridge

17. Moutsopoulos HM, Klippel JH, Pavilidis N, Steinberg AD, Chu FC, Tarpley TM. (1980) Correlative histologic and serologic abnormalities of sicca syndrome in systemic lupus erythematosis. *Arthr Rheum* **23** : 36-40

18. Alspaugh MA, Talal N, Tan EM (1976) Differentiation and characterization of autoantibodies and their antigens in Sjögren's syndrome. *Arthr Rheum* **19:** 216-222.

19. Alspaugh MA, Jensen FC, Rabin H, Tan EM (1979) Lymphocytes transformed by EB virus: induction of nuclear antigen reactive with antibody in rheumatoid arthritis. *J Exp Med* **147** :1018–1027

20. Venables PJW, Pawlowski T, Mumford PA, Brown C, Crawford DH, Maini RN (1988). Reaction of antibodies to rheumatoid arthritis nuclear antigen with a synthetic peptide corresponding to part of Epstein-Barr nuclear antigen 1. *Ann Rheum Dis* **47** : 270–279

21. Venables PJW, Roffe LM, Erhardt CC, Maini RN, Edwards JMB, Porter AD (1981) Titers of antibodies to RANA in rheumatoid arthritis and normal sera. *Arthr Rheum* **24** : 1459–1464

22. Shillitoe EJ, Daniels TE, Whitcher JP, Strand CV, Talal N, Greenspan JS (1982) Antibody to cytomegalovirus in patients with Sjögren's syndrome as detected by enzyme-linked immunosorbent assay. *Arthr Rheum* **25** : 260–5

23. Moutsopoulos HR, Skopouli FN, Sarras AK, Tsampoulas C, Mavridis AK, Constantopoulos SH, Maddison PJ (1985), Anti-Ro (SS-A) positive rheumatoid arthritis (RA) a clinicoserological group with a high incidence of D-penicillamine side-effects. *Ann Rheum Dis* **44** :215–219.

24. Venables PJW, Ross MGR, Charles PJ, Melsom RD, Griffiths PD, Maini RN (1985) A sero-epidemiological study of cytomegalovirus and Epstein-Barr virus in rheumatoid arthritis and sicca syndrome. *Ann Rheum Dis* **44** : 742–746

25. Wolf H, Haus M, Wilmes E (1984) Persistence of Epstein-Barr virus in the parotid gland. *J Virol* **51** : 795–798

26. Fox RI, Pearson G, Vaughan JH. (1986) Detection of Epstein-Barr virus associated antigens and DNA in salivary gland biopsies from patients with Sjögren's syndrome. *J Immunol* **137** : 3162–3168.

27. Venables PJW, Teo CG, Baboonian C, Hughes RA, Griffin BE, Maini RN. Persistence of EBV in salivary gland biopsies from patients with Sjögren's syndrome and healthy controls. **Submitted**

28. Whittingham S, McNeilage J, and McKay IR. (1985). Primary Sjögren's syndrome after infectious mononucleosis. *Ann Int Med* **102** : 490–497.

29. Lindahl G, Hedfors E, Klareskog L, Forsum U (1985) Epithelial HLA-DR expression and T lymphocyte subsets in salivary glands in Sjögren's syndrome. *Clin Exp Immunol* **61** : 475–482

30. Adamson TC, Fox RI, Frisman DM, Howell FV (1983) Immunohistologic analysis of lymphoid infiltrates in primary Sjögren's syndrome using monoclonal antibodies.*J. Immunol* **130** : 203–208

31. Horsfall AC, Venables PJW, Allard SA, Maini RN. Co-existent anti-La antibodies and rheumatoid factors bear distinct idiotypic markers. *Scand J Rheumatol* **(in press)**

32. Horsfall AC, Venables PJW, Mumford PA, Allard SA, Maini RN. Distribution of idiotypes in human autoimmune disease. *Biochem Soc Trans* **16 :** 341

33. Fox RI, Bumol T, Fantozzi R, Bone R, Schreiber R. Expression of histocompatibility antigen HLA DR by salivary epithelial cells in Sjögren's syndrome. *Arthr Rheum* **29** : 1105–1111.

34. Plater-Zyberg C, Maini RN, Lam K, Kennedy TD, Janossy G (1985) A rheumatoid arthritis B-cell subset expresses a phenotype similar to that in chronic lymphatic leukaemia. *Arthr Rheum* **28** : 971–976

POLYMYALGIA RHEUMATICA & GIANT CELL ARTERITIS

B L Hazleman
Consultant Rheumatologist
Addenbrooke's Hospital
Cambridge CB2 2QQ

In recent years there has been an increasing tendency to consider giant cell arteritis (GCA) and polymyalgia rheumatica (PMR) as closely related conditions. The two conditions form a spectrum of disease and affect the same patient population and frequently occur together in the same individual.

Polymyalgia Rheumatica

Polymyalgia rheumatica is a clinical syndrome of the middle aged and elderly characterised as follows:

- Pain and stiffness in the neck, shoulder and pelvic girdles.

- Accompanied by systemic features such as low grade fever, fatigue, weight loss.

- The Erythrocyte sedimentation rate is almost always elevated.

- A dramatic response to small doses of corticosteroids is typical.

Giant Cell Arteritis

- A vasculitis of unknown aetiology which occurs primarily in older individuals.

- Other terms that are commonly used include temporal arteritis, cranial arteritis and granulomatous arteritis.

- It is important to recognise arteritis early in its course because treatment with corticosteroids relieves symptoms and prevents blindness and other complications due to occlusion or rupture of involved arteries.

CLINICAL FEATURES

Age, sex and onset

The mean age at onset of giant cell arteritis and polymyalgia rheumatica is approximately 70 years, with a range of about 50 to more than 90 years of age. Women are affected about twice as often as men.

The onset of the disease can be dramatic and some patients can give the date and hour of their first symptom. Equally, the onset can be insidious and in most instances the symptoms have been present for weeks or months before the diagnosis is established. Constitutional symptoms, including fatigue, anorexia and weight loss and depression, are present in the majority of patients and may be an early or even an initial finding and can lead to delay in diagnosis.

POLYMYALGIA RHEUMATICA

The onset is commonest in the shoulder region and neck with symmetrical involvement of the shoulder and pelvic girdles. Involvement of distal limb muscles is unusual. Stiffness is usually the predominant feature, is particularly severe after rest, and may prevent the patient getting out of bed in the morning. The muscular pain is often diffuse and movement accentuates the pain; pain at night is common. Muscle strength is usually unimpaired, although the pain makes interpretation of muscle testing difficult. There is tenderness of involved structures with restriction of shoulder movement if diagnosis is delayed. An improvement of shoulder range is rapid with oral corticosteroid therapy, unlike that seen in frozen shoulder.

Rarity of Synovitis

It has been suggested that both axial and peripheral synovitis can occur. Most consider that peripheral synovitis is uncommon in PMR; when it occurs it is transient, non-erosive, and non-deforming. There is no confirmatory evidence that axial synovitis occurs often.

GIANT CELL ARTERITIS

There are a wide variety of symptoms, but most patients have clinical findings related to involved arteries at some stage of their illness.

Headache is the most common symptom and is present in two-thirds or more of patients. It usually begins early in the course of the disease and may be the presenting symptom. The pain is severe and usually localised to the temple but it may be occipital or be less defined and precipitated by brushing the hair. It can be severe even when the arteries are clinically normal and conversely may subside even though the disease remains active. Scalp tenderness is common, particularly around the temporal and occipital arteries, and may disturb sleep. The vessels may be thickened, tender and nodular with absent or reduced pulsation.

Ophthalmic Features

Visual disturbances have been described in 25-50% of cases, although the incidence of visual loss is now less than 10%. This is probably because of earlier recognition and treatment. Blindness may be the initial presentation of GCA but tends to follow other symptoms by several weeks.

Visual symptoms are an ophthalmic emergency, for if GCA is identified and treated urgently blindness is almost entirely preventable. Visual loss is usually sudden, painless and permanent. There is a risk of the second eye becoming involved if the patient is not treated rapidly.

Other arteritic symptoms

Pain on chewing, due to claudication of the muscles of mastication, occurs in up to two-thirds of patients. Tingling in the tongue, loss of taste, and pain in the mouth and throat can also occur, presumably due to vascular insufficiency.

Clinical evidence of large artery involvement is present in 10-15% of cases. Bruits may be heard over large arteries and there may be tenderness, particularly over the subclavian artery.

RELATIONSHIP BETWEEN POLYMYALGIA RHEUMATICA AND GIANT CELL ARTERITIS

It is difficult to maintain a practical distinction between polymyalgia rheumatica and giant cell arteritis by clinical or histological criteria. Patients originally suffering from polymyalgia rheumatica have later had symptoms of cranial arteritis and in patients with polymyalgia rheumatica who have no symptoms or signs of arteritis, positive temporal artery biopsies are found in 10-15%.

LABORATORY FINDINGS

The erythrocyte sedimentation rate (ESR) is usually greatly elevated and provides a useful means of monitoring treatment, although it must be appreciated that some elevation of the ESR may occur in otherwise healthy elderly people. Establishing a raised ESR is the key investigation although a normal ESR is occasionally found in patients with active biopsy-proven disease. Quantification of acute phase proteins is no more helpful than the ESR in the assessment of disease activity. Anaemia, usually of a mild hypochromic type, is common and resolves without specific treatment but a more marked normochromic anaemia occasionally occurs.

Abnormalities of thyroid and liver function have also been well described. Cases of hypothyroidism and hyperthyroidism have been reported. Raised serum values for alkaline phosphatase have been found in up to 70% of patients with polymyalgia rheumatica and transaminases may be mildly elevated. Abnormal isotope liver scans may also occur.

DIAGNOSIS

The diagnosis of polymyalgia rheumatica is initially one of exclusion. The differential diagnosis (Table) in an elderly patient with muscle pain, stiffness and a raised ESR is wide because the prodromal phases of several serious conditions can mimic it.

TABLE: DIFFERENTIAL DIAGNOSIS IN POLYMYALGIA RHEUMATICA

1. Neoplastic Disease
2. Joint Disease
   a) osteoarthritis, particularly of cervical spine
   b) rheumatoid arthritis
   c) connective tissue disease
3. Multiple Myeloma
4. Leukaemia
5. Lymphoma
6. Muscle disease
   a) polymyositis
   b) myopathy
7. Infections eg bacterial endocarditis
8. Bone disease, particularly osteomyelitis
9. Hypothyroidism
10. Parkinsonism
11. Functional

Polymyalgia rheumatica can usually be differentiated from late onset rheumatoid arthritis by the absence of prominent peripheral joint pain and swelling. In patients with polymyositis, muscular weakness is the predominant factor limiting movement, whereas in polymyalgia rheumatica pain causes limited function. It is important to try to distinguish between the aches and pains of osteoarthritis and the very different symptoms of polymyalgia.

The diagnosis of giant cell arteritis should be considered in any patient over the age of 50 years who has recent onset of headache, transient or sudden loss of vision, myalgia, unexplained fever or anaemia or high erythrocyte sedimentation rate. Because the symptoms and signs may vary in severity and be transient, patients suspected of having GCA must be questioned carefully about recent as well as current symptoms. The arteries of the head, neck and limbs should be examined for tenderness, enlargement, thrombosis and bruits. A previous history of headaches, scalp tenderness, jaw claudication and other symptoms may not at first be mentioned by the patients.

Temporal artery biopsies need not be carried out routinely in patients with polymyalgia rheumatica if clinical evidence for giant cell arteritis is absent. Blindness is uncommon in such patients.

Physicians vary greatly in their reliance on temporal artery biopsy findings in giant cell arteritis. Some feel that the false negative rate (probably due to the focal involvement) diminishes the value of the procedure and prefer to start steroid treatment on the basis of the typical history and physical examination. Others emphasise the value of a positive histological diagnosis especially later where side effects of steroid treatment have developed.

MANAGEMENT

Introduction

Corticosteroids are mandatory in the treatment of GCA, because they reduce the incidence of complications such as blindness and rapidly relieve symptoms. Most use steroids to treat PMR, because although non-steroidal anti-inflammatory drugs will lessen the painful symptoms, they are not as effective as corticosteroids and do not prevent arteritic complications. The response to steroids is usually dramatic and occurs within days.

Corticosteroid treatment has improved the quality of life for patients, although there is no evidence that therapy reduces the duration of the disease. A fear of vascular complications in those patients with a positive biopsy often leads to the use of high doses of corticosteroids. Recent studies have emphasised the importance of adopting a cautious and individual treatment schedule and have highlighted the efficacy and safety of lower doses of prednisolone.

Management Techniques

Initially the steroids should be given in a sufficient dosage to control the disease and then maintained at the lowest dose which will control the symptoms and prevent ischaemic complications. Where arteritis is strongly suspected there should be no delay in starting therapy while awaiting histological confirmation as the temporal artery biopsy will still show inflammatory changes for several days after corticosteroids have been started and the result is unlikely to alter therapeutic decisions. If the temporal (or other) artery biopsy shows no arteritis but the clinical suspicion of the disease is strong, corticosteroid treatment should still be commenced. The great danger is delaying therapy as blindness may occur at any time.

There are few prospective clinical trials to help decide on the correct initial dose. In practice, most studies report using 10-20 mg prednisolone/day to treat polymyalgia and 40-60 mg/day for giant cell arteritis because of the higher risk of arteritic complications. Some ophthalmologists suggest an initial dose of at least 60 mg as they have seen blindness occur at a lower dose, but this has to be balanced against the potential complications of high dosage in this age-group. Once initial symptoms are controlled weekly decrements of no more than 5 mg have been proposed. The reduction is more gradual when 10 mg is reached. It is suggested that 1 mg every 2-4 weeks is sufficient. These dosages are suggestions only and not to be interpreted rigidly as individual cases vary greatly.

Clinical relapse may occur without a rise in ESR and the ESR may rise without corresponding symptoms. Fortunately complications are rare and the activity of the disease seems to decline steadily. Relapses are more likely during the initial 18 months of treatment and within one year of withdrawal of steroids; patients should be asked to report back urgently if arteritic symptoms occur. There is no reliable method of predicting those most at risk, but arteritic relapses in patients who presented with polymyalgia rheumatica are unusual.

Controversy exists over the expected duration of the disease. Most European studies within the last 20 years report that between one third and one half of patients are able to discontinue steroids after 2 years of treatment although shorter disease duration has been reported from the Mayo Clinic in the USA. The consensus view seems to be that stopping treatment is feasible from two years onwards. The risks of relapse, particularly with arteritic complications, have to be balanced against the risks of steroid related side effects: between one fifth and a half of patients may experience serious side effects.
Patients who are unable to reduce the dosage of prednisolone because of recurring symptoms or who develop serious steroid-related side effects pose particular problems. Azathioprine has been shown

to exert a modest steroid sparing effect and recent reports suggest that methotrexate may be more effective.

CONCLUSIONS

The overall strategy should be to use an adequate dose of prednisolone for the first month to obtain good symptomatic control with a fall in ESR, then to aim for maintenance doses of less than 10 mg after six months. The exact doses will need to be adjusted to the needs of the individual patients, but a possible schedule is 15 mg prednisolone/day for PMR, to reduce the dose to about 7.5-10 mg/day by 6-8 weeks. Patients with GCA should be treated with 40 mg daily for the first month unless visual symptoms persist, when higher doses (60-80 mg) may be needed. A suitable dose reduction would be to 20 mg prednisolone/day at about 8 weeks.

Reduction of prednisolone dose on alternate days once doses of less than 5 mg are reached makes withdrawal easier, e.g. 4/5 mg alternate days. The addition of a non-steroidal agent at this stage may reduce some of the minor muscular symptoms that patients develop as steroids are reduced. Some patients, however, find it impossible to reduce the dose below 2-3 mg/day and this level of maintenance dose is probably safe.

Polymyalgia rheumatica and giant cell arteritis are amongst the more satisfying diseases for clinicians to diagnose and treat because the unpleasant symptoms and serious consequences of these conditions can be almost entirely prevented by corticosteroid therapy. Unfortunately there is no objective means of determining the prognosis in the individual and decisions concerning duration of treatment remain empirical, and require careful supervision.

REFERENCE

Giant Cell Arteritis and Polymyalgia Rheumatica. Ed. Hazleman and Bengtsson. Bailliere's Clinical Rheumatology, Vol 5, No.3, 1991.

May 1992

RAYNAUD'S PHENOMENON

J J F Belch
Lecturer in Medicine & Rheumatology
University Department of Medicine
Royal Infimary
Glasgow

INTRODUCTION

Man is a tropical creature, more able to lose heat than to retain it. When naked and at rest, his neutral environmental temperature is 28°C. With an 8°C fall in temperature, his metabolic rate must double or his body temperature will drop. In fact, 70% of man's energy requirements are devoted to the maintenance of body temperature. Man's response to cold, that is the putting on of clothes, allows him to live in temperate areas; despite this, there are people who respond abnormally to cold and suffer from diseases such as chilblains, cold urticaria, winter itch (prurigo hiemalis) and Raynaud's Phenomenon. Of these, Raynaud's Phenomenon (RP) remains the least understood and most difficult to treat.

CLINICAL SYMPTOMS

It is now over 120 years ago that Maurice Raynaud first described his syndrome of episodic digital ischaemia provoked by cold and emotion. Classically, there is pallor of the affected digits, followed by cyanosis and rubor. The pallor reflects decreased arterial flow, the cyanosis the deoxygenation of the static venous blood, and the rubor reactive hyperaemia following the return of flow. The original definition requires modification; it is now thought that the triphasic colour change is not essential for diagnosis. Furthermore, stimuli other than cold and emotion can produce vasospasm, for example trauma (especially sustained pressure), hormones and chemicals (including those in cigarette smoke). However, cold is most frequently implicated, although it should be noted that it is the *change* that provokes an attack; vasospasm can occur when sunbathing at high temperatures if a cooler wind blows (1). It is not only the digits that are affected; the nose, ear lobes and tip of tongue can also be involved. Recent evidence supports a hypothesis of systemic vasospasm. There are abnormalities of myocardial perfusion in RP which are related to spasm of the coronary arteries, and vasospasm in the oesophagus has been reported. Some researchers have speculated that the kidney and lung lesions seen in severe RP associated with systemic sclerosis may be accounted for in the same way. RP exists in varying degrees of severity in 5-10% of the population and, if severe, causes pain, digital ulceration, and even gangrene. It affects women 9 times as commonly as men. The conditions frequently associated with Raynaud's Phenomenon are listed in Table 1.

NOMENCLATURE

In 1932, Allen & Brown (2) emphasised the wide spectrum of disorders with which Raynauds may be associated. They classified patients with associated disease as having RP, and those without as having Raynaud's Disease (RD). In recent years the development of more sensitive laboratory procedures has revealed that greater than one half of patients with Raynauds have an associated systemic disease. Furthermore, long-term studies have shown that Raynauds may be the precursor of systemic illness by many years; because of this the American author, Porter (1), suggested that the terms "disease" and "phenomenon" be entirely abandoned and the term "Raynaud's Syndrome" (RS) be used. Unfortunately not all Americans use this terminology and Europeans have largely opted for a different approach, which can make assessment of reports from different centres difficult. For this report the European terminology has been used – i.e. RP subdivided into RS + associated disorder and RD = idiopathic primary.

TABLE 1: ASSOCIATED DISEASES

A Immunological and connective tissue disorder
- Progressive systemic sclerosis
- Systemic lupus erythematosus
- Rheumatoid arthritis
- Mixed connective tissue disease
- Dermatomyositis and polymyositis
- Hepatitis B antigenaemia

B Occupational
- Vibration White Finger
- Vinyl chloride workers
- Cold injury (frozen-food packers)
- Ammunition (nitrates) workers (outside work)

C Obstructive arterial disease
- Atherosclerosis
- Thoracic outlet syndromes (including cervical rib)
- Emboli

D Drug induced
- Beta blockers
- Ergot and other anti-migraine drugs
- Cytotoxics
- Bromocriptine
- Sulphasalazine

E Miscellaneous
- Cold agglutinins
- Cryoglobulinaemia
- Thyroid disease (myxoedema)
- Neoplasm
- Chronic renal failure
- Idiopathic Raynaud's Disease

PATHOPHYSIOLOGY (Table 2)

Hand and digital blood flow is diminished during an attack of Raynauds; however, the mechanism by which this is produced is unclear. As these patients can vasodilate in response to rewarming, increased sympathetic tone has been implicated (3). Direct evaluation of the sympathetic nervous system is not possible, however, and measurement of catecholamines during spasm has produced conflicting results. In addition, symptoms of RP can return after an apparently successful sympathectomy.

Lewis (4) postulated a local arterial hypersensitivity to cold. This work was supported by a later proposal of a relative lack of ß adrenegic sensitivity of the vessels, allowing uncontrolled vasoconstriction in response to normal quantities of cold induced catecholamines.

Lafferty *et al* (5), have put forward a theory explaining the sex difference seen in Raynauds sufferers. Peripheral blood flow fluctuates greatly from one moment to the next: such fluctuations can be made to "entrain" or "lock on" to periodic hot and cold stimuli applied to the contralateral hand. The degree of entrainment produced provides a sensitive objective measure of severity of RP. Lafferty investigating the blood flow patterns induced by thermal entrainment in RP, suggested a failure of histaminergic post-sympathetic vasodilatation may be one of the fundamental pathophysiological defects. He further demonstrated Raynauds-type blood flow patterns in normal women at the time of ovulation. Oestrogen increases the sensitivity of small arteries to adrenaline and noradrenaline, and he was able to correlate the changes in blood flow with an increase in urinary oestrogen metabolites. Lafferty suggests that RD is caused by an exaggerated vascular response to normal (or possibly abnormal) fluctuations in female sex hormones.

TABLE 2: SUGGESTED ABNORMALITIES IMPORTANT IN THE PATHOGENESIS OF RAYNAUD'S PHENOMENON

Plasma	Vessel Wall	Blood Cells
Hormones	Sympathetic innervation	White Cell
Viscosity	Immune complexes	Red Cell
	Fibrinolysis	Platelet
	Factor VIII	
	Prostacyclin	

i) Auto-immunity

Subjects with RS, however, often show evidence of auto-immunity and other immunological abnormalities. Experimental studies in animals suggest that immune complexes may play an important role in the pathogenesis of the vascular lesions. An association has been found between RS and immune complexes in vinyl chloride disease; increased levels of phagocytosed immune complexes have been found in circulating leucocytes of RS patients, correlating with systemic involvement and severity of vasospasm (6). Immune complexes deposited in the endothelial lining of blood vessels may promote vascular damage; in addition, immune complexes cause platelet aggregation and the resulting platelet clump might further obstruct the microcirculation.

ii) Leucocyte adherence

Although leucocyte migration and chemotaxis has been shown to be normal, the PMNs are abnormally adherent. A layer of adherent cells over the endothelial surface will decrease blood flow and this may also be important in RP. In addition, there is increased PMN chemiluminescence reflecting increased oxygen free radical generation. Such free radicals have been shown to produce vasospasm in experimental animals.

iii) Hyperviscosity

Hyperviscosity of plasma and whole blood has been detected in RP, particularly at low temperatures (7). However, recent studies in moderately affected patients fail to show a significant increase. The fact that RP is rare in other hyperviscosity states, such as polycythaemia and other paraproteinaemias, suggests that viscosity is not a major pathogenic factor. It is now generally accepted that hyperviscosity occurs with any end-stage chronic vascular disease, irrespective of its aetiology, and can be regarded as a consequence rather than a cause of the disease.

iv) Erythrocytes

The red cell's diameter is greater than that of the smaller capillaries, so flow in the microcirculation may be critically dependent on red cell deformability. This is decreased in some RP patients (8). Cold temperatures will reduce red cell deformability further, as will the acidosis present in cold ulcerated fingers.

v) Fibrinolysis and factor viii

The baseline fibrinolytic status is reduced and plasma fibrinogen levels raised. These abnormalities may aggravate the disease through deposition and poor clearance of vascular fibrin (9). However, these findings may reflect endothelial damage, as plasminogen activator is produced by the endothelium and any disease at this site would result in diminished activator production and a subsequent decrease in fibrinolysis. Similarly, increased levels of blood clotting factor VIII have been detected in RP. Factor VIII is also produced by the endothelium, but in contrast to plasminogen activator, noxious stimuli such as vasospasm and ischaemia increase production. Such an increase can further contribute to the micro-vascular obstruction through its activity in the coagulation cascade and through its ability to aggregate platelets. Factor VIII R Ag may be a fairly specific marker for vasculitis.

vi) Prostacyclin and platelets

Another endothelial product, the important vasodilator and antiplatelet agent prostacyclin (PGI_2) has also been investigated. Platelet aggregation has been reported as being increased in RP (7) and platelet aggregates may block the small digital vessels. Platelets also release vasoconstrictor substances such as thromboxane A_2 and serotonin, and this may further aggravate the symptoms of RP. Interestingly, levels of the stable metabolite of PGI_2 have been recorded as being elevated. This apparent paradox is explained by platelet resistance to the anti-aggregating effects of PGI_2, which is augmented at cold temperatures (10).

Alterations in coagulation and rheology might account for the decrease in blood flow in RP. However, most of these abnormalities have only been reported in patients with RS, and not in primary RD (the exception to this is F.VIII R Ag which may be the most sensitive marker of endothelial damage). It is likely, therefore, that these changes are a consequence rather than a cause of the disease. However, this may be unimportant as adherent white cells, hard red cells, platelet clumps and fibrin deposition contribute to impaired blood flow, and their correction may produce clinical improvement.

TREATMENT OF RAYNAUD'S PHENOMENON

i) Mild Disease

Much can be done for patients with mild disease without the need for drugs. Stopping cigarette smoking can produce immediate symptomatic benefit, as can change of occupation and withdrawal of drugs known to be associated with RP. In the USA, biofeedback techniques have proven successful in some patients, but this requires a very well-motivated patient. It has also been suggested that rotating the arms of 80rpm can be effective!

Advice on cold avoidance is very important. Achieving this aim is difficult, but practical solutions to the problem are many and varied. Electrically-heated gloves and socks are, for some, the perfect solution; a belt-worn rechargeable battery pack provides power for up to 3 hours and wires concealed beneath the clothing give a normal appearance. Financial restraints on hospitals in some areas mean they can be difficult to obtain, but these garments are very popular with patients, although infrequently irritation of digital ulcers by the added heat has been noted. Chemical hand warmers (obtainable from local sports shops) provide a satisfactory alternative source of heat for about 6 hours. "Comfort shoes" can be useful for RP affecting the feet; the padded soles keep the feet warm and relieve the pressure on the toes which can result in vasospasm.

Many patients are apprehensive about their disease; the disappearance of the blood supply during vasospasm is frightening, patients fear the onset of gangrene and the loss of digits. Reassurance is often required, and information regarding the self-help group "The Raynaud's Association" is often gratefully received. For current patient literature on this and other diseases, apply to the ARC.

ii) Sympathectomy

Assessment of the published results is extremely difficult as most studies have been uncontrolled with indiscriminate patient selection and short follow-up. Longer studies show a higher relapse rate (11) and an especially poor response in RS associated with a connective tissue disorder. Most workers feel sympathectomy is not now indicated for upper limb Raynauds. In contrast, it still has an important place in the treatment of Raynauds for the feet. This discrepancy between upper and lower limbs is not understood, but lower limb sympathectomy can produce rewarding results. The surgeon has not however been totally discharged in his responsibilities in the upper limb. New techniques have been developed where simple skin grafting and removal of infected nails have enabled severe long-term ulcers to heal. In systemic sclerosis, the tightness of the skin over the fingertip also contributes to the decreased blood flow. Operation to remove part of the bone of the terminal phalanx and relieve this pressure, has proved useful.

iii) Intra-arterial Reserpine

The effects are short-lived and the potential for arterial damage high. It is now rarely used and reserved only for severe and intractable spasm.

iv) Vasoactive Drugs

The current use of vasodilators in RP remains controversial as most studies have been uncontrolled. Encouraging results have, however, been obtained with inosital nicotinate (Hexopal). Its postulated mode of action is via release of the vasodilator nicotinic acid. Successful controlled studies have recently been published (12) and these, combined with objective evidence of increased tissue blood flow, suggest that this agent may be useful in mild disease. Inexplicably the drug may take up to 3 months to produce an effect so treatment should be given for at least this period of time. Work with other vasodilators has proved disappointing, with side-effects being a limiting factor.

v) Nifedipine

The calcium antagonist nifedipine has been shown to be effective in some RP patients in a number of well-controlled double-blind studies (13). It has been suggested that nifedipine exerts its beneficial effect in RP via peripheral vasodilation, but more recently antiplatelet effects and suppression of neutrophil function have also been demonstrated. The starting dose is usually 10mg 3 tid, although some patients who are abnormally sensitive to the drug, do better on 5mg 3 tid. This can be increased to 20mg 3 tid, often given as the slow release preparation, "Adalat Retard". Side-effects are minimal and typical of other vasodilators, eg headaches and dizziness. These are usually transient and often disappear with continued treatment. Although not 100% effective, this drug is so well-tolerated that it is rapidly becoming the first-line drug treatment for RP. One worrying feature, however, is that it has not been passed for use in pregnancy: as the majority of RP patients are women of child-bearing age, advice on pregnancy avoidance must be given.

Newer calcium antagonists are now being assessed in Raynauds and some but not all (14) may also be useful.

vi) Prostaglandin Infusion

The vasodilator antiplatelet prostaglandins PGE_1 (15) and PGI_2 (16) may also have a role in the management of RP. These drugs have to be given by intravenous infusion (PGE_1 by central line) and therefore require at least hospital attendance, if not admission. A regimen of weekly intermittent 5-hourly PGI_2 infusions with slow incremental increases in dosage to a maximum of 7ng/kg/min allows attendance on an outpatient basis. Success has also been reported with 3-day infusions but this requires patient admission. Side-effects of both PGE_1 and PGI_2 are vasodilatory, that is headache, flushing and nausea. Blood pressure should be monitored throughout the infusion. Although these PGs are vasodilators and antiplatelet agents, these effects are short-lived and do not explain the long duration of response. It has been reported that they increase red cell deformability and fibrinolysis, and decrease white cell aggregation and adhesion – all features which could be useful in a patient with RP.

Unfortunately, these treatments are not cures and repetition with the attendant problem of intravenous administration is required. This means that, in practice, PG treatment is usually reserved for patients with intractable digital ulceration. Alternative approaches to PG therapy are being assessed, such as the development of oral and transdermally absorbed analogues, and this may allow more prolonged release. However, the long-term effects on bone and tumour growth must first be established.

As PGE_1 and PGI_2 are endogenous local hormones, an attractive concept is to stimulate the body's own production of vasodilatory PGs by administering the appropriate precursor essential fatty acids. Evening primrose oil (EPO) contains gamma linoleic acid. This is metabolised to di-homo-gamma-linoleic acid which is the precursor of PGE_1. Study results of EPO, however, have been somewhat disappointing: although clinical improvement has been reported in some patients, no improvement in objective measures of blood flow has been documented (17). In addition, as this preparation is not available on prescription, it is expensive for the patient. Further controlled work is essential in this area.

vii) Plasma Exchange

Plasma exchange has been used successfully in the treatment of some patients with RP (18), producing improved digital artery patency and a prolonged clinical benefit. The mechanism by which these effects occur are poorly understood but may involve changes in platelet function, blood rheology and circulating immune complexes. All evidence points to removal of some specific plasma factor during exchange. This form of treatment is, however, time-consuming and expensive. In the long-term it is hoped to remove the particular plasma factor and re-infuse the patient's own plasma. As response to treatment is far from universal, this form of therapy is again reserved for patients with severe intractable ulceration.

SUGGESTED FLOW DIAGRAM FOR TREATMENT OF RP

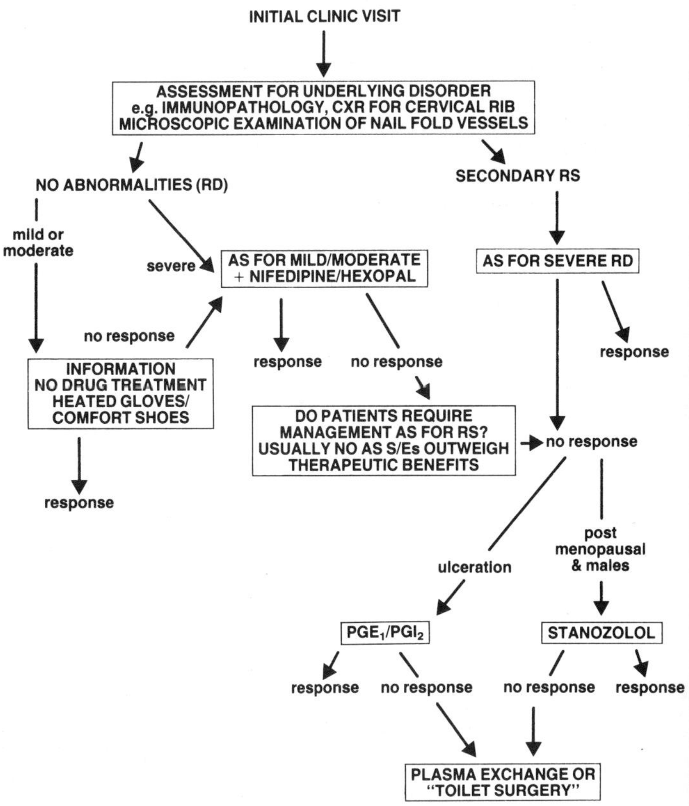

INITIAL CLINIC VISIT

ASSESSMENT FOR UNDERLYING DISORDER
e.g. IMMUNOPATHOLOGY, CXR FOR CERVICAL RIB
MICROSCOPIC EXAMINATION OF NAIL FOLD VESSELS

NO ABNORMALITIES (RD)

SECONDARY RS

mild or moderate

severe

AS FOR MILD/MODERATE + NIFEDIPINE/HEXOPAL

AS FOR SEVERE RD

no response

response

INFORMATION
NO DRUG TREATMENT
HEATED GLOVES/
COMFORT SHOES

response

no response

response

DO PATIENTS REQUIRE MANAGEMENT AS FOR RS?
USUALLY NO AS S/Es OUTWEIGH THERAPEUTIC BENEFITS

no response

ulceration

post menopausal & males

PGE_1/PGI_2

STANOZOLOL

response

no response

no response

response

PLASMA EXCHANGE OR "TOILET SURGERY"

viii) Drugs that affect viscosity, fibrinolysis and red cell deformability

The administration of low molecular weight Dextran has been reported to alleviate RP, as has ancrod (a defibrinating agent). However, both require parenteral administration and the development of antibodies to ancrod may limit its application. Likewise, troxerutin (Paroven) has been shown to be beneficial in a small pilot study. Unfortunately, no follow-up studies have been reported with these three agents and in general their application is disappointing.

The work with stanozolol has proved more exciting. Stanozolol (Stromba) is an anabolic steroid which enhances fibrinolysis and lowers fibrinogen levels. Initial work in RP suggested that it produced an increase in hand blood flow, improvement of symptoms and healing of digital ulcers (9). However patients with RD and normal fibrinogen levels also seem to benefit, suggesting that this drug's mode of action may not be fully understood. The drug is given in a dose of 5mg bd and the beneficial effects can take up to 3 months to appear. Side-effects are those usually associated with anabolic steroids, including the virilisation of females and altered liver function. Although liver neoplasia has never been reported with stanozolol (and it has been given over many years) this treatment is usually reserved for severely affected males and postmenopausal women who have normal liver function.

ix) Recent Advances

Recent pilot studies of other therapeutic approaches have shown some interesting results. Local application of glyceryl trinitrin cream appeared clinically beneficial (19). A high incidence of vasodilator side-effects have precluded widespread use of this treatment though low dose studies are under way.

Dazoxiben, the orally administered thromboxane synthetase inhibitor, has also been studied. It lowers plasma thromboxane A_2, the most important vasoconstrictor and platelet aggregant known, and initially there were some encouraging results from pilot studies. As has often been the case with RP, however, the initial promise has not been sustained by later studies. Ketanserin, a serotonin receptor antagonist, antagonises both the vasoconstricting and platelet aggregatory effects of serotonin. Oral ketanserin has been suggested as a new approach in the treatment of RP. Although early results from controlled studies have proved conflicting (20, 21), treatment with ketanserin seems reasonably free from side-effects, apart from a possible interaction with concomitant diuretic therapy. The results from a current multicentre study are eagerly awaited.

There have been a few uncontrolled reports regarding the angiotensin converting enzyme (ACE) inhibitor, Captopril. Single-blind studies have shown an increase in cutaneous blood flow in a proportion of patients treated with this drug (22). The reason for the vasodilator action of Captopril is unclear but may be related to the accumulation of vasodilator kinins. Controlled double-blind studies should be carried out to establish its place in RP. However, patients with renal disease may develop renal failure and nephrotic syndrome on ACE inhibitors, and as patients with systemic sclerosis and systemic lupus erythematosus may have renal impairment, it is unlikely that this drug will be suitable for these patients.

CONCLUSION

The wide variety of associated disorders, the variation in response from individual patients, and the difficulty in making accurate assessment of the therapeutic response, has led to confusion in the evaluation and management of RP. Treatment should be based on conservative medical management with nifedipine, stanozolol, plasma exchange and prostacyclin appearing the most promising for severe disease (see figure). However, further studies of the newer approaches are required and it should be remembered that the final prognosis of RS will be determined by that of any underlying disorder.

REFERENCES

1. Porter JM, Rivers SP, Anderson CJ, Baur GM. Evaluation and management of patients with Raynaud's Syndrome. *Am J Surg* 1981; **142**: 183-9.
2. Allen EV, Brown GE. Raynaud's Disease: a critical review of minimal requisites for diagnosis. *Am J Med Sci* 1932; **183**: 187-200.
3. Medlowitz M, Naftchi N. The digital circulation in Raynaud's Disease. *Am J Cardiol* 1959; **4**: 580-4.
4. Lewis T. Raynaud's Disease and pre-ganglionic sympathectomy. *Clin Sci* 1938; **3**: 320-36.
5. Lafferty K, De Trafford JC, Potter C, Robert VC, Cotton LT. Reflex vascular responses in the finger to contralateral thermal stimuli during the normal menstrual cycle: a hormonal basis to Raynaud's Phenomenon? *Clin Sci* 1985; **68**: 10-15.
6. Dowd PM, Kirby JD, Holborow EJ, Cooke ED, Bowcock SA. Detection of immune complexes in systemic sclerosis and Raynaud's Phenomenon. *Br J Dermatol* 1981; **105**: 179-88.
7. Firkin BG. *Involvement of platelets in non-haematological disorders and thrombosis.* In: The Platelet and its Disorders (ed. BG Firkin), MTP Press Ltd., Lancaster 1984; pp167-94.
8. Kovacs IB, Sowemimo-Coker SO, Kirby JDT, Turner P. Altered behaviour of erythrocytes in scleroderma. *Clin Sci* 1983; **65**: 515-9.
9. Ayers ML, Jarret PEM, Browse ML. Blood viscosity, Raynaud's Phenomenon and the effect of fibrinolytic enhancement. *Br J Surg* 1983; **68**: 51-54.
10. Belch JJF, O'Dowd A, Forbes CD, Sturrock RD. Platelet sensitivity to a prostacyclin analogue in systemic sclerosis. *Brit J Rheum* 1987; **24**: 346-50.
11. Hansteen V. Medical treatment in Raynaud's Disease. *Acta Chir Scan* 1976; **465**: 87-91.
12. Murphy R. The effect of inositol nicotinate (Hexopal) in patients with Raynaud's Phenomenon. *Clin Trial J* 1985; **22(6)**: 521-9.
13. Kahan A. Nifedipine in the treatment of Raynaud's Syndrome. *Ann Int Med* 1981; **94(4)**: 546.
14. Rhedda A, McCans J, Willan AR, Ford PM. A double blind placebo controlled crossover randomised trial of Diltiazem in Raynaud's Phenomenon. *J Rheum* 1985; **12(4)**: 724-7.
15. Clifford PC, Martin MFR, Sheddon MF, Kirby JD, Baird RN, Dieppe PA. Treatment of vasospastic disease with prostaglandin E_1. *Br Med J* 1980; **281**: 1031-4.
16. Belch JJF, Newman P, Drury JK, McKenzie F, Capell HA, Leiberman P, Forbes CD, Prentice CRM. Intermittent epoprostenol (prostacyclin) infusion in patients with Raynaud's Syndrome. *Lancet* 1981; **i**: 313-5.
17. Belch JJF, Shaw B, O'Dowd A, Saniabadi A, Sturrock RD, Forbes CD. Evening primrose oil (Efamol) in the treatment of Raynaud's Phenomenon: a double-blind study. *Thrombos Haemostas* 1985; **54(2)**: 490-4.
18. O'Reilly MJG, Talpis G, Robert VC, White JM, Cotton LT. Controlled trial of plasma exchange in treatment of Raynaud's Phenomenon. *Br Med J* 1979; **i**: 1113-5.
19. Franks AG. Topical glyceryl trinitrate as adjunctive treatment in Raynaud's Disease. *Lancet* 1982; **i**: 76-7.
20. Roald OK, Seem E. Treatment of Raynaud's Phenomenon with ketanserin in patients with connective tissue disorders. *Br Med J* 1984; **289**: 577-9.
21. Longstaff J, Gush R, Williams EH. A controlled study of ketanserin in Raynaud's Phenomenon. *AGM British Society of Rheumatology* 1984; **60a**.
22. Trubestein G, Wigger E, Trubestein R. Treatment of Raynaud's Syndrome with Captopril, *Dtsch Med Wochenschr* 1984; **109**: 857-60.

VASCULITIS

D G I Scott
Consultant Rheumatologist
Norfolk & Norwich Hospital
Hon Sen Lecturer
The London Hospital Medical College

I. DEFINITION AND CLASSIFICATION

"Vasculitis" is the term used to describe a heterogeneous group of uncommon diseases characterized by inflammatory cell infiltration and necrosis of blood vessel walls. This may arise *de novo* (eg polyarteritis nodosa) or as a secondary feature of an established clinical disease such as rheumatoid arthritis or systemic lupus erythematosus.

The consequences of such vascular inflammation depend upon the size, site and number of blood vessels involved. Muscular arteries may develop focal or segmental lesions. The former (affecting part of the vessel wall) may lead to aneurysm formation and possible rupture; segmental lesions (affecting the whole circumference) are more common and lead to stenosis or occlusion with distal infarction. Haemorrhage or infarction of vital internal organs are the most serious problems of systemic vasculitis and explain the poor prognosis of untreated polyarteritis nodosa (1) or of arteritis complicating rheumatoid arthritis (2-4). Small vessel vasculitis by contrast most commonly affects the skin and rarely causes serious internal organ dysfunction. Widespread systemic small vessel vasculitis may cause problems, especially in the kidney, when sufficient numbers of adjacent vessels are affected with significant release of inflammatory mediators or where overall perfusion is threatened.

Classification is confusing; there is considerable clinical overlap between the different vasculitic syndromes and usually the cause of the vasculitis is unknown. Even where there seems to be a known aetiological agent there is still difficulty with classification. For example, hepatitis BsAg has been associated with cutaneous vasculitis (5,6), cryoglobulinaemic vasculitis (7), glomerulonephritis (8) and arthritis (9) as well as polyarteritis (10, 11). A similar picture is now emerging with the vasculitis associated with HIV infection (12). Diagnosis still requires histological confirmation in most cases so the classification I use (13) is based on the size of the predominant vessel involved and the type of inflammatory change (Table 1). This classification also reflects different therapeutic approaches (14). Diseases in Group 1 are usually treated with immunosuppressive drugs (especially cyclophosphamide) as well as steroids; Group 2 are often managed conservatively with steroids only in selected cases, and Group 3 are usually controlled adequately with steroids alone.

TABLE I: CLASSIFICATION OF VASCULITIS

1. Systemic necrotizing arteritis (involving predominantly medium and small arteries)
   - (a) polyarteritis nodosa group
     - eg. classical PAN, microscopic PAN, infantile PAN, Kawasaki disease, arteritis of RA, SLE, Sjögren's etc.
   - (b) with granulomatosis
     - eg. Wegener's
     - Churg-Strauss vasculitis
     - granulomatous angiitis of the central nervous system
2. Small vessel vasculitis (syn. hypersensitivity, leucocytoclastic, allergic)
   - eg. Henoch-Schönlein purpura
   - essential mixed cryoglobulinaemia
   - vasculitis of RA, SLE, Sjögren's etc
   - drug-induced vasculitis
3. Giant cell arteritis (involving predominantly large arteries)
   - eg. temporal arteritis
   - Takayasu's arteritis
   - aortitis associated with RA, ankylosing spondylitis etc.

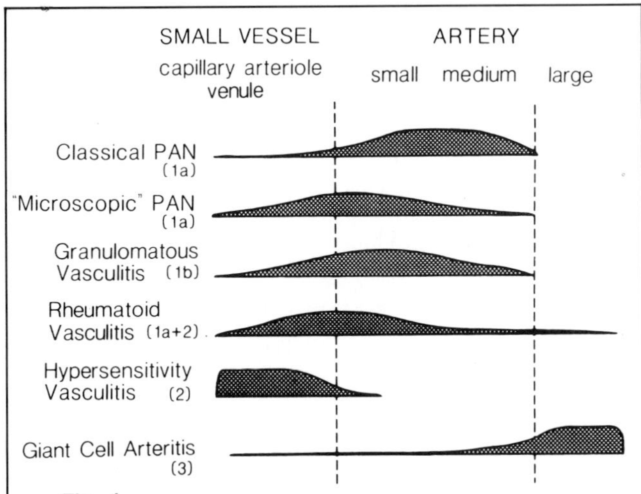

Fig. 1.
Relationship between vessel size and classification (shown in parentheses).

There is still considerable overlap even between these broad classification groups as is shown in Fig. 1. Although there is little overlap between Groups 2 and 3, a wide range of vessels can be involved in the systemic necrotizing arteritides (Group 1). For example, up to 20% of patients with polyarteritis nodosa have palpable purpura (small vessel vasculitis of the skin) stressing the importance of interpreting histology in an appropriate clinical context. Also, rheumatoid arthritis may be complicated by small vessel vasculitis (nail-fold infarcts), necrotizing arteritis (like polyarteritis nodosa) and more rarely aortitis or Takayasu's arteritis.

DIAGNOSIS

This requires a high index of suspicion and a combination of clinical and laboratory changes, and is usually confirmed by biopsy and/or angiography. Vasculitis should be included in the differential diagnosis of any multi-system disease, active glomerulonephritis, ischaemic signs and symptoms especially in a young person, palpable purpura or other nodular or necrotic skin lesions, mononeuritis multiplex and fever without an established cause (15).

CLINICAL FEATURES

The broad spectrum of clinical features associated with systemic vasculitis can be seen by examining specific diseases in more detail. Table 2 shows the main clinical features in 98 patients with systemic rheumatoid vasculitis seen over the last 10 years. These patients have widespread systemic involvement reflecting the inflammatory rheumatoid disease process as well as vasculitis. Most patients have chronic erosive seropositive and nodular disease and often a history of other extra-articular manifestations (4). A similar broad spectrum of clinical involvement is seen in polyarteritis nodosa and Wegener's granulomatosis (Table 3). These diseases can present at any age (mean 55-60) with only a slight male predominance and we are seeing an increasing number of patients (particularly women) presenting with typical polyarteritis nodosa in their seventies.

TABLE 2: CLINICAL FEATURES IN 98 PATIENTS WITH SYSTEMIC RHEUMATOID VASCULITIS

Organ	% Involvement	Characteristics
Skin	92	Nail-fold/nail-edge infarcts, leg and sacral ulcers, rash, peripheral gangrene*
Nodules	87	Subcutaneous rheumatoid nodules
Systemic	83	Weight loss, hepatosplenomegaly
Nervous system	44	Sensorimotor* and central nervous system
Lung	39	Fibrosing alveolitis, pleurisy
Heart	36	Pericarditis, arrhythmia, coronary arteritis*
Kidney	20	Haematuria* and/or proteinuria*
Eye	19	(Epi)Scleritis, Sjögren's
Gut	10	Abdominal pain,* colitis

* Features strongly suggesting arteritis

TABLE 3: CLINICAL FEATURES IN POLYARTERITIS (PAN) AND WEGENER'S GRANULOMATOSIS

	PAN	Wegener's
Mean age (years)	58	54[1]
Male : female	1.5:1	2:1
Kidney	85	80
Joints	65	65
Neuropathy	40[2]	30
Skin	50	45
Lung	30	90*
Heart	20	20
Abdomen	45	20
Eyes	15	50*
Ears	10	50*
Sinuses	?	95*

1. Local (non-renal) Wegener's mean age = 41 years
2. Increased in non-renal polyarteritis
* Major difference between PAN and Wegener's

LABORATORY

ROUTINE

Leucocytosis is common especially in the systemic necrotizing arteritis group with the exception of systemic rheumatoid vasculitis. Eosinophilia may occur with any vasculitic syndrome but is characteristic in Churg-Strauss vasculitis. The ESR and CRP levels are usually raised and CRP is useful for monitoring disease activity (17). (High CRP levels in rheumatoid vasculitis may of course reflect arthritis as well as vasculitis.) Renal involvement is one of the most important factors affecting prognosis, especially in polyarteritis nodosa and Wegener's granulomatosis. Early detection is vital and simple assessments (urinary sediment and serum creatinine) are essential early investigations in any patient in whom vasculitis is suspected. Immunological tests are helpful in specific diseases. Complement levels are usually low in systemic rheumatoid vasculitis but normal or raised in polyarteritis and Wegener's granulomatosis. Immune complexes including cryoglobulins are commonly detected in all the systemic vasculitides but their pathogenic role in these is often not established. Rheumatoid factor containing immune complexes are probably important in rheumatoid vasculitis (18), IgE immune complexes in Churg-Strauss vasculitis (19), and IgA immune complexes in Henoch-Schonlein purpura (20).

FACTOR VIII-RELATED ANTIGEN

This protein is present in endothelial cells and platelets so can reflect endothelial (and therefore vascular) damage. This includes non-inflammatory vascular conditions, including Raynaud's phenomenon, venous thrombosis and surgery as well as vasculitis. However, levels of Factor VIII RAg tend to be highest in diseases associated with systemic arteritis (21) and serial levels may be particularly useful in long-term assessment of disease activity. In the absence of any histological proof of vasculitis and in the appropriate clinical setting the finding of a very high level of Factor VIII-related antigen may be a useful aid to diagnosis.

ANTINEUTROPHIL CYTOPLASMIC ANTIBODY (ANCA)

One of the most interesting advances in the understanding of vasculitis in recent years has been the association of ANCA with systemic vasculitis. Although originally reported as specific to Wegener's granulomatosis (22, 23) high titres of IgG ANCA are now also found in other systemic vasculitides especially with renal involvement, including microscopic polyarteritis (24). IgM anti-ANCA have been found in patients with Kawasaki disease and in systemic vasculitis dominated by pulmonary haemorrhage (25). Persistently high levels of ANCA, despite treatment, suggest a high risk of relapse of vasculitis so serial measurements are particularly useful in complicated patients (Lockwood, personal communication). The role of ANCA in the aetiology of vasculitis is not established but it is directed against a sub-unit of alkaline phosphatase and the antigen is found on the surface of endothelial cells suggesting a possible pathogenetic role.

HISTOLOGY

The best site for confirming a diagnosis of vasculitis depends on the pattern of organ involvement, eg. sural nerve biopsy for neuropathy, skin biopsy for rash etc. Small vessel vasculitis and necrotizing arteritis may co-exist so multiple biopsies and/or angiography may be necessary in difficult cases.

The kidney is the most important organ involved and renal biopsy the most useful investigation. Significant bleeding is rare despite the possible puncture of arteritic aneurysms. Renal biopsy should be considered as a medical emergency when there is evidence of significant renal involvement shown by deteriorating glomerular function (rising serum creatinine) and an "active" urinary sediment (microscopic haematuria, proteinuria, casts etc.), as severe renal failure can develop within days especially in patients with polyarteritis nodosa and Wegener's granulomatosis. Urgent (non-emergency) biopsy is also indicated in the presence of stable or normal renal function if there is persistent haematuria or proteinuria to assess the severity of kidney involvement as well as for diagnostic purposes. The commonest finding is a focal segmental necrotizing glomerulonephritis, sometimes called microscopic polyarteritis but as this is accompanied by necrotizing arteritis at other sites including the kidney in up to 40% of patients, this term is often inappropriate. Crescents are common especially in Wegener's granulomatosis. Immunohistology shows a surprising absence of significant glomerular immune complex deposition in polyarteritis and Wegener's (16) in contrast to small vessel vasculitides such as systemic lupus erythematosus and Henoch-Schönlein purpura.

The value of "blind biopsy" of clinically uninvolved tissue is questionable. In the absence of renal involvement, Dahlburg *et al* recommend muscle biopsy as the most valuable safe procedure in systemic vasculitis (26) and a rectal biopsy is sometimes helpful in systemic rheumatoid vasculitis (27).

ANGIOGRAPHY

Angiography should include the coelic axis as well as both renal arteries where changes (especially aneurysms) are detected in up to 70% of cases of polyarteritis (28). Angiograms can only demonstrate the size and distribution of blood vessels involved and are not diagnostic of any specific disease. They have been reported in patients with drug abuse, atrial myxoma, thrombotic thrombocytopenic purpura and bacterial endocarditis as well as all the diseases in Group 1.

PROGNOSIS AND TREATMENT

The size of vessel involved and the presence (or absence) of renal involvement are the most important factors affecting prognosis. Despite recent therapeutic advances, up to 40% of patients with polyarteritis, 20 to 30% with systemic rheumatoid vasculitis and 10 to 20% with Wegener's granulomatosis (29-33) die within a year of diagnosis. Although the terminal event is now more commonly sepsis than uncontrolled vasculitis, the importance of renal involvement on the mortality of polyarteritis is shown by comparing those whose serum creatinine is more than 500 mmol/1 (47% mortality) with those whose creatinine is less than 500 mmol/1 (15% mortality) at the time of diagnosis (34), stressing the danger of any delay in diagnosis. A similar picture is seen in Wegener's granulomatosis where in addition there may be significant morbidity from nasal, laryngeal or pulmonary involvement.

Significant renal damage is rarer in patients with systemic rheumatoid vasculitis. In these patients arteritis (clinical or biopsy) is associated with a higher mortality (44%) than small vessel disease (20%), where cardiac disease (restrictive pericarditis, aortic regurgitation) is a common cause of death (35). The prognosis for diseases in Groups 2 and 3 is much more favourable. Less than 10% of patients with Henoch-Schönlein purpura develop significant renal involvement and of these only a few develop chronic renal disease. Some patients with essential mixed cryoglobulinaemia develop typical polyarteritis years after presentation (36). Giant cell arteritis and Takayasu's arteritis are rarely fatal but may be associated with significant morbidity (eg blindness and ischaemia).

TREATMENT

Cyclophosphamide is now established as the treatment of choice for Wegener's granulomatosis with a "remission rate" of 92% (37). Similar successes have been reported in polyarteritis nodosa (38) and systemic rheumatoid vasculitis (39).

Localised granulomatous lesions may be resistant to cytotoxic drugs or radiotherapy and systemic Wegener's granulomatosis can relapse after years of apparent control on cyclophosphamide (40). Long-term cytotoxic therapy and continued monitoring is essential especially in Wegener's granulomatosis. It seems that the majority of patients can be "controlled" by cyclophosphamide but that "cure" is rarely achieved. Other reported therapeutic options include cyclosporin and trimethoprim (41-43).

Polyarteritis by contrast is usually more short-lived with fewer relapses. So long as renal function has not been significantly compromised and the patient responds to treatment, cyclophosphamide can be discontinued within six to nine months, suggesting a significant cure rate in this disease. Systemic rheumatoid vasculitis shows more similarities with Wegener's granulomatosis with a tendency to relapse (4).

TABLE 4: CYCLOPHOSPHAMIDE TREATMENT REGIMENS[1]

1. **Continuous oral**

cyclophosphamide 2mg/kg/day
prednisolone 40-60mg/day reduce to 20mg/day by month 3
10mg/day by month 6
alternate day by month 9
withdraw cyclophosphamide 9-12 months[2]

2. **Intermittent intravenous**[3]

cyclophosphamide 15mg/kg)
methylprednisolone 1gm) – every 2 weeks x 6
increase interval between injections to 3 weekly (x2), monthly (x3)
withdrawal cyclophosphamide 9-12 months[2]

3. **Intermittent oral**[3]

cyclophosphamide 5mg/kg/day)
prednisolone 100-200mg/day) – 3 consecutive days
interval between treatments as in 2
withdrawal cyclophosphamide 9-12 months[2]

1. adjust dose if significant renal impairment,
2. longer treatment often necessary in Wegener's and rheumatoid vasculitis or change to azathioprine 2mg/kg/day,
3. add H_2 antagonist, especially in rheumatoid vasculitis, encourage high fluid intake (3 1./day) during cyclophosphamide treatment.

The most appropriate cytotoxic regimen is unknown. We favour intermittent cyclophosphamide therapy because of the risk of significant bladder toxicity with continuous oral cyclophosphamide as described by Fauci *et al* (37). Some currently used cyclophosphamide regimens are listed in Table 4. Steroid therapy alone cannot be recommended because of the high risk of relapse and because of the long-term complications (44).

Small vessel vasculitis may respond to simpler remedies, especially removal of inciting antigens, including drugs, infectious agents and environmental antigens. Other cases respond well to low-dose (less than 15mgm per day) steroids or other agents such as dapsone. Giant cell arteritis also usually responds to systemic steroids alone although Takayasu's arteritis occasionally requires additional cytotoxic therapy.

CONCLUSIONS

"Vasculitis" covers a very wide range of diseases and cytotoxic therapy must only be considered in the appropriate clinical setting. It is particularly important to define, where possible, involvement of arteries as in polyarteritis, Wegener's and some cases of rheumatoid vasculitis where early investigation and treatment is vital. Renal vasculitis is the most important complication associated with a particularly poor prognosis.

The development of newer laboratory tests such as ANCA and Factor VIII-related antigen has helped both with diagnosis and monitoring. Early aggressive immunosuppressive treatment (eg cyclophosphamide plus steroid) results in significant improvement in prognosis but many patients require prolonged treatment and under careful supervision. Until there is a clear understanding of the pathogenetic mechanisms involved in each vasculitic disease, cytotoxic therapy will be the mainstay of treatment. Future therapeutic developments such as the use of specific monoclonal antibodies and/or specific antibiotics would be warmly welcomed to replace the present, somewhat blunderbuss, immunosuppressive approach.

REFERENCES

1. Frohnert P P, Sheps S G. 1967. Long-term follow up study of peri-arteritis nodosa. *Am J Med* **43: 8-14.**
2. Schmid F R, Cooper N S, Ziff M, McEwan C. 1961. Arteritis in rheumatoid arthritis. *Am J Med* **30:** 56-83.
3. Bywaters E G L, Scott J T. 1963. The natural history of vascular lesions in rheumatoid arthritis. *Journal of Chronic Diseases* **16:** 905-914.
4. Scott D G I, Bacon P A, Tribe C R. 1981. Systemic rheumatoid vasculitis: a clinical and laboratory study of 50 cases. *Medicine (Baltimore)* **60:** 288-297.
5. Gower R G, Sausker W F, Kohler P F, Thorne G E, McIntosh R M. 1978. Small vessel vasculitis caused by hepatitis B virus immune complexes. *Journal of Allergy and Clinical Immunology.* **62** :222-228.
6. Neumann H A M, Berretty P J M, Reinders-Folmer S C C. 1981. Hepatitis-B surface antigen deposition in the blood vessel walls of urticarial lesions in acute hepatitis-B. *Br J Dermatol.* **104:** 383-388.
7. Levo V, Gorevic PD, Kassab H J, Zucker-Franklin D, Franklin E C. 1977. Association between hepatitis-B virus and essential mixed cryoglobulinaemia. *N Eng J Med.* **296:** 1501-1504.
8. Combes B, Stastny P, Shorey J, Eigenbrodt E H, Burrera A, Hull A R et al. 1971 Glomerulonephritis with deposition of Australia antigen-antibody complexes in glomerular basement membrane. *Lancet* **2:** 234-237.
9. Onion D H, Crumpacker C S, Gilliband B C. 1971. Arthritis of hepatitis associated with Australia antigen. *Ann Intern Med* **75:** 29-33.
10. Gocke D J, Hsu K, Morgan C, Bombardieri S, Lockshin M, Christian C L. 1970. Association between polyarteritis and Australia antigen. *Lancet* **2:** 1149-1153.
11. Sergent J S. 1980. Vasculitis associated with viral infections. *Clinics in Rheumatic Diseases* **6:** 339-350.
12. Seifert M. The Rheumatology of HIV infection. *Reports on Rheumatic Diseases (Series 2):* Topical Reviews 1989 no. 11.
13. Scott D G I, *Vasculitis.* In: Scott J T, ed. Copeman's textbook of the rheumatic diseases. 6th ed. Edinburgh: Churchill Livingstone, 1986: 1292-324.
14. Scott D G I. 1988. Classification and treatment of systemic vasculitides. *Brit J Rheum* **27:** 251-257.
15. Haynes B F, Allen N B, Fauci A S. Diagnostic and Therapeutic Approach to the Patient With Vasculitis. *Medical Clinics of North America* 1986; **70:** 355-368.
16. Adu D, Howie A J, Scott D G I, Bacon P A, McGonigle R J S, Michael J. 1987. Polyarteritis and the kidney. *Quarterly Journal of Medicine* **62:** 221-37.
17. Hind C R K, Savage C O, Winearls C G, Pepys M B. 1984. Objective monitoring of disease activity in polyarteritis by measurement of serum c-reactive protein concentration. *Br Med J* **288:** 1027-1030.
18. Scott D G I, Bacon P A, Allen C, Elson C J, Wallington T. 1981 IgG rheumatoid factor, complement and immune complexes in rheumatoid synovitis and vasculitis: comparative and serial studies during cytotoxic therapy. *Clinical and Experimental Immunology* **43:** 54-63.
19. Chauhan A, Scott D G I, Neuberger J M, Gaston J S H, Bacon P A. 1989. Churg-Strauss vasculitis and ascaris infection. *Annals of the Rheumatic Disease* (in press).
20. Levinsky R J, Barrat T M. 1979. IgA immune complexes in Henoch-Schönlein purpura. *Lancet* **2:** 110-3.
21. Woolf A D, Wakerley G, Wallington T B, Scott D G I, Dieppe P A. 1987 Factor VIII related antigen in the assessment of vasculitis. *Annals of Rheumatic Disease* **46:** 441-47.
22. van der Woude F J, Rasmussen N, Lobatto S, et al. 1985. Autoantibodies against neutrophils and monocytes: Tool for diagnosis and marker of disease activity in Wegener's granulomatosis. *Lancet* **1:** 425-429.
23. Gross W L, Ludeman G, Kiefer G et al. 1986. Anti-cytoplasmic antibodies in Wegener's granulomatosis. *Lancet* **1:** 806.
24. Lockwood C M, Bakes D, Jones S, et al. 1987. Association of alkaline phosphatase with an autoantigen recognised by circulating anti-neutrophil antibodies in systemic vasculitis. *Lancet* **1:** 716-720.
25. Savage C O S, Winearls C G, Jones S et al. 1987. Prospective study of radioimmunoassay for antibodies against neutrophil cytoplasm in diagnosis of systemic vasculitis. *Lancet* **1:** 1389-1393.
26. Dahlberg P J, Lockhart J M, Overholt E L. 1989. Diagnostic studies for systemic necrotizing vasculitis: sensitivity, specificity and predictive value in patients with multisystem disease. *Archives of Internal Medicine* **149:** 161-165.
27. Tribe C R, Scott D G I, Bacon P A. 1981. The place of rectal biopsy in the diagnosis of systemic vasculitis. *Journal of Clinical Pathology* **34:** 843-850.
28. Chatel A, Gornier T H, Brigot J M, Toulg C, Helenon C H. 1979. L'arteriographie dans la periarterite noueuse. *Journal of Radiologie* **2:** 113-120.
29. Cupps T R, Fauci A S. 1981. *The vasculitides,* Major problems in internal medicine, Vol XXI. Saunders, Philadelphia.
30. Leib E S, Restivo C, Paulus H E. 1979. Immunosuppressive corticosteroid therapy of polyarteritis nodosa. *Am J Med* **67:** 941-947.
31. Pinching A J, Lockwood C M, Pussell B A et al. 1983. Wegener's granulomatosis: Observations on 18 patients with severe renal disease. *Quarterly Journal of Medicine* **52:** 435-460.
32. Savage C O S, Winearls C G, Evans D J et al. 1985. Microscopic polyarteritis: Presentation, pathology and prognosis. *Quarterly Journal of Medicine* **56:** 467-483.
33. Geirsson A J, Sturfelt G. Trudesson L. 1987. Clinical and serological features of severe vasculitis in rheumatoid arthritis: prognostic implications. *Annals of the Rheumatic Diseases* **46:** 727-733.
34. Adu D, Beaman M, McGonigle R J S, Michael J, Howie A J, Scott D G I, Bacon P A. The clinical spectrum of polyarteritis and Wegener's granulomatosis. Conference proceedings (in press) from Seminar in Advanced Rheumatology, Bad-Ragaz, Switzerland. 3rd-6th November, 1988.
35. Bacon P A, Scott D G I. La vascularite rheumatoide. 1987. In: Sang J, ed. Polyarthrite rheumatoide. Aspects actuels et perspectives. Paris: Med-Sciences Flammerion 27-43.
36. Gorevic P D, Kassab H J, Levo Y, et al. 1980. Mixed cryoglobulinaemia: clinical aspects and long-term follow up of 40 patients. *Am J Med* **69:** 287-308.
37. Fauci A S, Haynes B F, Katz P, Wolff S M. 1983. Wegener's granulomatosis: prospective clinical and therapeutic experience with 85 patients for 21 years. *Annals of Internal Medicine* **98:** 76-85.
38. Fauci A S, Haynes B F, Katz P. 1978. The spectrum of vasculitis. Clinical, pathologic, immunologic and therapeutic implications. *Annals of Internal Medicine* **89:** 660-676.
39. Scott D G I, Bacon P A. 1984. Intravenous cyclophosphamide and methylprednisolone in treatment of systemic rheumatoid vasculitis. *Am J Med* **76:** 377-384.
40. Satoh J, Miyasaka N, Yamada T, Nishido T, Okuda M, Kuroiwa T, Shimokawa R. 1988. Extensive cerebral infarction due to involvement of both anterior cerebral arteries by Wegener's granulomatosis. *Annals of the Rheumatic Diseases* **47:** 601-611.
41. DeRemee R A, McDonald T J, Weiland L H. 1985. Wegener's granulomatosis: Observations on Treatment with Antimicrobial Agents. Mayo Clin Proc **60:** 27-32.
42. Israel H L. 1988. Sulfamethoxazole – Trimethoprim Therapy for Wegener's Granulomatosis. *Archives of Internal Medicine* **148:** 2293-2295.
43. Borleffs J C C, Derksen R H W M, Hené R J. 1988. Wegener's granulomatosis and Cyclosporine. Transplantation Proceedings Vol XX, No. 3, Suppl 4 (June) pp 344-345.
44. Conn D L, Tompkins R B, Nichols W L. 1988. Glucocorticosteroids in the Management of Vasculitis – a Double Edged sword? *The Journal of Rheumatology* **15:** 1181-183.

BEHÇET'S SYNDROME

C G Barnes
Consultant Physician
Department of Rheumatology
The Royal London Hospital

HISTORY

There is little doubt that Behçet's syndrome was first described by Hippocrates in the 5th Century B.C. (1). It was then recognised under various titles in ancient China and in the late 19th and early 20th centuries in Europe. Hulusi Behçet, Professor of Dermatology in Istanbul, in 1937 described the triple symptom complex which came to bear his name (2,3). He described the classical triad of oral and genital ulceration and inflammatory eye disease. The fourth major manifestation of skin involvement was added later.

Historically, this led to three questions - how may the condition be diagnosed, should it be known as Behçet's 'disease' or 'syndrome' and where should it be classified in the spectrum of disease?

The debate on the use of the title 'disease' or 'syndrome' stems from the two different, but probably complementary, views of whether this can be regarded as a single unified diagnosis (disease) or arising from a series of possible aetiologies leading to a common set of clinical manifestations (syndrome). In the absence of known and proven aetiopathogenesis (see below) and in view of the geographical variability of the condition many still prefer to use the term Behçet's syndrome (BS).

The classification of the syndrome in the wider spectrum of medicine has also produced two principal views. One is that it should be grouped with the seronegative spondarthritides. This arises from the involvement of mucous membranes, skin, eyes, the gastrointestinal and genito-urinary tracts, and joints. However, this view is no longer held by most authorities because of the clear difference of these lesions in BS from those in the seronegative spondarthritides and the different histocompatibility spectrum. The more acceptable classification is with the vasculitides because of the clinical and histological findings of both arterial and venous vasculitis.

The classification of the syndrome into sub-groups, particularly by our Japanese colleagues, merely emphasizes the major clinical manifestation in the individual patient. Hence,these patients are classified as having, for example, vasculo-Behçet's, neuro-Behçet's, occulo-Behçet's etc. Secondly Lehner sub-divides BS into mucocutaneous, arthritic, neurological and ocular types depending on the spectrum of manifestations present in the individual patient with the description of different immunological abnormalities in these sub-groups.

DIAGNOSIS

Painful oral aphthous ulceration may be regarded as the hallmark of the condition. However, it is known that this occurs in approximately 20% of the general population being somewhat more frequent in females by a ratio of approximately 4:3 (4). It is also recognised that 2-3% of patients with BS may not have oral ulceration (5).

In the absence of any totally reliable diagnostic test the diagnosis depends first on the knowledge and hence suspicion of the syndrome. Then the grouping together of sufficient clinical features allows a reliable diagnosis to be made.Traditionally these features have been sub-divided into major and minor manifestations largely dependent on the clinical frequency of their occurrence, occasionally with available histology, rather than on their pathological severity (Table 1). Thus vasculitis itself, either clinical or histologically proven, falls into the list of minor manifestations as does arthritis although the latter may be present in 45-60% of patients (6,7,8).

Table I. MANIFESTATIONS OF BEHÇET'S SYNDROME

Major	Minor
Oral ulceration	Arthritis/arthralgia
Genital ulceration	Vasculitis
Skin lesions	Gastrointestinal ulceration
- erythema nodosum	Central nervous system lesions
- pustules/folliculitis	- brainstem syndrome
- ulceration	- meningoencephalitis
- hypersensitivity (pathergy)	- headache, confusion, coma
Eye lesions	- epilepsy
- uveitis ± hypopyon	- psychoses
- retinitis	Cardiovascular lesions
	Pleuropulmonary lesions
	Epididymitis
	Family History

Therefore, this has led to a number of diagnostic criteria being recommended, dating back to 1946, of which five sets have remained in use, namely those of Mason & Barnes from the UK (9), the Behçet's Disease Research Committee of Japan (8,10), O'Duffy from the USA (11), Dilsen from Turkey (12) and Chang & Zheng from China (13). These diagnostic criteria sets have very considerable similarities with the possible exception of that from O'Duffy which depends on the presence of vasculitis. The others require the grouping together of major and minor criteria and it is interesting to note that those from China dated 1980 were derived totally independently from, and without any knowledge of, the other sets.

More recently the International Study Group for Behçet's Disease undertook a study of the prevalence of the manifestations of BS by collecting data on 914 patients from 7 countries from which International Criteria for the diagnosis of Behçet's disease were derived (5/Table 2). It must be stressed that these criteria, which may be regarded as diagnostic or for classification of the syndrome, are not principally for the diagnosis of the individual case which depends on the clinical acumen of the clinician. They are to ensure that studies of BS in different centres are based on comparable groups of patients.

Earlier sets of diagnostic criteria accepted the inclusion of the minor features of BS in the scheme of diagnosis. The new International Criteria not only demand the presence of oral ulceration but include only the accepted major criteria and the pathergy test (see below) which gave a high relative value (combined sensitivity and specificity) (Table 3). Thus, whereas vasculitis and epididymitis are highly specific when present they have a low sensitivity and are, therefore, unhelpful in diagnostic terms. At the same time the International Study Group agreed a more precise definition of various manifestations (Table 2). Even though it is recognised that approximately 2-3% of patients with BS do not have mouth ulceration it is nevertheless appropriate that in terms of multicentre, international, epidemiological, laboratory and therapeutic studies the presence of mouth ulceration is mandatory. The loss of approximately 2% of patients from such studies is less important than ensuring comparability of data.

Table 2. International Criteria for Diagnosis (Classification) of Behçet's Disease (5)

Recurrent oral ulceration	- major,minor or herpetiform - observed by physician or patient - recurrences at least thrice in any 12 month period
PLUS TWO OF:	
Recurrent genital ulceration	- aphthous or scarring - observed by physician or patient
Eye lesions	- anterior uveitis - posterior uveitis - cells in vitreous on slit lamp examination, OR, - retinal vasculitis observed by ophthalmologist
Skin lesions	- erythema nodosum observed by physician or patient - pseudofolliculitis or papulopustular lesions, OR, - acneiform nodules observed by physician in post-adolescent patients not on corticosteroid treatment.
Positive pathergy test	- read by physician at 24-48 hours

(Findings applicable only in absence of other diagnosis).

Table 3.

	Sensitivity	Specificity	Relative value
Genital ulcers	77	95	172
Eye lesions	60	93	153
Pathergy test	58	90	148
Folliculitis, papulopustular lesions, acneiform nodules	70	76	146) Sensitivity 81)
Erythema	44	95	139) Specificity 75)
Sub-cutaneous thrombophlebitis	16	95	111) Rel. Value 156
Deep-vein thrombosis	13	96	109
Epididymitis	8	100	108
Arterial occlusion and/or aneurysm	3	98	101
CNS involvement	10	89	99
Arthralgia	56	38	94
Family history	20	73	93
Gastrointestinal features	9	82	91
Arthritis	38	38	76

Relative value = sensitivity + specificity
from: International Study Group for Behçet's Disease 1990 (5)

EPIDEMIOLOGY

Formal epidemiological surveys of the prevalence of the syndrome are few. The maximum reported incidence is in the Far East where a prevalence of 1/10,000 of the general population has been reported from Japan. However the prevalence varies considerably even in Japan being maximal in the northern island of Hokkido and lowest in Kyushu (14). There is a suggestion that the prevalence, and the severity, of the syndrome is decreasing progressively as shown by repeated epidemiological studies in Japan (10). In the United Kingdom a prevalence of 0.064/10,000 has been reported from Yorkshire (15) and a lower prevalence of 1:800,000 has been reported from the United States (16). More recently a survey in rural northern Turkey showed a prevalence of 19/5,131 (17).

Sporadic reports of Behçet's disease have appeared over the years from other countries throughout Asia. More recently large numbers of patients have been diagnosed in Iran and in mainland China, and because of this reported distribution of patients the nickname 'The Silk Route Disease' has been coined, the suggestion being that the disease followed the medieval silk route between the Far East and Europe. There is also considerable variation in the prevalence of individual features of the syndrome. Thus a high incidence of gastrointestinal lesions is reported from Japan (8) but these are rare in Mediterranean and European populations. Similarly pulmonary lesions are reported from Europe but rarely in Japan. Familial aggregations of the syndrome are well recognised and recorded, although familial lone recurrent oral ulceration is more common.

The sex ratio of patients also varies from country to country. In Turkey, for example, there is a marked male predominance, men have more severe disease, and Turkish patients tend to have a younger age of onset and a higher incidence of eye disease (18). In Japan it was initially reported that the disease was more prevalent in females but even that now has been shown to vary in different parts of the country, the female preponderance being highest in the southern part of Japan and reversing to male preponderance in the north.

It is now well established that the disease is associated with a high prevalence of the HLA-B5(51) antigen in association with DR7 and DRw52. This association was initially noted in Japan, and subsequently in Turkey, and almost certainly is associated with the high incidence of inflammatory eye disease in patients with BS in those and other countries.

AETIOPATHOGENESIS

The aetiology of the disease remains unknown. Behçet himself and other workers at the time suggested a viral aetiology but this, over the years, was not confirmed. More recently, however, the HSVI genome has been detected in the lymphocytes of patients with Behçet's syndrome and HSVI antigen has been detected in immune complexes which are known to be a frequent finding in the condition (19).

There have been suggestions from Japan that exposure to toxic chemicals (organophosphorus and organochlorine compounds) may precipitate the disease and more recently there has been considerable interest in the possible role of streptococcal infections particularly with *S.sanguis* (10).

Immune complexes have regularly been detected in patients with Behçet's syndrome. Increased chemotaxis and motility of polymorphonuclear leucocytes has been detected and variable results on phagocytic activity have been reported.

RECURRENT ORAL ULCERATION (ROU)

The three principal forms of ROU, major, minor and herpetiform, may all occur in BS and no one form may be considered as typical or diagnostic of BS (20). Minor ulceration is defined as that which usually lasts up to 14 days and heals without scarring whereas major ulceration may last for weeks with loss of tissue and hence results in deep scarring. Both may commence with a palpable, red, tender nodule before mucosal ulceration occurs. Herpetiform ulceration starts as tiny blisters which coalesce and enlarge.

Recurrence is defined as ulceration which develops at least thrice in any twelve month period. Although oral ulceration is painful and may affect the buccal mucosa, soft palate and fauces, and is the most common feature of BS it is not usually the feature which leads the patient to seek medical advice (9). It is suggested that local trauma may precipitate ulceration.

GENITAL ULCERATION

Like oral ulceration this too is painful, may heal with scarring and occurs in approximately 80% of patients (5). In the female the vulva and vagina may be involved and in the male the scrotum is more often the site of ulceration than is the shaft of the penis. Again the ulcer is heralded by the appearance of a painful, tender nodule. Ulceration and pustule formation may also occur in the groins and perineum, and around the anus, at which sites they are also classified as genital lesions. Occasionally rectocolic or vesico-vaginal fistulae may develop. Exacerbations of genital ulceration may occur immediately before or during menstruation or immediately after pregnancy.

SKIN LESIONS

Erythema nodosum is probably the most characteristic skin lesion with an underlying vasculitis (21). Papulopustular lesions and acneiform nodules are also frequently present and do not differ in appearance from those occurring spontaneously in adolescence. At one time it was thought that comedones were not present in BS but this is not so.

EYE LESIONS (22)

Inflammatory eye lesions are the commonest form of serious morbidity in BS and may lead to blindness. Eye involvement usually develops within the first two years of the development of the full syndrome (23). Anterior uveitis, with or without hypopyon, (iridocyclitis) is the most frequent lesion and is relatively easily treated. More serious, in terms of impairment of visual acuity in the short and long term, is posterior uveitis and retinal vasculitis (uveoretinitis). Some authorities find that retinal vasculitis, to some degree, accompanies all cases of posterior uveitis and may be detected by slit lamp examination and fluorescein fundus angiography. This is accompanied by cells visible in the aqueous and vitreous. The retinal vasculitis may lead to vitreous haemorrhage, retinal haemorrhages and exudates, vascular occlusion, new vessel formation and retinal/optic nerve atrophy. Severe reduction in visual acuity has been recorded in between 50-85% of patients after 4 years of ocular disease.

VASCULITIS

The inflammatory involvement of blood vessels, both arteries and veins, may be considered as the principal pathological feature of the condition. Nevertheless clinical evidence of vasculitis, other than erythema nodosum or of the retina as discussed above, occurs in a minority of patients. Extensive reports of vascular involvement include arterial and venous occlusion at many sites including of the venae cavae, limb vessels and carotid arteries, and aneurysm formation of the popliteal and pulmonary arteries in particular (6,14,24).

Inflammatory vasculitis of the vessel wall, without the presence of giant cells, is present histologically and the presence of anticardiolipin (antiphospholipid) antibodies has not been confirmed after an initial suggestion that an increased incidence of these antibodies could be detected.

Many <u>pulmonary lesions</u> of non-specific type have been reported but the major concern is haemoptysis which may precede severe haemorrhage. This results from the rupture of an area of vasculitis or of an aneurysm of a large branch of the pulmonary artery into the bronchial tree and may be fatal (25, 26).

Similarly <u>central nervous system lesions</u> (see below) including the brain stem syndrome, transverse myelitis and headaches are probably all on the basis of vasculitis.

ARTHRITIS

An inflammatory arthritis is shown to be present in

approximately 45% of patients when a large number of case reports are combined (7). The arthritis is mon-articular or oligo-articular affecting up to five joints at a time, of which the knees are most commonly involved. Pain, swelling and stiffness of affected joints with clinical synovitis, confirmed histologically, indicates the true inflammatory nature of the arthritis. Various reports describe the arthritis as chronic, self-limiting or episodic, and although it is usually non-destructive, loss of cartilage and pannus formation with erosive damage have been demonstrated radiologically and histologically (6,8,9,27,28,29).

There still remains some controversy as to whether or not sacroiliitis is a feature of the arthritis of BS. With the exception of one large series in which sacroiliitis and ankylosing spondylitis is reported as occurring in up to 63% of patients, only occasional and sporadic cases have been reported from other centres. It was on the basis of this one series that it was suggested that Behçet's syndrome should be classified with the seronegative spondarthritides but in view of the overall lack of evidence of sacroiliitis, the different spectrum of skin, eye and bowel disease, and the difference in histocompatability typing, BS should no longer be considered as being categorised as a seronegative spondarthritis.

The histology of the synovium reveals an acute inflammatory reaction confined to the superficial zone of the synovium only. There is little, if any, synovial lining cell hyperplasia and the synovium is replaced by a dense acute inflammatory reaction, resembling granulation tissue, thus consisting of vascular elements and polymorphonuclear leucocytes without an excess of lymphocytes. Only a very small minority of specimens have been shown to contain any excess of plasma cells or of lymphoid follicle formation. One may therefore debate whether this represents 'ulceration' of the synovial surface (28,30).

GASTROINTESTINAL LESIONS

Ulcerative lesions of the gastrointestinal tract, other than oral ulceration itself, are recorded in many surveys but particularly those from Japan and the Far East (8). Such ulcerative lesions may occur from the oesophagus through the stomach and throughout the small and large intestines but our Japanese colleagues regard involvement of the caecum as typical. Such lesions therefore lead to abdominal pain, diarrhoea, gastrointestinal haemorrhage and occasionally perforation of the gut (6,8,10).

CENTRAL NERVOUS SYSTEM (CNS) (8,31,32)

Neurological involvement in Behçet's syndrome has been reported in a widely varying proportion of patients from 3-42%. More recent surveys suggest a prevalence of 10-12% in patients in Japan and Turkey (8,31). Included is a wide range of neurological symptoms and clinicopathological findings. Although CNS involvement is uncommon in the United Kingdom it is valid to pay considerable attention to these lesions because of the serious morbidity that they cause. Headache is frequent but more serious manifestations are probably based on vasculitic lesions and therefore include pyramidal and brain stem lesions, cranial nerve palsies and epilepsy. CT scans demonstrate localised lesions in the pyramidal tracts or mid-brain, and cerebral atrophy. Histological findings include perivascular infiltration of acute and chronic inflammatory cells, necrotic foci, foci of demyelination in the brain stem, and localised fibrotic lesions. Various psychiatric symptoms have been recorded including personality changes, disturbance of consciousness and hallucination.

THE PATHERGY TEST

The pathergy test is regarded by some authorities as specific to the syndrome. However, even after a number of years' discussion, there is still some debate as to how the test is best performed.

A 21-gauge needle is inserted through sterilised skin on the flexor aspect of the forearm to the sub-dermis either vertical or at a 45° angle to the surface and is withdrawn. A positive test consists of the formation of an erythematous papule or vesicle; which may ulcerate, at the needle-prick site after 48 hours. It has been shown that multiple needle-pricks on the forearm of an individual patient may produce positive results at some sites and negative at others and hence in the past it has been recommended that multiple tests should be performed.

An incidence of positive tests of up to 80% has been reported in various surveys, including from Turkey, and it is notable that in a recent epidemiological survey this test was positive in only 33% of patients and that the test was less commonly positive in milder disease (17). The pathergy test is rarely positive in European patients (33,34).

More recently it has been suggested that the test is more frequently positive when blunt needles are used (35). This may have considerable relevance to the interpretation of previous reports where the older type of re-sterilised steel needles were used (these frequently being relatively blunt) compared with surveys which have used sharper disposable needles. This may also explain the observation that the test is becoming less frequently positive over the years in Turkey where sharp disposable needles have only recently been in common use.

Dieppe and his colleagues have shown that the intradermal injection of monosodium urate crystals causes local and systemic responses. This technique has therefore been used to investigate patients in Leeds, London and Istanbul. It was shown that the intradermal injection of 2.5 mgs monosodium urate crystals (compared with Dieppe's original method using 10 mgs) regularly causes a positive skin reaction in all patients. Classical pathergy test performed at the same time, particularly in British patients, showed no such positive reactions and therefore this response to monosodium urate is different from the pathergy test itself. It appears to represent an augmented response to intradermal injection of these crystals in patients with BS (36).

TREATMENT (Table 4)

The treatment of BS may be divided broadly into three categories: symptomatic, the treatment of ophthalmic lesions and of vasculitis. However, there is a wide variation of opinion regarding appropriate drug treatment. There is nevertheless a wide consensus (37) that non-steroidal anti-inflammatory agents are effective in controlling inflammatory arthritis, and that systemic corticosteroids are beneficial in the treatment of intra-cranial hypertension, of the pyramidocerebellar syndrome and of gross disabling orogenital ulceration. Similarly it is agreed that no systemic treatment is required for eye disease that has been quiescent for 2 years and that colchicine is beneficial in treating erythema nodosum.

There is still a widely held opinion that colchicine represents a basic background treatment indicated for all patients with Behçet's syndrome but the evidence for this remains unproven.

There are relatively few controlled trials of treatment in Behçet's syndrome. Colchicine has been demonstrated to affect beneficially erythema nodosum and arthralgia only (38), levamisole has been shown to be ineffective, azathioprine (39) and cyclosporine have been shown to treat effectively severe inflammatory eye disease. There are large numbers of reports of uncontrolled studies with colchicine, various immunosuppressives (azathioprine, chlorambucil and cyclophosphamide) and cyclosporine in particular.

Symptomatic Treatment

Symptomatic treatment is usually all that is required for the majority of patients. This may be divided into treatment of orogenital ulceration and of arthralgia/arthritis.

Orogenital ulceration is usually successfully treated by topical applications of corticosteroids, usually triamcinolone acetonide in oral paste (Adcortyl in Orabase). Applications should be commenced as soon as the initial tender erythematous nodule at either site is detected when the ulceration may either be aborted or at least rendered less severe. Occasionally mouth washes, or gargles, of a soluble steroid preparation, such as 5 mgs soluble prednisolone (Prednesol) dissolved in 100-150 mls water and not swallowed, may be necessary.

It is uncommon that orogenital ulceration is sufficiently severe to require treatment with either systemic corticosteroids or even thalidomide.

Symptomatic treatment with simple or anti-inflammatory analgesics is normally all that is required for arthritis and arthralgia. Occasionally aspiration of, and corticosteroid injection into, an actively inflamed joint, such as a knee, is indicated. There is no good evidence that any more potent medication has any beneficial effect on the more severe forms of arthritis but these patients are few in number and formal studies, therefore, have not been possible.

Inflammatory eye disease

Anterior uveitis, with or without hypopyon, is usually treated with topical or sub-conjunctival injections of corticosteroids and mydriatics. Occasionally oral corticosteroids are required but this form of eye disease is usually of relatively minor significance.

Panuveitis, posterior uveitis and retinal involvement are of more serious import. Treatment with systemic corticosteroids, by oral or pulsed intravenous administration, cyclosporine and immunosuppressives are all recommended.

Thus, in the event of severe and sight-threatening eye disease the acute inflammatory reaction of the uveal tract should be brought under control with either low dose cyclosporine (<5 mgs per kg per day) or high dose systemic corticosteroid or pulse intravenous methylprednisolone 1,000 mgs on three occasions (usually on alternate days). These forms of treatment may be combined with azathioprine 2.5 mgs per kg body weight per day to maintain remission of disease. It has recently been demonstrated that azathioprine may prevent recurrences of, and *de novo,* eye disease in male patients (39).

Other, uncontrolled, studies have suggested that the use of cyclophosphamide or chlorambucil may have similar effects.

Vasculitis

The treatment of the vasculitis of Behçet's syndrome is no different from that of vasculitis in any other disease. Thus treatment is with a combination of corticosteroids and immunosuppressives, orally or intravenously.

TABLE 4. Summary of drug treatment

DRUG	DOSE	INDICATION
Simple analgesics Anti-inflammatory analgesics		arthralgia/arthritis
Colchicine	1.5mg/day	arthralgia erythema nodosum ? ulceration and eye lesions
Corticosteroids		
- topical	Triamcinolone acetonide oral paste	oral and genital ulceration
	Eye drops/ ointment	mild anterior uveitis
- oral	Prednisolone 10-100 mg/day	inflammatory eye disease, vasculitis, gross orogenital ulceration
- pulsed IV	Methylprednisolone 1000 mg thrice on alternate days	severe inflammatory eye disease, severe vasculitis and central nervous system lesions
Immunosuppressives		
- azathioprine	2.5 mg/kg/day	inflammatory eye disease, vasculitis, severe ulceration
- cyclophosphamide	IV 1-1.5g/month 500 mg/week (+mesna 200mg)	severe inflammatory eye disease, severe vasculitis
	oral 1.5-2mg/kg/day	inflammatory eye disease, vasculitis
- chlorambucil	0.2mg/kg/day	inflammatory eye disease
- methotrexate	7.5 -15mg/week week	inflammatory eye disease
Cyclosporine	3-10 mg/kg/day	acute eye disease
Anti-platelet agents	e.g. aspirin	thrombophlebitis
Thalidomide	200-400 mg/day	gross oral ulceration

REFERENCES

1. Feigenbaum, A. Description of Behçet's syndrome in the Hippocratic third book of endemic diseases. *Br. J. Ophthalmol.* 1956; **40:** 355-357.

2. Behçet, H. Uber rezidiverende, aphthose durch ein Virus verursachte Geschwure am Mund, am Auge und an dem Genitalen. *Derm. Woch.* 1937; **105** : 1152-1157.

3. Behçet, H. Some observations on the clinical picture of the so-called triple symptom complex. *Dermatologica* 1940; **81**: 73-78.

4. Sircus, W., Church, R., Kelleher, J. Recurrent ulceration of the mouth. *Quart. J. Med.* 1957; **26:** 235-249.

5. International Study Group for Behçet's Disease. Criteria for diagnosis of Behçet's disease. *Lancet.* 1990; **335**: 1078-1080.

6. Shimizu, T., Ehrlich, G.E., Inaba, G., Hayashi, K. Behçet Disease (Behçet Syndrome) *Sem. Arth. Rheum.* 1979; **8:** 223-260.

7. Barnes, C.G. Behçet's syndrome - joint manifestations and synovial pathology. In Lehner, T., Barnes, C.G. (eds). "Behçet's Syndrome: clinical and immunological features" London. *Academic Press* 1979; 199-212.

8. Inaba G. Behçet's Disease. In Vinken, P.J., Bruyn, G.W., Klawans, H.L., (eds.) *Handbook of Clinical Neurology* Elsevier Science Publishers, Amsterdam. 1989; **12:** 593-610.

9. Mason, R.M., Barnes, C.G. Behçet's syndrome with arthritis. *Ann. Rheum. Dis.* 1969; **28**: 95-103.

10. Mizushima, Y. Recent research into Behçet's disease in Japan. *Int J. Tissue. React.* 1988; **10**: 59-65.

11. O'Duffy, J.D. Criterès proposés pour le diagnostique de la maladie de Behçet et notes therapeutiques. *Rev. Med.* 1974; **36:** 2371-2379.

12. Dilsen, N., Konice, M., Aral, 0. Our diagnostic criteria for Behçet's disease - an overview. In Lehner, T., Barnes, C.G. (eds.). Recent Advances in Behçet's Disease. London, *Royal Society of Medicine Services. International Congress and Symposium Series No.* **103,** 1986; 177-180.

13. Zhang, X-Q (in Chinese). *Chin. J. Intern. Med.* 1980; **19:** 15-20.

14. Shimizu, T. Behçet's Disease: a systemic inflammatory disease. In: *Vascular Lesions of Collagen Diseases and Related Conditions.* Tokyo. University of Tokyo Press 1977, 201-211.

15. Chamberlain, M.A. Behçet's syndrome in 32 patients in Yorkshire. *Ann. Rheum. Dis.* 1977; **36:** 491-499.

16. O'Duffy, J.D. Summary of international symposium on Behcet's Disease, Istanbul. *J. Rheumatol.* **5:** 229-231.

17. Yurdakul, S., Gunaydin, I., Tuzun, Y. et al. The prevalence of Behçet's syndrome in a rural area in northern Turkey. *J. Rheumatol.* 1988; **15:** 820-822.

18. Yazici, H., Tuzun, Y., Parzali, H. et al. Influence of age of onset and patient's sex on the prevalence and severity of manifestations of Behçet's syndrome. *Ann. Rheum. Dis.* 1984; **43:** 783-789.

19. Lehner, T. The role of a disorder in immunoregulation associated with herpes simplex virus type I in Behçet's disease. In Lehner, T., Barnes, C.G. (eds.). Recent Advances in Behçet's Disease. London, *Royal Society of Medicine Services. International Congress and Symposium Series No.* **103,** 1986; 31-36.

20. Cooke, B.E.D. Oral ulceration in Behçet's syndrome. In 143-149.

21. Chun, S.I., Su, W.P., Lee, S., Rogers, R.S. Erythema nodosum-like lesions in Behçet's syndrome: a histopathologic study of 30 cases. *J. Cutan. Pathol.* 1989; **16:** 259-265.

22. Dinning, W.J. An overview of ocular manifestations. In Lehner, T., Barnes, C.G. (eds) "Recent Advances in Behçet's Disease" London. *Rôyal Society of Medicine Services International Congress and Symposium Series No.* **103,** 1986, 227-233.

23. Yazici, H., Tuzun, Y., Pazarli, H., Yurdakul, S., Yalçin, B., Muftuoglu, A. Behçet's disease as seen in Turkey. *Haematologia* 1980; **65:** 381-383

24. Muftuoglu, A. U., Yurdakul, S. Yazici, H. et al. Vascular involvement in Behçet's disease - a review of 129 cases. In Lehner, T., Barnes, C.G. (eds) "Recent Advances in Behçet's Disease" London. *Royal Society of Medicine Services International Congress and Symposium Series No.* **103**, 1986, 255-260.

25. Efthimiou, J., Spiro S.G. Pulmonary involvement in Behçet's syndrome. In Lehner, T., Barnes, C.G. (eds) "Recent Advances in Behçet's Disease" London. *Royal Society of Medicine Services International Congress and Symposium Series No.* **103**, 1986, 261-266.

26. Efthimiou J., Johnston, C., Spiro, S.G., Turner-Warwick, M. Pulmonary disease in Behçet's syndrome. *Quarterly J. Med.* 1986; **58:** 259-280.

27. Yurdakul, S., Yazici, H., Tuzun, Y. et al. The arthritis of Behçet's disease: a prospective study. *Ann. Rheum Dis.* 1983; **42:** 505-515.

28. Vernon-Roberts, B., Barnes, C.G., Revell, P.A. Synovial pathology in Behçet's syndrome. *Ann. Rheum. Dis.* 1978; **37:** 139-145.

29. Gow, P., Lehner, T., Panayi, G. Joint manifestations in Behçet's syndrome and in recurrent oral ulceration. In Lehner, T., Barnes, C.G. (eds). "Behcet's Syndrome: clinical and immunological features" London. *Academic Press* 1979, 223-239.

30. Gibson, T., Laurent, R., Highton, J., Wilton, M. et al. Synovial histopathology in Behçet's syndrome. *Ann. Rheum. Dis.* 1981; **40:** 376-381.

31.Siva, A., Ozdogan, S., Yazici, H. et al. Headache, neuropsychiatric and neurocomputerized tomography findings in Behçet's syndrome. In Lehner, T., Barnes, C.G. (eds) "Recent Advances in Behçet's Disease" London. *Royal Society of Medicine Services International Congress and Symposium Series No.* **103,** 1986, 247-254.

32. Inaba, G. Clinical features of neuro-Behçet's syndrome. In Lehner, T., Barnes, C.G. (eds) "Recent Advances in Behçet's Disease" London. *Royal Society of Medicine Services International Congress and Symposium Series No.* **103**, 1986, 235-246.

33. Davies, P.G., Fordham, J.N., Kirwan, J.R., Barnes, C.G., Dinning, W.J. The pathergy test and Behçet's syndrome in Britain. *Ann. Rheum. Dis.* 1984; **43:** 70-73.

34. Yazici H., Chamberlain, M.A., Tuzun, Y., Yurdakul, S., Muftuoglu, A.U. Comparative study of the pathergy reaction among Turkish and British patients with Behçet's disease. *Ann. Rheum. Dis.* 1984; **43:** 74-75.

35. Dilsen, N., Konice, M., Aral, 0., Ocal, L. How can we increase the sensitivity of the skin pathergy test in Behçet's disease? *2nd Mediterranean Symposium on Behçet's Disease,* Madrid, 1990, abs. RT-3.

36. Cakir, N., Yazici, H., Chamberlain, M.A., Barnes, C.G., et. al. The response to intradermal injection of monosodium urate crystals in Behçet's disease. *Ann Rheum. Dis* 1991; in press.

37. Yazici, H., Barnes, C.G. A survey of treatment in Behçet's syndrome. *Book of Abstracts, Behçet's Disease 5th International Conference*, Rochester, Minn, U.S.A. 1989.

38. Aktulga, E.,Altac, M., Muftuoglu, A., Ozyazgan, Y. et al. A double-blind study of colchicine in Behçet's disease. *Haematologica* 1980; **65:** 399-402.

39. Yazici, H., Pazarli, H., Barnes, C.G. Tuzun, Y. et.al. A controlled trial of azathioprine in Behçet's syndrome. *New. Engl. J. Med.* 1990; **322:** 281-285.

40. Yazici, H., Barnes, C.G. Practical Treatment Recommendations for the Pharmacotherapy of Behçet's Disease. *Adis Press,* New Zealand 1991: in press.

September 1991

THE RHEUMATOLOGY OF HIV INFECTION

M Seifert
Consultant Physician
Rheumatology Department
St Mary's Hospital
London

Since the first description of the disease now called Acquired Immune Deficiency Syndrome (AIDS) (1) this devastating disorder has gripped the attention of the medical and lay press and there is seldom a day when it is not mentioned. A vast amount of time and effort has been devoted to unravelling the mysteries of AIDS and consequently new light has been shed on basic phenomena in virology and immunology. It has been estimated that 5-10 million people around the world have been infected with the virus causing AIDS and yet we have no knowledge of how many of these will develop the disease and die.

From its first discovery in homosexuals (2) AIDS has been described in intravenous drug users (3), recipients of blood or blood products (4), children born to mothers at risk (5), the heterosexual sexual partners of patients with AIDS (6) and in Africans (7).

The clinical manifestations of infection with the human immunodeficiency virus (HIV) are broad and range from the absence of symptoms to the immunosuppression associated with AIDS itself.

TABLE I. SUMMARY OF CLASSIFICATION SYSTEM FOR HIV INFECTIONS

Group I	Acute infection (transient symptoms with seroconversion)	
Group II	Asymptomatic infection	
Group III	Persistent generalised lymphadenopathy	
Group IV	Other manifestations	
	A	Chronic constitutional disease
	B	Neurological disease
	C	Specified secondary infections
	D	Specified secondary cancers
	E	Other conditions

Table 1 shows The Centre for Disease Control in Atlanta classification of the disease, and the rheumatological problems that may occur when there is infection with HIV are included under Group IV E. (8).

THE VIRUS AND ITS EFFECTS

The discovery that infection with HIV caused AIDS was reported in 1983 (9) and the subsequent recovery of this virus from patients with the disease and its related conditions confirmed this (10). Further identification of antibodies to the virus in populations at risk from AIDS (11) and those inadvertently the recipients of blood products (12) have underlined the infectious spread of the disease.

The virus is a retrovirus resembling a group of lentiviruses that cause infection in sheep (VISNA) and horses (infectious anaemia virus) (13). The same sub-family of retroviruses, the caprine arthritis encephalitis virus, causes arthritis in goats (14).

A retrovirus encodes its genetic information in RNA and uses a unique viral enzyme called reverse transcriptase to allow a double stranded DNA copy of the viral RNA to be made (i.e. at one step in the cycle of replication genetic information flows from RNA to DNA in a "retro" direction). The first step in the infection of the target cell by HIV is the binding to the CD4 antigen receptor sites present on the cell surface (15). T cell lysis occurs and T4 lymphopenia develops. HIV may also chronically infect macrophages, B cells infected with the Epstein-Barr virus (which are increased in patients with AIDS), and certain other T cells, these may not necessarily be destroyed. Abnormalities in the activation and immunoregulation of B cells also occur with the development of hypergammaglobulinaemia. There is an inability to mount an antibody response to new antigens and the usual diagnostic serological tests are consequently unreliable.

RHEUMATOLOGICAL MANIFESTATIONS OF HIV INFECTION

There are now a number of reports in the literature outlining the various rheumatological problems that have been recognised in patients infected with HIV. With the overwhelming complications of advanced disease some of these problems tend to remain in the background whilst the physician is faced with devastating destruction of the brain, lung and gut. Nonetheless there must be an awareness of the rheumatological presentations of HIV infection as these may be the first signs of this infection.

TABLE 2. SUMMARY OF THE CHARACTERISTIC IMMUNOLOGICAL ABNORMALITIES ASSOCIATED WITH INFECTION WITH HIV
Lymphopenia
Selective T4 cell deficiency
Decreased or absent delayed cutaneous hypersensitivity to both recall and new antigens
Elevated serum immunoglobulins, predominantly IgG and IgA in adults and including IgM in children
Increased spontaneous immunoglobulin secretion by individual B lymphocytes.

HIV itself has not yet been implicated as the cause of arthritis, although the virus has been cultured from synovial fluid and this must remind rheumatologists of the potential hazard in aspirating joints in HIV infected patients (16). Table 3 lists the present rheumatic diseases found in HIV infected patients. New syndromes are likely to be claimed although it is probable that patients infected with HIV will develop the wide spectrum of rheumatic diseases seen in any young active population (17). Whilst HIV infection has not been claimed to produce rheumatic disease *per se*, there is no doubt that inflammatory polyarthritis is increasingly recognised in populations normally relatively free of such disease such as Africans in Zambia (Christopher Conlan personal communication) and Zimbabwe (18).

Acute joint effusions occurring in HIV infected patients must be aspirated and opportunistic infections are likely to be missed unless the microbiologist is alerted. Sporothrix schenckii (19) and Cryptococcus neoformans (20) have both been cultured from the synovial fluid of patients with HIV infection.

The development of an acute polyarthritis as a presentation of HIV infection has been reported with the majority of these patients having a reactive arthritis and found to be HLA-B27 positive (21). An exacerbation of psoriasis and polyarthritis has been described in patients previously only mildly affected in which the psoriasis has become severe and uncontrollable as the symptoms of immunodeficiency developed (22). Reactive arthritis and psoriatic arthritis developing *de novo* with the diagnosis of asymptomatic HIV infection and the subsequent deterioration of these diseases with the development of AIDS is also recognised (23). The fact that this occurs in the presence of profound immunodeficiency and with a depletion of CD4 positive (helper) T lymphocytes suggests that these cells may not be important in the pathogenesis of the arthritis in these patients.

SJÖGREN'S SYNDROME

Arthralgia associated with bilateral parotid glandular enlargement, keratoconjunctivitis sicca or xerostomia has been found as a consequence of HIV infection (24). Some of these patients have benign cystic lymphoepithelial lesions on parotid gland biopsy and other salivary gland biopsies show heavy lymphoplasmacytic infiltrates in the interstitium. Antinuclear antibodies are negative.

TABLE 3. RHEUMATOLOGICAL MANIFESTATIONS OF HIV INFECTION	
Group 1	Opportunistic joint infections
Group 2	Reactive arthritis Psoriatic arthritis
Group 3	Sjögren's syndrome Necrotising vasculitis SLE-like syndromes Polymyositis
Group 4	Arthralgia and polyarthritis

NECROTISING VASCULITIS AND SLE

Although in the presence of marked deficiency of cellular immunity, HIV infection is increasingly recognised as being associated with immune disorders. There are well documented reports of polyarteritis nodosa, lymphomatoid granulomatosus, leucocytoclastic vasculitis and primary angiitis of the central nervous system (25). As well as vasculitis, other similarities exist between HIV infection and SLE such as autoimmune thrombocytopenia, lymphadenopathy, splenomegaly, peripheral neuropathy, pleural effusions and lung lesions. The presence of anticardiolipin antibodies may be associated with the deterioration in the clinical course of the disease (26) and false positive HIV antibody tests may occur in SLE.

POLYMYOSITIS

Muscle disease is recognised as an early complication of infection with HIV. Polymyositis has been reported as an early manifestation of this infection with patients presenting with profound muscle weakness and elevated creatinine phosphokinase. In these reported cases viral antigens have been found in the lymphoid cells surrounding muscle fibres (27).

ARTHRALGIA

Generalised weight loss, fever and malaise associated with aches and pains in mostly large joints is frequently seen, and although backache from osteomyelitis due to mycobacteria or fungal infection is reported, this arthralgia may just be symptomatic of the infection itself. Severe intermittent joint pain lasting twenty-four hours and without evidence of synovitis has also been found (17).

MANAGEMENT

Precautions must be taken when handling specimens of synovial fluid and synovium from patients infected with HIV. Patients attend routine rheumatology out-patient clinics and often require help from physiotherapists and occupational therapists.

Non-steroidal drugs are frequently used to control inflammation and pain in affected joints but the use of steroids should be avoided until more information is available because of reports of exacerbation of Kaposi's sarcoma (28). There are no clear guidelines on intra-articular steroids and on the whole they should be used with caution because of their systemic effect and certainly if opportunistic infection is suspected in joint effusions. Methotrexate has been found to profoundly accelerate AIDS and azathioprine can cause fatigue and weight loss (21). Sulphasalazine may be helpful in controlling the inflammatory arthritis and the chronic diarrhoea, but this has not been evaluated.

The inhibitor of reverse transcriptase, azidothymidine (AZT) is now licenced for use and is being used in the treatment of early HIV infection. The main side-effect of AZT is anaemia and myelosuppression. It may also interact with aspirin, paracetamol and other non-steroidal anti-inflammatory drugs.

CONCLUSIONS

Rheumatologists in future will increasingly encounter patients infected with HIV in their routine clinics. A number will appear fit and complain only of minor rheumatological problems but others will be profoundly ill with extensive psoriasis and acute painful polyarthritis. Across this spectrum other rheumatological manifestations of HIV infection will appear. In a recent series of fifty patients presenting with rheumatic lesions only eleven were known to be HIV positive prior to the development of the arthritis. Twenty-two patients had an acute peripheral non-erosive arthritis, and of these eleven had psoriasis or keratoderma blenorrhagica (29).

The pathogenic mechanisms behind this arthritis are still not known, but the possibility that it is the result of a reactive arthritis to opportunistic infection or even the HIV itself demands vigorous pursuit.

REFERENCES

1. Pneumocystis pneumonia – Los Angeles. *MMWR* 1981. **30**:250-252.
2. Update on Kaposi's sarcoma and opportunistic infections in previously healthy persons – United States. *MMWR* 1982 **31**:294-301.
3. Opportunistic infections and Kaposi's sarcoma among Haitians in the United States. *MMWR* 1982 **31**:353-61.
4. Possible transfusion-associated acquired immune deficiency syndrome (AIDS) – California. *MMWR* 1982 **31**:652-4.
5. Unexplained immunodeficiency and opportunistic infections in infants – New York, New Jersey, California. *MMWR* 1982 **31**:665-8.
6. Immunodeficiency among female sexual partners of males with acquired immune deficiency syndrome (AIDS) – New York. *MMWR* 1983 **31**:697-8.
7. Clumeck N, Mascart-Lemone F, de Maubeuge J, Brenez D, Marcelis L. Acquired immune deficiency syndrome in black Africans. *Lancet* 1983. **1**:642.
8. Selick R M, Jaffe H W, Solomon S L, Curran J W. CDC Definition of AIDS. *N Engl J Med* 1986 **315**:761.
9. Barré-Sinoussi F, Chermann J C, Rey F, et al. Isolation of a T-lymphotrophic retrovirus from a patient at risk for the acquired immune deficiency syndrome (AIDS). *Science* 1983 **220**:868-71.
10. Gallo R C, Salahuddin S Z, Popovic M, et al. Frequent detection and isolation of cytopathic retroviruses (HTLV-III) from patients with AIDS and at risk for AIDS. *Science* 1984 **224**:500-3.
11. Antibodies to a retrovirus etiologically associated with acquired immunodeficiency syndrome (AIDS) in populations with increased incidences of the syndrome. *MMWR* 1984 **33**:377-9.
12. Curran J W, Lawrence D N, Jaffe H, et al. Acquired immunodeficiency syndrome (AIDS) associated with transfusions. *N Engl J Med* 1984 **310**:69-75.
13. Rabson A B and Martin M A. Molecular organization of the AIDS retroviruses. *Cell* 1985 **40**:477-80.
14. Crawford T B, Adams D S, Cheevers W P and Cork L C. Chronic arthritis in goats caused by a retrovirus. *Science* 1980 **207**:997-9.
15. Dalgleish A G, Beverley P C L, Clapham P R, Crawford D H, Greaves M F and Weiss R A. The CD4 (T4) antigen is an essential component of the receptor for the AIDS retrovirus). *Nature* 1984 **312**:763-7.
16. Withrington R H, Cornes P, Harris J R W, et al. Isolation of HIV from synovial fluid of a patient with reactive arthritis. *Br Med J* 1987 **294**:484-5.
17. Berman A, Espinoza L R, Diaz J D, et al. Rheumatic Manifestations of Human Immunodeficiency Virus Infection. *Am J Med* 1988 **85**:59-64.
18. Davis P, Stein M, Latif A and Emmanuel J. HIV and polyarthritis. *Lancet* 1988 **i** 936.
19. Lipstein-Kresch E, Isenberg H D, Singer C, Cooke O and Greenwald R A. Disseminated sporothrix schenkii infection with arthritis in a patient with acquired immunodeficiency syndrome. *J Rheumatol* 1985 **12**:805-8.
20. Ricardi D D, Septowitz D V, Berkowitz L B, et al. Cryptococcal arthritis in AIDS patients. *J Rheumatol* 1986 **13**:455-9.
21. Winchester R, Bernstein D H, Fischer H D, et al. The co-occurrence of Reiter's syndrome and acquired immunodeficiency. *Ann Intern Med* 1987 **106**:19-26.
22. Duvic M, Johnson T M, Rapini R P, Freeze T, Brewton G and Rios A. Acquired immunodeficiency syndrome associated psoriasis and Reiter's syndrome. *Arch Dermatol* 1987 **123**:1622-32.
23. Forster S R, Seifert M H, Keat A C, et al. Inflammatory joint disease and human immunodeficiency virus infection. *Br Med J* 1988 **296**:1625-7.
24. Ulirsch R C and Jaffe E S. Sjögren's syndrome like illness associated with the acquired immunodeficiency syndrome-related complex. *Hum Pathol* 1987 **18**:1063-8.
25. Calabrese L H, Yen-Liebeman B, Estes M, et al. Systemic necrotizing vasculitis and the human immunodeficiency virus (HIV) (abstr). *Arthritis Rheum* 1988 **31**:141.
26. Mizutani W T, Woods V L, McCutchan J A, et al. Anticardiolipin antibodies in human immunodeficiency virus (HIV) infected gay males may be associated with a deteriorating clinical course (abstr). *Arthritis Rheum* 1988 **31**:142.
27. Dalakas M C, Pezeshkpour G H, Gravell M and Sever J L. Polymyositis associated with AIDS retrovirus. *JAMA* 1986 **256**:2381-83.
28. Schlkhafer E P, Grossman M E, Faging Bell K. Steroid induced Kaposi's sarcoma in a patient with pre-AIDS. *Am J Med* 1987 **82**:313-317.
29. Rowe I F, Forster S M, Seifert M H and Keat A C S. Rheumatic lesions in individuals with human immunodeficiency virus (HIV) infection (abstr). *Br J Rheumatol* 1987 **27**:2.

HYPERMOBILITY SYNDROME

R Grahame
Professor of Clinical Rheumatology
United Medical & Dental Schools of Guy's and St Thomas' Hospitals
Guy's Hospital
London SE1 9RT

INTRODUCTION

The hypermobility syndrome (HMS) is a commonly occurring (and frequently overlooked) entity, which causes much suffering in the community. Medical students are taught to examine for *loss* of joint range of movement (if they are taught to examine joints at all). It is not surprising, therefore, that doctors - specialists and generalists alike - commonly fail to recognise joint laxity, the hallmark of which is *increased* joint range, ie hypermobility. In consequence, much suffering is misdiagnosed, is inappropriately or inadequately treated, or (most likely of all) passes unrecognised. This is a much neglected area in rheumatology.

HOW IS HYPERMOBILITY RECOGNISED?

The 9-point 'Beighton' scoring system (Fig 1), which requires the subject to be able to perform a series of passive manoeuvres, is widely used and has withstood the test of time. It is a useful and simple screening procedure, which can be used both in the clinic and in epidemiological studies (1). Its main shortcoming is that it is an 'all-or-none' test, giving a reasonable estimate of the widespread (or otherwise) nature of the joint laxity, but no indication whatsoever of its degree. A semi-quantitative modification devised by Contompasis giving a 56-point range gives a much wider indication of joint laxity, which both covers the normomobile and even dips into the hypomobile range.

IS IT INHERENT OR ACQUIRED?

The answer is that it can be either. Generalised joint laxity is a genetically-determined disorder of connective tissue. The precise identity of the putative gene(s) responsible is currently under intense scrutiny (see below). Acquired hypermobility can be achieved by dint of intensive training as is seen in ballet dancers. It is also observed in pregnancy, acromegaly, hyperparathyroidism and chronic alcoholism. The generalised inherent variety is a feature

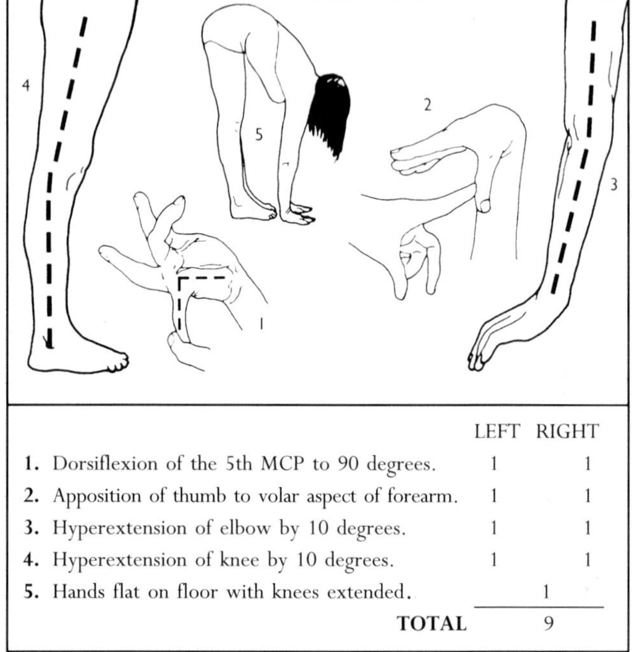

		LEFT	RIGHT
1.	Dorsiflexion of the 5th MCP to 90 degrees.	1	1
2.	Apposition of thumb to volar aspect of forearm.	1	1
3.	Hyperextension of elbow by 10 degrees.	1	1
4.	Hyperextension of knee by 10 degrees.	1	1
5.	Hands flat on floor with knees extended.	1	
	TOTAL	9	

Figure 1. Indicators of hypermobility. The 9-point Beighton score.

common to a number of heritable disorders of connective tissue (HDCTs) including the Marfan syndrome (MFS), the Ehlers-Danlos syndrome (EDS), osteogenesis imperfecta (OI), and homocystinuria. Most of these disorders are rare, but the commonly encountered hypermobility syndrome is the exception.

HYPERMOBILITY SYNDROME DEFINED

The term 'hypermobility syndrome' (HMS) was coined by Kirk, Ansell and Bywaters in 1967 (2) as the occurrence of musculoskeletal symptoms in hypermobile subjects in the absence of demonstrable systemic rheumatological disease, ie in apparently otherwise normal individuals. Subsequent studies in several different countries have established that:

1. there are overlap features with other rarer and more serious HDCTs, in particular the Marfanoid habitus (without ectopia lentis) (Fig 2) and stretchy skin (Fig 3).
2. it is a benign disorder without life-threatening complications, such as disecting aortic aneurysm.
3. in most pedigrees a dominant mode of inheritance is seen.
4. symptoms arise as a result of connective tissue laxity and/or fragility.

HOW COMMON IS HYPERMOBILITY?

There have been few epidemiological studies of joint laxity. The data that are available point to the presence of generalised joint laxity in a substantial proportion

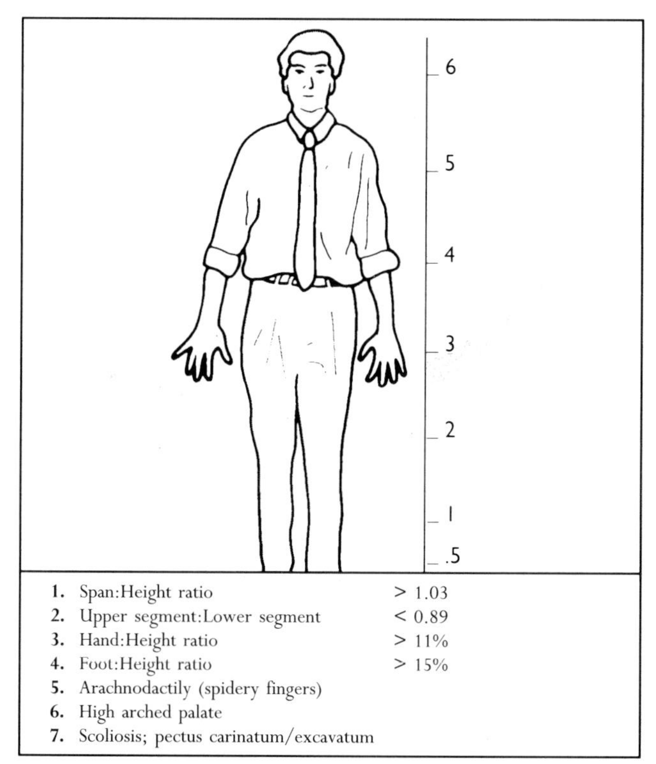

	Criterion	Value
1.	Span:Height ratio	> 1.03
2.	Upper segment:Lower segment	< 0.89
3.	Hand:Height ratio	> 11%
4.	Foot:Height ratio	> 15%
5.	Arachnodactily (spidery fingers)	
6.	High arched palate	
7.	Scoliosis; pectus carinatum/excavatum	

Figure 2. Criteria for Marfanoid habitus.

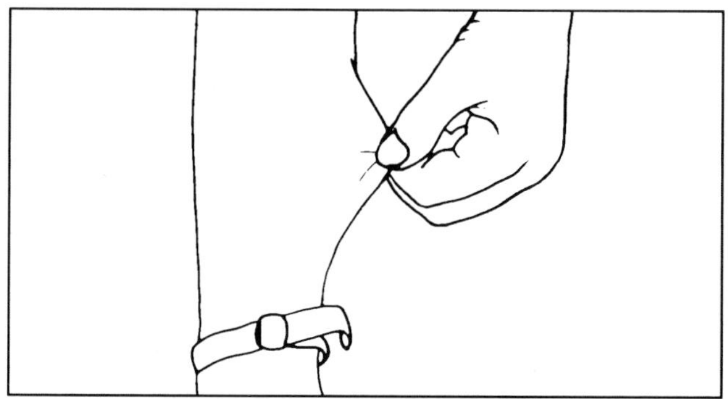

Figure 3. Skin hyperextensibility.

of healthy individuals in all populations studied. Joint laxity diminishes with age and is greater in females than in males. There are also ethnic variations, with Asians showing the greatest range of joint mobility followed by Negroes and Caucasians in descending order. Following the publication of a study of 660 North American music students of all ages in which 47% of males and 78% of females showed at least one hypermobile joint, we now know that 'pauci-articular hypermobility' is even more highly prevalent in otherwise healthy subjects than the generalised variety (3).

HOW COMMON IS THE SYNDROME?
(ie hypermobility + the symptoms)

As far as the population as a whole is concerned, this is a totally unknown quantity. There is a strong impression that the overwhelming majority of hypermobiles suffer no ill effects, and that symptoms tend to occur in those in the top 5-10% of the range of joint mobility.

The question of clinic prevalence is a little clearer. A diagnostic survey of 9275 new referrals to one large London general rheumatology clinic revealed that HMS was more frequently diagnosed than ankylosing spondylitis, crystal synovitis or psoriatic arthritis, comprising 3.25% of all female and 0.63% of all male referrals (4). Thus HMS (provided that it is recognised) is seen to be one of the major causes of morbidity within the field of rheumatic diseases.

HOW DOES IT PRESENT?

HMS presents in a profusion of locomotor and non-locomotor guises. The common and recurring theme is trauma inflicted on a locomotor system genetically imperfect and thus ill-adapted to sustain the additional demands imposed on it by unaccustomed physical activity or acute injury. The result is connective tissue failure in its various forms.

In clinical terms the following conditions are common modes of presentation (5).

Articular Manifestations

The articular features comprise:

1 Myalgia and arthralgia. These are often very troublesome and occur in the absence of any identifiable cause. Their severity is often influenced by the phases of the menstrual cycle, and by changes in the weather.

2 Soft tissue lesions as are commonly seen in everyday practice but with greater frequency. These arise from trauma or overuse and include epicondylitis, tendonitis, capsulitis, plantar fasciitis and carpal tunnel syndrome.

3 Anterior knee pain (so-called chondromalacia patellae) is often associated with genu recurvatum, laxity of the cruciate and collateral ligaments and recurrent patellar subluxation or dislocation (see 6 below).

4 Acute articular and periarticular traumatic lesions such as traumatic joint synovitis, tenosynovitis or bursitis; and/or capsular, ligament, tendon or muscle tears.

5 Chronic monoarticular or polyarthritis which may mimic other forms of arthritis, notably adult rheumatoid arthritis or juvenile chronic arthritis. For reasons given above these may be poly-, pauci- or mono-articular. These are frequent sources of mis-diagnosis, generating unnecessary anxiety, and provoking inappropriate (even hazardous) treatment.

6 Recurrent dislocation or subluxation, notably of the shoulder, patello-femoral, or metacarpophalangeal joints. A common complaint is a sensation of 'the joint slipping out of place and back again', with or without pain. Another, is audible (and sometimes disconcerting) clicking emanating from a hypermobile joint.

7 Temporo-mandibular dysfunction associated with displacement of the intra-articular disc. This gives rise to a clicking jaw, pain on chewing, and, occasionally, an inability to close the mouth requiring manual reduction by the patient.

8 Premature osteoarthritis. This is based on anecdotal rather than firm epidemiological data. The author has encountered widespread and advanced OA even involving joints uncommonly affected by OA eg the shoulders) occurring in hypermobile women as early as their mid-thirties.

9 Spinal disorders. Congenital anomalies such as spina bifida occulta and transitional vertebrae are more frequent in hypermobile subjects than in controls (6). Low back pain, either acute or chronic, is a frequent presenting and recurring symptom. This may be traced to a variety of traumatic lesions of vertebrae (notably partes interarticulares defects with or without spondylolisthesis), intervertebral disc prolapse (with or without root compression). In addition back pain to soft tissue trauma is commonly encountered in the younger hypermobile subject. The term, 'loose back syndrome' has been applied to the occurrence of back pain in female hypermobile subjects for which no structural cause has been identified. In older people lumbar spondylosis or spinal stenosis may be found. Similar problems arise in relation to the cervical spine, to which hypermobile subjects appear to be particularly vulnerable.

10 Bone fragility leading to a predisposition to fracture, especially stress fractures, may manifest in those hypermobile subjects indulging in demanding physical pursuits. It should be stated that the defect is not gross (as it is in another HDCT, osteogenesis imperfecta), since bone mineral measurements by DEXA scan in HMS patients taken as a whole are not significantly lower than in normals (7). Another association which can be explained on the basis of reduced tensile strength of bone is idiopathic protrusio acetabulae.

11 Marfanoid habitus with long slender extremities (Fig 2) is seen in HMS patients in the absence of other features of the true Marfan syndrome such as aortic root dilatation (8) or lens dislocation (ectopia lentis) (Atkinson et al personal communication).

Extra-Articular Features in the HMS

These illustrate the ubiquitous nature of collagen and other connective tissue fibrous proteins and the widespread effects that ensue when they are defective. They comprise:

1 Skin hyperextensibility (Fig 3), fragility, striae and the formation of papyraceous (paper-like) scars.

2 Mitral valve prolapse. When the association with MVP was first observed by the use of echocardiography in the 1970s, it was considered to be of serious import (6). Recent studies employing state-of-the-art technology have established that true (hemo dynamically significant) MVP is probably barely more highly prevalent in HMS subjects than in the population as a whole (8).

3 Visceral problems may arise from weakening of the body's supporting structures eg rectal and uterine prolapse, spontaneous pneumothorax, hernia and varicose veins.

WHAT IS THE UNDERLYING DEFECT?

Early studies in HMS patients pointed to collagen as the likely site of the genetic abnormality as evidenced by a disturbance in the balance between the two major collagen types in skin (types I and III) (9); by increased urinary hydroxyproline excretion (10); and by the production of abnormally small diameter dermal collagen fibres viewed by scanning electron microscopy. It has now been established that mutations in the genes (COL1A1 and COL1A2) that encode the chains of type I collagen are responsible for most cases of osteogenesis imperfecta (OI) (11) and in Ehlers-Danlos syndrome type VII (arthrochalasis multiplex congenita) (12). A similar linkage to structural collagen genes was not forthcoming in the HMS (13) nor in the Marfan syndrome (MFS). Two recent important and exciting discoveries unequivocally link a mutant fibrillin gene on chromosome 15 to MFS (14) on the one hand, and a second fibrillin mutation on chromosome 5 to a related disorder, congenital contractural arachnodactyly, on the other (15). Studies are currently underway to determine whether similar mutations can be invoked in the pathogenesis of HMS.

SELF-HELP GROUPS IN THE UK

British Coalition of the Heritable Disorders of Connective Tissue

Marfan Association	Ehlers-Danlos Support Group	Hypermobility Syndrome Assn
Diane Rust	Valerie Burrows	Jane Butler
6 Queens Road	1 Chandler Close	10 Wolfester Terrace
Farnborough	Richmond	Sparkford
Hants GU14 6DH	N Yorkshire DL10 5QQ	Somerset BA22 7JE
Tel: 01252 547441	Tel: 01748 823 867	Tel: 01935 851344

Figure 4.

HOW CAN THESE PEOPLE BE HELPED?

A 5-Point Programme

1 Establish the correct diagnosis

HMS sufferers benefit greatly from being told that they *do not* have a serious potentially crippling disease like rheumatoid arthritis or juvenile chronic arthritis. Many will already have been told that they do! They can then be spared the anguish of living with that diagnosis as well as the futility (and dangers) of taking slow-acting anti-rheumatoid drugs which can have no beneficial effects (only adverse ones) in this condition. Many will rejoice to learn that their symptoms *are* taken seriously, *are* diagnosable, and (hopefully) *are* treatable. The likelihood is that, in the absence of physical signs (hypermobility having been overlooked!), their symptoms will have been attributed to 'psychogenic rheumatism'. They will either have accepted this assessment or go from specialist to specialist seeking help. Orthodox medicine having failed her, the hapless patient may end up seeking the (dubious) benefits of alternative medicine.

2 Inform the patient

So now you can tell them what they *have* got. Take a detailed family history and construct a pedigree. This will almost certainly bring to light other affected members of the family and help to demonstrate the hereditary nature of the condition. It may also help to distinguish HMS from EDS, MFS and OI in patients manifesting features of overlap. The ARC patient leaflet on Hypermobility is an extremely useful educational resource for patients, their families and friends. For symptomatic HMS patients with local problems a range of other appropriate ARC patient leaflets is available. Patients may wish to be put in touch with the appropriate self-help group (see Fig 4).

3 Treat the treatable

Many of the conditions seen in the HMS are soft tissue lesions which abound in everyday clinical practice (but more so!). They are easily identifiable by clinicians trained in locomotor medicine. They can be treated along conventional lines to good effect, using a variety of techniques - rest, splinting, local corticosteroid injection, physiotherapeutic techniques as appropriate. A word of caution here; it is important to remember that the tissues are less robust and require greater care in handling, especially in using passive mobilisation or other manipulative techniques. For the same reason it is prudent when using local steroid injections to use the minimal dose and to avoid depot preparations and repeated injections. Many of the other clinical problems encountered (as listed above) eg back pain, cervical spondylosis, osteoarthritis etc will, of course, be amenable to a range of conventional treatments.

4 Where the source of pain is more elusive...

Arthralgia, myalgia and/or back pain (in the absence of an identifiable cause) is a common occurrence in the HMS. One of the imponderables is why some HMS patients develop pain for the first time in adult life, while others have their most difficult time in adolescence. The pathogenesis of such pains is obscure and they are difficult to treat.

On the whole while analgesics may help, NSAIDs are disappointing, as are most types of conventional physiotherapy.

By asking HMS patients to keep an activities diary and noting what they do and when, it may be possible to identify factors which provoke or exacerbate symptoms. In such cases (even minor) adjustments to the life-style can be therapeutic.

Some patients obtain relief from arthralgia when joints are restored to their *hypermobile* range. This is the basis of the series of stretching exercises, which patients can perform by themselves. They are illustrated in the ARC Hypermobility leaflet. Others may be helped by a variety of other techniques eg TENS machine, acupuncture, hydrotherapy or balneotherapy.

There is a subset of patients whose pain defies all attempts at relief, despite rigorous attention to this programme. Not surprisingly, they become frustrated and depressed. Such patients pose a major therapeutic challenge. Such unfortunate individuals deserve all the ingenuity, sympathy and support that the health team can muster.

5 Encourage and pursue research

Encourage and pursue research into the clinical, molecular genetic, epidemiological, and therapeutic aspects of this group of disorders. Recent advances in understanding the genetic defects in Marfan syndrome have unleashed an unprecedented display of international collaboration in basic biomedical research, which bodes well for the future.

REFERENCES

1. Beighton P, Solomon L, Soskolne C. Articular mobility in an African population. *Ann Rheum Dis* 1973; **32:** 413-8.
2. Kirk JH, Ansell BA, Bywaters EGL. The hypermobilty syndrome. *Ann Rheum Dis* 1967; **26:** 419-25.
3. Larsson L-G, Baum J, Mudholkar GS. Hypermobility: features and differential incidence between the sexes. *Arthrit Rheum* 1987; **30:** 1426-30.
4. Grahame R. Clinical manifestations of the joint hypermobility syndrome. *Revmatolgia* (USSR) 1986; **2:** 20-4
5. Beighton P, Grahame R, Bird HA. *Hypermobility of Joints* 2nd Edition. Berlin, Heidelberg, New York: Springer-Verlag, 1989.
6. Grahame R, Edwards JC, Pitcher D, et al. Clinical and echocardiological study of patients with the hypermobility syndrome. *Ann Rheum Dis* 1981; **40:** 541-6
7. Ryan PJ, Fogelman I, Child A, Grahame R. Bone mineral density in Joint Hypermobility Syndrome (HMS). *Brit J Rheumatol* 1992; **Supp 2:** 64
8. Mishra M, Chambers JBC, Jackson G, Child A, Grahame R. Cardiac abnormalities in Joint Hypermobility Syndrome (HMS). *Brit J Rheumatol* 1992; **Supp 2:** 63
9. Child AH. Joint Hypermobility Syndrome: inherited disorder of collagen synthesis. *J Rheumatol* 1986; **13:** 239-42
10. Gage JP. Collagen biosynthesis related to temporomandibular joint clicking in childhood. *J Prosthetic Dent.* 1985; **53:** 714-717
11. Tsipouras P, Ramirez F. Genetic Disorders of Collagen. *J Med Genet* 1987; **30:** 428-432
12. Steinmann B, Tuderman L, Peltonen L at al. Evidence for a structural mutation of procollagen type 1 in a patient with the Ehlers-Danlos syndrome type VII. *J Biol Chem* 1980; **255:** 8887-8893
13. Henney AM, Brotherton DH, Child AH, Humphries SE, Grahame R. Segregation analysis of collagen genes in two families with joint hypermobility syndrome. *Brit J Rheum* 1992; **31:** 169-174
14. Kainulainen K, Pulkkinen L, Savolainen A, Kaitila I, Peltonen L. Location on chromosome 15 of the gene defect causing Marfan syndrome. *N Eng J Med* 1990; **323:** 935-939
15. Lee B, Godfrey M, Vitale E, Hori H, Mattei M-G, Sarfarazi M, Tsipouras P, Ramirez F, Hollister DW. Linkage of Marfan syndrome and a phenotypically related disorder to two different fibrillin genes. *Nature* 1991; **353:** 330-334

SUGGESTIONS FOR FURTHER READING

1. Grahame R. The Hypermobility Syndrome: a review. *Ann Rheum Dis* 1990; **49:** 199-200
2. Beighton P, Grahame R, Bird HA. *Hypermobility of Joints.* 2nd Edition. Berlin, Heidelberg, New York: Springer-Verlag, 1989
3. *Joint Hypermobility* ARC leaflet for patients
4. Ed Peter Royce and Beat Steinmann. *Connective Tissue and its Heritable Disorders. Molecular, Genetic and Medical Aspects.* Wiley Liss - New York, Chichester, Brisbane, Toronto, Singapore 1993
5. Turner-Stokes L. Treatment and control of chronic arthritis and back pain. *Topical Reviews* Jan 1993 No **23** ARC Reports on Rheumatic Diseases

September 1993

OSTEOPOROSIS AND THE FAMILY DOCTOR

A St J Dixon
Consultant Rheumatologist
Royal National Hospital for Rheumatic Diseases
Bath

DEFINITION

Osteoporotic bone is more porous than it should be when viewed under the microscope. The marrow spaces are enlarged, the medullary trabecular bone is sparse and the cortical bone is thin from loss of the bone mineral hydroxyapatite and the collagenous protein matrix. Because of this, bones are weak and fracture easily. Many different processes contribute. Age-related bone loss begins in the third decade, slowly at first, more rapidly later, until a man of 80 may have only half the bone mineral he had at 30. Additionally, women experience an acceleration of bone loss starting as oestrogen levels decline before the menopause and continuing for about ten years after it (Fig 1). Osteoporosis is made worse by lack of exercise, immobilisation or paralysis, by corticosteroid or thyroid hormone excess and by the effects of chronic illnesses and dietary deficiencies. Histologically, osteoclast activity outpaces osteoblast activity. Metabolically, there is a negative calcium balance and an increase in bone collagen breakdown products in the urine.

PREVALENCE SOCIAL AND ECONOMIC IMPACT

In the absence of a single specific marker for osteoporosis, prevalence has to be measured by the number of osteoporosis-related fractures. Crush fractures of the spine are generally recognised as osteoporotic but osteoporosis-related limb fractures are often not perceived as such, although it has been estimated that osteoporosis contributes to the majority of fractures in the elderly.

Spinal crush fractures may be multiple; they heal with loss of height and permanent deformity and often cause chronic pain and disability requiring constant medical and family care. Limb fractures if set correctly heal in the normal time and do not lead to long-term disability. Fractures of the proximal femur (hip fractures) are in a class of their own, since they always need hospitalisation and have been estimated to cost the country £500m per annum. They carry a high fatality rate – at least 20% within six months. Fifty percent of survivors lose independence and require long-term care.

PUBLIC AND PROFESSIONAL AWARENESS OF OSTEOPOROSIS

As a result of media campaigns and publicity (including this report!) there is now awareness that osteoporosis is preventable and in most instances treatable. For example, one long-term case/control study of postmenopausal women has shown that the relative risk of hip fracture can be cut to one third by hormone replacement therapy (HRT). There is similar evidence for spinal osteoporosis.

Figure 1

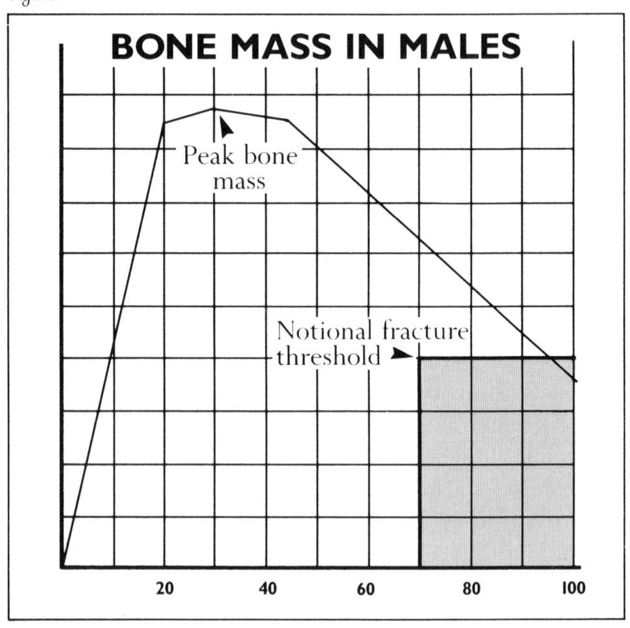

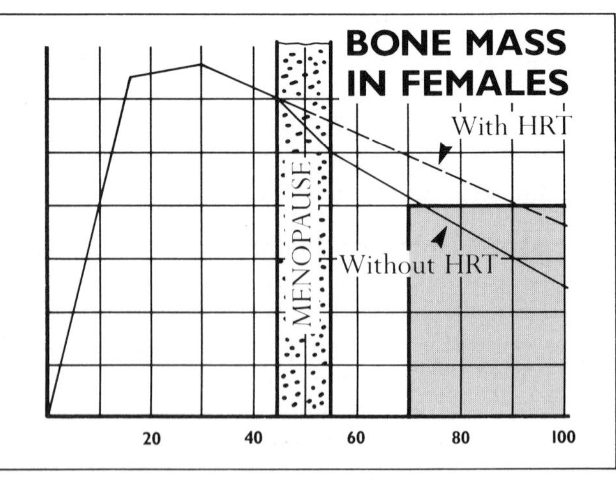

Total Bone Mass in Men & Women

Males develop a bigger skeleton during the years of growth, have a higher peak bone mass and only cross the notional fracture threshold in old age, on average.

Females have smaller skeletons, lower peak bone mass, suffer acceleration of bone loss around the menopause (unless given Hormone Replacement Treatment) and cross the fracture threshold in their seventies, on average.

PRESENTATION AND PREVENTION

There is a tendency for osteoporosis to run in families. Because of this or as a result of publicity, women concerned about their future health will ask their doctor for advice on prevention. Others may come because osteoporosis has been diagnosed on X-rays taken for some other reason. Practices which include Well Woman clinics and nurse counsellors may be better able to supervise HRT if this is considered suitable.

A search through a practice diagnostic index can detect others who may need preventative treatment. Oophorectomy entails a high risk of osteoporosis as does hysterectomy (since on average, ovarian function ceases within three years of removal of the womb). Currently only about a quarter of such women are given hormone replacement and then only for an inadequate duration, although without it osteoporosis is virtually inevitable.

The register might also reveal others at high risk. These would include those on long-term corticosteroid or thyroxine treatment and those who have already had repeated fractures. Osteoporosis, usually mixed with some osteomalacia (separately treatable with Vitamin D) is also inevitable in primary biliary cirrhosis and alcoholic liver disease and in malabsorption states as after gastrectomy or coeliac disease. Less common causes are anorexia nervosa, Cushing's syndrome, hyperprolactinaemia, Turner's syndrome and any other cause of precocious loss of ovarian function.

OSTEOPOROSIS IN MEN

Men are affected in the ratio of one man to every ten women. Osteoporosis in women is postmenopausal or idiopathic in all but 20%. In contrast, in men an underlying cause is present in over 50% and should be sought. Alcoholism, corticosteroid therapy, hypogonadism and bone tumour related osteoporosis are the commonest findings.

DETECTION AND SCREENING FOR THOSE AT RISK

Ordinary X-rays are inefficient for detecting early osteoporosis. Some 30% of bone mineral must be lost before it can be diagnosed with certainty. X-rays are chiefly useful in excluding other bone diseases. Modern dual energy X-ray apparatus (DEXA) can measure with precision bone density in those sites which matter most (lumbar spine and femoral neck) and have rendered earlier methods obsolescent. Serial measurements can detect significant changes in six months. Population norms exist by which subjects may be divided into three groups – those with a high bone density who are not at risk, those with a very low density who require treatment and an intermediate group for whom repeat measurement is desirable to assess the rate of change. The rate of bone loss can also be measured biochemically. Specific methods of measuring bone collagen breakdown products will soon be available. At present, there are only about 50 DEXA in the country, many of which are used privately or for research, so that NHS use has to be restricted to those known to be at high risk. Clearly this will change as more equipment becomes available and screening for all women at the menopause can be foreseen.

PREVENTION IN CHILDHOOD AND YOUNG ADULT LIFE: WHAT CAN BE DONE?

The aim is to achieve and maintain a high peak bone mass so that despite the inevitable later age-related bone loss there is always enough reserve bone strength to resist trivial trauma. This means a balanced diet, adequate calcium, regular exercise and avoiding smoking and excess alcohol. Most dietary calcium comes from milk products (other than butter and cream). The other main sources are the water supply (usually about 100 mg/litre) and pulses and vegetables. Milk intolerance due to lactase deficiency – said to affect about 5% of people – can be countered by Lactaid, a proprietory yeast derived enzyme which converts lactose to galactose and glucose in milk overnight in the refrigerator. Cows' milk allergy can sometimes be overcome with goats' or sheep's milk products. The National Osteoporosis Society's recommended daily allowance of calcium is 800 mg for children, 1200 mg for teenagers and 1000 mg for adults, with extra during pregnancy and lactation. In the elderly and in postmenopausal women not on HRT extra calcium is needed to compensate for poor utilisation. (A pint of milk contains about 700 mg of calcium.)

Exercise builds and maintains strong bones and muscles. Animal experiments suggest exercise should be regular, should involve all parts of the skeleton, be fairly intense and preferably weight-bearing but need not be of the sort involved in long days of manual labour. For the sedentary, climbing upstairs instead of taking the lift or a brisk walk each morning to the bus or shops may suffice. Children and young adults need regular use of playgrounds and sports facilities. Exercise is beneficial at any age and probably works through the increased pull of muscles on bones. It has been shown to increase bone density in the young and middle-aged but not in the very old. Benefit in the elderly is probably through increased strength, confidence and balance resulting in fewer falls.

Prevention of postmenopausal osteoporosis depends on HRT. Not all women will want it or tolerate it. Not all will need it. Those least at risk will tend to be overweight (as adipose tissue contributes to postmenopausal circulating oestrogens). Women with primary osteoarthritis are also less at risk, since they tend to have dense, rigid bones. Conversely, a previous fracture indicates an increased risk.

ESTABLISHED OSTEOPOROSIS OF THE SPINE

The first vertebrae to collapse are usually in the lower dorsal or upper lumbar region. One wedged vertebra is not an uncommon finding in routine X-rays without a remembered history of pain or a fall. Two or more wedged vertebrae always suggest osteoporosis. In the Acute Vertebral Crush Fracture syndrome, tenderness is central and localised. Pain is more diffuse and symmetrical and may radiate to the front of the body or legs depending on the vertebral level. All movements, even coughing, are painful. There is no neurological impairment although testing for straight leg raising may bring on pain. The age of onset is 55 plus, lower in those at special risk, eg on corticosteroids. A 'slipped disc' is a common misdiagnosis. The differential diagnosis includes other causes of spinal collapse – chiefly cancer or myeloma. If the diagnosis is clear (usually because there has been a previous episode at another level) it is inhumane to transfer the patient to hospital if home care can be arranged. The patient should be nursed in a semi-sedentary position for as short a time as possible. Analgesics may include opiates initially. Later, paracetamol or co-praxamol are usually sufficient. Pain will improve in two to four weeks, occasionally longer. Spinal braces are unhelpful. Long-term treatment to prevent further deterioration can be started at this time.

LATE SPINAL OSTEOPOROSIS

In untreated spinal osteoporosis a series of crushed and wedged vertebral bodies lead to spinal shrinkage and kyphosis. Up to 25 cm of height may be lost. The classical picture is of an elderly woman with a smooth thoracic kyphosis, difficulty in holding her head up, a short trunk compared to her legs or arm span, 'concertina creases' around a protruding abdomen and loss of space between the rib margin and the pelvic brim (Fig 2). Breathlessness, hiatus hernia symptoms and pelvic floor weakness with incontinence reflect the cramping of the viscera in the reduced thoracic and abdominal cavities. Spinal pain, although not always a feature, is usually dominant. It arises from continued vertebral micro-fractures and collapse from strains on ligaments and posterior spinal joints caused by the altered body shape and probably from obstruction and congestion of spinal and nerve root venous plexuses. There may also be neck pains and tension headaches reflecting the difficulty in holding the head up to maintain forward gaze. Pain can arise from impaction of ribs on the pelvic brim and sometimes from accompanying osteomalacia. If further deterioration of bone density can be stopped (for example, by HRT or other drugs) remarkable functional recovery can occur.

Rehabilitation in severe spinal osteoporosis starts with non weight-bearing hydrotherapy exercises progressing to dry land physiotherapy designed to improve muscle strength, posture and confidence. Pelvic floor exercises help incontinence. Adaptations to home and to car seats can restore ability to manage and to drive. The National Osteoporosis Society can provide guidance on dress design for women to improve morale by disguising ugly humped backs.

PREVENTING HIP FRACTURE

A few hip fractures precede a fall – the weakened femoral neck cracks and the sufferer drops to the ground. In most, however, it is the fall which causes the fracture. Falls in the elderly generally occur indoors and from a standing height. Seasonal increases are due to icy or slippery pavements or to poor domestic lighting. Falls have extrinsic or intrinsic causes. The former are exemplified by grandmother coming to visit the family

Figure 2

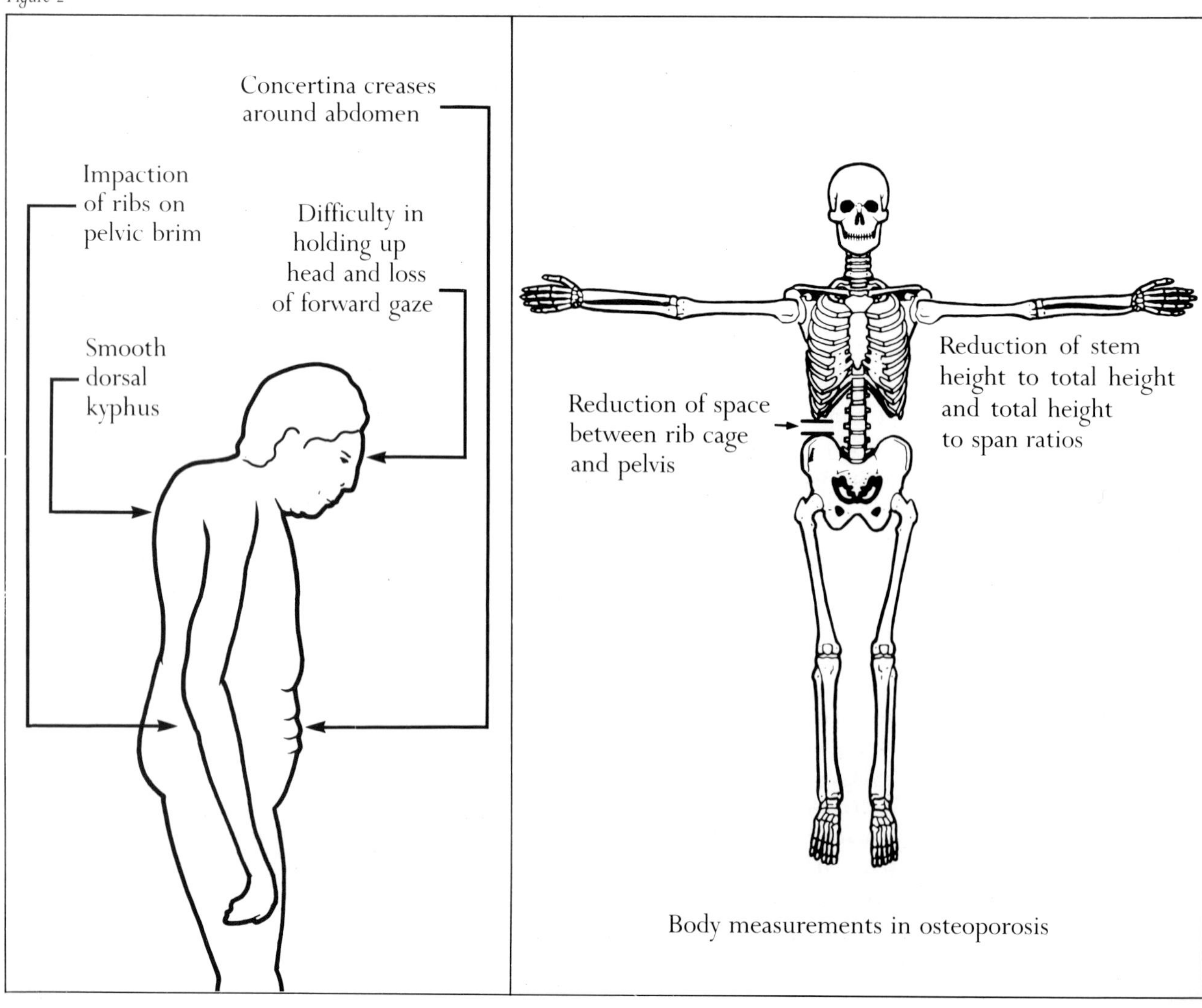

Body measurements in osteoporosis

and tripping over a child's toy left in a dark passage. Or at a railway ticket counter queue when a suitcase is put down to get out money and the elderly person who has just got her ticket backs away from the counter and is brought down by the obstruction. Most such extrinsic hazards are preventable, eg by installing good lighting, by tacking down or removing loose carpets, by carrying a stick or umbrella for additional balance. Other falls have intrinsic causes, such as muscle weakness, arthritis, impaired balance or eyesight. There may be temporary disturbances of attention or consciousness such as 'lazy sinus' and Stokes Adams attacks leading to dysrhythmia. Antihypertensives and diuretics cause postural hypotension and drop attacks. The elderly are often oversensitive to antidiabetics giving hypoglycaemic attacks. Reviewing the drug list or referring the patient for a cardiac pacemaker may help prevent such falls.

AFTER THE HIP FRACTURE

The Royal College of Physicians (January 1989) published recommendations to improve the outcome of hip fractures. Its report found that hip fracture patients spent too long lying on hard trolleys in casualty or X-ray departments developing pressure sores and pneumonia. Operations were frequently delayed and performed by inexperienced surgeons and anaesthetists at night without adequate previous medical assessment and preparation. Post-operative rehabilitation was inadequate and co-ordination of discharge from hospital with general practitioner and carers lacking. A survey one year later has found no improvement. The toll in mortality, residual morbidity and unnecessary dependency continues.

TREATMENTS FOR OSTEOPOROSIS

Not all treatment comes out of a bottle of tablets. Stopping smoking, reducing alcohol intake, getting the elderly out in the sun occasionally: these are life-style changes which can be important. Corticosteroids may need to be reduced or withdrawn. All patients on thyroid medication should have regular blood checks to see if the dose needs reduction.

HRT – This is now available as calendar packs of pills, as medicated adhesive patches or as implants. For women without a womb, continuous oestrogen treatment suffices. For those with an intact womb, balanced HRT is necessary with a progestogen being given for ten to twelve days per monthly cycle. The general rule is to start treatment at the lowest dose possible and gradually to increase guided by symptoms and, when available, blood oestrogen and FSH levels. Some women will tolerate one preparation but not another. HRT will stop, or slow, bone loss at any age although the longer after the menopause the less is the effect. It can be started up to the age of 65 – up to 70 is recommended in America – and should be continued for at least ten years. Even a short exposure to HRT will reduce the relative risk of hip fracture later. It should be preceded by general physical, pelvic and breast examinations, to ensure that there are no contra-indications before treatment is started. There is evidence that HRT also reduces the risks of heart attacks and strokes and these benefits far outweigh any (disputed) possible increase in the long-term breast cancers rate.

Calcitonin – Available as salcatonin (Calsynar). This is effective, usually well tolerated, but must be given by injection, usually two or three times a week to start with. It is expensive.

Bisphosphonates – Etidronate (Didronel) is the only one currently available for prescription under the NHS at the prescriber's discretion as it currently awaits a full product licence for osteoporosis. Four hundred mg is given daily for two weeks and repeated every three months. Calcium supplements equivalent to 500 mg of calcium are taken nightly. Etidronate should be given in the middle of a six-hour fast, as food reduces absorption. It is a practical alternative for women for whom HRT is inappropriate or not tolerated.

Anabolic steroids – Stanazolol tablets and nandralone decanoate in oil depôt injections are available. Both may be masculinising and usually cannot be continued for more than three years.

Fluoride – Given as tablets or capsules of 20 mg of sodium fluoride, it will improve spinal density and reduce the frequency of further spinal fractures, but may increase the risk of limb fractures. This may be a matter of dose so this should be kept to 40 mg a day, covered with calcium supplements, which should be taken at least 4 hours spaced before or after the fluoride.

Vitamin D – About 400-500 international units per day is the normal requirement, and can be given to the elderly or disabled who do not get out in the sun. More than this is not helpful and large doses may be harmful.

More detailed information on aspects of osteoporosis and treatment can be obtained from the National Osteoporosis Society at P O Box 10, Radstock, Bath, BA3 3YB.

January 1991

PAGET'S DISEASE OF BONE

D C Anderson
Department of Medicine
Chinese University of Hong Kong
Prince of Wales Hospital
Shatin
New Territories
Hong Kong

INTRODUCTION

Paget's disease, also described originally by Sir James Paget as 'osteitis deformans' (1) is a chronic, potentially disabling focal bone disease of uncertain aetiology, characterised by dramatically increased osteoclastic and secondary osteoblastic activity. Its incidence varies widely across the world, being particularly high in the United Kingdom, especially parts of the North-West, where the incidence in a radiological survey 15 years ago was found to be as high as 8% in some towns, in men over the age of 55 years (2). Lower levels were found elsewhere in the UK (about 2% in Aberdeen), with a moderate incidence in France and very low levels in Scandinavia (3). Other hot spots include New Zealand, parts of Australia, and the plain round Buenos Aires (4); there is a moderate incidence in America. In many parts of the world the incidence is unknown, but it is exceedingly rare in China, Hong Kong and Japan, although when it does occur it appears to be the same disease.

The disease is seen in all races, and it is unclear whether the wide range in incidence is due to variation in exposure to the aetiological agent, and/or to variation in susceptibility to it. Such variation might be genetic or acquired (as for example through Vitamin D deficiency early in life or at the time of initial exposure to the putative infectious agent). A number of genetic studies have failed to reveal any very impressive HLA associations (5). The close racial similarity between native British (high incidence) and Norwegians (very low incidence) for example, as well as the comparable incidences among black and white Americans suggests that the variations in disease incidence are mainly environmental. There is a strong clustering of the disease within families, with an expectation of Paget's disease among siblings of an affected case of about 7 times higher than the background (odds ratio of 7), but this could also be environmental (5). Within a family with more than one individual affected, the disease varies enormously in its distribution and severity between family members, just as it does among unrelated individuals.

There are some peculiar variants of the disease. A related condition, which appears to be of dominant inheritance, is seen in an extended family in Belfast, and has been named 'familial expansile osteolysis' (6); in this disease there is both generalised and focal excessive bone resorption. So-called juvenile Paget's disease is atypical in its early onset and more generalised in nature. Finally, in Avellino in Northern Italy a form exists characterised by the frequent occurrence of osteoclastomas of jaw, a form of bone tumour that is otherwise exceptionally rare in Paget's disease (7).

PATHOPHYSIOLOGY

Osteoclasts are the multi-nucleated giant cell tunnelling machines of bone. Every medical student is familiar with the picture of Sir James Paget's first case, with extensive bone involvement and massive bony deformity in a deaf old man with a massively thickened skull. Today we still see such cases, but in terms of understanding how the disease develops we have to look much earlier, and particularly at the interface between Pagetic and normal bone. In such cases it has been well documented by serial radiographs that the disease advances through bone at a speed of about 12mm per year (8). This is particularly well seen on X-rays of the skull showing the picture of osteoporosis circumscripta, where the disease is initially particularly osteolytic and so shows up as a clear interface between the diseased and the normal bone, and thus the disease advance can be measured, (or could before old X-rays were so readily and rapidly destroyed!).

HISTOLOGY

Most of the information on the histological appearance of Paget's disease in vivo is derived from transiliac bone biopsies taken from the iliac crest. These are best conducted using local anaesthesia (10ml 1% lignocaine in 1:200,000 adrenaline), with skin, subcutaneous tissues and periosteum anaesthetised on the outside. On the inside of the ilium the periosteum is anaesthetised in like fashion via a 19-gauge needle directed to the predicted site of the biopsy hole through muscle, keeping close to the bone. Using a Lalor biopsy drill, despite the vascularity of the bone, a sample can be obtained safely by an experienced operator, provided the patient's coagulation state is first checked and found to be normal. This is only justified with the patient's consent and either in case of genuine doubt concerning the diagnosis, or as part of an approved research protocol. It is of course only relevant in the 70% or so of cases with pelvic involvement.

The **bone structure** itself is highly abnormal, most dramatically seen under crossed polarised light, which reveals a mosaic of chopped-up lamellar and true woven bone (9,10), the result of many repeated and apparently random cycles of aggressive resorption and bone formation. At the advanced stage of disease in which most patients present, there is a marked increase in bone mass per unit volume, as well as thickening and expansion of the bone. The **bone surface** has a great increase in number and size of osteoclasts, with probably a hundred-fold increase in osteoclast mass in some cases. This bone resorption is closely followed by bone formation, which remains coupled at the local level. Since with effective treatment directed against the osteoclast (see below) the osteoblasts lay down normal lamellar bone again and eventually return to a normal state in which most bone surfaces are quiescent, we may presume that the primary abnormality lies within the osteoclasts.

Numerous studies have apparently identified inclusion bodies in Pagetic osteoclasts (11), and these have been repeatedly attributed to infection by one or more paramyxoviruses. However, the specificity of these particles, thought to be due to viral nucleocapsids, is in some doubt, and there certainly remains the possibility that they are the result of some normal osteoclast product, rather than viral infection. The time is certainly ripe for a critical re-examination of the ultrastructural changes in the bone cells in Paget's disease.

EVIDENCE FOR AN INFECTIOUS (VIRAL) AETIOLOGY (Fig 1)

This might best be described as circumstantial but persuasive! First, we need to consider how the osteoclasts normally function, and so how they might be uniquely susceptible to persistent local infection, if certain criteria for the infecting organism were to be met.

Briefly, the osteoclast is a multi-nucleated bone-resorbing machine, that carries out its function most elegantly in the tunnelling process through compact cortical bone that leads to the formation of the Haversian systems. Much evidence points to a greater efficiency of this process in the presence of larger cells, a possible consequence of the need for the osteoclast to stick to the bone surface by means of a sealing ring, under which it pumps its protons to a pH of 4 or less, and proteolytic enzymes (acid hydrolases). This dissolves mineral and destroys matrix, a process which appears to be completed by macrophages, which may also lay down a cement line for osteoblasts to attach to. The coupling process appears to result from a stimulus either from the osteoclasts direct, or from the creation of a hole, for osteoblast precursors to divide and lay down new bone concentrically.

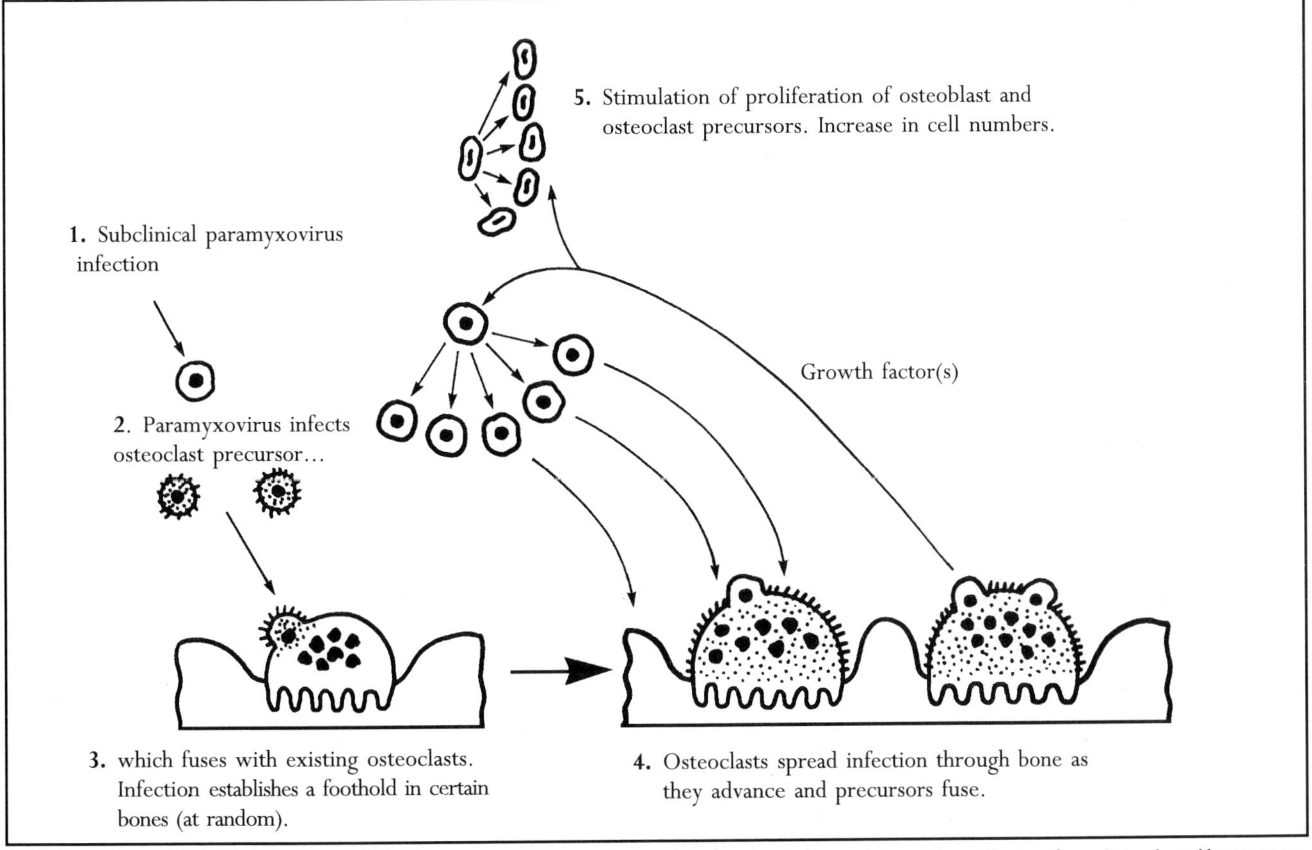

Figure 1. Model to suggest how a persistent virus coding for a cell fusion protein (spikes) might lead to Paget's disease, with excessive proliferation of osteoclast and osteoblast precursors. Redrawn from: Anderson D C. Handb. Exp. Phamacol Vol 107, Eds Mundy & Martin, Springer-Verlag 1993, p426, by kind permission of Springer-Verlag.

The osteoclast becomes multinucleated by the process of precursors fusing with one another; presumably this necessitates the production of a fusion protein for insertion into the cell surface membrane. One of the attractions of the paramyxovirus hypothesis is that such viruses make cells fuse by producing their own fusion protein, so leading to the formation of syncytial plaques. The spread through and damage to tissues caused by these viruses results in no small measure from this property. Thus a single infection of marrow precursors might be followed by selective sequestration and persistence of the virus in the osteoclast, in a site now relatively or absolutely hidden from the immune system.

It was the EM and some immunocytological evidence implicating paramyxoviruses which led us 10 years ago to look for evidence of an non-human source, possibly a domestic animal. In brief, our study and one from New Zealand show that Paget's disease patients have a particularly high incidence of exposure to domestic dogs (12-14). 22% of our patients and 7-17 % of two groups of controls, know they had close contact with a dog with distemper (the dog equivalent of measles) (13). Finally, we have direct evidence, based on the techniques of in situ hybridisation and the polymerase chain reaction (PCR), for the presence at least in two thirds of cases, of canine distemper virus (CDV) (15,16). However, the PCR findings have so far not been confirmed, and as far as I know in situ hybridisation has not been tried, by others. We do have definite evidence that in the dog, CDV can infect the osteoclast, and suggestive evidence that the virus may cause a bone disease, metaphyseal osteopathy in the dog (17). There is no evidence of a humoral immune response to CDV in Paget's patients (18).

In summary, the case against canine distemper must be said to be 'not proven', and a fresh approach is clearly needed. It has to be admitted, too, that CDV infection of dogs was ubiquitous 30-60 years ago (when we infer that the disease must have started) and still is, not just in the UK but in many parts of the world such as China where Paget's is rare. It seems probable that other factors, such as close proximity with sick pet animals (part of the family in many UK households), virus persistence in a damp climate and possibly host susceptibility through vitamin D deficiency at the time of infection, might all be implicated in the high incidence in the North West of England. We may never know.

THE CLINICAL SPECTRUM AND DIAGNOSIS OF PAGET'S DISEASE

(See Refs 19-20)

Clinical spectrum

The diagnosed cases are in any community the tip of the iceberg of this disease - probably less than 5%. In large part this must be because through most of its history, and in most cases throughout life, the disease is asymptomatic. This is not to belittle Paget's disease, because there is no doubt that it can be responsible for great disability of long-standing, or fatal complications such as bone sarcomas.

The disease picks out anything from one up to 20-30 bones, apparently at random, with a propensity for larger bones and those with a very large surface to volume ratio, such as the vertebrae and pelvis. This may simply be a function of the initial number of active osteoclasts available for fusion with an infected precursor, at the presumed time of onset of the disease; once in a bone, the disease is apparently free to spread throughout its length. Smaller bones and those with more cortical bone, would obviously have fewer cells to become infected.

It is convenient to think of the disease as having four phases as follows; a phase of **initial infection** (?) (probably clinically silent); a phase of **asymptomatic advance** through affected bones; a phase of **progressive deformity**; and finally one of **late complications**. The problem is that inevitably a clinical description becomes anecdotal, since every case is, literally, unique in its extent and distribution.

The clinical spectrum; generalisations and anecdotes!

Some useful **generalisations** are as follows. **Pain** in or possibly related to a Pagetic bone should always be assumed to be due to the disease, regardless of whether or not there is an incremental fracture, and the patient treated accordingly. It is often dull and boring in nature, and not relieved by analgesics. **Deformity** depends upon the stresses to which that bone is subjected; forward bowing and loss of the sharp anterior border of the tibia is common, and lateral and forward bowing of the femur; basilar invagination of the skull. **Superficial bones** are the only ones in which a confident diagnosis can be made on clinical grounds alone. Some bones are therefore greatly **over-represented in the examination setting**; these include the skull, radius, maxilla and tibia. For any bone it is always instructive to ask where the disease started; here the deformity is greatest, and it does affect the nature of the deformity, for instance in the tibia, which bows differently according to which end is affected first. **Unusual accompaniments** can produce bizarre and unique features; for example involvement of the frontal bone and sinusitis, leading to gross frontal bossing with 'inflation' of the front of the head; or gross bowing of the right humerus in a man whose occupation involved unusual stresses on this particular bone. **Primary malignant tumours of bone**; over the age of forty, probably more than half are associated with and develop in underlying Pagetic bone. There is probably more **non-specific malaise** associated with Paget's disease than doctors give credit for. **High output cardiac failure** is exceptionally rare, although the bone is highly vascular, and in cases of 'mega-Paget's' cardiac output is moderately increased.

Table I.
Distribution of lesions on bone scan

(from Ref 9; data of Meunier & Kanis)

	France (Lyon) (863 lesions)	England (Sheffield) (1,287 lesions)
Pelvis	72%	71%
Lumbar spine	58%	51%
Femora	55%	49%
Thoracic spine	45%	43%
Sacrum	44%	28%
Skull	42%	38%
Tibiae	35%	25%
Humeri	31%	17%
Scapulae	24%	19%
Cervical spine	14%	16%
Ribs	12%	11%
Clavicles	11%	5%
Face	11%	4%
Calcaneum	10%	9%
Patellae	7%	6%
Hands	6%	3%
Feet	5%	8%

Diagnosis

This is most commonly suspected on the basis of finding an elevated level of **serum alkaline phosphatase**; this depends upon the number of bones affected and the stage of development (presumptive duration) of the disease. As a marker it is therefore of variable value. Urinary hydroxyproline (HOP) or HOP/creatinine ratio adds nothing to the diagnosis, and no other measure of bone resorption or formation will, I suspect, add to our clinical armamentarium in the future!

X-ray is reliable when the disease is advanced. Particularly reliable is the finding of generalised expansion and deformity of a long bone, generally more marked at one end than the other, and with a **lytic leading edge (blade of grass appearance)**. Likewise in long bones the pattern of **incremental fractures**, stacked one above the other on the inner aspect of the cortex of the outer concavity of an expanded and 'fuzzy' tibia or femur is diagnostic. **Osteoporosis circumscripta**, strangely, which is only seen in the skull, possibly because of the paucity of muscle attachments, is a highly diagnostic finding. Particularly fascinating is the occasional case where the disease has clearly arrested on coming to an unclosed suture, demonstrating the incompetence of the osteoclast in eating through anything other than calcified tissue.

Bone scans, which are carried out with 99-Technetium-labelled bisphosphonate, are very helpful in the diagnosis. The finding of a bone or bones of random distribution, showing intense and uniform uptake over a considerable length is diagnostic. Whenever a radiological skeletal survey is considered it should be dismissed in favour of the much cheaper and more informative bone scan, with subsequent X-ray, if desired, of 'hot' bones. **Skeletal surveys are never justified.**

RECENT ADVANCES IN TREATMENT OF PAGET'S DISEASE (See Refs 20 and 21)

There can be few diseases that were previously so resistant to treatment where advances over the past 25 years, and especially the past decade have been so dramatic. I shall concentrate here on the latest bisphosphonates, and rather peremptorily dismiss their competitors. **Calcitonin** was a big advance over analgesics and placebos in its day, but it is expensive, only ever modestly effective, is a nuisance however it is given, and often causes symptoms. Nasal insufflation may be better tolerated than injections, but it is still simply a means of sedating the disease, and offers no prospect of stamping it out. **Mithramycin**, although sometimes highly effective is too toxic to be considered in the face of the bisphosphonates.

The bisphosphonates (Fig 2)

In order to work our way through the plethora of bisphosphonates a few generalisations may be helpful. They were first developed as **analogues of pyrophosphate, an inhibitor of bone mineralisation**, to inhibit ectopic calcification. They are all equipotent in this regard, the first to be developed being disodium etidronate. Where they differ dramatically is in the capacity of the R2 sidechain to augment their potency in inhibiting bone resorption. **Etidronate** is relatively weak, so high doses have to be given with the inevitable attendant risk of inhibiting mineralisation, wherever bone is being laid down. Bone is laid down at an exceptional rate in Pagetic bones, so here the mineralisation defect is greatest. In the UK at least, few if any doctors experienced in Paget's disease are now using etidronate, although it is the only bisphosphonate licensed for this condition! **Dichloromethylene bisphosphonate** is better in this regard than etidronate, but as far as I know there is no prospect of it being licensed for Paget's disease in the UK, and it has a less favourable mineralisation/resorption profile than pamidronate.

Pamidronate is the present front-runner among available treatments for the disease, but it is definitely not the last word; it is likely to be superseded at least for the resistant case, by even more potent bisphosphonates, such as alendronate. Used properly (vide infra) it is possible with one or more courses to induce a full biochemical remission (SAP falling to normal) in 90% of cases in whom the SAP is initially elevated. Somewhere in the region of 10-15% of cases can be put into permanent remission; our experience suggests that when this occurs it is usually after the first course, and we suspect that there may be a sub-population of patients who are especially responsive.

Name	Chemical Formula	Approx Relative Anti-Osteoclastic Potency
pyrophosphate	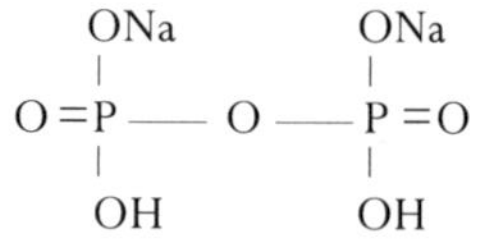 ONa ONa O=P — O — P=O OH OH	
etidronate	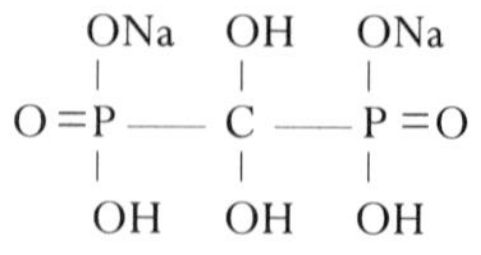 ONa OH ONa O=P — C — P=O OH OH OH	1
clodronate	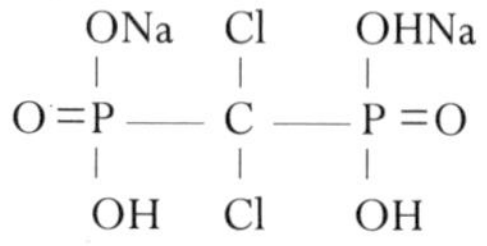 ONa Cl OHNa O=P — C — P=O OH Cl OH	10
pamidronate	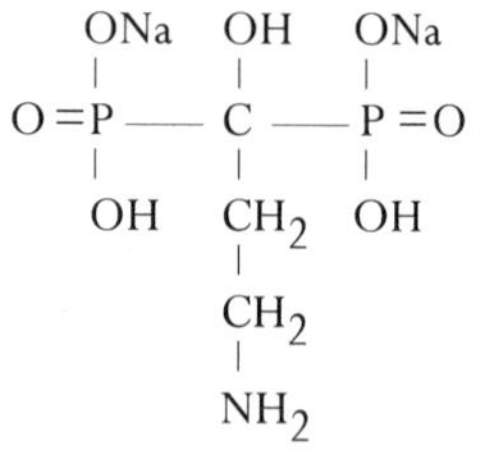 ONa OH ONa O=P — C — P=O OH CH_2 OH CH_2 NH_2	100
alendronate	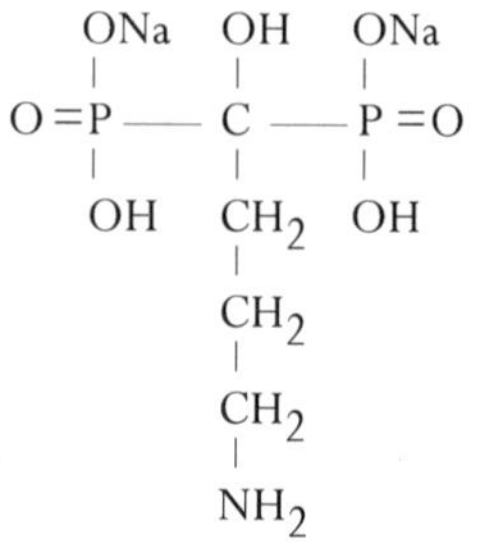 ONa OH ONa O=P — C — P=O OH CH_2 OH CH_2 CH_2 NH_2	1000

Figure 2. Structure of four of the major bisphosphonates (disodium salts), and their approximate relative potencies as inhibitors of bone resorption.

The drug is only available commercially as an IV preparation, and must be given diluted in saline because it is highly irritant. Many regard this formulation as a nuisance, but since the drug can be given as a short series of infusions, spaced out at intervals of 1-2 weeks, and on average does not have to be repeated for 2 years or so there are advantages for a well organised hospital-based unit. There are very good reasons for expertise to be concentrated in such centres, which are generally run by rheumatologists or endocrinologists. Compliance can be assured, there are no unpleasant GI side-effects, and the precise dose given is known. We recommend that a series of infusions be given as follows; if the SAP is below 500 IU/l, a 30mg infusion over two hours, followed by three of 60mg, each over four hours. If the SAP exceeds 500 IU/l we use six 60mg infusions. The infusions are spaced out at 2-week intervals. The drug is extremely well tolerated, although patients may experience a pyrexial response and increased bone pain after the first one or two doses (22). In fact there is no clearly-established most effective dose regime, but total doses of less than 180mg are undoubtedly sub-optimal. This raises the question as to what markers of response should be followed and when.

Assessment of response

All generalisations are false, but the following are reasonably justifiable.

1) The biochemical response is maximal at about six months, and SAP, although an index of formation rather than resorption, is a necessary and sufficient biochemical marker.

2) Bone scans, when informative (ie when they show extremely 'hot' bones) are the most sensitive; they should not be repeated until six months after therapy. If 'hot spots' remain, then the disease is still focally active and will eventually relapse, regardless of the biochemistry.

3) X-rays are most informative when there is lytic disease, but should be used highly selectively.

4) Although clinical benefit results in at least two thirds of symptomatic cases, it is difficult to prove scientifically, and is a relatively insensitive marker, in view of the variation in bones affected, distribution and severity of disease. However, biochemical relapse is generally associated with a return of symptoms.

5) Bone biopsy will provide histological evidence of the degree of response, but of course only samples one piece of the skeleton, and is useless when the pelvis is not involved.

Who should be treated with pamidronate, and how aggressively?

Experienced clinicians in this field vary from the complacent to the gung-ho! My own feeling is that all young patients, and those of any age with symptoms that **may** be due to the disease, merit treatment. Furthermore, I believe that it is cost-effective to give doses (see above) that are effective, rather than doses known to be sub-optimal. For retreatment, higher doses, with individual infusions of up to 180mg over six hours may be given.

Predicting the future; the promise of the newer bisphosphonates

The bisphosphonates exert their beneficial effects in Paget's, as in malignant hypercalcaemia, bone metastases and osteoporosis (for which conditions they are being primarily developed by drug companies) by inhibiting the osteoclasts. There is good evidence for alendronate that it binds to bone beneath the osteoclasts, and is concentrated on the resorbing bone surface (23). The drugs then seem to make the bone unrecognisable to the osteoclast, and they may act simply by breaking the vicious cycle whereby resorbing osteoclasts call for more recruits, in the form of dividing and proliferating precursors. It is to be hoped that the more potent bisphosphonates will improve the response rate to that currently seen in a small minority of patients with pamidronate, namely apparent biochemical roentgenological, histological and clinical cure.

REFERENCES

1. Paget J. On a form of chronic inflammation of bones (osteitis deformans). *Med Chir Trans Lond* 1877; **60**: 37-63.

2. Barker D J P, Chamberlain A T, Guyer P B et al. Paget's disease of bone: the Lancashire focus. *Br Med J* 1980; **280**: 1105-7.

3. Barker D J P. The epidemiology of Paget's disease of bone *Br Med Bull* 1984; **40**: 396-400.

4. Mautalen C, Pumarino H, Blanco M C, et al. Paget's Disease: the South American experience. *Sem Arthr Rheum* 1994; **23**: 226-7.

5. Siris E. Epidemiological aspects of Paget's disease: family history and relationship to other medical conditions. *Sem Arthr Rheum* 1994; **23**: 222-225.

6. Osterberg P H, Wallace R G H, Adams D A et al. Familial expansile osteolysis. *J Bone Joint Surg* 1988; **70**: 255-260.

7. Jacobs T P, Michelsen J, Polay J S et al. Giant cell tumor in Paget's disease of bone. Familial and geographic clustering. *Cancer* 1979; **44**:742-747.

8. Maklugue B, Malghem J. Dynamic radiological patterns of Paget's disease of bone. *Clin Orth Rel Res* 1987; **217**: 126-151.

9. Meunier P J, Coindre J, Edouard C M et al. Bone histomorphometry in Paget's disease. Quantitative and dynamic analysis of Pagetic and non-Pagetic bone tissue. *Arthritis Rheum* 1980; **23**: 1095-1103.

10. Richardson P C, Anderson D C, Denton J et al. Changes in bone morphology following treatment of Paget's disease of bone with APD in Takahashi HE (ed). *Bone morphometry*, 1990, Nishimura/Smith-Gordon, Niigata, pp235-238.

11. Harvey I, Viral aetiology of Paget's disease of bone: a review. *J Roy Soc Med* 1984; **77**: 943-948.

12. O'Driscoll J B, Anderson D C, Past pets and Paget's disease. *Lancet* 1985; **2**: 919-921.

13. O'Driscoll J B, Buckler H M, Jeacock J, et al. Dogs, distemper and osteitis deformans: a further epidemiological study. *Bone Miner* 1990; **11**: 209-216

14. Holdaway I M, Ibbertson H K, Wattie et al. Previous dog ownership in Paget's disease. *Bone Miner* 1990; **8**: 53-58

15. Gordon M T, Anderson D C, and Sharpe P T. Canine distemper virus localised in bone cells of patients with Paget's disease. *Bone* 1991; **12**: 195-201.

16. Gordon M T, Mee A P, Anderson D C et al. Canine distemper virus transcripts sequenced from Pagetic bone. *Bone Miner* 1992; **19**: 159-174.

17. Mee A P, Gordon M T, May C et al. Canine distemper virus transcripts detected in the bone cells of dogs with metaphyseal osteopathy. *Bone* 1993; **14**: 59-67.

18. Gordon M T, Mee A P and Sharpe P T. Paramyxoviruses and Paget's disease. *Sem Arthr Rheum* 1994; **23**: 232-234.

19. Singer F R, Wallach S, (eds). *Paget's disease of bone; clinical assessment, present and future therapy*. Elsevier 1991.

20. Kanis J A. *Pathophysiology and treatment of Paget's disease of bone*. Martin Dunnitz, 1991.

21. Cantrill J A, Anderson D C. Treatment of Paget's disease of bone. *Clin Endocrinol* (Oxf) 1990; **32**: 507-518.

22. Anderson D C, Richardson P C, Kingsley Brown J et al. Intravenous pamidronate: evolution of an effective treatment strategy. *Sem Arthr Rheum* 1994; **23**: 273-275.

23. Sato M, Grasser W, Endo et al. Bisphosphonate action. Alendronate localisation in rat bone and effects on osteoclast ultrastructure. *J Clin Invest* 1991; **88**: 2095-2105.

September 1994

REFLEX SYMPATHETIC DYSTROPHY

A L Herrick
Lecturer/Consultant Rheumatologist
University of Manchester Rheumatic Diseases Centre
Hope Hospital
Salford

INTRODUCTION AND DEFINITION

As with many conditions or spectra of conditions attracting a variety of names (Table 1), reflex sympathetic dystrophy (RSD) is poorly understood and often ill-defined. To complicate matters further, it can be very difficult to treat and can have devastating effects in severely affected individuals, its most characteristic feature being persistent, often burning pain.

The first description of what we now recognise as RSD was by Mitchell and colleagues, who graphically reported the plight of soldiers who developed the condition as a complication of peripheral nerve injury resulting from gun-shot wounds of the American Civil War (1). The term 'RSD' was coined by Evans almost 50 years ago (2). Recent years have witnessed increasing interest in the definition, pathophysiology, and management of RSD. It is now recognised that RSD is not a distinct entity but should be considered rather as a descriptive term which does not imply aetiology. At the VIth World Congress on Pain the following definition for RSD in the light of current knowledge was suggested (3):

'RSD is a descriptive term meaning a complex disorder or group of disorders that may develop as a consequence of trauma affecting the limbs, with or without an obvious nerve lesion. RSD may also develop after visceral diseases, and central nervous system lesions, or, rarely, without an obvious antecedent event. It consists of pain and related sensory abnormalities, abnormal blood flow and sweating, abnormalities in the motor system and changes in the structure of both superficial and deep tissues ('trophic' changes). It is not necessary that all components are present. It is agreed that the term 'reflex sympathetic dystrophy' is used in a descriptive sense and does not imply specific underlying mechanisms'.

Table 1.
Some of the terms used to describe what are now considered under the definition of 'RSD'

Sudeck's atrophy
Causalgia (minor or major)
Shoulder-hand syndrome
Post-traumatic dystrophy
Post-traumatic osteoporosis
Chronic traumatic oedema
Algodystrophy
Algoneurodystrophy
Post-traumatic angiospasm
Post-traumatic spreading neuralgia
Painful osteoporosis

The terminology in the literature surrounding RSD can be confusing. The term 'causalgia' relates to severe burning pain following a major peripheral nerve injury, usually traumatic (4), and patients with causalgia form a sub-group within the above definition of RSD. Sometimes used is the term 'sympathetically mediated pain'. This does not completely equate with RSD but two points need to be made in this respect:

1. 'Sympathetically mediated pain' may form a sub-group within the broader definition of RSD, without marked thermoregulatory or trophic changes (5). It seems likely that sympathetically mediated pain in many instances develops into 'full-blown' RSD. This pain should respond to sympathetic blockade.

2. While certain cases of RSD are believed by some workers to be 'sympathetically independent', as discussed later it seems likely that the sympathetic nervous system plays a role in the majority of cases of RSD, although the importance of this may vary between patients. One school of thought is that the sympathetic nervous system is important early on in the pathogenesis of RSD, but that the pain later becomes 'sympathetically independent'(6).

PREVALENCE AND PRECIPITATING FACTORS

RSD, especially in its more minor forms, is not rare. Its reported incidence depends on how carefully it is looked for. For example, careful prospective

Table 2.
Clinical features of RSD

- **Pain** (usually commencing distally, often 'burning')
- **Tenderness** (often hyperaesthesia, allodynia)
- **Oedema**
- **Vasomotor and sudomotor changes**
- **Weakness, tremor, muscle spasm**
- **Dystrophic changes of nail and skin**
- **Contractures**

studies have found incidences after Colles' or tibial fractures of up to 37%, whereas earlier work had suggested that RSD complicated fewer than 2% of fractures (7,8). While RSD used to be regarded as a syndrome of older age groups, patients of any age may be affected and RSD is now increasingly recognised in children (9).

RSD can complicate many conditions other than fractures (10) and this is more widely acknowledged as clinical awareness of RSD increases. 'Precipitating factors' can be broadly divided into three groups: trauma including fractures, central nervous system or spinal disorders, and visceral lesions such as myocardial infarction. However, in some cases no underlying cause can be found and this is especially true in children (9).

Recent studies examining these issues include a carefully conducted prospective study of 100 patients in which an incidence of RSD after traumatic brain injury of 12%, occurring in the spastic upper extremity, was reported (11). Of particular interest to rheumatologists and orthopaedic surgeons is that RSD can occur after lumbar spine surgery, arthroscopy, and in conditions associated with bone fragility (12-14).

Much has been written about certain personality traits being associated with RSD. There is no doubt that many patients with RSD demonstrate marked behavioural changes but the question is whether these are a contributory cause, or a result, of the RSD. Opinion varies, but two recent reviews suggest that as yet there is no definite evidence that certain personality traits actually predispose to the development of RSD (15,16). Neurogenic pain can undoubtedly induce illness behaviour, which often results in patients with RSD being disbelieved by doctors. This increases their distress.

CLINICAL FEATURES

RSD generally affects the extremities: hand and wrist, knee, or foot and ankle are most commonly involved although occasionally a whole limb is affected as, for example, in that variant described as shoulder-hand syndrome when shoulder, hand and wrist are all involved. Not infrequently there may be bilateral involvement (17).

The clinical features of RSD are summarised in Table 2. These are important because RSD is predominantly a clinical diagnosis: although investigations as discussed below can aid in diagnosis, in themselves they are rarely conclusive. Variation in diagnosic criteria as well as in the terminology of RSD has hampered progress in its understanding and treatment, and this is an area currently being addressed (3).

The main clinical feature of RSD is persistent pain, often described as a burning. It may begin in the extremity then spread proximally in a non-dermatomal distribution, and generally it is different in character from the pain of the condition which precipitated the RSD, for example the pain immediately following an injury. The terms 'allodynia' and 'hyperpathia' are often used in relation to RSD. These mean, respectively, pain provoked by a stimulus which does not under normal circumstances produce pain, and an exaggerated reaction to a painful stimulus, especially if repetitive. Tenderness which is often generalised usually accompanies the pain and also often oedema.

Vasomotor and sudomotor changes may be prominent. Colour and temperature changes are variable. The affected area may be red, mottled or cyanotic. Often warm in the early stages of RSD, the limb may then become cool. Increased sweating is common. There may be a prominent motor component with tremor, weakness, or sometimes muscle spasm.

The evolution of RSD is sometimes divided into three stages (4,18,19), although it is often difficult to separate out these stages in any one individual. All the features described above are typical of stage 1 ('acute'), when vasomotor changes may be predominantly vasodilatory and the limb initially warm. Stage 2 ('dystrophic') is characteristically associated with continuing pain and vasomotor changes with a tendency for the limb to be cool, and early dystrophic changes of skin and nails with the onset of contractures. Stage 3 ('atrophic') may bring a diminution of the pain and vasomotor changes but increased disability which is now predominantly due to irreversible atrophic changes and contracture, and sometimes ankylosis. Durations of three to six months for each of Stages 1 and 2, and variable (up to years) for Stage 3 have been quoted but again, these are variable. Not all patients progress to Stages 2 and 3 and there is some doubt as to how useful this clinical staging is.

RSD has also been classified as 'definite' (pain, tenderness, oedema, vasomotor and sudomotor changes), 'probable' (pain, tenderness, and either vasomotor and sudomotor changes or swelling), 'possible' (vasomotor or sudomotor changes) and 'doubtful' (unexplained pain and tenderness) (20). The important point seems to be to have a high index of suspicion of RSD, for, as discussed below, this has implications for management.

DIFFERENTIAL DIAGNOSIS

The differential diagnosis is that of a swollen, tender limb extremity. Trauma, cellulitis, inflammatory arthritis and malignancy might be considered, but a careful history will usually allow the diagnosis to be made, especially if there is a background of trauma or other precipitating factor for RSD.

INVESTIGATIONS

There is no 'diagnostic test' for RSD but X-rays and isotope bone scans may be helpful. Characteristic and well described radiographic abnormalities are patchy osteoporosis of the affected extremity (most marked juxta-articularly but which is often diffuse) and sometimes erosive changes (21). Isotope bone scanning (delayed imaging) shows increased uptake which is not confined to the periarticular areas (22). Three phase imaging has been described in RSD as showing patterns which vary depending on the clinical stage of RSD at which the patient is studied. In a study of 181 patients, what were defined as blood pool, early and delayed fixations were all increased in patients studied within the first 20 weeks of development of RSD, whereas patients examined later showed normal or reduced uptakes during different phases, the pattern of which depended upon the clinical staging (23). Regarding measurement of bone density, a recent study has shown that reduction in bone density, as measured by a radiographic scoring system and single photon absorptiometry, was greater and more prolonged after Colles' fractures complicated by RSD than after Colles' fractures without RSD (24).

Thermography, by detecting assymmetries in limb temperature, can aid in the diagnosis of RSD (25). However, its use is limited by its availability. Measurements of skin blood flow and temperature can usefully document the effectiveness of sympathetic blockade, but these remain mainly research tools at present (26).

PATHOPHYSIOLOGY

This is not fully understood and is an area of much current debate and complex hypotheses (5,6,10,27-9). Several factors must play a role to account for the fact that a minority of individuals, in response to what may be a relatively trivial insult (or with no predisposing injury or condition at all) develop the severe pain of RSD, in association with oedema, autonomic and trophic changes.

It seems likely that both peripheral and central mechanisms are involved. After an initial noxious stimulus, nociceptors are activated. Roberts' hypothesis, which is often quoted and highlights the role of both low-threshold mechanoreceptors and central dorsal-horn mechanisms in the pathogenesis of RSD, suggests that:

1. The initial nociceptive stimulus activates unmyelinated (C) nociceptors at the site of injury, and as a result wide dynamic range (WDR) neurones in the dorsal horn are activated and sensitised.

2. These sensitised WDR neurones can now be activated by input from low threshold mechanoreceptors. This would explain the phenomenon of allodynia.

3. As low threshold mechanoreceptors can be activated by sympathetic efferent activity as well as by light touch, then a vicious cycle can be perceived incorporating the concept of 'sympathetically mediated pain' (27).

While this theory usefully emphasises the importance of both peripheral and central mechanisms in the pathogenesis of RSD, it is now felt unlikely that WDR neurone sensitisation occurs, but that other central mechanisms are important (6). Whatever the mechanism, it seems probable that alteration of central information processing results (5).

Regarding the peripheral sensitisation of receptors in RSD, it is now believed that the alpha-1 adrenoreceptor may play an important role here. Campbell et al, with particular reference to peripheral nerve injury, point out how sympathetic activity may activate not only mechanoreceptors, but also nociceptors directly (28). They suggest that alpha-adrenergic receptors may become expressed on nociceptors in certain cases of soft tissue or nerve injury, and that these receptors can be activated by sympathetic discharge through release of noradrenaline. This is in keeping with their observation that patients with sympathetically mediated pain may experience relief with drugs interfering with alpha-adrenergic function. Again we have a vicious cycle, this time incorporating pain (caused initially by trauma), sympathetic discharge, noradrenaline release, alpha-adrenoreceptor activation and further nociceptor activity. Janig has highlighted this concept of a vicious cycle involving sympathetic activity and an abnormal state of afferent neurones in the pathophysiology of RSD, and believes that the sympathetic nervous system is fundamentally involved (5). The fact that many patients do respond to sympathetic blockade does support an important role for the sympathetic nervous system in the majority of patients.

Evidence supporting the role of the alpha-1 adrenoreceptor includes exacerbation of the pain of RSD by injection of noradrenaline, and its relief by intravenous administration of the alpha-adrenergic antagonist phentolamine (29). This phentolamine test can be used diagnostically: pain relief after phentolamine suggests that the pain is sympathetically maintained and that the patient is likely to benefit from sympathetic blockade (29,30).

Clearly the situation is highly complex and many different and interacting mechanisms may be involved as well as those already mentioned. For example, it has been suggested that the coupling between sympathetic postganglionic axons and afferent axons in the periphery may lead not only to afferent impulse activity to the spinal cord but also to antidromic activity which could in turn lead to a 'neurogenic' inflammatory component and to blood flow abnormalities in the periphery, both of which are in keeping with the clinical picture of RSD (5). The peripheral blood flow dysregulation which occurs in RSD may in turn contribute to the vicious cycles of

Table 3. Approaches to treatment of RSD

Physiotherapy
Sympathetic blocks
Paravertebral (stellate or lumbar)
Regional intravenous
Epidural blocks
Drug treatment
Alpha-blockers
Calcium channel blockers
Ketanserin
NSAIDs
Calcitonin
Corticosteroids
Anticonvulsants
Antidepressants
Transcutaneous nerve stimulation
Surgical sympathectomy
Dorsal column stimulation

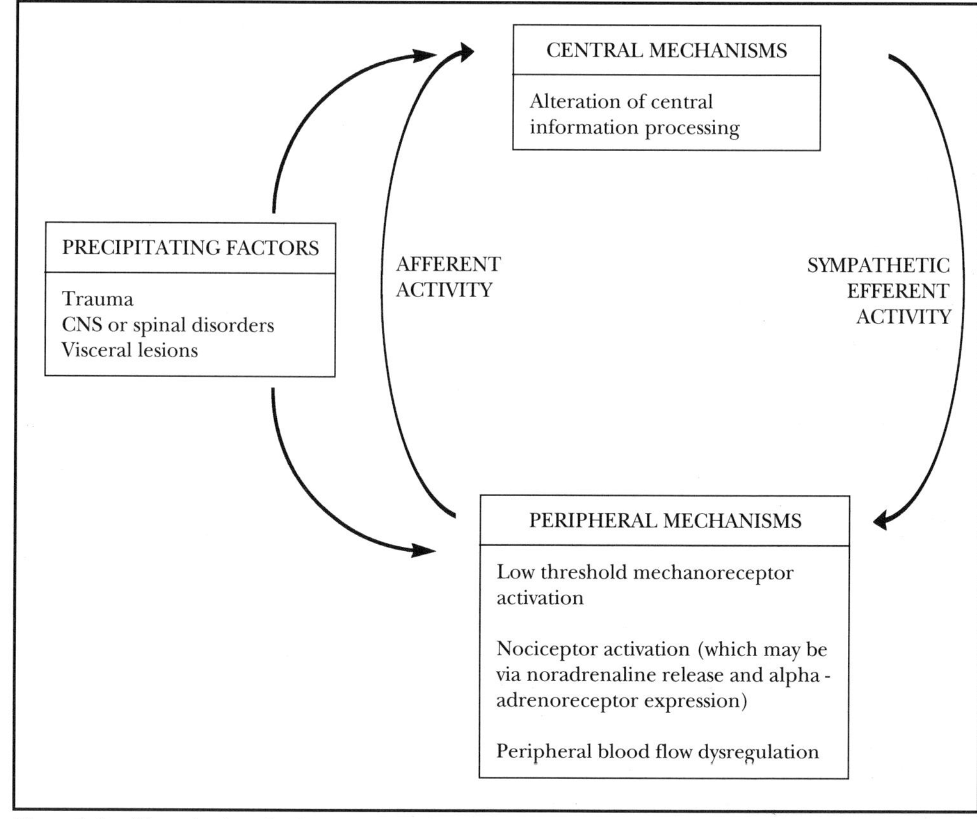

Figure 1. Possible mechanisms for the 'vicious cycle' of RSD

RSD by various mechanisms including impaired venous return and increased interstitial pressure (31).

In summary, there are many hypotheses (Figure 1), but no one unifying and accepted theory to explain all the clinical features of RSD.

MANAGEMENT

Early clinical suspicion and diagnosis is the key to successful management of RSD. It is recognised that once RSD has progressed to a late stage with marked atrophy and scarring, then treatment is unlikely to be successful. In this respect preventative measures are important, and early mobilisation of patients with possible predisposing conditions, for example after injury, should be encouraged.

Treatment options are outlined in Table 3. As with most conditions in which a multiplicity of treatments has been suggested, treatment is often unsuccessfuland a substantial proportion of patients are left with pain and major functional disability. At the other end of the spectrum many RSDs remit spontaneously. Any guidelines for the treatment of RSD must be interpreted cautiously, for very few controlled trials of treatment have been undertaken and those which do exist often involve very small patient numbers and end-points may be subjective. Very few of the trials which do exist are placebo-controlled. The variation in diagnostic criteria and outcome measures between reports further complicate the issue. Much of the experience of treatment is essentially anecdotal.

It is generally accepted that physiotherapy is an important part of management, either alone or in combination with other treatment modalities. The emphasis should be on mobilization of the affected part. Continuous passive motion (CPM) may be helpful, especially in RSD affecting the knee.

Sympathetic blockade is recommended in management of RSD and a prompt response to stellate or lumbar sympathetic blockade is sometimes used as an aid to diagnosis. However, sympathetic block is not always successful in alleviating the features of RSD. There are two main methods of performing sympathetic blockade: paravertebral block or regional intravenous blockade. To consider first paravertebral blocks, generally a series of local anaesthetic blocks is given, the frequency 'titrated' to the patient's response. Lumbar sympathetic blocks were suggested to be an effective form of treatment for lower limb RSD compared to conservative management when 28 of 43 patients treated by sympathetic nerve block improved, but this was largely a retrospective study (32).

Intravenous guanethidine blocks compared favourably to stellate ganglion blocks in a randomised trial of parallel group design of 19 patients with upper limb

RSD (33). The intravenous block leads to a high concentration of guanethidine being applied directly to the sympathetic nerve endings in the treated extremity, producing a noradrenergic neurone block. An advantage of this intravenous 'Bier's block' technique is that while not without its hazards and requiring very careful supervision (34), it does not require the expertise necessary for stellate or lumbar sympathetic block. This technique has also been used with apparent benefit using reserpine (35) and bretylium (36) with lidocaine. As with sympathetic ganglion blocks, the intravenous blocks can be repeated as necessary, the effect of the first block usually lasting around 2 days with subsequent blocks lasting longer (37).

Epidural blocks have also been used, but have the disadvantage of blocking not only sympathetic fibres. A recent randomised cross-over study of 15 patients with long-standing lower limb RSD (median duration 34 months), so far reported only in abstract form, found little difference between guanethidine blocks and epidural anaesthesia, and benefit only in a minority of patients (38).

While multiple drug treatments have been suggested for the treatment of RSD as shown in Table 3, few have been substantiated in adequate clinical trials. Corticosteroids have been advocated for the treatment of RSD (39) and one placebo-controlled trial did suggest that 30mg of prednisolone daily conferred benefit (40). Calcitonin was reported to produce more rapid pain relief than physiotherapy alone in a trial of parallel group design of 24 patients, but any benefit was marginal (41). A randomised double-blind trial of nasal calcitonin reported no significant clinical benefit from 400iu daily (42). Because of the recent interest in the alpha-1 adrenoreceptor in the pathogenesis of RSD, alpha-blockers may be an appropriate choice of treatment (43,44), but again, randomised prospective trials are required. Other vasodilators have also been tried (45,46).

Transcutaneous nerve stimulation has been reported to be effective in some patients wih RSD and was helpful in 9 of 10 children in an uncontrolled study (47). Acupuncture has also been suggested (48). Surgery may be helpful in a small number of selected cases: in patients experiencing good but short-term relief from sympathetic blockade then chemical or surgical sympathectomy may be warranted. Spinal cord stimulation has also been tried (49). As mentioned earlier, many patients with RSD demonstrate marked pain behaviour emphasising how the approach to the patient with RSD should ideally be multidisciplinary (50).

THE FUTURE

Basic scientific and clinical research into RSD must continue in parallel. RSD, however, is a difficult condition to study. As with so many disorders which may fall within the province of the rheumatologist, RSD covers a broad spectrum of disease and disability, placebo-controlled clinical trials involving adequate patient numbers are difficult to mount, and clinical progression or improvement is not always easy to measure. However, steps are being taken to encourage and facilitate the study of RSD and it is likely that the increasing clinical interest shown in it will continue.

REFERENCES

1. Mitchell SW, Moorehouse GR, Kenn WW. *Gunshot Wounds and Other Injuries of Nerves.* Philadelphia: JB Lippincott Co., 1864.

2. Evans JA. Reflex sympathetic dystrophy. *Ann Int Med* 1947; **26**: 417-26.

3. Janig W, Blumberg H, Boas RA, Campbell JN. The reflex sympathetic dystrophy syndrome: Consensus statement and general recommendations for diagnosis and clinical research. In: Bond MR, Charlton JE, Woolf CJ, eds. *Proceedings of the VIth World Congress on Pain.* Amsterdam: Elsevier Science Publishers, 1991: 373-6.

4. Bonica JJ. Causalgia and other reflex sympathetic dystrophies. *Adv Pain Res Therapy* 1979; **3**: 141-66.

5. Janig W. The sympathetic nervous system in pain: physiology and pathophysiology. In: Stanton-Hicks M, ed. *Pain and the Sympathetic Nervous System.* Massachusetts: Kluwer Academic Publishers, 1990: 17-89.

6. Schwartzman RJ: Reflex sympathetic dystrophy and causalgia. *Neur Clin* 1992; **10**: 953-73.

7. Atkins RM, Duckworth T, Kanis JA. Features of algodystrophy after Colles' fracture. *J Bone Joint Surg* (Br) 1990; **72-B**: 105-10.

8. Sarangi PP, Ward AJ, Smith EJ, Staddon GE, Atkins RM. Algodystrophy and osteoporosis after tibial fractures. *J Bone Joint Surg* (Br) 1993; **75-B**: 450-2.

9. Bernstein BH, Singsen BH, Kent JT et al. Reflex neurovascular dystrophy in children. *J Pediatrics* 1978; **93**: 211-5.

10. Abram S. Incidence - hypothesis - epidemiology. In: Stanton-Hicks M, ed. *Pain and the Sympathetic Nervous System.* Massachusetts: Kluwer Academic Publishers, 1990: 1-15.

11. Gellman H, Keenan MAE, Stone L, Hardy SE, Waters RL, Stewart C. Reflex sympathetic dystrophy in brain-injured patients. *Pain* 1992; **51**: 307-11.

12. Sachs BL, Zindrick MR, Beasley RD. Reflex sympathetic dystrophy after operative procedures on the lumbar spine. *J Bone Joint Surg* 1993; **75-A**: 721-5.

13. Rodeo SA, Forster RA, Weiland AJ. Neurological complications due to arthroscopy. *J Bone Joint Surg* 1993; **75-A**: 917-26.

14. Karras D, Karargiris G, Vassilopoulos D, Karatzetzos C. Reflex sympathetic dystrophy syndrome and osteogenesis imperfecta. A report and review of the literature. *J Rheumatol* 1993; **20**: 162-4.

15. Lynch ME. Psychological aspects of reflex sympathetic dystrophy: a review of the adult and paediatric literature. *Pain* 1992; **49**: 337-47.

16. Bruehl S, Carlson CR. Predisposing psychological factors in the development of reflex sympathetic dystrophy. *Clin J Pain* 1992; **8**: 287-99.

17. Kozin F, McCarty DJ, Sims J, Genant H. The reflex sympathetic dystrophy syndrome. I. Clinical and histological studies: evidence for bilaterality, response to corticosteroids, and articular involvement. *Am J Med* 1976; **60**: 321-31.

18. Steinbrocker O, Argyros TG. The shoulder-hand syndrome: present status as a diagnostic and therapeutic entity. *Med Clin of N Am* 1958; **42**: 1533-53.

19. Wilson PR. Sympathetically mediated pain: diagnosis, measurement, and efficacy of treatment. In: Stanton-Hicks M, ed. *Pain and the Sympathetic Nervous System.* Massachusetts: Kluwer Academic Publishers, 1990: 90-123.

20. Kozin F. Reflex sympathetic dystrophy syndrome. *Bulletin on the Rheumatic Diseases* 1986; **36**: 1-8.

21. Kozin F, Genant HK, Bekerman C, McCarty DJ. The reflex sympathetic dystrophy syndrome. II. Roentgenographic and scintigraphic evidence of bilaterality and of periarticular accentuation. *Am J Med* 1976; **60**: 332-8.

22. Atkins RM, Tindale W, Bickerstaff D, Kanis JA. Quantitative bone scintigraphy in reflex sympathetic dystrophy. *Br J Rheumatol* 1993; **32**: 41-5.

23. Demangeat J, Constantinesco A, Brunot B, Foucher G, Farcot J. Three-phase bone scanning in reflex sympathetic dystrophy of the hand. *J Nucl Med* 1988; **29**:26-32.

24. Bickerstaff DR, Charlesworth D, Kanis JA. Changes in cortical and trabecular bone in algodystrophy. *Br J Rheumatol* 1993; **32**: 46-51.

25. Perelman RB, Adler D, Humpreys M. Reflex sympathetic dystrophy: electronic thermography as an aid to diagnosis. *Ortho Review* 1987; **16**: 53-8.

26. Irazuzta JE, Berde CB, Sethna NF. Laser Doppler measurements of skin blood flow before, during, and after lumbar sympathetic blockade in children and young adults with reflex sympathetic dystrophy syndrome. *J Clin Monit* 1992; **8**: 16-9.

27. Roberts WJ: A hypothesis on the physiological basis for causalgia and related pains. *Pain* 1986; **24**: 297-311.

28. Campbell JN, Raja SN, Meyer RA. Painful sequelae of nerve injury. In: Dubner R, Gebhart GF, Bond MR, eds. *Proceedings of the Vth World Congress on Pain.* Amsterdam: Elsevier Science Publishers, 1988; 135-43.

29. Campbell JN, Meyer RA, Raja SN. Is nociceptor activation by alpha-1 adrenoreceptors the culprit in sympathetically maintained pain? *APS Journal* 1992; **1**: 3-11.

30. Arner S. Intravenous phentolamine test: diagnostic and prognostic use in reflex sympathetic dystrophy. *Pain* 1991; **46**: 17-22.

31. Blumberg H, Griesser HJ, Hornyak ME. Mechanisms and role of peripheral blood flow dysregulation in pain sensation and edema in reflex sympathetic dystrophy. In: Stanton-Hicks M, Janig W, Boas RA, eds. *Reflex sympathetic dystrophy.* Massachusetts: Kluwer Academic Publishers, 1990: 81-95.

32. Wang JK, Johnson KA, Ilstrup DM. Sympathetic blocks for reflex sympathetic dystrophy. *Pain* 1985; **23**: 13-7.

33. Bonelli S, Conoscente F, Movilia PG, Restelli L, Francucci B, Grossi E. Regional intravenous guanethidine vs. stellate ganglion block in reflex sympathetic dystrophies: a randomised trial. *Pain* 1983; **16**: 297-307.

34. Hannington-Kiff JG. Intravenous regional sympathetic block with guanethidine. *Lancet* 1974; **i**: 1019-20.

35. Rocco AG, Kaul AF, Reisman RM, Gallo JP, Lief PA. A comparison of regional intravenous guanethidine and reserpine in reflex sympathetic dystrophy. A controlled, randomised, double-blind cross-over study. *Clin J Pain* 1989; **5**: 205-9.

36. Hord AH, Rooks MD, Stephens BO, Rogers HG, Fleming LL. Intravenous regional bretylium and lidocaine for treatment of reflex sympathetic dystrophy: a randomised, double-blind study. *Anesth Analg* 1992; **74**: 818-21.

37. Hannington-Kiff JG. Intravenous regional sympathetic blocks. In: Stanton-Hicks M, Janig W, Boas RA, eds. *Reflex sympathetic dystrophy.* Massachusetts: Kluwer Academic Publishers, 1990: 113-24.

38. Pountain GD, Chard MD, Smith EM, Hazleman BL, Jenner JR, Hughes DL. Comparison of guanethidine blocks and epidural analgesia in longstanding algodystrophy of the lower limb. *Br J Rheumatol* 1993; **32 (ABS Suppl 2)**: 53.

39. Kozin F, Ryan LM, Carerra GF, Soin JS. The reflex sympathetic dystrophy syndrome. III. Scintigraphic studies, further evidence for the therapeutic efficacy of systemic corticosteroids, and proposed diagnositic criteria. *Am J Med* 1981; **70**: 23-30.

40. Christensen K, Jensen EM, Noer I. The reflex sympathetic dystrophy syndrome. Response to treatment with systemic corticosteroids. *Acta Chir Scand* 1982; **148**: 653-5.

41. Gobelet C, Meier J, Schaffner W, Bischof-Delaloye A, Gerster J, Burckhardt P. Calcitonin and reflex sympathetic dystrophy syndrome. *Clin Rheumatol* 1986; **5**: 382-8.

42. Bickerstaff DR, Kanis JA. The use of nasal calcitonin in the treatment of posttraumatic algodystrophy. *Br J Rheumatol* 1991; **30**: 291-4.

43. Abram SE, Lightfoot RW. Treatment of long-standing causalgia with prazosin. *Reg Anaesth* 1981; **6**: 79-81.

44. Ghostine SY, Comair YG, Turner DM, Kassell NF, Azar CG. Phenoxybenzamine in the treatment of causalgia. Report of 40 cases. *J Neurosurg* 1984; **60**: 1263-8.

45. Prough DS, McLeskey CH, Poehling GG et al. Efficacy of oral nifedipine in the treatment of reflex sympathtic dystrophy. *Anesthesiol* 1985; **62**: 796-9.

46. Moesker A, Boersma FP, Scheijgrond HW, Cortvriendt W. Treatment of posttraumatic sympathetic dystrophy (Sudeck's atrophy) with guanethidine and ketanserin. *Pain Clinic* 1985; **1**: 171-6.

47. Kesler RW, Saulsbury FT, Miller LT, Rowlingson JC. Reflex sympathetic dystrophy in children: treatment with transcutaneous electric nerve stimulation. *Pediatrics* 1988; **82**: 728-32.

48. Fialka V, Resch KL, Ritter-Dietrich D, et al. Acupuncture for reflex sympathetic dystrophy. *Arch Int Med* 1993; **153**: 661-5.

49. Robaina FJ, Dominguez M, Diaz M, Rodriguez JL, De Vera JA. Spinal cord stimulation for relief of chronic pain in vasospastic disorders of the upper limbs. *Neurosurgery* 1989; **24**: 63-7.

50. Raj P, Cannella J, Kelly J, McConn K, Lowry P. Multi-disciplinary management of reflex sympathetic dystrophy. In: Stanton-Hicks M, Janig W, Boas RA, eds. *Reflex sympathetic dystrophy.* Massachusetts: Kluwer Academic Publishers, 1990: 165-72.

May 1994

THE MANAGEMENT OF LOW BACK PAIN - A PERSONAL VIEW

I Haslock
Consultant Rheumatologist
Middlesbrough General Hospital

Pain in the back is the commonest rheumatological symptom leading to consultation with a general practitioner. It is a symptom which induces negative feelings in both doctor and patient and the outcome of treatment is often unsatisfactory. Why is this so? Firstly, the diagnosis of back pain should be based on a good history and a competent physical examination. Although history taking is improving, examination of the locomotor system by general practitioners remains inadequate, and that of the spine grossly inadequate. Without proper use of this essential diagnostic tool, subsequent management is doomed to failure. Secondly, the consultation takes place in an arena of nihilism on both sides. The patient has been schooled by press publicity, especially that extolling alternative medicine, and previous experience to expect neither cure for his problems nor sympathy with them. The doctor is aware of his own inadequacies in both diagnosis and treatment, but attempts to push the 'blame' for inadequacies in outcome towards the patient. This is often expressed as a suspicion that most patients with back pain are malingering. There appears to be no evidence that any but the most tiny proportion of patients present with spurious symptoms; one of the most important steps on the road to diagnosis and treatment of back pain must be the assumption that all patients presenting with such pain have a pathological cause for their symptom, and that failure to ascertain its nature is the doctor's fault not the patient's.

Practice Point

IT MUST ALWAYS BE ASSUMED THAT PATIENTS WITH BACK PAIN HAVE A PATHOLOGICAL CAUSE FOR THEIR SYMPTOMS

Thirdly, there are great areas of uncertainty regarding both the cause and the appropriate treatment of much back pain. Some well-defined symptom complexes with validated methods of treatment exist. However, even after the most meticulous clinical and technological investigation the precise cause of many patients' symptoms will elude us. The description of the approach to back pain which follows will be based on the pragmatic view that we must maximise our chances of identifying these well defined symptom-complexes, minimise our chances of overlooking serious pathology such as malignancy, and treat those patients without well-defined disease empirically, but in as sympathetic and logical a fashion as is possible.

History

The objective of history taking is to find out about the onset, site, radiation and type of pain. Exacerbating and relieving factors are important, and all the facts must be recorded. If the pain is not described in the records, but, simply recorded as 'LBP', a patient with recurrent sciatica who subsequently presents with a spinal secondary might well be dismissed as having a further episode of the same 'LBP'.

Historical findings aiding diagnosis include a sudden onset during a specified action, such as lifting, or a history of classic sciatic radiation of pain, which are strongly suggestive of a mechanical cause. True sciatic pain is often exacerbated by actions which increase intrathecal pressure, such as coughing, sneezing or straining at stool. The inappropriate prescription of opiate analgesics, especially dihydrocodeine, implies either a lack of understanding of the patient's problem or an indifference to it. Severe morning stiffness with relief by exercise might indicate inflammatory disease. A family history of seronegative spondarthritis might arouse suspicion of this strongly hereditary group of diseases.

In contrast, pain of slow onset with no relief from changes in posture or activity might lead to suspicion of a systemic cause for the back pain. All leg pain is not sciatica. Sacro-iliac pain is frequently referred to the thigh. Claudicant pain in the legs indicates a vascular cause for the pain, either peripheral vascular disease, an aneurism or 'cord claudication'. In older patients the co-existence of hip or knee osteoarthritis can lead to a false diagnosis of 'sciatica' if the history and examination are inadequate.

Practice Point

PAIN IN THE BACK WITH PAIN IN THE LEG DOES NOT OF NECESSITY INDICATE 'SCIATICA'.

A history of back pain must be set in the context of a general history. This will partly be aimed at ascertaining symptoms implying neurological problems arising from spinal disease, such as change in bladder control. Other questions will explore the possibility of the back pain being part of a more generalised disease. Loss of weight, change in bowel habit, prostatism or gynaecological symptoms, should lead to suspicion of malignancy. Dyspepsia requires consideration of a posterior penetrating ulcer; pancreatic carcinoma is another important visceral cause of back pain. The practitioner must always ask the question 'Is this patient iller than I would expect him to be from his back symptoms alone?'. The history is not complete until this question is satisfactorily answered.

Examination

At a recent consensus conference on the management of common locomotor problems, the only area of major dispute between the general practitioner participants and the attending rheumatologists lay in the area of examination. In discussion, it eventually emerged that the main reason for general practitioners belittling the role of examination, and in some cases rationalising its non-use, was a knowledge of their own inadequacies in examining the locomotor system. A subsidiary reason was difficulty in performing an adequate examination within the physical and temporal contraints imposed by their practice organization. Neither of these reasons should be allowed to detract from the fact that in the diagnosis of back pain, as in all diseases of the locomotor system, a good clinical examination is the single most important action which will be undertaken.

Practice Point

EXAMINATION IS THE MOST IMPORTANT DIAGNOSTIC PROCEDURE THAT WILL BE UNDERTAKEN. IT IS AN ABSOLUTE OBLIGATION OF EVERY PRACTITIONER TO ENSURE THAT HIS EXAMINATION TECHNIQUE IS IMMACULATE AND THAT ADEQUATE TIME AND SPACE IS AVAILABLE DURING CONSULTATION FOR A FULL, DETAILED EXAMINATION

The patient must be undressed for an adequate examination. He should first be examined standing. The spine should be straight and the paraspinous contours symmetrical. The two sides of the pelvis should be at equal heights. Alterations may be due to a structural abnormality, such as a structural scoliosis or leg length discrepancy, or local areas of muscle spasm. Spinal posture is important. While diminished lumbar lordosis may be an early sign of ankylosing spondylitis, it is much more frequently simply a sign of generally bad spinal posture. This is especially found in young people and is a frequent cause of back pain rather than simply a sign of it. An extra deep lumbar lordosis, often associated with obesity, may also produce back pain. In both cases the source of the pain is probably ligamentous.

Movement should be observed from behind so that true spinal movement can be observed. One of the most confusing signs is observation of the finger-floor distance on forward flexion. The ability to touch the floor with the fingers depends on hip movement as much as spinal movement; this is regularly demonstrated by patients with ankylosing spondylitis who are able to touch the floor easily despite having a fused spine provided their hip movement is normal and their hamstrings are stretchable. Movements should be full in range for the patient's age, and symmetrical. Restriction of movement in all planes raises the suspicion of ankylosing spondylitis, though patients with non-specific back pain also show this pattern. Decrease in one movement, usually forward flexion, is typical of mechanical pain. Increased movement, usually demonstrated as the ability to place the palms flat on the floor with the legs straight, is a sign of hypermobility which is a common and underdiagnosed cause of back pain, especially in women. Asymmetry of side-flexion is associated with facet joint abnormality.

The patient should then be examined lying on his back, the ease with which he moves to the couch from the standing posture being part of the examination. Straight leg raising is examined, and a sciatic stretch test performed by sharply dorsiflexing the foot at the limit of the straight leg raise. If there is any doubt about the patient's cooperation with straight leg raising, ask him to sit up with his legs straight in front of him; ability to do this implies straight leg raising of about 80 degrees. Hip and knee movements can be examined in conjunction with straight leg raising. There is controversy as to the validity of the many tests of sacro-iliac pain which exist. None has been shown to have unequivocal validity, and there is, in any case, considerable doubt regarding the diagnosis of sacro-iliac strain or mal-alignment to which use of such tests may lead. Power, reflexes and sensation in the legs should be tested, especially the area of the sacral roots. The pulses in the legs and feet should be palpated. Finally the supine position gives opportunity for abdominal examination both for signs of disease such as malignancy (eg, a hard liver) or an aortic aneurism. Renal tenderness should also be sought as some back pain is of renal origin. The patient then rolls to the prone position for completion of the neurological examination, especially the femoral stretch test, and local palpation of the spine, paraspinous areas and pelvis. This last is of limited value, although identification of the painful area does improve empathy with the patient, and severe local vertebral tenderness may enhance suspicion of malignancy or vertebral crush fracture due to osteoporosis.

For straightforward cases, this is all the

examination that is necessary. Clues obtained by this time may require further examination using special techniques. Suspicion of leg-length discrepancy can be confirmed by measurement. A hypermobile spine should lead to a search for hypermobile peripheral joints. Suspicion of malignancy should lead to a full physical examination including rectal and vaginal examination. If a seronegative spondarthritis is suspected, chest expansion should be measured and the peripheral joints and skin examined.

Although the majority of patients do have some underlying cause for their pain, there is a small proportion in whom the symptoms will be exaggerated, sometimes grossly. Histories containing dramatic descriptions of agonising pain make the practitioner suspicious, although he should also consider the possibility that his relationship with his patient is such that the patient feels a need to exaggerate symptoms in order to gain the practitioner's attention. Examination is usually the discriminator, where inappropriate, diffuse and exaggerated tenderness, tremulous, restricted movements, including those distant from the site of pain, and discrepancies between the ease of movement exhibited in actions such as undressing or getting onto the couch contrasts with gross restriction during formal examination. In such cases, it is inappropriate to dismiss the patient without exploring the psycho-social reasons producing such reactions and taking appropriate therapeutic action. It is particularly inappropriate for such patients to be sent for physiotherapy, as this both reinforces the patient's illness behaviour and insults the professionalism of a colleague.

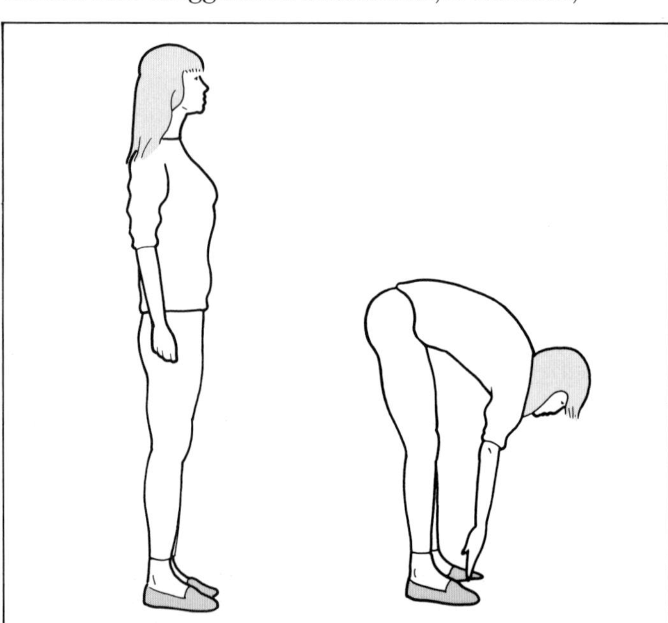

Normal bending. Ability to touch the toes is provided by a combination of flexion of the vertebrae and movement of the hip joints.

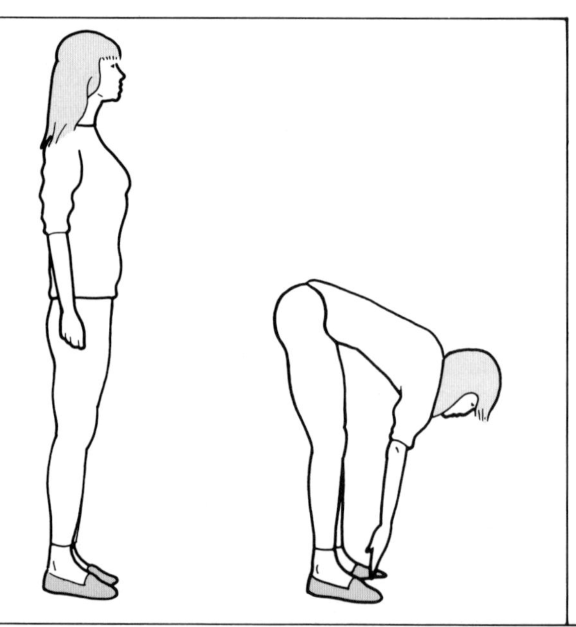

A patient with rigid vertebrae, due for example to ankylosing spondylitis, may still be able to touch his toes because of hip flexion alone.

Investigation

One reason for the primacy of physical examination in the diagnosis of back pain is the restricted amount of information derived from investigations. A low haemoglobin and raised ESR or plasma viscosity would confirm suspicion of an inflammatory or malignant process. A raised alkaline phosphatase could indicate Paget's disease or advanced malignancy and a raised acid phosphatase carcinoma of prostate. Suspicion of myeloma would be confirmed by immunoelectrophoresis and urine examination. X-rays are of diagnostic value in only a minority of patients. Spondylolisthesis may be found in patients with pain exacerbated by exercise and often associated with symptoms in both thighs. Minor congenital abnormalities at the lumbo-sacral junction are common, occurring in about 5% of the population. They have no proven association with symptoms, although abnormal joints which become the site of osteoarthritis may be symptomatic. Middle-aged and elderly patients often show signs of lumbar spondylosis, but there is a poor correlation between the radiological findings and symptoms. Paget's disease, osteoporotic crush fractures or malignancy may be seen in more elderly patients. If a seronegative spondarthritis is suspected, an AP film of the lumbar spine centred on the dorso-lumbar junction plus an X-ray of the pelvis should be obtained. Interpretation of lumbar spine films from X-ray reports is impossible. No practitioner should ask for X-rays unless he is going to view them himself and, preferably, show them to the patient. The greatest value of X-rays often lies in showing them to the patient and interpreting them with the help of a model lumbar spine.

Practice Point

NO PRACTITIONER SHOULD REQUEST SPINAL X-RAYS UNLESS HE IS GOING TO VIEW THEM PERSONALLY, NOT JUST READ A REPORT, AND PREFERABLY SHOW THEM TO THE PATIENT

More complex investigations should only be undertaken where a specific intervention is likely to be made. Thus the diagnosis of a prolapsed disc should be confirmed by myelography or CT scanning before surgery is contemplated. These investigations may be particularly helpful where a central disc protrusion is suspected. Spinal canal stenosis has probably been under-diagnosed in the past. The symptoms are of chronic low back pain increased by exercise. Radicular signs in both legs are common. Two useful symptoms are the need to bend forward (which increases the canal diameter) when hurrying, eg, to cross a road, and an ability to cycle for long distances when walking is severely impaired, again due to altered canal alignment. CT scanning is particularly appropriate in diagnosing this condition.

Treatment

Treatment will depend on whether one of the defined symptom complexes has been identified, or whether, as is the majority outcome, the diagnosis appears to be of non-specific low back pain. Suspicion of malignant disease, aortic aneurism or intra-abdominal or retroperitoneal pathology should lead to urgent referral. A clinical diagnosis of a seronegative spondarthritis should lead to prescription of an appropriate NSAID and instruction in simple home exercises, probably followed by non-urgent referral for advice by a rheumatological team.

True acute sciatica should be assumed to be due to disc prolapse in the first place. If neurological signs are intense, especially if there is bladder disturbance, an urgent surgical opinion should be sought. Lesser degrees of this condition can be treated by rest at home. This should be with the patient lying on his back on the floor or other similar hard surface. The legs may need supporting. Rest is inadequate unless this posture is adopted for 23 hours 50 minutes per day. Specialist help should be requested if ten days of this regime, supplemented by adequate analgesia, fails to alleviate the symptoms. Facet joint lesions are best treated by manipulation or mobilisation techniques either carried out by the practitioner himself or by a physiotherapist. All practitioners should have open access to physiotherapy services.

> **Practice Point**
>
> ALL GENERAL PRACTITIONERS SHOULD HAVE OPEN ACCESS TO PHYSIOTHERAPY SERVICES BUT THIS DOES NOT MEAN THAT OVER-REFERRAL SHOULD TAKE PLACE. TEACHING REGARDING POSTURE AND SPINAL EXERCISES SHOULD BE PART OF EVERY PRACTITIONER'S ARMAMENTARIUM AND SHOULD NOT REQUIRE REFERRAL

Patients with hypermobility should be taught an isometric exercise regime and encouraged to persist with it on a lifelong basis. Osteoporotic patients should undertake a moderate, mobilising exercise regime once their acute pain has passed, and all elderly people, especially women, should be encouraged in a lifestyle of adequate exercise and adequate calcium intake to minimise the progression of this disease. Patients in whom the pain is felt to arise from Paget's disease should have a specialist appraisal before specific therapy is instituted.

The majority of the remaining patients require reassurance that no serious disease is going on. This can only be given by a practitioner who is confident in his clinical diagnostic ability, especially in the competence of his clinical examination. There is a need in most patients to correct their posture and teach them to strengthen their paraspinous and abdominal muscles by isometric exercises. Correct lifting, carrying, working and sitting must be taught. The obese should lose weight and the flabby improve their overall musculature. Everyone must learn that abusing an ill-prepared body is bound to lead to recurrent problems. Adequate analgesia should be offered, occasionally supplemented by short-term night sedation to allow sleep. All patients should be treated with empathy and understanding: it is the absence of these which leads many patients to attend alternative practitioners with their spurious promises of cure.

It has been shown that 75% of acute episodes of low back pain get better within two weeks. The practitioner treating patients with low back pain should always have this optomistic prognosis in the forefront of his mind. Providing his personal capabilities are sufficient for him to confidently identify the small minority of patients with severe disease, he should be able to alleviate the symptoms in the majority, and help with advice and encouragement to reduce the risk of recurrence, without recourse to any skills apart from his own.

Conclusion

This account of low back pain is a personal and pragmatic approach which is not aligned to any of the many dogmatic systems which abound in this area of practice. One area in which dogmatism is justified, however, is in demanding of all practitioners who treat back pain, which is, after all, one of the commonest ailments with which they will deal, competence in its clinical assessment and a practice organization which allows both time and space for this assessment to be carried out. Given these essentials, the majority of patients can be managed with simple help and advice well within the competence of every practitioner.

REFERENCE:
Standards in Rheumatology: A suggested management plan for some common conditions in rheumatology. Royal College of General Practitioners North of England Faculty. The Medicine Group (UK) Ltd 1987, Oxford, 1987.

May 1988

ACUTE NECK PAIN - DIFFERENTIAL DIAGNOSIS AND MANAGEMENT

J A Mathews
Physician
Department of Rheumatology
St Thomas' Hospital
London

INTRODUCTION

The neck is often admired for its aesthetic properties but its main function is to connect the head with the trunk. Its stability depends mainly upon the spine which in the cervical region has seven vertebrae. These articulate with each other through a system of joints of unusual complexity. Not only is each pair of vertebrae separated by the usual intervertebral disc and pair of apophyseal joints, but in the cervical spine the bodies articulate by an additional pair of synovial joints at their postero-lateral aspects. The need to move the head, to communicate, breathe and eat, places an almost continuous demand on this system and the wonder is that this does not lead to even more frequent problems.

The cervical spine provides a protective passageway for structures vital to life. The blood supply of the brain partly depends on the vertebral arteries which pass through the cervical vertebrae, and the spinal cord is enclosed in the spinal canal. These features indicate the crucial importance of the cervical spine. It thus occupies a uniquely important place in the system of joints of the body.

Most cervical problems are mechanical and mainly affect the joints and associated ligaments and muscles. The term cervical spondylosis is used to describe the pathology. Less common, but more serious, is an extension of this involving nerve roots, the vertebro-basilar circulation, and the spinal cord itself. Uncommon but very important is inflammatory or neoplastic disease.

HISTORY

Most patients with neck problems complain of pain and stiffness. Mechanical disturbances are often associated with a history of some unaccustomed activity, or a sustained awkward posture. It is not necessary for there to be a specific injury. Spondylosis is most common in the low cervical region. The pain is usually felt low in the neck, and often radiates to the occiput, trapezius, and interscapular areas. This distribution may be due to dural irritation. Shoulder abduction can also be painful leading to the erroneous diagnosis of a shoulder joint lesion.

The symptoms are usually aggravated by neck movement and relieved by rest. The story is often episodic; indeed this feature is reassuring as more sinister pathological processes often produce symptoms that are relentless and progressive. Patients sometimes report a "whiplash" injury from a road traffic accident. This affects the issue in that it often implies that there are medicolegal proceedings in the offing.

Nerve root involvement sometimes follows, most commonly C7, with very severe pain radiating dorsally down the forearm to the hand and fingers.

SIGNS

The cervical spine may be held in or pulled by muscle spasm into an unusual angle, "torticollis". Movements normally occur quite freely and are examined in three planes; flexion/extension, rotations and lateral flexions. These are usually painfully restricted in an asymmetrical pattern. When pain and paraesthesiae are intermittent, useful confirmation of their origin can sometimes be obtained by "over-pressure". Extension or lateral flexion is gently reinforced by the examiner's hand and sustained to see if symptoms are reproduced. If the 7th cervical nerve root is involved motor, reflex or sensory

	Symptoms	Signs
articular	intermittent neck pain	asymmetrical restriction of neck movement
dural	pain occiput vertex trapezius deltoid interscapular	rarely pain on shoulder abduction or external rotation
nerve root (usually C7)	severe pain upper arm dorsum forearm dorsum hand to index & middle fingers	weakness triceps finger & wrist extensors absent triceps reflex sensory impairment

signs may occur. The weakness involves triceps, wrist and finger extension, the triceps reflex is diminished or absent, and there may be the appropriate impairment of skin sensation in the C7 dermatome.

The presence of bilateral symptoms or signs, or involvement of more than one nerve root is a feature of great importance, often signifying a more severe or serious pathology. Bladder symptoms and long tract signs indicate spinal cord compression. Any of these are a warning to handle with care.

INVESTIGATIONS

In a patient with a classical and short history, say up to 3 weeks, no investigation is necessary. In all other circumstances a cervical spine X-ray should be seen. Its main purpose is to help exclude serious pathology. The lateral view may be entirely normal, but frequently shows some reversal of the normal gentle lordosis. Very commonly spondylotic changes are seen at the C5/6, C6/7 levels with characteristic loss of joint space, posterior and anterior osteophyte formation, and sometimes distortion of the vertebral bodies (Fig 1). Oblique views often show encroachment into intervertebral foramina by osteophytes (Fig 2). Clearly these changes will have taken months to develop and do not delineate the cause of recent symptoms. They indicate an underlying pathological process, an exacerbation of which is presumed to have led to recent symptoms and signs.

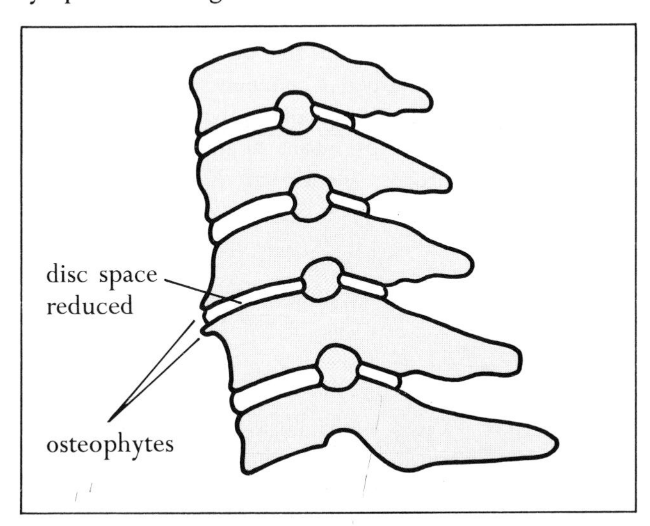

Figure 1. X-rays may show loss of the normal gentle lordosis, loss of disc space, and anterior and posterior osteophyte formation.

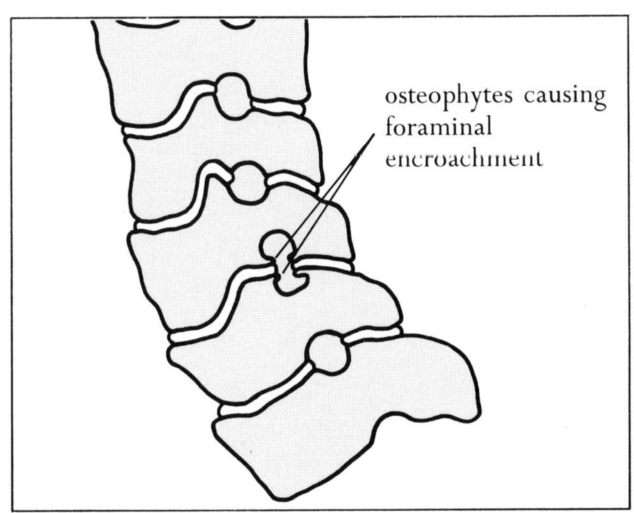

Figure 2. Oblique views may highlight the osteophytes encroaching in the intervertebral foramen.

The antero-posterior X-ray is much maligned. It is said to be so rarely helpful as not to be cost-beneficial. However without it one would not see cervical ribs, and might miss destructive neoplastic or infective pathology in the lateral aspects of the cervical spine. Possibly it is not needed as a routine but experience suggests that the A-P view is necessary when there is root pain or a neurological deficit.

Spondylotic changes are reported to occur in about half of the population over the age of 50 years. A very common cause of patient anxiety and consequent consultations is the worrying wording used in X-ray reports: "degeneration", "osteoarthritis", "severe spondylosis". Terms like these when read by patients lead to understandable anxiety. The clinician will need to assess the actual symptoms and signs and reassure the patient as appropriate.

DIFFERENTIAL DIAGNOSIS

It goes without saying that in patients with mechanical problems there are no features of systemic illness, clinically or on investigation. However a wide range of disorders can present with or be accompanied by acute neck pain. These need to be considered.

Infection can lodge either in the cervical spine or retropharyngeal space. The patient will usually, but not always, be unwell. The pain is constant and movement symmetrically restricted. The ESR will be raised early, but bone and joint X-ray changes are late. Destruction of a vertebral body may be seen on lateral views; sometimes a pair of vertebrae and the intervening disc are affected. Inflammatory processes may extend into the retropharyngeal space which can be seen through the mouth, or the soft tissue shadow demonstrated on the lateral X-ray.

Non-infective inflammation occurs in a wide range of connective tissue disorders, most commonly in rheumatoid arthritis. The upper cervical spine synovial tissue is affected leading to ligamentous weakness, and frequently to joint instability. Antero-posterior atlanto-axial subluxation occurs in about one quarter of hospital rheumatoid patients. Destruction of the lateral processes of the atlas can lead to vertical subluxation. Sub-axial lesions may also occur. For example, destructive inflammation, most often at C4/5, can lead to anterior slippage of C4 with compression of the anterior spinal artery by the upper posterior border of C5. All of these problems can prejudice the cervical spinal cord.

Ankylosing spondylitis classically commences in the sacro-iliac joints, but sometimes the cervical stiffness is the presenting feature. The diagnosis will be apparent clinically on spinal examination. The spondylitic spine is osteoporotic and fragile and can be the site of a pathological fracture. This can be fatal due to severe spinal cord compression.

Polymyalgia rheumatica and giant cell arteritis can also present with neck symptoms. Classically they occur in the elderly. The pain is of sudden or gradual onset, and the stiffness is symmetrical. The problem usually also affects the shoulders and sometimes the lumbar spine and pelvic girdle. Temporal artery involvement may be obvious but occipital arteritis can cause neck pain and stiffness and is more difficult to diagnose. An ESR is always worth doing in elderly patients with acute neck pain.

Neoplasms are usually secondary – to breast, bronchus, kidney, etc. Pain is unrelenting and the spine held rigid. The diagnosis is suspected on the history and signs, and confirmed by X-ray (antero-posterior and lateral views), bone scan, or biopsy.

CLINICAL FEATURES

Reassuring
- intermittent symptoms
- pain confined to articular and dural distribution
- neurological features confined to a single root

Worrying
- constant or progressive symptoms
- neurological features bilateral or involving more than one nerve root

TREATMENT

Episodes of acute neck pain are generally self-limiting and only require symptomatic treatment. The efficacy of rest cannot be gainsaid. It is to some extent automatic, and can be helped by a collar. Off-the-shelf collars can be very helpful but do need care in fitting. The height, front and back, needs to be checked so that the cervical spine is supported in a neutral position, and the circumference needs to be correct. The closer fitting and firmer the collar, the more effective it will be, and restriction of movement to one third can be obtained. Accurately fitted rigid collars, which take a purchase on chin and occiput, chest and thorax, can achieve a reduction of movement to 10%. These are cumbersome and take time to make, and should be reserved for patients at neurological risk. Occasionally pain will be so severe as to necessitate bed rest. A collar and analgesic/anti-inflammatory or muscle relaxant are all that are usually needed. Sometimes dramatic hastening of relief can be obtained by "manipulation". An experienced physiotherapist will usually exert manual traction followed by a rotation or lateral flexion movement. This can be repeated two or three times twice or thrice weekly, treatment being gauged by progress. A lesser form of manipulation is sometimes offered by less aggressive therapists consisting of "mobilisations". The cervical joints are repeatedly pressed through their ranges of movement. This is probably more applicable with older patients.

When root pain occurs cervical traction can be used. The physiotherapist applies traction with the patient lying or sitting, and using sufficient force to overcome gravity, as well as muscle and joint resistance. This can be given for up to half an hour several times a week. Particularly severe pain especially with nerve root involvement can be helped by bed rest with continuous traction. An epidural anaesthetic/steroid injection is rarely used. This is a procedure needing the aid of a specialised pain relief anaesthetist.

CONCLUSION

Most neck pain is episodic and of mechanical origin. Symptoms can be helped when necessary by rest in a collar, analgesics, or non-steroid anti-inflammatories. If an episode persists for more than three weeks or neurological features ensue, an X-ray and expert opinion is indicated.

September 1989

THE PAINFUL SHOULDER

B Hazleman
Consultant Rheumatologist
Addenbrooke's Hospital
Cambridge

Shoulder pain is a common complaint and usually the site of the lesion is apparent after a careful history and examination. The onset frequently follows excessive use or trauma. It is for this reason that it is often treated by rest, which leads to time off work sometimes for a seemingly trivial condition. By learning simple injection techniques one is able to shorten the recovery time by relieving symptoms and hasten a return of functional activity.

Movement is dependent on the unhampered gliding of the periarticular structures:- the musculo-tendinous rotator cuff, the subacromial bursa, and the tendon of the long head of the biceps muscle (fig. 1). It is the pathological changes in these tissues which are chiefly responsible for the conditions to be discussed. The innervation of the shoulder joint and its surrounding structures is mainly through the C5 nerve root. Pain in relation to disordered function is therefore felt over the C5 dermatome which is the area overlying the deltoid muscle. It is only with disorders of the acromioclavicular joint (C4) that pain is felt at the top of the shoulder.

Figure 1 Diagram of the shoulder showing the relationship of the shoulder joint, rotator cuff, sub-acromial bursa and acromioclavicular joint and common sites of pathology.

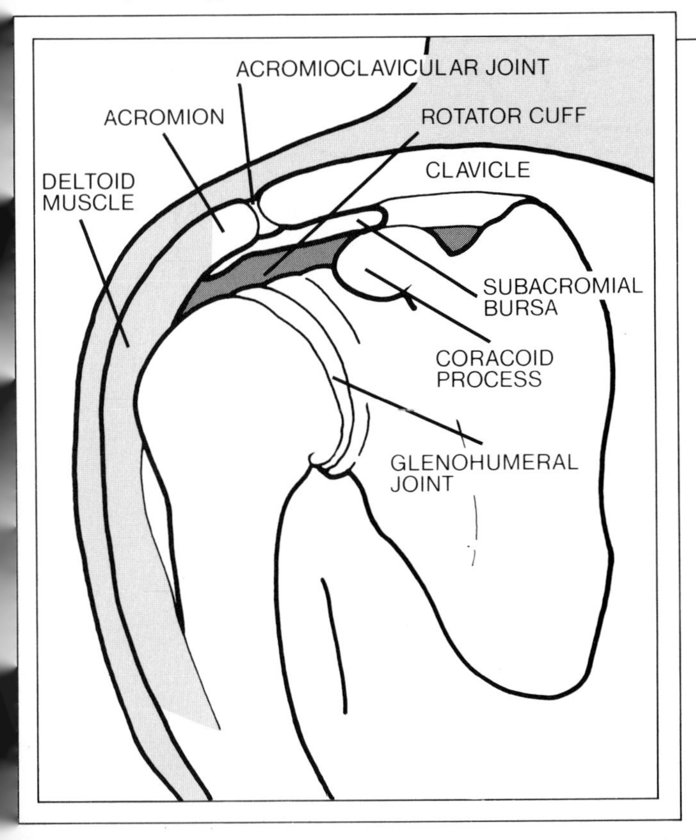

Night pain and inability to lie on the affected shoulder are common to all lesions, but careful clinical assessment with particular attention to the presence of a painful arc, location of tenderness, and manoeuvres that increase pain usually permit accurate diagnosis. Pain arising from a shoulder lesion can usually be produced by movement of the shoulder itself. There are several important extrinsic causes of shoulder pain that must be considered and excluded by history and examination. Movement of the neck should be tested followed by palpation of the supraclavicular fossae and examination of the respiratory and cardiovascular systems. The coracoid process is often tender in supraspinatus tendinitis, leading to confusion with bicipital tendinitis. Painful shoulders often follow or co-exist with stiff painful necks. Finding signs in the neck and appropriate neurological signs in the arm does not rule out an injectable lesion in the shoulder.

Rotator Cuff Tendinitis

Degenerative changes are prone to occur in the rotator cuff as a consequence of vascular and mechanical factors. It is persistent and recurrent stress that produces changes in the tendon and therefore tendinitis is seen particularly in occupations where excessive and repetitive movement of the shoulder occurs.

Supraspinatus Tendinitis

While any of the tendons of the rotator cuff may be affected by tendinitis, it most commonly involves the supraspinatus portion of the cuff close to its insertion to the humeral head. Pain and limitation of active (and sometimes passive) movement, especially abduction, occurs and a painful arc on abduction and tenderness over the tendon insertion may be noted.

Calcific Tendinitis

Some cases of supraspinatus tendinitis are associated with calcareous deposits visible on X-ray.

The deposits may remain asymptomatic or produce chronic symptoms with nagging discomfort in the region of the affected tendon. Occasionally the deposits may be extravasated into the subacromial bursa, giving rise to intense pain or loss of movement, severe tenderness, swelling and muscle spasm.

Infraspinatus and Subscapularis Lesions

These are less common and do not tend to calcify. While the symptoms are usually similar to those of supraspinatus tendinitis, pain induced by resisted external or internal rotation usually allows the correct diagnosis to be made.

Bicipital Syndromes and Subacromial Bursitis

Tendinitis of the long head of the biceps may lead to rupture of the tendon. Subacromial bursitis is almost always secondary to tendinitis or another adjacent lesion.

Acromioclavicular Joint Lesions

Injury to this joint is common in sportsmen; subluxation or dislocation of the joint occurs. Tenderness over the affected joint is common and pain is felt after 90° of abduction of the arm. Degenerative arthritis of this joint can occur and a 'spur' may impinge on the rotator cuff tendons.

Frozen Shoulder (Adhesive Capsulitis)

This condition may occur spontaneously but can follow other rotator cuff lesions or trauma. In addition, conditions that produce pain (eg the referred pain of myocardial infarction) or immobility (eg from stroke) of the shoulder or arm can predispose to its development. Severe night pain and pain on all movement develops and lasts for weeks. Pronounced restriction of all active and passive movements lasts 6 to 18 months before improvement. Arthrography may reveal a small, shrunken, thickened capsule. An external rotation is limited by greater than 50°.

Patients with even minor degrees of frozen shoulder may develop a secondary reflex sympathetic dystrophy syndrome – the shoulder-hand syndrome. Urgent treatment is required to avoid a useless hand.

TREATMENT
Rotator Cuff Tendinitis

Acute lesions should be treated initially by rest and analgesics with the local application of ice-packs 3-4 times a day for the first 24-48 hours. Non-steroidal anti-inflammatory drugs may be prescribed for periods of up to 2-3 weeks. Physiotherapy may be of benefit (particularly ultrasound). Codman's exercises (pendular and wall-climbing exercises) should be prescribed as part of the rehabilitative process. The importance of rest to the joint and surrounding structures must be stressed in order to avoid further inflammation. Aggravating exercises should be avoided for up to six weeks. Chronic or persistent cuff tendinitis often responds to corticosteroid injections, no more than 3 should be given.

Technique of Shoulder Injection

Once the technique of shoulder injection is learned any doctor should be capable of injecting the shoulder joint. Maximum relief of pain is usually achieved with 25-50mg. of hydrocortisone acetate or equivalent corticosteroid using routine aseptic precautions.

The most useful technique for non-specialised use is the posterior approach to the shoulder (Fig 2). It has a good chance of success when one is not too sure of the diagnosis, as it will help in lesions of the supraspinatus, infraspinatus and subscapularis tendons and in disorders of the glenohumeral joint. The patient sits with his back to the doctor who palpates the spine of the scapula, following it laterally until it turns forward to become the acromion process. He then with his forefinger finds the coracoid process. The line between the two marks the track of the needle. If the needle is advanced 1 inch

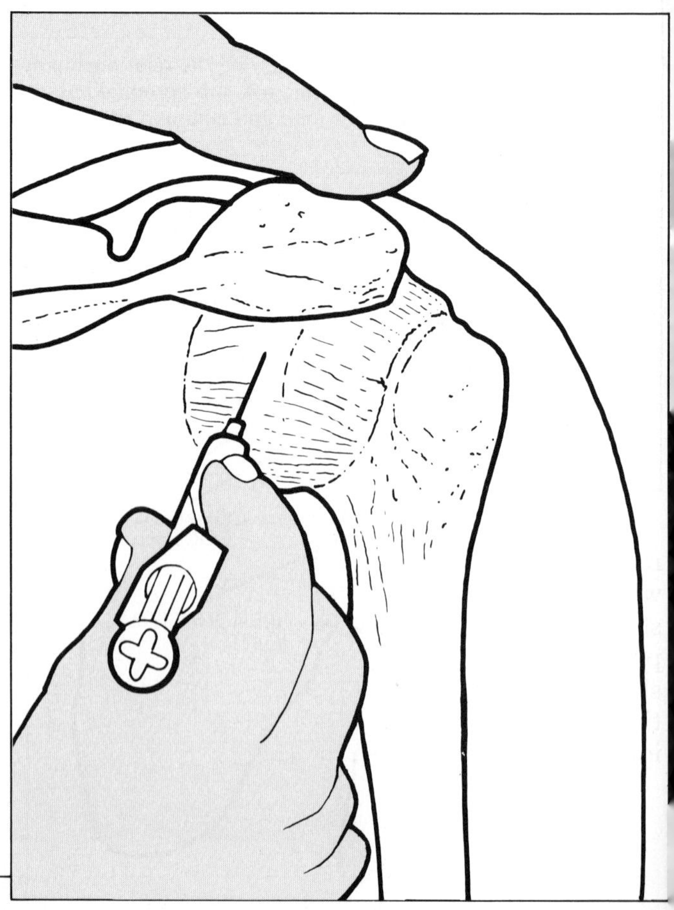

Figure 2 Injection of shoulder joint using the posterior approach.

below the acromion process there is no resistance and the tip of the needle is in the upper recess of the shoulder joint away from the head of the humerus and the cartilage of the glenoid cavity.

The lateral approach is best used for supraspinatus tendinitis. The patient is seated with his arm loosely at his side. The arm is not rotated. Palpate the most lateral point of the shoulder and advance the needle medially below the acromion process and slightly posteriorly along the line of the supraspinous fossa. Inject when 1 inch of the needle is inserted. It is important that the patient does not tense the muscles as it may then be difficult to inject. Injections into the subacromial bursa are difficult and fluoroscopic guidance may be required. A direct anterior approach in which the needle is inserted vertically beneath the acromion is preferred.

Figure 3 Injection of shoulder joint using the anterior approach.

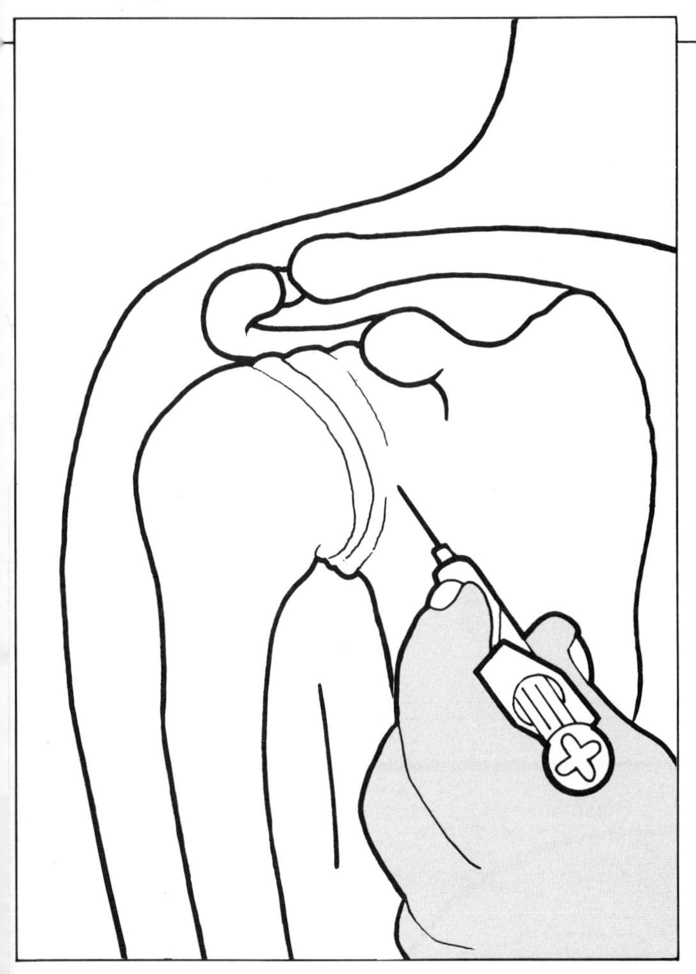

The anterior approach to the shoulder is a little more difficult (fig. 3). If the patient lies on his back with his forearm laid across the abdomen the shoulder is partially internally rotated. It is now possible to feel the coracoid process and the injection should be given just lateral to this in the direction of the joint line. Passive rotation of the arm will easily identify the head of the humerus.

The Acromioclavicular Joint

Pain arising from this joint is associated with tenderness on palpation and occasionally with swelling. The joint is a plane articulation, and therefore it is possible to inject it centrally from in front. The joint cavity is small and will seldom accept more than 0.5 ml of fluid. Acute lesions often settle with rest alone.

The Glenohumeral Joint

This is the true shoulder joint and the main physical sign of glenohumeral disease is limitation of external rotation of the arm. The glenohumeral joint is best approached from the posterior or anterior aspect. The ease of injection should determine that the needle is in the right place.

Injections of steroid into this joint can help the pain of the frozen shoulder and also reduce inflammation in inflammatory joint conditions.

Bicipital Tendinitis

Treatment is the same as other musculo-tendinous lesions. Injection of the tendon sheath with hydrocortisone should be performed with care as injection of the tendon may lead to rupture.

Pain Spots Around the Shoulder

Anatomical areas which are rich in pain nerve endings include the muscle-bone and ligament-bone junctions. Most pain spots around the shoulder are at these entheses. The tender areas are usually located along the scapula margin or along the spine of the scapula. They frequently respond to a weak lignocaine-corticosteroid mixture (eg hydrocortisone, 10mg diluted with 5-10ml of 1% lignocaine). Painful tender spots around the shoulder are often referred from the neck and in these patients the discomfort is unrelated to shoulder movements.

CONCLUSION

The shoulder is one of the most rewarding joints to treat and the finding of a limited or painful movement can be explained from a basic knowledge of functional anatomy. The shoulder joint depends very much on its surrounding soft tissues for its stability and function and the rotator cuff tendons occupy a central role; it is with lesions of these structures that steroid injections are likely to be of particular benefit.

January 1988

CARPAL TUNNEL SYNDROME

C Hawkins, H Currey, P Dieppe

PERIPHERAL NERVES ARE VULNERABLE TO MECHANICAL COMPRESSION AT POINTS WHERE THEY TRAVEL THROUGH CONFINED SPACES: ONE OF THE MOST IMPORTANT EXAMPLES OF SUCH AN "ENTRAPMENT NEUROPATHY" IS MEDIAN NERVE COMPRESSION AT THE WRIST. IT IS EXTREMELY COMMON, READILY DIAGNOSED ON HISTORY AND PHYSICAL SIGNS ALONE, AND TREATMENT IS HIGHLY EFFECTIVE.

Morbid Anatomy

The bones of the wrist form a concavity on the palmar aspect. This is bridged over by the flexor retinaculum to form the carpal tunnel *(Fig. 1)*. Through this tunnel run the flexor tendons to the fingers and the median nerve. Any enlargement of the contents of this confined space compresses all its contents. The sensory fibres of the median nerve are most susceptible to pressure; the motor fibres are less vulnerable. Tendon function may also be compromised by severe pressure. The median nerve supplies sensation to the radial 3½ digits, and motor fibres to the muscles of the thenar eminence – opponens pollicis and abductor pollicis brevis *(Fig. 2)*.

Aetiology

Anything which increases bulk within the carpal tunnel may compress the nerve. Thus fluid retention, obesity, bony lesions, arthritis of the wrist, infiltrative disorders and other space-occupying lesions may all be responsible.

THE CAUSES OF CARPAL TUNNEL SYNDROME

1. Most cases are "primary" and idiopathic.

2. A few cases are "secondary" to some other disorder.

	LOCAL CAUSES:	SYSTEMIC CAUSES:
COMMON:	Arthritis of the wrist (especially RA) Fractures *(scaphoid or Colles')* Trauma	Fluid retention (including pregnancy and the "Pill")
RARE:	Other bony and soft-tissue lesions in the wrist	Myxoedema Acromegaly Amyloidosis Scheie's syndrome

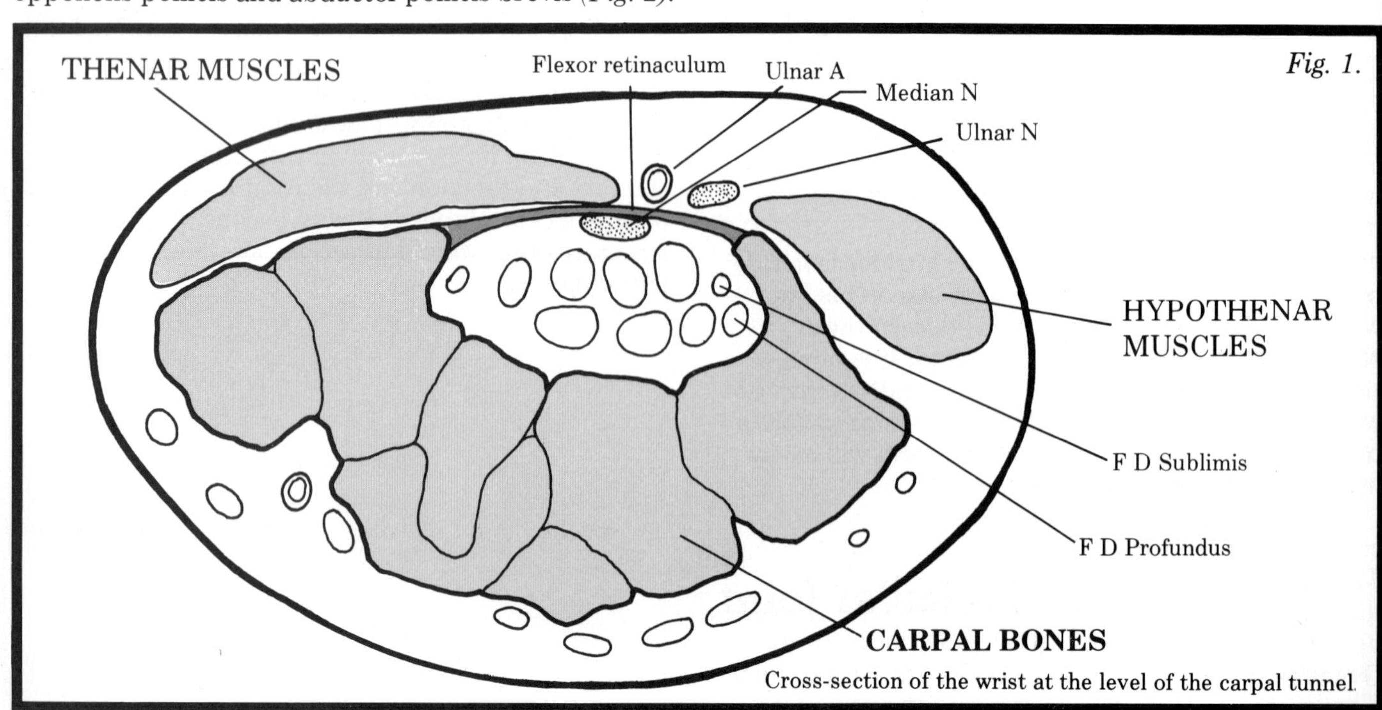

Cross-section of the wrist at the level of the carpal tunnel.

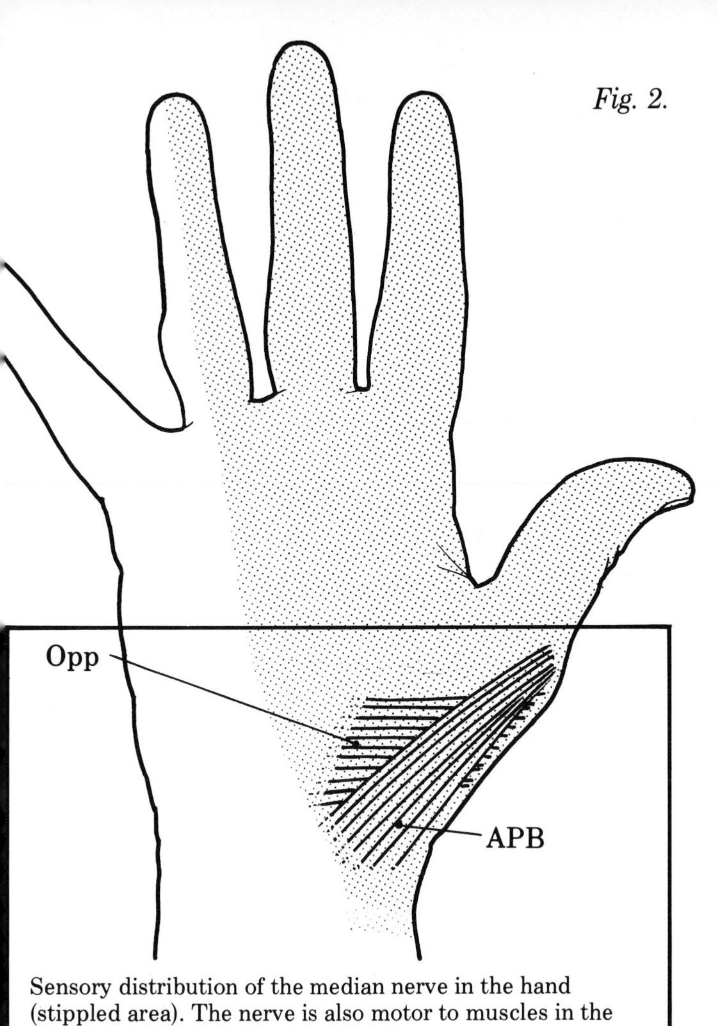

Sensory distribution of the median nerve in the hand (stippled area). The nerve is also motor to muscles in the thenar area. The two muscles most conveniently tested clinically are abductor pollicis brevis (APB) and opponens (Opp).

Most cases are idiopathic, occurring principally in middle-aged women. Obesity and fluid retention may contribute. Wrist synovitis, previous fractures *(scaphoid or Colles')* and recurrent trauma are common causes. Myxoedema, pregnancy, the contraceptive "Pill", and heart failure are less important. Very rare factors include primary amyloidosis, acromegaly and Scheie's syndrome.

Practice Point:
Beware of carpal tunnel as the presentation of rheumatoid arthritis or some other arthropathy.

Symptoms

THE TYPICAL CASE: A middle-aged woman complains of being woken at night by an unpleasant numb, tingling sensation in one or both hands. She may remember that it affects mainly the thumb, index and ring fingers. A highly characteristic feature is that the patient will usually have learned that relief can be obtained by hanging the arm out of bed and wringing the hand. In advanced cases pain may be severe and the patient may complain of interference with fine finger movements, inability to feel small objects such as pins when trying to pick them up, and wasting of the muscles at the base of the thumb.

LESS COMMON FEATURES: Pain, discomfort or parasthesiae may persist through the day. The sensory symptoms are not always confined to the distribution of the median nerve – pain often spreads up the forearm and may affect the little finger. Occasionally patients present with sensory loss or motor symptoms as the only complaint.

The diagnosis is often missed when carpal tunnel syndrome complicates an orthopaedic or rheumatological condition at the wrist. The typical symptoms are then superimposed on other features of the primary lesion.

Practice Points:
Pain spreading up the forearm may be due to carpal tunnel syndrome.
Beware of carpal tunnel syndrome complicating other symptomatic wrist disease. Ask specifically for night pain, tingling and numbness in the median nerve distribution.

Physical Signs

In mild cases there are no abnormal physical signs. Three types of signs may be present:

1. Reproduction of pain and parasthesiae by compressing the carpal tunnel can be attempted in several ways. Tinel's sign achieves this by percussion over the nerve at the wrist. A similar result may be achieved by sustained full flexion *(Phalen's sign)* or extension of the wrist.
2. Sensory signs (unlike symptoms) are confined to the distribution of the median nerve *(Fig. 2)*. Blunting of light touch and pinprick are common. "Splitting of the ring finger" (sensation better on the ulnar than the radial side) is almost pathognomonic of carpal tunnel syndrome.
3. Motor signs appear later with wasting of the muscles of the thenar eminence and loss of power in the involved muscle. Figs. 3a and b illustrate techniques for testing power in these muscles.

Two tests for motor power in muscles innervated by the median nerve in the hand: (a) Opponens muscle. The examiner attempts to separate the tightly opposed tips of the thumb and little fingers. (b) Abductor pollicis brevis. The patient places the back of his hand flat on a table, then raises the thumb vertically upwards, starting from a position beside the palm. The examiner resists this upward movement.

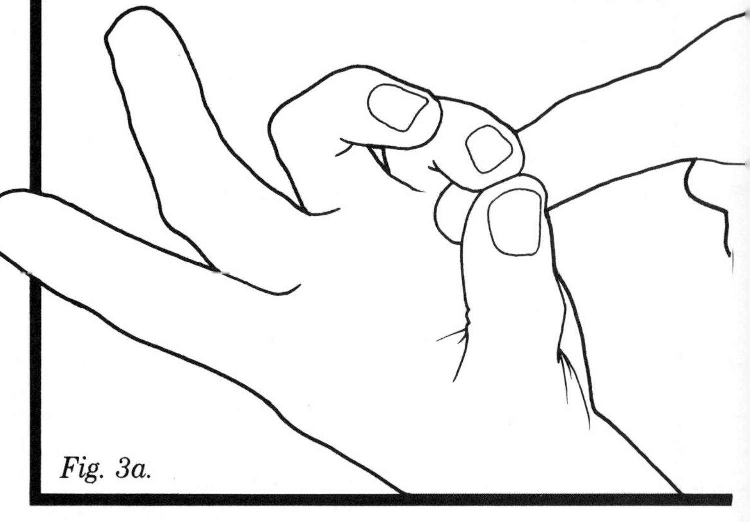

Fig. 3a.

Practice Point:
If the history is typical, carpal tunnel syndrome can be confidently diagnosed in the absence of any physical signs.

PHYSICAL SIGNS IN CARPAL TUNNEL SYNDROME (4 grades of severity)

No abnormal signs

Symptoms reproduced by compressing tunnel *(Tinel's sign, Phalen's sign).*

Sensory impairment in nerve distribution

Wasting and weakness of thenar eminence muscles.

Investigations

In most cases special investigations are unnecessary. The indications for investigation are either suspicion of some primary local or generalised disorder, or atypical signs or symptoms causing diagnostic uncertainty.

If a primary cause is suspected the investigations will be those most appropriate for the particular condition. A radiograph and ESR are probably the most useful "screening" tests. If the diagnosis is uncertain electrical nerve conduction studies can be performed. When the nerve is stimulated just above the wrist there is delay in arrival of the motor impulse at the thenar eminence; conversely a sensory stimulus applied to the index finger is delayed or unrecordable above the wrist.

Practice Points:

Investigations are usually unnecessary.
Maintain a high degree of suspicion of carpal tunnel syndrome complicating the compromised "rheumatic" hand in rheumatoid arthritis, osteoarthritis and other arthropathies.
If in doubt arrange electrical studies.

Course and Prognosis

In the common, idiopathic case, symptoms may wax and wane over many months or years. They sometimes settle spontaneously; alternatively nocturnal discomfort may become progressively more obtrusive and unpleasant.

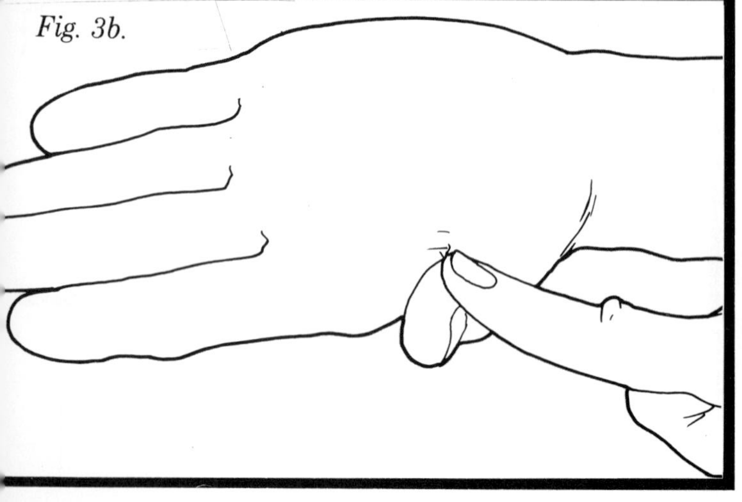
Fig. 3b.

The risk of progression is greater if there is an underlying cause such as an arthropathy, when diagnosis is often delayed.

The condition is reversible when sensory features alone are present. When motor signs appear recovery may be delayed or incomplete in spite of adequate treatment.

Practice Point:

The condition should be treated before motor signs appear in order to avoid irreversible changes.

Management

Secondary cases sometimes respond to treatment of the primary disorder *(e.g. a diuretic for oedema)*, but in most cases one of three local procedures is necessary:

Splints:

In mild cases, dominated by nocturnal symptoms, a light resting wrist splint, holding the wrist in the neutral position, may be all that is required. Immediate relief may occur (incidentally confirming the diagnosis), and after using a night splint for a few weeks, the condition often resolves completely.

Local injections:

Injection of a small quantity of a long-acting steroid preparation is often effective in mild cases and may lead to lasting resolution of symptoms.

Surgery:

Severe cases, patients with motor involvement, and those who have not responded to splints or injections may require surgical decompression of the carpal tunnel. Division of the flexor retinaculum is a simple and highly effective procedure. An unexpected cause is occasionally revealed at surgery, and material should therefore be sent for histology.

TREATMENT OF CARPAL TUNNEL SYNDROME

Wrist splints

Local corticosteroid injection

Surgical decompression

Practical Procedure:

Injection of the carpal tunnel *(Fig. 4)*.

As with any local injection, care must be taken to maintain sterile conditions. Locate the palmaris longus (the prominent superficial flexor tendon in the middle of the wrist – not always present). Mark a spot just to the radial side of this tendon on the distal of the two flexor creases on the palmar side of the wrist. Position the patient on the couch (in case of a faint) with the wrist relaxed and slightly extended (it may help to rest it across a pillow). After cleaning the skin insert a short, narrow gauge needle at the marked entry site and direct it at 45° towards the fingers.

Insert for about 6mm (the length of a short 23 gauge needle). Carefully inject a minute amount of long-acting steroid. If the needle or the initial tiny injection causes severe pain or parasthesiae withdraw the needle (you may be in the nerve, although in severe cases the procedure itself may result in pain due to high pressure in the carpal tunnel). If not, inject up to 0.2ml of steroid without local anaesthetic. After the procedure warn the patient that symptoms may be worse for the first 24-48 hours. (The increased volume may cause temporary exacerbation). No special precautions are required afterwards, although it is sensible to avoid over-use for the first 48 hours.

Fig. 4.

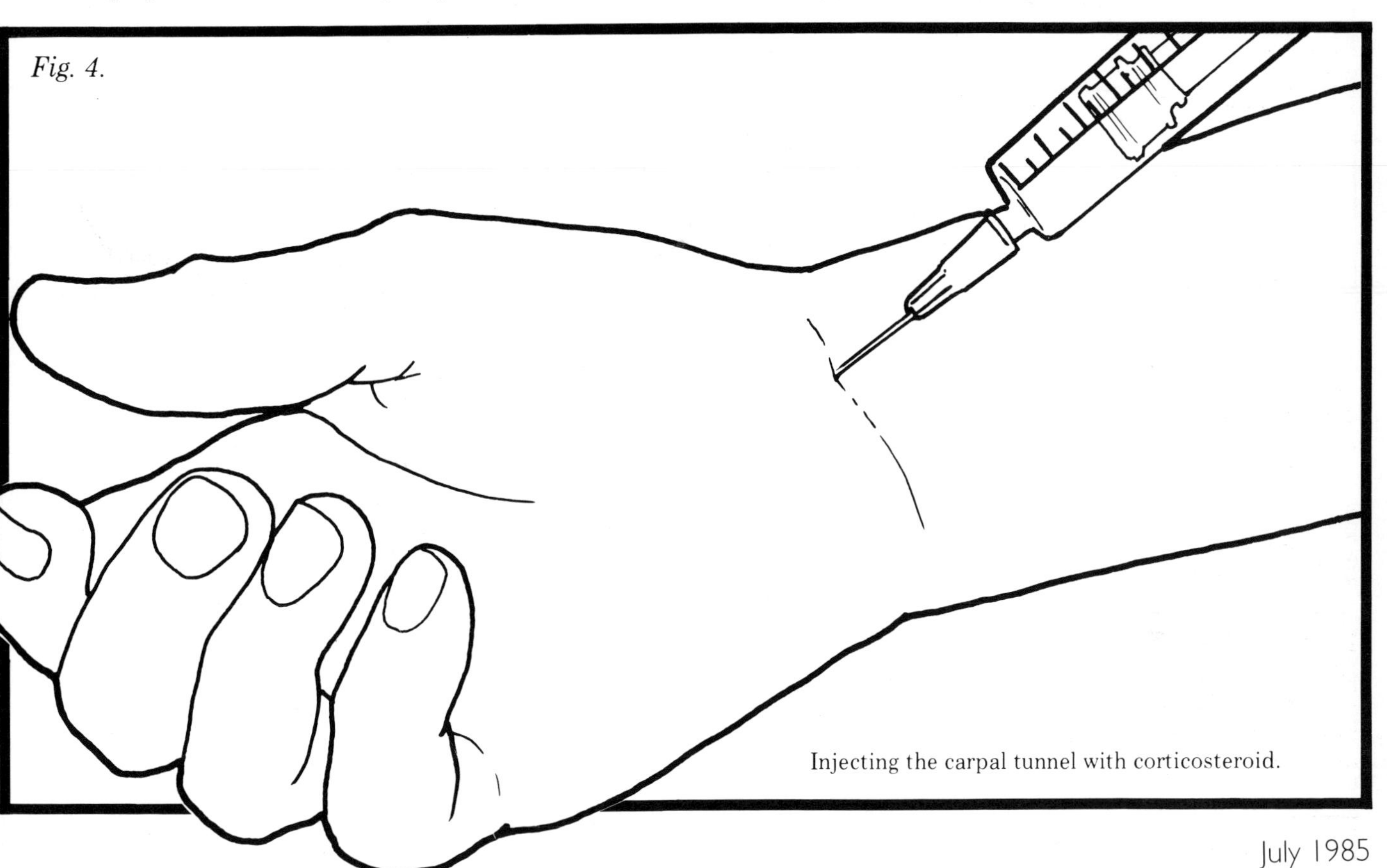

Injecting the carpal tunnel with corticosteroid.

July 1985

TENNIS & GOLFER'S ELBOW

D N Golding
Rheumatology Unit
Princess Alexandra Hospital
Harlow

Two common minor rheumatic complaints present as pain around the elbow joint: "tennis elbow" (lateral epicondylitis) on the outer aspect, and "golfer's elbow" (medial epicondylitis) on the inner side. Both conditions can be confidently diagnosed on the history and physical signs, and both can usually be cured by the general practitioner without the patient needing a hospital referral.

One of the first good descriptions of tennis elbow was given by Renton in 1830, who claimed to cure it by inserting needles into the brachioradialis muscles – a form of acupuncture? In 1882 Morris called it "lawn tennis arm", but it soon became clear that tennis was only one of many causes of this condition. However, the name "tennis elbow" has stuck, and is used to describe a condition characterised by unilateral pain and tenderness around the lateral epicondyle. Elbow pain is sometimes due to a similar condition localised to the medial epicondyle, when it is called "golfer's elbow". Occasionally the two coexist, or there is bilateral involvement; but in general bilateral elbow pain, or pain with tenderness at more than one site, suggests another condition. The local damage and inflammation at tendon insertions, which characterises tennis and golfer's elbow, must be distinguished from elbow pain secondary to arthritis of the joint itself or referred pain from the cervical spine.

Clinical Features

Tennis elbow is uncommon under 40 or over 60 years of age (Boyd and McLeod 1973). The pain is variable, from mild discomfort on using the arm to aching severe enough to prevent sleep. The pain is aggravated by gripping and twisting and the tenderness of the epicondyle is noticed by the patient whenever he knocks the elbow. In tennis elbow the pain radiates down the supinator muscle on the posterolateral aspect of the forearm, in golfer's elbow it radiates across the flexor aspect of the belly of the forearm. Indeed, referred pain is sometimes felt only in these regions and not in the elbow itself. Paraesthesiae in the arm do not occur in "primary" epicondylitis, but usually indicate proximal nerve root pressure due to cervical spondylosis, to which the pains and tenderness around the elbow is

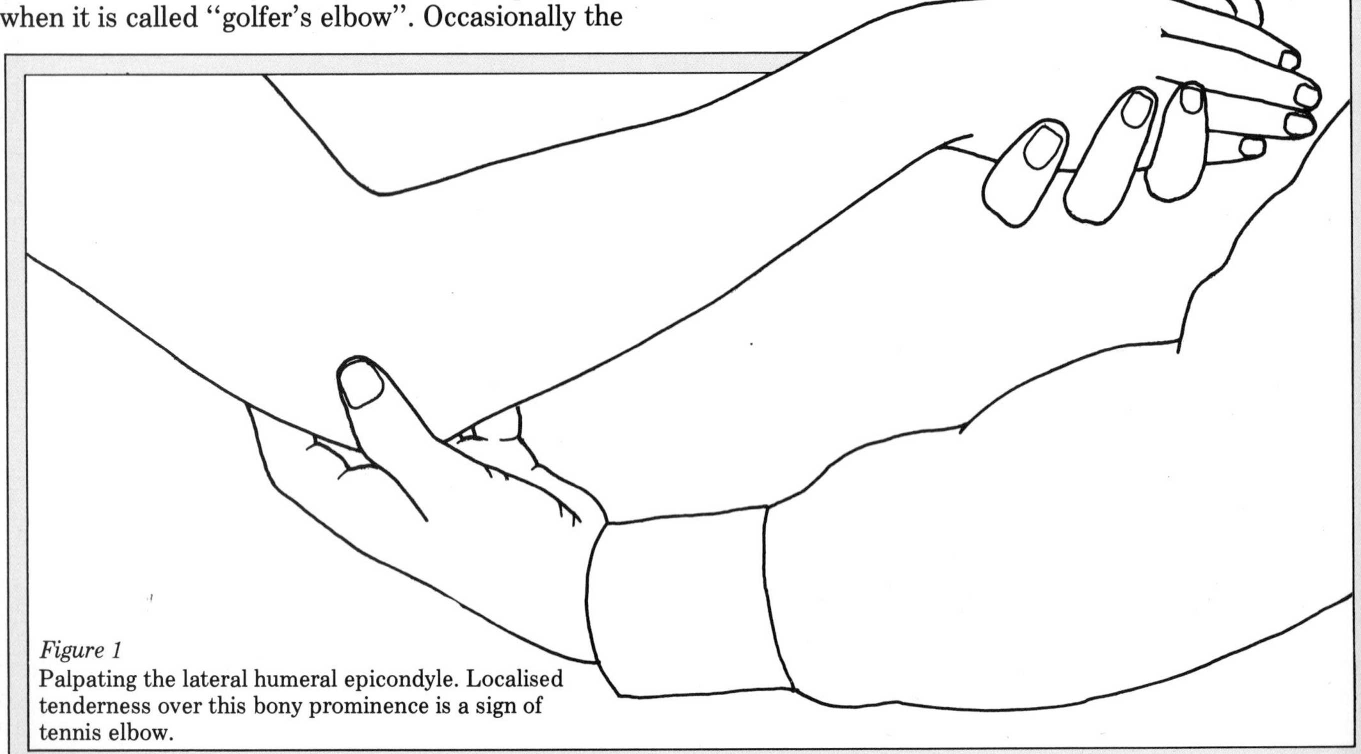

Figure 1
Palpating the lateral humeral epicondyle. Localised tenderness over this bony prominence is a sign of tennis elbow.

"secondary". However, paraesthesiae of the hands may be due to concomitant carpal tunnel syndromes which occasionally accompany tennis elbow.

Clinical examination shows a normal elbow joint which moves freely and without pain, though it may appear slightly stiff on passive movement due to resistance by the patient. The elbow joint itself is not swollen but occasionally there is a little localised soft-tissue swelling over the medial or lateral epicondyle, which is tender on palpation, the degree of tenderness depending on the severity of the epicondylitis *(Fig. 1)*. In atypical cases the tenderness is maximal above the epicondyle, over the supracondylar ridge, or sometimes over the humeral head. In severe or moderate cases of tennis elbow, pain is reproduced by forced radial deviation of the wrist, the elbow being held in the extended position. In tennis elbow there is pain on resisted extension of the wrist *(Fig. 2)*, in golfer's elbow resisted flexion of the wrist is painful *(Fig. 3)*. Pain on resisted flexion of the third finger, the elbow being extended, and hypoalgesia over the dorsum of the first interdigital web is said to denote an "atypical tennis elbow" due to radial nerve entrapment, as will be described later. The diagnosis of tennis and golfer's elbow is entirely clinical, though when an "atypical" or "secondary" epicondylitis is suspected further investigations are required. Radiographs of the elbow are normal (unless there is underlying osteoarthritis, to which epicondylitis is secondary); very occasionally there is a slight periosteal reaction of the epicondyle, or a fleck of calcium, usually representing hydroxyapatite crystals at the site of the common flexor or extensor origin. Thermography shows a "hot spot" over the epicondyle and analysis of the gradient across the abnormal area correlates well with severity, but this investigation is not normally required and is useful mainly for investigation purposes, such as assessing response to various treatments.

As already mentioned, the diagnosis of tennis or golfer's elbow is nearly always clinical. The following features suggest that the symptoms are due to some underlying disorder:

1. Bilateral "epicondylitis" (or the presence of both golfer's and tennis elbow).
2. Tenderness not localised to the epicondyle.
3. Paraesthesiae, painful limitation of neck movements or depression of deep reflexes in the arm, suggesting cervical nerve root pressure.
4. Failure to respond to local steroid injection.
5. Injection only temporarily successful, followed by recurrence within a few weeks.
6. Clinical or radiological evidence of localised arthritis (usually osteoarthritis) of the elbow.

Figure 3 Testing for pain on resisted flexion of the wrist. If the patient has golfer's elbow this provokes pain over the medical humeral epicondyle (see over).

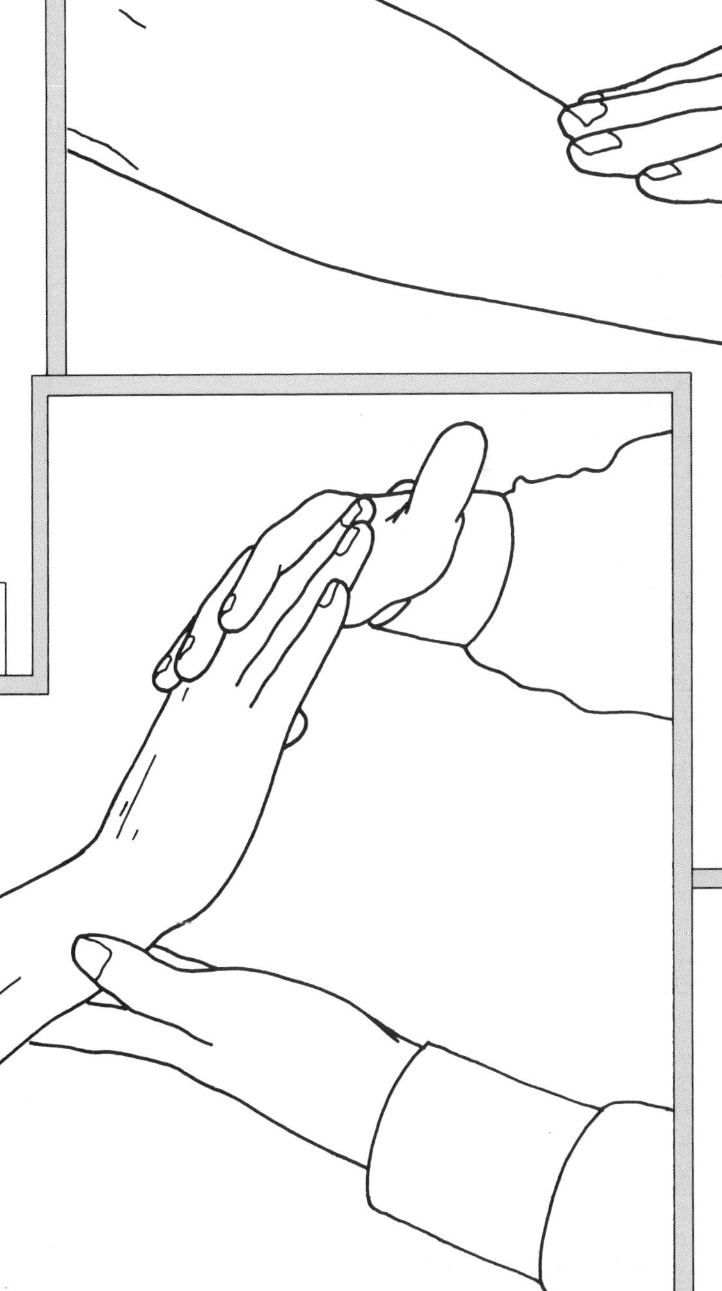

Figure 2 Testing for pain on resisted extension of the wrist. If the patient has tennis elbow this provokes pain over the lateral humeral epicondyle.

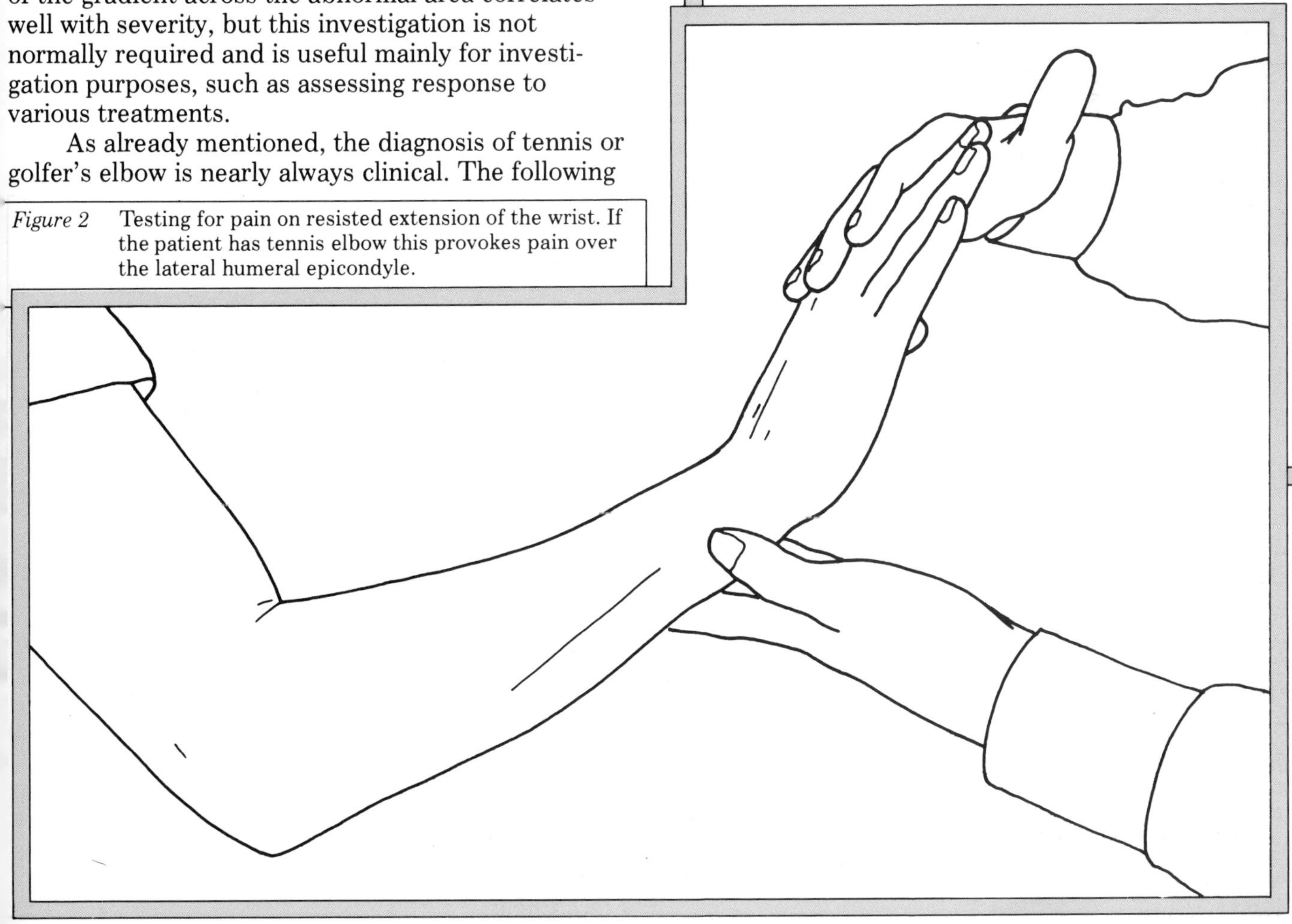

7. Evidence of generalised arthritis (e.g. rheumatoid arthritis).
8. Evidence of gout, supported by a high serum uric acid. Warm, red overlying skin of the elbow suggests soft-tissue gout (otherwise it may indicate cellulitis).

Course. Tennis and golfer's elbow are usually self-limiting, but symptoms may persist for well over a year. Standard treatment with local steroid injection (see below) usually gives immediate relief, but follow-up of patients has shown that recurrence is not uncommon: in 60% of patients the disability is prolonged, even after apparently successful initial therapy.

Pathogenesis

The common tennis or golfer's elbow is usually due to an *enthesopathy*, a lesion at the site of tendinous insertion into bone at the point where the common tendon originates from the lateral or medial humeral epicondyle. The cause is unknown, but occupational strains may be important, as it occurs in those who are continually gripping and twisting, such as carpenters and dentists. Varying occupational types have been described – for example, the term "gaoler's elbow" has been coined for those developing the condition from repeatedly opening and closing heavy cell doors! In spite of the name, only 5% of cases occur in tennis players, and it is said to be common in players who have hypermobile joints. A "real tennis" elbow can result from the strong chopping strokes of real tennis and it has been ascribed to table tennis, badminton and other racket games.

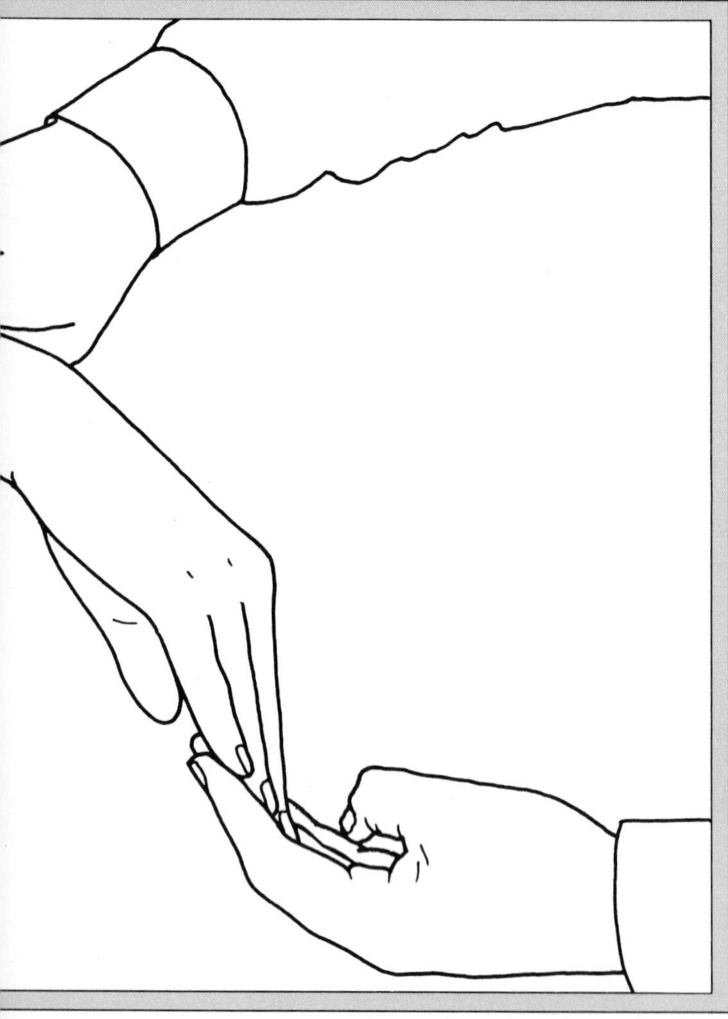

The enthesopathy primarily involves the extensor carpi radialis brevis component of the common extensor origin. A tear can be seen in many patients with tennis elbow who come to surgery. Several anatomical varieties – tenoperiosteal, muscular, tendinous and supracondylar, have been described depending on the points of maximum local tenderness. Other lesions have been found at operation: radiohumeral bursitis, a subperiosteal haematoma, or partial tear of the lateral ligament of the elbow. Some resistant cases of pain resembling tennis elbow arise from entrapment of a twig of the radial nerve known as "the anterior interosseous nerve syndrome". It is said that this can be detected by finding hypoalgesia to pinprick over the distribution of the radial nerve, i.e. the dorsum of the web of the corresponding thumb. Radial nerve entrapment may be confirmed by electrical conduction studies: measuring the terminal sensory latency and comparing it with the opposite (unaffected) side.

As already mentioned, pain like tennis or golfer's elbow may be secondary to proximal nerve-root pressure from cervical spondylosis or disc lesions and to underlying arthritis of the elbow joint. The author believes that gout involving the soft tissues may sometimes mimic tennis elbow (Golding and Thompson, 1962).

Management

Many tennis and golfer's elbows respond to one, or perhaps two, *local injections of corticosteroid* (usually triamcinolone 20mg or methylprednisolone) mixed with a local anaesthetic such as 2% lignocaine into the point of maximal tenderness at the common flexor origin (in golfer's elbow) or common extensor origin (in tennis elbow) *(Fig. 4)*. Hyaluronidase may be included in the injection "cocktail" to help spread the steroid around the inflamed tissue. The injection is given slowly into the tenoperiosteal area, finally gently infiltrating the periosteum itself. It is inadvisable to repeat the injection more than once or twice as there is a risk of atrophy of the overlying skin. Many patients have increased pain for a few hours, occasionally for a day or two after the injection and should be warned about this. After the injection the elbow should probably be rested as far as possible for two or three weeks, avoiding activities which previously caused pain. A *wrist splint* can be provided to prevent strain on the common flexor or extensor origin incurred by flexion and extension of the wrist. Firm strapping of the forearm muscles just distal to the elbow joint, or the use of one of the commercially available *elbow splints* such as the "Medisplint" may be tried. This can be effective in preventing recurrences (if worn during activities which provoked pain), or even as a primary method of treatment.

When steroid injections are ineffective or only partly effective (or should the patient refuse injection) *ultrasound therapy* to the area sometimes provides relief, but is much less reliable than steroid injection. While exercises to strengthen the forearm muscles are often prescribed in the USA, in the UK emphasis is generally placed on resting the elbow rather than exercising it.

If there is little or no response to one or two steroid injections and a course of ultrasound, one must review the possibility of *some other cause* for the pain. There may be a good response to intermittent neck traction when cervical spondylosis is responsible. Median nerve conduction tests will identify associated carpal tunnel syndrome. Ulnar nerve conduction tests may throw light on a persisting golfer's elbow because ulnar neuritis or entrapment at the elbow is sometimes associated with medial epicondylitis. In patients with rheumatoid arthritis general treatment of this condition is required as well as local treatment of the epicondylitis and the same is true of gout.

The long-lasting or recurrent tennis elbow may have become "chronic" due to fibrosis of the common extensor origin, and the tendon is felt to be thickened. Here deep massage and friction combined with ultrasound is helpful, or fibrous adhesions can be broken by manipulating the elbow under anaesthetic (forcible extension and pronation of the forearm). At the same time a local steroid injection is given to avoid re-activation of acute inflammation.

Surgical treatment of tennis or golfer's elbow is only required very occasionally, when the condition is absolutely resistant to conservative treatment and severe enough to handicap the patient. Various operations have been advocated: division of the tendon at the epicondyle (tenotomy); open ablation of the origin of the extensor carpi radialis brevis from the periosteum, capsule and attached lateral ligament, sometimes followed by shaving of the exposed lateral epicondyle; or Z-plasty of the extensor carpi radialis brevis in its lower third to relieve tension on the common extensor origin. Other procedures include denervation of the common origin and excision of part of the annular ligament. Radial or posterior interosseous nerve entrapment can be relieved when this is thought to be a factor responsible for persistent tennis elbow.

Figure 4 The first line of treatment for tennis elbow is an injection of corticosteroid and local anaesthetic down to and around the lateral humeral epicondyle, exactly at the site of maximum tenderness.

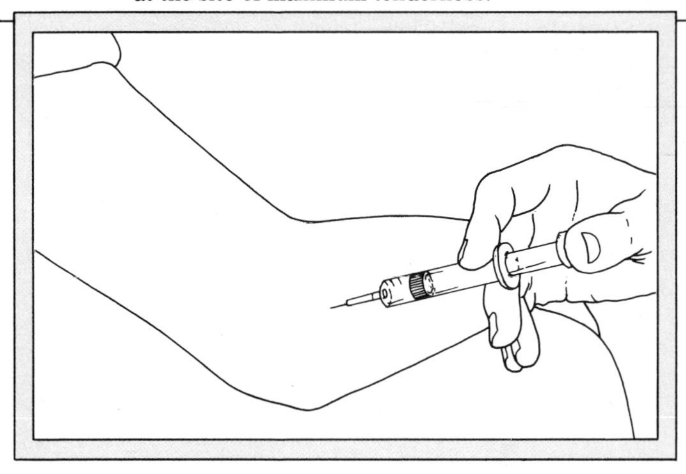

REFERENCES

1. Boyd H.B. and McLeod A.C. (1973). Journal of Bone and Joint Surgery, **55A**, 1183.
2. Golding D.N. and Thompson M. (1962). Proceedings of the Royal Society of Medicine, **55**, No. 5, 406-408 (Section of Physical Medicine 14-16).
3. Morris H. (1882). Lancet, **2**, 557.
4. Renton J. (1830). Edinburgh Medical Journal, **34**, 100.

THE PAINFUL FOOT

J Black
State Registered Chiropodist
Clinical Associate
The Orthopaedic Foot Clinic
Western Infirmary
Glasgow

The foot remains one of the most complex mechanical structures in the body. Even with modern sophisticated methods of evaluation, much of the function of the foot is shrouded in mystery. In a normal lifespan most feet will cover 100,000 miles or the equivalent of walking three times around the earth's surface. Apart from the mechanical considerations, which respond to variations in anatomical structure, feet also reflect the state of our general health and will mirror systemic conditions such as diabetes, rheumatoid arthritis, peripheral vascular disease and neurological conditions with complications being manifest in the feet.

In order to understand basic foot pathology it is sensible to divide the foot into three distinct areas: 1 the hindfoot – comprising the ankle and subtalar joints; 2 the midfoot – made up of the talo-navicular joint and the calcaneo-cuboid articulation together with the joints of cuneiforms and metarsals one, two and three and the joints of the cuboid and the fourth and fifth metatarsals; and 3 the forefoot – made up of the metatarsals, the metatarsophalangeal joints and the toes *(Fig 1)*. Each of these areas of the foot is subject to its own specific disorders and the commonest are highlighted here.

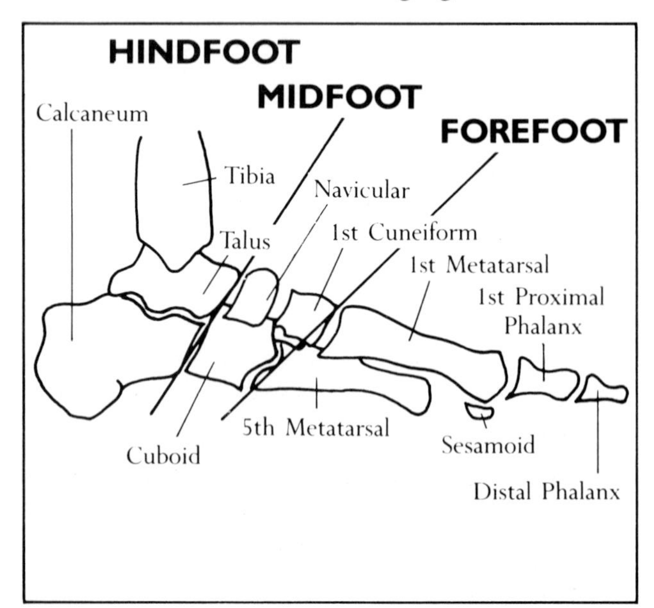

FIG 1: Three basic divisions of the foot

THE HINDFOOT

When considering the hindfoot one must evaluate the function of both the ankle and subtalar joints together as they are closely linked anatomically and functionally. Any condition affecting one joint will quite frequently provoke a compensatory change in the other. Most conditions affecting the ankle tend to be traumatic in origin. Inversion sprains of the ankle are by far the most common with the lateral ligaments being strained during forcible inversion of the subtalar joint *(Fig 2)*. Quite frequently inversion sprains of the ankle result from malalignment between the forefoot and the hindfoot which sees the forefoot everted in relation to the hindfoot, such that in order to place the forefoot on the ground the hindfoot must invert or supinate. When this happens on uneven ground or with excessive force, the velocity of the inversion can cause a violent sprain of the ankle. Repeated ankle sprains often indicate such malalignment problems. Immobilisation may be necessary with below knee walking plasters or strapping. Ice is useful especially in the early stages and rest often a necessity.

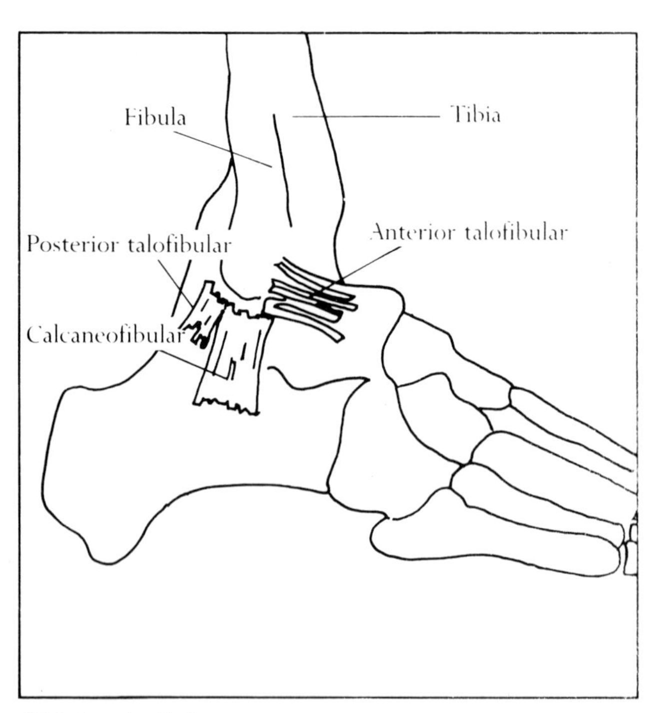

FIG 2: Lateral ankle ligaments

Assessment of the ankle joint is simple and Fig 3 illustrates evaluation of dorsiflexion and plantar flexion necessary for normal walking. Many injuries of the ankle joint result from sport and accurate history of the mechanics of the injury will lead to a conclusive diagnosis. Limitation of ankle joint motion has profound effects on locomotion and compensatory motion has to be found either in the subtalar joint or in the knee. Excess pronation is a frequent method of compensation *(Fig 4)*,and this often leads to tibialis posterior tendinitis manifested by pain at the insertion of the muscle on the plantar aspect of the navicular and radiating under and behind the medial malleolus and up the inner aspect of the lower leg along the margin of the tibia.

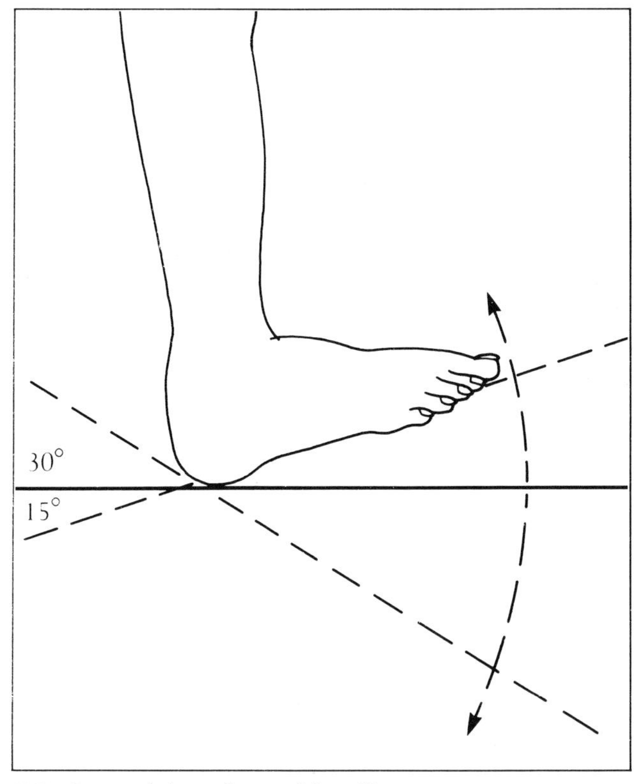

FIG 3: Dorsi and plantar flexion of the ankle

Congenital anomalies affecting the hindfoot such as talipes equinus are evident from birth and require orthopaedic referral. Tarsal conditions, the most common being the calcaneal navicular bar, rarely manifest themselves till early teens when the foot develops a flattened appearance. It can also be accompanied by peroneal spasm which can be exquisitely painful. This sometimes requires surgical intervention but if movement is present orthoses (supports) often offer adequate relief. Flat feet by themselves may not be due to any inherent pathology and require no treatment whatsoever other than reassurance of over-anxious parents.

Achilles tendinitis and plantar fasciitis with associated heel pad pain are also conditions which commonly affect the hindfoot. Mechanical causes are frequently implicated and should not be forgotten when advocating a treatment regime.

THE MIDFOOT

Most problems occur as a result of injury or overuse. The ability of the foot to cope with levels of stress to which individuals subject their feet depends on the amount of compensation available in the midtarsal joints. Strain of the plantar fascia is a common problem with people whose job demands long periods of standing or individuals who put on a lot of weight over a relatively short period. Tendinitis of tibialis anterior, tibialis posterior and the peronei are frequently overuse problems and are best treated by understanding the cause. Orthotic control offers the best form of management. Exostoses around the margins of the joints, in particular on the dorsal aspect of the foot, are common. Certain types

> **PRACTICE POINT**
> If The Foot Does Not Fit The Shoe Then It Is Reasonable To Get The Shoe To Fit The Foot.

of footwear which avoid pressure on these areas provide the best way of dealing with the problem, although in severe cases surgical intervention may be the only solution. Ganglions often appear in this area as well, but are rarely problemmatical. Midfoot pain is often chronic with symptoms persisting for prolonged periods. If associated with poor foot mechanics orthoses will reduce movement and offer the best form of relief.

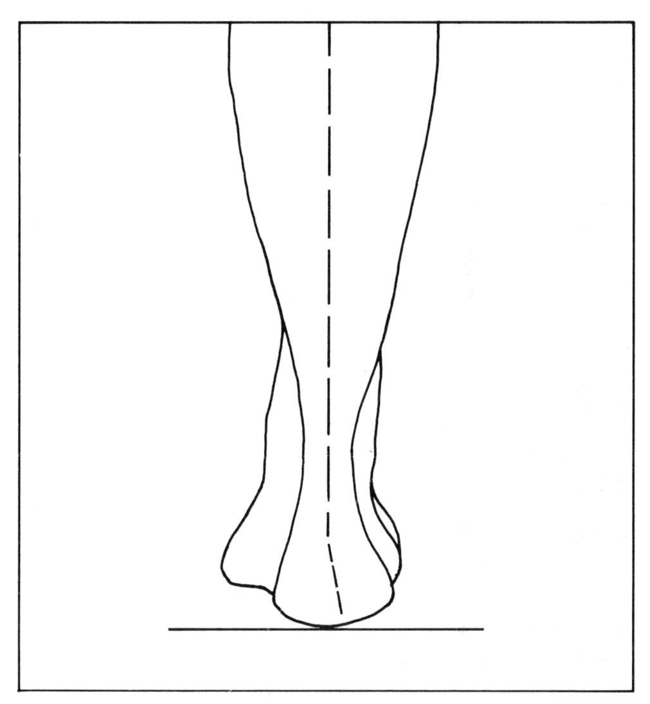

FIG 4: Pronated foot with calcaneal eversion

THE FOREFOOT

The forefoot presents many problems, frequently associated with bad footwear. Toe deformities and hallux valgus are the most common. Corns and inflamed bursae are added complications. Most forefoot problems can be adequately managed by a State Registered

> **PRACTICE POINT**
> State Registration Is The Only Qualification For Chiropodists Working In The NHS.

Chiropodist. Surgical intervention may be necessary and many chiropodists can now perform digital surgery on a day care basis using local anaesthesia. More complex surgery remains the province of the orthopaedic surgeon, but this too can be carried out under local anaesthetics.

Ingrown toenails still present as a common problem but they can be adequately dealt with by the chiropodist who has the necessary expertise.

Verrucae and athlete's foot are conditions which predominate in people who use communal changing areas such as swimming baths and sports centres. Verrucae can be distinguished from corns because they are normally painful on lateral compression, whereas corns are painful on direct pressure. Corns also occur over weight bearing areas while verrucae can occur anywhere on the plantar surface. Verrucae are frequently painful first thing in the morning or after retiring to bed, whereas corns are most painful when subjected to direct pressure from footwear. Both conditions are common in the young. If verrucae are not troublesome it is sometimes wise just to ignore them. Effective foot hygiene cannot be overstressed. Potassium permanganate footbaths and the use of appropriate fungicides are generally efficacious and provided they are used for two to three months after the symptons have disappeared the condition should disappear. However patients and clinicians often forget current footwear as a continuing source of infection: furry slippers or boots should be discarded.

Examination

Examination of the foot demands not only an accurate history of the complaint, but also the need to compare the foot of which the patient complains with what may be considered the normal foot. Many practitioners do not even ask patients to remove their shoes and stockings before either writing a prescription or referring their patient to the orthopaedic surgeon or the chiropodist for a second opinion. Nor is it adequate to examine the foot in isolation. When examining feet we do so not only with the patient seated but we must ask the patient to stand and examine the position of the feet from in front of the patient and from behind. This way we will be able to get an overall impression of the basic structure of the foot but also its relationship with the legs. It may well be that the patient's complaint stems from postural abnormalities of the trunk rather than within the foot itself and therefore examining the feet without being able to see the legs including the knees will not allow the practitioner to come to a reasonable diagnosis.

The symptoms of which the patient complains should be considered in context. Does the pain only occur during weightbearing? How long ago was the onset? Does it radiate? Is there any swelling? Are there any colour changes of note? Are the feet cold? Are there any abnormalities of gait? Are these symptoms merely confined to the feet or are there other symptoms related to other body systems which we should be taking into account?

Joint mobility or the lack of it should be considered. There should be 30° of plantar flexion and some 15° - 20° of dorsiflexion available in the ankle joint for normal locomotion. Inversion at the subtalar joint should be twice that of eversion *(Fig 5)* and the midtarsal joints should allow the forefoot to assume a position relative to the hindfoot where the transverse planes of both are parallel. The first metatarsal phalangeal joint and the joints of the lesser toes should move freely and without pain.

DIAGNOSIS AND TREATMENT

Treatment will of course depend on the nature and severity of the symptoms; however for generalised foot care the services of the State Registered Chiropodist will be able to maintain feet in a healthy state. In principle the feet should never be treated in isolation. Care should always be taken to ensure that the complaints of the patient are not part of a systemic condition.

> **PRACTICE POINT**
> The Foot is a Systemic Mirror And Should Always Be Examined If Some Systemic Illness Is Suspected.

For example, rheumatoid arthritis can present itself as pain in the metatarsophalangeal joints, but it is not uncommon for this to be labelled as 'metatarsalgia' until a proper examination reveals tenderness and thickening of some of these joints. Pain and tenderness of the calcaneum – either inferior or posterior at the insertion of the Achilles tendon – can be a feature of Reiter's disease or other forms of inflammatory arthritis, which may also produce an asymmetrical sausage-shaped swelling of one or more toes. Involvement of the first metatarsophalangeal joint by acute gout is of course well known, but sometimes gouty arthritis can be less dramatic than classical fiery podagra.

> **PRACTICE POINT**
> It Is Much More Effective If All The Core Services Work Together In The Primary Care Team.

Where possible it is best if the chiropodist, orthopaedic surgeon, diabetic specialist and rheumatologist work in harmony to provide an integrated service.

CONCLUSION

Many patients suffering from painful feet tend to feel that their complaints are not taken seriously and yet 43% of school children by the age of fifteen have some form of foot deformity. 83% of elderly over the age of seventy five have serious problems with their feet which decrease their mobility and thus place ever increasing burdens on other branches of the social services. Keep patients' feet in good order and they maintain their independence and their quality of life for very much longer.

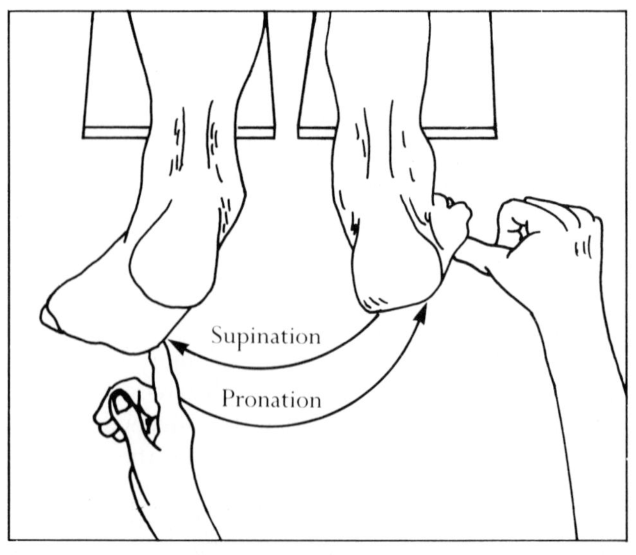

Fig 5: Evaluation of the subtalar joint

THE MANAGEMENT OF ACUTE SOFT-TISSUE INJURIES IN SPORT

C Murray-Leslie
Consultant Rheumatologist
Derbyshire Royal Infirmary

Sport for all means sports injuries for all, and doctors are now seeing soft-tissue injuries in individuals of widely varying age, fitness and athletic ability. It is therefore useful for family doctors to be conversant with the treatment of athletic injuries and to understand the principles of fitness training and warming up in the prevention of injury and its recurrence.

Any serious competitive athletic activity requires adequate and sensible physical preparation. Such physical training seeks to increase muscle strength and endurance, increase the speed and co-ordination of muscle action and finally increase and maintain cardiorespiratory fitness. It is important that muscles should be developed symmetrically on each side of the body, for example both quadriceps muscles in footballers, and the non-dominant side in throwing sports.

The overall successful management of acute sports injuries requires:

1. **An accurate history.**
2. **A physical examination with an emphasis on function.**
3. **An accurate anatomical and pathomechanical diagnosis including identification of any contributory faults in technique or equipment.**
4. **Recognition of serious injury requiring orthopaedic management.**
5. **Adequate initial treatment to reduce bleeding, swelling and pain.**
6. **Adequate functional rehabilitation of the injured part.**
7. **Maintenance of overall muscular and cardiorespiratory fitness throughout.**
8. **The involvement of an experienced and interested physiotherapist.**

TREATMENT AND REHABILITATION

The treatment plan will vary according to the site and severity of the injury, but it is important that the athlete should not return to competitive activity until s/he is fully recovered and has full function without pain. Any medical or athletic dishonesty in this respect risks recurrence of injury and the possibility of a chronic problem.

Immediate Treatment of Injury (up to 48 hours)

The majority of acute muscle and joint injuries should be treated as soon as possible by:

1. The individual desisting from sport followed by **resting** the injured part.
2. The application of **ice** with **compression** of the injured part, but avoiding heat or massage.
3. **Elevation** of the limb.

This regimen is aimed at reducing swelling, local bleeding and pain, and can be remembered by the mnemonic R.I.C.E (Fig 1). Initially assessment of acute injury can be difficult and is often best repeated after 24 or 48 hours.

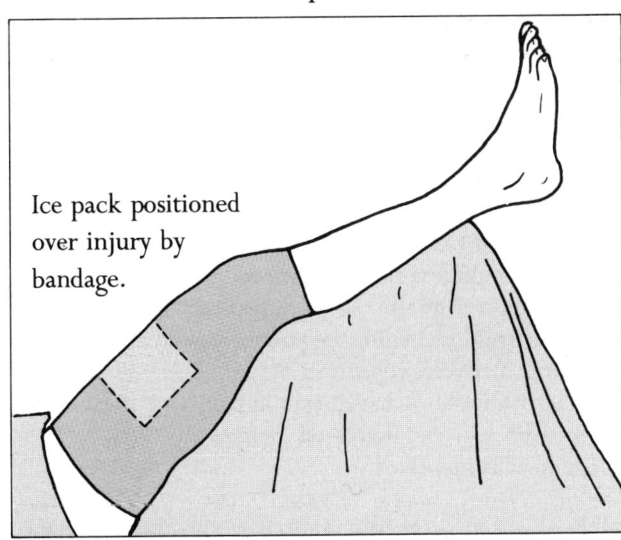

Figure 1. Injured quadriceps muscle treated by elevation, cooling and compression with an elastic bandage.

Rest

As a rule the athlete should rest the affected part for 24-48 hours avoiding all loading on the injured area.

Cooling (Ice)

In the first 24 hours after injury ice packs, crushed ice, a packet of frozen peas or even cold running water can be applied to traumatised tissue. To be effective ice should not be applied for more than 10 minutes at a time as prolonged cooling causes vasodilatation and is counter-productive.

PRACTICE POINT

Ice or ice packs should never be directly applied to the skin and bandage or towelling must always be interposed.

Compression

Compression can be applied simultaneously with cold, and this can be done conveniently by using an elastic bandage under tension to hold an ice pack in position. The bandage should extend about 20 cm above and below the injury.

Elevation

An injured leg should be elevated for 24-48 hours when there has been substantial swelling and bleeding. Ideally an injured leg should be maintained at an elevation of 45° from the horizontal.

Non-Steroidal Anti-Inflammatory Drugs

These may be useful in a wide variety of injuries to reduce inflammation and pain in the acute stage.

PRACTICE POINT

Corticosteroid injections have no place in the treatment of acute soft-tissue injuries in sport and may be injurious.

Treatment after 48 Hours

Once bleeding has ceased and swelling stabilised then, depending upon the nature and severity of the injury, treatment to promote healing and increase function may be undertaken.

Heat

This can be applied to superficial and deep tissues in various ways (hot packs, infra red lamps, short wave, etc.). Heat relieves pain and muscle spasm and reduces joint stiffness, making movement easier. It may also promote healing by increasing blood flow.

Exercise

The resumption of exercise needs to be under the supervision of an interested and experienced physiotherapist. The guiding principle is that exercise is gradually increased and care taken not to produce pain. For many joint and muscle injuries isometric exercises can start immediately. Initially muscle contractions are made slowly to avoid exceeding the pain threshold and adequate rest given between repetition of the contractions. Once muscle contractions have become pain free the number performed can be increased before the resistance to movement is increased.

Once resisted isometric exercises can be performed without pain, dynamic exercising can be gradually introduced. Slow, active, gentle stretching of joints and the maintenance of the fully stretched position for 6-8 seconds is important and should be carried out once static muscle contractions are no longer painful.

Immobilisation of Joints

This may be required for the healing of more serious ligamentous or tendon injuries, but should only be applied on specialist medical advice and it should be remembered that the detraining effect of immobilising a joint in an athlete even for a short time is considerable.

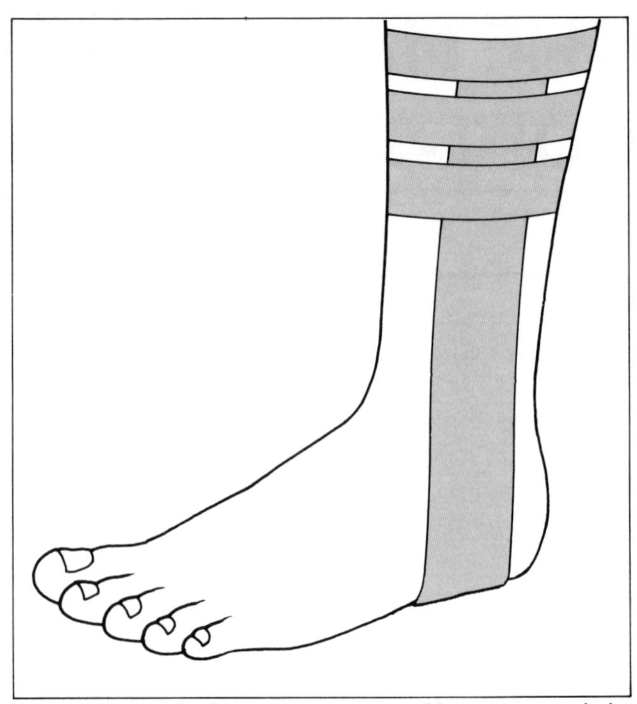

Figure 2. A non-stretch adhesive stirrup to prevent ankle inversion over which a 'figure of 8' strapping can be applied.

Functional Support of Joints

A number of supporting devices of dubious efficacy exist. However taping of joints with in-elastic adhesive tape can be of value in protecting the ankle joint following lateral ligament injury or where there has been a tendency to recurrence of injury (Fig 2). To be effective, strapping has to be tight and is therefore best avoided in the acute stages of an injury. In addition it should only be applied by an experienced practitioner.

INJURY TO MUSCLES

These are predisposed to by lack of warming up before sport, poor fitness, poor technique, fatigue and previous injury. Muscle tears may be complete or incomplete and are inevitably accompanied by bleeding. This may lead to haematoma formation or widespread extravasation of blood into the subcutaneous tissues. Intermuscular bleeding may lead to bruising some distance from the site of injury, which may be misleading. Intramuscular haematoma and complete muscle rupture require long and careful rehabilitation.

INJURY TO TENDONS

Partial and complete rupture of both small and large tendons can occur during sport. Often older athletes are affected and tears often involve areas of tendons with a relatively poor blood supply, such as 2-5 cm from the calcaneal attachment of the Achilles tendon and 1-2 cm from the humeral attachment of the supraspinatous tendon.

Complete rupture of a tendon leads to loss of function. In the case of the Achilles tendon a sudden 'giving' sensation and pain is followed by very little pain but an inability to run and difficulty in walking. A palpable gap may be felt in the tendon and the individual is unable to stand on his toes other than occasionally by the use of the toe flexors. Additionally there is an increase in the range of passive dorsiflexion at the ankle and squeezing the calf fails to transmit pull to the calcaneum.

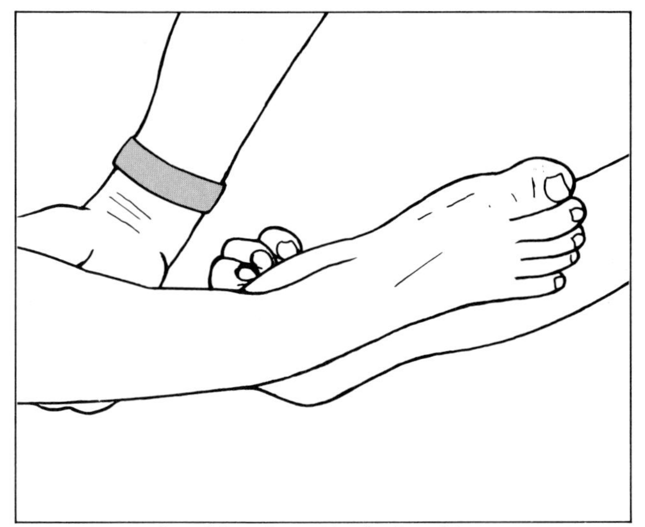

Figure 3. Testing the stability of an ankle after lateral ligament sprain.

Figure 4. A wobble board for balance and co-ordination training after ankle injury.

Partial rupture of the Achilles tendon also produces a painful sensation of tearing but tendon function remains intact. There will however be local tenderness, pain on stretching the tendon and sometimes an area of swelling.

Surgical repair is recommended for complete tears of the tendon followed by immobilisation of the ankle for four to six weeks as this gives a shorter overall recovery and there is a reduced recurrence rate compared to treatment by immobilisation alone. Partial tears are usually treated conservatively by a period of rest and immobilisation of the ankle followed by a regimen of increasing exercise.

SPRAINED ANKLES

Eighty percent of injuries to the ankle are ligamentous strains with the majority affecting elements of the lateral ligament. However other injuries occur including rupture of the medial ligament (deltoid), disruption of the tibio-fibular syndesmosis and fracture. Ankle injuries may occur singly or in combination and the extent of an injury may not be immediately apparent. Certainly the amount of immediate swelling does not indicate the severity or extent of the injury. The doctor's primary task is to determine whether joint instability is present (Fig 3) and whether fracture is likely, both of which will require x-ray examination and orthopaedic assessment. Rehabilitation of ankle injuries involves not only exercises for muscular strength, but most importantly exercises for co-ordination and balance (Fig 4).

KNEE INJURIES

As with the ankle, soft-tissue injuries of the knee are common in contact sports. All ligamentous injuries of the knee are potentially serious as they may affect joint stability. Where there is any possibility of complete rupture, the patient must be seen by an orthopaedic surgeon. Injuries to the knee ligaments and meniscal cartilages may occur singly or in combination and the full extent of ligamentous injuries can be easily overlooked. Immediate and rapid swelling of the knee within the first 30 minutes after injury suggests haemarthrosis which can be easily confirmed by aspiration and indicates significant injury. Sometimes full examination may have to be delayed for 24-48 hours after injury because of pain and muscle spasm and even then it may have to be undertaken under anaesthetic.

To determine the ligamentous integrity of the knee, medial and lateral stability is assessed with the knee straight and in 20°-30° flexion. The anterior drawer sign is carried out to determine anterior stability of the knee both with the knee at 90° of flexion and also at 10°-20° of flexion. The knee is also inspected for posterior subluxation of the tibia and the posterior drawer sign is performed testing the integrity of the posterior cruciate ligament (Fig 5). Quadriceps wasting can occur very rapidly after knee injuries and efforts to maintain and improve the strength of these muscles should begin as soon as possible. Usually static tightening of the quadriceps can be practised from the time of injury.

Figure 5a. Posterior subluxation of right tibia from posterior cruciate injury.

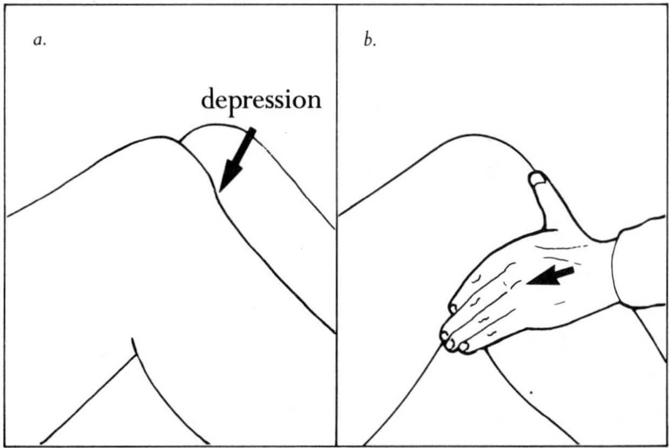

Figure 5b. Examination of posterior cruciate ligament with posterior drawer test.

HELPFUL ADDRESSES:

British Association of Sport and Medicine
c/o National Sports Medicine Institute
The Medical College of St Bartholomew's Hospital
Charter House Square
London EC1M 6BQ

Association of Chartered Physiotherapists in Sports Medicine
81 Heol West Plas
Coity
Bridgend
Mid Glamorgan CF35 6BA

WORK-RELATED SYNDROMES

H A Bird
Senior Lecturer in Rheumatology
University of Leeds

INTRODUCTION

Work-related syndromes involving the musculoskeletal system are not new. The currently fashionable "repetitive strain injury" was first described around 1700 and folklore perpetuates conditions such as "Upholsterer's hand" and "Fisherwoman's finger". Such vivid descriptions detract from the fundamental problem of most work-related syndromes which is that repetitive over-use, better termed "mis-use", can produce symptoms at any site in the musculoskeletal system once a certain threshold of activity is exceeded. Our own interest has been in the occupational ills of musicians but the principles that lead to their occurrence can be applied equally well to any other occupation.

THE IMPORTANCE OF A DETAILED OCCUPATIONAL HISTORY

Recording the job title alone is not enough. The physician should enquire carefully about the nature of the work and may sometimes need to visit the workplace. Factors contributing to musculoskeletal symptoms are well recognised and are summarised under the headings of movement, posture and organization.

1. Movement

The task performed should be analysed in terms of the force applied, the direction in which it is applied, the speed required and the frequency. These simple details may help clarify the level of experience of the worker (inexperience often produces excessive force for the task), whether they were aggressive or relaxed and whether the tools provided were adequate. Tools may need to be power assisted and the implement tailored to each individual's hand and frame.

2. Posture

The body should be supported in a position of optimum function, the standing worker able to work at maximum mechanical advantage. The sedentary worker requires support for the back and feet. For jobs requiring hand function, the forearm should be inclined slightly downwards and the wrists should not be flexed. The thumb should not be used excessively in proportion to the other fingers.

3. Organization

Movements and posture have to be integrated with the work organization. The speed of working may be independent or dependent, as in a conveyor line. The worker may be on a fixed salary or receiving an incremental bonus. Training may not have been given and further supervision may be inadequate. There should be access to an adequate complaints procedure to avoid delay in the reporting of industrial injury.

DIVERSITY OF EMPLOYMENT

Women tend to be more dexterous than men and more frequently work part-time. The occupational history should seek strains experienced during the period a part-time worker is at home. Employees on production lines, such as electronics assembly, are particularly susceptible to repetitive strain of the upper limbs. Keyboard operators, usually sedentary, are likely to mis-use the back and the fingers. Low temperatures, outside work in wet conditions and vibration all exacerbate symptoms.

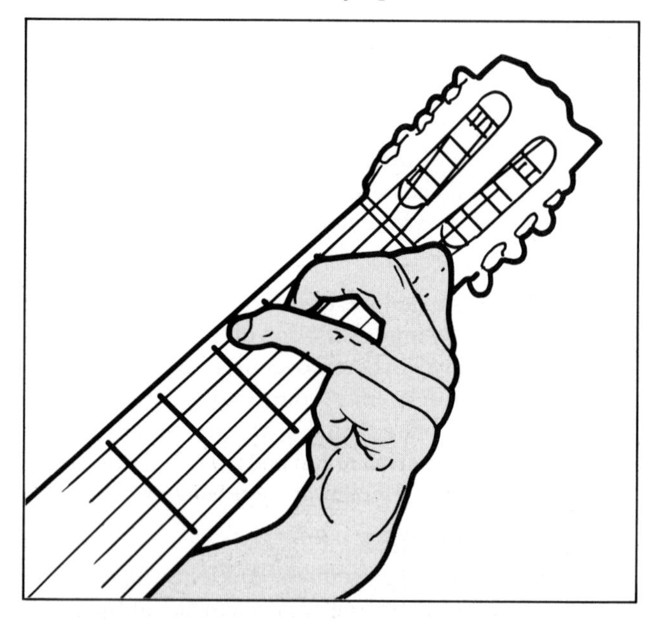

The occupational ills of musicians can be similarly predicted. For keyboard players and wind players problems are equally distributed between left and right arms. Pianists suffer wrist and finger problems. Woodwind players, who hold a heavy instrument rigidly for long periods at a mechanical disadvantage, suffer upper arm strains. String players have the most diverse symptoms. The functions of the arms in string players is quite different. The bowing arm is susceptible to wrist and shoulder strain; the hand that stops the strings develops finger problems, most marked in classical guitar players where the hand is subjected to most stretch. Double-bass and cello players have posture problems and back strain.

MUSCULOSKELETAL COMPLAINTS THAT ARE EASILY IDENTIFIABLE

Sometimes the occupation produces a well defined syndrome for which there is a specific treatment. The remedy should be accompanied by alteration of the working environment so the precipitating stimulus does not recur.

A. Carpal Tunnel Syndrome

This is common amongst seamstresses, grocers, butchers and clerical workers. Excessive force required for finger pinch grip, a "clothes wringing" repetitive motion or vibration are all likely ergonomic risk factors. Diagnosis is based on history and examination. Treatment is with local hydrocortisone injection and subsequent avoidance of the precipitating factor. Sometimes it may be necessary to proceed to EMG studies and surgery.

B. Epicondylitis at the elbow

This is not confined to golf and tennis players. It occurs in occupations where the forearm is twisted against resistance and local tenderness at the epicondyle is often evident upon examination. Treatment is with rest, intra-lesional hydrocortisone and avoidance of precipitating factors.

C. Tenosynovitis in the hand

This is most common with repetitive flexion and extension of the thumb or fingers, particularly in typists, or when an electronic production line is accelerated. Mothers attending to their new-born babies are also at risk! The most commonly involved tendon is that of abductor pollicis longus (De Quervain's syndrome). The condition may respond to infiltration of the offending tendon with hydrocortisone and lignocaine.

The speed of a conveyor belt may be slowed down.

D. Capsulitis of the shoulder

Restriction of movement in all directions (frozen shoulder) appears more frequently than the more local supraspinatus tendonitis. Treatment may be by physiotherapy or injection as described in an earlier ARC report.(1)

CHRONIC SYMPTOMS WITHOUT PHYSICAL SIGNS

Unfortunately such clearly defined symptoms are seen in only a small minority of work-related problems. The majority of patients describe more diffuse aching, stiffness or tiredness, often of muscle and occasionally of joints, invariably in relation to work. Examination may reveal non-specific muscle tenderness or restriction of movement at affected joints but often few or no localising signs are found. As chronicity establishes

Mothers attending to new-born babies are at risk from De Quervain's syndrome.

itself, the patient becomes depressed. Anxiety may be a feature, particularly if the patient's livelihood depends upon their ability to continue with their occupation. In an "open access" musicians' clinic, many patients attend at times of personal stress. For students this may be related to examinations; for a professional musician it may be related to a new appointment.

The patient's story should be believed and persistence in history taking may be required. In one example, an outbreak of shoulder pain affecting the majority of violinists in an orchestra had initially been ascribed either to hysteria or to a viral infection. Enquiry revealed that symptoms occurred only when an opera of unusual length was performed in one of three theatres. The slope of the orchestral pit in this theatre was of a different angle compared to the others, necessitating an unusual posture of the neck and shoulders in order to see the conductor!

A chronic condition may be precipitated by an acute event of this sort. If the working conditions are not conducive to interest the occupational illness may become self-perpetuating, even leading to litigation against the employer.

AETIOPATHOGENESIS OF THE CHRONIC CONDITION

Chronic occupational conditions have been given various names. Repetitive strain injury implies a condition arising entirely because of repetitive strain; primary fibromyalgia syndrome (fibrositis) is a more diffuse disorder sometimes associated with localised trigger points in muscle at which pressure precipitates symptoms. A more specific term for this is myofascial pain syndrome.

The aetiology of these conditions is not known but recent observations include the following:

(a) A muscle biopsy study on patients with over-use syndrome has shown specific pathological changes (increased Type 1 fibres; decreased Type 2 fibres); not seen in volunteer controls.

(b) Abnormal EEG patterns during sleep and even nocturnal apnoea occur in primary fibromyalgia. It is not yet clear whether the sleep disturbance causes the fibromyalgia or vice versa.

(c) Occasionally symptoms have been exacerbated by a low grade hyperventilation with fluctuating hypocarbia.

TREATMENT

The most important thing is to identify the precipitating occupational factor and to prevent it, or at least to ameliorate it. Although management may be prepared to slow down the speed of a conveyor belt, the professional musician is unlikely to wish to stay away from his instrument for the 3-6 months rest that may be required to alleviate symptoms. If the work environment cannot be improved, it becomes important to identify particular trigger factors.

Modification of the occupation

If 15 minutes playing a particular composition invariably brings on symptoms in a musician, rational therapy is to insist that practising of this composition is reduced to 10 minutes. Alternatively a different finger technique may be used for the difficulty. A dancer may be required to adopt a different (rather than less exacting) style of dance. An athlete may benefit from concentrating on a different event.

Physiotherapy

Physiotherapy may complement modification at work. The optimum physiotherapy varies and the scientific rationale for its use is not always clear but we have found heat or cold (both of which can be improvised at home), shortwave diathermy and interferential all to be of value in some patients.

Drug Therapy

(a) Analgesics

This is a rational approach. Paracetamol in a dose of 500 mg or 1000 mg taken on an "as required" basis is probably best. The patient anticipates the trigger factor and takes paracetamol up to one hour before in the hope of preventing symptoms. Co-proxamol (dextropropoxyphene + paracetamol), Co-dydramol (dihydrocodeine + paracetamol) and codeine are less satisfactory for long-term use but may occasionally be required.

(b) Anti-inflammatory drugs

Their use is less rational unless there is a clear inflammatory component. Nevertheless, they sometimes help. A drug of short half-life such as ibuprofen in a dose of 200 mg or 400 mg should be taken up to one hour before the trigger factor.

(c) Antidepressants

A controlled trial has shown that amitriptyline, usually 50 mg taken each night is more effective than placebo in relieving the symptoms of chronic fibromyalgia syndrome.

Complete Rest

If these simple measures fail, consideration should be given to a prolonged period of rest from the offending activity, sometimes up to 6 or 12 months. This may require special arrangements with the employers. This remedy is least attractive to performers who will have to weigh up the disadvantage of loss of their performing skills with the advantage of possible (though not always certain) cure of their repetitive strain injury.

OCCUPATIONAL HEALTH ASPECTS

The family practitioner should work in close collaboration with the employer's occupational health service. The expense of improving working conditions may be offset by a reduction in the amount of sick leave requested. In Australia a diagnosis of "repetitive strain injury" confers upon the employee the right to a lump sum payment for work-related disease from the National Workers Compensation System. A recent Australian epidemic of "repetitive strain injury" has proved so costly that the Royal Australian College of Physicians has suggested that the alternative term "regional pain syndrome" would lead to less litigation and perhaps earlier rehabilitation.

REFERENCE

(1). Hazleman B., The Painful Shoulder, *Reports on Rheumatic Diseases* (Series 2), 1987, Practical Problems No. 7.

FURTHER READING

Littlejohn GO (1986). Repetitive Strain Syndrome: An Australian Experience. *Journal of Rheumatology*, **13**, 1004-1006.

Fry HJH (1986). Overuse Syndrome in Musicians: Prevention and Management. *Lancet*, **ii**, 728-731.

Scudds RA and McCain GA (1988). The Differential Diagnosis of Primary Fibromyalgia Syndrome (Fibrositis). *Internal Medicine for the Specialist*, **9**, 83-103.

January 1989

RHEUMATIC COMPLAINTS IN THE PERFORMING ARTS

H A Bird
Senior Lecturer in Rheumatology
University of Leeds
R Grahame
Professor of Clinical Rheumatology
University of London
Director
Dancers' Clinic
Guy's Hospital
London

INTRODUCTION

'Performing Arts Medicine' is attracting increasing attention. The subject includes problems as diverse as medical afflictions of the larynx in singers and actors, adequate function of the ear in actors and musicians and 'stage fright' in almost any performer. This review deals only with the musculoskeletal system which, in practice, restricts it mainly to the consideration of dancers and musicians.

MUSCULOSKELETAL PROBLEMS IN DANCERS

Dancers depend on healthy flexible joints and strong muscles for the performance of their art. They also require the right kind of physique, the correct technique and adequate stamina. When they lack any of these crucial attributes the dancer is at risk of injury. Another predisposing factor is too much joint flexibility. Joint laxity or double-jointedness is now considered to be a benign, hereditary, multi-system disorder of connective tissue characterised by a degree of weakness and fragility of collagen-bearing tissues - ligament, tendon, muscle, bone, cartilage, and skin. Because laxity of the spine, hips and ankles facilitates the impressive range of movement demanded of dancers (they do not have to work at it!), it acts as a positive selection factor for entry into ballet school. Thereupon joint hypermobility ceases to be an asset and becomes a liability. For not only are injuries more likely to occur because of the collagen defect, their healing tends to be more protracted.

Another 'risk factor' in female dancers is an inadequate diet. Ballet dancers have a lower body mass, are shorter in stature and have longer arms than the general population. To a large extent this somatotype is considered to be the aesthetic ideal for the ballerina, and is the basis on which they are selected. However maintaining this 'ideal shape', almost invariably entails a grossly unhealthy dietetic restriction leading to carbohydrate, calcium and vitamin deficiencies. Delayed menarche or recurrent amenorrhoea is a common occurrence, providing another contributary factor (oestrogen deficiency) in the pathogenesis of stress fractures.

THE RANGE OF INJURY ENCOUNTERED

Acute soft-tissue injuries are extremely common, but many of these are avoidable. A sudden loss of balance, a faulty technique (sometimes on the part of a partner), inadequate warm-up, dancing on a hard unsprung floor, working under pressure or just feeling run down can result in injury. More serious injuries include a dislocation (eg of shoulder, patella or MTP joint), an acute low back injury, a meniscus tear or a complete tendon rupture (eg tendo Achilles or flexor hallucis longus). A more common occurrence is an incomplete tear of a ligament, a muscle or a tendon-bone attachment. Despite their relatively trivial nature, these last mentioned lesions can, in common with the more serious injuries, threaten the future career and livelihood of the dancer if inadequately treated and allowed to become chronic. Back, neck and ankle are the most frequent injury sites, followed by the foot, groin/ hip, knee,thigh/calf in descending order. Although most available data refer to classical ballet, contemporary dance appears to be no less hazardous.

Overuse injuries are, in effect, chronic soft-tissue injuries. They too are commonplace amongst dancers, and for reasons similar to those cited for acute injuries. Examples include the 'shin splint syndrome' (traction injury of the origins of the long extensors and/or flexors of the foot); and tenosynovitis (even stenosing tenosynovitis) of the flexor tendon sheaths behind the medial malleolus notably that of flexor hallucis longus. Usually, when spotted early, these conditions will be relieved by appropriate reduction of the workload falling on the affected part. However, treatment with ultrasound, local hydrocortisone injections (AVOID INJECTING INTO TENDONS) or sometimes even surgical intervention may be required in more severe or intractable cases.

Fractures (in particular stress fractures) may occur in the lower limbs eg femoral neck, tibial shaft and the tarsal and metatarsal bones. These can give rise to pain lasting for several months and seriously impairing the ability to dance. In spite of the finding of localised pain and tenderness, a conventional X-ray may be normal. In such cases the condition can easily be spotted on a scintiscan.

Some problems peculiar to dancers

1 **'Poor turnout'.** In order to swing the leg high in the air it is anatomically essential for the dancer to achieve maximal lateral hip rotation (a 'flat turnout' - every dancer's goal - is when the feet are in line but pointing away from one another). Where turnout is 'poor', an attempt is made to compensate for this by 'turning out' at the foot, thereby creating chronic tortional strain on the medial knee and ankle ligaments. Once the problem has been identified it may then be possible to concentrate on increasing turnout at the hip, thereby reducing the strain distally.

2 **Dancing *en pointe*** is highly unphysiological. It may give rise to a variety of problems - discomfort, bruising, recurrent

nail-shedding, bunions, callouses, premature epiphyseal fusion (leading to toe-shortening) and even osteoarthritis of the 1st MTP joint. These problems may be minimised by introducing point work gradually; after the age of 11 years; after the child

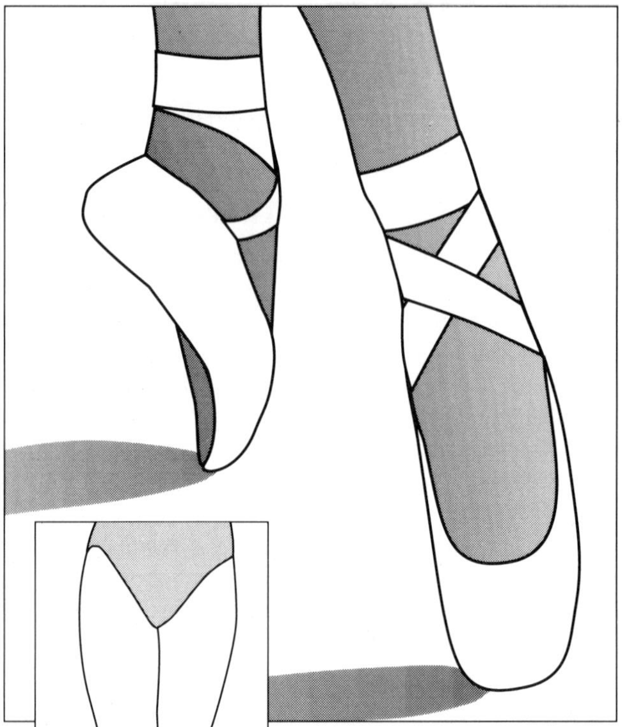

Fig 2 En Pointe

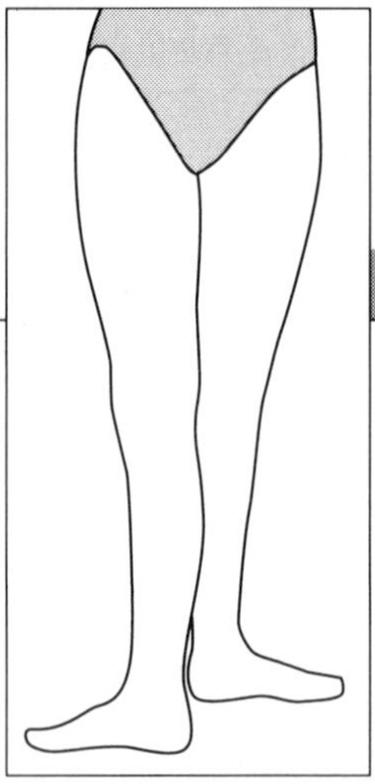

Fig 1 Turnout

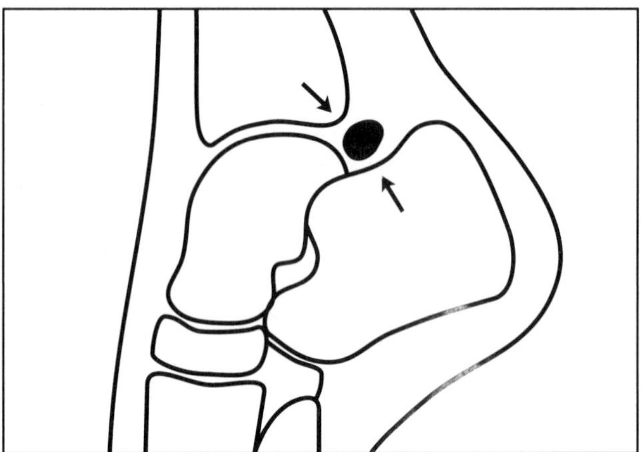

Fig 3 The os trigonum can become caught between the lower tibia and the upper calcaneum when the foot is pointed.

has been dancing for no less than 3 years and already displaying sufficient muscle strength; and wearing the correct boxed-toe shoe.

3 **Os trigonum compression.** This normally inoffensive small bone (an unfused epiphysis of the posterior tubercle of the talus) may become caught between the tibia and the calcaneum when the ankle is maximally plantarflexed. Attempting to dance *en pointe* becomes extremely painful, even impossible. Fortunately, if recognised, the problem can be cured by excision of the os trigonum.

4 **Male dancers.** An occupational hazard of male dancers entails the frequent lifting up and down of their female partners. This renders them liable to spinal problems - eg back strain, intervertebral disc prolapse, partes interarticulares defects with or without spondylolisthesis. They are also prone to shoulder injuries including supraspinatus tendonitis and dislocation. Although these are known associations of joint laxity, it should be pointed out that in contrast to their female partners, male dancers in general do not exhibit generalised ligamentous laxity.

A recent large survey revealed that in the UK professional dancers are more likely to consult a physiotherapist than a doctor for relief of their complaints. The reason they give is that doctors often fail to appreciate the seriousness of their injuries and the potentially crippling effect on their careers. They also go to osteopaths and chiropractors.

Prompt and appropriate treatment of an acute injury reduces the risk of it becoming chronic. Much is known about ways of minimising the risk of dance injury. If these were more widely known, then many needless injuries could be prevented.

MUSCULOSKELETAL PROBLEMS IN MUSICIANS: PROBLEMS ASSOCIATED WITH PARTICULAR INSTRUMENTS

Wind Instruments

For the oboe and clarinet, a major problem is the need to hold a relatively heavy instrument in an awkward position away from the body for long periods of time. Symptoms thereby induced in the arms can be relieved by hanging the instrument from the neck. Bassoon players may also be at risk of back strain. The even more awkward position at which a flute or piccolo is held is compensated by the lightness of the instrument. Modern key systems ensure that large stretches of the fingers are not often required. The problems on brass instruments are similar though correspondingly greater as these are heavier though this may be compensated by a lesser duration of playing that is required from brass players in a typical orchestral score. Apart from the trombone, both hands have similar functions.

Keyboard Instruments

Sitting for long periods in awkward postures can cause strain on the back but the more common problems in keyboard players are encountered in the forearm and at the wrists, mainly because the hands have to be supported for long periods of time in a position of mechanical disadvantage. Such symptoms can be accentuated when greater force is required to perform on heavier keyboards. Some music may require considerable lateral stretch of the fingers. Symptoms tend to be symmetrical in both hands.

Percussion

A good drum roll places considerable strain on the wrist but otherwise percussion players are not particularly susceptible to symptoms.

Strings

The stringed instruments produce the greatest diversity of complaints because, unlike other instruments, the hands have quite different functions. For the violin and viola, symptoms of the shoulder and elbow are restricted to the bowing arm. Symptoms attributable to the flexor and extensor tendon apparatus affecting the fingers and wrists occur almost exclusively in the hand that is used on the strings. This pattern of symptoms persists in cellists and bass players who in addition may be susceptible to neck and back problems if posture is poor. Classical guitar players probably require the greatest span of all between the fingers.

THE RANGE OF INJURY ENCOUNTERED

1. Around 70% of symptoms encountered in musicians can be classified as overuse injuries (repetitive strain disorder).

2. 20% of musicians develop localised rheumatic syndromes such as epicondylitis (tennis and golfer's elbow), tenosynovitis, carpal tunnel syndrome or frozen shoulder, the features and management of which have been described in earlier ARC reports.(1)

3. Around 5% of musicians are found to have some degree of joint hypermobility and are therefore susceptible to injuries similar to those seen in dancers, largely confined to the fingers.

4. Less than 5% of patients referred will have one of the many varied sorts of arthritis, occurring by chance in a musician. This is not necessarily serious - with careful rheumatological management it is surprising how many patients with quite severe generalised osteoarthritis or rheumatoid arthritis affecting the hands are able to continue playing. The relatively slow progression of such arthritides allows plenty of time for the acquisition of the minor changes in technique that may be required.

REPETITIVE STRAIN DISORDER

The term 'overuse syndrome', better described as 'misuse' which attracts attention to the need for an altered technique, is probably the same. Although fashionable, these syndromes are not new. Clinical findings differ little from those described by Poore in his 'Clinical lecture on certain conditions of the hand and arm which interfere with the performance of professional acts, especially piano playing (Br Med J, 1887; i: 441 - 4).

The term repetitive strain disorder is best restricted to the symptoms that are initiated by a particular repetitive mechanical act. This movement may be technically demanding and often places the fingers or limb at a mechanical disadvantage. A further characteristic is that symptoms only occur when a certain threshold of total activity is exceeded. Symptoms are relieved by rest in the early stages though with time, symptoms will occur more frequently when the threshold of activity required to produce them may fall. Pain, tenderness and sometimes parasthesiae that are initially diffuse later localise at the site of a particular tendon or enthesis (the point at which the tendon joins the bone) that can be predicted anatomically from the particular repetitive action that causes symptoms . Later physical signs such as swelling and synovial proliferation may appear.

It is best to tackle the problem early. Analysis of performance normally allows the player to identify the particular movement that produces symptoms. In discussion with a sympathetic teacher, technique may be altered to cause less strain when the movement is executed though sometimes it will be necessary to avoid the particular piece or pieces that produce the symptoms. For a complete beginner, the change to an alternative instrument is occasionally needed. For the more experienced player, avoidance of the styles of particular composers may be required.

Many cases respond to such simple measures but for others periods of enforced rest may be necessary. If symptoms invariably occur after one hour, the session should be divided into two 30 minute periods or, even better, four fifteen minute periods allowing adequate rest between each spell of playing. Occasionally, avoidance of music making for two or three weeks is required. The player then returns for no more than five minutes at a time, gradually building up the capacity to practice over a period of months rather than weeks or years. Exceptionally, a period of complete rest (with abstinence from writing, carrying and holding any heavy object) is recommended though opinions vary on the value of this since the resultant problems of disuse atrophy often outweigh the therapeutic gain.

Some musicians have found physiotherapy and relaxation techniques, including the Alexander technique helpful. Analgesics may also be prescribed to be taken on an 'as required' basis and are probably more rational in this condition than anti-inflammatory drugs. It is unusual for muscle relaxants or beta-blockers to help and intra-lesional steroid injections are only of value if there are clinical signs of tenosynovitis or proliferative synovitis.

FURTHER READING

Textbook of Performing Arts Medicine, Eds. Robert Thayer Sataloff, Alice G. Bradfornbrener & Richard J. Lederman. New York, Raven, 1990, pp 432

REFERENCES

(l) Carpal Tunnel Syndrome, The Medical Editors, Practical Problems:1, in Reports on Rheumatic Diseases (Series 2), publ. Arthritis and Rheumatism Council, London (1985). Tennis and Golfer's Elbow, D N Golding, Practical Problems: 2, in Reports on Rheumatic Diseases (Series 2) publ. Arthritis and Rheumatism Council London (1986). Work-Related Syndromes, H A Bird, Practical Problems:11 in Reports on Rheumatic Diseases (Series 2) publ. Arthritis and Rheumatism Council London (1989).

May 1991

NON-STEROIDAL ANTI-INFLAMMATORY DRUGS - USE & ABUSE

P W Thompson
Consultant Rheumatologist
Poole Hospital NHS Trust
Longfleet Road
Poole Dorset BH15 2JB
and Honorary Senior Lecturer
Royal London Hospital Medical College
London E1 2AD

C Dunne
Senior Registrar in Rheumatology
East Dorset Hospitals

MODE OF ACTION

A NSAID will suppress the classical features of inflammation (dolor, calor, turgor and erythema). Although originally thought to act by inhibiting prostaglandin synthesis it is now clear that the mode of action involves many pathways in the production of inflammatory mediators as well as interaction between inflammatory cells (Figure 1, after Forrest and Brooks)(1).

PHARMACOKINETICS & FORMULATIONS

Most NSAIDs are completely absorbed from the gastrointestinal tract. They bind strongly to plasma proteins and are predominantly cleared by the liver, metabolites being excreted in the urine. Some drugs are absorbed in their active form whereas others (pro-drugs) are converted by hepatic metabolism to active drugs.

They can be divided into two groups according to their half-life. Long half-life (>12 hours) drugs eg piroxicam, tenoxicam and azapropazone are taken once or twice daily but plasma concentrations may

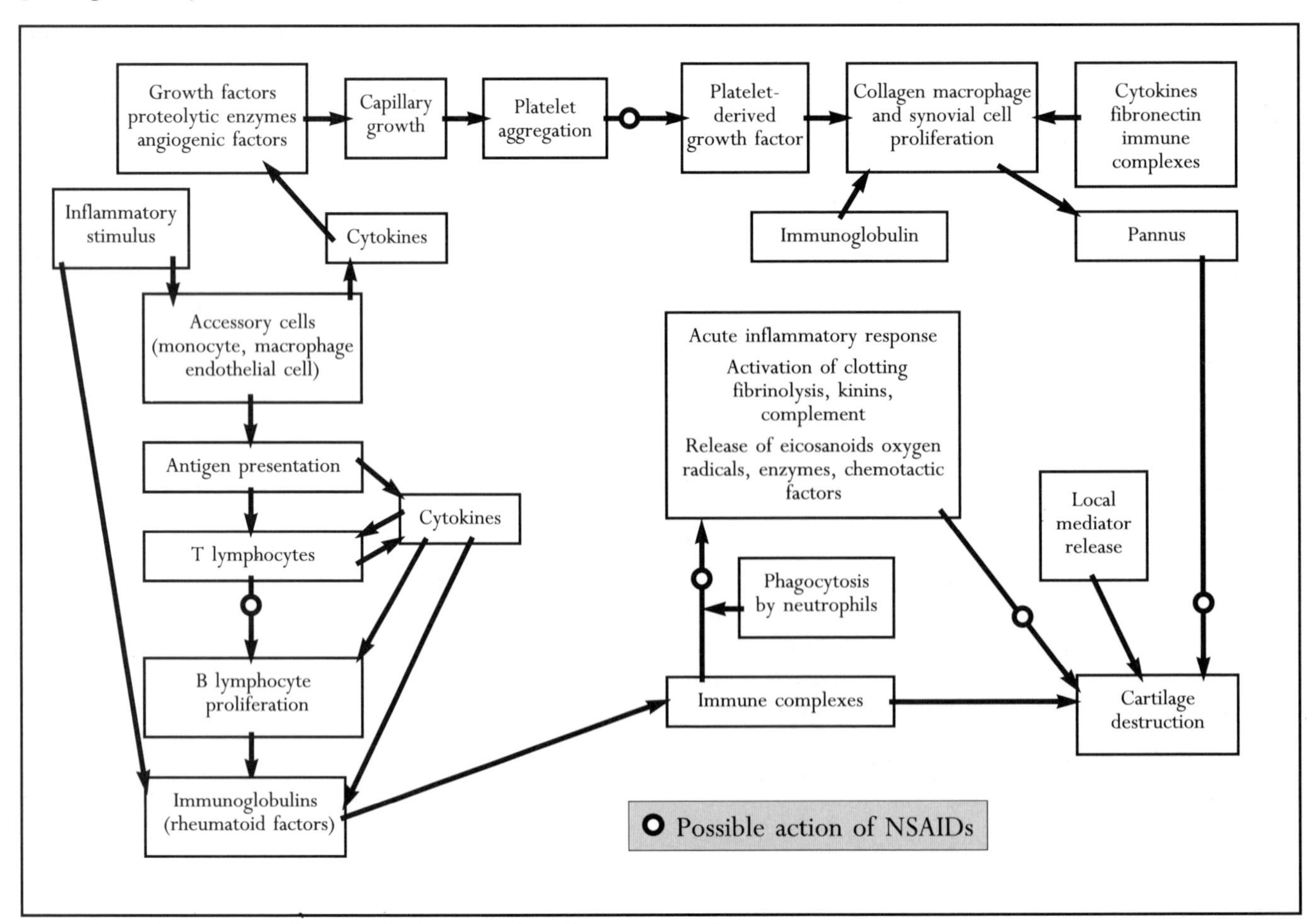

Figure 1. Probable modes of action of NSAIDs in the inflammatory pathways.

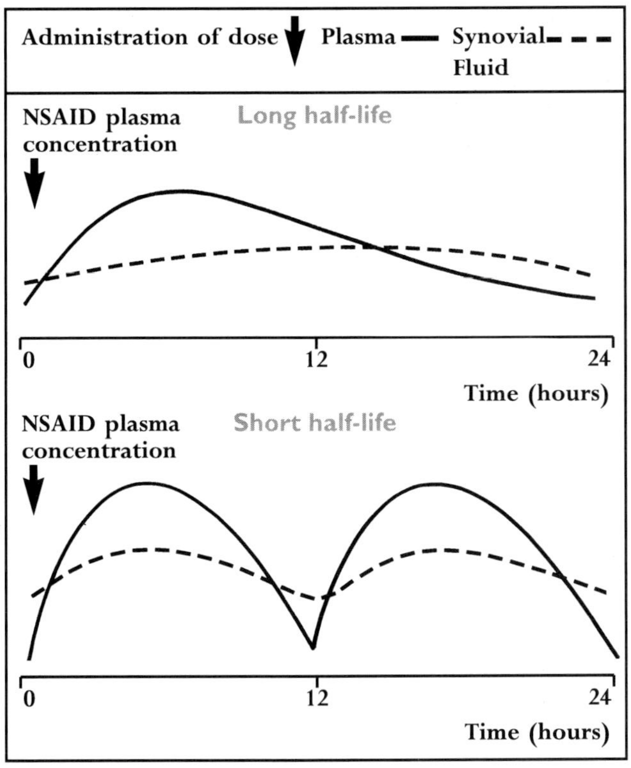

Figure 2. Plasma and synovial fluid NSAID concentrations in rheumatoid arthritis.

build excessively, particularly in elderly patients, increasing the risk of side effects. It should be noted that, despite quite large fluctuations in plasma levels with short half-life drugs (<6 hours), synovial fluid concentrations are more constant (Figure 2).

Modern formulation includes several slow release compounds. NSAIDs can also be given as suppositories, by intra-muscular injection or topically.

VARIABILITY OF RESPONSE

Huskisson et al (2) first demonstrated marked individual variability of response to NSAIDs in rheumatoid arthritis. This has been confirmed subsequently but the causes for these differences are uncertain. By implication if there is a poor response to one NSAID others should be tried.

Table 1. Indications for the use of NSAIDs

Acute (conditions requiring only a short course)

Arthritides
- Gout
- Pseudogout (acute pyrophosphate arthritis)
- Acute inflammatory flare of osteoarthritis

Sports injuries
Post-operative pain relief
Renal colic
Dysmenorrhea

Chronic (conditions usually requiring prolonged treatment)

Rheumatoid arthritis
Ankylosing spondylitis
Psoriatic arthritis
Other connective tissue diseases featuring polyarthritis

INDICATIONS FOR TREATMENT

NSAIDs are indicated in situations where joint or soft tissue inflammation causes pain, stiffness and swelling. This ranges from the acute sports injury such as a sprained ankle to the chronic inflammation seen in rheumatoid arthritis and ankylosing spondylitis (Table 1). NSAIDs have a role in post-operative pain relief and renal colic. In the acute situation a short course is usually all that is needed. A few days' treatment will quickly control most acute arthritides after which the dose can be reduced or the drug stopped altogether minimizing the risk of serious adverse reactions. In the chronic situation where long term treatment is needed the initial dose should be low and it may be necessary to try several drugs before finding the most effective and best tolerated for the patient.

Rheumatologists consider it appropriate to treat mechanical conditions such as osteoarthritis and degenerative disc disease with simple analgesics. However, there is no doubt that in some situations these conditions have an acute inflammatory flare and an NSAID will confer symptom relief in the short term.

In treating patients with destructive inflammatory arthritides it is important to remember that suppression of symptoms and signs of inflammation by NSAIDs will not limit the damaging effects of synovial proliferation. NSAIDs do not suppress the acute phase response measured by the ESR or C-reactive protein and are not disease modifying drugs. In a progressive erosive arthritis with evidence of a persisting acute phase response, disease modifying agents such as gold, d-penicillamine and methotrexate should be considered.

Table 2. Common adverse reactions with NSAIDs

Gastrointestinal (both stomach and small bowel may be affected)
- Indigestion
- Ulceration
- Perforation
- Haemorrhage

Renal
- Acute renal failure
- Hypertension
- Cardiac failure

Hepatic
- Transient and reversible rise in transaminases

Hypersensitivity
- Rashes
- Bronchospasm

Haematological
- Thrombocytopenia
- Neutropenia
- Red cell aplasia
- Haemolytic anaemia

**Table 3.
The most important drug interactions (after Tonkin and Wing)**

Drug affected	NSAID	Effect
Diuretics and antihypertensives	All (?sulindac)	Reduced (sodium retention)
Oral anticoagulants	All	Increased (potential risk of GI bleed)
Lithium	All	Increased (reduced renal clearance)
Anticonvulsants	All	Increased (displaced protein binding)
Digoxin	All	Increased (reduced renal clearance)

ADVERSE EFFECTS AND DRUG INTERACTIONS

The most important reactions reported to the Committee for Safety of Medicine for 1980-1993 are shown in Table 2 (3). Gastric upsets are common with peptic perforation and haemorrhage not infrequent causes of death, and common causes of morbidity. Renal dysfunction mediated by inhibition of prostaglandin driven glomerular filtration is also potentially hazardous. These side effects are dose related and much more common in elderly people. Dizziness and headaches are a common feature and prevent the use of these drugs in many patients. Remember that bronchospasm may be precipitated in asthmatic patients.

Common drug interactions are shown in Table 3 (from Tonkin and Wing (4)). Important interactions occur with diuretic and hypotensive agents that may result in acute renal failure. The potential interaction between NSAIDs and low dose methotrexate highlighted by some pharmacists is not a practical problem at the doses used in rheumatoid arthritis.

WHICH NSAID?

There is an ever increasing number of NSAIDs with multiple formulations. It is impossible to be dogmatic about the use of individual drugs. It is suggested that the practitioner familiarize him/herself with five or six drugs from different classes (Figure 3). The report from the Committee for Safety of Medicines (3) recommends that ibuprofen be used as first drug and it is emphasized that the individual response to a particular NSAID may be very different in apparently similar clinical conditions.

Some NSAIDs are useful in particular situations. Indomethacin is noted for its effect in ankylosing spondylitis and gout. Colchicine is used in acute gout and its side effect profile is not very different from NSAIDs although it is not a NSAID. Sulindac is reported to have a renal sparing effect and may be useful in patients with impaired renal function.

Topical preparations are now available for several drugs. They are more efficacious than placebo and may occasionally be useful for painful osteoarthritic joints where they can be rubbed on as necessary. Local skin sensitivity may occur and there is some absorption into the circulation leading occasionally to systemic side effects.

Suppositories are useful in reducing the risk of gastric irritation by direct effect of the drug on the gastric mucosa. However, there is still a risk of gastric ulceration mediated via the circulation and local irritation of the rectum occurs, even leading to rectal bleeding on occasions.

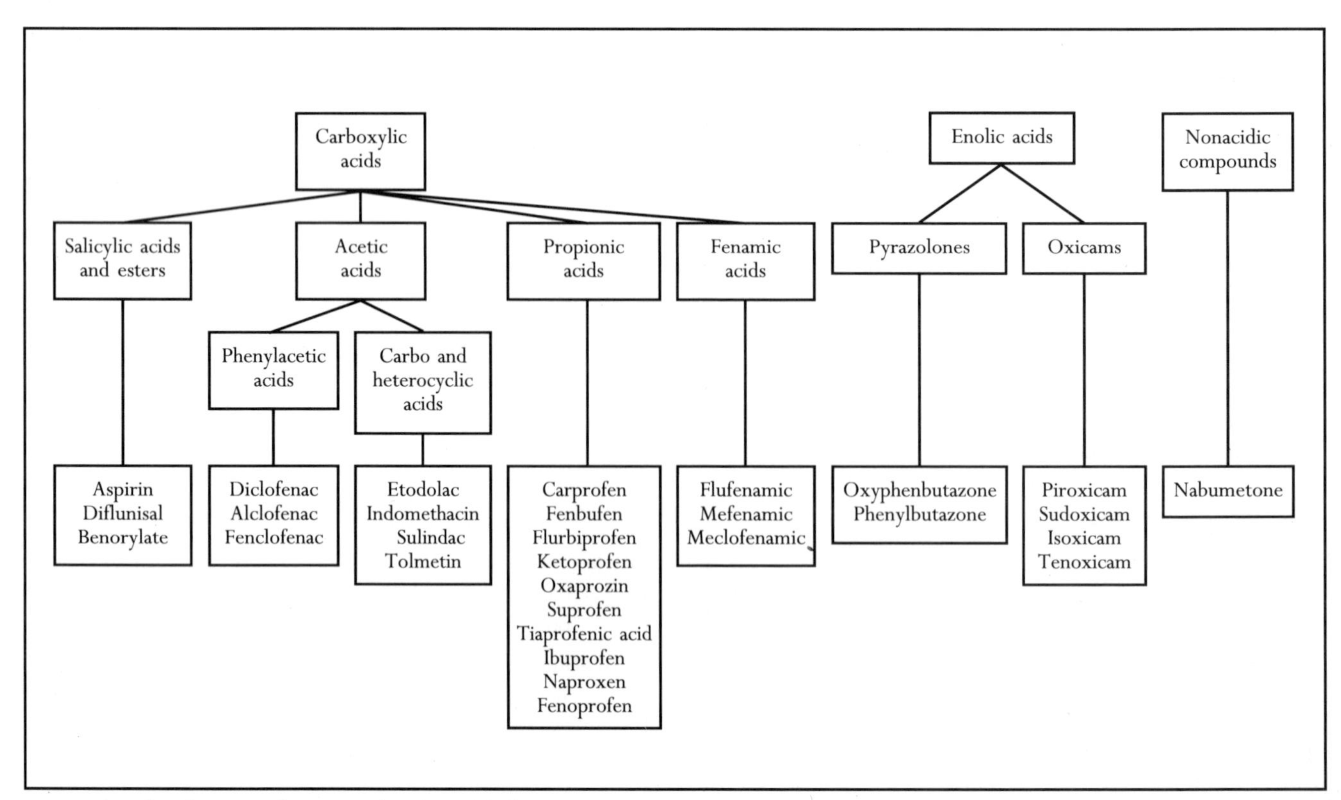

Figure 3. Classification of NSAIDs by chemical class.

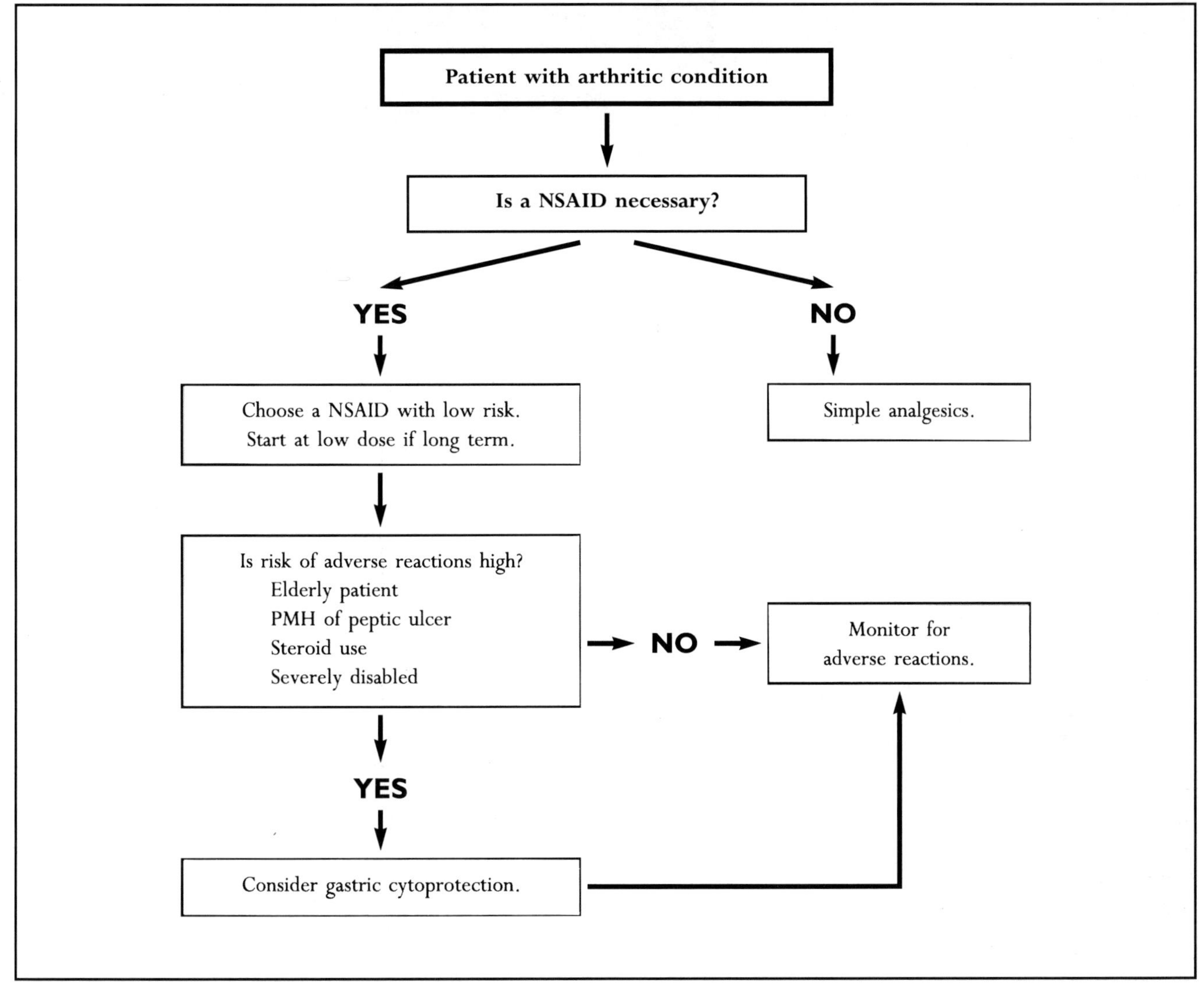

Figure 4. A treatment algorithm to minimize adverse reactions.

PRACTICE POINT

In the treatment of chronic inflammatory arthritides it is advisable to try several NSAIDs sequentially. The patient is then able to choose the one found most useful.

MINIMIZING ADVERSE REACTIONS

Figure 4 shows a treatment algorithm to reduce the frequency of adverse reactions. Often simple analgesics can be used successfully. If a NSAID is deemed necessary then start with a drug known to have a low risk such as ibuprofen. Start treatment with a low dose and consider a slow release formulation. Be particularly careful of renal function in the elderly patient taking diuretics and introduce the NSAID slowly. In patients with active peptic ulcer disease NSAIDs are contraindicated. In patients with a history of peptic ulcer it is wise to consider gastric cytoprotection. Probably H_2 receptor antagonists are most useful in patients with a history of duodenal ulcer and prostaglandin analogues for patients with a history of gastric ulceration. Combination drugs are beginning to appear but their role for long term prophylaxis in the patient who has not suffered previous peptic ulceration has yet to be proved. Some authorities would recommend concurrent treatment in patients over sixty-five years with disability or taking corticosteroid therapy in whom the risk of serious adverse gastro-intestinal effects is high.

REFERENCES

1. Forrest M, Brooks PM. Mechanism of action of non-steroidal anti-rheumatic drugs. *Bailliere's Clin Rheumatol*, 1988; **2**: 275-94.

2. Huskisson EC, Woolf PC, Baume HW, Scott J, Franklyn S. Four anti-inflammatory drugs – responses and variations. *Br Med J*, 1974; **1**: 1084-9.

3. Current problems in pharmacovigilance. Committee for Safety of Medicines, 1994; **20**: 9-11.

4. Tonkin AL, Wing LMH. Interactions of non-steroidal anti-inflammatory drugs. *Bailliere's Clin Rheumatol*, 1988; **2**: 455-83.

January 1995

MONITORING DRUG THERAPY IN RHEUMATOID ARTHRITIS: EFFICACY

R Butler
Consultant Rheumatologist
The Robert Jones & Agnes Hunt Orthopaedic Hospital
Oswestry
Shropshire

INTRODUCTION

The use of drugs forms an important part of the management of rheumatoid arthritis but other measures such as physiotherapy, occupational therapy assessment, education, intra-articular steroid injection and surgery all form part of the overall management programme.

ANALGESIC AND NON-STEROIDAL ANTI-INFLAMMATORY DRUGS

Simple analgesics are useful but non-steroidal anti-inflammatory drugs (NSAID) often give greater symptomatic relief since their anti-inflammatory properties will improve manifestations of rheumatoid synovitis such as joint swelling and morning stiffness. NSAID are generally preferable when there is evidence of active inflammatory arthritis but analgesics may be adequate if the disease is relatively quiescent. Both classes of drugs can be used on an as-required basis to control symptoms.

Gastrointestinal irritation, rashes and CNS symptoms are well-recognised side-effects of NSAID and these drugs may impair renal function, especially in patients with pre-existing renal disease. They may also reduce the efficacy of diuretics, beta-blockers and hypoglycaemic agents and potentiate warfarin. One should therefore avoid prescribing an NSAID where a simple analgesic would suffice and review the need for an NSAID regularly in the light of changes in disease activity and symptomatology. However rheumatoid arthritis is a chronic painful condition and NSAID should not be withheld if they are needed to make the patient's life tolerable.

SECOND-LINE ANTI-RHEUMATIC DRUGS

These are also known as specific anti-rheumatic drugs, slow-acting anti-rheumatic drugs, disease-modifying anti-rheumatic drugs (DMARD) and remission-inducing drugs (RID): none of these terms is entirely satisfactory. Commonly used preparations include intramuscular gold, auranofin, penicillamine, sulphasalazine and hydroxychloroquine; methotrexate and azathioprine are also used fairly frequently. The choice of preparation will be influenced by the severity of disease, presence of extra-articular or concurrent disease, ability to monitor for possible adverse reactions and the individual rheumatologist's preference.

The aim of second-line drug therapy is to suppress synovial inflammation and so abolish the symptoms and signs of active arthritis; symptoms arising from established deformity and secondary degenerative joint disease will not respond. Because of the potential toxicity of these drugs decisions regarding when to start, change or stop second-line therapy depend upon careful clinical assessment.

TABLE 1. MEANS OF ASSESSING DISEASE ACTIVITY IN RHEUMATOID ARTHRITIS
Duration of morning stiffness
Visual analogue pain score
Number of swollen joints
Number of tender joints
Walking time
Grip strength
Laboratory measures e.g. ESR and CRP
X-rays
Health assessment questionnaires

HOW TO ASSESS RHEUMATOID ARTHRITIS?

The activity of rheumatoid arthritis can be assessed in a number of ways *(table 1)*. Changes in the different measures tend to occur in parallel but no single method can be regarded as ideal and it is best to use several. Serial measurements provide sound clinical data on which to base decisions regarding therapy.

Early morning stiffness. Morning stiffness is a characteristic feature of active rheumatoid arthritis and tends to increase during exacerbations of disease. Patients can generally give a fair estimate of the duration of morning stiffness.

Pain. Pain can be assessed by several methods but the visual analogue score (VAS) has proved both practical and useful. This consists of a 10cm line at one end of which is written 'no pain' and at the other 'worst possible pain' or a similar phrase. The patient makes a mark at a point on this line to represent their current level of pain. Thus a mark 7.5mm along the line would give a VAS score of 75%.

Number of swollen joints. A count of the number of swollen joints can provide a useful guide to the extent and activity of rheumatoid arthritis. The degree of swelling in individual joints can also be assessed by measurement of joint circumference on a serial basis. This is most often performed on knee joints or on proximal interphalangeal joints.

Number of tender joints. The Ritchie articular index is commonly used in rheumatology units to assess the activity of rheumatoid arthritis. Joints are squeezed gently and the degree of discomfort graded according to the response. The scores for each joint are added to give a total score. Clearly this method will vary according to the pressure exerted by the examiner and the pain threshold of the patient but serial measurements recorded by a single examiner on a given patient can give valuable information.

Walking time. Serial measurements can be made of the time taken to walk a given distance, typically 50 feet. This reflects lower limb function rather than disease activity overall but may be helpful.

Grip strength. This can be measured with a modified sphygmomanometer. It is of little value in late disease since relatively little change occurs when there is marked deformity of the fingers.

Laboratory measures. The erythrocyte sedimentation rate (ESR), plasma viscosity and C-reactive protein (CRP) tend to be high during phases of active disease and to fall with successful treatment or spontaneous remission but exceptions do occur. These tests can be used to monitor the efficacy of second-line drug therapy and to help select patients for such therapy, but laboratory data must be considered in the context of the overall clinical picture. Other laboratory measures appear to offer no great advantage.

X-rays. Progressive deforming arthritis is usually associated with widespread periarticular erosion of bone. A favourable outcome is much more likely if the erosive process can be arrested and the ability to prevent erosions has been regarded as the yardstick against which the efficacy of second-line drug therapy is judged. A relatively simple method of assessment is the Larsen technique which uses a series of standard films for different joints. The patient's X-rays are compared with the standard films and scored according to the standard film which they most closely resemble.

Health status questionnaires. Measures such as those discussed above provide an indirect reflection of the patient's functional capacity. Several questionnaires have been developed which assess ability to wash, dress, walk, perform household activities etc. The Stanford health assessment questionnaire (HAQ) has been modified for use in British patients and the HAQ score has been shown to reflect changes in disease activity and improvement resulting from effective drug therapy or joint replacement surgery.

WHEN TO START SECOND-LINE DRUG THERAPY?

This decision is largely made on clinical grounds since we do not have a reliable genetic or laboratory marker at present which will identify patients destined to develop progressive disabling arthritis. Patients with widespread joint swelling and tenderness, prolonged morning stiffness, fatigue, weight loss and functional impairment are clearly candidates for second-line drug therapy *(table 2)*. How soon such therapy is started will depend on the individual patient and physician as well as on the severity of the arthritis but failure to respond to NSAID and conservative measures within 3 months is commonly regarded as an indication for second-line drug therapy. It may be instituted sooner if there is intolerance of NSAID or in the presence of extra-articular manifestations of rheumatoid disease.

TABLE 2. POSSIBLE INDICATIONS FOR SECOND-LINE DRUG THERAPY
Persistent synovitis despite NSAID
Progressive disability despite NSAID
Progressive deformity
Intolerance of NSAID
For steroid-sparing effect
Erosive disease
ESR >30mm/hour or CRP >20mg/l
Extra-articular disease

Widespread erosive disease is associated with functional impairment and the appearance of erosions is commonly regarded as an indication for second-line drug therapy. Patients with a positive test for rheumatoid factor do worse than those without. Patients with an ESR consistently greater than 30mm/hour or a CRP greater than 20mg/l seem to be at particular risk of erosive disease, and whereas these abnormalities by themselves may not constitute an indication for second-line therapy such patients should be observed closely.

WHEN TO CHANGE SECOND-LINE DRUG THERAPY?

These drugs are called slow-acting agents and there is some delay between the initiation of therapy and a clinical response (*figure 1*). It is important to warn the patient of this so as to avoid false expectations. The decision as to how long to persist with a given second-line drug can be difficult: it should not be abandoned before it has had a chance to work but one should not persist with a drug if the clinical response is inadequate. Few patients will respond within 1 month but if a response has not occurred by 7 months it is unlikely to do so later. As a rule of thumb it is reasonable to persist with a given drug for at least 3-4 months but if a satisfactory response is not apparent by 6-7 months then an alternative should be tried.

Because of the delay between the onset of therapy and a response there is often a temptation to change drugs prematurely but this should be resisted. Measures which can be used to help patients during this difficult phase include the use of resting splints and a programme of physiotherapy, perhaps as a hospital in-patient, and the use of intra-articular and possibly systemic steroids as well as analgesics and NSAID.

In some patients a partial response occurs or a satisfactory clinical response is followed by a relapse. The decision to change to an alternative agent will depend upon the activity of the arthritis but will involve consideration of previous responses and adverse reactions to other second-line drugs and concurrent medical problems. The results of serial assessments of disease activity and functional capacity as described above may help since evidence of deterioration will prompt a change in therapy. Progressive erosive disease indicates inadequate control of the disease and persistently raised values for ESR and CRP often indicate an incomplete response to therapy.

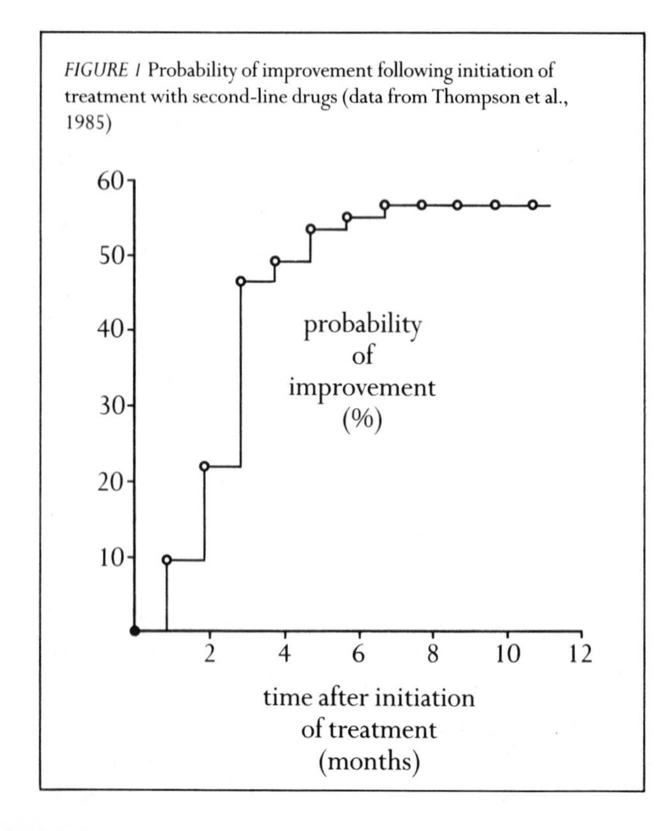

FIGURE 1 Probability of improvement following initiation of treatment with second-line drugs (data from Thompson et al., 1985)

WHEN TO STOP SECOND-LINE DRUG THERAPY?

Adverse reactions to second-line drugs are not uncommon and may require discontinuation of therapy. This topic is dealt with fully in a later article and will not therefore be discussed here. Sometimes second-line drug therapy has to be discontinued because patients default from follow-up or will not have the blood tests necessary to monitor the safety of these drugs.

In those patients in whom complete remission occurs one has to decide whether to continue second-line drug therapy or discontinue it. Most rheumatologists have seen patients in remission in whom withdrawal of a second-line drug has been followed by a severe relapse which has proved unresponsive to re-introduction of the drug. For this reason there is a tendency to continue maintenance treatment or certainly to withdraw it cautiously over 6-12 months or longer. This decision has to be taken on an individual basis and will clearly be influenced by factors such as the patient's attitude to medication or a desire for pregnancy.

CONCLUSIONS

The use of drugs in patients with rheumatoid arthritis has to be considered against the natural history of the disease which typically runs a fluctuating course over many years. Analgesic and NSAID preparations can make the patient's life more tolerable but these drugs are not without side-effects and their use should be reviewed on a regular basis. Second-line drugs should not be discarded prematurely but equally one should not persist too long with a given drug if the clinical response is inadequate. Rational decisions regarding changes to second-line drug therapy are greatly helped by careful serial assessment of disease activity.

REFERENCES

Scott DL, Spector TD, Pullar T, McConkey B
What should we hope to achieve when treating rheumatoid arthritis?
Annals of the Rheumatic Diseases 1989, **48:** 256-61

Thompson PW, Kirwan JR, Barnes CG
Practical results of treatment with disease-modifying anti-rheumatoid drugs.
British Journal of Rheumatology 1985, **24:** 167-75

July 1990

MONITORING DRUG THERAPY IN RHEUMATOID ARTHRITIS: TOXICITY

P Brooks
North Shore Hospital
St Leonards
NSW 2065
Australia

INTRODUCTION

Although non-steroidal anti-inflammatory drugs (NSAIDs) and slow-acting anti-rheumatic drugs (SAARDs) are extremely useful in the management of rheumatic diseases, adverse reactions to these drugs are common. Some of these adverse drug reactions are due to the known pharmacological effects of the drugs while others are attributed to hypersensitivity or idiosyncratic reactions. For NSAIDs, examples of the former would be the gastrointestinal reactions or functional renal impairment while hepatocellular or skin reactions are often due to idiosyncrasy or hypersensitivity. Many of the drug reactions are relatively mild and, with dose reduction, patients may be continued on the drug. However, some are severe and can (rarely) lead to death.

NSAIDS

Gastrointestinal

The major adverse drug reactions of NSAIDs are seen in Table 1. The most common adverse reactions occur in the gut. The true incidence of significant gastrointestinal bleeding associated with ingestion of NSAIDs is not known but is probably between 3 and 7 per thousand per year. The relative risk of developing a peptic ulcer complication while on an NSAID is between 1.5 and 3 – not a high risk – but significant when large numbers of the population are taking these drugs. It has been pointed out that a relative risk of only two or three in users of NSAIDs is compatible with these drugs being the direct cause of 20-30% of all cases of ulcer complications. Up to 50% of patients attending a hospital rheumatology clinic might have an erosion or small gastric ulcer on endoscopy. Interestingly, only about 50% of these patients will complain of any indigestion. Iron deficiency anaemia might be the presenting feature and blood loss from either the upper or lower GI tract should be sought in this situation. There is a suggestion that elderly women may be particularly at risk from developing gastrointestinal complications of NSAIDs and this group of patients should be followed carefully. Symptoms and signs of peptic ulceration should be searched for, together with any fall in haemoglobin.

TABLE 1. ADVERSE REACTIONS OF NSAIDS

Gastrointestinal	Indigestion, nausea, gastric erosions, peptic ulceration, small bowel ulceration, hepatitis
Renal	Acute renal failure, hypokalaemia, fluid retention, hypertension, interstitial nephritis, papillary necrosis
Skin	Photosensitivity, erythema multiforme, urticarial, maculopapular, vesicular or exfoliative reactions
Respiratory	Bronchospasm
Haematological	Thrombocytopenia, agranulocytosis, aplastic anaemia, haemolytic anaemia
Central effects	Headache, dizziness, confusion

Hepatocellular damage has been reported with most NSAIDs although there does seem to be a slightly higher frequency of liver reactions with sulindac and diclofenac. However, these reactions are rare and routine monitoring of liver function tests is not called for.

Renal

Functional renal impairment is commonly observed, particularly when non-steroidal anti-inflammatory drugs are being commenced. Great care must be taken in those patients who have hypertension, volume depletion, congestive cardiac failure, hepatocellular insufficiency or underlying renal impairment. Interstitial nephritis has been reported with many NSAIDs but rarely causes permanent damage. Occasionally acute renal failure occurs but again this is unusual in someone with normal renal function. NSAIDs can interfere with the control of hypertension in patients receiving diuretics, betablockers and angiotensin-converting enzyme inhibitors. Both the diuretic and antihypertensive action of frusemide are antagonised by NSAIDs although they have less effect on the direct action of the thiazides. Patients with hypertension or congestive cardiac failure should be observed carefully in the first two to three weeks after NSAID therapy is introduced.

Skin

Stevens-Johnson syndrome and toxic epidermal necrolysis are rare complications of NSAID therapy but photosensitivity reactions are relatively commonly reported. They are seen with all NSAIDs and there is inadequate information on relative incidence.

Respiratory Effects

Between 2% and 20% of adult asthmatics have a high sensitivity to aspirin and these subjects may also be at similar risk from other NSAIDs. Occasionally bronchospasm occurs as part of an anaphylactoid reaction to an NSAID. Asthmatic patients should be monitored carefully when NSAIDs are introduced and they should be encouraged to use a peak flow meter at regular intervals for the first two or three days of therapy.

Haematological

The most common haematological adverse reactions of NSAIDs are thrombocytopenia, agranulocytosis, aplastic anaemia or haemolytic anaemia. Iron deficiency anaemia from chronic blood loss is commonly associated with peptic or lower gut ulceration. NSAID induced inhibition of platelet cyclo-oxygenase results in reduced platelet adhesiveness and prolongation of bleeding time. Whereas aspirin acetylates platelets and inhibits cyclo-oxygenase for their life span, the action of other NSAIDs is reversible and the effect has generally worn off by 24 hours. Even with aspirin, bleeding abnormalities return to normal within about four days, since when the aspirin has been ceased new platelets are produced which function normally. This has important implications in terms of how long these agents have to be ceased prior to surgery. The recommendation should be aspirin three to four days but other NSAIDs 24 hours, except in the case of piroxicam which appears to inhibit platelet function for approximately three days.

Central Effects

Indomethacin is commonly associated with headache and dizziness but other NSAIDs can also produce these features. Interestingly, some of the nausea associated with NSAIDs may be on a central basis rather than irritation of gastric mucosa.

SLOW-ACTING ANTI-RHEUMATIC DRUGS

The most common side-effects of SAARDS are shown in Table 2. Adverse reactions with hydroxychloroquine are usually mild. Pruritic skin rash, increased pigmentation or bleaching of the hair can occur and the drug should be ceased. The major side-effects are seen in the eyes: impaired reading ability, poor distant vision and night blindness. These can disappear if the dose is reduced. Macular pigmentation can occur but severe maculopathy associated with irreversible visual impairment is extremely rare at a dose of 400 mg a day or less. Eyes should be checked at 4-6 monthly intervals by an ophthalmologist.

The adverse reactions of D-penicillamine and gold follow a similar spectrum. Skin rashes, proteinuria and haematological effects are most common. Proteinuria occurs in between 10% and 30% of patients on gold and D-penicillamine while skin rashes are also frequent. While on gold, patients should be questioned carefully about itchiness of the skin and examined carefully for a dry, scaly rash. If this occurs, intramuscular gold should be ceased. A full blood count and a check of urine for protein should be done before each injection. The results should be marked in a booklet which is held by the patient so that any downward trend in the platelet count or white cell count can be picked up before it reaches a critical level. In this case the gold is ceased and the blood count watched carefully. All the side-effects

TABLE 2.
MAJOR SIDE-EFFECTS OF SAARDS

DRUG	SIDE-EFFECTS	ACTION
HYDROXYCHLOROQUINE	Skin	Cease
	Gut	Reduce dose
	Leukopenia	
	Eyes – subjective	Reduce dose
	– objective	Cease
GOLD – Intramuscular	Dermatitis (30%)	Cease
	Stomatitis	Cease (may restart)
	Proteinuria	Cease
	Thrombocytopenia, Leukopenia, Aplasia	Cease
– Oral	As for IM Gold although less frequent	
	Diarrhoea	Reduce dose
D-PENICILLAMINE – Early	Rash (Maculopapular)	Cease (can restart)
	Nausea, Loss of taste	Reduce dose
	Mouth Ulcers	Cease (can restart)
	Proteinuria (<3g/24 hours)	Reduce dose
	Proteinuria (>3g + oedema)	Cease
– Late	Drug Induced Lupus	Cease
	Myasthenia Gravis	Cease
	Pemphigus	Cease
	Goodpastures	Cease
– At any time	Thrombocytopenia	Cease Restart at lower dose
	Pancytopenia	Cease
SALAZOPYRIN	Nausea, Dyspepsia	Reduce dose
	Skin Rashes	Cease (restart)
	Allergic Reactions (Hepatitis, Pulmonary Eosinophilia)	Cease
	Macrocytosis	Add Folic Acid
	Haemolytic Anaemia, Pancytopenia	Cease
	Reduced Sperm Count	Continue
METHOTREXATE	Hepatic Fibrosis, Blood Dyscrasia	Cease
CYCLOPHOSPHAMIDE	Haemorrhagic Cystitis	Cease
	Pancytopenia	Cease

seen with intramuscular gold can also occur with oral gold but are less frequent and usually less severe. Diarrhoea, however, is dose related although patients developing diarrhoea are often able to continue auranofin, albeit at a lower dose.

Side-effects of D-penicillamine can be divided into those that occur early in treatment, late in treatment or at anytime. Early rashes are usually maculopapular in nature and the drug may be restarted. Nausea, anorexia and a blunting of taste also occur early and tend to disappear if the drug is continued. Isolated proteinuria, less than 3 gm a day, can well disappear with time despite continuation of D-penicillamine. Proteinuria in excess of 3 gm daily plus oedema or haematuria are usually an indication to cease the drug. Late adverse reactions such as drug-induced lupus, myasthenia gravis, a pemphigus-like reaction with blistering or Goodpastures syndrome all require drug cessation. Thrombocytopenia or pancytopenia can occur at any time during the treatment. Thrombocytopenia is quite common and usually reverses quickly once the D-penicillamine is ceased. In this situation the drug can usually be restarted at a lower dose. If pancytopenia occurs the drug should be ceased and not restarted.

Salazopyrin is gaining increasing popularity for the treatment of rheumatic diseases. Nausea, dyspepsia and skin rashes are quite common and usually disappear despite continuing the drug. Macrocytosis is an indication for folic acid replacement. Haemolytic anaemia or pancytopenia are rare and if they occur the drug should be ceased. Most men on salazopyrin exhibit a reduced sperm count. The patient should be warned about this but there is no reason to discontinue the drug.

Methotrexate has been associated with hepatic fibrosis but in rheumatological doses this is unusual unless there is underlying liver damage such as previous hepatitis or a history of heavy alcohol intake. Blood dyscrasias rarely occur and again are usually seen in those with reduced renal function or underlying folate deficiency. The immunosuppressive drugs cyclophosphamide and azathioprine have a significant incidence of neoplasia in the long term or demonstrate short term blood dyscrasias. Cyclophosphamide can also cause haemorrhagic cystitis, while azathioprine can be associated with hepatitis.

Monitoring of Patients on SAARDs

There have been no studies which really address the question as to how often patients should be monitored when on these drugs. Guidelines for routine practice are summarised in Table 3. Patients on hydroxychloroquine should have their visual fields checked by an ophthalmologist every 4-6 months or earlier if they notice any visual deterioration. Patients on intramuscular gold should receive a full blood count and a urinalysis for blood and protein prior to every injection (weekly or monthly depending on the frequency of injections). Patients taking D-penicillamine should have a full blood count and urinalysis for blood protein at second weekly intervals when changing doses but can reduce this to every 1-3 months once their dose is stable. For patients taking salazopyrin, blood counts and liver function tests should be done every two weeks for the first three months and then at the routine clinic visit. Patients taking methotrexate should have full blood counts and liver function tests at weekly intervals for the first month and then at 1-2 monthly intervals after that. Great care should be taken with elderly patients who have reduced renal function and who are taking other drugs which might interact. For any of these agents, it is important to look at trends in the full blood count and liver function parameters rather than absolute figures. Patients should carry with them a booklet of results (often produced by the pharmaceutical manufacturers) in which their results can be recorded serially. It is much more important to look at a trend in results rather than having an absolute cut-off point for ceasing therapy.

Although adverse reactions of NSAIDs or SAARDs are a common cause of the drug having to be ceased, serious side-effects can be reduced to a minimum by carefully explaining to the patient the need to report adverse events early.

TABLE 3. MONITORING OF PATIENTS ON SAARDS

Drug	Test	Frequency
HYDROXY-CHLOROQUINE	Visual Fields	4-6 monthly
GOLD	Full Blood Count Urine	Prior to each injection
D-PENICILLAMINE	Full Blood Count Urine	2nd weekly when changing doses or every 1-3 months
SALAZOPYRIN	Full Blood Count Liver Function	Every 2 weeks for first 2-3 months then at routine patient's review
METHOTREXATE	Full Blood Count Liver Function	Every 2 weeks for 2 months then every 3 months

PRACTICE POINTS

Gastric erosions or ulcers are common in rheumatoid patients on NSAIDs and are often asymptomatic.

Care should be taken with NSAIDs in patients who have hypertension, volume depletion, congestive cardiac failure, hepatocellular insufficiency or underlying renal impairment. Patients on gold and D-penicillamine should be encouraged to test their urine each week.

Patients taking slow-acting anti-rheumatic drugs should be clearly told about common side-effects and encouraged to report them early.

October 1990

LOCAL CORTICOSTEROID INJECTIONS - GENERAL ASPECTS AND UPPER LIMB

D N Golding
Consultant Rheumatologist
West Essex Rheumatology Unit
Princess Alexandra Hospital
Harlow
Essex

GENERAL ASPECTS AND UPPER LIMB

Corticosteroids may be used systemically or by injection into or around joints. Systemic steroids are only occasionally needed for rheumatoid arthritis, but steroid injections may well alleviate pain and swelling and, in conjunction with appropriate non-steroidal drug therapy and splinting, are very important in the treatment of this condition. Injection of steroids into soft tissues is often the treatment of choice in disorders such as tenosynovitis, tennis elbow, rotator cuff lesions of the shoulders and ligamentous lesions of the knees and ankles.

It has been known that hydrocortisone is active in reducing inflammation ever since cortisone was discovered in 1948. At first hydrocortisone acetate was used for intra-articular injections; later synthetic derivatives were found to give more potent and long-lasting effects. Steroid injections are now amongst the most important tools of the rheumatologist and increasing numbers of general practitioners are discovering the feasibility and value of these injections. As far as technique is concerned, observation of a rheumatologist skilfully injecting joints and soft tissues is all that is needed.

Intra-articular steroids are rapidly taken up by synovial cells and clinical improvement is often seen within hours and usually maintained for several weeks or months. Sometimes pain and swelling is reduced for a much longer period, and there may never be a recurrence of synovitis, particularly in the case of small joints of the fingers and toes. Soft-tissue inflammatory lesions respond readily and often permanently.

Indications for Steroid Injections

Using an aseptic 'no-touch' technique, steroid injections are very safe and (unless there is evidence of nearby sepsis, which should always preclude injections) joint infection is extremely rare. Injections are useful for:

(1) Inflammatory synovitis, especially when one or only a few joints are involved. In addition to. rheumatoid arthritis, injections can be useful in reactive arthritis, connective tissue disorders (such as SLE), psoriatic arthritis and other types of seronegative spondarthritis and the inflammatory stages of osteoarthritis.

(2) Soft-tissue inflammatory lesions. These may be divided into: (a) Juxta-articular lesions: ligamentous strain, bursitis, inflamed cysts (such as Baker's cyst at the back of the knee) and capsular lesions, such as frozen shoulder in the painful acute stages. (b) Extra-articular lesions: tendon lesions (such as rotator cuff disorders of the shoulder) and tenoperiosteal lesions (enthesopathies) such as tennis elbow.

Contra-indications to Steroid Injections

Complications of steroid injection are rare. The risk of septic arthritis is greatest when a blood-borne infection gets into a joint already damaged with arthritis in a debilitated patient. Aseptic necrosis involving a weight-bearing joint is most likely to occur when frequent injections are given into a joint, but can occur spontaneously in weight-bearing joints involved with severe, erosive arthritis, as in the knee where crumbling and collapsing bone results in severe valgus or varus deformity. As regards tendon sheaths, most regard injections as safe; though some orthopaedic surgeons believe that they predispose to weakening and even rupture of tendons. Aggravation of inflammation following steroid injection is commonly seen in soft-tissue lesions and the patient should be warned to expect an increase in pain for some hours. Hypersensitivity reactions occur rarely in atopic individuals (chills, fever and urticarial rashes) - the offending allergen is probably not the steroid but resides within the vehicle in which the steroid is dissolved.

PRACTICE POINT

Here is a step-by-step way to give steroid injections:

1. (Optional). Mark the injection spot. In soft-tissue lesions, the site of injection is often at the point of maximum tenderness.
2. Wash the hands, preferably with an antiseptic soap, then dry thoroughly.
3. Load the syringe and, using a no-touch technique, attach the needle and withdraw the steroid (recommended steroid preparations are given below). For soft-tissue lesions, if local anaesthetic is not included in the steroid preparation, 2 ml. of 2% lignocaine should be mixed with the steroid. If it is desired that the steroid should spread around the tissues (as in shoulder capsulitis), an ampoule of hyaluronidase (Hyalase) 1500 l.u. can be added to help spreading.
4. Prepare the skin by swabbing with iodine, isopropyl alcohol or similar antiseptic. In sensitive areas (and particularly where the patient is unduly nervous) skin analgesia is provided by 'freezing' the area with ethyl chloride or P.R. spray.
5. Aspirate any obvious effusion.
6. Inject the steroid into the joint or the soft-tissue lesion.
7. Dispose of the syringe with the attached needle in a container for disposable instruments.

Technique of Steroid Injection

It is always advisable to aspirate initially any obvious joint effusion. This relieves discomfort due to mechanical tension and allows examination of the synovial fluid, particularly important if there is any possibility of septic arthritis or gout.

Corticosteroid Preparations for Injection

Hydrocortisone is still occasionally used but the following are more powerful volume for volume:

STEROID	AVAILABILITY
Prednisolone acetate (Deltacortil, Deltastab)	vials 25 mg./ml.
Methyl prednisolone acetate (Depo-Medrone)	vials 40 mg./ml.
Triamcinolone hexacetonide (Lederspan)	vials 20 mg./ml. and 5 mg. /ml .
Prednisolone phosphate (Codelsol) (soluble, clear)	vials 16 mg./ml.
Dexamethasone phosphate (Decadron) (soluble, clear)	vials 4 mg./ml.

The author's preferences for routine use in soft-tissue lesions are methyl prednisolone (marketed mixed together with lignocaine as 'Depo-Medrone with Lidocaine' ampoules) and triamcinolone for intra-articular injection. In patients who have previously had severe post-injection pain one of the soluble preparations may be less likely to cause as much discomfort. *

Steroid Injections for Upper Limb Disorders- The Shoulder

The shoulder consists of two joints (glenohumeral and acromioclavicular joints) along with the subdeltoid (subacromial) bursa and the rotator cuff common insertion of the supraspinatus, infraspinatus, subscapularis and teres minor muscles (see fig. 1) . Pain in the shoulder can be easily classified on a clinical basis.

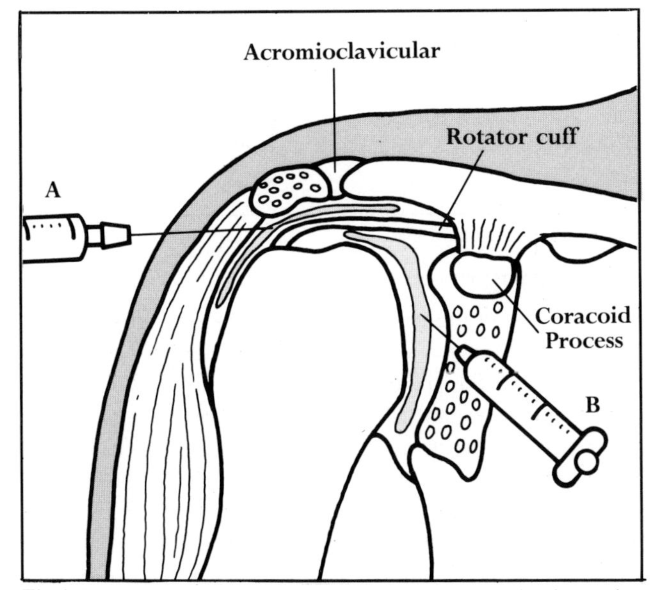

Fig.1 The shoulder region. Injection of subdeltoid(A) and glenohumeral joint(B)

** Opinions differ. Some prefer to use 2% lignocaine to anaesthetise the skin and subcutaneous tissue, followed (using a second syringe through the same needle) by corticosteroid into the joint or tissue to be injected.*

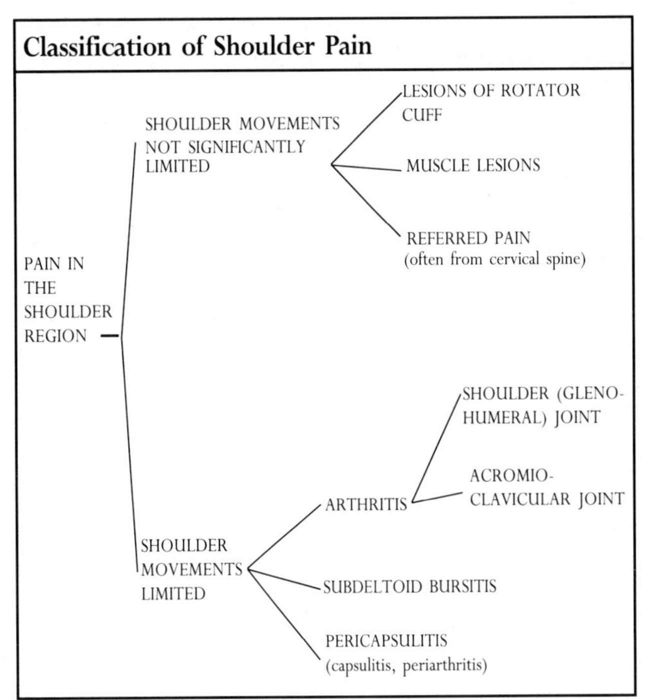

Using this simple classification one can sort out the common varieties of shoulder pain. Osteoarthritis of the shoulder joint is uncommon; rheumatoid arthritis involves the shoulder only as part of established rheumatoid disease; there is often diffuse swelling of the shoulder in subdeltoid bursitis; and in capsulitis (frozen shoulder) all movements are restricted (and painful in the acute stages). Calcium (hydroxyapatite) salts may be deposited within the subdeltoid bursa or in the vicinity of the insertion of degenerate tendons as seen on X-ray.

Rotator cuff lesions are often, though not always, locally tender and therefore amenable to local steroid injection, the cuff being reached via a lateral approach, the needle being directed medially from a point between the tip of the acromion and the head of the humerus (see fig. 1). Physiotherapy by itself is often insufficient but if there is considerable shoulder stiffness (as in chronic lesions) the injection can be followed by gentle passive exercises.

In rheumatoid arthritis of the shoulder (glenohumeral) joint pain often responds to an intra-articular steroid injection. The joint may be injected either from behind, the needle directed from a point below the acromion, (easily palpated) towards the coracoid process; or from the front (see fig. 1).

Arthritis of the acromioclavicular joint is usually degenerative (OA), sometimes rheumatoid. Pain and tenderness are both localised to the joint (not referred down the upper arm, as in most shoulder lesions). The joint can be injected directly from above, using just a small amount (0.5 ml.) of steroid.

Subdeltoid bursitis is easily aspirated and then injected, using a lateral or anterior approach. A severe variety of this condition is known as the Milwaukee Shoulder, where there is a subdeltoid effusion containing hydroxyapatite crystals and a tear of the rotator cuff which leads to upward subluxation of the head of the humerus.

Capsulitis of the shoulder (commonly known as 'frozen shoulder') goes through three clinical stages. In the initial 'acute stage' the shoulder is very painful, with limitation of active and passive movements in all directions. This is followed by the 'subacute stage', where there is moderate pain and movements are still restricted; then the 'chronic stage', where the pain has largely subsided, but movements remain restricted for several months or longer. In the acute and subacute stages three or four steroid injections around the capsule combined with lignocaine and hyaluronidase to help spreading, often (though not always) relieve the pain, but sometimes two or three such injections may be required at 2 or 3-weekly intervals. Even so shoulder movements remain stubbornly restricted and resolution of movements may be very slow - if this unduly handicaps the patient, one can attempt to free the shoulder by distending the bursa with 20-50 mls N-Saline. Otherwise a manipulation under anaesthetic together with a steroid injection can accelerate resolution of movements. When a frozen shoulder comprises part of a 'shoulder-hand syndrome' (which sometimes follows cardiac infarction, bypass operations or pulmonary disorders), with pain, swelling and vasodilation of the corresponding hand (later the hand becoming pale and atrophic) a steroid injection into the carpal tunnel, as well as injections for the shoulder capsulitis, may help relieve hand pain.

THE ELBOW

The three joints of the elbow are the humero-ulnar, the radiohumeral and the superior radio-ulnar. Pain arising in or around the elbow is either:

PERIARTICULAR - soft-tissue inflammation (enthesopathy) at the common extensor origin laterally (tennis elbow) or common flexor origin medially (golfer's elbow), or olecranon bursitis at the back of the elbow, or **ARTICULAR** - can be degenerative, inflammatory or infective arthritis.

Steroid injections into the common extensor or flexor origins are very helpful in most cases of tennis or golfer's elbow. Should this not be the case, the condition may be secondary to another disorder (which itself requires treatment) such as cervical spondylosis or disc lesion with root involvement, or underlying elbow arthritis. Again, a tennis elbow may turn out to be a soft-tissue manifestation of rheumatoid arthritis, gout or a spondyloarthropathy. Steroid injections in acute tennis elbow are often painful and patients should be warned about the possibility of post-injection pain. 1-2 ml. of steroid are injected at the site

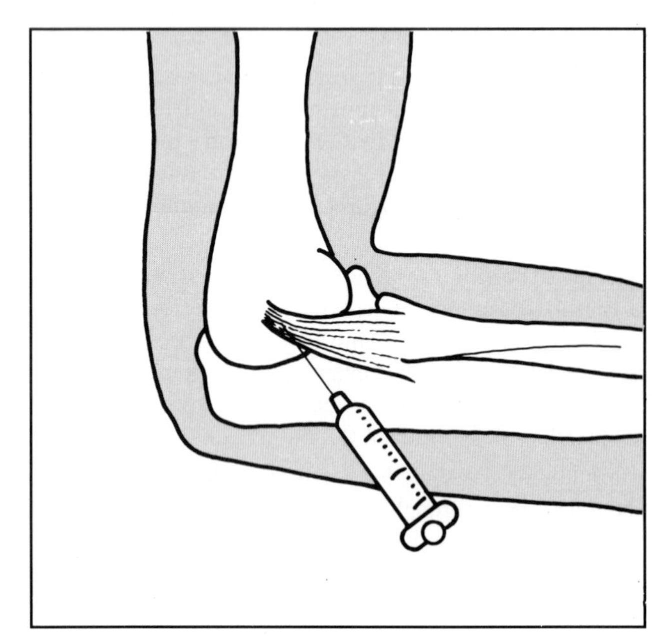

Fig. 2 Injection site for tennis elbow

of maximum tenderness into the tendon origin and then gradually into the tenoperiosteal junction (see fig. 2). Sometimes tenderness is maximal over the radial head, possibly due to inflammation of a small bursa adjacent to the radio-ulnar joint. Multiple tender points around the common extensor origin may imply that the pain is referred from 'above', ie the cervical spine. In golfer's elbow, tenderness is over the medial epicondyle, injected in the same way. Also, a golfers' elbow may accompany an ulnar nerve lesion at the elbow, in which case a steroid injection into the common flexor origin may give considerable relief of pain.

The bursa in olecranon bursitis (student's elbow) is painful if inflamed, and aspiration of the bursa and injection of steroid is usually helpful. In the event of recurrence surgical excision of the bursa is a simple procedure.

Arthritis of the elbow can respond to intra-articular steroid injection. The posterolateral approach is best: with the elbow flexed at 70°, locate the depression between the olecranon and the lateral epicondyle at the posterolateral aspect of the joint, then direct the needle in a forward and slightly downward plane (fig. 3).

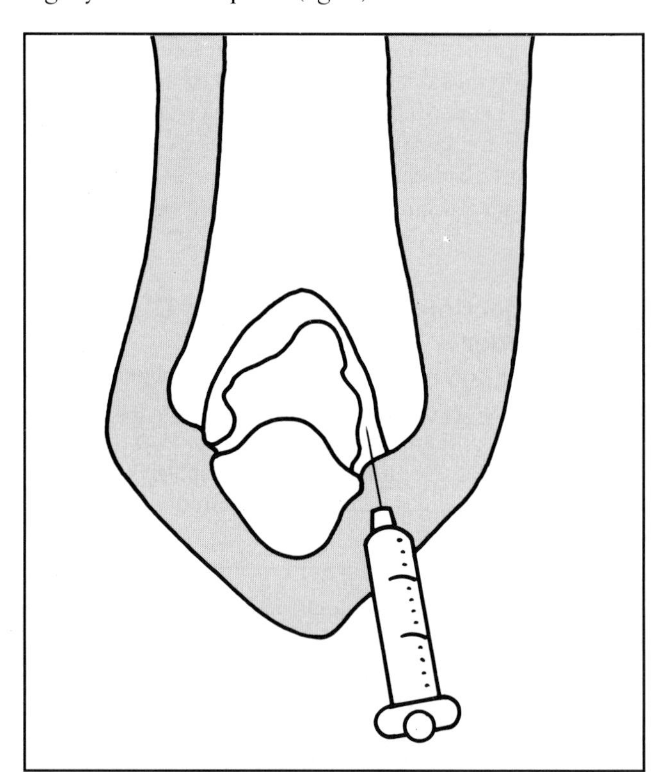

Fig.3 Injection of elbow joint

THE WRIST

Tenosynovitis of the tendon sheaths around the wrist is either traumatic, idiopathic or associated with rheumatoid arthritis. A lump is often visible and palpable (wrongly called a ganglion) but aspiration may be difficult as here the synovial fluid is extremely viscous. Steroid injections into tendon sheaths are often effective. Acute radial tenosynovitis is usually rapidly alleviated by a single steroid injection into the sheath. However, in chronic radial tenosynovitis (sometimes called de Quervain's disease) surgical treatment is often required, especially when this is related to occupational repetitive trauma.

There is a difference of opinion as to whether the carpal tunnel syndrome should be treated initially by local steroid injection, as some believe that surgical release is normally advisable, except in the mildest cases. There is no doubt that, should the condition be a result of median nerve compres-

SOFT–TISSUE DISORDERS AROUND THE WRIST

On anterior aspect of wrist	tenosynovitis of a flexor tendon or the common flexor sheath carpal tunnel syndrome
On posterior aspect of wrist	– tenosynovitis of extensor tendons
On lateral (radial) aspect of wrist	– tenosynovitis of common tendon sheath of extensor pollicis brevis/abductor pollicis longus

ARTHRITIS OF WRIST JOINTS

Wrist (radio-carpal) joint

Inferior radio-ulnar joint

First carpo-metacarpal joint (at thumb base)

sion by flexor tenosynovitis at the front of the wrist, a steroid injection into the tendon sheath may well abolish symptoms. Again, carpal tunnel syndrome is sometimes temporary, as when resulting from fluid retention during pregnancy. Otherwise the severity and progress of this condition seems to depend on the degree of median nerve compression - which can be ascertained by nerve conduction tests. Mild degrees of median nerve compression often respond temporarily, and sometimes permanently to a steroid injection, but most severe lesions require surgical decompression. The tunnel can be injected either in the mid-line above the distal wrist-crease, directing the needle slightly downwards towards the palm; or into the palm 1/2 inch distal to the wrist crease, directing the needle towards the wrist. (Note: pain and paraesthesiae in the median nerve distribution on insertion of the needle may indicate that the nerve has been touched and the needle should be withdrawn slightly. Similar symptoms may occur afterwards and do not necessarily imply that the median nerve has been touched

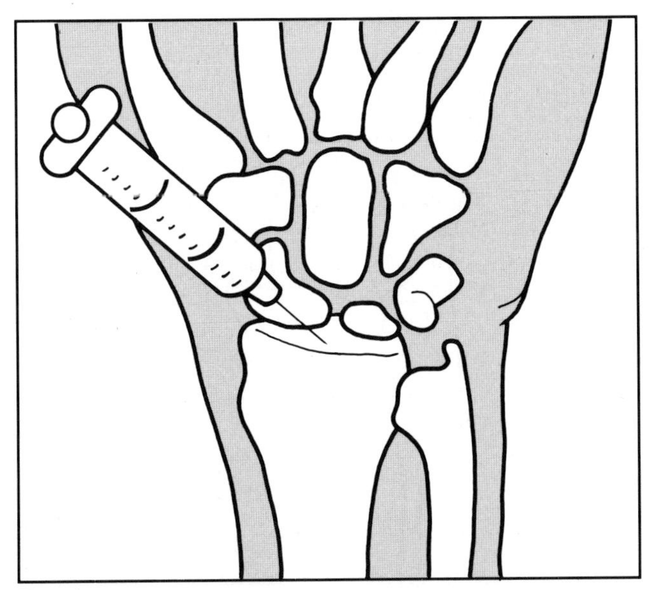

Fig. 4 Injection of wrist joint

but merely that the injected fluid has increased the pressure in an already tense carpal tunnel.)

Arthritis of the wrist joint is usually rheumatoid (sometimes secondary osteoarthritis, following injury or a fracture). Probably because the wrist is constantly moving steroid injections may not be as effective as injections into other non-weight bearing joints. Indeed splinting is often the most effective way to alleviate wrist pain, but if persistent it is worth trying an injection using a dorsal approach at the level of the ulnar styloid and pointing the needle slightly upwards (fig. 4). The inferior radio-ulnar joint often communicates with the wrist-joint and so can be injected alternatively (or as well), using a medial approach just above the ulnar styloid.

Osteoarthritis of the first carpo-metacarpal joints at the thumb-bases often responds to a steroid injection. The needle is introduced on the anterolateral aspect of the wrist, just below the base of the thumb metacarpal.

The Finger-Joints

Steroid injections are very effective in tenosynovitis of the finger-tendons and arthritis of the small finger-joints. Prior desensitization of the skin with ethyl chloride or other anaesthetic spray is recommended, as injections into small finger joints can be painful. The patient should be seated, with hands resting on a table. Many rheumatologists inject the metacarpophalangeal and interphalangeal joints of the fingers from the dorsal aspect. However, the writer finds that the palmar approach, using only a small amount of steroid (such as 0.2 ml. triamcinolone) and a very fine-bore needle is easier. The stalwart rheumatoid patient may allow several metacarpophalangeal and interphalangeal joints to be injected at one sitting. It is also possible to inject terminal interphalangeal joints of the fingers in osteoarthritis or psoriatic arthritis, but not usually advisable to attempt to inject into painful Heberden's nodes (adjacent to the terminal interphalangeal joints) - here, an anti-inflammatory drug is often useful.

FURTHER READING Local Injection Therapy in Rheumatic Diseases. Dixon A.St.J. and Graber J., EULAR Publishers, Basle 1983.

September 1991

LOCAL CORTICOSTEROID INJECTIONS - THE LOWER LIMB

D N Golding
Consultant Rheumatologist
West Essex Rheumatology Unit
Princess Alexandra Hospital
Harlow
Essex

THE REGION OF THE HIP

The hip region consists of the hip-joint, the groin, the trochanters and the ischial tuberosity. Pain in this region may be due to:

Referred pain from the lumbar spine (usually from the upper lumbar region)
Referred pain from the sacro-iliac joints (sacro-iliitis)
Osteoarthritis of the hips
Other types of hip arthritis: rheumatoid arthritis, ankylosing spondylitis involving the hips
"Transient synovitis" of the hips: this may be an early symptom of inflammatory arthritis, but often no underlying cause is apparent and there is full recovery
Perthes' disease: a form of avascular necrosis of the hip occurring in children or adolescents
Adolescent coxa vara ("slipped femoral epiphysis")
Osteomalacia: hip pain and associated weakness (pseudomyopathy) is not uncommon in this condition.
Bursitis around hips: psoas, trochanteric and ischial bursitis.
(Note: Pain arising from hip-joint may be referred to the medial thigh or knee).

Injection Therapy

Local steroid injections are not useful for most of these hip disorders, exceptions being the various types of bursitis around the hips, especially trochanteric and ischial bursitis. Injections into the hip-joints are technically very difficult, and any relief provided is usually transient. However bursitis, either secondary to underlying arthritis, as a direct result of trauma or with no particular cause, is important as there is a good response to a local injection into the bursa.

Trochanteric bursitis is characterized by pain and tenderness localized to the area around the greater trochanter, some 10 cms. below the level of the anterior superior spine. The tender, inflamed bursa is palpated over the greater trochanter and injected via a lateral approach.

Ischial bursitis causes pain in the lower buttock on sitting. Again it may be a primary bursitis, or secondary to a lumbar disc or other disorder.

Practice Point

The commonest causes of pain in the hips are as follows:
1. Osteoarthritis of the hip.
2. Pain referred from the upper lumbar spine (usually a disc lesion or area of osteoarthritis).
3. Bursitis around the hips, especially trochanteric and ischial bursitis.

While steroid injections are not appropriate for osteoarthritis of the hip, they often give immediate relief in bursitis.

THE KNEE

There are many possible causes of pain felt in or around the knee: (figure 1)

1. Patello-femoral osteoarthritis (or chondromalacia patellae)
2. Medial or lateral ligament strain
3. Arthritis of the knee-joint proper, either degenerative (osteoarthritis) or inflammatory.
4. Popliteal bursitis (Baker's cyst): painful swelling behind knee.
5. Internal derangements of knee (eg cartilage injury).
6. Osteochondritis of tibial tubercle (Osgood-Schlatter's disease).
7. Tender fat pads (panniculitis) around the knee.
8. Osteochondritis dissecans - bone infarction, leading to detachment of fragment from medial femoral condyle.
9. Pre-patellar bursitis.
10. Pain referred to the knee, usually from either hip-joint disease or a lesion of the upper lumbar spine.

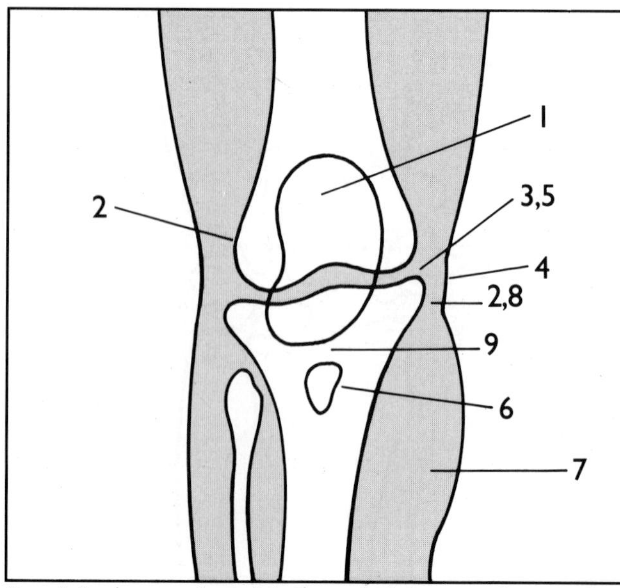

Figure 1. Structures in and around the knee, with which pain may be associated.

Injection Therapy

Local injections are useful in the following conditions causing knee-joint pain.

Ligamentous strain pain is often secondary to underlying osteoarthritis of the knee, even at an early stage. Medial ligament strain is easily detected by local tenderness at either or both the superior and inferior attachments of the ligament. Local injections of steroid/lignocaine at these points are often effective in relieving pain. (Note: medial or lateral ligamentous pain is not necessarily associated with valgus or varus deformity of the knee, but if this is present local injections are obviously less likely to be of long-lasting benefit.)

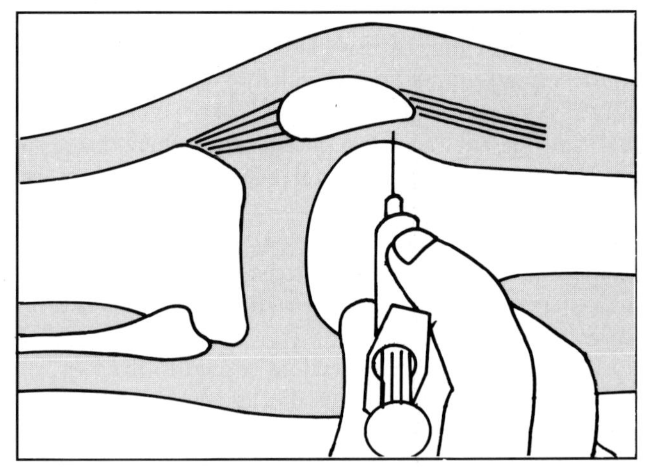

Figure 2. Injection of knee joint (in extension)

Inflammatory arthritis and synovitis of the knee - A swollen knee should first be aspirated and the synovial fluid examined for bacteria and crystals. If very turbid or purulent, steroid should not be introduced until sepsis has been excluded by appropriate bacteriological examination. The knee-joint is easily entered on the medial or lateral side between the patella and femur with the knee extended (see fig. 2): entry can be shown by aspiration of synovial fluid. If there is fixed flexion deformity of knees (as in established rheumatoid arthritis) injection is often easier antero-medially below the patella, just beside the patellar tendon (see fig. 4).

Popliteal bursitis (Baker's cyst) may be part of synovitis and secondary to knee arthritis, in which case the cyst communicates with the joint and so can be reached by injecting it. Otherwise the cyst can be directly aspirated (and injected) from the posterior aspect of the knee, the patient lying prone. If there is rupture of the joint capsule and herniation of synovial membrane downwards between the calf muscles, a large"rheumatoid cyst of the calf" may cause painful swelling of the leg (this can be misdiagnosed as phlebitis, but sometimes both are present - local thrombophlebitis results from compression of superficial veins by the prolapsed cyst).

Pre-patellar bursitis ("housemaid's knee") often responds to an injection into the bursa, which lies anterior to the patellar ligament.

THE ANKLE

In addition to the ankle (talo-calcaneal) joint itself, other structures around this joint can become inflamed. These include the peroneal tendons behind the lateral malleolus, the long extensor tendons in front of the ankle, the posterior tibial tendon behind the medial malleolus and the Achilles tendon at the back. Pain in this region usually arises from synovitis or arthritis of the ankle, or from tenosynovitis affecting the sheaths of any of these tendons.

Injection Therapy

The ankle-joint is injected from the front, just medial to the tibialis anterior tendon (see fig. 5). The needle is directed posterolaterally and rather obliquely, tangential to the slope of the talus. Adjoining tendon sheaths may be injected, remembering that a painful ankle in rheumatoid arthritis is often due to tenosynovitis of the medial or lateral tendons rather than arthritis.

THE HEEL

Pain in the heel can be classified as (a) pain beneath the heel, (b) pain behind the heel.

Pain beneath the heel is most often due to plantar fasciitis. When unilateral this is usually primary ("idiopathic"), but when bilateral it is often associated with arthritis of the foot joints (rheumatoid or seronegative B27-positive spondarthritis as in Reiter's disease or psoriatic arthritis). Atypical gout is a rare cause of plantar fasciitis. Spurs of the calcaneum ("simple" spurs) are often seen radiologically in the common primary plantar fasciitis. In patients with heel pain it is also important to exclude the possibility of pain referred from the lower lumbar spine, due to involvement of an S_1 or S_2 nerve-root by a 5th lumbar disc prolapse.

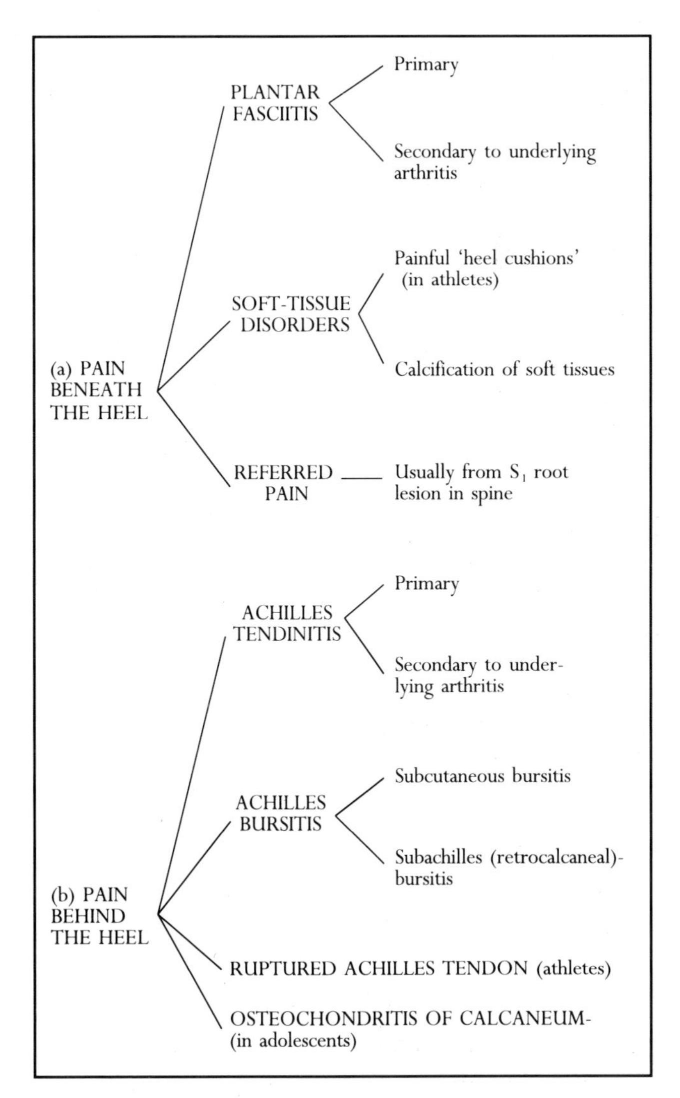

Figure 3. The causes of heel pain

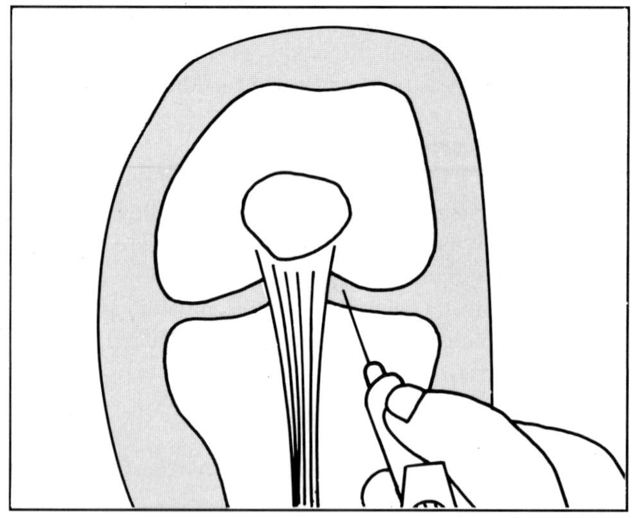

Figure 4. Injection of knee joint (in flexion)

Like plantar fasciitis, Achilles tendinitis or bursitis may be "primary", or secondary to underlying arthritis. Gouty bursitis may occur, and indeed tophi are occasionally found on the Achilles tendon itself. Before injecting the Achilles bursa, it is useful to attempt aspiration to see if the synovial fluid (normally very viscous) shows inflammatory features (ie turbidity, high white cell count or crystals of urate, pyrophosphate or hydroxyapatite). In Achilles tendinitis the tendon itself is inflamed, tender and often swollen. This large tendon is covered by a thin paratenon (not by a proper tendon sheath), so (unlike bursitis) no attempt should be made to inject steroid into it for fear of subsequent rupture.

Injection Therapy

Plantar fasciitis often, though not always, responds to one or two injections of a steroid/lignocaine/hyaluronidase mixture given into the point of maximum tenderness - usually medially at the origin of the plantar fascia. After the injection, arrange for a patient to have a sorbo-rubber insert in the heel of the shoe. Then it is important to try to correct obvious predisposing causes, such as obesity and pes planus - for which combined valgus and varus arch supports are helpful. When plantar fasciitis is secondary to underlying inflammatory joint disease (often bilateral), local treatment must be accompanied by systemic treatment of the underlying arthritic disorder.

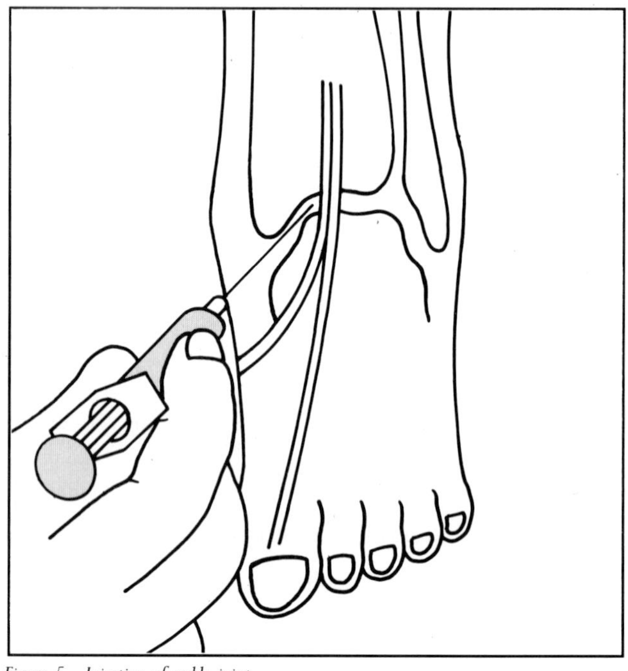

Figure 5. Injection of ankle joint.

It has been already stressed that the Achilles tendons themselves must never be injected though it should be noted that steroid injections are often effective in sub-Achilles bursitis.

THE FOOT

Along with correction of abnormal foot mechanics, such as pes planus, steroid injections are helpful for many painful foot disorders. In this context the heel, plantar fascia, ankle-joint and various foot joints (talocalcaneal, mid-tarsal, metatarsophalangeal and interphalangeal) must all be considered.

Pain in the feet may be classified as follows:
(a) Mechanical pain associated with foot deformities (eg pes planus, pes cavus, hallux valgus)
(b) Pain due to trauma or chronic foot-strain: previous fractures (including stress fractures of metatarsals), sprains or strains of the foot joints.
(c) Arthritis of foot and toe-joints: osteoarthritis, rheumatoid arthritis, seronegative spondarthritis, gout.
(d) Osteochondritis: may involve the metatarsal heads or navicular bone.
(e) Tenosynovitis affecting tendons related to the foot.
(f) Pain from vascular disorders affecting the feet (atheroma and Raynaud's phenomenon).
(g) Pain from neurological disorders affecting the feet, especially peripheral neuropathy (as in diabetes) and the tarsal tunnel syndrome (compression neuropathy of the posterior tibial nerve).

Injection Therapy

Ligamentous strains of the foot and the various types of arthritis often respond well to steroid injections given into the site of maximum tenderness.

The metatarsophalangeal joints are commonly involved in rheumatoid disease, leading to dropping of the anterior arches, widening of the forefoot and sometimes splaying of the toes, so that arch supports and larger sizes of shoes are required. As when injecting finger joints, the author's preference is to inject the metatarsophalangeal joints from the plantar aspect, tangentially to the joint. Initial spraying with a cold solution, such as ethyl chloride, is appreciated as these injections can be quite painful and only a small amount (0.5 ml) of steroid solution is required.

The first metatarsophalangeal joint (big toe) is involved by osteoarthritis or by gout (acute or chronic stages). Acute gout normally responds to NSAID's. In chronic gout or osteoarthritis of the big toe pain can often be relieved by a steroid injection, but often surgical treatment is required.

Osteoarthritis or rheumatoid arthritis of the other foot joints (intertarsal, tarsometatarsal, subtaloid- and mid-tarsal) can be painful and sometimes a "lump" appears on the instep (due to dorsal subluxation of a tarsal bone) It is not generally realised that these joints can be usefully injected, and even though specific joints may be difficult to enter, pain can be relieved by infiltration of the surrounding soft tissues. The subtaloid joint is best injected from the lateral aspect, at a level just above the tip of the lateral malleolus, the needle pointing towards the first metatarsal head. However, rheumatoid involvement of this joint leads to progressive valgus deformity below the ankle (pes plano-valgus) and when this is pronounced injection becomes technically very difficult.

Tenosynovitis of the anterior or posterior tibial tendon sheaths must be recognised as causes of pain in the rheumatoid foot, as these sheaths are readily injected with steroid.

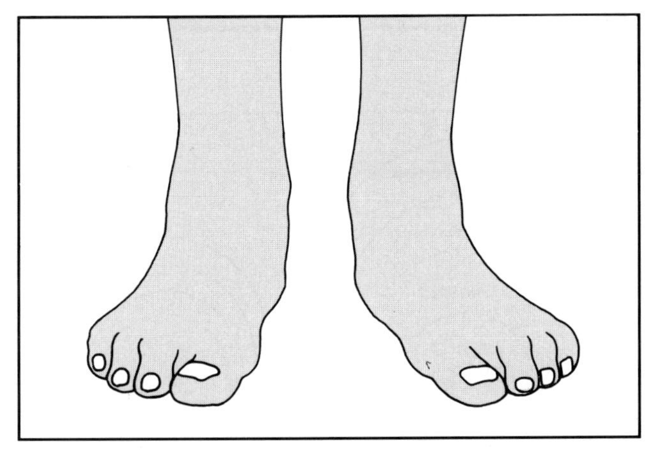

Figure 6. Valgus ankles in patient with rheumatoid arthritis.

A note on Corticosteroid Injections

Please note that further discussion of preparations to be injected and methods of injection appears in part I of this series: General Aspects and Upper Limb

Reference

The most comprehensive account of local steroid injections can be found in No.4 of the Eular monograph series (edited by A. St. J. Dixon and J. Graber) - published by Eular Publishers, Basle, Switzerland (1983).

January 1992

TREATMENT & CONTROL OF CHRONIC ARTHRITIC AND BACK PAIN

L Turner-Stokes
Consultant in Rehabilitation Medicine
Northwick Park Hospital
Harrow

INTRODUCTION

Acute pain functions as a biological early warning system, signalling tissue damage. Musculoskeletal pain may arise from bones, joints or soft tissues by a variety of different mechanisms which may be principally divided into 'inflammation' and 'mechanical derangement'. Careful clinical assessment to identify as far as possible the origin of pain in an arthritic patient is therefore fundamental to management, so that the correct treatment modalities may be applied.

The management of chronic pain, however, is rarely that simple. Waddell et al (1) applied the following 'Illness Behaviour Model' to the study of low back pain: "Most low back pain starts with a physical problem in the spine. Psychological disturbances are secondary to this physical disorder. The most important psychological disturbance is distress which presents clinically as illness behaviour. Disability then arises from a combination of physical disorder, distress and illness behaviour". This Glasgow Illness Model is illustrated in figure 1. Conventional medicine has largely ignored the illness behaviour component of low back pain, which probably accounts for its poor results. Symptoms and signs of illness behaviour should be clearly distinguished from those of physical disease. Physical treatment may then be directed at physical disease but management must include treatment for distress and illness behaviour in their own right (2).

The first part of this report will review current methods of providing pain relief. The second part reviews the cognitive behavioural strategies which are now increasingly used to combat pain and disability.

Although emphasis is given to the management of chronic pain, many conditions are punctuated by acute-on-chronic episodes so that acute measures may also be required to return the patient to *status quo*.

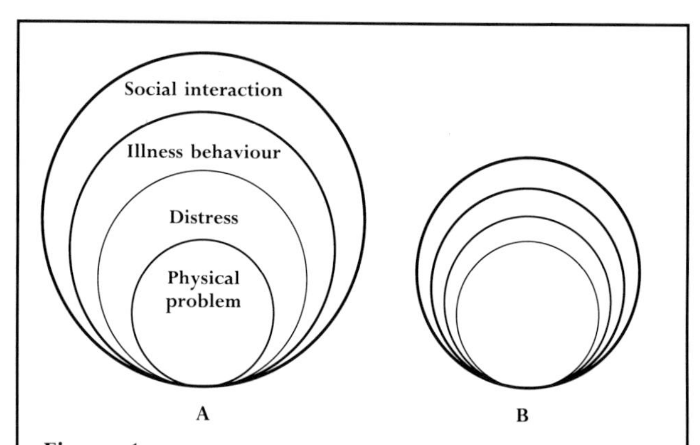

Figure 1
The Glasgow Illness Model. Diagrammatic representation of the physical, psychological and behavioural components of illness and the variation of their relative importance in different individuals.
(Adapted with permission from Waddell 1992)

PRE-TREATMENT ASSESSMENT

Before embarking on any pain relief programme, careful clinical assessment and investigation should be undertaken to rule out simply remediable causes for pain.

Active inflammatory arthritis requires aggressive management. If synovitis is restricted to one or two joints, local measures such as intra-articular injection, synovectomy etc may be appropriate. More widespread synovitis, however, may require disease-modifying anti-rheumatic drugs, either singly or in combination. Surgical intervention should be considered for severe degenerative joint damage; isometric exercise programmes to build up supporting musculature, and if necessary external splinting or support to encourage physical activity. In the context of back pain, CT myelography (or MRI scanning if available) to exclude surgically remediable lesions, such as disc prolapse, should be undertaken in the early stages. Chronicity is a poor prognostic factor in terms of treatment outcome.

PAIN RELIEF INTERVENTIONS

I. Pills and potions

Non-steroidal anti-inflammatory drugs (NSAIDs)

NSAIDs inhibit cyclo-oxygenase, thus impeding the production of inflammatory prostaglandins. If tolerated, they generally provide effective pain relief in arthritis. This holds true not only for inflammatory forms, but for osteoarthritis (3) as well. Where gastro-intestinal intolerance precludes cheaper prepara-

TABLE 1. THE RELATIVE MERITS OF REST AND EXERCISE

	EXERCISE	REST
Pain	Painful in early stages	Reduces pain by: - relieving loading - destimulating nociceptors
Physical Effects	Enhances blood supply and nutrition, preventing ischaemia Restores articular function, bone and muscle strength thereby preventing contactures	Too much rest causes: - ischaemia - osteopenia - muscle wasting - contractures
Mood	Enhances endorphin production - boosting mood - decreasing distress	Reduces endorphin production, causing: - depression - distress, frustration - boredom
Disability and Illness Behaviour	Ability enhances positive feedback. Increased independence Reduced illness behaviour	Emphasises disability Reinforces dependence, sick role and abnormal illness behaviour

tions, the use of pro-drugs such as fenbufen or nabumetone may be justified. In elderly patients with renal impairment, NSAIDs can precipitate renal failure by reducing renal perfusion, and should only be used with the utmost caution.

Simple analgesics

Centrally-acting analgesics may reduce perception of pain but, with the exception of paracetamol, tend to cause sedation and constipation. Combinations of paracetamol with dextropropoxyphene (Co-proxamol, codeine (Co-codamol) or dihydrocodeine (Co-dydramol) are frequently prescribed but often reported by the patients to be unhelpful.

Narcotic analgesics suppress natural endorphin production They induce tolerance and dependence and have no place in the management of chronic arthritic pain, where they merely compound pre-existing problems with addiction.

Tricyclic antidepressants

The increased incidence of anxiety and depression among chronic pain sufferers is not the only justification put forward for the use of tricyclic antidepressants in these patients. A reported synergistic effect with centrally-acting analgesics and the stimulation of endorphin production (4) lend support in theory. In practice, however, they are often disappointing and in the absence of clear benefit should be discontinued after six months.

Muscle relaxants

Centrally acting muscle relaxants such as carisoprodol, methocarbamol or anticholinergics (eg orphenadrine) may be used to reduce paravertebral spasm in acute spinal pain (5) but their place in the chronic setting is less clear. The most common side-effect of muscle relaxants is drowsiness, which in turn may reduce awareness and motivation for rehabilitation.

Benzodiazepines are now known to be strongly addictive with dangerous side-effects on withdrawal. Like narcotic analgesics they have no place in the management of chronic musculoskeletal pain.

2. General Measures

Homeopathic remedies and diet

Since many patients ask about the importance of diet, cod-liver oil etc, the theory behind this will be discussed briefly.

The normal western diet contains significant amounts of poly-unsaturated animal fats. These are broken down to fatty acids, predominantly arachidonic acid or 'eicosatetranoic acid' (the tetra refers to the degree of unsaturation, ie the number of double bonds). Fatty acids are further metabolised to form prostaglandins and in this case the PG2 series, which are potent mediators of inflammation. NSAIDs inhibit cyclo-oxygenase, one of the enzymes in this pathway, thereby reducing the production of inflammatory prostaglandins.

By contrast, the metabolism of fish oils produces larger amounts of eicosapentanoic acid, and in turn prostaglandins in the PG3 series. These tend to be less inflammatory than the PG2 series. Substitution of fish oil for animal fat in the diet could theoretically reduce inflammation, but in practice fat-free diets are difficult to tolerate and the quantity of substituted fish oil even more so. A single dose of cod-liver oil daily will have little effect, other than providing a useful source of vitamin D.

Evening primrose oil is metabolised down a different pathway to form eicosatrienoic acid and thence the PG1 series. Some of these prostaglandins have a mild anti-inflammatory effect. However it is worth remembering that cyclo-oxygenase inhibitors will depress prostaglandin production in this pathway as well, so NSAIDs could negate the effect of evening primrose oil if taken concurrently.

Diet

A daily diet which is low in animal fat but contains adequate minerals and vitamins holds several advantages over and above the theoretical reduction of inflammatory prostaglandin production. A diet of white meat and fish in exchange for red meat, low fat dairy products in exchange for full fat ones, and plenty of green vegetables helps to keep body-weight down, to ensure adequate intake of iron, calcium and vitamin D (which is especially important in the face of immobility), and very often to encourage in the patient a sense of self-help and control over their symptoms.

Bed rest versus physical exercise

The relative merits of rest and exercise are laid out in Table 1.

Bed rest
The last two decades have seen a clear change in medical opinion regarding the advisability of bed rest. There is no evidence to show that bed rest is beneficial; even for acute arthritis or back pain, but ample evidence of its deleterious effects. During bed rest, 3% of muscle strength is lost per day (6), resulting in decreased physical fitness. Periods of bed rest should be kept to an absolute minimum. Even in septic arthritis, patients may remain ambulant although non-weight bearing on the affected joint.

In the chronic setting, prolonged rest can lead to osteopenia, contractures, depression, loss of the work habit and difficulty in starting rehabilitation. Early mobilization and return to work should be vigorously encouraged. There is no evidence that this increases the likelihood of future episodes of back pain (1).

Patients with chronic pain tend to have low levels of physical activity. This leads to a reduction in cardiovascular fitness which can be as disabling as the pain itself. Physical exertion in this context tends to result in muscular pain, reinforcing the belief that exercise makes the pain worse and so further reducing activity levels.

Exercise
Increased physical activity promotes bone and muscle strength and improves the flow of nutriments into intervertebral discs. It also increases endorphin levels in the cerebrospinal fluid, leading to an increased sense of well-being and a reduction in pain perception (7). Exercise also provides demonstrable benefit in preventing future back injuries (8).

Patients are therefore taught to exercise in a programme that encompasses three main areas:

1. General exercise to improve physical fitness: patients are encouraged to take regular non-jarring exercise such as swimming, cycling, walking.

2. Back care and joint protection information: including the necessary adjustments to their home, workplace and habits to avoid exacerbation of the problem.

3. Remedial exercise programme: such as quadriceps drill for arthritis in the knees, extension or isometric flexion exercises for the spine.

The remedial part of the programme should be tailored to the individual's patient's requirements and supervised in the early stages to ensure correct execution. Passive extension exercises (eg Mackenzie) may help to milk back a herniated disc and therefore be helpful in the acute setting, but may exacerbate chronic low back pain due to spinal stenosis, spondylolysthesis or facet osteoarthropathy. For these conditions isometric flexion exercises (eg Williams) are often preferable (9). If weight-bearing is intensely painful, hydrotherapy may be tolerated more easily than dry-land exercise.

Corset and Braces
Lumbar corsets reduce the gross range of movement, increase intra-abdominal pressure, and may help to reduce intra-discal pressure (10). In the short-term, a corset can be helpful in reminding the patient to maintain correct posture and facilitate return to work. In this case it may be used *providing* it is left off as soon as possible. Long-term use leads to disuse atrophy of the muscles which support the back, and should be avoided; instead, these muscles should be built up with remedial exercise.

Some patients with chronic pain syndromes become dependant on cervical collars, corsets or braces as externally visible expressions of their disability. Supervised 'weaning' from these should be undertaken slowly, but firmly, in a multidisciplinary setting. Sudden withdrawal is likely to result merely in switching from one prop to another.

3. Physical Techniques

Spinal manipulative techniques are aimed at increasing mobility, breaking adhesions, readjusting the vertebra and reducing muscle spasm and pain. Controlled studies show a significant short-term improvement but no long-term effect (7). Other physical techniques such as the local application of heat, cold, ultrasound, shortwave may also have a place in reducing acute muscle spasm but there is no evidence that they alter the natural history of back pain, and their main use should be to facilitate the early introduction of an exercise programme, which the patient is taught to continue at home.

4. Counterstimulation

Transcutaneous Electrical Nerve Stimulation (TENS)
TENS uses electric stimulation of the afferent nervous system in order to modulate pain perception. It is shown to be effective in acute and chronic pain(11) and may be used as an adjunct to other treatment modalities. In particular it may prove helpful in affording the patient some measure of control over their pain.

Acupuncture and local injection techniques
The art of acupuncture is rapidly gaining popularity in the West, both in its ancient Chinese form and in the Westernised version of 'trigger-point acupuncture' where local trigger-points of tenderness are stimulated. Stimulation may be achieved by dry needling alone or by injection of the site with local anaesthetic and/or steroid. In the face of chronic pain, benefit is usually short-lived. As with manipulation, though, the window may still be effective if it paves the way to further rehabilitation (7).

Acupuncture has proved effective for myofascial pain, but peripheral osteoarthritis and back pain respond less favourably (12).

5. Specific injection techniques

a) for arthritis pain
Intra-articular injection of steroids may reduce active synovitis and may also be helpful, even in the absence of overt inflammation, for patients with osteoarthritis (13).

Local nerve blocks may relieve pain from severe destructive arthritis which is not amenable to surgical treatment - for example supra-scapular nerve blocks for chronic intractable shoulder pain (14).

Regional sympathetic blockade has been used in rheumatoid arthritis to try to reduce the pro-inflammatory effects of the sympathetic nervous system (15) but the effect may be too short-lived to be of benefit.

b) for spinal pain

Discography should be regarded as a purely diagnostic test. The most important feature is its reproduction of the patient's pain and it has been used to assess proper needle placement for chemonucleolysis.

Facet joint injection has been used in the conservative management of low back pain. It appears to be more effective with high volume injections, and it is suggested that much of the benefit may be derived from extravasation into the epidural space (16).

Epidural injections Many different techniques have been advocated for epidural injection but none of them has been shown to provide long-term relief in the chronic setting (17).

One of the common difficulties in assessing the efficacy of injection techniques is to differentiate the benefit of simple needle placement with that of local injection of anaesthetic, steroids or both; and to determine what counts as placebo control. In the final analysis, though, none of them give long term benefit except where short term benefit can be capitalised on with further rehabilitation.

TABLE 2.

AN INTEGRATED PAIN REHABILITATION PROGRAMME SHOULD INCLUDE:

Assessment - to identify components of physical disorder, distress and illness behaviour

Explanation - a thorough explanation in language the patient can understand, including the physical and behavioural components of their disability

Reduction of pain - using analgesia, physical interventions (ice/heat, manipulation, TENS, acupuncture etc), strategies to reduce distress, anxiety and illness behaviour - advice on self-help and establishing patient's control of lifestyle

Recovery of function - physical objectives include recovery of normal muscle tone and joint flexibility, illness behaviour objectives include resuming self-care and light daily activities

Rehabilitation - a graded return to normal activities (including work, social and leisure) at pre-morbid level and withdrawal from medication

Preventative aftercare - including weight reduction, ergonomics at work and play, postural re-training, continuing aerobic exercise

CHRONIC PAIN MANAGEMENT

This report has so far covered interventions for trying to *relieve* patients of their pain. There is a group of patients, however, in which all these techniques will fail. Efforts must then be concentrated on helping patients to cope better *despite* their pain. It is not necessary, or even advisable, to separate these two approaches. Table 2 suggests a format for an integrated pain rehabilitation programme. If the propensity for developing a chronic pain syndrome is perceived in the early stages, a multidisciplinary approach which combines pain relief techniques with positive coping strategies may provide a better outcome. Since recognition is all-important, salient features of some common chronic pain syndromes will be discussed.

Persistent pain following trauma

Trauma may strike at all ages, but can be particularly devastating to the young, who may be disabled for the rest of their lives. Pain may persist long after injured tissues have healed, and when no longer functioning to signal on-going tissue damage, it can be extremely difficult to treat. The severity of the injury has little bearing on the severity of the pain syndrome. Socio-economic sequelae, depression, a sense of injustice, litigation may all contribute, but the individual strands are often very difficult to disentangle.

Myofascial pain syndrome This is characterised by trigger-points (local areas of irritability). There is a generally consistent pattern of referred pain from these trigger points and varying degrees of musculoskeletal dysfunction and sleep disturbance (18). This regional pain syndrome may be contrasted with the more generalised muscle pain characterising fibromyalgia, although both conditions form part of the same spectrum of non-specific muscular pain (19). Common sites for trigger points are in the inter-scapular and trapezius muscles on the posterior thoracic wall. This syndrome commonly follows whiplash injuries and there may be other associated symptoms, such as paraesthesiae, numbness, dizziness and fatigue. Pain relief interventions may include counter-stimulation of trigger points eg by local injection, acupuncture or TENS, but the king-pin of treatment should be a programme of stretching exercise, aerobic conditioning and postural retraining, combined if necessary with a cognitive behavioural approach.

Sympathetically maintained pain This is a group of disorders in which proximal trauma leads to a distal pattern of continuous burning pain, with hyperalgesia and allodynia in the painful area (18). It includes causalgia (following a traumatic nerve lesion) and reflex sympathetic dystrophy (RSD). Local abnormal sympathetic activity is often observed, with changes in temperature and colour and sweating patterns. Later the affected part become cold, pale and wasted. Contractures and osteopenia appear (so-called Sudek's atrophy). Sympathetic ganglion blockade (eg stellate ganglion block) or intravenous guanethidine blocks may be helpful in the early stages but should be combined with active physiotherapy to improve function. A relationship between RSD and emotional stress is increasingly appreciated, together with the need for intervention on this level. RSD not uncommonly presents in childhood, when it will often necessitate family therapy.

A cognitive behavioural approach to chronic pain management

In addition to their pain, patients with arthritis have to cope with deformity and disfiguration, physical disability and its socio-economic consequences for them and their families, not to mention the unpredictable course of the disease with its flares and remissions. Anxiety and depression may increase the perception of pain and result in pain behaviour and reduced attempts to engage in activities of daily living. Increasing dependence on relatives and friends may strain relationships and lead to increased social isolation. Family members cast into a caring role may become over-protective, endorsing passive behaviour in the patient, and reinforcing their feelings of worthlessness.

Cognitive behavioural programmes emphasize the fact that the responsibility for pain and disability most appropriately belongs to the patient. They aim to increase patients' belief in their own ability to control pain as well as improving coping skills such as physical relaxation, stress management, pacing activities and self-assertion. A multi-disciplinary approach should include input from the various remedial disciplines: a) physiotherapy - to encourage remedial exercise and general physical fitness, b) occupational therapy - encouraging independence in daily living activities, c) psychology - to teach coping skills and their application, and d) medical - to supervise drug withdrawal, provide realistic information concerning their disease as well as to endorse the approach as a whole.

Even though pain intensity remains unchanged, cognitive behavioural programmes have proven effective in increasing work, social and leisure activities in patients with rheumatoid arthritis (20) and in reducing pain behaviour and anxiety (21).

Similar programmes have been applied across the spectrum of chronic pain and in particular for management of disabling spinal pain and were recently reviewed by Jensen et al (1991) (22). Currently, a lack of uniformity in method confounds comparison and there is a need for better measures for parameters such as coping, beliefs and adjustment. This is undoubtedly an area of rehabilitation which will make an important contribution over the coming decades.

REFERENCES

1. Waddell G. A new clinical model for the treatment of low back pain. *Spine* 1987;**12**: 632-644
2. Vernon. Commentary: A model of incorporating the illness behaviour model in the management of low back pain. *J Manipulative and Physiological Therapeutics* 1991; **6**: 379-89
3. Bollet AJ. Analgesic and anti-inflammatory drugs in the therapy of osteoarthritis. *Seminars in Arthritis and Rheumatism* 1981; **11**: 130-2
4. Brown RS, Bottomley WK. The utilization and mechanism of action of anti-depressants in the treatment of chronic facial pain: a review of literature. *Anaesth Prog* 1990; **37**: 223-9
5. Elenbaas JK. Centrally-acting oral musculoskeletal relaxants. *Am J Hosp Pharm* 1980; **37**: 1313-1323
6. Chase JA. Outpatient management of low back pain. *Orthopaedic Nursing* 1992; **11**: 11-20
7. Fast A. Low Back Disorders: Conservative Management. *Arch Phys Med Rehabil* 1988; **69**: 880-891
8. Cady LD, Bischoff DP, O'Connell ER, Thamoas PC, Allan JH. Strength, fitness, and subsequent back injuries in fire-fighters. *J Occup Med* 1979; **21:** 269-272
9. Kendall PH, Jenkins JM. Exercises for backache; a double-blind controlled trial. *Physiotherapy* 1968; **54**: 154-7
10. Frymoyer J. Back pain and sciatica. *New Eng J Med* 1988; **318:** 291-300
11. Melzack R. Prolonged relief of pain by brief intense transcutaneous somatic stimulation. *Pain* 1975; **1**: 357-373
12. Junnila SYT. Long term treatment of chronic pain with acupuncture: *Acupuncture and electrotherapeutics Res Int J* 1987; **12:** 23-36
13. Dieppe PA, Sathapapayavongs B, Jones HE, Bacon PA, Ring EFJ. Intra-articular steroids in osteoarthritis. *Rheumatology and Rehabilitation 1980*; **19**: 212-7
14. Emery P, Bowman S, Wedderburn L, Grahame R. Suprascapular nerve block for chronic shoulder pain in rheumatoid arthritis. *Br Med J* 1989; **299**: 1079-80
15. Levine JD, Fye K, Heller P, Basbaum AI, Whiting-O-Keefe Q. Clinical response to regional intravenous guanethidine in patients with rheumatoid arthritis. *J Rheumatol* 1986; **13**: 1040-3
16. Moran R, O'Connell D, Walsh MG. The diagnostic value of facet joint injectionS. *Spine* 1988; **13**: 1407-1410
17. El-Khoury GY, Renfrew DL. Percutaneous procedures for the diagnosis and treatment of lower back pain: diskography, facet joint injection and epidural injection. *AJR* 1991; **157**: 685-91
18. Ashburn MA, Fine PG. Persistent pain following trauma. *Military Medicine* 1989; **154**: 86-9
19. Fricton JR, Awad E. *Myofascial pain and fibromyalgia*. New York. Raven Press 1990
20. Randich SR. Evaluation of pain management program for rheumatoid arthritis patients. *Arthritis Rheum* 1982; **25**: S11 (Abstract)
21. Bradley LA, Young LD, Anderson KO et al. Effects of psychological therapy on pain behaviour of rheumatoid arthritis patients. *Arthritis Rheum* 1987; **30**:1105-1114.
22. Jensen MP, Turner JA, Romano JM, Karoly P. Coping with chronic pain: a critical review of the literature. *Pain* 1991; **47**: 249-283
23. Wadell G. Understanding the patient with backache. In *The Lumbar Spine and Back Pain*, Ed MIV Jayson, Churchill Livingstone 1992.

January 1993

WHAT CAN PHYSIOTHERAPY OFFER?

R Grahame
Consultant Rheumatologist
Guy's Hospital
London

R Cooper
Principal
School of Physiotherapy
Guy's Hospital
London

Introduction

Despite the strides made in rheumatology in the last two decades and the shift in emphasis from physical to medical treatment, physiotherapy remains a frequently used tool in the treatment of a broad range of rheumatic conditions. In-patients or out-patients referred by hospital consultant or general practitioner are likely to be treated within the hospital ward and department, or in the Community. Detailed assessment allows the setting of realistic objectives and the choice of appropriate methods. The physiotherapist expects the referring doctor to make an accurate diagnosis, and he or she works in collaboration with the doctor and other paramedical professionals.

What do physiotherapists do that is applicable to rheumatic diseases?

1. Make splints to rest joints thereby preventing and/or treating deformities and contractures.
2. Teach and supervise exercises that improve joint movement and muscle strength, thereby restoring useful function.
3. Apply "soothing" measures including short-wave, ultrasound, interferential, laser, infra-red and hydrotherapy. (These warm the diseased tissues thereby inhibiting muscle spasm and enabling restorative exercise to be more readily performed). Experimentally, ultrasound has been shown to accelerate the healing of traumatic skin lesions in the rabbit (1) and to stimulate protein synthesis by fibroblasts in tissue culture (2). Clinically, ultrasound has been demonstrated to stimulate the healing of varicose ulcers in man (3).
4. Apply mobilisation and manipulation to restore mobility to "stuck" joints by passive manoeuvres using controlled force in increasing degrees.
5. Counsel on:-
   (i) Care of the locomotor system (especially the back) during and after an episode of injury or disease.
   (ii) The prevention of injury or disease by instructing at-risk groups, e.g. nurses and heavy-manual workers in the care of the back; instructing on the importance of a good posture in adolescence.

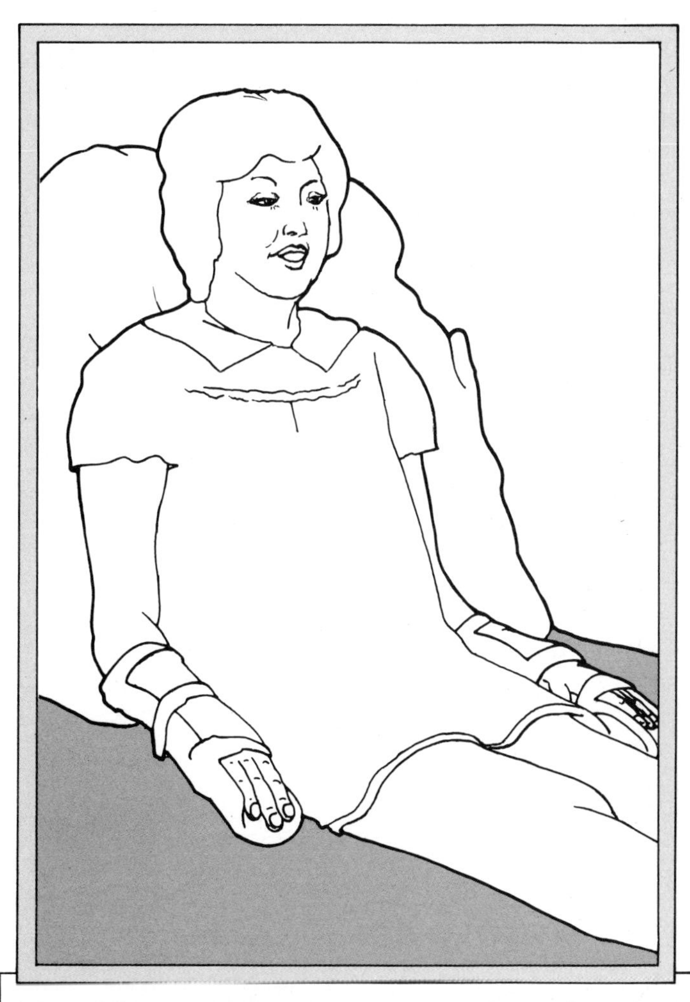

1. Immobilisation of inflamed joints (wrists and fingers) is achieved here by plaster-of-Paris resting splints held in place by "Velcro" straps. These splints can easily be removed for eating, etc.

How do physiotherapists work?

Physiotherapists have been working in close co-operation with the medical profession since the end of the 19th Century. There are now 22,000 physiotherapists working in the U.K. within the National Health Service and the private sector. Their ethical code does not permit advertisement, and treatments are initiated by reference from a medical practitioner. The physiotherapist will require a clinical diagnosis with relevant history and details of any contra-indications to treatment, and will then plan the treatment after making his or her own assessment of the patient's problem. Many NHS physiotherapists nowadays work in the Community, perhaps attached to a Health Centre or group practice. Their role may be advisory or counselling as opposed to the treatment role predominantly played by hospital physiotherapists. They also treat patients in Day Centres and Residential Homes.

Is physiotherapy effective?

The choice of treatment is largely decided by intuition or based on experience, and research to evaluate methods of treatment is still scanty, despite its needs having been the subject of comment in a series of reports on the paramedical professions in the 70's. The undergraduate and second-degree courses, to which physiotherapists are increasingly gaining access, should help to stimulate research, and practising physiotherapists themselves are increasingly aware of this need. However, experience suggests that even used empirically the various methods of treatment used by the physiotherapists do have an effect in relieving pain and stiffness, restoring strength and improving function.

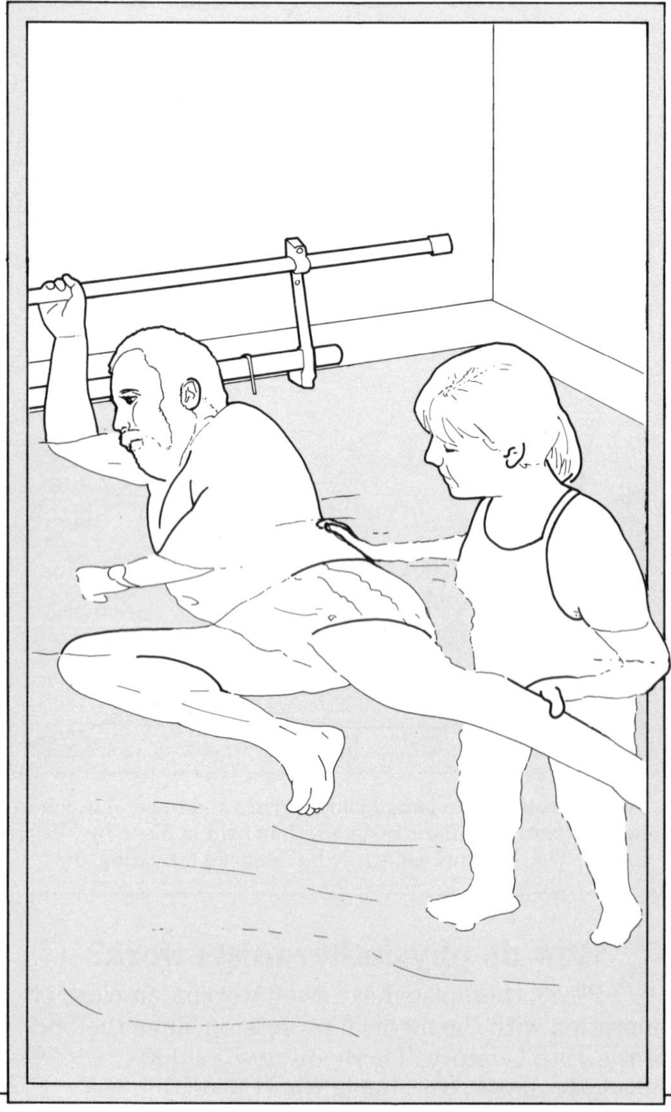

2. The buoyancy and warmth of a therapy pool is ideal for mobilising stiff joints and exercising weak, weight-bearing muscles.

Relationship with other paramedical groups

The complementary role played by physiotherapists with other members of the rehabilitation team including doctors, occupational therapists, social workers, and speech therapists is demonstrated on rounds and case conferences where valuable interactions can be made, ideas exchanged, and therapeutic strategies mature. Regrettably, the team concept sometimes has little more than lip service paid to it, but where it works as a reality it harnesses and concentrates ideas greatly to the benefit of the patient.

3. Here the physiotherapist is preparing the splint shown in 1 by moulding the wet plaster to the patient's forearm, wrist and hand.

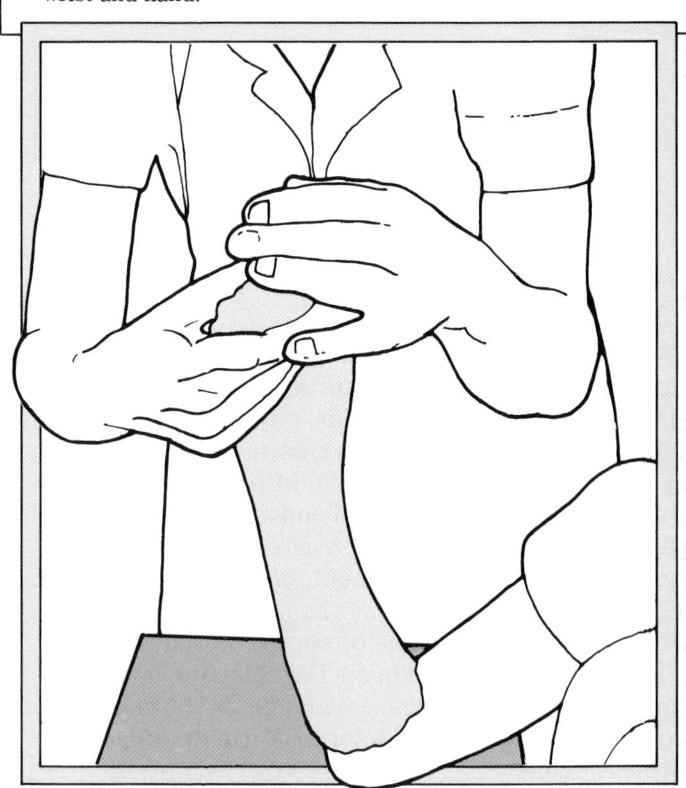

Physiotherapy and the Rheumatic Diseases

Acute arthritis (active inflammatory joint diseases, e.g. flaring rheumatoid arthritis)

The care of patients confined to bed for treatment of acutely painful, inflamed joints, whether at home or in hospital, demands close collaboration between the nurse and physiotherapist in order to help prevent pressure sores and the chest and vascular complications of prolonged recumbency. Making resting splints for inflamed joints is usually the responsibility of the physiotherapist, and these must be well fitting and skilfully designed to achieve their purpose of providing support and rest in a good functional position for the joint.

To prevent other joints stiffening during a period of bed rest, a programme of generalised exercises will be devised which can be supervised during the day by a physiotherapist and by a nurse or other care giver when the physiotherapist is not present. Isometric exercises will help minimise atrophy of muscles which control the immobilised joints. Gradually as inflammation subsides a progressive scheme of graded activity will be introduced and the patient may well benefit from hydrotherapy at this stage. Early restoration of function will be the goal, and involvement of and collaboration with the occupational therapist and other members of the rehabilitation team is particularly important.

Chronic arthritis (osteoarthritis or long-standing relatively inactive rheumatoid arthritis)

The changes that have taken place in joints may be very disabling; although these may be irreversible the symptoms which they produce can often be eased by a regimen of simple active exercises – aimed at increasing the range of joint movement, reversing contractures that may have developed and restoring muscle function to the optimum. Aids such as walking sticks or a walking frame may be introduced with appropriate instruction in their use and sensible advice given about modifying the patient's life-style in order to minimise demands made on damaged joints. At the same time the occupational therapist will be able to suggest and supply gadgets to help the patient's daily activities.

Deformity in chronic arthritis

Flexion contractures of the knee should be treated energetically by active quadriceps exercises and serial splinting by means of back slabs made of plaster-of-Paris; these are replaced weekly as the contracture diminishes. Prior to joint replacement of the hip or knee, physiotherapists can play an important role in providing pre-operative muscle-strengthening exercises, and in encouraging postoperative ambulation. In the treatment of the many varieties of joint subluxation that can occur, e.g. the metatarsophalangeal joints, a combined approach with physiotherapist, occupational therapist, orthotist and chiropodist is often effective.

Back pain

An acute episode of back pain may resolve with bed rest but there is a practical limit to the completeness of the rest and the length of time that it can be tolerated. If at the end of a week the pain persists, more active measures may be required. For many, a temporary corset is adequate. So called "facet joint dysfunction" may be alleviated by passive movement and repeated gentle oscillatory mobilising techniques precisely localised to the appropriate level. Traction, sustained or rhythmical, exercise regimens to stretch tight structures and strengthen supporting muscles all have their place in the therapist's repertoire though it appears from trials that placebos can often be as effective as other therapeutic treatments (4, 5, 6). In the presence of nerve root compression "active" (i.e. manipulative) treatments are best avoided for fear of exacerbations; isometric flexion exercises may then be helpful.

"Back schools" have developed in which a short course of advice with teaching of good posture, lifting skills and self care helps the patient to look after himself and avoid subsequent episodes.

4. Selection and training in the use of walking aids is one of the physiotherapist's skills. Frames such as this are invaluable for those with serious walking problems. For patients with a poor grip these gutter supports for the forearms help to support the body weight.

Ankylosing spondylitis

One of the most important contributions that the physiotherapist makes in the field of rheumatic diseases is in treating ankylosing spondylitis, as physiotherapy – in the form of intensive courses of spinal mobilising exercises – remains an important element of management. Ankylosing spondylitis "clubs" have a supportive function and provide weekly exercises in the pool and gymnasium under a physiotherapist's direction supplementing the patient's own daily exercise programme which is so essential in this condition.

Neck pain

This again may be long standing and chronic (as in cervical spondylosis) or short-lived and acute (as in whiplash injury) and may be accompanied by referred pain and paraesthesiae in the upper limb. As with corsets for low-back pain, collars have their advocates and their place in the treatment of this troublesome condition. Advice on posture may be helpful. Traction, manipulation or localised oscillatory mobilisation may all be successfully used on different occasions and physiotherapists can often help patients presenting with these problems. Again, if neurological signs or symptoms are present, forceful manipulative procedures should be avoided for fears of inducing cord or nerve-root damage, and a collar or perhaps cervical traction tried instead.

Trauma and over-use

The most widespread form of self-limiting pain arising in the locomotor system is due to trauma, either the acute sudden injury variety or the more insidious effects of over-use of tissues occasioned by unaccustomed or repetitive physical activity, e.g. jogging, aerobics or house decorating in the unwary and untrained.

Traditionally, acute trauma to soft tissue is treated by rest, ice, compression and elevation ("RICE"). This must soon be followed by activity if prolonged invalidism is to be avoided. The use of ultrasound is a valuable adjunct in the treatment of muscle and ligamentous injuries. Early movement and guarded functional use of the injured part will prevent post-traumatic adhesions and stiffness and in the case of the shoulder, progression to "frozen shoulder" (adhesive capsulitis). Over-use injuries include tennis and golfer's elbow, carpal tunnel syndrome, rotator cuff lesions (supraspinatus and bicipital tendinitis) plantar fasciitis, tenosynovitis, bursitis etc. They may be treated by ultrasound and friction (deep massage) as an alternative to the use of local steroid injections. Carpal tunnel syndrome and tennis and golfer's elbow are featured separately in Reports 1 and 2 of the present series of Practical Problems.

REFERENCES

1. Dyson, M., Pond, J.B., Joseph, J., Warwick, R. The stimulation of tissue regeneration by means of ultrasound. *Clin. Sci.* 1968; **35:** 273-85.
2. Harvey, W., Dyson, M., Pond, J.B., Grahame, R. *The 'in vitro' stimulation of protein synthesis in human fibroblasts by therapeutic levels of ultrasound.* Excerpta Medica, International Congress Series No. 363, Proceedings of the Second European Congress on Ultrasonics in Medicine, Munich 12-16 May, 1975, Excerpta Medica, Amsterdam – Oxford, p10-21.
3. Dyson, M., Franks, C., Suckling, J.. Stimulation of healing of varicose ulcers by ultrasound. *Ultrasonics* 1976; **14:** 232.
4. Davies, J., Gibson, T., Tester, L. The value of exercises in the treatment of low-back pain. *Rheum. Rehab.* 1979; **18:** 247-252.
5. Coxhead, C.E., Inskip, H., Mead, T.W., North, W.R.S., Troup, J.D.G. Multi-centre trial of physiotherapy in the management of sciatic symptoms. *Lancet* 1981; **1:** 1065-1068.
6. Gibson, T., Harkness, J., Blagrave, P., Grahame R., Woo, P., Hills, R. Controlled comparison of short-wave diathermy treatment with osteopathic treatment in non-specific low-back pain. *Lancet* 1985; **1:** 1258-1260.

May 1986

WHAT CAN OCCUPATIONAL THERAPY OFFER?

P Jeffreson
Occupational Therapist
Rheumatology Unit
Robert Jones & Agnes Hunt Orthopaedic Hospital
Oswestry

INTRODUCTION

Occupational therapy is playing an increasingly prominent role in the treatment of rheumatic diseases. People who suffer from these diseases, especially rheumatoid and osteoarthritis, require practical answers to everyday problems such as difficulty in dressing, getting about the home or to the shops, at work and preparing and eating food. The occupational therapist can assist in their return to functional independence by providing special equipment and by teaching people how to approach their problems in an active, positive way and thus learn how to help themselves.

WHAT DO OCCUPATIONAL THERAPISTS DO THAT IS APPLICABLE TO RHEUMATIC DISEASES?

1 Assess and provide practical solutions to problems encountered during activities of daily living and work.

2 Assess the home or work environment and recommend equipment and adaptations to restore a person's independence.

3 Make splints to rest and protect joints and to assist useful movement.

4 Run patient education sessions; for example, joint protection and pain management for rheumatoid arthritis.

5 Counsel patients on coming to terms with their disease.

6 Assess upper limb function to determine if splints or joint replacement surgery would be of benefit.

7 Carry out remedial activities to increase joint movement and muscle strength.

8 Liaise with Social Services and GPs to ensure coordination of activities.

Treatment is individually tailored to each person following detailed assessment to highlight problem areas.

WORK AND ACTIVITIES OF DAILY LIVING

Advice is given about alternative working methods and positions. Through use of specialist equipment a person may be able to perform a task previously made impossible or very painful through disease. Essential equipment is loaned, additional items may be purchased or the occupational therapist can advise on where it may be obtained. All hospital occupational therapy departments keep essential items in stock for loan or sale. Social Services occupational therapy stores have a more comprehensive loan system.

In many areas there are advice centres where people with disabilities can go to receive qualified advice and to try out equipment.

Some occupational therapy departments run a work assessment and work-tolerance training service.

Figure 1. Detailed assessment to analyse problems and try out different equipment. This can be specialised such as an ergonomic knife and large-handled plug, or an easily available item such as an electric tin opener. Microwave cooking saves lifting and cleaning heavy saucepans.

Figure 2. Poor grip can be helped by enlarging handles and extending levers, as on cutlery, keys and taps. Difficulty reaching can be overcome by using longer handles on combs and shoe horns.

HOME ASSESSMENT

Advice and help are given for difficulties such as managing steps and stairs; getting in and out of the bath; on and off the toilet, bed or chair; reaching cupboards and cooker and so on. Possible solutions include the provision of a half-step at the house entrance; banister rails; a stairlift; a bath seat (static or assisted); a raised toilet seat; a chair raise unit etc. Assessments are carried out by both Health Service and Social Services occupational therapists. Hospital occupational therapists refer adaptations to Social Services unless the patient wishes to pay for it him or herself.

Information is given on financial assistance and help with obtaining Government grants.

Figure 3. A stairlift.

SPLINTS

These are individually tailored and made from a variety of materials, including thermoplastics. They are most commonly made for people with rheumatoid arthritis.

Splinting aims to:

1 rest and support painful, swollen joints.

2 place joints in the best functional position to overcome the disabling effects of deformity.

3 reduce the risk of further deformities occurring.

4 provide post-surgical positioning and stabilisation of the hand using dynamic outrigger splints. For example, following metacarpo-phalangeal joint replacement surgery or extensor tendon repair.

Detailed advice is given to the patient about the purpose of the splint and it is checked at regular intervals for comfort and efficacy.

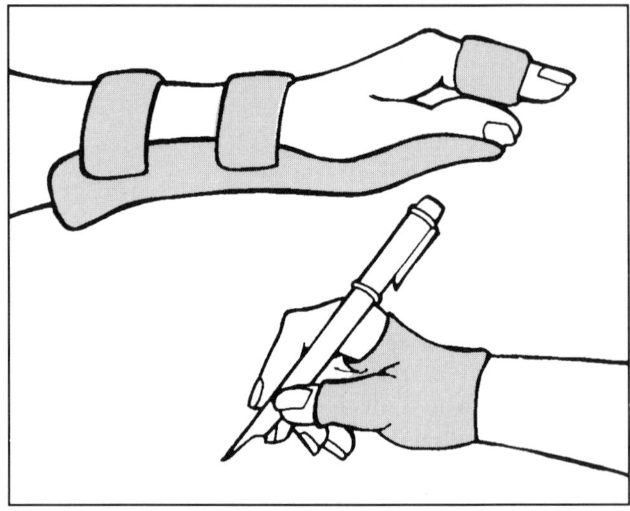

Figure 4. A resting splint (top) and a working splint.

PATIENT EDUCATION

This is important for people with rheumatoid arthritis and is most effective if started early in the course of the disease. Education is often carried out in groups which provide a supportive atmosphere for exchange of information.

The following are two examples of education topics.

1. **Joint protection and energy conservation** in rheumatoid arthritis. Subjecting joints to unnecessary strain whilst doing daily tasks can contribute towards joint deformity. Learning different ways of doing things and caring for their joints is a positive way for people to help conserve energy, reduce pain and the deforming effects of the disease. Examples (see figure 5):

a saving energy by sitting to do tasks

b using lever taps to prevent strain on finger joints

c raising bowl in sink by placing it on an upturned bowl to prevent back strain

d using power grip to hold saucepan and resting it on bowl to reduce wrist strain.

2. **Pain management.** This most usually involves use of relaxation exercises and creative visualisation technique. It is very popular with patients.

COUNSELLING

Occupational therapists are trained in basic counselling skills and some go on to further post-graduate training. Counselling to help people come to terms with disease is rarely a primary reason for referral, but is often part of a treatment programme, especially for those with rheumatoid arthritis.

UPPER LIMB FUNCTIONAL ASSESSMENT

Systematic, measured testing is done for upper limb function which helps to determine efficacy of splinting and surgery. It is an important tool in determining which joints or soft tissue structures are the primary cause of functional loss since it is not always the most deformed joints which lose most function. Patients and surgeons can then gain more insight into possible outcomes of any procedures being considered.

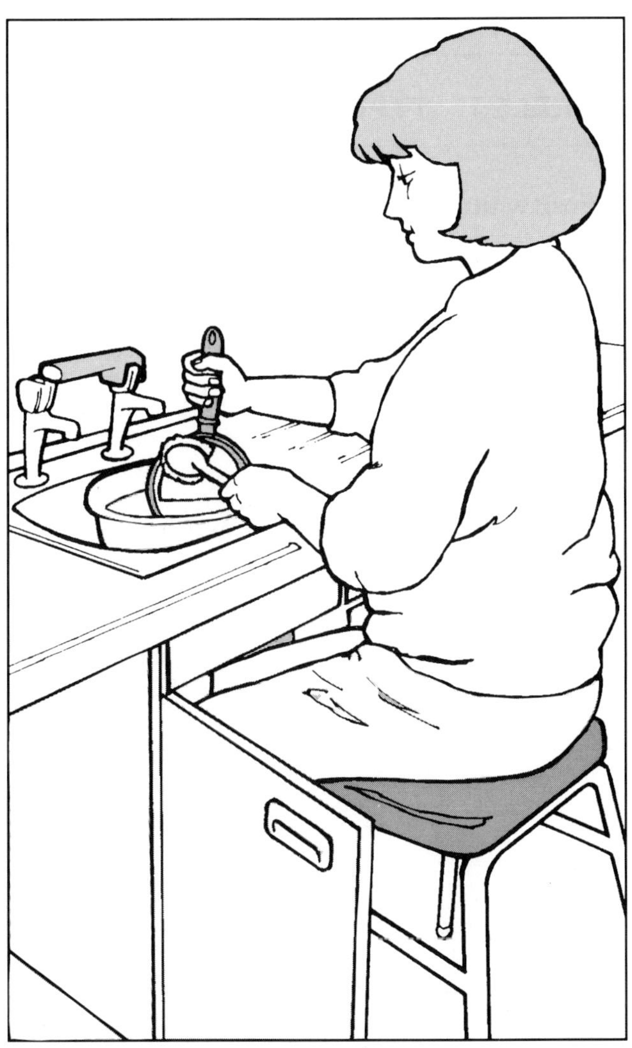

Figure 5. Joint protection and energy conservation.

REMEDIAL ACTIVITIES

These aim to increase muscle strength and joint range of movement in stiff, weak limbs or following surgery. The emphasis is on upper limb function and work is often carried out in conjunction with physiotherapists. Activities include the use of therapeutic putty, adapted board games, printing, computers and crafts.

REFERRAL TO OCCUPATIONAL THERAPY

Occupational therapists work in Health and Social Services. Some hospitals have specialist rheumatology units and can offer the full range of services. Some receive referrals directly from general practitioners and other health workers in the community, others through consultant rheumatologists and orthopaedic surgeons. Social Services deal mainly with special equipment and home adaptations. Occupational therapists also work in Disability Resource Centres which the patient can approach directly. National HQ will advise of the nearest regional centre: The Disabled Living Centres Council, 286 Camden Road, London N7 0BJ Tel. 0171 700 1707.

SUMMARY

Many people suffering from rheumatic diseases search for alternative, less painful ways of doing daily tasks. Occupational therapy can help these people regain their independence through practical advice and treatment leading to an improved quality of life.

FURTHER READING

1 Unsworth, H. Coping with rheumatoid arthritis (1986). Published by Chambers, Edinburgh. An excellent book for patients and practitioners containing lots of practical advice and information.

2 Melvin, J L. Rheumatic disease in the adult and child: Occupational Therapy and Rehabilitation (1989). Published by S A Davis Co., Philadelphia.

3 Ward, A B. Footwear and Orthoses. ARC Practical Problems Sept 1992, No 22. Describes some of the splints made by occupational therapists.

4 ARC video, Help is at Hand, explains the role of the occupational therapist and demonstrates some useful gadgets for people with rheumatoid arthritis.

September 1993

FOOTWEAR & ORTHOSES

A B Ward
Consultant Physician
Department of Rehabilitation Medicine
Haywood Hospital
Stoke-on-Trent ST6 7AG

Special footwear and orthoses (devices worn outside the body supporting and aiding the function of that part) are commonly prescribed by rheumatologists and orthopaedic surgeons and it is vital that GPs and specialists should understand their importance and know how to get one for their patients. Doctors should be given basic training in orthotics at both undergraduate and postgraduate level in order to realise their potential value.

A team approach (doctor, therapist and orthotist) is judged most likely to ensure appropriate prescription since it is important that both the orthotist and the patient know what the orthosis is aiming to do. If the patient does not wear the device, the whole process has failed, no matter how technically good the appliance is, so the doctor must first estimate the patient's compliance. Some orthoses are highly complex and costly. More 'in-house' manufacture is thus highly desirable to address both issues, and this will be further encouraged by improvements in orthotist training.

Orthoses are suitable for diseases of the musculoskeletal and central nervous systems and for peripheral nerve insults, including nerve compression syndromes. This report will be a simple overview and some of the footwear and orthoses are described in Table 1.

FOOTWEAR

Foot pain is one of the commonest presentations to GPs and rheumatologists and in rheumatoid arthritis this may be due to joint disease or to nerve injury from unsupported weight-bearing structures. Prevention of subtalar subluxation is important in early disease in order to prevent pain distally later and the wearing of good footwear is a cheap and effective way to help this.

Footwear has never commanded much attention from the medical profession and many doctors do not realise how prescribing comfortable shoes can transform the lives of people with rheumatic diseases. The development of depth shoes has increased the range of shoes available and there is now less need for surgical shoes to be individually made.

TABLE 1. TYPES OF ORTHOSES

Footwear	Insoles Shoe modifications Bespoke shoes
Supports	Collars Lumbar Supports/Belts Epicondylitis Clasps
Splints	Static/Resting - prevent movement and support joints Working & Lively - help to increase function in a limb

Insoles

Medial Longitudinal Arch Supports
These are used for simple flat feet, for lateral plantar nerve compression and also to help prevent subtalar valgus subluxation as commonly occurs in rheumatoid arthritis.

Metatarsal Domes
This device sits in the shoe and transfers weight away from the metatarsal heads to the metatarsal shafts, thus relieving the pain from metatarsophalangeal joint disease and subluxation. A larger size of shoe may be needed to prevent callosities on the dorsum of the toes and Plastazote temporary domes should first be tried to assess their efficacy.

Heel Insoles

Indications are traumatic heel and leg pain and plantar fasciitis and occasionally a hole needs to be cut out under the tender point. To prevent heel pain, shock absorbing pads are useful (eg Sorbothane, Viscolast).

Modified Shoes

Shoe Raises

These are used to correct unequal leg lengths. The amount of raise needed is half the leg length difference, in order to maintain a normal swing phase in walking. Differences of less than 1cm are probably not worth correcting in this way.

Depth Shoes

These are enhanced footwear for people with deformed feet. Lightweight with a non-slip sole and a wide opening to allow easy fitting, they are fairly cheap to produce and cater for most deformities. Sufficient space is available to fit an insole, but this should be checked first (see figure 1).

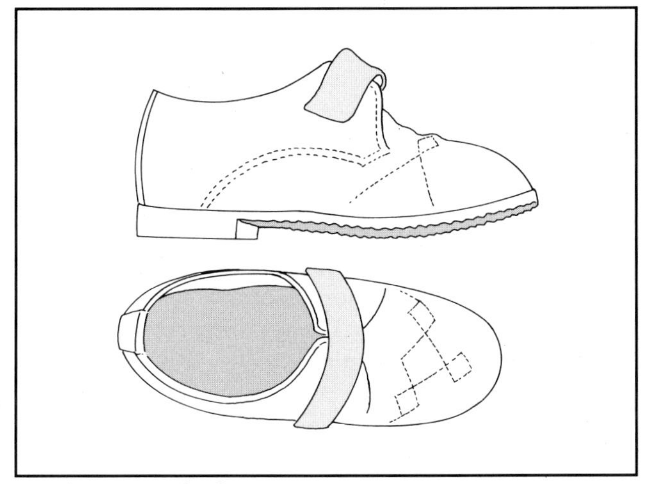

Figure 1. Depth shoes.

Bespoke Shoes

Individually designed to fit people with difficult feet, they can fulfil a variety of functions from tough working shoes to comfortable lightweight items. They are very expensive to make and therefore the casts should be checked against the patient's feet before manufacture.

SUPPORTS

Collars

Used to reduce pain by supporting the neck, they do not truly prevent movement, no matter how strong the materials used. For effective immobilisation skull or halo traction should be used. Collars should be comfortable, although this may be difficult to achieve in hot weather. They are useful to reduce muscle spasm in the few days after a whiplash injury to the neck and every patient with rheumatoid disease should wear one in preparation for surgery, highlighting to the anaesthetist the risk of vertebral and cord damage during intubation.

Corsets

The commonest indication is for acute lumbar disc protrusion with muscle spasm, especially during the mobilisation phase after bed rest. They are usually uncomfortable to wear and are often discarded, but constantly remind the wearer to protect the back and more importantly hold in the anterior abdominal wall (1). Some patients wear corsets for years, unable to do without them. In addition, polythene jackets are used with variable success for the pain of osteoporotic vertebral collapse and to prevent the effects on respiration of increasing truncal weakness, as seen in muscular dystrophies, etc.

Epicondylitis Clasp

These are worn on the proximal forearm to decrease the load on the extensor and flexor muscle origins in tennis and golfer's elbow respectively, by transferring the effective origin point of the muscle to a point under the clasp through a tight grip over the muscle belly. Since this protects the enthesis (the point of attachment of tendon to bone) at the lateral or medial humeral epicondyle patients are often able to work or play tennis while wearing a clasp.

SPLINTS

It is possible to make splints for anything from simple thumb pain to a brachial plexus injury. The aims and functions of splintage (2) are described in Table 2 and they can generally be grouped as follows:

a) Resting splints

These immobilise and are thus often used at night to rest joints. Help may be required to put them on and take them off, particularly if bilateral splints are used, and they may interfere with daily function too much. Care thus needs to be taken before prescribing them. An example of such a splint is a paddle splint incorporating the wrist and small joints of the hand for patients with active rheumatoid arthritis.

TABLE 2. FUNCTIONS OF A SPLINT
Stabilize Joints
Reduce pain and inflammation through immobilisation
Place the limb in best functional position
Protect joints leading to confident usage
Prevent or reduce further deformity

b) Working or lively splints

These allow a limb to work in some functional way and may incorporate a moving part, either free-moving or against resistance. Stabilising one joint may result in better functional use of the whole limb. Excessive deformity of a joint contraindicates the wearing of a lively splint, since rubbing of the underlying skin during use and impairment of the mechanical function of the device may occur. For instance, in a knee, a valgus or varus deformity of 20 degrees is usually the maximum for which a splint can be tolerated.

c) Serial splinting

Used to increase the range of movement in a contracted joint, there is now less need for this because doctors and therapists are more aggressive with joint injection, active physiotherapy, etc. Serial splinting still has its place in rehabilitation and will reduce even very large contractures when accompanied by active treatment. The limb is straightened as much as is comfortable and the splint applied. Splints should be bivalved 48 hours after application and physiotherapy given daily. The splint is then changed every 7-10 days for a straighter splint until the objective is achieved.

There is a whole range of commercially made orthoses for commoner problems. Below are some types of splint commonly seen in rheumatological practice.

Resting Wrist and Hand Splints

Made of Orthoplast and used to relieve acutely inflamed joints, they are useful as night-resting splints. The wrist should be held in 10 degrees of extension.

Working Wrist Splints

The Futura wrist splint is probably the best known in the UK. There is a metal bar on the volar surface resting the wrist, but full use of the hand is allowed. It is useful in carpal tunnel syndrome, or inflammatory arthritis and repetitive strain injuries and is washable (see figure 2). An individually-made Orthoplast or polythene splint may be necessary if the wrist is deformed.

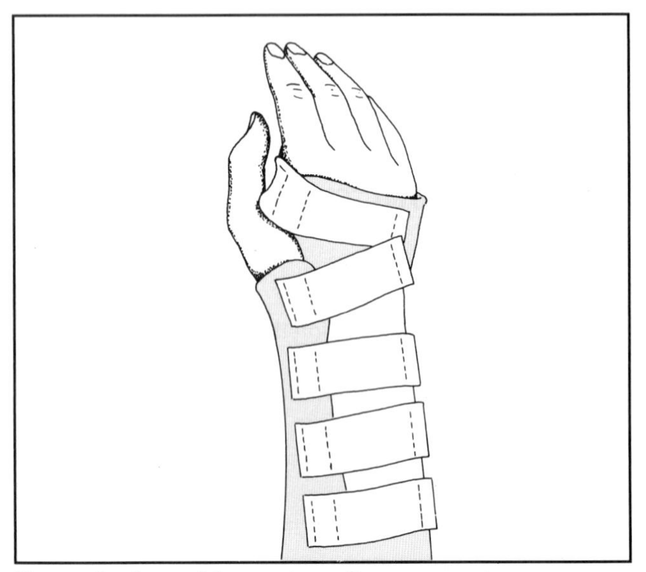

Figure 2. A working wrist splint.

Working Hand Splints

Ulnar digital drift in rheumatoid arthritis is difficult to correct through splintage unless a cumbersome device is used. However, splints should be used following extensor tendon rupture to preserve function. An Opponens splint is used for the painful carpometacarpal joint of the thumb in generalised osteoarthritis.

Knee Splints

These stabilise knees with collateral ligament or cruciate ligament dysfunction (or both). See Table 3.

TABLE 3. KNEE SPLINTS

Collateral Ligament Injuries	
Mild	Simple Knee Corset (eg Neoprene) allowing patient to exercise quads and hamstrings
More Severe	Hinged Corset (eg Cinch Splint)
With Deformity	Under 20°, Full Knee Orthosis (eg TVS) Over 20°, little will help
Cruciate Ligament Injuries	Require more complex stabilisation. Braces (eg Donjoy) prevent antero-posterior movement.
Disrupted Knees	Straight leg polythene jacket (eg Polya)

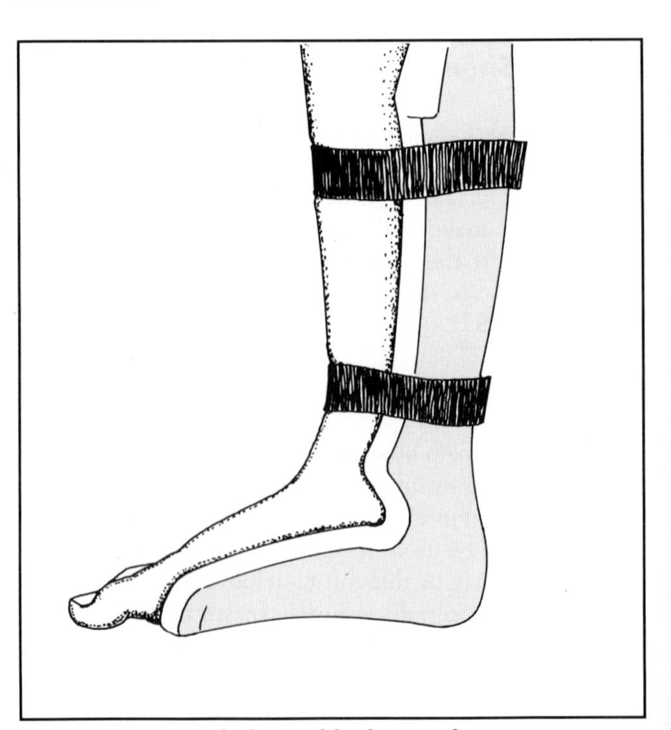

Figure 3. An Ortholon ankle-foot orthosis.

Ankle-Foot Orthoses

The main indications are foot drop from a lateral popliteal nerve palsy and stroke, which can be helped by an Ortholon orthosis (see Figure 3). Ankle and subtalar joint instability may also be helped by this and it may incorporate insole corrections. It is lightweight, but not particularly strong, cracking when given severe usage by otherwise fit people or when subjected to severe spasticity. A leg iron caliper may then be required, fixed to the heel of the shoe from a strap at the upper calf.

HOW TO GET ORTHOSES & FOOTWEAR

These are available through the hospital surgical appliance department where there is a qualified orthotist, who at present is usually the employee of a surgical appliance company. Units are starting to employ their own orthotists on the potential savings from greater 'in-house' manufacture of items. The acquisition of wholly committed orthotists to the rehabilitation services is to be welcomed: it will allow the development of a genuine professional relationship between them, clinicians and therapists.

Referral may be from GPs directly or through hospital specialists, depending on local practice. Many physiotherapy departments and A&E departments also have a supply of the more commonly used items.

Maintenance

Most commercially made splints are washable as are those made from thermoplastics and polythene, etc. If in doubt, ask the orthotist. For mechanical maintenance the splint should be referred back to the orthotist for on-site repairs and modifications.

SUMMARY

Orthoses are indicated for patients with a whole range of conditions. Increased interest from the medical profession will raise the standard of orthotics and will allow the new generation of orthotists to provide a highly regarded service.

REFERENCES

1. Jayson M I V, Degenerative Disease of the Spine and Back Pain, Clin Rheum Dis, 1976; 2: 557-585.

2. Clarke A, Allard L, Braybrooks B, Rehabilitation in Rheumatology, Martin Dunitz, London 1987 p221-243.

September 1992

ANTIBODIES TO CELLS & CONNECTIVE TISSUE DISEASES

R M Bernstein
Consultant Rheumatologist
Manchester Royal Infirmary
Manchester

Advances in autoantibody research are shedding new light on the connective tissue diseases. Relatively few in number, the antibodies to cellular antigens are of value in management and the recognition of new syndromes.

INTRODUCTION

We all harbour the ability to make autoantibodies against our own cells and tissues. Low levels may accelerate the removal of cellular debris by the reticulo-endothelial system (1), and some autoantibodies have close structural relationships with antibodies to bacteria. In the connective tissue diseases, the checks and balances are disturbed, and autoantibodies reach high titres, accounting for a considerable proportion of the circulating immunoglobulin. Yet this is no release of the flood-gates. Only a few autoantibodies are synthesised in abundance in each condition. Whether a consequence of the peculiar way each antibody might damage the body or an enigmatic clue to aetiology, this remarkable disease specificity is the basis of the clinical value of autoantibody testing. This review concerns some of the newer antibodies to cellular antigens found chiefly in autoimmune rheumatic disease (Table I) (2). Organ-specific autoimmunity (to thyroid and pancreatic islet cells, for instance) is excluded. The clinician's request may be precise – for antibodies to DNA or cardiolipin, perhaps – but, when he asks for "ENA", a whole series of antibodies is involved: what follows may help with their interpretation.

ANTINUCLEAR ANTIBODY

The ANA is a simple screening test for autoimmune disease, but for every positive result in a case of systemic lupus erythematosus (SLE) many more will arise because of drug therapy, old age, chronic infection, rheumatoid arthritis, or another autoimmune disease. At least 5% of patients with SLE are ANA-negative, as are about a quarter of patients with other connective tissue diseases. Many of these ANA-negative cases can be picked up by one of the tests described below.

High titres of ANA are more likely to be significant, and the pattern of ANA staining may be helpful. This is particularly so when large tissue culture cells are used as the substrate for immunofluorescence rather than frozen tissue sections. Homogeneous staining is frequent in SLE, drug-induced lupus and chronic active hepatitis, and this type of ANA gives rise to the LE cell phenomenon. Speckled staining is perhaps more frequent in overlap syndromes, and nucleolar staining may suggest scleroderma. However, several antibodies give similar staining patterns, and such results are only useful in conjunction with the whole clinical picture.

Anti-centromere antibody may be an exception: recognised by its speckled staining of chromosomes in tissue culture cells, it is found almost exclusively in patients with severe Raynaud's phenomenon related to a relatively benign form of scleroderma known as CREST syndrome (calcinosis, Raynaud's phenomenon, oesophageal dysmotility, sclerodactyly, telangiectasia) (3) Thus the finding of this antibody indicates a relatively good prognosis in systemic sclerosis but a guarded one in a patient with Raynaud's phenomenon.

TABLE I.

ANTIBODY DISEASE ASSOCIATIONS IN THE CONNECTIVE TISSUE DISEASES (% FREQUENCY)

ANTIBODY	SLE	MCTD	PRIMARY SJÖGREN'S SYNDROME	MYOSITIS	PSS	RA	PBC	CAH	OTHER
Ro	24	17	75	8	4	3	6	4	<1
La	9	3	42	1	1	–	1	–	–
Sm	4-30*	3	–	–	–	–	–	–	–
RNP	23	100	4	14	3	–	–	–	–
Jo-1	<1	3	–	25	1	–	–	–	–
PL-7	–	–	–	5	–	–	–	–	–
PL-12	–	–	–	3	–	–	–	–	–
PM-Scl	–	–	–	11	3	–	–	–	–
Ku	6	–	–	3	–	–	–	–	–
Scl-70	–	–	–	–	20	–	–	–	–
Centromere +	2	–	–	–	29	–	8	–	<1
Multiple Nuclear Dots +	2	–	2	–	–	–	13	–	–
XR	–	–	–	–	–	–	10	24	–
SL	6	3	2	–	–	3	1	–	–
Ribosomal	3	–	2	–	1	–	–	–	–
PCNA	3	–	–	–	–	–	–	–	–
PL-4	2	–	–	–	–	–	–	–	–

* Sm in 4% of white patients and 30% of black and Chinese.
+ detected by immunofluorescence.
SLE = systemic lupus erythematosus; MCTD = mixed connective tissue disease;
PSS = progressive systemic sclerosis; RA = rheumatoid arthritis;
PBC = primary biliary cirrhosis; CAH = chronic active hepatitis.

Adapted from reference 2.

LE CELLS

The LE cell (4) is a neutrophil leucocyte that has phagocytosed the nucleus of a dead cell. The test depends on opsonisation of the nuclear material by homogeneous-pattern ANA (antibody to DNA and histones). Anti-DNA assays have superseded it in the diagnosis of SLE.

ANTI-DNA ANTIBODIES AND SYSTEMIC LUPUS ERYTHEMATOSUS

Antibodies to double-stranded DNA usually indicate a diagnosis of SLE, but positive results occasionally arise in rheumatoid arthritis, chronic active hepatitis, systemic sclerosis and chronic infections such as malaria. In drug-induced lupus the rise is usually slight. Only about 70% of patients with SLE are positive (partly because the normal range has to be set quite high to exclude non-specific results in other conditions). A sudden rise or fall in titre sometimes heralds a flare, and complement-fixing anti-DNA antibodies may cause nephritis, but there are so many exceptions that decisions about treatment are best made on clinical grounds, rather than the test results (5).

ANTI-PHOSPHOLIPID ANTIBODIES, THROMBOSIS AND ABORTION

Phospholipids are an important constituent of cell membranes, including platelets and blood vessel walls. High levels of anti-phospholipid antibody are associated with thrombosis and recurrent abortion (6). It is thought that the antibody exaggerates platelet aggregation either by a direct effect on platelets or by inhibiting the release of prostacyclin from vascular endothelium (7). First discovered as the false positive Wassermann reaction and then as the lupus anticoagulant (a paradoxical term based on the prolongation of clotting tests *in vitro*), the measurement of antiphospholipid (or "anticardiolipin") antibodies is now becoming widely available by the ELISA and radioimmunoassay techniques. Raised levels of antibody are found in 40% of patients with SLE, but it is chiefly the top 10% (and particularly those with IgG antibodies) who are at greatest risk of complications such as deep venous thrombosis, pulmonary embolism, renal vein thrombosis, Budd-Chiari syndrome (rare), premature stroke, myocardial infarction, mesenteric ischaemia, pulmonary hypertension, and placental insufficiency resulting in abortion (8).

Often there are other clues to the diagnosis of this thrombotic syndrome. The platelet count may be *reduced* to around 60-100 x 10^9/1, and hypertension (sometimes labile) and livedo reticularis are common, at least in patients prone to arterial thrombosis. Increasingly, cases are seen where there is no other clinical evidence of SLE, and the antinuclear antibody may be negative. Indeed, over 10% of myocardial infarction in young men and 10% of recurrent abortion are a consequence of this autoimmune disease (7; 9). Recognition is important because of the high risk of multiple thrombotic events. The level of antiphospholipid antibody may fluctuate, so a normal test should be repeated later if the index of suspicion is high.

Treatment is difficult. Venous thrombosis and pulmonary embolism can be controlled by anti-coagulation, but there is a high rate of recurrence if anticoagulation is discontinued. Prednisolone at a daily dose of about 40mg together with a small dose of aspirin has led to successful pregnancy in women with many previous abortions, but in some cases treatment must begin before conception: management of such pregnancies is currently the subject of clinical trials. Corticosteroid therapy, immunosuppression, control of blood pressure, anticoagulation and anti-platelet agents all have a role in the prevention of arterial thrombosis. Steroids are effective (in that withdrawal of steroid therapy has been known to lead on to a stroke), but the dose and the risk/benefit ratio of long-term treatment are still unknown.

ANTIBODIES TO SOLUBLE CELLULAR ANTIGENS

Many laboratories are now testing for antibodies to extractable nuclear antigens (ENA) present in a simple saline extract of cells (2; 10-12). Some of these antigens are cytoplasmic, so the term ENA is not strictly accurate). This set of antibodies is detected by the formation of precipitin lines between drops of serum and cell extract placed in wells cut in a gel. Reference sera are used to seek lines of identity, and in this way a dozen or more different antibodies can be recognised. With purification of the antigens quantitative assays are now under way, revealing still closer disease associations and fluctuations in the antibody levels (13). The arcane nomenclature (Ro, La, Sm, RNP and so on) is based on patients' names, disease associations and crude biochemical analysis, and for some there are synonyms (Ro/SSA, La/SSB).

In clinical practice these antibodies are of growing importance for several reasons: they are much more closely associated with disease than the ordinary ANA test; some are positive when the ordinary ANA is negative; and most show remarkable clinical associations with particular syndromes within the connective tissue diseases. Some of these are termed "disease subsets" (like the thrombotic syndrome in SLE), and others "overlap syndromes", the best known being mixed connective tissue disease (MCTD). Overlap syndromes vary in severity from patient to patient, but usually there is some combination of Raynaud's phenomenon, myositis, arthritis, scleroderma, sicca syndrome and pulmonary fibrosis. In the early stages any distinction between them may seem academic, but evidence is growing for major differences in outcome, ranging from full recovery to pulmonary fibrosis, pulmonary hypertension, scleroderma or central nervous system disease. Long-term follow-up will better define these overlap syndromes, but already the identification of a particular autoantibody can be used as a piece in the jigsaw of clinical features and laboratory findings that leads to diagnosis and to an informed approach to follow-up. The more important precipitating antibodies are summarised in Table II, and their relationships with particular disease subsets and overlap syndromes are discussed below.

TABLE II

CLUES TO DIAGNOSIS

Antibody:	Clinical interpretation:
ANA	Autoimmune disease, chronic infection, drugs, ageing.
DNA	SLE, rarely other.
Cardiolipin	Recurrent thrombosis and abortion ± SLE.
"ENA"	A set of antibodies: see below.
Ro (= SSA)	Primary Sjögren's syndrome, SLE, subacute cutaneous LE, congenital heart block.
LA (= SSB)	As with anti-Ro. In SLE the course is often milder.
Sm	SLE, with racial variation.
RNP	SLE, mixed connective tissue disease, Raynaud's phenomenon, swollen fingers, myositis.
Jo-1, PL-7, PL-12	Myositis and fibrosing alveolitis with Raynaud's, sicca, arthralgias.
PM-Scl (= PM1)	Myositis-scleroderma overlap.
Ku	SLE, myositis-scleroderma overlap.
SL, ribosomal, PCNA, PL-4	Chiefly SLE.
XR	Chronic active hepatitis.
Centromere (ANA pattern)	CREST syndrome ± primary biliary cirrhosis.
Multiple nuclear dots (ANA pattern)	Primary biliary cirrhosis, usually with sicca syndrome.
Mitochondria	Primary biliary cirrhosis.
Neutrophil alkaline phosphatase	Wegener's granulomatosis, microscopic polyarteritis nodosa.

ANTI-Ro (SSA), SLE, SICCA SYNDROME AND CONGENITAL HEART BLOCK

Anti-Ro is a relatively common antibody, found in 75% of patients with primary Sjögren's syndrome and up to 30% of those with SLE, but it is uncommon (5% or less) in the other systemic autoimmune conditions. Since anti-Ro-positive patients may be ANA-negative, detection of anti-Ro is a useful additional screening test, simply requiring the use of a spleen extract rather than the thymus used for most other precipitating antibodies. Patients with primary Sjögren's syndrome and anti-Ro are at increased risk of nervous system involvement and cutaneous vasculitis (14), while in lupus there is a dermatological form, usually ANA-negative but anti-Ro-positive, termed subacute cutaneous LE (15). The majority of anti-Ro-positive lupus patients have no specific features related to this antibody. However, anti-Ro antibody is associated with congenital heart block. It has been known for some years that a third of mothers delivering a child with congenital atrio-ventricular block have a connective tissue disease, usually SLE or primary Sjögren's syndrome. It is now clear that over two-thirds of all the mothers carry anti-Ro, and the antibody is transferred across the placenta to the infant (16). Some babies exposed in this way are born with heart block, and a few even have transient rash and hepatosplenomegaly, but it must be emphasised that only a minority of mothers with the antibody produce babies with heart block, and it may be another antibody or even occult virus infection that leads to the fibrosis of conducting tissue responsible for this permanent condition. It is not usually serious unless other cardiac defects are present.

ANTI-La (SSB) and SICCA SYNDROME

La antibody usually occurs in association with anti-Ro but is less common, being found in just under half the cases of primary sicca (Sjögren's) syndrome and 10% of SLE. In SLE, it often indicates a milder course, with rash but no renal disease, going on to sicca syndrome later (17). Lymphocytic infiltration leading to dryness of exocrine glands, most obvious in the lacrimal and salivary glands, is an important sign of systemic autoimmune disease. Anti-Ro and anti-La usually indicate that the sicca syndrome is "primary" or secondary to SLE, rather than rheumatoid arthritis, autoimmune liver disease or another connective tissue disorder. Arthritis is often a feature in these patients, and although rheumatoid factor may be strongly positive, the joint disease is rarely destructive or crippling. Sometimes the sicca features are still sub-clinical when the disease presents, but a high IgG level may be a clue and should stimulate a request for antibodies to Ro and La.

ANTI-Sm, SLE AND RACIAL VARIATION

Sm antibody is sometimes found in SLE, and like anti-DNA antibody it is now an American classification criterion for the disease. However, there is racial variation in its frequency: whilst common in black and Chinese cases, it is rarely encountered in white patients with lupus.

ANTI-RNP AND MIXED CONNECTIVE DISEASE

Anti-RNP antibody is found in a quarter of patients with SLE and somewhat less often in systemic sclerosis, primary Sjögren's syndrome and polymyositis. Particularly high titres, with bright speckled ANA staining, are found in a group of patients who lack anti-DNA antibodies but have certain clinical similarities; for these cases the term "mixed connective tissue disease" has been coined (18). Invariably these patients have severe Raynaud's phenomenon and swollen fingers, usually together with some of the features of SLE, scleroderma, sicca syndrome, myositis and rheumatoid arthritis. Renal disease is much less common than in SLE, and follow-up suggests that the inflammatory features eventually settle down (sometimes with the antibody disappearing), leading to recovery or more often an end stage with features of scleroderma. MCTD is still a controversial concept (19), for even in typical SLE anti-RNP antibody is associated with Raynaud's phenomenon and an increased frequency of myositis, while other patients with the antibody have Raynaud's phenomenon only. Certainly it is not the only overlap syndrome, and its severity can vary. At one time it was taught that MCTD is a benign condition particularly responsive to corticosteroid therapy. In fact, the 10-year mortality, 5-10%, is a little worse than in SLE, and injudicious use of steroids adds infection, osteoporosis and other cushingoid side-effects to the later fibrotic illness. Myositis, depression, psychosis, pleurisy and other inflammatory involvement may require steroid therapy, but the development of interstitial lung disease, pulmonary hypertension and oesophageal dysmotility is not prevented. As in systemic sclerosis, a histamine-H2 antagonist will diminish reflux oesophagitis and the risk of stricture. There is as yet no evidence that calcium-antagonist vasodilators can prevent the development of pulmonary hypertension, but they may be of limited value for the Raynaud's phenomenon. The immunoglobulin level is often two to three times normal, largely anti-RNP, and fluctuates with the degree of inflammation: it is tempting to speculate that this plays some role in the underlying microvascular disease and spasm.

Jo-1, PL-7, PL-12, PM-ScL AND Ku IN MYOSITIS

An overlap syndrome somewhat similar to MCTD but with a different pace and presentation has been recognised through studies of Jo-1 antibody (20; 21). The presentation is usually with myositis or pulmonary fibrosis: 80% of cases have both, and either involvement can be aggressive. Joint pains and Raynaud's phenomenon usually enter the picture; sicca syndrome and sometimes sclerodactyly develop later; occasionally there is full-blown lupus or systemic sclerosis with additional autoantibodies detectable. Anti-Jo-1 antibody is found in 25% of cases of myositis in rheumatological practice, but it is not found in childhood myositis and seems to be rare in the myositis associated with malignancy. Two uncommon antibodies, PL-7 and PL-12, are associated with the same syndrome and directed at antigens closely related to Jo-1 in the cell (22-24). Further antibodies, unrelated to the Jo-1 specificity, are anti-PM-Scl and anti-Ku: both seem to be associated with a myositis-scleroderma overlap, in which the emphasis moves from early myositis to later acrosclerosis and calcinosis, often again with pulmonary fibrosis. These antibodies are closely related to myositis syndromes, but anti-Ku also occurs in SLE. Follow-up will show just how far these overlap syndromes differ one from another, but already the detection of anti-Jo-1 and the other antibodies is a warning of chronic multisystem disease with the focus on muscle and lung.

ANTI-ScL-70 IN SCLERODERMA

Anti-Scl-70 antibody is specific for progressive systemic sclerosis and detectable in over 20% of cases (25). These patients have diffuse skin involvement and an increased risk of pulmonary fibrosis (26; 27). Contrast this with anti-centromere ANA and the more indolent CREST syndrome, where severe pulmonary hypertension may eventually develop. In a patient with Raynaud's phenomenon, the presence of either antibody suggests progression to scleroderma.

FURTHER AUTOANTIBODIES IN SLE

SLE is not a blizzard of innumerable auto-antibodies, but a few more precipitins do occur, with frequencies of 3-10%. These include the SL, PCNA, Ku, ribosomal and PL-4 systems (2). Antibodies to PCNA and PL-4 are rare but specific for SLE, whereas the others are less restricted. Statistical analysis suggests more CNS disease with anti-ribosomal antibody, more non-infective fever with anti-SL and more renal disease with PL-4.

ANTIBODIES TO NEUTROPHIL ALKALINE PHOSPHATASE IN VASCULITIS

Once invariably fatal, Wegener's granulomatosis (a form of vasculitis) is now controllable with steroids and cytotoxic therapy. Early diagnosis is vital but often delayed. The recent discovery of autoantibodies to neutrophils – specifically to alkaline phosphatase – in Wegener's granulomatosis and microscopic polyarteritis nodosa, is a step forward in diagnosis, in the monitoring of disease activity, and perhaps in understanding the pathogenesis of systemic vasculitis (28).

TABLE III

INTRACELLULAR ANTIGENS IN THE LIFE OF THE CELL

Antigen	Identity	Function
Histones	Structural proteins	Packaging of DNA.
Scl-70	Topoisomerase I	DNA supercoiling.
PCNA	35K protein	Cell proliferation/DNA synthesis.
Ku	60K, 80K proteins	DNA binding.
Nucleolar speckled	RNA polymerase I	Transcription of rRNA.
RNP	U1-ribonucleoprotein particle	RNA processing
Sm	Several U-ribonucleo-protein particles	RNA processing
Jo-1, PL-7, PL-12	Aminoacyl-tRNA synthetases	Protein synthesis
Ribosomal RNP	Ribosomal P proteins and rRNA.	Protein synthesis
La	46K protein	Transport of RNA polymerase III transcripts.
Ro	60K protein	RNA transport or translation control?

AUTOANTIGENS IN THE LIFE OF THE CELL

In parallel with their clinical evaluation, autoantibodies are proving powerful tools for molecular biologists. There are more than 10,000 intracellular macromolecules, yet under half of 1% are autoantigens. Of these a few are nucleic acids (notably DNA itself), while most are proteins. Often the antigen is part of a macromolecular complex with other protein and nucleic acid components (2). In such a complex, one or another component can be antigenic in different patients (29), suggesting that it is the whole particle that somehow incites the antibody response. It is hard to see how this could be a fortuitous cross-reaction with a foreign immunogen (the rheumatic fever model of molecular mimicry), but a virus infecting the cell might bind to a cellular component so rendering it immunogenic (22). As shown in Table III, most of the antigens have vital roles in the replication of DNA and the synthesis of proteins. For instance, histones are structural proteins around which the DNA is coiled and supercoiled; the Scl-70 antigen is an enzyme, topoisomerase I, that unwinds the supercoils so that the DNA can be replicated or transcribed (31), and the proliferating cell nuclear antigen is involved in DNA synthesis (32). One of the nucleolar antigens is an RNA polymerase, and Sm and RNP are small ribonucleoprotein particles that cut out redundant sequences from RNA transcripts (33). The "myositis antigens" Jo-1, PL-7 and PL-12 are three of the enzymes that pair up amino acids with their appropriate transfer RNAs ready for protein synthesis (translation) at the ribosomes (22-24).

CLUES TO AETIOLOGY

The function of each antigen is probably irrelevant to the *pathogenesis* of autoimmune disease because there is little evidence that antibodies enter cells, but these functions may throw light on *aetiology*. The hypotheses linking virus infection with autoimmunity to particular cellular antigens are well worth reading, as is the recent work showing very close structural similarities between autoantibodies to DNA and cardiolipin and antibodies to common bacterial antigens (22; 34-36). Undoubtedly some autoantibody-disease associations will be explained by the particular damaging effects of the antibody (e.g. immune complexes of DNA and anti-DNA in nephritis), but in other cases the link may be at an earlier stage, with an aetiological agent inciting both the disease and the accompanying autoantibody response.

January 1987

REFERENCES

1. Grabar P. Autoantibodies and the physiological role of immunoglobulins. *Immunol Today* (1983) **4:** 385-389.
2. Bernstein RM, Bunn CC, Hughes GRV, Francoeur AM, Mathews MB. Cellular protein and RNA antigens in autoimmune disease. *Mol Biol Med* (1984) **2:** 105-120.
3. Moroi Y, Peebles C, Fritzler M, Steigerwald JC, Tan EM. Autoantibody to centromere (kinetochore) in scleroderma sera. *Proc Natl Acad Sci USA* (1980) **77:** 1627-1631.
4. Hargraves MM, Richmond H, Morton R. Presentation of two bone marrow elements: the "Tart" cell and the "L.E." cell. *Proc Mayo Clin* (1948) **23:** 25-28.
5. Hughes GRV. *The Connective Tissue Diseases.* (1979) 2nd ed. Oxford: Blackwell Scientific Publications.
6. Harris EN, Gharavi AE, Boey ML, Patel BM, Mackworth-Young CG, Loizou S, Hughes GRV. Anticardiolipin antibodies: detection by radioimmunoassay and association with thrombosis in SLE. *Lancet* (1983) **ii** 1211-1214.
7. Carreras LO, Defreyn G, Machin SJ, Vermylen J, Deman R, Spitz B, Van Assche A. Arterial thrombosis, intra-uterine death and "lupus" anticoagulant. Detection of immunoglobulin interfering with prostacyclin formation. *Lancet* (1981) **i:** 244-246.
8. Harris EN, Gharavi AE, Hughes GRV. Anti-phospholipid antibodies. *Clin Rheum Dis* (1985) **11:** 591-609.
9. Hamsten A, Norberg R, Bjorkholm M, De Faire U, Holm G. Antibodies to cardiolipin in young survivors of myocardial infarction: an association with recurrent cardiovascular events. *Lancet* (1986) **i:** 113-116.
10. Anderson JR, Gray KG, Beck JS, Kinnear WP. Precipitating autoantibodies in Sjögren's disease. *Lancet* (1961) **ii:** 456-460.
11. Tan EM. Autoantibodies to nuclear antigens: their immunobiology and medicine. *Adv Immunol* (1982) **33:** 167-240.
12. Reichlin M. Current perspectives on serological reactions in SLE patients *Clin Exp Immunol* (1981) **44:** 1-10.
13. Venables PJW, Charles PJ, Buchanan RRC, Yi T, Mumford PA, Schrieber L, Room GRW, Maini RN. Quantitation and detection of isotypes of anti-SS-B antibodies by ELISA and Farr assays using affinity purified antigens. An approach to the investigation of Sjögren's syndrome and systemic lupus erythematosus. *Arthritis Rheum* (1983) **26:** 146-155.
14. Alexander EA, Provost TT. Ro (SSA) and La (SSB) antibodies. *Springer Semin Immunopath* (1981) **4:** 253-273.
15. Maddison PJ. ANA-negative SLE. *Clin Rheum Dis* (1982) **8:** 105-119.
16. Scott JS, Maddison PJ, Taylor PV, Esscher E, Scott O, Skinner RP. Connective tissue disease autoantibodies to ribonucleoprotein, and congenital heart block. *N Engl J Med* (1983) **309:** 209-212.
17. Wasicek CA, Reichlin M. Clinical and serological differences between systemic lupus erythematosus patients with antibodies to Ro versus patients with antibodies to Ro and La. *J Clin Invest* (1982) **69:** 835-843.
18. Sharp GC, Irvin WS, Tan EM, Gould RG, Holman HR. Mixed connective tissue disease – an apparently distinct rheumatic disease syndrome associated with a specific antibody to an extractable nuclear antigen (ENA). *Amer J Med* (1972) **52:** 148-159.
19. Alarcon-Segovia D. Mixed connective tissue disease – a decade of growing pains. *J Rheumatol* (1981) **8:** 535-540.
20. Yoshida S, Akizuki M, Mimori T, Yamagata H, Inada S, Homma M. The precipitating antibody to an acidic nuclear protein antigen, the Jo-1. in connective tissue disease: a marker for a subset of polymyositis with interstitial pulmonary fibrosis. *Arthritis Rheum* (1983) **26:** 604-611.
21. Bernstein RM, Morgan SH, Chapman J, Bunn CC, Mathews MB, Turner-Warwick M, Hughes GRV. Anti-Jo-1 antibody: a marker for myositis with interstitial lung disease. *Brit Med J* (1984) **289:** 151-152.
22. Mathews MB, Bernstein RM. Myositis autoantibody inhibits histidyl-tRNA synthetase: a model for autoimmunity. *Nature Lond* (1983) **304:** 177-179.
23. Mathews MB, Reichlin M, Hughes GRV, Bernstein RM. Anti-threonyl-tRNA synthetase, a second myositis-related autoantibody. *J Exp Med* (1984) **160:** 420-434.
24. Bunn CC, Bernstein RM, Mathews MB. Autoantibodies to alanyl-tRNA synthetase and tRNA Ala coexist and are associated with myositis. *J Exp Med* (1986) **163:** 1281-1291.
25. Douvas AS, Achten M, Tan EM. Identification of a nuclear protein (Scl-70) as a unique target of human antinuclear antibodies in scleroderma. *J Biol Chem* (1979) **254:** 10514-10522.
26. Bernstein RM, Steigerwald JC, Tan EM. Association of antinuclear and antinucleolar antibodies in progressive systemic sclerosis. *Clin Exp Immunol* (1982d) **48:** 43-51.
27. Catoggio LJ, Bernstein RM, Black CM, Hughes GRV, Maddison PJ. Serological markers in progressive systemic sclerosis: clinical correlations. *Ann Rheum Dis* (1983) **42:** 23-27.
28. Lockwood CM, Bakes D, Jones S, Whitaker K, Moss D, Savage C. Association of alkaline phosphatase with an antigen recognised by sera from patients with systemic vasculitis. (Personal communication)
29. Bernstein RM, Neuberger JM, Bunn CC, Callender ME, Hughes GRV, Williams RS. Diversity of autoantibodies in primary biliary cirrhosis and chronic active hepatitis. *Clin Exp Immunol* (1984e) **55:** 533-560.
30. Habets WJ, Moet MM, van de Pas J, van Venrooij WJ. Characterisation of nuclear and cytoplasmic autoimmune antigens. In: Peeters J, ed. *Protides of the Biological Fluids* (1985) Oxford, Pergamon, **33:** 199-204.
31. Shero JH, Bordwell B, Rothfield NF, Earnshaw WC. High titres of autoantibodies to topoisomerase I (Scl-70) in sera from scleroderma patients. *Science* (1986) **231:** 737-740.
32. Mathews MB, Bernstein RM, Franza R, Garrels JI. The identity of the "proliferating cell nuclear antigen" and "cyclin". *Nature (Lond)* (1984) **309:** 374-376.
33. Lerner MR, Boyle JA, Mount SM, Wolin SL, Steitz JA. Are snRNPs involved in splicing? *Nature (Lond)* (1980) **283:** 220-224.
34. Plotz PH. Autoantibodies are anti-idiotype antibodies to antiviral antibodies. *Lancet* (1983) **ii:** 824-826.
35. Walker EJ, Jeffrey PD. Polymyositis and molecular mimicry, a mechanism of autoimmunity. *Lancet* (1986) **ii:** 605-607.
36. Sela I, El -Roeiy A. Isenberg DA, Kennedy RC, Colaco CB, Pinkhas J. Shoenfeld Y. A common anti-DNA idiotype in sera of patients with active pulmonary tuberculosis. *Arthritis Rheum* (1986) **29:** in press.

ANTIPHOSPHOLIPID ANTIBODIES: THEIR CLINICAL SIGNIFICANCE

G R V Hughes
R A Asherson
M A Khamashta
Lupus Research Unit
The Rayne Institute
St Thomas' Hospital
London SE1 7EH

HISTORY

The presence of circulating anticoagulants in patients with systemic lupus erythematosus (SLE) was first documented by Conley and Hartman in 1952 *(1)*. An increased risk of paradoxical thrombosis in patients with these endogenous anticoagulants was recognised by Bowie *et al* in a report from the Mayo Clinic in 1963 *(2)*. Feinstein and Rapaport in 1972 first used the term 'lupus anticoagulant' (LA). Placental infarctions leading to repeated abortions were subsequently described in the late 1970s but it was not until the early 1980s that the significance and relationships of the LA to other antiphospholipid antibodies (aPL) were clarified *(3-6)*. It has now become clear that these antibodies identify an important subset of patients manifesting a variety of clinical events, most of which are associated with hyper-coagulability and vascular occlusions.

DETECTION OF aPL

aPL may be detected by one or more of the following tests: the LA test, the solid phase anticardiolipin (aCL) assay, and, occasionally, the standard test for syphilis (STS).

Although it is known that LA react with phospholipids, the precise epitope(s) with which LA react are not known. The present hypothesis is that they interact with the phospholipid portion of the prothrombin activator complex of the clotting cascade, as evidenced by their effect on routine coagulation tests (prolongation of the activated partial thromboplastin time, the Russell viper venom time and, less frequently, prolongation of the prothrombin time) *(7)*.

In 1983, we described a sensitive and reliable technique of solid phase radioimmunoassay for the detection of aCL *(5)*. Subsequently, it was found that other negatively charged phospholipids such as phosphatidylserine, phosphatidylinositol and phosphatidic acid could also be used as antigen in the solid phase assays (ELISA or RIA) *(6,8)*. The aCL assay, unlike the LA test, is more sensitive, has less observer error, and can be performed on stored sera.

There are subtle differences (not explained by different sensitivities of the various assays) between LA and aCL:

- LA activity may be abolished by steroid administration whereas aCL levels may remain unaffected *(9)*.
- 30% of patients may have one antibody without the other *(10)*.
- Recently, some authors have shown that aCL and LA define separate subgroups of phospholipid binding antibodies, thus explaining the discordance often seen between the two tests *(11)*.

CLINICAL ASPECTS

Patients with elevations of IgG aCL and/or the presence of LA are at increased risk for the development of vascular occlusions, specially under conditions listed in Table 1.

TABLE 1. RISK FACTORS FOR THROMBOSIS IN PATIENTS WITH aPL

1. Prolonged bed rest.
2. Post-surgical procedures.
3. Oral contraceptives (oestrogen).
4. Pregnancy and puerperium.
5. Active SLE.
6. Renal disease.
7. Anticoagulation problems: – Warfarin discontinuation eg. for biopsies, surgery. – Warfarin resistance – Poor compliance
8. Other risk factors eg. hypertension, smoking, etc.

a) Frequency of occurrence

The lack of standardisation of the LA and aCL tests make prevalence figures difficult to estimate. Most studies quote the frequency of the LA to be 6-10% and aCL 20-50% in patients with SLE *(12-14)*. Clearly, aPL are not limited to patients with SLE and have been described in other autoimmune, drug induced, malignant and infectious disorders (Table 2). However, the majority of these patients have low titre positive tests, often transient and of little clinical importance. In SLE, up to one third of patients with the LA and about 50% of patients with moderate to high positive IgG aCL have a history of thrombosis and/or recurrent miscarriages *(15)*. When aPL are encountered in connective tissue diseases other than SLE, aCL alone are usually demonstrable without a positive LA test.

b) The antiphospholipid syndrome (APS)

We introduced this term to identify patients with aCL

TABLE 2. CLINICAL CONDITIONS ASSOCIATED WITH aPL

1) Autoimmune diseases	3) Infections
Systemic lupus erythematosus	Bacterial (tuberculosis, leprosy, syphilis)
Rheumatoid arthritis	Protozoan (Pneumocystis carinii)
Scleroderma	Viral (AIDS, hepatitis, rubella, EBV)
Dermatomyositis-Polymyositis	4) Lymphoproliferative disorders
'Overlap' syndromes	Hairy cell leukaemia
2) Drug exposure	Malignant lymphoma
Chlorpromazine	Waldenstrom's macroglobulinaemia
Procainamide	5) Miscellaneous disorders
Hydralazine	Epithelial malignancies (prostate, bronchus)
Quinidine	No underlying disease (elderly).
Antibiotics	
Phenytoin	

TABLE 3. CRITERIA FOR THE APS

Clinical	*Laboratory*
Venous thrombosis	IgG aCL (moderate/high levels)
Arterial thrombosis	IgM aCL (moderate/high levels)
Recurrent foetal loss	Positive LA test
Thrombocytopenia	

Patients with the syndrome should have at least one clinical plus one laboratory finding during their disease. aPL test must be positive on at least two occasions more than 3 months apart.

TABLE 4. PRESENTATION OF THE APS

Venous thrombosis: Deep venous thrombosis (lower limb, axillary or subclavian veins), mesenteric, renal, hepatic, splenic, caval, cerebral venous thrombosis, retinal and pulmonary thromboembolism.

Arterial thrombosis: Strokes, transient ischaemic attacks, multi-infarct dementia, 'pseudo-multiple sclerosis'.

Recurrent foetal loss

Haemocytopenias: Particularly thrombocytopenia.

Livedo reticularis

Cardiac associations: Valve lesions, particularly mitral and aortic incompetence, pseudoinfective endocarditis ('vegetations' – ie clot on valve), intracardiac thrombus simulating atrial myxoma, myocardial infarctions, multiple small coronary occlusions – 'pseudocardiomyopathy'.

Neurological associations: Guillain-Barre syndrome, transverse myelitis, chorea, global amnesia.

Others (less common): Ischaemic necrosis of bone, splinter haemorrhages, pulmonary hypertension and Addison's disease.

or the LA, who have clinical features associated with these antibodies (Table 3). A high proportion of patients manifesting the APS do not suffer from classical lupus, according to the revised 1982 criteria for the classification of SLE *(16)*. These patients have been characterised as suffering from 'lupus-like' disease, which is probably merely a variant of lupus itself, and a 'primary' APS *(17)*.

c) **Presentation of the APS**

The most frequent forms of presentation of the APS are shown in Table 4.

d) **Special situations**

Sneddon's syndrome:

The combination of *livedo reticularis,* cerebrovascular disease and hypertension was first described by Sneddon in 1965. The association of *livedo* with strokes in patients with aPL prompted studies of these antibodies in patients with Sneddon's syndrome *(17,18)*. In our prospective study of patients with *livedo reticularis,* 43% had aCL *(19)*.

'Pseudo-infective' endocarditis:

Non-infective vegetations, which are caused by intracardiac thrombus formation may mimic infective endocarditis, particularly if they are superimposed on previously damaged valves *(20)*. When accompanied by splinter haemorrhages, diagnostic and therapeutic problems arise in the persistently culture negative patient. *(21)*.

Addison's disease/hypoadrenalism:

First documented in 1989, there have now been several patients reported with this complication. Interestingly, most documented cases have been males, and have a history of previous venous thromboses. As hypoadrenalism has occurred in some cases on anticoagulation therapy, adrenal haemorrhage has been diagnosed. Others (biopsy proven) have been shown to have occlusion of adrenal vessels and have suffered haemorrhagic infarction of both adrenal glands. The condition should be suspected in any patient with a history of previous venous thrombosis who develops abdominal pain either spontaneously, following vigorous exercise or post-operatively *(22)*.

Multi-infarct dementia:

These patients develop dementia either following a diagnosed stroke with hemiparesis/hemiplegia, or in the absence of neurological signs. Diagnosis is usually made by computed tomographic brain scan. Anticoagulant therapy may prevent further cerebral damage *(23)*.

'Pseudo-multiple sclerosis':

In some patients with bizarre, transient/recurrent cerebral/neurological signs aPL have been detected in the absence of other immunological abnormalities.

Chorea:

A large number of case reports have now been published, relating aPL to the development of this condition either spontaneously, in lupus patients, or perhaps appearing for the first time in the puerperium or during pregnancy (**'chorea gravidarum'**) *(24,25)*. A number of patients with this complication were found to go on to develop cerebrovascular occlusions such as strokes, and prophylactic anticoagulant therapy may be indicated for this complication.

Ischaemic necrosis of bone:

Isolated cases of patients with aPL who presented with ischaemic necrosis of bone in the absence of steroid therapy have occurred, suggesting that this uncommon complication in SLE may, in some, be associated with aPL and thrombosis *(26,27)*.

Pulmonary hypertension:

A number of patients with pulmonary hypertension have aPL *(28)*. These include patients with recurrent deep vein thrombosis and pulmonary thromboembolism, some patients with SLE and pulmonary hypertension and a small number (5-10%) of patients with 'primary' idiopathic pulmonary hypertension.

Splinter haemorrhages:

Splinter haemorrhages affecting subungual areas of fingers or toes have been described particularly accompanying *amaurosis fugax (29)*. They have also been seen in some patients with aPL who have become pregnant or have been given oral contraceptives.

The recently highlighted association with heart valve disease *(20)* further emphasises the diagnostic similarities with bacterial endocarditis.

Vasculitis:

The vast majority of patients with aPL associated vascular occlusive events have shown no evidence of inflammatory vasculitis *(30)*. As vasculitis is more frequent in SLE than aPL related complications, this combination, when it occurs, is probably coincidental.

TABLE 5. POTENTIAL CAUSES OF BLEEDING IN PATIENTS WITH LA

- Specific factor inhibitors
  - Factor VIII inhibitor
  - Factor II inhibitor
- Thrombocytopenia
- Platelet dysfunction
- Uremia
- Concomitant drug administration (eg. aspirin)

Bleeding:

It became evident over the years that the LA was associated not with bleeding but, paradoxically, with thrombosis. However, when bleeding does occur, it has been usually ascribed to the presence of other coagulation abnormalities. (Table 5).

Idiopathic thrombocytopenic purpura (ITP):

aCL have been detected in up to 30% of ITP patients. This finding raises the possibility that patients with the APS may present only with severe thrombocytopenia and may then go on to develop foetal loss or thrombosis later in their disease course *(31)*.

TABLE 6. PROPOSED MECHANISMS OF ACTION OF aPL

1) Decreased prostacyclin production
2) Decreased fibrinolysis
3) Decreased protein C and thrombomodulin
4) Decreased protein S
5) Decreased antithrombin III
6) Increased platelet activation and aggregation

MECHANISMS OF ACTION

Although several hypotheses (Table 6) have suggested a pathogenic role for aPL, there is no conclusive evidence, so far, that these antibodies are the direct cause of thrombosis and foetal loss *(32,33)*.

Recently, two groups of investigators, working independently, have found that affinity purified aCL bound to liposomes that contained negatively charged phospholipids only in the presence of plasma or serum, which indicated the requirement of a 'cofactor' – referred to as aCL cofactor *(11,34)*. This cofactor was purified and its properties closely resemble those of beta-2-glycoprotein I (apolipoprotein H). These authors have shown that aCL cofactor was essential for aCL to bind to liposomes that contained cardiolipin or phosphatidylserine. Galli *et al* have also shown that the aCL cofactor is an apparent antigen for aCL when coated on a microtitre plate in the absence of any phospholipid *(34)*. Furthermore, Krilis *et al* found that increased cofactor levels correlate with thrombotic events (personal communication). These findings are likely to open new avenues of research on the mechanisms of aPL associated thrombosis.

TREATMENT

The asymptomatic patient probably does not require any treatment. However, in those conditions listed in Table 1, prophylaxis may be required either with aspirin, warfarin or low dose heparin (5000 U/12 h).

The treatment of patients with clinical manifestations remains controversial, and no controlled trials have yet been published *(35)*. Patients with a history of venous thrombosis should probably receive long term anticoagulants in the face of positive aCL in high/moderate titres. In the presence of arterial occlusion, oral anticoagulation should once again be administered.

Most advocate the use of low-dose salicylates, though again, there is little in the way of controlled trials.

Prednisolone/immunosuppressives should only be used if required for the underlying condition such as SLE.

Warfarin resistance has been encountered in several patients, who may require up to 20 mg/day of warfarin to achieve an international normalised ratio (INR) within a therapeutic range. The INR in patients with aPL should be kept at a level of 3-4. Any levels below this may result in vascular occlusions. Levels should therefore be closely and carefully monitored and patients instructed to increase their dosage should the INR fall below the levels required.

In some patients with severe extensive occlusions, eg. threatened gangrene, intravenous prostacycline, plasma exchange and fibrinolytic agents have been tried, though their use is experimental.

Over the past three years, there has been a re-evaluation of the significance of aPL in pregnancy. Whilst an increased rate of foetal wastage is seen in this group, experience suggests that with close monitoring, this can be significantly reduced. In view of this finding, many of the high dose prednisolone treatment strategies are being re-evaluated.

On the basis of the current knowledge, the presence of aPL in the absence of a previous history of foetal loss or thrombosis is not an indication for treatment. In those with two or more foetal losses or miscarriages, several therapeutic approaches have been proposed (Table 7). A number of uncontrolled studies reporting favourable pregnancy outcomes and similarly treatment failures have been reported with most of these therapeutic regimens *(36)*. Controlled, prospective and multicentre trials of treatment at risk subjects are currently under way.

CONCLUSIONS

We have described a syndrome characterised by venous and/or arterial thrombosis, recurrent foetal loss, often accompanied by thrombocytopenia, associated with presence of aPL. This syndrome is seen in patients with SLE and the closely related 'lupus-like' disease, ie. lupus patients not conforming to the 1982 revised American Rheumatism Association classification criteria for SLE. It is also seen in a group of patients who do not manifest any of the major clinical or serological features of SLE, the majority of whom do not appear to progress to classical lupus. These patients have been characterised as suffering from a 'primary' APS.

One of the clinical gains from this newly-described association is the recognition that not all disease manifestations in SLE (eg. cerebral involvement) are inflammatory, and that treatment directed towards thrombotic events may be more appropriate in this sub-set of patients.

TABLE 7. THERAPEUTIC REGIMENS FOR PREGNANCY FAILURE ASSOCIATED WITH aPL

1. No treatment.
2. Low dose aspirin.
3. Low dose prednisolone.
4. Low dose aspirin plus low dose prednisolone.
5. Low dose aspirin plus high dose prednisolone.
6. Low dose prednisolone plus azathioprine.
7. Full dose subcutaneous heparin.
8. Intravenous high dose immunoglobulin.
9. Plasma exchange plus low dose prednisolone.

REFERENCES

1. Conley CL, Hartman C. A haemorrhagic disorder caused by circulating anticoagulants in patients with disseminated lupus erythematosus. *J Clin Invest* 1952; **31:** 621-622

2. Bowie EJ, Thompson JH, Pascussi CA, Owen CA. Thrombosis in systemic lupus erythematosus despite circulating anticoagulants. *J Lab Clin Med* 1963; **62:** 416-430

3. Boey ML, Colaço CB, Gharavi AE, et al. Thrombosis in systemic lupus erythematosus: striking association with the presence of circulating lupus anticoagulant. *Br Med J* 1983; **287:** 1021-1023

4. Hughes GRV. Thrombosis, abortion, cerebral disease and lupus anticoagulant. *Br Med J* 1983; **287:** 1088-1089.

5. Harris EN, Gharavi AE, Boey ML, et al. Anticardiolipin antibodies: detection by radioimmunoassay and association with thrombosis in systemic lupus erythematosus. *Lancet* 1983; **ii:** 1211-1214

6. Harris EN, Gharavi AE, Loizou S, et al. Cross-reactivity of antiphospholipid antibodies. *J Clin Lab Immunol* 1985; **16:** 1-6

7. Harris EN, Antiphospholipid antibodies. *Br J Haematol* 1990; **74:** 1-9

8. Gharavi AE, Harris EN, Asherson RA, Hughes GRV. Anticardiolipin antibodies: isotype distribution and phospholipid specificity. *Ann Rheum Dis* 1987; **46:** 1-6

9. Derksen RHWM, Hasselaar P, Blokzijl L, et al. Coagulation screen is more specific than the anticardiolipin antibody ELISA in defining a thrombotic subset of lupus patients. *Ann Rheum Dis* 1988; **47:** 364-371

10. Lockshin MD, Qamar T, Druzin ML, Goei S. Anticardiolipin antibody, lupus anticoagulant and fetal death. *J Rheumatol* 1987; **14:** 259-262

11. McNeil HP, Chesterman CN, Krilis SA. Anticardiolipin antibodies and lupus anticoagulants comprise separate antibody subgroups with different phospholipid binding characteristics. *Br J Haematol* 1989; **73:** 506-513

12. Alarcón-Segovia D, Delezé M, Oria M, et al. Antiphospholipid antibodies and the antiphospholipid syndrome in systemic lupus erythematosus. A prospective analysis of 500 consecutive patients. *Medicine (Baltimore)* 1989; **68:** 353-365

13. Cervera R, Font J, López-Soto A, et al. Isotype distribution of anticardiolipin antibodies in systemic lupus erythematosus: prospective analysis of a series of 100 patients. *Ann Rheum Dis* 1990; **49:** 109-113

14. Love PE, Santoro SA. Antiphospholipid antibodies: anticardiolipin and the lupus anticoagulant in systemic lupus erythematosus (SLE) and in non-SLE disorders. *Ann Intern-Med-* 1990; **112:** 682-698

15. Harris EN, Asherson RA, Hughes GRV. Antiphospholipid antibodies – autoantibodies with a difference. *Ann Rev Med* 1988; **39:** 261-271

16. Harris EN. Syndrome of the black swan. *Br J Rheumatol* 1987; **26:** 324-326

17. Asherson RA, Khamashta MA, Ordi-Ros J, et al. The 'primary' antiphospholipid syndrome: Major clinical and serological features. *Medicine (Baltimore)* 1989; **68:** 366-374

18. Levine SR, Langer SL, Albers JW, Welch KMA. Sneddon's syndrome: an antiphospholipid antibody syndrome? *Neurology* 1988; **38:** 798-800

19. Asherson RA, Mayou SC, Merry P, Black MM, Hughes GRV. The spectrum of livedo reticularis and antiphospholipid antibodies. *Br J Dermatol* 1989; **120:** 215-221

20. Khamashta MA, Cervera R, Asherson RA, et al. Association of antibodies against phospholipids with heart valve disease in systemic lupus erythematosus. *Lancet* 1990; **335:** 1541-1544

21. Asherson RA, Tikly M, Staub H, et al. Infective endocarditis, rheumatoid factor, and anticardiolipin antibodies. *Ann Rheum Dis* 1990; **49:** 107-108

22. Asherson RA, Hughes GRV. Addison's disease and primary antiphospholipid syndrome. *Lancet* 1989; **ii:** 874

23. Asherson RA, Mercy D, Philips G, et al. Recurrent stroke and multi-infarct dementia in systemic lupus erythematosus associated with antiphospholipid antibodies. *Ann Rheum Dis* 1987; **46:** 605-611

24. Asherson RA, Derkston RWHM, Harris EN, Hughes GRV Chorea in systemic lupus and lupus-like disease: association with antiphospholipid antibodies. *Seminars Arth Rheum* 1987; **16:** 253-9

25. Khamashta MA, Gil A, Anciones B, et al. Chorea in systemic lupus erythematosus: association with antiphospholipid antibodies. *Ann Rheum Dis* 1988; **47:** 681-683

26. Asherson RA, Jungers P, Liote F, Hughes GRV. Ischaemic necrosis of bone associated with the lupus anti-coagulant and antibodies to cardiolipin. *Proc. of The XVI Congress of Rheum, Sydney, Australia* 1983; **373.**

27. Lavilla P, Khamashta MA, Valencia ME, Puig JG, Vazquez JJ. Necrosis osea avascular en el lupus eritematoso sistemico. *Rev Mex Reumatol* 1988; **3:** 118-122

28. Asherson RA, Oakley CM. Pulmonary hypertension in SLE. *J Rheumatol* 1986; **13:** 1-5

29. Asherson RA. Subungual splinter haemorrhages: a new sign of the antiphospholipid coagulopathy? *Ann Rheum Dis* 1990; **49:** 268

30. Lie JT. Vasculopathy in the antiphospholipid syndrome: thrombosis or vasculitis, or both? *J Rheumatol* 1989; **16:** 713-715

31. Harris EN, Gharavi AE, Hegde U, et al. Anticardiolipin antibodies in autoimmune thrombocytopenic purpura. *Br J Haematol* 1985; **59:** 231-234

32. Khamashta MA, Asherson RA, Hughes GRV. Possible mechanisms of action of the antiphospholipid binding antibodies. *Clin Exp Rheumatol* 1989; **7 (suppl 3):** 85-89

33. Hasselaar P, Derksen RHWM, Blokzijl L, et al. Risk factors for thrombosis in lupus patients. *Ann Rheum Dis* 1989; **48:** 933-940

34. Galli M, Comfurius P, Maassen C, et al. Anticardiolipin antibodies (ACA) directed not to cardiolipin but to a plasma protein cofactor. *Lancet* 1990; **335:** 1544-1547

35. Lockshin MD. Anticardiolipin antibody. *Arthritis Rheum* 1987; **30:** 471-472

36. Walport MJ. Pregnancy and antibodies to phospholipids. *Ann Rheum Dis* 1989; **48:** 795-797

METHODS AVAILABLE FOR EVALUATING BONE MINERAL CONTENT

H A Bird
Senior Lecturer in Rheumatology
University of Leeds
V Wright
Professor of Rheumatology
University of Leeds

TRABECULAR AND CORTICAL BONE:-

The skeleton comprises 80% cortical bone, mainly in the appendicular skeleton and 20% trabecular or cancellous bone, mainly in the axial skeleton. The relative proportions of the two types of bone varies with site. Bone is a dynamic organ and the pattern of age-related bone loss (in which breakdown outweighs synthesis) differs for cortical and trabecular bone. The cortical component of long bones is resorbed from the endosteal surface, but this is partly offset by new bone formation at the periosteal surface which produces a widening of such bones with age. With age 20-30% cortical bone is lost in a slow continuous process. Trabecular bone has a much higher surface area to volume ratio, so is more sensitive to change on resorption or **formation. 50% of trabecular bone is lost with age and such** loss may be rapid though often self-limiting. Although there is less trabecular bone, it probably contributes relatively more to the strength of bone because of its different physical properties. Changes here may provide more sensitive indicators of certain early metabolic changes than changes in cortical bone.

BONE STRUCTURE

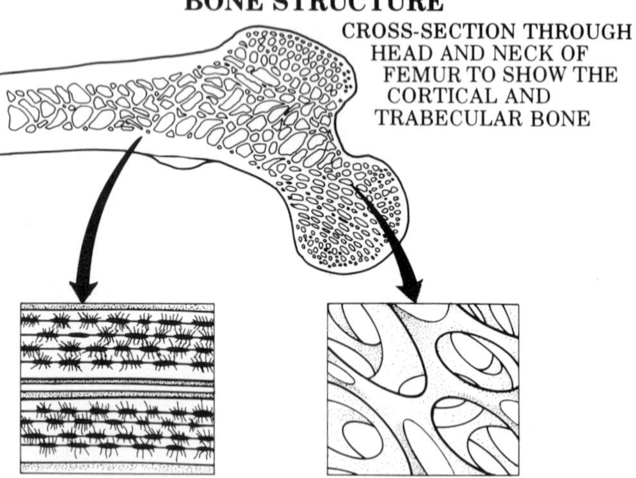

80% (APPENDICULAR)
COMPACT (CORTICAL) BONE
A central harversian (canal) with neurovascular lundle is surrounded by tight sheets of lamella bone interspersed with cells.

20% (AXIAL)
SPONGY (TRABECULAR) BONE
Consists of lacework of mineralised separated by large demineralised spaces.

BONE CHANGES IN RHEUMATIC DISEASES:-

Patients with pain in joints or bone may be referred to rheumatology clinics. In many metabolic bone diseases, fractures tend to occur at sites that contain relatively large amounts of trabecular bone [1,2]. Osteoporosis, a decrease in bone mass, is the commonest metabolic disorder of the skeleton and may be drug (e.g. prednisolone) induced.

The variation in bone structure may become even more pronounced in patients with rheumatic diseases. Localised areas of Paget's disease may occur, osteoarthrosis is associated with increased bone density around affected joints and rheumatoid arthritis produces osteopenia around inflamed joints. Qualitative assessment may be made by bone biopsy, usually at the iliac crest which may reveal an unexpected variety of pathology[3]. Bone histochemistry is likely to increase knowledge in the future[4], but discussion centres on the extent to which a single bone biopsy mirrors changes occurring at distal parts of the skeleton. Bone structure is under hormonal control but no differences in either 25-OHD_3 levels or 1,25-OHD_3 levels have been found in plasma when a degenerative is compared with an inflammatory arthritis[5,6]. However, increased bone metabolism has been demonstrated in rheumatoid arthritis by the method of whole body retention of ^{99}Technetium diphosphonate[7].

Simple bone radiographs are not sufficient to diagnose early bone loss because significant loss in bone mass may precede radiological change [2]. There has therefore been recent interest in non-invasive methods that improve sensitivity in the measurement of bone mineral content, though all of these expose the body to a small amount of radiation[8,9].

RADIOGRAMMETRY:-

This measures the thickness of the cortex of the metacarpal bones using a standard A-P X-ray on **industrial fine-grain film. From such measurements** various indices of cortical bone volume are calculated. Radiogrammetric results may be compared with a large normal population and are usually precise and reproducible[10,11,12]. Small changes in periosteal cortical resorption are shown by serial measurements, but the method does not measure absolute bone mineral content and can only be applied to the appendicular skeleton where it is of most value in measuring serial change.

PHOTODENSITOMETRY:-

This uses the bone mineral image on standard radiographic film as an indicator of photon absorption by bone and therefore indirectly measures bone mineral content[13]. The degree of film whitening is measured by a photodensitometer or by a chemical assay of the amount of silver on the exposed film. Calibration of each film is achieved by simultaneous exposure to a reference aluminium alloy wedge with a similar degree of X-ray absorption as bone.

SINGLE-ENERGY PHOTON ABSORPTIOMETRY:-

This measures mineral content in the appendicular skeleton, usually at the radius. A mono-energetic photon **source, such as ^{125}I is coupled in a yoke with a sodium** iodide scintillation counter detector. The difference in photon absorption between bone and soft tissue allows calculation of the total bone mineral content found in the scan path. This is inversely related to the measured transmission count rate. The method has been well used and validated [14,15,16], but accurate repositioning of the subject for repeat measurements lowers the reliability. A further refinement is the use of a multi-wire proportional counter as a detector to produce a transmission image of the bone being irradiated[17].

PHOTON ABSORPTIOMETRY

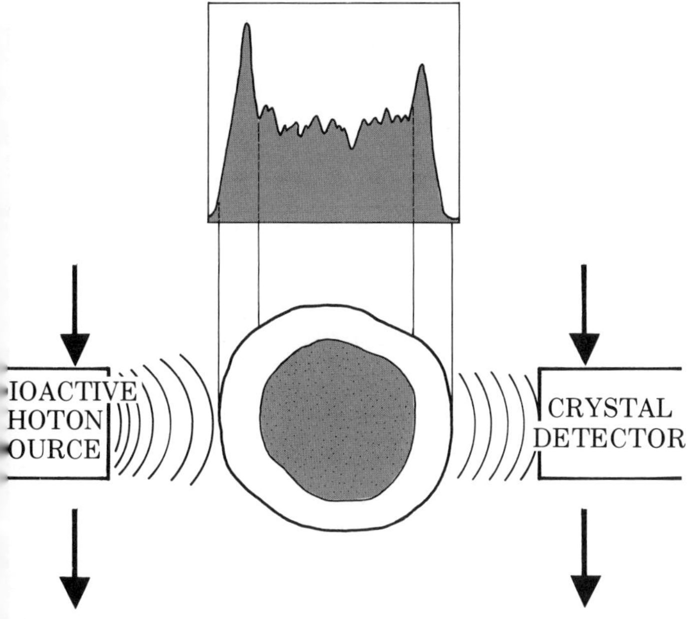

THE RADIOACTIVE SOURCE EMITS PHOTONS WHICH ARE DETECTED BY A CRYSTAL ON THE OTHER SIDE OF THE LIMB. THE SOURCE AND DETECTOR MOVE ACROSS THE LIMB TO SCAN THE AREA. PHOTONS ARE ABSORBED BY BONE, RESULTING IN AN ABSORPTION TRACING WHICH SHOWS PEAKS OVER THE DENSE CORTICAL BONE.

DUAL-ENERGY PHOTON ABSORPTIOMETRY:-

This is a modification of single-energy photon absorptiometry for use on the axial skeleton. A radioisotope is used that emits photons at two different energy levels. This eliminates the need for a constant soft tissue thickness across the scan path allowing use in areas such as the spine. The signal produced is independent of the soft tissue components scanned. The method is significantly more expensive than the single-energy technique. The isotope used is usually ^{153}Gadolinium[18,19,20].

COMPUTED TOMOGRAPHY:-

This method utilises quantitative data generated by computer-based tomography imaging devices[21]. Bone mass can be measured in any area of interest such as a vertebral body. A numeral reference standard such as K_2HPO_4 solution is required for calibration and a scout view is needed for localisation. A single or a dual-energy technique may be used. Data from scans of small volumes (3-4 cubic centimeters) are quantified and averaged and used in conjunction with calibration data to calculate mineral equivalents expressed in milligrams of K_2HPO_4 per cc. Total, cortical or trabecular bone mineral can be calculated.

COMPTON SCATTERING TECHNIQUE:-

This method utilises the scattering of a beam of gamma rays into a detector; the level of activity detected is a function of the density of the bone target. Two orthogonal photon beams are employed. The density measurement is the density of both organic and inorganic components of bone. An advantage is that the technique can be located entirely within weight-bearing trabecular bone, but several technical problems require resolution and to date it has not been possible to distinguish osteoporotic from normal individuals by this method[22].

NEUTRON ACTIVATION ANALYSIS:-

This uses a source of high-energy neutrons to activate body ^{48}calcium to ^{49}calcium. The subsequent decay back to ^{48}calcium can be measured using a gamma radiation counter to provide a measurement of total body calcium. On the assumption that 98% of body calcium is found in the skeleton, this technique approximates to total skeletal calcium content. The method requires complex costly apparatus and is only available in a small number of institutions. Patients are placed in a claustrophobic counting chamber that may prove inaccessible to some with arthritis[23,24,25].

SAFETY ASPECTS:-

The choice of method for evaluating bone mineral content may depend upon availability of apparatus. Nevertheless, investigators should be aware of the relative safety and cost before making a choice. The radiation exposure to the local tissues and to the gonads of each method is shown in the Table, where comparison is made with the radiation exposure of routine chest X-ray and examination of the lumbar spine by standard X-ray views.

Radiogrammetry and photodensitometry involve small doses of radiation with negligible gonad or bone-marrow radiation, both being performed at peripheral sites. Photon absorptiometry involves the least radiation of all, there being no scatter from use at peripheral sites[26]. Thus the dose to ovaries is 2 mrad and to bone marrow less than 0.2 mrad. For assessments on vertebral bodies the dose of radiation is larger and less well defined. Single-energy computed tomography involves 200-250 mrad exposure – localised to a 10 cm region of the upper abdomen[27]. With careful supervision dosage to gonads may be as low as 10 mrad. The highest radiation occurs with neutron activation analysis though proportionally smaller doses are involved if partial body irradiation techniques are used.

The cost of assessments will vary according to the equipment and manpower available. For running costs, photodensitometric techniques are the cheapest followed by single-energy and then dual-energy photon absorptiometry. The costs of computed tomographic methods and neutron activation analysis are much higher.

PRECISION AND RELIABILITY:-

These are also shown in the Table for each of the methods. "Precision" is the reproducibility of the test on repeated determinations, the percentage figure showing the average degree of variation when the test result is performed several times on the same specimen. Single-energy photon absorptiometry and dual-energy computed tomography are seen to be slightly less precise than other methods.

"Reliability" provides an index of the correlation between the method and reference standards. The percentage figure shows the degree of difference between the bone mineral content estimated by the test and the bone mineral content calculated by reference to standard ash weights. Again, single-energy computed tomography is the least reliable, but there is not much to choose between methods.

ADVANTAGES AND DISADVANTAGES OF THE METHODS:-

Radiogrammetry, photodensitometry and single-energy absorptiometry are used in the appendicular skeleton. The methods are of limited use in assessing metabolic bone diseases that involve areas with a greater proportion of trabecular bone such as the spine. Photodensitometry has technical problems relating to radiographic technique and methods of film processing. Some feel the method has therefore been superseded by photon absorptiometric techniques. The single-energy photon absorptiometry requires careful positioning of the bone site and the theory requires a uniform soft tissue thickness surrounding the bone.

Dual-energy photon absorptiometry and computed

COMPARISON OF TECHNIQUES AVAILABLE

	Radiation Exposure			
Technique	Local Tissue	Gonads	Precision	Reliability
Chest X-ray	30 mrad	negligible		
X-ray series of lumbar spine	600 mrad	considerable		
Radiogrammetry	100 mrad	negligible		
Photodensitometry	100 mrad	negligible	1-4%	6%
Photon absorptiometry				
single energy	2-5 mrad	negligible	3-5%	1-4%
dual energy	5-15 mrad	2 mrad	1-3%	4-6%
Computed tomography				
single energy	200-250 mrad	Variable (may be as low as 10 mrad)	1-3%	8% (less in elderly)
dual energy			3-5%	2-4% (less in elderly)
Neutron activation analysis	300-5000 mrad	not available	2-3%	6%

tomography are more suited to assessment of trabecular bone loss in the spine. The amount of bone scanned in dual-energy photon absorptiometry differs with the size of the skeleton and must be subsequently normalised. Attenuation of extra-osseous calcification or vascular structures with calcification may contribute to inaccurate measurements. Computed tomography may be used to measure cancellous or cortical bone or an integrated sum of both. The method can identify the absolute mineral content of a specific volume of bone. The reliability of single-energy computed tomography is variable and depends on the fatty tissue of the trabecular bone marrow. This is relevant in osteoporotic subjects since fat concentration in marrow rises with age leading to spuriously low values for mineral content. Dual-energy computer tomography allows a more reliable determination of bone mineral content independent of fat or water variation but at the expense of reduced precision and an increased radiation dose. The use of age-related regression analysis for calculating mineral content may reduce inaccuracies[28].

Findings from computer tomography and dual photon absorptiometry are precise and correlate fairly well with measured ash weights for isolated bone. Of the two, photon absorptiometry tends to correlate better with the results from neutron activation analysis which might be seen as the ultimate standard for total skeletal calcium measurement in the few centres where it is available.

DISTRIBUTION OF MINERAL VERSUS QUANTIFICATION:-

The discussion above implies that the methods can be ranked in terms of safety, precision and lack of errors for the measurement of quantitative mineral content. However, this global quantification will only provide limited information. Bone is constantly being remodelled according to patterns of stress and the mechanical needs of the body and a more composite view of mineral distribution is obtained by the simultaneous recording of mineral content at several sites. In practice, those sites more susceptible to clinical pathology have tended to be the best studied. These comprise the forearm (easily accessible), the vertebral body and the femur, particularly the femoral neck. The methods considered are those most frequently used in the UK.

THREE SITES SUSCEPTIBLE TO BONE PATHOLOGY AND METHODS USED TO ASSESS BONE DENSITY AT THESE SITES

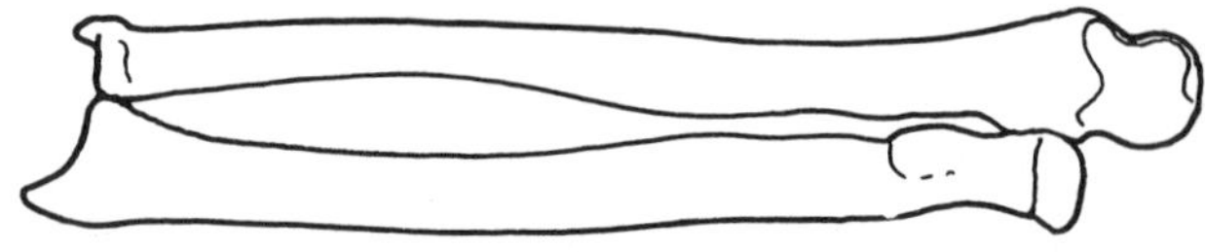

THE FOREARM
PHOTON ABSORPTIOMETRY

THE FEMUR
RADIOGRAMMETRY
(Photon Absorptiometry)
C T SCANNING

VERTEBRAL BODIES
C T SCANNING
(Dual Photon Absorptiometry)

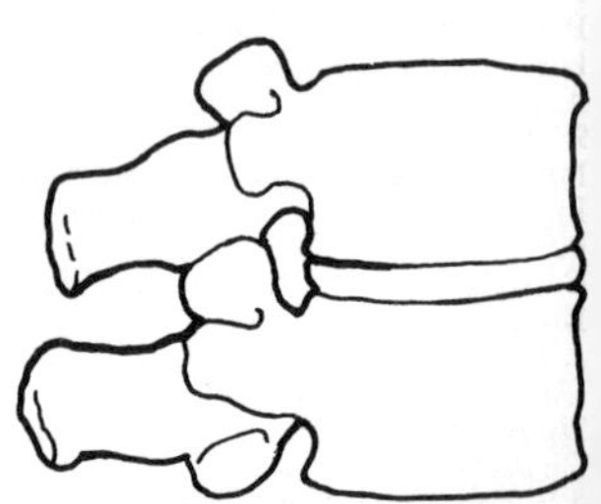

Forearm: Bone mineral content is usually assessed by single photon absorptiometry. The value obtained at any site reflects both trabecular and cortical bone there. The distal radius is mainly trabecular bone whilst proximal sites are mainly cortical. Precision is less for distal sites because of errors in positioning. Cortical bone at the metacarpal is usually assessed by radiogrammetry. Comparison of patients with fractured forearm and normal controls suggests that loss of cortical metacarpal bone is a better indicator of patients at risk of fracture than forearm bone loss, so the two sites are probably complementary in the information they convey[29].

Vertebral body: Visual assessment of vertebral density from X-ray may be misleading as over 50% of the bone has to be lost before change is apparent. Dual photon densitometry and CT scanning are only occasionally available in the UK. Osteophytosis occurring in degenerative joint disease of the spine produces spurious measurements with dual photon densitometry, which probably makes CT scanning the method of choice in spite of the higher exposure to radiation.

Femur: This accessible site offers a compromise of a weight-bearing peripheral bone that is frequently subject to fracture. Cortical bone measurement can be performed by radiogrammetry and trabecular bone is assessed by Singh grade. In this subjective method[30] X-rays of the femoral neck are taken and the trabecular pattern compared with standard radiographs graded from 1-6. Using a combination of cortical measurements and Singh grade it is possible to discriminate patients with femoral neck fracture from normal controls[31]. Dual photon absorptiometry and CT scanning allow a more accurate estimation of bone status if they are available.

CONCLUSIONS:-

Longitudinal studies employing metacarpal radiogrammetry, single photon absorptiometry of the forearm and dual photon absorptiometry or CT scanning of the spine have shown that bone loss occurs at different rates in different parts of the skeleton. Assessment at a single site conveys limited information and may even give a totally false impression of overall mineral loss. Irrespective of site, trabecular bone may be lost more rapidly than cortical bone. Neutron activation analysis which measures total body calcium (98% of which is skeletal) is largely a measure of cortical bone which comprises 80% of the skeleton. It is possible for considerable change and loss in trabecular bone not to impinge on the results from neutron activation analysis. Total body calcium measured by this method correlates better with mineral content of the femur than with mineral content of the radius or ulna[25], perhaps because the femur is a larger part of the total cortical bone.

There seems to be an argument for measuring locally, particularly at the site where fractures occur, and there would be theoretical advantages in special purpose CT scanners (currently under development) that measure both cortical and trabecular bone separately. This might allow prediction of those at risk of fracture.

The other practical problem is to measure with sufficient precision to detect losses of bone mineral content of a few per cent per year. Trials of drugs that might be effective on the skeleton inevitably have to span several years. There is a need for greater precision to detect more rapid change over a shorter period before being able to adjudicate on the best drugs to prevent loss of bone mineral in clinical trials. One experimental approach, microfocal radiography[32], is a sophisticated variant of radiogrammetry. No doubt other radiological methods for the still more sophisticated quantitation of mineral content will be developed.

REFERENCES

1. COHN, S.H. (1982).
Techniques for determining the efficacy of treatment of osteoporosis.
Calcif.Tissue Int. **34:** 433-438.
2. JOHNSTON, C.C., EPSTEIN, S. (1981).
Clinical, biochemical, radiographic, epidemiologic and economic features of osteoporosis.
Orthopaedic Clinics of North America.
12: 559-569.
3. BIRD, H.A. (1979).
Bone biopsy in the investigation of bone pain and fractures.
Rheum.&Rehab. **18:** 38-42.
4. CONFERENCE REPORT. (1984).
Assessment and treatment of bone disease.
Ann.Rheum.Dis. **43:** 660-661.
5. BIRD, H.A., PEACOCK, M., STORER, J.H., WRIGHT, V. (1980).
Comparison of serum 25-OH vitamin D concentrations in rheumatoid arthritis and osteoarthrosis.
Br.Med.J. **1:** 1416.
6. BIRD, H.A., WRIGHT, V., HENNES, U., THEISS, E. (1982).
Comparison of serum 1, 25-Dihydroxycholecalciferol concentrations in rheumatoid arthritis and osteoarthrosis.
Ann.Rheum.Dis. **41:** 257-258.
7. RAJAPAKSE, C., THOMPSON, R., GRENNAN, D.M., WINSTON, B.M., PATEL, P., NUTTALL, P.M., MURPHY, J. WEISS, J.B. (1983).
Increased bone metabolism in rheumatoid arthritis as measured by the whole-body retention of $^{99}Tc^{m}$ methylene diphosphonate.
Ann.Rheum.Dis. **42:** 138-141.
8. HEALTH AND PUBLIC POLICY COMMITTEE, AMERICAN COLLEGE OF PHYSICIANS. (1984).
Position paper: radiologic methods to evaluate bone mineral content.
Ann.Int.Med. **100:** 908-911.
9. RECKER, R.R. (1982).
Non-invasive measurements of bone loss.
In: Non-invasive Bone Measurements: Methodological Problems. (Eds.) Dequeker, J. and Johnston, C.C. Oxford – Washington D.C., IRL. pp. 1-13.
10. BARNETT, B., NORDIN, B.E.C. (1960).
A radiological diagnosis of osteoporosis.
Clin.Radiol. **11:** 166-174.
11. SAVILLE, P.D. (1965).
Changes in bone mass with age and alcoholism.
J.Bone.Jt.Surg. **47A:** 492-499.
12. DEQUEKER, J. (1970).
Pattern of development and loss of bone with age.
Lancet. **1:** 359-360.
13. WEST, R.R. (1973).
The estimation of total skeletal mass from bone densitometry measurements using 60 keV photons.
Br.J.Radiol. **46:** 599-603.
14. CAMERON. J.R., SORENSON, J. (1963).
Measurement of bone mineral in vivo: an improved method.
Science. **142:** 230-232.
15. SMITH, D.M., NANCE, W.E., KANG, K.W., CHRISTIAN, J.C., JOHNSTON, C.C. (1973).
Genetic factors in determining bone mass.
J.Clin.Invest. **52:** 2800-2808.
16. MAZESS, R.B. (1971).
Estimation of bone and skeletal weight by direct photon absorptiometry.
Invest.Radiol. **6:** 52-60.
17. HORSMAN, A., READING, D.H., CONNELLY, J., BATEMAN, E, GLASGOW, W., McLACHLAN, M.S.F. (1977).
Bone mass measurement using a xenon-filled multi-wire proportional counter as detector.
Phys.Med.Biol. **22:** 1059-1072.
18. KROLNER, B., PORS-NIELSON, S.P. (1980).
Measurement of bone mineral content (BMC) of the lumbar spine.
1: Theory and application of a new two-dimensional dual photon attenuation method.
Scand.J.Clin.Lab.Invest. **40:** 653-663.
19. RIGGS, B.L., WAHNER, H.W., DUNN, W.L., MAZESS, R.B., OFFORD, K.P., MELTON, L.J. (1981).
Differential changes in bone mineral density of the appendicular and axial skeleton with ageing.
J.Clin.Invest. **67:** 328-335.
20. DUNN, W.L., HEINZ, M.S., WAHNER, H.W., RIGGS, B. (1980).
Measurement of bone mineral content in human vertebrae and hip by dual photon absorptiometry.
Radiology. **136:** 485-487.
21. GENANT, H.K., BOYD, D.P. (1977).
Quantitative bone mineral analysis using dual energy computer tomography.
Invest.Radiol. **12:** 545-551.
22. COHN, S.H. (1982).
Intercomparison of techniques for the non-invasive measurement of bone mass.
In: Non-invasive Bone Measurements: Methodological Problems. (Eds.) Dequeker, J. and Johnston, C.C. Oxford – Washington D.C., IRL. pp. 21-22.
23. ANDERSON, J., OSBORN, S.B., TOMLINSON, R.W.S., NEWTON, D, RUNDO, J., SALMON, L., SMITH, J.W. (1964).
Neutron activation analysis in man in vivo. A new technique in medical investigation.
Lancet. **2:** 1201-1205.
24. HARRISON, J.E., McNEILL, K.G., HITCHMAN, A.J., BRITT, B.A. (1979).
Bone mineral measurements of the central skeleton by in vivo neutron activation analysis for routine investigation in osteopenia.
Invest.Radiol. **14:** 27-34.
25. HORSMAN, A., BURKINSHAW, L., PEARSON, D., OXBY, C.B., MILNER, R.M. (1983).
Estimating total body calcium from peripheral bone measurements.
Calcif.Tissue Int. **35:** 135-144.
26. EL-KHOURY, G.Y., USTA, H.Y (1982).
Measurement of bone mineral content using computed tomography.
Iowa Ortho.J. **2:** 97-100.
27. GENANT, H.K., CANN, C.E., ETTINGER, B., GORDAN, G.S. (1982).
Quantitative computed tomography of vertebral spongiosa – a sensitive method for detecting early bone loss after oophorectomy.
Ann.Int.Med. **97:** 699-705.
28. GENANT, H.K., CANN, C.E., BOYD, D.P. (1983).
Quantitative computed tomography for vertebral mineral determination.
In: Clinical Disorders of Bone and Mineral Metabolism. (Eds.) Frame, B., Potts, J.T. New York. Excerpta Medica. pp.40-47.
29. FRANCIS, R.M. (1985).
Personal Communication.
30. SINGH, M., NAGRATH, A.R., MAINI, P.S. (1970).
Changes in trabecular pattern of the upper end of the femur as an index of osteoporosis.
J.Bone Jt.Surg. **52A:** 457-467.
31. HORSMAN, A., NORDIN, B.E.C., SIMPSON, M., SPEED, R. (1982).
Cortical and trabecular bone status in elderly women with femoral neck fracture.
Clin.Ortho.Related Res. **166:** 143-151.
32. BUCKLAND-WRIGHT, J.C. (1983).
X-ray assessment of activity in rheumatoid disease.
Br.J.Rheum. **22:** 3-10.

THE USE OF THE DIAGNOSTIC TISSUE BIOPSY IN RHEUMATOLOGY

A Freemont
Senior Lecturer in Osteoarticular Pathology
Department of Rheumatology
University of Manchester

In most surgical and some medical specialities, a "tissue diagnosis" made on biopsy material is considered the definitive diagnostic investigation. Rheumatology is one medical speciality in which, until recently, the diagnostic biopsy was less commonly employed. The reasons for this are very complex and relate to factors such as the nature of rheumatological practice, and the availability of other laboratory investigations, notably immunoserology.

Within recent years 3 major events have altered the potential importance of biopsy-based diagnosis in rheumatology. The first is the introduction of new techniques into osteoarticular pathology; the second the increased use of the "day case" biopsy; and the third the enlightened approach of the ARC with its sponsorship of training posts in this branch of pathology. The importance of the latter is that specialist units are developing in many regions which will act as a repository of technical and interpretive skills that would not otherwise be available. This will result in increased access for rheumatologists to a specialised pathological opinion and a greater contact with the speciality for trainee pathologists.

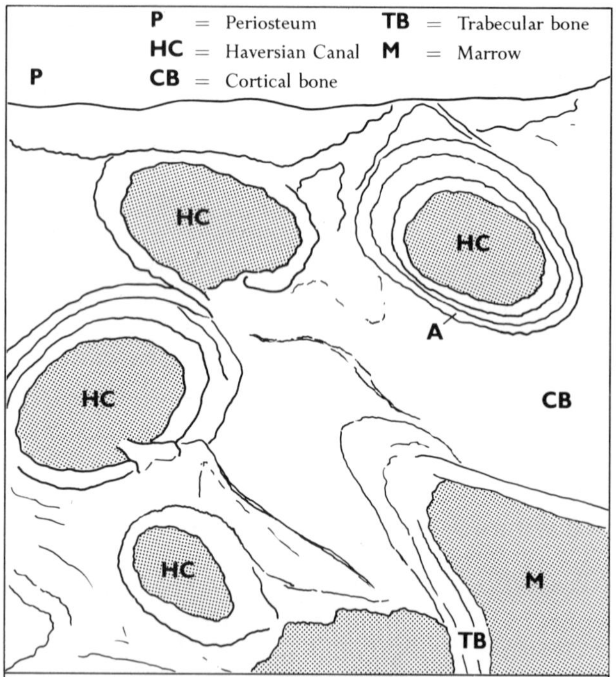

P = Periosteum, HC = Haversian Canal, CB = Cortical bone, TB = Trabecular bone, M = Marrow

Tetracycline fluorescence in a bone biopsy. Most fronts bear a double label. The distance between labels (A) can be used to derive the rate of mineralisation. A decrease in (A) may be the only evidence of osteoporosis.

Even with access to the appropriate technology and sufficient throughput of material, rheumatological pathology still poses more interpretive challenges than many other branches of pathology but the scope for contributing to patient diagnosis and management is now very much greater. For maximum information to be extracted from every biopsy there has to be a close relationship between the pathologist and the clinician. The latter contributes both clinical data (including necessary feedback) and the tissue sample. But to do so effectively she or he must understand the scope and limitations of the pathological technique and supply the appropriate tissue in the correct way. This review will discuss the techniques available to the histopathologist and their applications in the field of rheumatology. As the major aim of this overview is to demonstrate the scope of biopsy pathology in disease diagnosis, only the techniques most commonly employed for this purpose will be discussed.

PRINCIPLES OF TISSUE PROCESSING AND STAINING

In order to fully understand the requirements of the histopathologist it is necessary to appreciate the ways in which tissue is handled within the laboratory.

In very general terms the principles of light microscopy (by far the most commonly used analytical system) require that the specimen be cut sufficiently thinly to allow the passage of light through the tissue and that the component of the tissue under study be rendered visible.

The conventional thickness for tissue sections is between 3 and 6ums, although for certain investigations the thickness may be as little as 1um and as great as 20um. It is impossible to cut fresh tissue at this thickness. In order to produce usable sections it is necessary to support the tissue. This is achieved in two main ways. The first is to harden the tissue by changing its chemical structure. Although this step is sometimes omitted, fixation, as this process is known, has other advantages including prevention of autolysis and tissue breakdown by micro-organisms. The most widely used fixative is the protein cross-linking aldehyde formaldehyde. This is an excellent fixative but has limitations notably in taking up to 24hrs for fixation to occur and dramatically changing the structure of tissue proteins. Many other fixatives are available but they are less commonly employed. Even tissue hardened in this way cannot be sectioned to the correct thickness. To achieve this it is necessary to replace the tissue water with a harder material. The most commonly used support is "paraffin wax", a mixture of plastics and waxes. The other major support medium is solidified water, the basis of the "frozen section".

Once sectioned the tissue has to be "stained". This requires that a visible reaction product be formed. Usually this is a coloured product but sometimes a visible product can be achieved in other ways such as the production of visible light by illuminating a fluorochrome with UV radiation.

The overwhelming majority of tissue sections are stained using coloured dyes which react with components of the tissue in a more or less specific way. The most commonly used stains are haematoxylin and eosin. These are general stains selective for no single component of the tissue. With them the structure of the tissue and the arrangement and appearances of the cells are more important to the interpretation than the distribution of specifically stained components. Other conventional stains react more specifically with components of the tissue such as elastic or reticulin revealing as they do the amount and distribution of the substance under study.

Nowadays much more specific methods are available for identifying molecules within tissues. Of these the most commonly employed is immunohistochemistry (1) in which antibodies are attached to specific antigens in the tissue section. A disclosing system, usually an enzyme or fluorescein, is linked to the antibody which is used to produce a visible reaction product localised to the site of the original antigen. In this way it is possible to identify extra- or intra-cellular molecules and specific cell types by demonstrating surface or cytoplasmic molecules specific to that cell. Most stains work well in formalin fixed wax embedded tissue (conventional processing) but the protein crosslinkage induced by formalin fixation and other stages in processing so alter the structure of tissue molecules as to interfere with their antigenicity and prevent antibody binding. Techniques are available for improving antibody binding in conventionally processed tissue but the majority of antibodies still give best results in frozen sections.

A whole variety of other less frequently used techniques are available, but of these the only ones used regularly in diagnostic histopathology are enzyme histochemistry and electron microscopy.

Enzyme histochemistry exploits the fact that in frozen sections, and to a lesser extent conventionally processed tissues, naturally occurring enzymes are still active and can be made to act on chemicals that resemble their natural substrate to produce a stable visible reaction product.

Electron microscopy uses an electron, rather than a photon, beam to examine the tissue. The very short wavelength of the electron beam allows much greater resolution in suitably thin sections (<100nm) permitting the tissue to be examined at much higher magnifications (2).

SITES OF BIOPSY

In 1988 the 8 rheumatologists within the North Western Region who regularly send material to this laboratory, which specialises in osteoarticular pathology, provided either directly or indirectly approximately 1200 of the 2100 specimens processed. Of these biopsies 22% were of synovium, 21% skin, 12% muscle, 8% salivary glands, 6% tenosynovium, 5% subcutaneous tissue, 5% articular surfaces, 4% mucous membranes, 4% arteries, 4% "metabolic bone" biopsies, 3% amputations (usually digits), 2% entheses, 1% ligaments, and 4% others. Other specialist pathologists have received biopsies from other sites from this same clinician group which include (in numerical order) bowel, bone marrow and lymph node, liver, kidney, lung and pleura, nerve, heart and brain.

INDIVIDUAL TISSUES

Individual tissues have different handling requirements and yield different information. These are discussed below and summarised in the Table.

a) Synovium and tenosynovium (3)

Synovial changes in disease are remarkably focal within any one joint or tendon sheath. Multiple biopsies are therefore advised. Some diseases, including mycobacterial infections, villonodular synovitis and crystal deposition disease have distinctive histological appearances but in many respects the diagnostic yield of synovial biopsy is low. This is largely because despite being possible usually to distinguish between inflammatory and non-inflammatory arthropathies within each group the synovial appearances are often similar. Subtle changes allow certain arthropathies such as rheumatoid disease, SLE, AS, Behçets disease and OA to be diagnosed in a small but significant proportion of cases. At present there is little advantage in using other than routinely processed and stained tissue.

b) Skin and mucous membranes

Although a variety of rheumatological diseases have manifestations in the skin, biopsy is most commonly performed in 2 circumstances; for the diagnosis of SLE and vasculitis. The best specimen is an elipse of skin 1.0 × 0.5 cm taken down to the subcutaneous fat (full thickness skin biopsy). The advantage of this type of specimen is first that an elipse can be divided into samples for frozen section and routine processing and second a full thickness biopsy allows disorders such as eosinophilic fasciitis, scleroderma and larger vessel vasculitis to be diagnosed. Because skin varies with age and site, it is essential that the pathologist is notified of these data.

In the identification and differentiation of various diseases such as SLE, dermatomyositis, discoid lupus and the whole spectrum of the vasculitides, immunofluorescence on frozen sections using polyclonal antibodies against various immunoglobulin heavy chains, C3 and fibrinogen yields the maximum data and is cheap and simple (4).

c) Muscle (5)

The introduction of various instruments for muscle biopsy under local anaesthesia means that it is as simple and painless as a liver biopsy and just as useful. Sufficient muscle can be obtained to allow most disorders of interest to the rheumatologist to be diagnosed. We process all tissue for frozen sectioning and on this routine stains and enzyme histochemistry are always performed. If necessary a similar panel of those fluorescein labelled antibodies used on skin can be employed for the diagnosis and classification of vasculitis, as can other forms of immunohistochemistry for categorising cellular infiltrates. The specimen can be divided to provide a specimen for electron microscopy if needed although in rheumatological practice this is rarely required. The most common reasons for muscle biopsy in this unit are for the diagnosis of inflammatory, steroid-induced and neurogenic myopathies. Although a unit such as this, involved in the diagnosis of all aspects of locomotor and connective tissue disease, cannot offer as comprehensive a service as a laboratory specialising in muscle pathology, the range of questions being asked in rheumatology is relatively narrow and a basic morphological and enzyme histochemical assessment is usually adequate for the task.

d) Salivary glands (6)

The diagnosis of Sjögrens syndrome can be made with some confidence on routinely processed biopsies of labial salivary glands.

e) Subcutaneous tissue (7)

Subcutaneous tissue is biopsied most commonly to identify subcutaneous nodules, diagnose panniculitis and demonstrate amyloid deposition.

Rheumatoid nodules have a characteristic appearance particularly when viewed between crossed polarisers and are rarely confused with other lesions. Immunohistochemistry has little to add to their diagnosis. Amyloid however, although usually diagnosed by conventional staining techniques lends itself to demonstration using immunohistochemistry. Fortunately the residual amount of antigenically intact amyloid protein is such that after formalin fixation sufficient remains for detection using antibody-based techniques. This is certainly the case with immunoglobulin light chains, amyloid A and beta-2 microglobulin but, in this laboratory, for the demonstration of P protein frozen sections are necessary.

f) Articular surfaces (8)

Ideally demonstration of articular surface abnormalities necessitates sectioning the whole specimen. Modern processing equipment designed to permit high biopsy throughput does not lend itself to sectioning large pieces of tissue eg. intact slabs of femoral head. However, in purely diagnostic terms, the amount of new information obtained from the examination of these specimens, removed usually therapeutically for joint failure is small and providing the specimen is carefully sampled important but possibly clinically unsuspected conditions such as aseptic necrosis, Pagets disease, osteomyelitis and intraosseous vasculitis, should not be overlooked.

g) Arteries (9)

Arteries are biopsied to make the diagnosis of arteritis. Unfortunately the urgency to start treatment often means that the biopsy is undertaken some time after initiating therapy. Such are the changes that can occur naturally in normal arteries particularly in the elderly that unless a mural inflammatory cell infiltrate, mural necrosis or gross segmental fibrosis of the vessel wall are seen the biopsy appearances are not helpful. The result is that biopsy after treatment has started is almost invariably a waste of time.

Immunofluorescent studies for immunoglobulin and complement deposition may be informative. A positive result occurs surprisingly infrequently, even in overt vasculitis, and although we perform this investigation on every artery it is of help in less than 5%.

TABLE I: THE PROCESSING AND STAINING TECHNIQUES USED IN THIS LABORATORY FOR EXAMINING DIFFERENT TISSUES, TOGETHER WITH THE DISEASES FOR WHICH THEY ARE MOST COMMONLY BIOPSIED.

TISSUE	PROCES Co	PROCES FS	STAINING Co	STAINING IP	STAINING IF	STAINING EH	DISEASES
Synovium	*	-	*	?	-	-	Granulomatous disease, PVNS, Some arthropathies.
Skin	*	*	*	?	*	-	SLE, Vasculitis, Dermatoses Fasciitis, Scleroderma
Muscle	-	*	*	?	?	*	Various myopathies, Vasculitis
Salivary gland	*	-	*	-	-	-	Sjögren's syndrome
Tenosynovium	*	-	*	?	-	-	As for synovium
Subcutaneous tissue	*	?	*	*	-	-	Subcutaneous nodules, Amyloid, Panniculitis
Articular surfaces	*	-	*	-	-	-	Articular disease, Aseptic necrosis, osteomyelitis, intraosseous vasculitis
	Bone requires decalcification						
Mucous membranes	*	*	*	?	*	-	As for skin
Arteries	*	*	*	-	*	-	Vasculitis
Metabolic bone biopsies	Special techniques for embedding, sectioning, Staining and Examining						Osteoporosis, Osteomalacia, Hyperparathyroidism, Renal and Endocrine Osteodystrophies
Amputations	*	-	*	-	-	-	Vascular disease, Infection
Entheses	*	-	*	-	-	-	Traumatic, inflammatory, Metabolic enthesopathies
	Decalcification						
Ligaments	*	-	*	-	-	-	Fibromatoses, Trauma
Bone marrow	*	-	*	?	-	-	Marrow suppression, Haematological disorders, As for bone and entheses
	Decalcification or Resin embedding						
Lymph nodes	*	*	*	*	-	?	Lymphadenopathy
Liver	*	-	*	-	-	-	Hepatic dysfunction, amyloid
Kidney	*	*	*	?	*	-	Glomerular and tubular disease vasculitis, amyloid
Bowel	*	-	*	-	-	-	Inflammation, Ulceration, Amyloid Vasculitis, Systemic sclerosis
Lung	*	-	*	-	-	-	Fibrosing alveolitis, vasculitis
Nerve	*	-	*	-	-	-	Neuropathy, Vasculitis, Amyloid
Heart	*	*	*	*	-	-	Cardiomyopathy, Valve lesions

KEY TO TABLE

PROCES = Processing
Co = Conventional (Processing – formalin fixed, wax embedded)
(Staining– specific and non-specific stains)
FS = Frozen section
IP = Immunoperoxidase or immunoalkaline phosphatase immunohistochemistry
IF = Immunoflourescence
EH = Enzyme histochemistry

h) "Metabolic" bone biopsies(10)

Bone is usually decalcified prior to processing and sectioning. Unfortunately much of the diagnostic information is then lost. To retain the maximum amount of data it is necessary to section the tissue "undecalcified". This requires that the biopsy is embedded in a much harder material than paraffin wax – usually a plastic resin. The tissue block is then so hard that it must be cut with a motorised microtome. The sections are then stained and examined in non-standard ways. The ultimate aim of these complex processing and examination techniques is to investigate the structure of bone matrix and the function of bone cells. Diseases that can be distinguished in this way include steroid and non-steroid induced osteoporosis, endocrine bone disease, osteomalacia, Pagets disease, renal osteodystrophy and hyperparathyroidism. The optimal biopsy is a 6-8mm diameter full thickness core biopsy of the iliac crest from a standardised area usually 2cm below and behind the anterior superior iliac spine. This is most commonly taken under local anaesthetic. Prior to biopsy the patient should be given 2 doses of tetracycline 10-15 mg/kg separated by an interval of 10 days. Tetracyclines are taken up into sites where bone is actively mineralising and can be visualised as a bright yellow green line at the interface between mineralised and non-mineralised bone matrix of unstained sections viewed in ultraviolet light. The tissue sections are not only examined qualitatively but also quantitatively using histomorphometry. This allows the severity of any abnormality to be defined and biopsies compared. The equipment required for processing, sectioning, staining, mounting and analysing the tissue are not standard histopathological equipment and are too expensive to be deployed in a district general hospital that may generate only 5-10 such biopsies annually. The technical and interpretive skills are also highly specialised and time consuming and again are not easily justified in a busy general histopathology department. It is usual therefore for such a service to be offered at a regional or subregional level in specialised laboratories.

i) Amputations

These specimens can be regarded as being very similar to articular surfaces. They are usually taken therapeutically for end stage disease. Almost all amputations received in this laboratory from rheumatology patients are ischaemic and/or infected digits and the most pressing concern is to establish the extent and type of the vascular occlusive disease and the infective process.

j) Entheses

The diagnosis of an enthesopathy is only rarely made on the basis of biopsy and although it is fairly straight-forward to differentiate traumatic, metabolic and inflammatory enthesopathies it is rarely necessary to establish the diagnosis histologically.

k) Other sites

The way in which these tissues are handled in the laboratory depends on the facilities available and the problem being addressed. In general terms conventional processing or a combination of this and immuno-histochemistry are employed for examining these tissues. Specific reasons for biopsying these tissues include the diagnosis of peptic ulceration, lymphadenopathy, drug-induced marrow suppression, fibrosing alveolitis, hepatic dysfunction, glomerular disease and cardiac valve abnormalities. In addition these tissues are biopsied to make less specific diagnoses such as vasculitis.

FUTURE ADVANCES

As stated earlier the past few years have seen major changes in the scope and application of diagnostic biopsy pathology to rheumatology, but what of the future? Within the next ten years there will be two major "advances" in the field. The first, and from the diagnostic viewpoint the most important, will be a faster turnround time for biopsy reporting. This will be technology led. We are already using microwave fixation which reduces the time needed for fixation from 24 hours to 50 seconds. Processing machines are available which will process tissue in 4-5 hours and modern communication systems allow printed information to be sent and received in an instant. With these advances there is the potential for a "same day" biopsy service to be offered with all the attendant implications for patient management. Secondly new technology will open new areas of diagnosis. Although at the moment *in-situ* hybridisation (11) appears to be of strictly limited value in diagnostic osteoarticular pathology the possibility of demonstrating viral genomic material or specific risk-bearing genes in tissue within 10 hours of receipt of the specimen offers a way in which modern mechanistic concepts of disease aetiology could be exploited diagnostically. Furthermore the ability to probe tissues quantitatively for evidence of cytokine production may give an objective basis for the reasoned use of new generations of drugs specifically targetted at these substances.

CONCLUSIONS

There is still relative underutilisation of histopathology in the diagnosis and assessment of rheumatological diseases. Modern techniques allow greater accuracy in diagnosis and have greatly improved the scope and value of rheumatological pathology. The future offers much especially more accurate and faster diagnosis and the possibility of using tissue pathology to tailor treatment.

REFERENCES

1. Goudie RB. Immunohistology in diagnostic histopathology In: Recent advances in histopathology 13. Ed. Anthony PP and MacSween RNM Churchill Livingstone, Edinburgh 1987 pp233-254

2. Bloodworth JMB, Azar A, Yodaiken RE. Symposium on electron microscopy in diagnostic pathology. Human Pathology 1975 **6:** 402-516

3. Revell PA. The synovial biopsy. In: Recent advances in histopathology 13. Ed Anthony PP and MacSween RNM. Churchill Livingstone, Edinburgh 1987 pp 79-93

4. Meyrick Thomas RH, Black MM, Bhogal B. The value of immunofluorescence techniques in the diagnosis of skin disorders. In: Recent advances in histopathology 12. Ed: Anthony PP and MacSween RNM, Churchill Livingstone Edinburgh 1984 pp 69-81

5. Weller RO. Muscle biopsy and the diagnosis of muscle disease. In: Recent advances in histopathology 12. Ed: Anthony PP and MacSween RNM, Churchill Livingstone Edinburgh 1984 pp 259-288

6. Mason DK, Chisholm DM. Salivary glands in health and disease. Saunders, Philadelphia 1975

7. Lever WF, Schaumberg-Lever G. Histopathology of the skin. 6th edition JB Lippincott Philadelphia 1983

8. Catto M. Locomotor System. In: Muirs textbook of pathology. Edward Arnold. London 1980 pp 874-941

9. Alarcon-Segovia D The necrotising vasculitides In: Clinics in Rheumatic Diseases. **6:** no 2 1980

10. Ellis HA. Metabolic Bone Disease In: Recent advances in histopathology 11. Ed. Anthony PP and MacSween RNM. Churchill Livingstone, Edinburgh 1981 pp 185-202

11. Gee CE, Roberts JI. In-situ hybridisation histochemistry: a technique for the study of gene expression in single cells. DNA 1983; **2:** 157-163

SYNOVIAL STRUCTURE & FUNCTION

J C W Edwards
Senior Lecturer in Rheumatology
The Middlesex Hospital Medical School
London

DEFINITION

Synovial tissue is usually defined as the soft tissue lining the cavities in joints, tendon sheaths and bursae (1). This definition has two drawbacks. It does not tell us how to recognise a bursa or how to distinguish a synovial tendon sheath from fibro-areolar tissue around tendon elsewhere. It does not indicate what, if any, basic biological properties link these tissues.

Synovium means "with egg", because synovial fluid is like glair (egg-white). However, Canoso and co-workers have shown that superficial bursae may contain little, if any, of the substance that makes the fluid glairy; hyaluronic acid (2). Even in joints and tendon sheaths, glairy fluid may be hard to find. The hyaluronic acid in synovial fluid probably represents a tiny percentage of the body total. It may be unwise to base a definition on the presence of this molecule.

Synovial tissue is often covered with a layer of cells. But again, in some areas these are absent. Clearly, there are dangers in a definition based on the presence of these cells. It is probably more useful to define synovial tissue as:

"Soft tissue, lining a blind space or potential space in connective tissue, which carries no surface epithelium or mesothelium, but which has a surface layer which is non-adherent and capable of retaining a discrete volume of fluid."

This definition distinguishes joint, tendon sheath and bursal cavities from other potential spaces in connective tissue. It rests on the idea that synovial fluid can only exist where there is an enclosing layer of tissue to hold it in one place. It can be tested by the practical means of injecting fluid into the space. The fluid will remain in a synovial space, but will track irregularly out of non-synovial spaces.

STRUCTURE OF SYNOVIAL TISSUE

Four elements of synovial tissue need consideration; the compact surface zone, the surface cell layer, packing tissue and the vasculature (1).

THE COMPACT ZONE

Normal synovial tissue has a smooth non-adherent surface. Whatever the size of the synovial structure, this surface is composed of a continuous sheet of tissue described by Key as the "compact zone" (3). The compact zone varies with the size and mechanics of a joint from a single sheet of flattened cells lying on a few wisps of collagen in a mouse knee to a sheet of fibrous tissue more than a millimetre thick in some parts of the human knee. In areas where the underlying tissue is densely fibrous, the compact zone is not distinct from the deeper fibrous tissue. Cells tend to be sparse in such fibrous areas, and there is no very clear distinction between these areas and fibrocartilage (3).

THE SURFACE CELL LAYER

Much of synovial tissue is covered by cells. These cells form an overlapping array which may form a clearly defined monolayer, or may merge with clusters of cells deeper in the tissue. In some areas, although there is a clear monolayer of cells, these are buried a few microns beneath superficial acellular matrix (3).

There has been debate as to whether the cells near the tissue surface are "ordinary connective tissue cells" or a distinct cell type (1). This begs a number of questions. Current evidence suggests that the origins of these cells are similar to other connective tissue cells, but that they are activated in rather different ways, because of their position at the surface. The distribution of cells with different properties is distinctly patchy, with clumps of phagocytic cells at one place, and virtually none at other sites, suggesting that activating stimuli vary from one place on the surface to another.

There is a working hypothesis that most cells of connective tissue (excluding lymphocytes, polymorphs, vessels etc.) can be divided into monocyte derived and tissue fixed cells, and that these two groups of cells have different potential activities (4). Monocyte derived cells often behave as typical macrophages, but expression of functional markers is very variable, and some appear to be more committed to antigen presentation. (Most connective tissue cells can become spiky or dendritic at times, and the term dendritic cell serves more to confuse than enlighten.)

The direct evidence for monocyte derived cells being present on synovial surfaces rests on kinetic experiments in rodents (5,6). However, the circumstantial evidence from histochemical studies is extensive. The recent demonstration of the absence of expression of a cell division marker Ki67 on cells with macrophage properties in diseased synovium adds further support to the idea that these cells are all monocyte derived and do not divide significantly in the tissue (7).

The intercellular matrix between the superficial cells differs from deeper matrix in the relative lack of collagen (8). Some collagen is present, however, probably as a mixture of type I and type III (9). The matrix contains fine fibrillar and amorphous material (8) some of which may be dermatan sulphate proteoglycan (1).

PACKING TISSUE

Beneath the compact zone, and in some cases continuous with it, is a variable amount of fatty, areolar or fibrous tissue (3). Apart from the fact that the type of tissue appears to vary according to the stresses and strains at different sites, it seems otherwise unremarkable.

THE VASCULATURE

The vasculature of synovial tissue varies considerably in precise distribution, but certain patterns seem to be common. Davies and Edwards described a prominent plexus of arterioles and venules within a few hundred microns of the tissue surface (10). This is present in both joints and tendon sheaths. It contains most of the red cells in the tissue and makes some synovium slightly pink.

This plexus gives rise to capillaries running up to within about ten microns of the surface. Some of the superficial capillaries in joint synovium have fenestrae (areas where the plasma membrane from opposite sides of the cell are fused to form a monolayer membrane or "window") (11). The number of fenestrae is relatively low, but it is of interest that a majority of them face the cavity (12).

Synovial tissue may carry a wide range of folds and projections, which may be finger-like, club-shaped, beaded or thread-like. The smallest projections carry no vessels. Slightly bigger projections have a central arteriole and venule. Large projections carry a fully developed plexus.

Schumacher made a detailed study of the vessels in monkey joint lining (13). He found relatively tall endothelium in some of the deeper venules, and also observed changes in these vessels after passive movement. It is still unclear as to whether there are any other special features of synovial vessels. However, this is an area of increasing interest with regard to lymphocyte traffic (14).

The vasculature of bursal walls is not well described and may differ significantly from other synovial tissue.

THE EXTENT OF THE TISSUE

Confusion about the definition of synovium may arise because the four elements described follow different structural rules. Whereas the thickness of the compact zone varies enormously, the depth of the vascular plexus is probably rather uniform. The presence and number of cells on the surface varies, not only with the type of tissue underneath, but from patch to patch in one area. Both the compact zone and the vessels may appear to be shared with adjacent structures such as epimysium or periosteum.

People differ in the thickness of tissue they include in the concept of synovium. Some concentrate on the surface cells and others on the surface capillaries. The "membrane" which can be identified by blunt dissection contains the compact zone *in toto*. However, a definition of synovium which is of value in the study of disease also has to include the tissue carrying the arterioles and venules. It is here that lymphocytes and plasma cells accumulate in the process we call synovitis. It is probably sensible to include in a definition of synovial tissue all the soft connective tissue whose structure and function is influenced by the presence of the synovial cavity, and this may mean very different things in different places (see figure 2)

FUNCTIONS OF SYNOVIAL TISSUE

Like other soft connective tissue, synovial tissue forms a **packing which allows movement of adjacent structures.** However, it achieves this through an unusual mechanism involving a pool of free interstitial fluid. The various elements of the tissue act together to allow this to come about (1).

THE COMPACT ZONE

The compact zone is structurally rather like a non-adherent surgical dressing. There are two functional components. The surface has the property of being permeable to water, protein and possibly large glycosaminoglycans, but sufficiently resistant to rapid fluid transit to retain a pool of fluid under the changing forces occurring during normal movement. Only in disease does this fail and the lining ruptures and empties. This behaviour relates partly to a surface pore size of about 0.07 microns (12) and partly to the viscosity of synovial fluid.

The rest of the compact zone, like the gauze backing of the dressing appears to act as a pliant fibrous support.

THE SURFACE CELL LAYER

Cells at or near the tissue surface appear to have two functions. They produce the hyaluronic acid found in synovial fluid. They also maintain the integrity and non-adherence of the tissue surface. This is probably achieved through molecules such as collagenase (for removing damaged collagen), plasminogen activator (for removing fibrin), fibronectin, collagens I and III and proteoglycan. The stimuli which encourage fibroblasts to make molecules such as collagenase and hyaluronate have been studied in detail (15, 16).

The mechanisms of joint lubrication are still under debate, but probably involve coating of hyaline cartilage by a glycoprotein called LGP-1. This molecule may well be synthesised by synovial surface cells.

PACKING

Joints are chiefly packed with soft tissue. Recent work on rabbit and human joints indicates that much of the articular surface is in direct contact with soft lining tissue or separated from it by a fluid film less than 50 microns thick. Larger collections of fluid tend to be limited to gaps between incongruous fibrocartilaginous discs and hyaline cartilage. The total volume in a rabbit knee is about 30 microlitres (12).

Although small, this amount of synovial fluid has an essential packing function. The resting joint cavity is at a pressure just below atmospheric (12). During movement the pressure in different parts of the cavity goes up or down. Excessive movements can generate a sufficient vacuum to release gas into the joint, which is what happens when people "crack" their finger joints. If joints contained less fluid than normal high vacuums would be expected to occur during normal movement, simply because the synovial tissue is not infinitely compliant. Moving a limb would be like trying to bend a pack of vacuum packed bacon – a remarkably difficult exercise.

Control of the volume of synovial fluid is not understood, but two main possibilities exist. Firstly, if synovial fluid volume falls, the pressure in the cavity drops and fluid is sucked into the cavity. If the volume rises the pressure rises and fluid is reabsorbed into the tissue. This passive mechanism may be supplemented by active control of hyaluronic acid production. If fluid volume drops the surface cells will be exposed to more mechanical stress and may produce more hyaluronate. By mechanisms which cannot be covered here in detail (1) this should favour retention of fluid in the cavity, and restore homeostasis.

THE VASCULATURE

All vascular beds in the body leak a small amount of water into the surrounding tissue. This water becomes lymph. Synovial tissue is unusual in that some of the water passes in and out of the cavity (and also the hyaline cartilage) before becoming lymph. During exercise and rest there are shifts of water in one or other direction (12) but there is no overall directional flow or circulation route as far as we know. This is quite distinct from the situation in a filtering organ such as the kidney or salivary gland, from which fluid is exported to the outside world.

Since there is no overall loss of fluid from synovial surfaces over a period of time, there seems no requirement for specialised fluid producing capillaries. It is intriguing that synovial capillaries have fenestrae, for which no good explanation has been found.

In joints, but probably not in tendon sheaths, and certainly not in bursae, synovial vasculature nourishes a tissue other than itself: the articular cartilage. It is often assumed that this process involves synovial fluid. Our observations on rabbit and small human joints suggest that in many areas the articular cartilage is so close to the lining tissue that any intervening synovial fluid is of doubtful relevance to molecular exchange. Nevertheless, during certain phases of exercise and rest a fine film of fluid may transude from the lining surface and pass over the cartilage under unknown hydrostatic gradients within the cavity. Levick has suggested that this sort of convective transport of small molecules may be important (12).

In other areas, where relatively large amounts of synovial fluid occur in the spaces between cartilage and fibrous meniscus or avascular fibrous synovial fronds, synovial fluid may provide the only adequate supply of nutrients, refreshed by convective exchange during movement. Other routes include those through cartilage matrix itself and exchange between opposite cartilage surfaces refreshed by contact with soft tissue during changes of position (1).

In practice, routes of cartilage nutrition probably vary from joint to joint and from place to place within a joint, and it may be misleading to consider synovial fluid as having a highly specialised function in this regard. It may simply be that the fluid reaches areas not provided for in other ways.

CHANGES IN DISEASE

Increased vascular permeability in inflamed synovial tissue leads to an imbalance in Starling forces with resulting tissue oedema and effusion (really a large pool of oedema).

A slight increase in oedema of synovial tissue during rest is probably responsible for so-called early morning stiffness. Drugs which limit the oedema associated with prostaglandin production are the most effective at reducing morning stiffness.

In joints in which worn cartilage and osteophytes set up friction the volume of synovial fluid is increased. The protein level is low, suggesting normal vascular

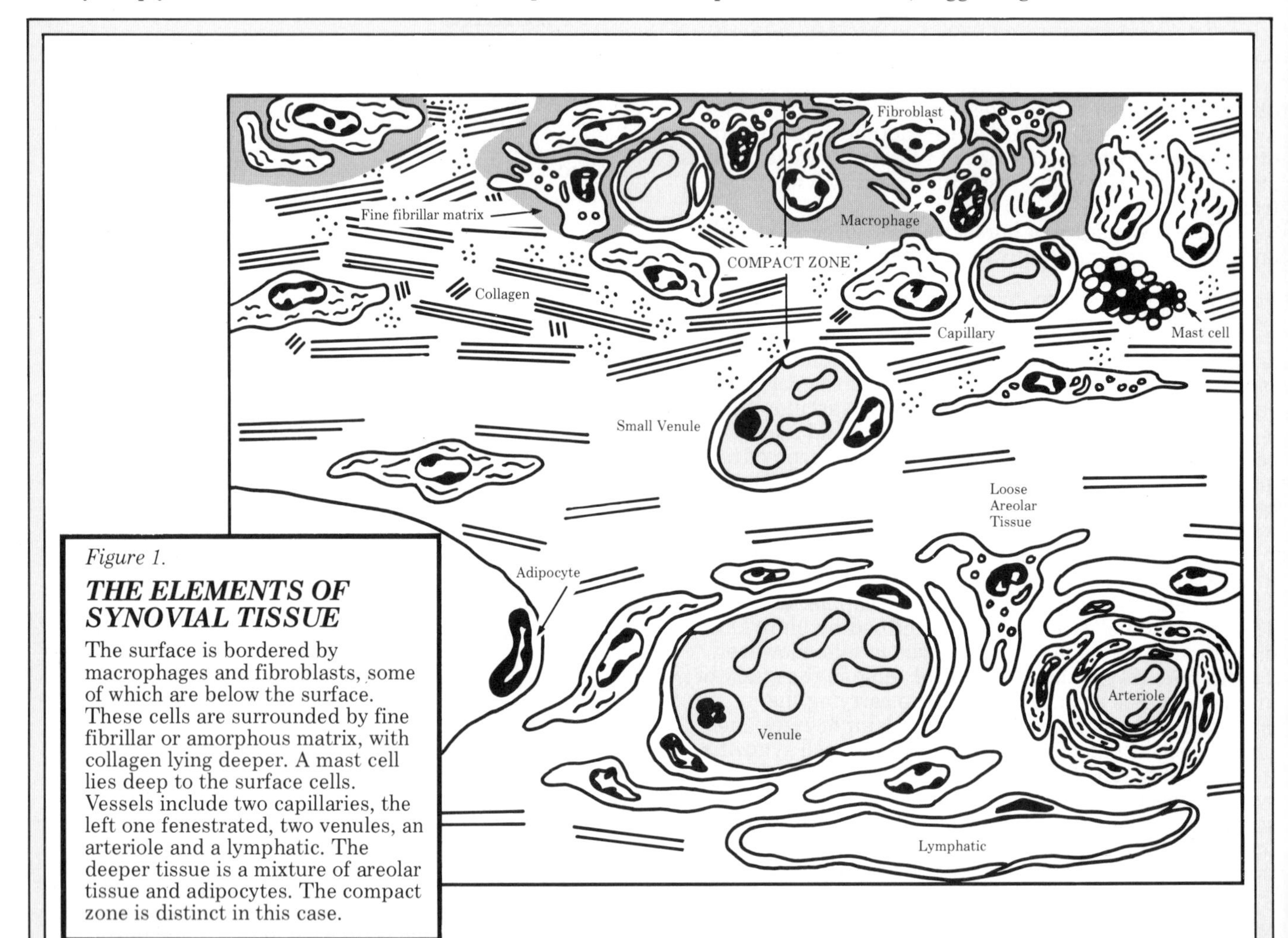

Figure 1.

THE ELEMENTS OF SYNOVIAL TISSUE

The surface is bordered by macrophages and fibroblasts, some of which are below the surface. These cells are surrounded by fine fibrillar or amorphous matrix, with collagen lying deeper. A mast cell lies deep to the surface cells. Vessels include two capillaries, the left one fenestrated, two venules, an arteriole and a lymphatic. The deeper tissue is a mixture of areolar tissue and adipocytes. The compact zone is distinct in this case.

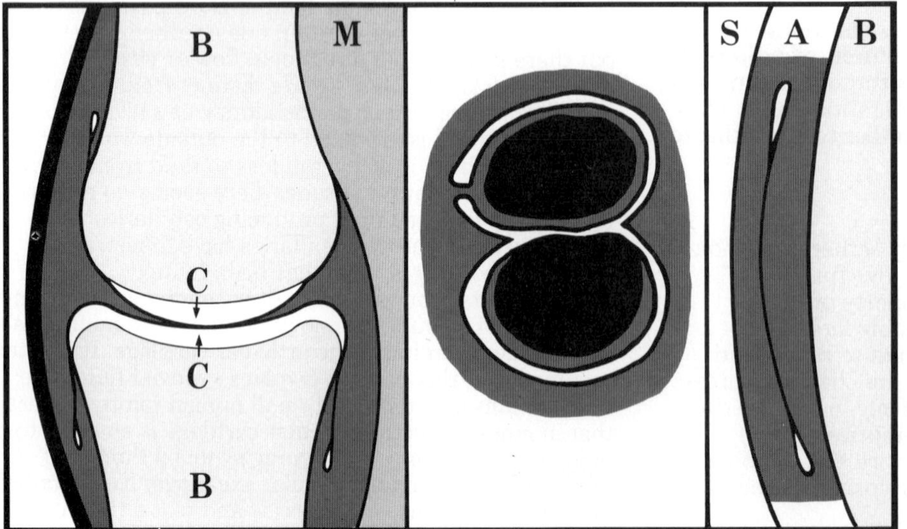

Figure 2.

SYNOVIAL STRUCTURES SEEN IN SECTION

Left: Synovium filling the space between bone (B), cartilage (C), tendon (solid black) and muscle (M) in a joint.

Middle: Synovium lining a tendon sheath. The upper tendon (solid black) has a visceral synovial layer and a mesotendon . The lower tendon has only a partial visceral layer.

Right: A bursal space lined by synovium in a layer of areolar tissue (A) between skin (S) and bone (B).

permeability, but the hyaluronic acid level is high. The implication is that friction stimulates hyaluronic acid production, but this fails to protect the soft tissue from further friction, excess hyaluronate accumulates, and with it excess fluid. Excess hyaluronate production may even be a primary phenomenon in some cases, possibly related to the formation of Heberden's nodes and articular cysts.

The influence of synovial tissue on cartilage integrity is extremely complex. Synovial tissue appears to provide the small molecules necessary for cartilage survival, but it also provides molecules such as interleukin 1 and proteases which may mediate cartilage destruction. The irony is highlighted by the co-culture experiments of Fell and Jubb, in which normal synovial tissue brought about the destruction of normal cartilage *in vitro* (17).

Despite an enormous literature on the possible mechanisms of cartilage degradation, no totally convincing theory has been put forward. This may be partly because a number of mechanisms contribute. (Possibilities include direct action of polymorph enzymes, or metalloproteinases from synovial fibroblasts and the indirect action of molecules such as interleukin 1 on both synovial fibroblasts and chondrocytes.) It may also indicate that we have yet to understand the way in which tissue geometry, mechanical stimuli and cell chemistry interrelate. Such problems, which exercise the minds of embryologists, have hardly been considered by students of joint disease. It may be that until we find ways of approaching such physico-chemical interactions we will continue to flounder in a quagmire of unconvincing biochemical hypotheses.

In the past, synovial tissue has often been considered as a rather irrelevant scrap of gristle, if it was mentioned at all. This review can only touch on a few basic aspects of the tissue now being actively investigated. What has become clear is that synovium holds the key to the processes of joint disease. In order to base our treatment on a rational approach to tissue physiology, much more detailed study is needed, covering aspects as diverse as molecular biology and fluid dynamics.

REFERENCES

1. Henderson B and Edwards JCW. *The Synovial Lining in Health and Disease.* (1987) Chapman and Hall.
2. Canoso JJ, Stack MT and Brandt K. Hyaluronic acid content of deep and subcutaneous bursae in man. (1983) *Ann. Rheum. Dis.* **42**, 171.
3. Key JA. *The synovial membrane of joints and bursae.* (1932) In special Cytology, II, 2nd edition., Paul B. Hoeber, New York, pp. 1055-76.
4. Van Furth R, Cohn ZA, Hirsch JG et al. The mononuclear phagocyte system. (1972) *Bull. World Health Org.,* **46**, 845.
5. Edwards JCW and Willoughby DA. Demonstration of bone marrow derived cells in synovial lining by means of giant intracellular granules as genetic markers. (1982) *Ann. Rheum. Dis.* **41**, 177.
6. Dreher R. Origin of synovial type A cells during inflammation. An experimental approach. (1982) *Immunobiol* **161**, 232.
7. *Personal communication,* P.A. Revell. Full publication in press 1987.
8. Ghadially FN. *Fine structure of synovial joints.* (1983) Butterworths, London.
9. Linck G, Stocker S, Grimaud JA and Porte A. Distribution of immunoreactive fibronectin and collagen (Type I. III. IV) in mouse joints. (1983) *Histochemistry,* **77**, 323.
10. Davies DV and Edwards DAW. The blood supply of the synovial membrane. (1948) *Ann. R. Coll. Surg. Eng.* **2**, 142.
11. Suter ER and Majno G. Ultrastructure of the joint capsule in the rat: presence of two kinds of capillaries. (1964) *Nature* **202**, 920.
12. Levick JR. *Synovial fluid and trans-synovial flow in stationary and moving normal joints.* In Articular cartilage and other intra-articular structures. (1987) Ed. H. Helminen. Pub. Wright, Potters Bar.
13. Schumacher HR. The microvasculature of the synovial membrane of the monkey: ultrastructural studies. (1969) *Arthr. Rheum.* XII, **4**, 387.
14 Jalkanen S, Steere AC, Fox RI and Butcher EC. A distinct endothelial cell recognition system that controls lymphocyte traffic into inflamed synovium. (1986) *Science.* **233**, 556-558.
15. Krane SM, Goldring SR and Dayer JM. Interactions among lymphocytes, monocytes and other synovial cells in the rheumatoid synovium. (1982) *Lymphokines* **7**, 75.
16. Castor CW, Roberts DJ, Hossler PA and Bignall MC. Connective tissue activation XXV. (1983) *Arthr. Rheum.* **26**, 522. (And preceding communications in this series.)
17. Fell HB and Jubb RW. The effect of synovial tissue on the breakdown of articular cartilage in organ culture. (1977) *Arthr. Rheum.* **20**, 1359.

January 1988

VIRAL AETIOLOGY OF ARTHRITIS

A M Denman
Head of the MRC Connective Tissue Diseases Research Group and Consultant Physician
Clinical Research Centre
Watford Road
Harrow
Middlesex

IDENTIFIABLE FORMS OF VIRAL ARTHRITIS

Short-lived monoarticular arthritis or polyarthritis commonly accompanies virus infections (1) (Table 1). The association with the characteristic clinical features of these infections usually makes the diagnosis easy to establish. Rising antibody titres are confirmatory especially when accompanied by detectable IgM antibody. Diagnostic difficulties may arise in infections where the arthritis precedes the appearance of other manifestations of infection; arthritis provoked by hepatitis A and B virus is a noteworthy example. With most virus infections the arthritis is rarely chronic or relapsing. Epidemics of acute viral arthritis have been recorded in areas where certain alphaviruses are endemic (2); these have been termed "O'Nyong'Nyong" in East Africa and "epidemic polyarthritis" in New South Wales and other parts of Australia. A viral cause is often suspected but not proven in patients with ephemeral arthritis. Retrospective diagnosis may be serologically possible as experience in "early synovitis" clinics has show. Some viruses which induce unusually severe or prolonged arthritis have attracted particular attention as possible causes of arthritis of unknown aetiology.

TABLE 1: VIRAL CAUSES OF ARTHRITIS (in order of current clinical importance)
rubella
parvovirus
alphaviruses (formerly arboviruses)
hepatitis A and B
echoviruses
coxsackieviruses
mumps
adenovirus
varicella zoster
Epstein-Barr virus
herpes simplex virus
cytomegalovirus
HIV?

RUBELLA VIRUS ARTHRITIS

Rubella virus provokes polyarthritis in 20-50% of adults after immunisation or natural infection (3). Usually the joint symptoms subside within 2-3 weeks but in some individuals persistent relapsing polyarthralgia or even overt polyarthritis ensues (4). However, it is exceptionally uncommon for patients with post-rubella arthritis to develop the characteristic joint or serological features of rheumatoid arthritis. Nevertheless, rubella virus infection has been incriminated in some forms of chronic arthritis in children and adults (5, 6). These patients have displayed neither rheumatoid factor nor progressive erosive disease. There is no compelling evidence incriminating rubella virus infection in most forms of chronic arthritis.

PARVOVIRUS INFECTION

Parvovirus infection provokes acute self-limited arthritis of large joints in both children and adults. Any association between chronic arthritis and parvovirus infection is problematical. In prospective studies patients with acute parvovirus arthritis have not developed chronic arthritis (7, 8). Serological evidence of recent parvovirus infection has been reported in two patients with rheumatoid arthritis (9) but this observation is the exception. Parvovirus has been reportedly isolated from a patient with severe rheumatoid arthritis, the agent eliciting a neurological disorder in neonatal mice (10). Polyclonal antibodies to the agent reacted with a synovial antigen unique to rheumatoid cells. These claims have not been confirmed.

EPSTEIN-BARR (EB) VIRUS

EBV has been implicated in the pathogenesis of rheumatoid arthritis almost solely on indirect grounds. A high percentage of patients have antibodies ("RANA") in high titre to a nuclear antigen expressed by EBV-infected cells but these antibodies are encountered in normal subjects (11). Moreover, RANA are detectable in rheumatoid arthritis patients lacking serological evidence of EBV infection (12). Nor is there any correlation between serological evidence of EBV infection and juvenile chronic arthritis (13).

There are also claims that host defence against EBV is aberrant in rheumatoid arthritis (Fig. 1). EBV principally establishes life-long infection of a small percentage of B lymphocytes. *In vitro* these cells give rise to lymphoblastoid cell lines. *In vitro* systems show that the proliferation of EBV-infected B cells is limited initially by interferons and non-specific cytotoxic cell populations and subsequently by specifically sensitized T lymphocytes. T cell immunity has been judged defective in rheumatoid arthritis because the *in vitro* proliferation of EBV-infected cells is inadequately opposed at all stages (14). Effective EBV-antibody production may also be impaired in some patients, the pattern of response resembling that noted in indisputable immuno-deficiency diseases (15). In consequence the *in vitro* synthesis of immunoglobulins by EBV infected lymphoblastoid cell lines is markedly different from other lines resulting particularly in the increased production of IgM. There is speculation that defective *in vivo* control of B cell proliferation leads to autoantibody production. However, a defective T cell response to EBV-infected B cells is not confined to rheumatoid arthritis and is noted in other forms of arthritis (17), ankylosing spondylitis (18) and scleroderma (19). There is a strong suspicion, therefore, that alleged abnormalities in handling EBV reflect non-specific disease activity rather than a defect peculiar to rheumatoid arthritis.

Fig. 1 Natural history of Epstein-Barr (EB) virus infection in relation to the rheumatic diseases

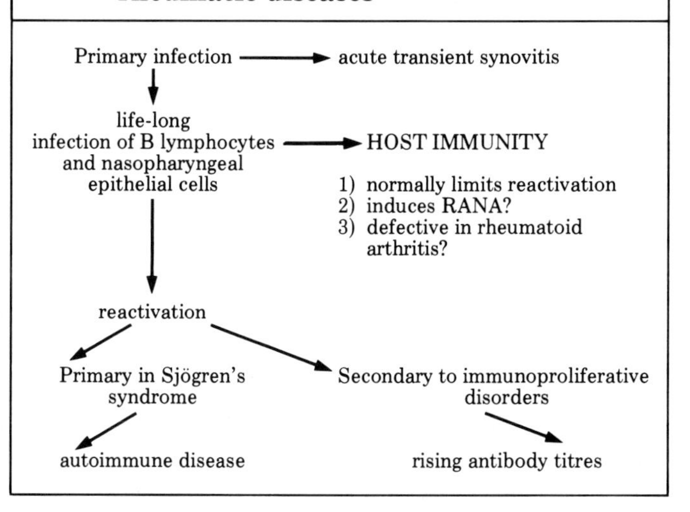

RETROVIRUS INFECTIONS

In most species retroviruses have been identified which induce malignant or immunodeficiency diseases. In addition, closely related lentiviruses have been detected which produce immunopathological disorders characterised by a long incubation period and slow progression. One such virus, caprine arthritis encephalitis virus (CAEV), produces immunoproliferative synovitis resembling rheumatoid arthritis in sheep and goats. Serological surveys indicate that asymptomatic infection is widespread although with marked national differences (20). The immunopathological events recall those encountered in the rheumatoid synovial membrane which in this instance stem from persistent infection (21, 22). The virus grows to low titre in certain macrophages, its replication being largely restricted by interferons produced by T lymphocytes in response to a factor secreted by infected macrophages. Interferons also induce Ia antigen expression by uninfected macrophages thereby attracting other lymphocyte populations.

In man also retroviruses have been identified which are responsible for leukaemias, lymphomas and immunodeficiency diseases. It is reasonable to predict, therefore, that agents analogous to CAEV cause immunopathological disorders. The close sequence homology between HIV and other lentiviruses emphasises that relatively minor structural differences influence the clinical features of infection (23, 24).

PATHOGENETIC MECHANISMS IN VIRAL ARTHRITIS

Elucidating the pathogenesis of the arthritis in recognised viral infections would be a useful step in searching for novel agents in arthritis of unknown aetiology. However, this has not proved a simple matter.

1) Local infection of joint cells

Local infection is the simplest explanation and is supported by isolating the infectious agent from synovial effusions (rubella virus) or identifying viral antigens in synovial effusion cells (arboviruses) synovial fluid (rubella virus, adenovirus) or synovial biopsies (hepatitis A and B virus). However, such observations do not establish that the responsible virus primarily infects cells peculiar to the synovial membrane or associated tissues. Rubella viral antigens have been detected in the chondrocytes of congenitally infected rabbits and so may have a special ability to grow in these cells (25). Rubella virus also persistently infects cultured human synovial cells (26).

Although infectious mononucleosis is occasionally associated with acute arthritis (Fig. 2), there is no evidence that EBV infects synovial cells. EBV-associated antigens have been detected in salivary gland biopsies from patients with Sjögren's syndrome but this also may represent non-specific viral reactivation (27).

2) Immune complexes

Viral antigens and anti-viral antibodies have been detected in immune complexes and cryoprecipitates in the serum and synovial effusions of patients with arthritis induced by arboviruses and rubella virus (28). However, it is difficult to determine whether preformed complexes reach the joints passively from the circulation or are formed *in situ* between locally synthesized antigens and antibodies generated locally or systemically.

3) Hypersensitivity reactions to viruses

Arthritis in viral infections is often associated with urticarial or other rashes and could be a manifestation of a systemic allergic response to disseminated virus. Thus most adults immunised with rubella virus are thought to be vulnerable to natural rubella infection because they lack anti-rubella antibodies detectable by standard screening techniques. Post-immunisation arthritis may develop predominantly in previously infected individuals whose antibodies can only be detected by more sensitive methods (29). If these antibodies only partially oppose viral replication sufficient viral antigen could be released to provoke a form of serum sickness arthritis.

4) Viral persistence in mononuclear cells

Many viruses persistently infect various lymphocyte and monocyte-macrophage populations. Arthritis could result from viral infection of such cells either resident in the synovial membrane or migrating there from the blood. Indeed, viral antigens have been detected in synovial monocytes in viral arthritis (30). Rubella virus has been identified in blood lymphocytes for up to eight years after infection and there is some correlation between persistent infection in this manner and chronic post-rubella arthritis in children and adults (4, 5). One can postulate that infected mononuclear cells migrating to the synovial membrane attract an immune attack by other lymphocytes.

DIRECT EVIDENCE FOR VIRAL INFECTION IN CHRONIC ARTHRITIS

There have been no convincing reproducible reports in any form of chronic synovitis of viral infections identified by classical isolation techniques or sophisticated methods for detecting viral products. Most earlier studies dealt with long-term fibroblast cultures established from synovial tissue and did not address more specialized synovial cells or infiltrating mononuclear cells (1). Recently freshly isolated or cultured lymphocytes and macrophages have been similarly investigated but with negative results (31). These include co-cultivation with cell lines susceptible to retroviruses screened for syncytia formation and reverse

Fig. 2 Arthritis in primary EBV infection

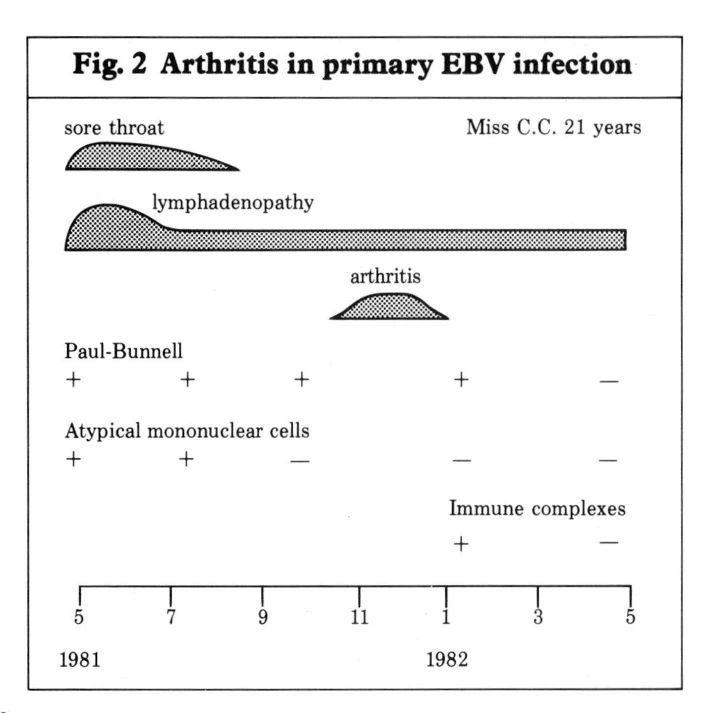

transcriptase production. Cytomegalovirus (CMV) has been isolated from cultured synovial cells of a patient with rheumatoid arthritis (32) but the latent CMV genome is present in several kinds of normal cell so that this observation is in itself of little significance. It must be stressed, however, that there has been little attempt to isolate and culture other synovial cell types with similar experiments in mind.

The genome of herpes simplex virus (HSV) has been detected in blood lymphocytes of patients with Behçet's syndrome (33) but the pathogenetic significance of this finding for arthritis and other disease features is unknown.

INDIRECT EVIDENCE FOR VIRAL INFECTION

Detecting local specific anti-viral responses in arthritic joints suggests, but does not prove, that these joints may harbour the provoking agent.

1) Local antibody responses

Higher antibody titres to HSV and respiratory syncytial virus are found in the synovial effusions of patients with seronegative arthritis or rheumatoid arthritis than in sera from the same patients (34). These findings do not constitute proof of local infection and may simply reflect local activation of B cells in a manner analogous to oligoclonal anti-viral antibody production in the CSF of patients with multiple sclerosis. In addition, there is evidence that synovial membrane and blood lymphocytes produce specific anti-influenza antibody equally briskly in response to systemic immunisation with influenza virus (35). There is no evidence that the immunising virus or related antigens localize to joints. Indeed, the well documented flares of arthritis secondary to intercurrent infections may result from the contribution of synovial lymphocyte populations to the systemic immune response (36).

2) Local lymphocyte responses

In vitro proliferative responses *in vitro* to viral antigens have been extensively investigated on the supposition that any enhanced responsiveness of synovial lymphocytes compared with blood lymphocytes may point to local infection by the stimulating agent. Support for this view comes from sequential studies of a patient with chronic polyarthritis attributed to rubella virus on the grounds that rubella virus could repeatedly be isolated from blood and synovial effusion lymphocytes; the joint lymphocytes consistently responded to *in vitro* challenge by rubella antigens (37). However, rheumatoid synovial lymphocytes respond to several viruses, the response often exceeding that induced in blood lymphocytes from the same patients (38, 39). These results are difficult to interpret because of the absence of any consistent pattern. Mumps virus for example induced a proliferative response by synovial lymphocytes regardless of the patients' clinical features. There is also a need to analyse a wider range of lymphocyte responses using well characterized viral antigens and assay systems. Evidently, too, these reactions may reflect systemic infections or immunological events unrelated to local infection. Thus, rheumatoid synovial lymphocytes commonly synthesize more alpha and gamma interferon *in vitro* than blood lymphocytes in response to viral stimulation, the pattern reflecting recent systemic infection by these viruses (40).

VIRUS-INDUCED AUTOIMMUNITY AND CHRONIC ARTHRITIS

Several theoretical mechanisms have been suggested by which virus infections might provoke auto-immune diseases (Table 2) (41). For these speculations to be relevant to the pathogenesis of chronic arthritis, it is necessary first to prove that autoimmunity contributes to the disease process and secondly to show that the autoimmune component is initiated or perpetuated by virus infection. There is still little evidence that the immunoproliferative reaction in rheumatoid or other forms of chronic synovitis is directed at local auto-

TABLE 2: POSTULATED MECHANISMS OF VIRUS-INDUCED AUTOIMMUNE DISEASE

Mechanism	Comments
1) Virus alters structure of host cell surface antigen whether expressed on surface (e.g. human receptors) or exported via cell membrane (e.g. hormones)	Little direct evidence in human disease but supported by experimental models
2) Virus alters rate of synthesis or expression of host antigen	No clinical evidence but shown in experimental models
3) Vertically transmitted viruses code for antigens expressed postnatally and therefore do not induce tolerance	Recent experimental evidence
4) Endogenous viral sequences activated when neighbouring genes transcribed, viral antigens are immunogenic	Experimental diabetes
5) Molecular mimicry: a) between host antigens and viral sequences b) between idiotypes of anti-viral antibodies and viral receptors	Sequence similarities identified and anti-idiotype antibodies induce experimental auto-immune diseases
6) Activation of immune system: a) virus grows in lymphocytes b) indirect activation by virus-induced mediators e.g. interferon-induced class 2 HLA antigens	EBV is good clinical and experimental example. Documented in organ-specific but could be secondary phenomenon
c) viral components directly activate lymphocytes	Established in HIV infections

antigens in a manner analogous with known organ-specific auto-immune diseases. Locally synthesized auto-antibodies and particularly rheumatoid factors may contribute to tissue damage but are of doubtful aetiological significance. It is even more speculative to invoke virus-induced auto-immunity although several attractive experimental models have been described.

GROWTH DISORDERS, VIRUS INFECTIONS AND ARTHRITIS

Persistent synovitis can be viewed as an abnormal proliferative disorder associated with a local immune response. Local production of several growth factors has been detected but whether these play a primary or secondary role is uncertain. Viruses could contribute to disordered growth in several ways. Abnormal growth could be initiated by the activation of proto-oncogenes with sequence homology for retroviruses either from mutation or the integration of exogenous retroviral sequences. However, the interpretation of proto-oncogene activation and expression is complicated by the realisation that these genes normally regulate cell division and differentiation (42). Thus, whilst unusually high levels of RNA transcription from some proto-oncogenes have been found in blood lymphocytes of patients with SLE, these changes may simply reflect a proliferative response to an unknown stimulus rather than a primary abnormality (43, 44). There is evidence in one animal model that susceptibility to an autoimmune disease is dependent on retrovirus gene activation (45, 46). Insulin dependent diabetes appears to develop in genetically susceptible inbred mouse strains because hyperglycaemia activates transcription from the preproinsulin gene complex. This also activates transcription of a neighbouring endogenous retroviral gene sequence which codes for the expression of a membrane antigen and which may initiate a T cell response.

CONCLUSIONS

1) Known virus infections of joints produce self-limited arthritis but there is little evidence that these viruses are involved in the pathogenesis of chronic arthritis.

2) Direct attempts to isolate viruses from chronically arthritic joints have been almost universally fruitless.
3) Indirect attempts to incriminate viruses in the pathogenesis of chronic arthritis have produced suggestive but not persuasive evidence.
4) Virus-induced autoimmune mechanisms are theoretically attractive but of unproven relevance.
5) Interactions between exogenous infections and genes regulating growth could contribute to the abnormal proliferative events characteristic of rheumatoid arthritis and related disorders.

REFERENCES

1. Phillips PE. Infectious agents in the pathogenesis of rheumatoid arthritis. *Seminars in Arthritis and Rheumatism* 1986; **16:** 1-10.
2. Bennett PH. Ross River virus infection – an acute polyarthritis caused by arbovirus. *J Rheum,* 1983; suppl. No. **10:** 34-6.
3. Tingle AJ, Allen M, Petty RE, Kettyls GD, Chantler JK. Rubella-associated arthritis. I. Comparative study of joint manifestations associated with natural rubella infection and RA 27/3 rubella immunisation. *Ann Rheum Dis* 1986; **45:** 110-14.
4. Tingle AJ, Chantler JK, Pot KH, Paty DW, Ford DK. Postpartum rubella immunisation: association with development of prolonged arthritis, neurological sequelae, and chronic rubella viraemia. *J Infect Dis* 1985, **152:** 606-12.
5. Chantler JK, Tingle AJ, Petty RE. Persistent rubella virus infection associated with chronic arthritis in children. *N Eng J Med* 1985; **313:** 1117-23.
6. Grahame R, Armstrong R, Simmons N, Wilton, JMA, Dyson M, Laurent R, Millis R, Mims CA. Chronic arthritis associated with the presence of intrasynovial rubella virus. *Ann Rheum Dis.* 1983; **42:** 2-13.
7. Reid DM, Reid TMS, Brown T, Rennie JAN, Eastmond CJ. Human parvovirus-associated arthritis: a clinical and laboratory description. *Lancet* 1985; **i:** 422-25.
8. White DG, Woolf AD, Mortimer PP, Cohen BJ, Blake DR, Bacon PA. Human parvovirus arthropathy. *Lancet* 1985: **i:** 419-21.
9. Cohen BJ, Buckley MM, Clewley JP, Jones VE, Puttick AH, Jacoby RK. Human parvovirus infection in early rheumatoid and inflammatory arthritis. *Ann Rheum Dis* 1986 **45:** 832-8.
10. Simpson RW, McGinty L, Simon L, Smith CA, Godzeski CW, Boyd RJ. Association of parvoviruses with rheumatoid arthritis of humans *Science* 1984: **223:** 1425-8.
11. Catalano M, Carson DA, Slovin SF, Richman DD, Vaughan JH. Antibodies to Epstein-Barr virus determined antigens in normal subjects and in patients with seropositive rheumatoid arthritis. *Proc. Natl. Acad. Sci. USA.* 1979; **76:** 5825-8.
12. Ferrell PB, Aitcheson CT, Pearson GR, Tan EM. Sero-epidemiological study of relationships between Epstein-Barr virus and rheumatoid arthritis. *J Clin Invest* 1981; **67:** 681-7.
13. Gear AJ, Venables PJW, Edwards JMB, Maini RN, Ansell BM. Rheumatoid arthritis, juvenile arthritis, iridocyclitis and Epstein-Barr virus. *Ann Rheum Dis.* 1986; **45:** 6-8.
14. McChesney MB, Bankhurst AD. Cytotoxic mechanisms in vitro against Epstein-Barr virus infected lymphoblastoid cell lines in rheumatoid arthritis. *Ann Rheum Dis.* 1986; **45:** 546-52.
15. Cohen JHM, Vischer TL, Carquin J, Blanchard F. A subset of rheumatoid arthritis patients with a pattern of Epstein-Barr virus antibodies similar to that found in primary and secondary immunodeficiency diseases. *Arth Rheum* 1985; **28:** 39-40.
16. Irving WL,Walker PR, Lydyard PM. Abnormal responses of rheumatoid arthritis lymphocytes to Epstein-Barr virus infection in vitro: evidence for multiple defects. *Ann Rheum Dis* 1985; **44:** 462-8.
17. Gaston JSH, Rickinson AB, Yao QY, Epstein MA. The abnormal cytotoxic T cell response to Epstein-Barr virus in rheumatoid arthritis is correlated with disease activity and occurs in other arthropathies. *Ann Rheum Dis* 1986; **45:** 932-936.
18. Robinson S and Panayi GS. Deficient control of in vitro Epstein-Barr virus infection in patients with ankylosing spondylitis. *Ann Rheum Dis* 1986; **45:** 974-77.
19. Kahan A, Kahan A, Kenkes CJ, Amor B. Defective Epstein-Barr virus specific suppressor T cell function in progressive systemic sclerosis. *Ann Rheum Dis* 1986; **45:** 553-560.
20. Dawson M, Wilesmith JW. Serological survey of lentivirus (maedi-visna/caprine arthritis encephalitis) infection in British goat herds. *Vet Rec* 1985; **117:** 86-9.
21. Narayan O, Sheffer D, Clements JE, Tennekoon G. Restricted replication of lentivirus. *J Exp Med* 1985; **162:** 1954-69.
22. Kennedy PGE, Narayan O, Ghotbi Z. Hopkins J, Gendelman HE, Clements JE. Persistent expression of Ia antigen and viral genome in visna-maedi virus-induced inflammatory .... *J Exp Med* 1985; **162:** 1970-82.
23. Gonda MA, Braun MJ, Clements JE, Pyper JM, Wong-Staal F, Gallo RC, Gilden RV. Human T-cell lymphotropic virus type III share sequence homology with a family of pathogenic lentiviruses. *Proc Nat Acad Sci (USA)* 1986; **83:** 4007-11.
24. Pyper JM, Clements JE, Gonda MA, Narayan O. Sequence homology between cloned caprine arthritis encephalitis virus and visna virus, two neurotropic viruses. *J Virol* 1986; **58:** 665-70.
25. London WT, Fuccillo DA, Anderson B, Seyer JL. Concentration of rubella virus in chondrocytes of rabbits congenitally infected with rubella. *Nature* 1970; **226:** 172-3.
26. Cunningham AL, Fraser JRE. Persistent rubella virus infection of human synovial cells cultured in vitro. *J Infect Dis* 1985; **151:** 638-45.
27. Fox RI, Pearson G, Vaughan JH. Detection of Epstein-Barr virus-associated antigens and DNA in salivary gland biopsies from patients with Sjögren's syndrome. *J Immunol* 1986; **137:** 3162-8.
28. Fraser JRE, Cunningham AL, Clarris BJ, Askov JG, Leach R. Cytology of synovial effusion in epidemic polyarthritis. *Aus. NZ J Med* 1981; **11:** 168-73.
29. Tingle AJ, Kettyls GD. Rubella arthritis induced by vaccination. *Infect Immun* 1983; **40:** 22-8.
30. Ansell BM. *Infective arthritis.* In: Copeman's Textbook of Rheumatic Diseases, edit. JT Scott. 6th edition. Churchill Livingstone, 1986; 1137-61.
31. Pelton BK, North M, Palmer RG, Hylton W, Smith-Burchnell C, Sinclair AL, Malkovsky M, Dalgleish AG, Denman AM. A search for retrovirus infection in SLE and RA. **(in preparation)**
32. Hamerman D, Greser I, Smith C. Isolation of cytomegalovirus from synovial cells of a patient with rheumatoid arthritis. *J Rheum* 1982; **9:** 658-64.
33. Bonass WA, Bird-Stewart JA, Chamberlain MA, Halliburton IW. *Molecular studies in Behçet's syndrome.* In: Recent Advances in Behçet's Disease, International Congress and Symposium Series No. 183 edit. Lehner T. Barnes CG, Royal Society of Medicine Services, pp.37-42.
34. Mims CA, Stokes A, Grahame R. Synthesis of antibodies, including antiviral antibodies, in the knee joints of patients with arthritis. *Ann Rheum Dis.* 1985; **44:** 734-6.
35. Pelton BK, Harvey AR, Denman AM. The rheumatoid synovial membrane participates in systemic anti-viral immune responses. *Clin Exp Immun* 1985; **62:** 657-61.
36. De Vere-Tyndall A, Bacon T, Parry R, Tyrrell DAJ, Denman AM, Ansell BM. Infection and interferon production in systemic juvenile chronic arthritis: a prospective study. *Ann Rheum Dis* 1984; **43:** 1-7.
37. Chantler JK, Da Roza DM, Bonnie ME, Reid GD, Ford DK. Sequential studies on synovial lymphocyte stimulation by rubella antigen, and rubella virus isolation in an adult with persistent arthritis. *Ann Rheum Dis* 1985; **44:** 564-8.
38. Ford DK,Da Roza DM, Reid GD. Chantler JM, Tingle AJ. Synovial mononuclear cell responses to rubella antigen in rheumatoid arthritis and unexplained persistent knee arthritis. *J Rheum* 1982; **9:** 420-3.
39. Ford DK, Da Roza DM. Further observations on the response of synovial lymphocytes to viral antigens in rheumatoid arthritis. *J Rheum* 1986; **13:** 113-7.
40. **In preparation.**
41. Oldstone MBA, Notkins AL. *Molecular mimicry.* In: Concepts in viral pathogenesis. II ed. Notkins AL, Oldstone MBA. Springer Verlag 1986; pp 195-202.
42. Kaczmarek L. Proto-oncogene expression during the cell cycle. *Lab Invest* 1986; **54:** 365-76.
43. Boumpas DT, Tsokos GC, Eleftheriades EG, Harris CC, Mark GE. Increased proto-oncogene expression in peripheral blood lymphocytes from patients with systemic lupus erythematosus and other autoimmune diseases. *Arth Rheum* 1986; **29:** 755-60.
44. Klinman DM, Mushinski JR, Honda M, Ishigatsubo Y, Mountz JD, Raveche ES, Steinberg AD. Oncogene expression in autoimmune and normal peripheral blood mononuclear cells. *J Exp Med* 1986; **163:** 1292-1307.
45. Leiter EH. Type C retrovirus production by pancreatic beta cells. *Am J Path* 1985; **119:** 22-32.
46. Leiter EH, Fewell JW, Kuff EL. Glucose induces intracisternal type A retroviral gene transcription and translation in pancreatic beta cells. *J Exp Med* 1986; **163:** 87-100.

September 1987

THE IMMUNOGENETICS OF RHEUMATOID ARTHRITIS

G S Panayi
ARC Professor of Rheumatology
Guy's Hospital
London

K I Welsh
Senior Lecturer in Molecular Genetics
Guy's Hospital
London

Rheumatoid arthritis (RA) is a disease whose aetiopathogenesis involves genetic and environmental factors. Regrettably, there has been very little progress in understanding the environmental factors. However, recent investigations have considerably advanced our knowledge of genetic susceptibility. Analysis of HLA linkage in multicase families with RA has suggested that genes outside the major histocompatibility complex (MHC) may be important (1). We shall review the contribution of both MHC and non-MHC genes to the development of RA.

THE CONTRIBUTION OF MHC GENES TO THE DEVELOPMENT OF RA

The application of serological, biochemical and molecular biological techniques has revealed the complexity of the HLA-D region located on the short arm of the sixth chromosome (Figure 1). In Figure 1[A] is shown the general arrangement of genes coding for the three types of MHC products, while Figure 1[B] shows a detailed map of the HLA-D region which is of immediate concern. This is subdivided into three regions: HLA-DP (most centromeric), HLA-DQ and HLA-DR. Each region consists of alpha and beta genes whose products associate at the cell membrane to form an alpha/beta heterodimer. This heterodimer is employed in presenting antigen to T cells which are then stimulated to mount an appropriate immune response.

The classical, serologically defined specificities HLA-DR1 . . . DR14 are heterodimers of the products of the DR beta and alpha genes. The initial HLA association

Figure 1. ***THE STRUCTURE OF THE HUMAN MHC REGION ON CHROMOSOME 6.***

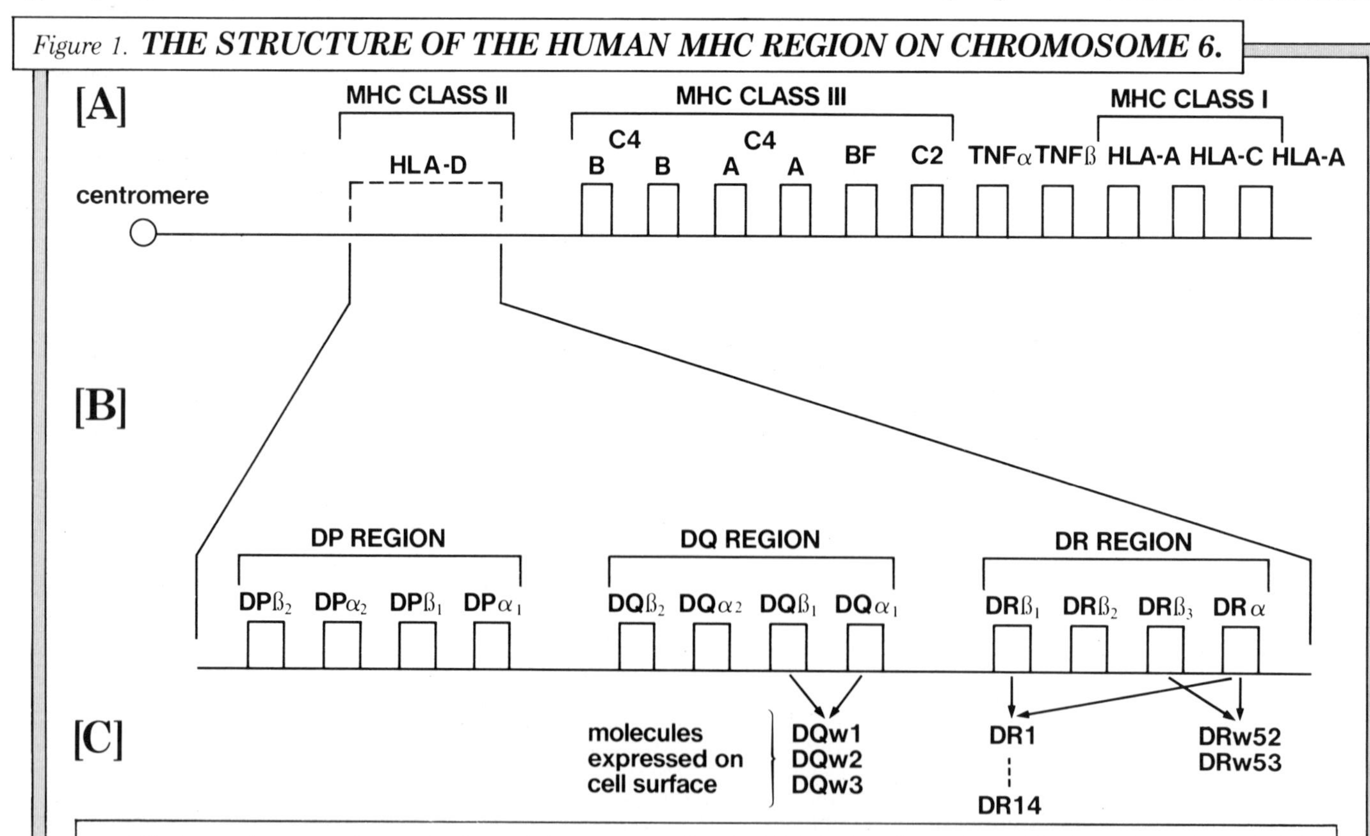

[A] shows the general organisation of the genes coding for MHC class I products (HLA-A, -B and -C), MHC class II products (HLA-D) and for MHC class III (complement components C4A, C4B, BF and C2). Note the presence of the tumor necrosis factor genes.

[B] shows a detailed map of the HLA-D region which has been simplified for clarity. The nomenclature employed is that recently recommended at the 10th International Histocompatibility Workshop.

[C] shows the associations of different alpha and beta chains which associate at the cell surface to form the serologically defined markers of relevance to RA.

with RA was, of course, HLA-DR4 (2,3). However, not all patients with RA are DR4 positive and in some populations (Israeli Jews, Indians, Spanish), RA is linked to HLA-DR1 rather than DR4. HLA-DR4 is linked to HLA-DRw53 which is a serologic specificity recognising a DR beta 3/DR alpha heterodimer. The additional serological marker for the extended DR4 haplotype is DQw3 which recognises a DQ beta/DQ alpha heterodimer.

How can one account for those cases of RA which are not linked to DR4? Class II MHC products can be defined by a mixed lymphocyte reaction (MLR) in which T lymphocytes proliferate to allogeneic DR antigens. Using homozygous typing cells as stimulators, it is possible to subdivide DR4 into a number of Dw MLR subtypes (Table 1). It is of interest to note that the Dw10 subtype, which is the predominant subtype found in Israeli Jews, is not a RA susceptibility subtype. How can one account for those cases of RA which are linked to DR1? Scrutiny of published DR1 sequences shows that they are identical to the Dw14 subtype of DR4 (4). Thus, one can postulate that shared epitopes on class II molecules (DR4, DR1) may confer susceptibility to RA. It is known that these epitopes reside on the third hypervariable region of DR beta 1 in a helical region that is critical for T cell recognition.

TABLE 1

MLR subtypes (Dw), ethnic origin and susceptibility to rheumatoid arthritis in HLA-DR4 positive individuals.

MLR subtype	Ethnic origin	susceptibility to RA
Dw4	White	+
Dw10	Jewish/Indian	–
Dw13	White	?
Dw14	White	+
Dw15	Japanese	+

\+ susceptible
– not susceptible

Support for this hypothesis comes from three sources. First, the aminoacid sequence homology between susceptibility Dw subtypes in the third hypervariable region of the DR beta molecule. Second, the derivation of T cell clones from MLR cultures specific for the Dw14 subtype which can recognise the Dw14 associated epitope on non-DR4 haplotypes (for example, DR1 positive) in patients with RA (5). Third, the monoclonal antibody 109d6 recognises an epitope encoded by a third hypervariable region sequence which is found preferentially in patients with RA whether DR4 or DR1 positive (4,6).

More recently, the HLA-DQw3.1 allele has been described as an additional susceptibility gene in patients with Felty's syndrome as well as DR4 positive patients with RA (8). However, in Japanese RA patients the DQw allele linked to DR4 is newly defined and different from the DQ beta linked to the DR4 haplotypes found in whites. This may mean that DQ beta is not directly related to susceptibility to develop RA.

THEORETICAL CONSIDERATION OF THE INFLUENCES OF MHC GENETIC MARKERS IN RA

In twin studies there is around 48% concordance of the disease in identical twins and around 10% in non-identical twins. This sets the upper limit of the potential ability of the pure genetic definition of "at-risk" (i.e. 48% of those defined as at risk will get RA). A very approximate influence of the MHC (excluding DP) can be assessed by studying the coincidence of the disease in HLA similar and HLA disparate non-identical twins, or by studying the coincidence of the disease in HLA similar and HLA disparate siblings of the probands in multi-case families. The findings are that around 17% of MHC "similar" and 5% of MHC "disparate" siblings will contract RA. Similar analyses can, of course, be carried out for assessing the influence of the sex of the individual, but there is insufficient data to apply the process to other genetic areas of interest.

What does the data from the MHC studies alone tell us? The difference between 48% and 17% is probably due to at least 3 contributing factors. Firstly, non MHC genes, which are shared in the identical twins but to a lesser extent in the other groups must play a considerable role in susceptibility. The two other candidates with a proven role are sex related and immunoglobulin genes (8,9). Secondly, those MHC region genes which were not known at the time of the original studies and are not in close linkage disequilibrium with the HLA-DR region, may play a significant role in susceptibility. Thirdly, there is the role of environmental factors. The upper limit of 48% on genetic determination proves the influence of the environment. It is probable that identical twins share a more similar environment than non-identical twins or normal siblings. The overall importance of the environment can also be illustrated by the elegant studies on the Xhosa tribe in South Africa. Tribal members have a high genetic susceptibility to the disease, but those living in their home village environment have a low or zero incidence of RA whilst those who have moved into the Soweto township for work have a prevalence similar to that of Northern Europeans.

Hence, genetic and environmental influences are closely linked and of approximately equal importance in the determination of the at-risk group. Further it appears that the MHC, followed by sex-linked genes, followed by IgH region genes, are, in that order, the major genetic factors. There may be several initiating agents which can activate a common disease process. This activation process may be under relatively tight genetic control.

NON-MHC GENES AND THE DEVELOPMENT OF RA

The role of non-MHC genes in the development of RA is supported not only by HLA-linkage studies in multi-case RA families but also by studies of families in which RA co-exists with autoimmune thyroid disease (10). These non-MHC genes could be immune or non-immune related; amongst the former may be included genes linked to immunoglobulins, complement and the T cell receptor, but no information is available regarding the latter.

(a) **Sex**

There is a 3:1 female-to-male ratio in RA and a proven influence of pregnancy on the disease process. There is, however, very little evidence to indicate why this is so. Using an argument, originally based on left-handedness, it has been proposed that autoimmune disease with a female bias might be influenced early in development by a testosterone linked process (11). In simple terms, the development of parts of the brain and the thymus can be influenced by testosterone levels. Females may therefore stand a higher chance of low-testosterone linked abnormal development processes. For example, the average female would be expected to have a poorer thymus-dependent induced tolerance to self than the average male. It has been well documented that many RA patients go into remission during pregnancy. However, although hormonal levels are important in autoimmune processes and RA can be significantly modulated during pregnancy, the reasons behind the increased susceptibility to RA in females are not accurately defined at present.

(b) **Immunoglobulin genes**

Genes coding for immunoglobulin heavy chains and for K and L chains are found on chromosomes 14, 2 and 22 respectively. No evidence is available regarding the involvement of K or L genes in susceptibility to RA (8). By the use of restriction fragment length polymorphism (RFLP), we and other colleagues (9,12) have produced

Figure 2. ***DIAGRAM OF THE HUMAN GENE IgH REGION ON CHROMOSOME 14q.***

The vertical rectangles (▌) represent the indicated genes; before each constant region genes (C) there is a switch region (S). Each switch region is designated according to the C gene which it regulates eg $S\mu$, $S\alpha$, and so on.

evidence that genes linked to the loci for the immunoglobulin constant region may influence susceptibility to RA. There are no clear-cut associations between Gm allotypes, genetic markers on the Fc molecule of the immunoglobulin heavy chain (IgH), and RA. However, the ability to analyse gene linkage at the DNA level by RFLP analysis has been used by Sakkas and colleagues (9) to study the role of IgH in disease susceptibility. The genetic structure of the IgH region, found to be telomeric on the long arm of the 14th chromosome, is shown in Figure 2. Two DNA probes were used, one for the switch region and another for the polymorphic marker D14S1. It was found that RA was significantly linked with the S alpha 1 and D14S1 regions. The tentative conclusion from this work is that a disease susceptibility locus must be located somewhere between these two regions. The fact that protein polymorphism studies using Gm allotypes and alpha-1-antitrypsin have, at best, given conflicting results suggests that the genetic susceptibility locus residing in this part of the 14q chromosome may be coding for a hitherto unsuspected disease susceptibility factor.

(c) **T cell receptor genes**

The T cell receptor (TcR) is a dimeric structure consisting of alpha and beta chains whose genes are located on different chromosomes. Using RFLP analysis with TcR alpha and TcR beta constant region probes no association with RA was found (12). Further work is needed using a variety of TcR probes and restriction endonucleases before it can be concluded that TcR genes are not involved in disease susceptibility to RA.

COMPLEMENT GENES

The MHC Class III genes (see Figure 1) coding for C4A, C4B, and C2 and their products have not been linked to RA. However, the BFss phenotype has been linked to seropositive RA (13).

SUMMARY AND CONCLUSIONS

Our knowledge of the molecular basis of the HLA-DR association with susceptibility to RA is now at the level of single amino acid substitutions and their possible effects on T cell function. Future developments will be directed at delineating the role of non-MHC genes in disease susceptibility. There is no general case for widespread clinical application of genetic marker determinations in RA at present, but the rate of advance in the field suggests that there is a case for its restricted applicability.

May 1988

REFERENCES

1. Go RCP, Alarçon GS, Acton RT, Koopman WJ, Vittor VJ, Barger BO (1987). Analysis of HLA linkage in white families with multiple cases of seropositive rheumatoid arthritis. *Arthritis Rheum*, **30,** 1115-1123.
2. Stastny P (1978) Association of B cell alloantigen DRw4 with rheumatoid arthritis. *N Engl J Med*, **298,** 869-871.
3. Panayi GS, Wooley PH (1977). B lymphocyte alloantigens in the study of the genetic basis of rheumatoid arthritis. *Ann Rheum Dis* **36,** 365-368.
4. Bell JI, Esters P., St John T, Saiki R, Watling D, Erlich HA, McDevitt HO (1985). DNA sequence and characterisation of human class II major histocompatibility complex beta chains from the DR1 haplotype. *Proc Natl Acad Sci (USA)* **82,** 3405-3409.
5. Goronzy J, Weyand CM, Fathman CG (1986). Shared T cell recognition sites on human histocompatibility leucocyte antigen class II molecules of patients with seropositive rheumatoid arthritis. *J Clin Invest* **77,** 1042-1049.
6. Lee SH, Gregersen PK, Shen HH, Winchester RJ (1987). Strong association of rheumatoid arthritis with the presence of a polymorphic Ia epitope defined by a monoclonal antibody: comparison with the allodeterminant DR4. *Rheumatol Int (suppl)* **4,** 17-23.
7. Singal DP, D'Souza M, Reid B, Bensen WG, Kassam YB, Adachi JD (1987). HLA-DQ beta-chain polymorphism in HLA-DR4 haplotypes associated with rheumatoid arthritis. *Lancet*, **2,** 1118-1120.
8. Sidebottom D, Grennan DM, Sanders PA, Read A (1987). Immunoglobulin lambda light chain genes in rheumatoid arthritis. *Ann Rheum Dis* **46,** 587-589.
9. Sakkas L, Demaine AG, Vaughan RW, Welsh KI, Panayi GS (1988). The association of DNA variants at or near the IgH locus with rheumatoid arthritis. *J. Immunogenetics*, **In press.**
10. Grennan DM, Dyer PA, Claque R, Dodds W, Smeaton I, Harris R (1983). Family studies in RA – the importance of HLA-DR4 and of genes for auto-immune thyroid disease. *J Rheumatol* **10,** 584-589.
11. Geschwind N **(1984)** *Immunological Association of Cerebral Dominence in Neuroimmunology*, eds P Bihun & F Spreaffiv, Raven Press, New York.
12. Sakkas L, Demaine AG, Welsh KI, Panayi GS (1987). Restriction fragment length polymorphisms for T cell receptor alpha and beta chain genes in rheumatoid arthritis. *Arthritis Rheum* **30,** 231-232.
13. Lanchbury JSS, Pal B, Papiha SS (1987). BF and C3 polymorphism in rheumatoid arthritis. *Human Hered.* **37,** 144-149.

MECHANISMS OF AUTOIMMUNITY

D A Isenberg
Professor of Rheumatology
Bloomsbury Rheumatology Unit
University College & Middlesex School of Medicine
Arthur Stanley House
50 Tottenham Street
London W1P 9PG

INTRODUCTION

Autoimmune disease exacts a heavy toll. Approximately one individual in forty will suffer from such a condition and the economic costs arising from them are staggering. It has been estimated, for example, that in the United States alone rheumatoid arthritis causes an annual economic deficit of approximately 1 billion dollars. Although this review will focus on the autoimmune rheumatic diseases, potential targets for autoimmune attack are to be found all over the body as Table 1 indicates. It is clear that autoimmune diseases arise as a result of the interaction between a variety or mosaic of factors, including inherited, hormonal and environmental (1). Whereas most of the factors associated with autoimmune diseases seem now to be defined and will be discussed in turn, much remains to be determined about precisely how they interact and give rise to disease.

A key issue for the immune system of any organism is to be able to distinguish between self components and foreign material. The ability to 'tolerate' self tissue is the result of a very sophisticated mechanism whose basis is not fully elucidated. It is evident that for an antigen to be tolerated it must encounter the lymphocytes, at a particular stage of their ontogeny. T cells and the thymus are clearly central to this mechanism. A detailed review of the mechanisms involved in T cell clonal anergy and deletion is found elsewhere (2). A breakdown in tolerance to self antigens in the presence of other factors appears to allow the development of a self destructive autoimmune disease.

GENETIC FACTORS

Genes encode MHC (major histocompatibility complex) determinants, complement components, antibody variable region genes, and the T cell receptors each of which may predispose to autoimmunity. The MHC genes play a significant role in most autoimmune diseases. The MHC links with rheumatoid arthritis have been the focus of particular attention (reviewed in 3). The HLA-DR4 and DR1 MHC alleles, especially the Dw14 and Dw4 subtypes of DR4 and the Dw1 subtype of DR1 are, in particular, associated with rheumatoid. These subtypes contain a

Table I.
POTENTIAL TARGETS FOR AUTOIMMUNE ATTACK

Organic Specific Autoimmune diseases	Overlapping Autoimmune Diseases	Systemic Autoimmune Diseases
Endocrine		
Type 1 (insulin dependent)	Dermatomyositis	Systemic lupus erythematosus
Diabetes mellitus	(skin and muscle)	Sjögren's syndrome
Addison's disease	Goodpasture's syndrome	Scleroderma
	(lungs and kidney)	Rheumatoid arthritis
		Wegener's granulomatosis
Haemotological		
Autoimmune thrombocytopenia		
Autoimmune neutropenia		
Pernicious anaemia		
('warm type' or cold		
agglutinin disease)		
Dermatological		
Pemphigus		
Pemphigoid		
Neuromuscular		
Myasthenia Gravis		
Multiple sclerosis		
Autoimmune polyneuritis		

Table 2.
GENES ASSOCIATED WITH SLE

WITH THE DISEASE ITSELF		WITH ITS AUTOANTIBODIES	
MHC Class II		**MHC class II**	
HLA A1, B8, DR3	- in Caucasians	HLA-DQα (glutamine position 34)	Ro and La
(relative risk - 10x approx.)		HLA-DQβ (leucine position 26) (DQw2.1; DQw6 DQw8; DQw4)	Ro and La
HLA DR2	- in Japanese		
Tumour necrosis factor α		HLA -DQβ (positions 71-77; DQw7,8,9,6)	Lupus anti-coagulant
		HLA-DQw6 (DQA1*0102 and DQB1*0602)	Sm
MHC Class III		HLA-DQw5 and DQw8	nRNP
C4A null alleles (hetero and homozygous)		HLA-DQB1 *0201 (DR3 linked) *0602 (DR2 linked) *0302 (linked to some DR4s)	dsDNA
Complete C4 deficiency (rare)			
T cell receptor		**T cell receptor**	
TCRα polymorphism		TCRβ	Ro

unique sequence of amino acids in the third hypervariable region of the ß1 chains (4). Caucasians who are A1 B8 DR3 positive are approximately 10 times more likely to develop systemic lupus erythematosus (SLE), than those who lack this set of HLA antigens (5). It has been suggested that the association of DR3 with lupus is related to its being in linkage disequilibrium with a null allele of C4A (in Caucasian populations at least). Homozygous deficiency of other complement genes are strikingly associated with lupus, lupus-like or other autoimmune disorders (6). Recent studies have also shown association of MHC class II genes with SLE and the expression of particular autoantibodies. These are reviewed in Table 2 and elsewhere (7).

The links between particular T cell receptor genes and autoimmunity are also being scrutinised. The T cell receptor (TCR) recognizing MHC molecules and antigen has been isolated and partially characterized. The antigen recognition unit comprises two disulphide linked subunits. Four distinct receptor genes, termed alpha, beta, gamma and delta encode these units. In most T cells the receptor contains a clonally distributed alpha-beta heterodimer while 1-10% contain a gamma-delta heterodimer (3). On theoretical grounds, it is likely that multiple TCR's may bind the same MHC molecules. The majority of work in this area has been undertaken in animal models of autoimmune diseases. For example, a major deletion of the T cell receptor Vß locus has been identified in the New Zealand White (NZW) mouse and this has been linked to the production of IgG anti-DNA antibodies in the New Zealand Black /NZW F1 lupus prone strain (8). More recently, in an analysis of T cell clones from patients with lupus nephritis (9) it was shown that these clones had limited diversity in their γδ TCR junctional regions, rather resembling the foetal γδ thymocytes early in ontogeny. However, most studies (though not all, see ref 7) using restriction fragment length polymorphisms (RFLP) and TCR constant region probes have shown no definite association with SLE. Similar discordant results have been reported in patients with rheumatoid arthritis. Thus an increased usage of Vß6, Vß13.2 and Vß14 have been described by various investigators (3). Further studies on much larger numbers of patients are awaited.

HORMONES

The notable preponderance of females in patients with virtually all autoimmune disorders indicates that the sex hormones must have a major 'permissive' role in stimulating the development of clinically overt disease. Sex hormones, via surface receptors on lymphocytes, can act directly on T cells especially those carrying the cytotoxic/suppressor phenotype. Oestrogen tends to inhibit these cells allowing increasing antibody production by B cells.

Abnormal oestrogen metabolism with a bias to the overproduction of oestrogens (and reduced androgen levels) has been found in lupus patients (reviewed in 2). Oral contraceptives with a high oestrogen content can exacerbate lupus, and postmenopausal women treated with hormone replacement are in danger of reactivating their disease. Paradoxically the balance of evidence suggests that oral contraceptives may protect against the development of rheumatoid arthritis (10). Sex hormones may thus modify immune responses.

The effects of pregnancy on autoimmune diseases are much more varied. Approximately three-quarters of patients with rheumatoid arthritis go into remission (but invariably relapse within a few weeks of parturition). In contrast, lupus patients may present during pregnancy or develop an exacerbation during pregnancy or the puerperium. However, most lupus patients (except those with renal disease) go through pregnancy without any untoward event, and on balance pregnancy in a lupus patient is a much greater threat to the foetus than to the mother.

It is also evident that both thymic hormones and vitamin D may affect the immune system. Vitamin D, for example, apart from its critical role in maintaining the plasma calcium level, is capable of inhibiting immunoglobulin production and B cell proliferation, regulating thymocyte proliferation and has major effects on both monocyte and macrophage function. Intriguingly it appears able to induce heat shock protein synthesis in monocytes.

AUTOANTIBODIES

Suggestions in the early part of this century by Paul Ehrlich and his colleagues to the effect that the immune system responds to foreign antigens but not to self antigens have had to be substantially revised. It is now clear that most individuals have the capacity to produce a range of autoantibodies (generally termed 'natural' antibodies). The binding specificities of such autoantibodies are usually directed against highly conserved molecules including cytochrome C, transferrin, myelin, actin, nucleic acids and cytoplasmic filaments. A number of hypotheses have been put forward as to their function, including suggestions that they play a role in disposing of degraded autoantigens, and that they prevent damaging autoimmunisation by blinding the immune system to environmental epitopes that cross react with autoantigens.

What is not clear is the precise relationship between natural autoantibodies and pathogenic autoantibodies. Whereas the former tend to be of the IgM isotype the latter are usually IgG, but whether the latter autoantibodies develop from the former by isotype switching or are separately derived is uncertain.

The appearance of certain autoantibodies is usually closely associated with the development of the autoimmune disease. These autoantibodies may be identified in pathogenic lesions associated with the disease, eg antibodies to DNA in the lupus kidney, antibodies to La (an RNA/protein combination) in the labial biopsy of Sjögren's patients, and their serum levels may fluctuate with disease activity. More direct evidence of the contribution of pathogenic autoantibodies to the disease process in man is harder to come by for obvious ethical reasons. Examples do however exist. Thus antibodies to platelet surface and red blood cell surface antigens are responsible for autoimmune thrombocytopenia and autoimmune haemolytic anaemia respectively. Neonatal lupus is strongly associated with the passage of autoantibodies to La or Ro (an RNA/protein combination) across the placenta. Neonatal myasthenia gravis due to antibodies to the acetyl choline receptor may also occur in this way.

A major issue in the past few years has been to try and determine whether patients with autoimmune diseases carry disease specific V genes encoding autoantibodies. Alternatively do at least some germline genes encode for autoantibodies? It has now been very clearly demonstrated that germline genes may indeed encode for autoantibodies, but that there is a distinct tendency for somatic mutation to occur (carrying the implication of antigen drive) and that this is an important mechanism in the production of more pathogenic autoantibodies.

CD5 POSITIVE B CELLS

There has been much interest in a subset of B cells carrying the marker CD5 which is usually associated with T lymphocytes. It has been suggested that these B cells constantly recognize and stimulate each other through their idiotypes (see below) and demonstrate a limited response to external antigens. However CD5 positive B cells seem to be associated with the increased production of certain mostly IgM autoantibodies, notably rheumatoid factor and ssDNA antibodies (reviewed in 11). These cells are increased in number in patients with rheumatoid arthritis and Sjögren's syndrome. In SLE they have been shown to produce IgG anti-DNA antibodies (12).

Figure 1

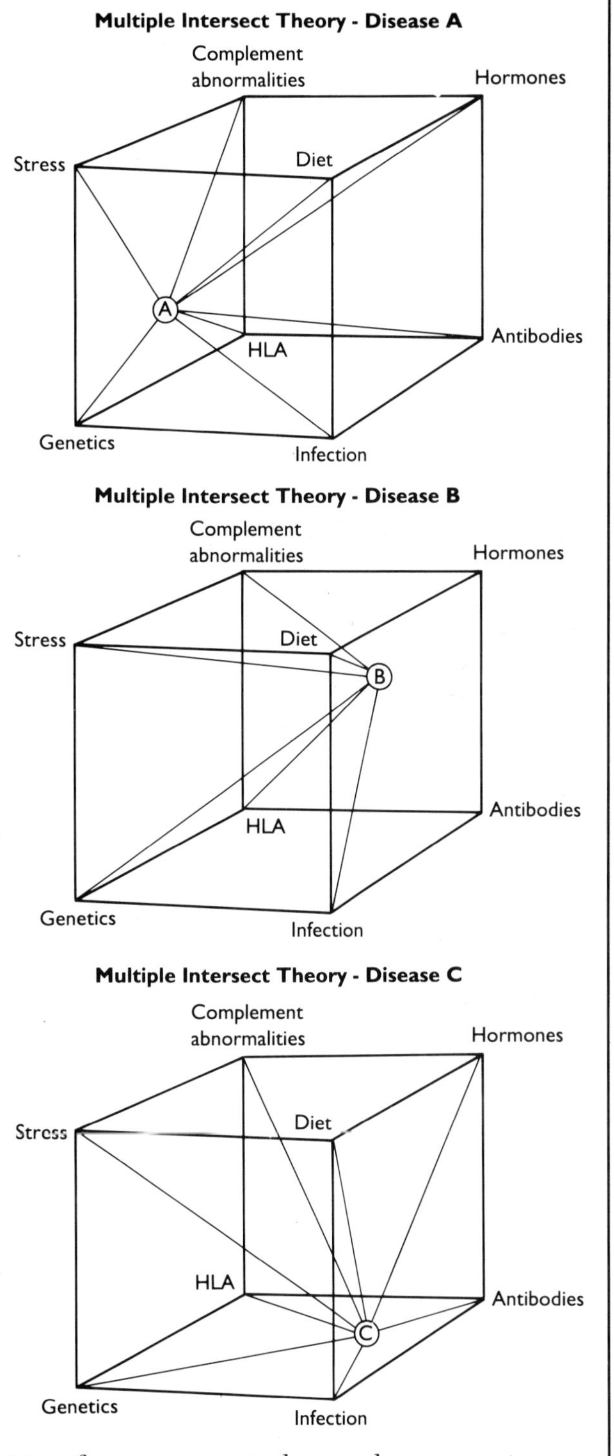

Many factors are required to produce an autoimmune disease. It may well be the way these factors combine or interact that determines which disease develops.

IDIOTYPES

Although antibodies are usually defined by the antigens with which they bind, another way of differentiating them is by identifying structures (known as idiotypes) in either of the hypervariable or framework regions of these molecules. Idiotypes may be present on either the heavy or light chain independently or require some component of heavy and light chains (conformational idiotype). Since idiotypes are, in essence, made up of amino acids it is reasonable to postulate that when the same idiotype is present in unrelated individuals, these individuals are likely to share the genes which encode the amino acids. Unexpected links between autoantibodies with different antigen binding specificities have been identified. For example antibodies to DNA, Sm and Ro may share a cross reactive idiotype as may human rheumatoid factors and anti-DNA antibodies. Idiotypes also link antibacterial and autoantibodies. Thus one idiotype, designated 16/6, has been identified on both anti-DNA and anti-Klebsiella K30 antibodies. That idiotypes may be associated with immunopathology is suggested by the fact that several of those described on anti-DNA antibodies, for example 16/6 and 3I, have been found to fluctuate with disease activity, and several have been found on immunoglobulins that are deposited in the skin and renal lesions of lupus patients (these data are reviewed in reference 13)

GLYCOSYLATION ABNORMALITIES

Although antibodies are thought primarily to consist of amino acids, the CH2 domains of antibodies are linked by bi-antennary oligosaccharide chains. It has recently been shown that in patients with rheumatoid arthritis (and Crohn's disease and tuberculosis) the IgG molecules have an increased number of biantennary oligosaccharide chains which lack the terminal galactose (and sialic acid) units (14). Intriguingly this abnormality (known as Gal 0), whilst not present in the first degree relatives of patients with rheumatoid arthritis, is present in some of their spouses, suggesting an environmental aetiology (15).

DRUG RELATED MECHANISMS

A number of therapeutic agents are now well recongnised to induce autoimmune disorders. Perhaps the best examples are hydralazine, isoniazid and chlorpromazine which cause a lupus-like syndrome as manifested mostly by skin rashes and joint pains. Most remarkable of all however is the ability of D-penicillamine, used in the treatment of rheumatoid arthritis, to induce seven different types of autoimmune disorder including a drug-induced form of lupus, myositis, myasthenia gravis, thrombocytopenia and haemolytic anaemia. Despite many efforts, the mechanisms of induction of these disorders remains uncertain. Amongst a variety of hypotheses suggested are a response to a drug or a metabolite which cross-reacts with host tissue; an immune reaction to a drug altered nuclear-protein conjugate; loss of tolerance following drug/protein interaction via activation; drugs acting as polyclonal activators or adjuvants in vivo; and effects on macrophage antigen recognition and processing. These concepts have been reviewed recently (16).

INFECTION

There is clearly an intimate link between infection, the immune system and autoimmunity. It is reasonable to postulate that the immune system has developed primarily to defend the organism against infectious diseases, and that the autoimmune process is the result of a subversion of this. Infectious agents are often thought of as triggers of any disorders. The onset of disease in many patients with myositis, diabetes, and to a lesser extent rheumatoid arthritis, seems to follow an infectious disorder eg a Coxsackie infection. The mechanisms by which this might occur are discussed later. It is also apparent in patients with systemic lupus erythematosus, that an apparently minor infection can trigger a transient exacerbation of the symptoms.

There is much interest currently in the possibility that a slow-growing form of mycobacterium might be the trigger or even the cause of rheumatoid arthritis (17). In contrast, other studies (18) have suggested that infections with Proteus mirabilis might be a trigger. Historically, rheumatoid arthritis is a condition of considerable interest, since it seems to have been almost unknown in Europe before the 19th century, which for a disease with a prevalence approaching 1% in urban societies strongly suggests that some form of organism is indeed able to trigger it.

TOXINS AND CHEMICALS

(Reviewed in detail in ref 1)

Toxins and chemicals may also be a factor involved in autoimmune responses. Perhaps the best documented example was the infamous 'Spanish oil' syndrome which affected approximately 20,000 people, causing the deaths of over 300. This resulted from a contamination of rapeseed oil which was sold as cooking oil. The two-part illness was characterised by an early acute phase with fever, rash, gastrointestinal upset and neurological features, followed by a more chronic phase in which the victims developed Raynaud's phenomenon and various features of both Sjögren's syndrome and scleroderma. A link between scleroderma and exposure to polyvinyl chloride (and a variety of other plastics and solvents) has also been well established. More recently, cigarette smoking has been found to be closely related to the clinical manifestations of Goodpasture's syndrome, and a variety of autoimmune phenomena including rheumatic symptoms have been linked with the use of silicone implants in breast mammoplasty operations.

STRESS

It is difficult to establish a direct correlation between stressful life events with initiation and/or exacerbation of autoimmune disorder. However most clinicians can quote examples from patients with lupus, rheumatoid arthritis or multiple sclerosis, in which the disease onset or flare seems to have a close temporal relationship with stressful life events, such as death, divorce, or failure to pass an examination.

AGE

It seems generally agreed that the immune response is probably maximal during puberty, declining progressively as the effect of senescence of both cellulor and humoral immune mechanisms become increasingly apparent. This process has been reported in both elderly experimental animals and humans. Production of autoantibodies, for example, increases with age (1). There appears to be a generally decreased immune responsiveness as the individual gets older. Although T cell functions appear to decrease with age, most B cell dependent responses remain relatively unchanged. However, alteration in the structure of the oligosaccharide chains which are attached to CH2 domains of IgG (see above) have also been shown to be age dependent (19). Despite these observations, the evidence that autoimmune disease increases with age is variable. There do appear to be peaks of incidence of both rheumatoid arthritis and myositis in the age group 50-60 but most other autoimmune disorders appear to occur before the age of 50, presumably reflecting the greater importance of the hormonal component.

DIET

The role of diet in the development of autoimmunity remains enigmatic. There are now a variety of studies showing that short term reduction of dietary fat and/or supplementation with fish oils may be beneficial for patients with rheumatoid arthritis and systemic lupus erythematosus. However, this is only indirect evidence of diet having a significant role in the aetiology of these conditions. Further studies are needed not least because patients themselves frequently suggest that certain items of food precipitate an exacerbation in their condition. Even if only a modest benefit in disease activity and reduction in drug therapy can be brought about by 'culinary compromise', changing the diet may have a role to play in the management of autoimmune disease.

CYTOKINES

Cytokines are potent poly peptides whose role is to mediate intra cellular signalling and thus to enable a coordinated immune response. There are a wide variety of cytokines including the interleukins (at least 12 have been identified), interferons (alpha, beta and gamma), tumour necrosis factor (alpha and beta), colony stimulating factors (eg granulocyte colony stimulating factor) and various other growth factors, including transforming growth factor. The relationship between cytokine activity and autoimmune disorders has been difficult to dissect because it is evident that different cells may produce the same cytokine, and different cytokines may have the same effects. Some cytokines inhibit immune reactions whilst others have apparently conflicting effects. They may be cytotoxic to a range of cell types. The subject is reviewed in detail elsewhere (20). Some particular cytokines are highlighted here.

Interleukin 1 is produced by a range of cells and acts on many different cell types. IL1 appears to upregulate the expression of adhesion molecules on cultured vascular endothelium which could contribute to the increased traffic of immune cells into inflammatory sites. It also causes fibroblast proliferation and collagen synthesis, leading to pannus formation. It is able to activate osteoclasts, causing bone resorption and induces the release of proteinases and proteoglycanases from chondrocytes. Over production of IL1 is thus thought to be associated with the tissue damage seen in patients with rheumatoid arthritis (reviewed in 21). Conflicting reports have appeared about the levels of IL1 in lupus patients. But important interactions between TNFα and IL1 have suggested that their release may be coordinated. TNFα is one of the most abundant cytokines seen in the rheumatoid synovium and it too can induce cartilage breakdown, bone resorption and synovial cell growth and fibroblast proliferation. In addition treating lupus-prone NZB/W F1 mice with high doses of TNFα can postpone the development of lupus nephritis.

IL2 has also been well characterized. It appears that it can only trigger an autoimmune disease which is mediated by a non-deleted T cell repertoire. Intriguingly IL2 appears to exert a beneficial effect on MRL/lpr mice and may result in the almost complete disappearance of cells bearing the lpr phenotype.

There has been much interest in IL6 which is known to cause the maturation of activated B cells into immunoglobulin producing cells. IL6 activity is significantly elevated in synovial fluid and serum from patients with rheumatoid arthritis. There appears to be a correlation between serum IL6 activity and serum levels of C-reactive protein. Intriguingly IL6 also appears to be linked to raised levels of agalactosyl IgG. Recently, IL6 levels have also been shown to be elevated in lupus and to correlate with disease activity.

It seems very likely that the factors described are indeed involved in the range of autoimmune diseases. It is however the way these factors interact which determines which particular disease the patient will develop. In Figure 1 a three dimensional model is shown which attempts to highlight this point. It is an extension of an original two dimensional concept suggested by Dr Michael Snaith, University of Sheffield.

Antigen

The role of antigen as a driving force is generally accepted to be of great importance in the organ-specific autoimmune disorders (eg thyroglobulin in autoimmune thyroid disease). Amongst the non organ-specific diseases, including most of the autoimmune rheumatic diseases, the role of antigen is not as clear cut though there are increasing 'suspicions' about DNA/histone and RNA/histone as antigens in SLE.

MECHANISMS

Molecular Mimicry

An increasing number of homologies between self and microbial antigens has been reported. Examples amongst bacteria include Klebsiella nitrogenase and HLA-B27 and Proteus mirabilis and HLA-DR4 whilst viral examples are EBV gp110 and Dw4 T cell epitope, HSV glycoprotein and the acetyl choline receptor and retroviral gag p32 and U-1 RNA (reviewed in ref 22). These examples of so-called molecular mimicry set the scene for potential T (or B) cell cross-reactions. However, the homologies ***per se*** whilst of interest, do not guarantee an autoimmune response or the clinical expression of an autoimmune disease, since the method and consequences of processing the proteins by the antigen presenting cells is likely to be critical.

The Role of Autoantibodies

The mechanisms by which autoantibodies play a major role leading to disease induction are complement dependent destruction of a target cell, opsonization, formation of immune complexes, blockade of receptor sites for their physiological ligands, and stimulation of self surface receptors.

Complement mediated cell lysis is uncommonly associated with autoantibodies. The best example is that of complement-fixing IgM autoantibodies which are associated with paroxysmal cold haemoglobinurea.

More frequently, as occurs in other kinds of autoimmune

haemolytic anaemia, the autoantibodies are unable to fix complement efficiently because the scattered spacing of the relevant autoantigen on the red blood submembrane does not permit the adjacent IgG molecules to cross-link by C1q. In the case of these haemolytic anaemias the autoantibodies opsonize the cells thus facilitating their phagocytosis.

Immune complex formation is a widely recognized event which may occur within the circulation and under certain conditions tissue deposition occurs or the complexes may occur within the tissues themselves. Systemic lupus provides a good example of both. For many years it was believed that circulating immune complexes consiting of DNA and anti-DNA antibodies were deposited in the tissues such as the kidney and the skin and that this was followed by the inflammatory events which led to tissue destruction. More recently, it has been suggested that antibodies to DNA bind by a so-called histone bridge to heparan sulphate associated with the glomerular basement membrane (23). Thus the immune complex is formed locally.

Antibodies binding to physiological cell surface receptors may in different situations either inhibit or stimulate them. The best example of inhibition occurs in myasthenia gravis where the anti-acetyl choline receptor antibodies blockade the receptor on the post synaptic muscle membrane. The cross linked receptors are internalised and reduced in number, thus leading to faulty triggering of muscle contraction. Similarly in insulin resistant diabetes there are autoantibodies to the insulin receptors which also interfere with the physiological function of the insulin reacting cells. In contrast in Graves' disease, the autoantibodies that bind to the receptors for the thyroid stimulating hormone (TSH)

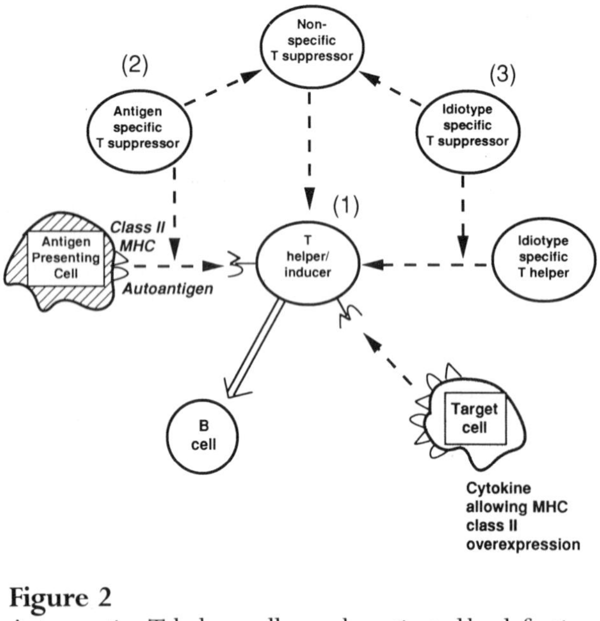

Figure 2
Autoreactive T-helper cells may be activated by defective response to non-specific (1), antigen specific (2) or idiotype specific (3) T suppressor cells or excessive surface expression of MHC class II molecules (and antigen) secondary to cytokine abnormalities de-repressing the class II genes. [Adapted with permission from Fig 14.14, Roitt I M, *Essential Immunology* 7th Edn, Blackwell Scientific, Oxford]

are themselves stimulatory. The anti TSH receptor autoantibodies cross link the receptor which is apparently fooled into thinking that the cell has been stimulated by TSH itself.

The driving forces behind polyclonal B cell stimulation which induces the hypergammaglobulinaemia detectable in most autoimmune diseases, have been explored recently. It has been shown, for example, (24) that lipopolysaccharides from gram-negative bacteria may cause polyclonal B cell activation in lupus-prone mice and that this can induce an exacerbation of their nephritis. Sobel et al (25) have shown that in the lupus-prone MRL/lpr mice as well as the presence of double negative T cells (ie $CD4^-$, $CD8^-$) an intrinsic B cell defect is essential for the production of autoimmunity. Further support for a primary defect in the B cell in this strain comes from the work of Strasser et al (26). They used a transgenic model in which a single disregulated gene (BCL2) which has the ability to prolong the B cell life-span, was able to induce hypergammaglobulinaemia and widespread evidence of systemic autoimmunity, including nephritis. Recently Watanabe-Kukunaga and colleagues (27) have shown that the lpr mice have defects in the Fas antigen gene. This gene produces a protein which is important in cell apoptosis, (programmed cell death) hence defects in the gene expression may lead to an increased number of autoantibody-producing B cells.

Some years ago Paul Plotz put forward the ingenious notion that an anti-idiotype might on occasion closely mimic an antigen. In his view antibodies to a viral epitope might induce the production of an anti-idiotypic antibody which could activate a cell surface site into which the virus itself might normally fit (28). Although this theory has never been fully confirmed, a recent study (29) has shown that a light chain fragment with an amino acid sequence very similar to a portion of RNP which was also an anti-idiotype to an anti DNA antibody, when injected into a healthy strain mouse, induced the production of both antibodies to DNA and RNP, together with evidence of glomerulonephritis.

The Role of T Cells

Induction of MHC class II antigens by interferon gamma may also be an important mechanism in the induction of autoimmune disease (22). This has been demonstrated in several disorders, including rheumatoid arthritis, thyroid disease and diabetes. The hypothesis is that interferon gamma can initiate an anti-self immune reaction by inducing MHC class II on the surface of tissue cells which leads to the activation of autoreactive T cells and direct evidence in favour of this idea comes from studies of monoclonal antibodies which block class II antigens and are able to suppress experimental forms of lupus, multiple sclerosis and myasthenia gravis.

There is however much evidence to suggest that T cells, notably T helper/inducers play a pivotal role in the development of autoimmunity (Figure 2). Furthermore as indicated earlier, the interaction of T cell and MHC-associated antigen peptide is probably a key event in many of these diseases. It may be that an environmental antigen (eg viral or mycobacterial component) when presented by a particular MHC allele, can elicit a T cell response that cross-reacts with an autoantigen. It has been postulated that heat shock proteins (hsp), immunodominant antigens of mycobacteria might, for example, be involved in the induction of autoimmunity in such a fashion (30). However, it seems more likely that some additional step such as, for example, overexpression of hsps on the surface of the human cells is also a prerequisite for an autoimmune disease to develop (31).

There is increasing evidence that helper (and suppressor) T cells are influenced by immunoglobulin idiotypes. This subject is reviewed elsewhere (23). Another possible influence is the so-called 'superantigens' (32). Superantigens are molecules which activate a large number of T cells. Their recognition does however appear to require MHC class II molecules and a T cell receptor. If there is a restriction in TCR gene usage, as discussed earlier, (ie V gene oligoclonality) since superantigens bind particular TCR Vβ gene products, it has been suggested that in some individuals RA may develop following activation of T cells by a Vβ specific superantigen (3). This activation would in theory initiate an immune response later perpetuated by cross-reactive autologous antigens.

SUMMARY

Autoimmune diseases continue to present a challenge in terms of understanding their aetiology and in providing effective treatment. The major factors involved in the development of these disorders have been identified. Determining the precise mechanism(s) by which they interact to cause disease remains an essential enigma which must be resolved in order to improve therapeutic strategies.

REFERENCES

1. Shoenfeld Y, Isenberg D. *The Mosaic of Autoimmunity*. Elsevier, Amsterdam 1987.

2. Schwartz R S, Datta S K. Autoimmunity and Autoimmune Diseases. Chapter in:*Fundamental Immunology* 2nd Edn. Ed. William E Paul, Raven Press Ltd, New York 1989.

3. Richardson B C. T cell receptor usage in rheumatic disease. *Clin Exp Rheum* 1992; **10**: 271-83.

4. Watanabe Y, Tokunaga K, Matsuki K et al. Putative amino acid sequence of HLA-DRβ chain contributing to rheumatoid arthritis susceptibility. *J Exp Med* 1989; **169**: 2263-8.

5. Worrall J G, Snaith M L, Batchelor F, Isenberg D A. SLE - a rheumatological view. *Quart J Med.* 1990; **275**: 319-30.

6. Morgan B P, Walport M J. Complement deficiency and disease. *Immunol Today* 1991; **12**: 301-6.

7. Arnett F C. Genetic aspects of human lupus. *Clin Immunol Immunopathol* 1992; **63**: 4-6.

8. Yanagi Y, Hirose S, Nagusawa R et al. Does the deletion within T cell receptor beta-chain gene of NZW mice contribute to autoimmunity in (NZB x NZW) F1 mice. *Eur J Immunol* 1986: **16**: 1179-82.

9. Rajapalan S, Mao C, Datta S K. Pathogenic autoantibody-inducing γ/δ T helper cells from patients with lupus nephritis express unusual T cell receptors. *Clin Immunol Immunopathol.* 1992; **62**: 344-50.

10. Spector T D, Roman E, Silman A J. The pill, parity and rheumatoid arthritis. *Arthritis Rheum* 1990; **33**: 782-9.

11. Watts R, Isenberg D A. Autoantibodies and antibacterial antibodies: from both sides now. *Ann Rheum Dis.* 1990; **49**: 961-5.

12. Suzuki N, Sakane T, Engleman E. Anti-DNA antibody production by CD5+ and CD5- B cells of patients with systemic lupus erythematosus. *J Clin Invest* 1990; **85**: 238-42.

13. Isenberg D A. DNA antibody idiotype 16/6 - an idiotypic system of some importance. *Ann De Med Interne* 1990; **141**: 57-63.

14. Radamacher T W, Parekh R B, Dwek R et al. The role of IgG glycoforms in the pathogenesis of rheumatoid arthritis. *Springer Seminars in Immunopathology* 1988; **10**: 231-49.

15. Sumar N, Colaço B, Bodman K et al. Abnormalities in the glycosylation of IgG in spouses of patients with rheumatoid arthritis. A family study. *J Autoimmunity* 1991; **4**: 907-14.

16. Adams L E, Hess E V. Drug-related lupus. Incidence, mechanisms and clinical implications. *Drug Safety Concepts* 1991; **6**: 431-49

17. Rook G, Stanford J. Slow bacterial infections or autoimmunity. *Immunology Today* 1992; **13**: 160-4.

18. Ebringer A, Ptaszinska T, Corbett M et al. Antibodies to proteus in RA. *Lancet* 1985; **2**: 305-7.

19. Parekh R, Isenberg D, Rook G, Roitt I, Dwek R, Rademacher T. A comparative analysis of disease associated changes in the galactosylation of serum IgG. *J Autoimmunity* 1989; **2**: 101-14.

20. Williams W, Ehrenstein M C, Isenberg D A. The Background to Autoimmunity. In: *The Handbook of Immunopharmacology*. Eds, E Davies & J Dingle. Academic Press, London. In press.

21. Brennan F M, Maini R N, Feldmann M. TNFα - A pivotal role in rheumatoid arthritis? *Brit J Rheum* 1992; **31**: 293-8.

22. Roitt I M. *Essential Immunology*. 7th Ed. Blackwell Scientific, Oxford 1991.

23. Brinkman K, Termaat R M, Berden J H M, Smeenk R T J. Anti-DNA antibodies and lupus nephritis: the complexity of cross-reactivity. *Immunol Today* 1990; **11**: 232-4.

24. Cavalla T, Granholm N A. Lipopolysaccharides from gram-negative bacteria enhances polyclonal B cell activation and exacerbates nephritis in MRL/lpr mice. *Clin Exp Immunol* 1990; **82** 515-21.

25. Sabel E S, Datagari T, Kaagiri K, Morris S C, Cohen P L, Eisenberg R A. An intrinsic B cell defect is required for the production of autoantibodies in the lpr model of murine systemic autoimmunity. *J Exp Med* 1991; 173: 1441-9.

26. Strasser A, Whittingham S, Vaux D L et al. Enforced BCL2 expression in B- lymphoid cells prolongs antibody responses and elicits autoimmune disease. *Proc Natl Acad Sci* USA. 1991; **88**: 8661-5.

27. Watanabe-Kukunaga R, Brannan C I, Copeland N G, Jenkins N A, Nagata S. Lymphoproliferative disorder in mice explained by defects in Fas antigen that mediates apoptosis. *Nature* 1992; **356**: 314-7.

28. Plotz P. Autoantibodies and anti-idiotypes to anti-viral antibodies. *Lancet* 1983; **2**: 824-6.

29. Puccetti A, Koizumi T, Migliorini P, Andre-Schwartz J, Barrett K, Schwartz R S. An immunoglobulin light chain from a lupus-prone mouse induces autoantibodies in normal mice. *J Exp Med* 1990; **171**: 1919-30.

30. Kaufmann S H E. Heat shock proteins and the immune response. *Immunol Today* 1990; **11**: 129-36.

31. Dhillon V, Latchman D, Isenberg D A. Heat shock proteins and systemic lupus erythematosus. *Lupus* 1991; **1**: 3-8.

32. Kishelow P, Swat W, Rocha B, von Boehmer H. Induction of immunological unresponsiveness in vivo and in vitro by conventional and superantigens in devloping and mature T cells. *Immunology Rev* 1991; **122**: 69-85.

September 1992

AUTOIMMUNITY TO CARTILAGE COLLAGENS

R B Clague, Consultant Physician
Noble's Hospital
Douglas
Isle of Man

K Morgan, Principal Scientific Officer
Department of Rheumatology
The Medical School
University of Manchester

INTRODUCTION

The synovial membrane in rheumatoid arthritis (RA) is a highly organised lymphoid tissue suggestive of a chronic hypersensitivity reaction to an exogenous or self antigen. The primary site of joint destruction is the articular cartilage, which also seems to be responsible for driving the immune response as synovitis within that joint usually subsides once the cartilage is completely destroyed (1). This suggests that exogenous antigens or autoantigens may be sequestered within the cartilage framework.

Investigation of the potential role of cartilage collagens in inciting and perpetuating arthritis was stimulated by Trentham and co-workers in 1977 (2) by the discovery that immunisation with native type II collagen induced an inflammatory arthritis in rodents. Since then, research on the biochemistry and immunology of the cartilage collagens has advanced rapidly, and modern immunological techniques have been applied to the measurement of this autoimmunity in experimental arthritis and human diseases.

BIOCHEMISTRY

The main structural proteins of all connective tissues within the body are collagens, of which at least 14 genetically distinct types have so far been described (3). Articular cartilage is a complex structure with chondrocytes synthesising an extracellular matrix of proteoglycan gel held within a collagen framework, which comprises 70% of its dry weight. There are at least 4 types of collagen found in articular cartilage in mature joints (Table 1). The other tissues of synovial joints contain many of the other collagen types, with types I, III and V collagen being present in bone and synovium. Type II collagen has a limited distribution within the body, being found only in the vitreous humour of the eye, the cartilage of the ear and the nucleus pulposus of the intervertebral disc as well as articular cartilage.

The basic structure of all native collagens is the triple helix in which three individual polypeptide α-chains twist together (Table 2). Short non-helical regions occur, which for type II collagen are at the amino- and carboxy- terminal ends of each α-chain. Pepsin extraction of collagens from articular cartilage removes these non-helical regions, and the different collagen types are purified by meticulous differential salt precipitation and extensive dialysis. Heat denaturation of the native collagen at 45°C causes uncoiling of the helix to produce three individual α-chains. Type II collagen is composed of three identical $\alpha1$(II) chains, but type XI is composed of three different α-chains [$\alpha1$(XI), $\alpha2$(XI) and $\alpha3$(XI) chains], though the $\alpha3$(XI) chain is biochemically similar to the $\alpha1$(II) chain of type II collagen.

Smaller fragments of each α-chain can be obtained by cyanogen bromide digestion producing CB-peptides of varying length. Type II collagen can be subdivided into a number of CB-peptides, with CB-8, CB-10 and CB-11 being the major peptides. The basic structure of the collagen molecule in the helical domains is a repeating glycine-X-Y triplet where X is often proline and Y is often hydroxyproline. The amino acid sequence of type II collagen is known, and small peptide sequences can be biochemically synthesised.

TABLE 1. CARTILAGE COLLAGENS

Type	Chain Composition	%
II	$[\alpha1(II)]_3$	85
VI	$[\alpha1(VI), \alpha2(VI), \alpha3(VI)]$	<2
IX	$[\alpha1(IX), \alpha2(IX), \alpha3(IX)]$	5
XI	$[\alpha1(XI), \alpha2(XI), \alpha3(XI)]$	8-10

TABLE 2. DIAGRAMMATIC REPRESENTATION OF ANTIGENIC COMPONENTS OF COLLAGEN

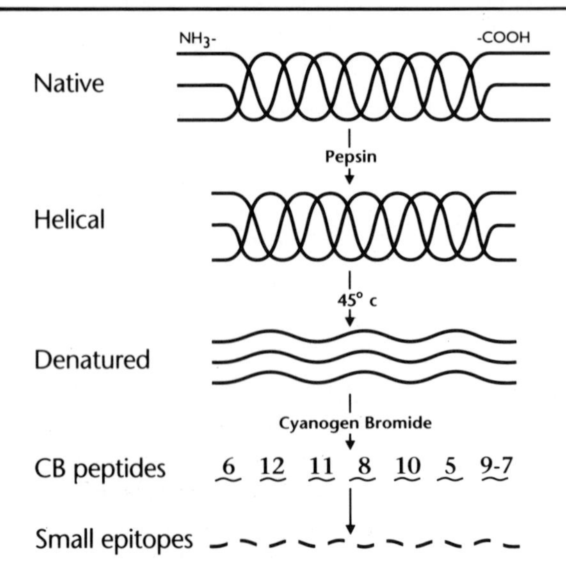

IMMUNOLOGICAL METHODS

The original studies on the measurement of antibodies to collagen were made using passive haemagglutination and semi-quantitative immunofluorescent assays, but these have now been replaced with solid-phase radioimmunoassays (RIA) and enzyme-linked immunosorbent assays (ELISA). The RIA and ELISA for collagen antibodies are not subject to interference by non-antibody proteins, and are highly sensitive techniques (4,5). There is, therefore, a need for standardisation of assays between different laboratories with reference to positive and negative sera (4).

Recently, immunoblotting techniques have been applied in the detection of antibodies to CB-peptides of collagen, though these techniques only give semi-quantitative results (6). Newer micro-solid-phase ELISA' s are being developed to measure antibodies to the small synthesised collagen peptides.

ANTIBODIES TO CARTILAGE COLLAGENS

RHEUMATOID ARTHRITIS (RA)

It is now generally accepted that the incidence of serum antibodies specific to native type II collagen is 10-15% in RA (7,8), though earlier studies suggested a much higher incidence (9,10). The antibody to native type II collagen can, in some patients, be detected at very high titre (1 in 5,000 dilution). The main class of these autoantibodies is IgG with IgA and IgM occurring in few patients. Serum antibodies to the other native cartilage collagens (types VI, IX and XI) have been less well studied, but are probably present in 2-3% of patients. Serum antibodies to denatured cartilage collagens are more frequent (15-25%), though there is more controversy about their incidence. The detection of antibodies to denatured type XI collagen is partly related to the biochemical similarity between the $\alpha 3$(XI) and $\alpha 1$(II) chains, but antibodies to the $\alpha 1$(XI) and $\alpha 2$(XI) chains have also been detected by immunoblotting (6).

Antibodies to native type II collagen have been found as early as two months after onset of symptoms in RA (personal observations), but published data have failed to show definite correlations with any clinical, investigative, immunological or radiological parameter (4,11). However, a retrospective longitudinal study in individual patients has shown a correlation with disease activity in some patients (12), especially when the complement binding IgG subclasses (IgG1 and IgG3) were measured (13). A recent prospective study over one year showed no relationship between antibody levels to type II collagen and any specific index of disease activity (14). However, antibody levels to denatured type II collagen declined over the year in the group of patients with inactive disease compared with the patient group with active disease, suggesting some involvement with the rheumatoid process. These studies confirm that autoimmunity to native type II collagen can remain at high and varying levels over long periods of time.

Serum antibodies may have less relevance to the severity of joint inflammation than antibodies localised to joint tissues. Indeed, the detection of cartilage-bound antibody is much higher (60-69%) than in sera, and can be demonstrated even in patients with no detectable serum antibodies to type II collagen (8,15). These autoantibodies can be synthesised by plasma cells in synovial membrane (16), are found in synovial fluid where they are capable of forming immune complexes (17), and can bind to cartilage in vitro (4). Wooley and colleagues (18) showed that the IgG subfraction from the serum of a patient with sero-negative RA but high levels of serum antibody to native type II collagen could bind to cartilage and induce a synovitis when injected into mice. The main IgG antibody subclasses produced are the complement binding IgG1 and IgG3 (13), indicating that the autoantibody could perpetuate joint inflammation by intra-articular complement activation.

Recent studies have looked at the finer specificity of these antibodies (6,8). Antibody binding to specific CB peptides, especially CB-11 but also CB-10 and CB-8, have been found by immunoblotting. Sequential serum samples from an individual patient have shown changes in both antibody class and binding to specific CB peptides with time (12). It may be that only by measuring specific antibody subclasses (e.g. IgG1 and IgG3) to specific epitopes on the collagen molecule that a true correlation with the degree of joint inflammation and potential damage will be obtained. Even then, it may be more important to look at the cartilage bound antibody rather than that found in the sera.

In RA, there is evidence that the persistence of antibody to native type II collagen is linked to HLA DR3 and/or DR7 class II MHC genes (11), whereas these autoantibodies only appear temporarily in early disease if these immune response genes are absent (eg HLA DR4 positive RA) (19). Other smaller studies have confirmed the lack of association with HLA DR4. The highest antibody titres to native type II collagen were associated with HLA DR3. Interestingly, a recent study has shown an association between the HLA phenotype 'A2,DR4' and high titres of antibody to denatured type II collagen, suggesting that a gene closely associated with HLA DR4 may regulate the antibody response to denatured type II collagen (20).

Antibodies to denatured type II collagen are less specific for RA and joint disease, as they are found in other arthritides and inflammatory conditions (10,21), though they can be synthesised in the synovial membrane (22). The difficulty of cross-reactivity with other denatured collagens probably accounts for the presence of these antibodies in non-articular inflammatory diseases. Further studies searching for antibody to specific type II collagen epitopes using more sophisticated immunological techniques may prove very rewarding.

RELAPSING POLYCHONDRITIS

Relapsing polychondritis is characterised by recurrent episodes of inflammation and destruction of cartilaginous tissues throughout the body. An immunological mechanism has been suggested by its association with other autoimmune diseases (23). Published studies suggest that serum antibodies to type II collagen are found in 33-67% patients, particularly in those with acute, active disease though the numbers studied are small (8, 24, 25). Terato et al found autoantibodies in thirteen out of twenty-six patients, though no clinical details on disease activity were given (8). They showed that purified antibodies from three patients mainly reacted to the CB-9-7 peptide of type II collagen, a reactivity rarely found in RA. Individual case reports also suggest that the antibody titre to native type II collagen correlates with disease activity. Thus autoantibodies to native type II collagen may be of diagnostic value in early active relapsing polychondritis.

Auricular lesions were noted in studies on native type II

collagen-induced arthritis in rats (26), but extra-articular cartilaginous lesions are not seen in RA patients with the autoantibodies. There is one description of nondeforming relapsing polychondritis associated with classical RA (27).

OTHER ARTHRITIDES

Serum autoantibodies specific for native type II collagen are found in a few patients with psoriatic arthritis (28, personal observation), juvenile chronic arthritis (29, personal observation), systemic lupus erythematosus (SLE) (10,21), generalised osteoarthritis (21, personal observation), and Paget's disease (21). Thus these autoantibodies are most frequent in RA compared with other arthritides but the number of patients studied in these other groups remains small.

Further studies on SLE are required as antibodies specific to the arthritogenic CB-11 peptide have been found in patients with the deforming non-erosive arthritis found in this disease (30). Antibodies to the collagen-like portion of C1q have been described in SLE (31) and could in theory cross-react with collagen, emphasising the complexity of this area.

CELL-MEDIATED IMMUNITY TO CARTILAGE COLLAGENS

Published data on cell-mediated immunity to collagen is sparse (28, 32, 33) and most refer to peripheral blood lymphocytes. Reactivity to denatured collagens is more frequent than to the native molecule and not restricted to RA. More importantly, T cell cloning of synovial lymphocytes in RA showed reactivity against native type II collagen in 2 out of 25 clones tested in a patient with high serum antibody levels to native type II collagen (34). The frequency of autoantigen reactive T cells in the samples was high and comparable to thyrocyte-specific T cell clones derived from the lymphocytic infiltrate in the thyroid of Graves disease. T cell clones reactive to type II collagen have also been isolated from normal individuals (35). It may be that T cell reactivity to cartilage collagens is actively suppressed in normal individuals, with breakdown of this suppression in RA.

ANIMAL STUDIES

Is there evidence therefore that this autoimmunity to cartilage collagens has pathogenic relevance in RA? Indirect evidence for this comes from studies of immunity to cartilage collagens in animals. Immunisation of rats or mice with types II, IX or XI collagen induces an inflammatory polyarthritis with features that resemble RA (2,36,37). The induction of arthritis is associated with the development of anti-collagen antibodies and T cell proliferative responses to the immunising cartilage collagen. More recently, a similar arthritis has been induced in monkeys with type II collagen (38).

The incidence, severity and chronicity of the arthritis depends on whether heterologous or autologous collagen is used for immunisation. Arthritis can also be induced by immunisation with the CB-11 peptide of type II collagen alone suggesting that at least one arthritogenic epitope is present within this peptide (39). The induction of arthritis is complement dependent (40), and the antibodies are complement fixing, cross-react with the animal's own type II collagen and bind to cartilage in the joints. Arthritis can be temporarily induced in naive rats by transfer of concentrated immunoglobulin from immunised arthritic rats (41). The production of antibodies to the immunising collagen is T cell dependent and once established, the progress of disease can be altered by treatments affecting T cell reactivity. Thus both T cell and B cell reactivities to collagen are important in the initiation and progression of collagen-induced arthritis.

The immune response to type II collagen in animals is under genetic control paralleling the human studies, and both MHC and non-MHC determinants may be important in the expression of arthritis (36,42). Antibodies binding to certain epitopes of the type II collagen molecule may be more important than others in arthritis induction. Thus in patients with RA, there may be arthritogenic and non-arthritogenic anti-collagen antibodies. Further studies on this animal model can help us to understand the role of various mediators in inflammatory arthritis in patients and may lead to novel methods of disease control.

CONCLUSIONS

The specificity and significance of autoimmunity to cartilage collagens in initiating RA should be questioned. The fact that it occurs in other forms of arthritis could indicate that it is a secondary phenomenon induced following the exposure of collagen epitopes to the immune system after initiation of cartilage destruction by another primary event, though it could play a significant role in perpetuating the joint inflammation and damage. Immunisation of susceptible animals with type II collagen can induce an immune response to this collagen and arthritis in the presence of specific immune response genes of the major histocompatibility complex (36,42, personal observations). These human and animal studies suggest a key role for specific class II molecules in the development of this autoimmunity.

The nature of autoimmunity to cartilage collagens is complex and intriguing. The application of further, newer immunological techniques (eg Western blotting, monoclonal antibodies, T cell cloning, T cell receptor analysis) will help to elucidate its role in arthritis. There is a wealth of immune reactions in the connective tissue diseases, yet here we have an autoimmune response with a pathogenic role in laboratory animals. The evidence points towards such a pathogenic role in chronic inflammatory arthritis, but it is likely to be only one of many potential pathogenic mechanisms in RA. Antibodies to collagens are currently the most relevant measurable autoantibodies against joint tissue, so may prove a further useful immunological marker in assessing new therapeutic regimes against joint destruction.

The relatively low incidence and lack of specificity of these autoantibodies for RA make their routine measurement in patients seem unattractive and unrewarding unless they have prognostic significance in being associated with more severe joint destruction. For the future, the measurement of antibodies to individual epitopes of cartilage collagens, rather than to the whole molecule, may prove more relevant in monitoring disease activity and joint destruction in the chronic inflammatory arthritides. The presence of autoantibodies to type II collagen does, however, have diagnostic and prognostic significance in early relapsing polychondritis.

May 1991

REFERENCES

1. Gardner DL. Pathology of rheumatoid arthritis. In: Scott JT, ed. Copeman's textbook of rheumatic diseases. 6th edn. Edinburgh: Churchill Livingstone, 1986;604-52.

2. Trentham DE, Townes AS, Kang AH. Autoimmunity of type II collagen: an experimental model of arthritis. J Exp Med 1977;857-67.

3. Grant M, Ayad S, Kwan AP, Bates GP, Thomas JT, McClure J. The structure and synthesis of cartilage collagens. In "The control of tissue damage" ed. Glavert, Elsevier Science Publishers BV. 1988;3-27.

4. Clague RB, Firth SA, Holt PJL, Skingle J, Greenbury CL, Webley M. Serum antibodies to type II collagen in rheumatoid arthritis: comparison of 6 immunological methods and clinical features. Ann Rheum Dis 1983;42:537-44.

5. Beard HK, Lea DJ, Ryvar R. Anomalous reactions in the haemagglutination assay for anti-collagen antibodies, studies on patients with rheumatoid arthritis or chronic low back pain. J Immunol Methods 1979;31:119-28.

6. Buckee C, Morgan K, Ayad S, Collins I, Clague RB, Holt PJL. Diversity of antibodies to type II collagen in patients with rheumatoid arthritis. Detection by binding to α-chains and cyanogen bromide peptides. Br J Rheumatol 1990;29:254-8.

7. Morgan K, Clague RB, Collins I, Ayad S, Phinn SD, Holt PJL. Incidence of antibodies to native and denatured cartilage collagens (types II,IX, and XI) and to type I collagen in rheumatoid arthritis. Ann Rheum Dis 1987;46:902-7.

8. Terato K, Shimozuru Y, Katayama K, Takemitsu Y, Yamashita I, Miyatsu M, Fujii K, Sagara M, Kobayashi S, Goto M, Nishioka K, Miyasaka N, Nagai Y. Specificity of antibodies to type II collagen in rheumatoid arthritis. Arthritis Rheum 1990;33:1493-1500.

9. Andriopoulos NA, Mestecky J, Miller EJ, Bradley EL. Antibodies to native and denatured collagens in sera of patients with rheumatoid arthritis. Arthritis Rheum 1976;19:613-7.

10. Stuart JM, Huffstutter EH, Townes AS, Kang AH. Incidence and specificity of antibodies to types I, II, III, IV and V collagen in rheumatoid arthritis and other rheumatic diseases as measured by 125I-radioimmunoassay. Arthritis Rheum 1983;26:832-40.

11. Klimiuk PS, Clague RB, Grennan DM, Dyer PA, Smeaton I, Harris R. Autoimmunity to native type II collagen - A distinct genetic subset of rheumatoid arthritis. J Rheum 1985;12:865-70.

12. Morgan K, Clague RB, Collins I, Ayad S, Phinn SD, Holt PJL. A longitudinal study of anti-collagen antibodies in patients with rheumatoid arthritis. Arthritis Rheum 1989;32:139-45.

13. Collins I, Morgan K, Clague RB, Brenchley PEC, Holt PJL. IgG subclass distribution of antinative type II collagen and antidenatured type II collagen antibodies in patients with rheumatoid arthritis. J Rheum 1988;15:770-4.

14. Stockman A, Rowley MJ, Emery P, Muirden KD. Activity of rheumatoid arthritis and levels of collagen antibodies: a prospective study. Rheumatol Int 1989;8:239-43.

15. Jasin HE. Autoantibody specificities of immune complexes sequestered in articular cartilage of patients with rheumatoid arthritis and osteoarthritis. Arthritis Rheum 1985;28:241-8.

16. Mestecky J, Miller EJ. Presence of antibodies specific to cartilage-type collagen in rheumatoid synovial tissue. Clin Exp Immunol 1979;22:453-6.

17. Clague RB, Moore LJ. IgG and IgM antibody to native type II collagen in rheumatoid arthritis serum and synovial fluid. Evidence for the presence of collagen-anticollagen immune complexes in synovial fluid. Arthritis Rheum 1984;27:1370-7.

18. Wooley PH, Luthra HS, Singh S, Huse A, Stuart JM, David CS. Passive transfer of arthritis in mice by human anti-type II collagen antibody. Mayo Clin Proc 1984;59:737-43.

19. Pereira RS, Black CM, Duance VC, Jones VE, Jacoby RK, Welsh KI. Disappearing collagen antibodies in rheumatoid arthritis. Lancet 1985;8453:501-2.

20. Rowley MJ, Tait B, Doran T, Emery P, Mackay IR. Associations between HLA and antibodies to collagen in rheumatoid arthritis. Ann Rheum Dis 1990;49:578-81.

21. Choi EKK, Gatenby PA, McGill NW, Bateman JF, Cole WG, York JR. Autoantibodies to type II collagen: occurrence in rheumatoid arthritis, other arthritides, autoimmune connective tissue diseases, and chronic inflammatory syndromes. Ann Rheum Dis 1988;47:313-322.

22. Rowley MJ, Williamson DJ, MacKay IR. Evidence for local synthesis of antibodies to denatured collagen in the synovium in rheumatoid arthritis. Arthritis Rheum 1987;30:1420-5.

23. Foidart JM, Abe S, Martin GR, Zizic TM, Barnett EV, Lawley TJ, Katz SI. Antibodies to type II collagen in relapsing polychondritis. N Engl J Med 1978;299:1203-7.

24. Ebringer R, Rook G, Swana GT, Bottazzo GF, Doniach D. Autoantibodies to cartilage and type II collagen in relapsing polychondritis and other rheumatic diseases. Ann Rheum Dis 1981;40:473-9.

25. Duke OL. Relapsing polychondritis. Br J Rheumatol 1988;27:423-5.

26. McCune WJ, Schiller AL, Dynesius-Trentham RA, Trentham DE. Type II collagen-induced auricular chondritis. Arthritis Rheum 1982;25:266-73.

27. Tishler M, Caspi D, Yaron M. Classical rheumatoid arthritis associated with nondeforming relapsing polychondritis. J Rheum 1987;14:367-8.

28. Trentham DE, Kammer GM, McCune WJ, David JR. Autoimmunity to collagen. A shared feature of psoriatic and rheumatoid arthritis. Arthritis Rheum 1981;24:1363-9.

29. Rosenberg AM, Hunt DWC, Petty RE. Antibodies to native and denatured type II collagen in children with rheumatic diseases. J Rheum 1984;11:425-31.

30. Choi EKK, Gatenby PA, Bateman JF, Cole WG. Antibodies to type II collagen in SLE: A role in the pathogenesis of deforming arthritis? Immunol Cell Biol 1990;68:27-31.

31. Antes U, Heinz H-P, Loos M. Evidence for the presence of autoantibodies to the collagen-like portion of C1q in systemic lupus erythematosus. Arthritis Rheum 1988;4:457-64.

32. Smolen JS, Menzel EJ, Scherak 0, Kojer M, Kolarz G, Steffen C, Mayr WR. Lymphocyte transformation to denatured type I collagen and B lymphocyte alloantigens in rheumatoid arthritis. Arthritis Rheum 1980;23:424-31.

33. Stuart JM, Postlewaite AE, Townes AS, Kang AH. Cell-mediated immunity to collagen and collagen α chains in rheumatoid arthritis and other rheumatic diseases. Amer J Med 1980;69:13-18.

34. Londei M, Savill CM, Verhoef A, Brennan F, Leech ZA, Duance V, Maini RN, Feldmann M. Persistence of collagen type II-specific T-cell clones in the synovial membrane of a patient with rheumatoid arthritis. Proc Natl Acad Sci USA 1989;86:636-40.

35. Lacour M, Rudolphi U, Schlesier M, Peter H. Type II collagen-specific human T cell lines established from healthy donors. Eur J Immunol 1990;20:931-34.

36. Wooley PH, Luthra HS, Stuart JM, David CS. Type II collagen-induced arthritis in mice. 1. Major histocompatibility complex (I region) linkage and antibody correlates. J Exp Med 1981;154:688-700.

37. Morgan K, Evans HB, Firth SA, Smith MN, Ayad S, Weiss JB, Holt PJL. $\alpha 1 \alpha 2 \alpha 3$ collagen is arthritogenic. Ann Rheum Dis 1983;42:680-83.

38. Stuart JM, Kang AH. Monkeying around with collagen autoimmunity and arthritis. Lab Invest 1986;54:1-3.

39. Terato K, Hasty KA, Cremer MA, Stuart JM, Townes AS, Kang AH. Collagen-induced arthritis in mice: localisation of an arthritogenic determinant to a fragment of type II collagen molecule. J Exp Med 1985;162:637-46.

40. Morgan K,Clague RB, Shaw MJ, Firth SA, Twose TM, Holt PJL. Native type II collagen-induced arthritis in the rat. The effect of complement depletion by cobra venom factor. Arthritis Rheum 1981;24:1356-62.

41. Stuart JM, Tomoda K, Yoo TJ, Townes AS, Kang AH. Serum transfer of collagen-induced arthritis. II. Identification and localisation of autoantibody to type II collagen in donor and recipient rats. Arthritis Rheum 1983;26:1237-44.

42. Griffiths MM, Eichwald EJ, Martin JH, Smith CB, DeWitt CW. Immunogenetic control of experimental type II collagen-induced arthritis. 1. Susceptibility and resistance among inbred strains of rats. Arthritis Rheum 1981;24:781-89.

ANTI-RHEUMATIC DRUGS & ARTICULAR CARTILAGE

R W Jubb
Department of Rheumatology
Selly Oak Hospital
Birmingham B29

INTRODUCTION

Articular cartilage is a living tissue. The chondrocytes within cartilage matrix respond to a variety of chemical and mechanical mediators. These cells can destroy or augment the matrix depending on the signals that they receive. In addition, the extra-cellular matrix is susceptible to products from the synovium, the synovial fluid, and the subchondral bone.

Many mechanisms can contribute to the destruction of the cartilage in arthritis. These include the production of abnormal matrix, the inhibition of matrix synthesis, and the catabolic effect of chondrocytic, and exogenous enzymes. The importance of these mechanisms has still to be elucidated for the two major forms of destructive arthritis; rheumatoid disease and osteoarthritis.

Current medical practice tends to treat symptomatic arthritis. Treatment is therefore directed towards relief of pain and improvement in joint function. The state of the cartilage is often of secondary interest and the effect that drugs might have on this tissue a tertiary consideration!

The evidence for potentially chondroprotective agents was fully reviewed in 1987 (1, 2). This review concentrates on subsequent publications on anti-rheumatic drugs and articular cartilage, although it should be remembered that any drug reaching the joint could modify its behaviour. Current evidence indicates that the biological activity of the chondrocytes is very different in normal, osteoarthritic and inflammatory cartilage. The effect of drugs has, therefore, been considered in this review by disease rather than by drug.

Sources of Evidence

Information about cartilage behaviour can be gained from animal and human tissues, which can be studied within the whole animal or after surgical removal. The most clinically relevant evidence remains that derived from patients while the least relevant is likely to be from dissected animal tissue. Insight into human cellular behaviour can be gained from animal studies but extrapolation is likely to be misleading. For example, in a recent report intra-articular steroids cause extensive loss of proteoglycan from articular cartilage (3), while in another study steroids have no detrimental effect on normal cartilage and protect the breakdown of cartilage in osteoarthritis (4). Both papers are animal studies and the discrepancy makes extrapolation to humans difficult. The explanation could be due to using different animals (horse and dog), different joints (radiocarpal and knee), different doses of the steroids (120mg/joint and 5mg/joint), or different methods of tissue analysis.

Cells can exhibit a biphasic response to a drug with inhibition of a cellular process at one concentration and stimulation of the same process at another (5). A relevant example is the observation that sub-therapeutic concentrations of non-steroidal anti-inflammatory drugs (NSAIDs) can stimulate the secretion of prostaglandins from human synoviocytes in culture rather than the expected inhibition (6). In another report, NSAIDs blocked the prostaglandin release from interleukin-1 stimulated cartilage while having no effect on the proteoglycan synthesis (7).

In tissue culture, the effect of drugs on cartilage metabolism can be monitored by more sophisticated methods that measure rates of matrix synthesis and depletion as well as the structure of the matrix components. For example, the amount of sulphate incorporated is taken as a measure of proteoglycan synthesis. It is generally presumed that an increase is 'good' while a decrease is 'bad', however, this rate of sulphation gives no information about the quality of the proteoglycan. Studies that use more detailed analyses of the matrix components will perhaps be of more help.

The behaviour of cartilage in tissue culture depends on the quality of the culture medium. Many culture systems fail to use chemically-defined medium; serum contains unquantified amounts of growth factors and other biologically active compounds which hinders interpretation and comparison of the results. The source and type of cartilage is often diverse ranging from chondrosarcoma cells to avian chondrocytes.

In animal models, the cartilage changes are monitored by morphological, histological and biochemical methods. These are then compared to the changes seen in human diseased cartilage.

In human studies, monitoring methods are limited. The opportunity for tissue analysis is restricted and there are no routine tests to measure the cartilage changes in arthritis. One reason is that the articular cartilage only accounts for a minority of the total body cartilage and there is evidence that extra-articular cartilage is involved in arthritis (8).

The best technique at the moment remains the radiological change in a particular joint.

EFFECT OF DRUGS ON NORMAL CARTILAGE

The effect of anti-rheumatic drugs on normal cartilage could be important. Many joint diseases affect only a limited number of joints and, hence, the use of certain drugs over prolonged periods of time could have a deleterious effect on the unaffected cartilage. Also, there are now several medical conditions where chondro-active drugs are used long-term; for example, low dose aspirin is used in the treatment of thrombotic vascular disease and oestrogens are being increasingly advocated as a prophylaxis for post-menopausal osteoporosis.

Tissue Culture

Proteoglycan synthesis, in culture experiments, has been studied in many papers. "Chondroprotective agents" such as extract of bone (matrigenin) (9), pentosan polysulphate (SP54) (8),glycosaminoglycan polysulphate (Arteparon) (8), and glycosaminoglycan-peptide complex (Rumalon) (10) have all been reported to increase the synthesis of proteoglycan by chondrocytes. Some drugs, including many non-steroidal anti-inflammatory drugs (11) have a neutral effect, while others such as hydrocortisone (12, 13), oestradiol (14), and salicylate (12) reduce proteoglycan synthesis.

Type II collagen is the major collagenous product from hyaline cartilage chondrocytes. Several anti-inflammatory drugs can inhibit its synthesis in culture including indomethacin, ketoprofen, ibuprofen and aspirin; etodolac and piroxicam were reported to cause no inhibition (15). Although human chondrocytes were used some were costal cartilage and others were from diseased knee joints (disease not specified).

Animal Studies

Articular cartilage in normal animals is susceptible to many drugs. Hydrocortisone reduces the proteoglycan in normal rabbit knee cartilage; an effect that is abrogated by pentosan polysulphate (13). Similar proteoglycan loss has been reported with corticosteroid injection into horse radiocarpal joints (3), whereas, as mentioned earlier, normal dog cartilage was unaffected by intra-articular steroids (4).

Over the past few years, Kalbhen has studied the effect of many anti-inflammatory drugs on the cartilage in the knee joint of normal hens (16). In this model many drugs induced destructive changes while a few (fenbufen, ketoprofen, diclofenac and tiaprofenic acid) caused no degeneration.

Dietary change alone can modify chondrocyte behaviour in some animals as illustrated by an inhibition of cartilage proteoglycan synthesis in rats fed a diet rich in fish oils (17); the extensive lay use of fish oil supplements could have more implications for joint behaviour than just the perceived suppression of inflammatory joint symptoms.

EFFECT OF DRUGS ON OSTEOARTICULAR CARTILAGE

In established osteoarthritis, the chondrocytes have formed clones of cells that are often actively releasing proteoglycan while between the cell clusters the matrix is devoid of proteoglycan and there are many empty lacunae suggesting a mixture of chondrocyte death and proliferation. The chondrocyte clusters reside in a disrupted cartilage matrix that is quite unlike normal cartilage.

The effect of drugs in osteoarthritis is an area of considerable research activity and major support from many pharmaceutical companies. It is in this disease that the concept of chondroprotection has received most interest.

Non-Steroidal Anti-inflammatory Drugs

Tissue Culture

Recent work continues to demonstrate differences between anti-inflammatory drugs. During organ culture of osteoarticular cartilage, the proteoglycan synthesis can be inhibited by salicylate (12) but not by tiaprofenic acid (12) or ketoprofen (18). Piroxicam downregulates the expression of interleukin-1 in organ culture of osteoarthritic synovial tissue (19), reminding us that the effect of drugs on the whole joint must be considered.

Animal Studies

Tiaprofenic acid has been used in the Pond-Nuki model of osteoarthritis (20). Cruciate ligament damage in the dog leads to cartilage changes similar to those of human osteoarthritis. Tiaprofenic acid, which was given from one week after the surgical rupture of the cruciate ligament, reduced both the degradation of proteoglycan and the histological grading after twelve weeks.

Clinical Studies

A clinical study has been reported recently using two non-steroidal anti-inflammatory drugs (21). One hundred and five patients, who were awaiting arthroplasty of the hip, were randomly allocated to take either indomethacin or azapropazone. They were then monitored for changes in symptoms and radiological alterations. Two observations were made; the patients taking indomethacin required operations sooner and the radiological loss of joint space was greater with this drug. It was suggested that the difference in inhibition of prostaglandin synthesis could be important. Unfortunately there was no control group which might have established if both drugs aggravated the progress of the osteoarthritis, rather than just suggesting a between treatment effect.

Corticosteriods

Traditionally, corticosteroids have only been used in osteoarthritis for the occasional intra-articular injection to reduce signs and symptoms of inflammation. Recent animal evidence might suggest an alternative role.

Animal Studies

When given prophylactically in the Pond-Nuki model, the degenerative changes were abrogated by exogenous hydrocortisone (4). Although this is a mechanical model for osteoarthritis, synovial changes do occur and hence the site of action of the steroid cannot be assumed to be the chondrocyte.

Clinical Studies
A large clinical study of osteoarthritis of the knee with effusion found that an intra-articular injection of betamethasone gave rapid relief of symptoms. This improvement was maintained for at least one year with additional injections (maximum of three injections in the year) (22). Unfortunately, there was no untreated control group for comparison nor any evidence that the cartilage had been modified.

"Chondroprotective Agents"
This term denotes a group of drugs that are prescribed extensively in some countries to treat osteoarthritis. They are used to modify both the symptoms and the final outcome of the disease. The two commonest drugs have been glycosaminoglycan polysulphate (Arteparon) and glycosaminoglycan-peptide complex (Rumalon). Others include sodium pentosan polysulphate (SP54), hyaluronates (Hylans), and superoxide dismutase (Orgotein).

Arteparon and Rumalon are extracts of bovine tissue; Arteparon is derived from lung and tracheal tissue while Rumalon is from cartilage and bone marrow. Neither are single chemical compounds and batch variation is a potential problem. Both are given by injection and the recent concern with bovine spongiform encephalopathy has raised a further worry (23). These compounds have been available for over twenty five years during which time they have been extensively investigated and are the subject of a detailed review (24). They are powerful proteinase enzyme inhibitors; it is probably these enzymes that are involved in the degradation of the cartilage matrix.

Animal Studies
The effects of chondroprotective drugs on animal models of osteoarthritis have been reported recently by several groups. Arteparon reduces the arthritic changes in the Pond-Nuki dog model (25) while sodium hyaluronate reduces the amount of soluble gylcosaminoglycan from articular cartilage in the same model (26). In the rabbit, the osteoarthritic changes in the partial menisectomy model are modified by Rumalon (27), and in the cruciate ligament model, tranexamic acid reduces the destructive changes (27); this compound is also an enzyme inhibitor and affects plasminogen activator.

Clinical Studies
Controlled clinical trial data is not strong. This is partly because both Arteparon and Rumalon became popular in Europe before rigorous clinical trials were common. Rejholec reported some long-term controlled studies from Prague in which both Arteparon and Rumalon influenced the osteoarthritic process (2). Symptoms, quality of life, ability to work, joint function, NSAID consumption and the incidence of surgical interventions were all significantly improved in comparison with controls. At the end of five years about 35% of the treatment groups showed no radiological progression compared to only 5% in the control group.

EFFECT OF DRUGS ON CARTILAGE FROM INFLAMMATORY ARTHRITIS
The inflammatory process in the synovium has profound effects on the metabolism of the chondrocyte and the stability of the cartilage matrix. Signals from a variety of cells can induce the cartilage to auto-destruct (29). In particular,certain cytokines (including interleukin-1 and tumour necrosis factor) convert the chondrocyte from a matrix synthesiser to a matrix destroyer. There is evidence, in culture, that other humoral agents (eg. insulin-like growth factor) can reverse the catabolism (30). The many cells in the synovium and synovial fluid release catabolic enzymes during inflammation that have a direct effect on the cartilage matrix. As mentioned earlier, it is possible that some of the biological activity of the chondroprotective agents is as an enzyme inhibitor. These drugs, however, have not been tested for therapeutic activity in inflammatory arthritis.

Animal Studies
The emphasis of drug therapy research in inflammatory arthritis has been to reduce the symptoms. A recent paper seems to confirm the widely held view that non-steroidal anti-inflammatory drugs do not reduce cartilage breakdown. Piroxicam, diclofenac and tiaprofenic acid all suppressed the signs of inflammation in an antigen-induced model of inflammatory arthritis, but did not affect the cartilage damage (31). In a similar model, indomethacin increased the loss of proteoglycan from the cartilage as well as reducing the synovitis (32), while steroids reduced the cartilage breakdown despite causing inhibition of proteoglycan synthesis in normal cartilage (31). This emphasises the difficulty of extrapolation from data on normal tissue behaviour to that of diseased tissue.

Clinical Studies
Monitoring cartilage changes in inflammatory arthritis remains a problem. As well as the problems encountered with degenerative arthritis, there is evidence that nonarticular cartilage is also affected (5). Second-line drugs have been shown to reduce the rate of formation of radiological damage (33). It is likely that such an action would also be beneficial to the cartilage, but firm data is awaited about the articular cartilage in this type of study. A report on the effect of methotrexate on interleukin-1 secretion and synthesis does not seem very encouraging, since the drug had no detectable effect on this cytokine in rheumatoid arthritis (34).

CONCLUSION
If preservation of cartilage in human arthritis is an objective, then there is no substitute for adequate clinical studies, even though, it is well recognised that the monitoring of therapy in arthritis is crude and often indirect. Animal and tissue culture studies are being used as evidence to recommend certain NSAID's as chondroprotective agents in the treatment of both rheumatoid and osteoarthritis. It must be clearly recognised that the clinical evidence is lacking and, as this review demonstrates, it is wrong to extrapolate such indirect evidence.

To improve our knowledge and understanding of chondro-active drugs in patients, there are three areas for further research. One, is to search for better tools to monitor human arthritis. Two, is to use the tissue culture and animal models to seek potentially more effective drugs. Three, is to sort out our present drugs with our present methods of assessment.

Despite many anti-arthritic drugs being around for more than twenty years our knowledge of their behaviour in human arthritis is still rudimentary. Slowly evolving diseases require long term studies. These studies need to be adequately controlled (if possible with placebo treatments), they must be of sufficient length to measure outcome, and they must be large enough to be statistically robust. At the moment, there are only a few such studies in progress and it will still be some time before the results are known. Even when these studies are complete there are many unanswered questions about the drugs we currently use to treat our patients with arthritis. Animal and tissue culture work is no substitute for clinical research; the two are complimentary and the clinical studies are ignored at our peril even though they are slow, cumbersome and not very exciting.

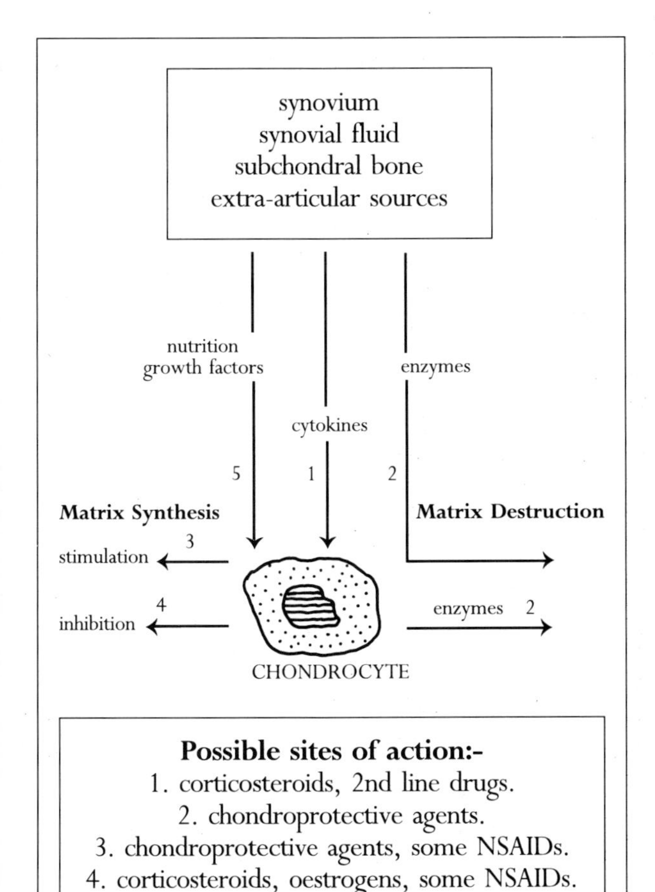

Anti-Rheumatic Drugs and Articular Cartilage Metabolism

REFERENCES

1. Laboratory evaluation of antiarthritic drugs as potential chondroprotective agents. D Burkhardt, P Ghosh *Sem Arth Rheum.* 1987; **17**, suppl1;3-34.

2. Long-term studies of antiosteoarthritic drugs: an assessment Rejholec V. *Sem Arth Rheum.* 1987; **17**, suppl1;35-53.

3. Changes in articular cartilage after intra-articular injections of methyl prednisolone acetate in horses. Chunekamrai S, Krook LP, Lust G, Maylin GA. *Am J Vet Res.* 1989; **50**; 1733-41.

4. Protective effects of corticosteroids on cartilage lesions and osteophyte formation in the Pond-Nuki dog model of osteoarthritis. Pelletier J-P, Martel-Pelletier J. *Arth Rheum.* 1989; **32**; 181-93.

5. Involvement of nonarticular cartilage as demonstrated by release of a cartilage-specific protein in rheumatoid arthritis. Saxne T, Heinegard D. *Arth Rheum.* 1989; **32**; 1080-6.

6. Enhanced prostaglandin E2 secretion by cytokine-stimulated human synoviocytes in the presence of subtherapeutic concentrations of nonsteroidal anti-inflammatory drugs. Lindsley HB, Smith DD. *Arth Rheum.* 1990; **33**; 1162-9.

7. Independent effects of interleukin-1 on proteoglycan breakdown, proteoglycan synthesis and prostaglandin E2 release from cartilage in organ culture. Arner EC, Pratt MA. *Arth Rheum.* 1989;**32**;288-97.

8. Evaluation of the effect of antiarthritic drugs on the secretion of proteoglycans by lapine chondrocytes using a novel assay procedure. Collier S, Ghosh P. *Ann Rheum Dis.* 1989; **48**; 372-81.

9. The effects of 'matrigenin' activity from bovine bone on the glycosaminoglycans of bovine articular cartilage in culture. A model for cartilage repair by bone derived factors. Brown S, Irwin D, Anastassiades T. *J Rheumatol.* 1989;**16**; 209-16.

10. Stimulation of protein-chondroitin sulphate synthesis by normal and osteoarthritic articular cartilage. Bollet AJ. *Arth Rheum.* 1968; **11**; 663-673.

11. Anti-Rheumatic Drugs and Cartilage. Gosh P. *Baillieres Clin Rheumatol.* 1988; **2**; 309-38.

12. In vitro effects of tiaprofenic acid, sodium salicylate and hydrocortisone on the proteoglycan metabolism of human osteoarthritic cartilage. Pelletier J-P, Cloutier J-M, Martel-Pelletier J. *J Rheumatol.* 1989; **16**; 646-55.

13. Pentosan polysulphate (Cartophen) prevents the hydrocortisone induced loss of hyaluronic acid and proteoglycans from cartilage of rabbit joint as well as normalises the keratan sulphate levels in their serum. Kongtawelert P, Brooks PM, Ghosh P. *J Rheumatol.* 1989; **16**; 1454-9.

14. Pharmacological actions of 17ß-oestradiol on articular cartilage chondrocytes and chondrosarcoma chondrocytes. Mackintosh D, Mason RM. *Biochem Biophys Acta.* 1988; **59**; 246-8.

15. Etodolac preserves cartilage-specific phenotype in human chondrocytes: effects on type II collagen synthesis and associated mRNA levels. Goldring MB, Sohbat E, Elwell JM, Chang JY. *E J of Rheum Infl.* 1990; **10**; 10-21.

16. The influence of NSAIDs on morphology or articular cartilage. Kalbhen DA. *Scand J Rheum. suppl.* 1988; **77**; 13-22.

17. Metabolic and ultrastructural changes in articular cartilage of rats fed dietary supplements of omega-3 fatty acids. Lippiello L, Fienhold M, Grandjean C. *Arth Rheum.* 1990; **33**; 1029-36.

18. In vitro influence of ketoprofen on the proteoglycan metabolism of human normal and osteoarthritis cartilage. Wilbrink B, Van Der Veen MJ, Huber J, Van Roy JLAM, Huber-Bruning O. *Agents and Action.* 1991; **32**; 154-159.

19. NSAID induction of interleukin-1/catabolin inhibitor production by osteoarthritic synovial tissue. JH Herman, WG Sowder, EV Hess.*J Rheumatol.* 1991; **18**; suppl 27; 124-126.

20. Treatment of osteoarthritis with tiaprofenic acid: biochemical and histological protection against cartilage breakdown in the Pond-Nuki canine model. DS Howell, JC Pita, FJ Muller, DH Manicourt, RD Altman. *J Rheumatol.* 1991; **18**, suppl 27; 138-142.

21. Effect of non-steroidal anti-inflammatory drugs on the course of osteoarthritis. S Rashad, P Revell, A Hemingway, F Low, K Rainsford, F Walker.*Lancet.* 1989; Sept **2;** 519-522.

22. A French controlled multicentre study of intraarticular orgotein versus intraarticular corticosteroids in the treatment of knee osteoarthritis: a one year follow-up.
B Mazieres, A-M Masquelier, M-H Capron. *J Rheumatol.* 1991; **18**,suppl 27; 134-137.

23. Bovine spongiform encephalopathy. Matthews WB. *Br Med J.* 1990; **300**; 412-13.

24. Chondroprotection.*Sem Arth Rheum.* 1987; **17**; no.2 (suppl 1).

25. Therapeutic treatment of canine osteoarthritis with glycosaminoglycan polysulfuric acid ester. Altman RD, Dean DD, Muniz OE, Howell DS. *Arth Rheum.* 1989; **32**; 1300-7.

26. Intraarticular sodium hyaluronate injections in the Pond-Nuki experimental model of osteoarthritis in dogs. Abatangelo G, Botti P, Del Bue M, et al. *Clin Orthop.* 1989; **241**; 278-85.

27. The effect of rumalon, a glycosaminoglycan protein complex, in partial menisectomy model of osteoarthritis in rabbits. Moskowitz RW, Reese JH, Young RG, Fein-Krantz D, Malemud CJ,.Caplan AI. *J Rheumatol.* 1991; **18**; 205-209.

28. Study of an inhibitor of plasminogen activator (tranexamic acid) in the treatment of experimental osteoarthritis.
E Vignon, P Mathieu, J Bejui, J Descotes, D Hartmann, LM Patricot, M Richard. *J Rheumatol.* 1991; **18**; suppl 27; 131-133.

29. The effect of synovial tissue on the breakdown of articular cartilage in organ culture. Fell HB, Jubb RW. *Arth Rheum.* 1977; **20**; 1359-1371.

30. Insulin-like growth factor 1 can decrease degradation and promote synthesis of proteoglycan in cartilage exposed to cytokines. Tyler JA. *Biochem J.* 1989; **260**; 543-8.

31. Impact of NSAID and steroids on cartilage destruction in murine antigen induced arthritis. Wim B van den Berg. *J Rheumatol.* 1991; **18**, suppl 27; 122-123.

32. Effect of indomethacin on swelling, lymphocytic influx, and cartilage proteoglycan depletion in experimental arthritis. Pettipher ER, Henderson B, Edwards JCW, Higgs GA. *Ann Rheum Dis.* 1989; **48**; 623-7.

33. Effects of hyroxychloroquine and sulphasalazine on the progression of joint damage in rheumatoid arthritis.
van der Heijde DMFM, van Riel PLCM, Nuver-Zwart IH, Gribnau FWJ, van de Putte. *Lancet.* 1989; **i**; 1036-8.

34. The effects of methotrexate on the production and activity of interleukin-1. Segal R, Mozws E, Yaron M, Tartakovsky B. *Arth Rheum.* 1989; **32**; 370-7.

January 1992

FREE RADICALS AND HYPOXIC-REPERFUSION INJURY

P Merry, ARC Research Fellow
M Grootveld, Lecturer in Clinical Chemistry
D R Blake, ARC Professor of Rheumatology
The London Hospital Medical College
London E1

INTRODUCTION

The development of an inflammatory synovitis such as rheumatoid arthritis (RA), more often than not results in a process that extends continuously over several years and often throughout the life of the patient. This dogged persistence is quite exceptional in medicine. In the last ten years there has been an explosion of interest in a mechanism of **free radical**-mediated inflammation termed **hypoxic-reperfusion injury,** the existence of which has been established in many disease states and organ systems[1]. In 1986 we proposed that the **persistence** of chronic synovitis could be explained by the occurrence of hypoxic-reperfusion injury in the joint. Such a mechanism has since been shown to occur[2,3]. In this report we look at the evidence.

FREE RADICALS

What is a free radical? Molecules achieve their stability by electron pairing and subsequent covalent bond formation. A free radical may be defined as an atom or molecule with one or more unpaired electrons, capable of independent existence They are denoted by a superscripted dot $R^{\bullet}$, and may have a positive or negative charge, or be neutral. Examples include the oxygen molecule, the hydrogen atom and most transition metals. The unpaired electron(s) that characterises an oxygen-derived free radical, confers a high level of instability and thus chemical reactivity on the molecule. Consequently, oxygen free radicals are often tissue damaging and usually only exist at low steady state concentrations *in vivo*[4].

Molecular oxygen – 0_2 – itself is a bi-radical, as it has two unpaired electrons and plays an important role as an electron acceptor. The addition of a single electron to 0_2 produces the superoxide radical – an anion- $0_2^{\bar{\bullet}}$ Superoxide is capable of participating in reaction sequences to produce other reactive oxygen species – for example the hydroxyl radical ($^{\bullet}OH$) and hydrogen peroxide (H_2O_2). These reaction sequences, and the involvement of transition metal catalysts are shown in the table.

TABLE I

[1] **Dismutation**
$$20_2^{\bar{\bullet}} + 2H^+ \rightarrow H_20_2 + 0_2$$

[2] **The reduction of iron (III) to iron (II)**
$$Fe^{3+} + 0_2^{\bar{\bullet}} \rightarrow \underbrace{(Fe^{3+}\text{-}0_2^{\bullet}/Fe^{2+}\text{-}0_2)}_{\textbf{perferryl species}} \rightarrow Fe^{2+} + 0_2$$

[3] **The iron-catalysed Haber-Weiss Reaction**
$$0_2^{\bar{\bullet}} + H_20_2 \xrightarrow[\text{catalyst}]{\text{iron-complex}} 0_2 + {}^{\bullet}OH + OH^-$$

[4] **The Fenton reaction**
$$Fe^{2+} + H_20_2 \rightarrow Fe^{3+} + {}^{\bullet}OH + OH^-$$

The hydroxyl radical is highly reactive; any produced *in vivo* will react with molecules at or within a few nanometres from its site of production. In biological systems iron does not exist in a 'free' state but exists in complexes with phosphate esters (such as ATP), carboxylic acids (eg citrate) and iron storage / transport proteins (ferritin, lactoferrin and transferrin). However a number of the low-molecular-mass iron complexes have the ability to catalyse the free-radical degradation of a wide range of biomolecules, including DNA. We have recently demonstrated that low-molecular-mass iron (III) is present as complexes with citrate in synovial fluid of patients with inflammatory synovitis: such iron will catalyse the formation of $^{\bullet}OH$

FREE RADICALS AND HEALTH

When polymorphonuclear leucocytes (PMNs) engulf microbes, they rapidly *consume* oxygen. This is referred to as the **respiratory burst,** a process which is not used for generating energy by mitochondrial oxidative phosphorylation which is responsible for the bulk of our inhaled oxygen usage. The oxygen consumption is utilised by PMNs to produce free radicals which are responsible for killing microbial pathogens. At least two enzymatic systems are responsible for this generation of microbicidal oxidants:- a) A plasma membrane bound NADPH oxidase system incorporating cytochrome-b-245[5]. b) The myeloperoxidase system; a haemoprotein located within the azurophilic granules, which in conjunction with a halide amplifies H_2O_2 dependant reactions. It is likely that there are further systems centred around the radical nitric oxide ($NO^{\bullet}$).

Evidence for the importance of free radical generation by PMNs comes from:- a) The demonstration that cells deprived of oxygen engulf but do not kill certain microbes efficiently, and, b) the syndrome of chronic granulomatous disease (CGD) in which the respiratory burst fails due to an inherited absence of cytochrome-b-245, resulting in persistent but selective bacterial infections.

FREE RADICALS AND TISSUE DAMAGE: THE EVIDENCE FOR THEIR INVOLVEMENT IN INFLAMMATORY SYNOVITIS

A consequence of uncontrolled production of free radicals is damage to biomolecules leading to altered function and disease. There is now much evidence both direct and indirect implicating radicals in the pathogenesis of inflammatory synovitis. Many cells present in the inflamed joint such as macrophages, neutrophils, lymphocytes and endothelial cells have the capacity, when isolated and stimulated, to produce free radicals: when stimulated in the environment of critical biomolecules such as lipids, DNA, proteins, carbohydrates, proteoglycans and glycosaminoglycans, they promote oxidative damage.

LIPID PEROXIDATION

The cell membrane, primarily composed of polyunsaturated fatty acids (PUFA), is a well studied target for radical attack, and the resultant process of lipid peroxidation (ie. rancidification) causes cell membrane damage (reviewed in 6)[6]. Polyunsaturated lipids undergoing the process of peroxidation give rise to the formation of the lipid breakdown products such as diene conjugates and thiobarbituric acid reactive substances (TBARS). These have become useful markers of oxidative damage to lipids.

Levels of TBARS in the synovial fluids of RA patients have been demonstrated to correlate with clinical severity of the disease. Additionally, examination of synovial fluid from patients with inflammatory and non-inflammatory joint effusions has demonstrated that conjugated dienes are present in both groups: the inflammatory group having significantly more (reviewed in 7)[7]. Radical attack on PUFAs leads to the generation of a chemotactic lipid recruiting further neutrophils.

PROTEIN OXIDATION

Exposure of proteins to free radicals will lead to denaturation, loss of function, cross-linking, aggregation and fragmentation[8]. There is much evidence of radical-mediated protein damage occurring in inflammatory synovitis. Immunoglobulin G (IgG) when exposed to free radicals *in vitro,* develops a characteristic autofluorescence (Ex 360nm, Em 454nm) and forms both monomeric and aggregated complexes. IgG with these characteristics is present in rheumatoid synovial fluid. Methionine residues on α-1-antitrypsin (the primary inhibitor of leucocyte elastase in serum) are oxidised to sulphoxide adducts by free radicals, rendering the molecule biologically inactive. Such radical-damaged α-1-antitrypsin is present in rheumatoid synovial fluid[9].

OXIDATION OF OTHER BIOMOLECULES

Free radicals also react with polysaccharides and induce fragmentation. The major macromolecule of synovial fluid, which accounts for its viscosity, is the glycosaminoglycan hyaluronate. Loss of synovial fluid viscosity is generally thought to be due to the depolymerisation of hyaluronate. *In vitro* experiments have shown that free radicals depolymerize hyaluronic acid producing lower synovial fluid viscosity[10].

There is also evidence linking free radicals with cartilage damage. It is known that •OH can degrade cartilage and that HOCI, derived from the myeloperoxidase – H_2O_2-C1 system, can attack proteoglycans, whilst H_2O_2 inhibits proteoglycan synthesis by cultured bovine articular cartilage. Injection of the hydrogen peroxide-producing enzyme, glucose oxidase, into mice or rat knees causes severe cartilage damage and chondrocyte death.

IRON AND INFLAMMATORY SYNOVITIS

Several observations suggest a role for iron-dependent radical reactions in promoting inflammatory joint disease. Animal studies show that a single injection of autologous blood into the rabbit knee produced synovitis and autologous blood will prolong a 'transient', though chronic, inflammatory reaction[11].

In active RA the inflamed synovium is subject to recurrent traumatic microbleeding and there is increased deposition of iron in the form of ferritin in the synovium[12], and iron capable of catalyzing the formation of •OH is present in synovial fluid, the concentration correlating loosely with parameters of disease activity[13]. In early RA, high levels of synovial iron predict a poor prognosis[12], whilst in RA, infusion of iron complexes is known to exacerbate synovitis, the effect appearing to be mediated by iron-promoted lipid peroxidation[14]. Mild nutritional iron deficiency significantly reduces the severity of adjuvant joint inflammation in rats without affecting the systemic components of the disease[15], and iron chelators are anti-inflammatory in a variety of animal models of inflammation[16].

THE OXYGEN PARADOX IN INFLAMMATORY SYNOVITIS

There is thus ample evidence implicating free radicals in the pathogenesis of inflammatory synovitis. However there is a quandary in that radical-mediated oxidative damage requires an adequate supply of oxygen. The oxygen tension in inflammatory synovial fluid is low; Lund-Oleson (1970)[17] found a mean value of synovial fluid pO_2 of 26 mmHg in 85 patients with RA. These observations might therefore suggest that cells within the joint may have a depressed, rather than increased, ability to generate free radicals. Edwards et al (1984)[18] investigated this concept *in vitro,* by examining the effect of altering the ambient O_2 concentration on the ability of stimulated rat PMNs to produce free radicals. They concluded that radical production by PMNs at an inflammatory site, such as an inflamed joint, may well be limited by the ambient O_2 concentration.

Therefore, in the relatively hypoxic environment of the

chronically inflamed joint, how are free radicals generated? In answer to this question, we speculated that radicals are generated within the inflamed joint by a hypoxic-reperfusion mechanism[19].

HYPOXIC-REPERFUSION INJURY

Ischæmia-induced tissue injury is recognised as a major factor in the pathogenesis of life-threatening diseases, for example coronary artery disease. It is now becoming clear that the mechanism of so-called ischæmic damage is not simple. It is certainly true that protracted ischæmia by itself, will ultimately produce tissue death. However, in some clinical situations a substantial part of the injury may be more properly termed **reperfusion** injury[1]. That is to say, much of the injury may occur not during the period of temporary hypoxia but rather during the period when oxygen is reintroduced to the tissue by the restoration of the blood supply. When this circumstance arises, free radicals may be generated in abundance due to the uncoupling of a variety of intracellular redox systems, and play a major role in producing microvascular and parenchymal damage.

Radical-promoted hypoxic-reperfusion injury was first demonstrated in the cat intestine. Transient ischæmia to the small bowel of the cat resulted in an increased intestinal capillary permeability and albumin clearance, which was magnified ten-fold on reperfusion. However, the increased intestinal capillary permeability that was observed during reperfusion was blocked by pre-dosing with the radical scavenging enzymes superoxide dismutase (SOD) or catalase, or allopurinol, a xanthine oxidase inhibitor[20]. Hypoxic-reperfusion injury has been applied to many disease states, including transient coronary or cerebral ischæmia, ischæmic acute renal failure, early renal and bone transplant rejection.

THE BIOCHEMISTRY OF HYPOXIC-REPERFUSION INJURY

One source of free radicals, established as a result of multiple investigations into hypoxic-reperfusion injury, is the xanthine oxidase/dehydrogenase enzymatic system[1].

The mechanism for the production of $O_2^{\bar{\bullet}}$ in post ischæmic tissues appears to be effected by changes in purine metabolism within ischæmic cells. During temporary ischæmia low oxygen concentrations halt mitochondrial oxidative phosphorylation, and cellular ATP production becomes dependent on anaerobic glycolysis. This is an inefficient means of ATP production from glucose and also results in the production of lactate. Increasing levels of lactate together with an increasing ratio of NADH to oxidised nicotinamide adenine dinucleotide (NAD^+), eventually lead to the inhibition of glycolysis. Moreover, intracellular ATP and adenosine diphosphate (ADP) levels, already reduced, fall further. This leads to raised levels of adenosine and of its breakdown products, including hypoxanthine and xanthine which are the substrates for the cytosolic xanthine oxidase/dehydrogenase enzyme system.

Xanthine oxidase, normally oxidises hypoxanthine and xanthine to uric acid. It is widely distributed among tissues and is predominantly located in the capillary endothelium[21]. The enzyme is synthesised as xanthine dehydrogenase (type 'D'), which transfers electrons to NAD^+. However, in ischæmic conditions a Ca^{2+}-dependent protease alters the enzyme critically, converting it to an oxidase ('O') form, which no longer transfers electrons to NAD^+, but to O_2 producing $O_2^{\bar{\bullet}}$. Upon reperfusion of temporarily ischæmic tissue, the 'O' form of the enzyme, supplied with oxygen as an electron acceptor and high levels of hypoxanthine, produces a flux of $O_2^{\bar{\bullet}}$ which may be converted either spontaneously or by the enzyme SOD to H_2O_2. In addition, the 'O' form of xanthine oxidase can mobilise iron from ferritin, by a mechanism largely dependent on the generated superoxide. The released iron has the ability to catalyse the formation of $^{\bullet}OH$ from $O_2^{\bar{\bullet}}$ and H_2O_2 via equations 3 and 4. The complement component C_5a, as well as the monocyte product tumour necrosis factor, α, also convert xanthine dehydrogenase to xanthine oxidase in a rapid and irreversible fashion[22]. Activated neutrophils acting on endothelial cells have a similar effect.

Hence, during ischæmia important biochemical changes occur within tissue:- i) A new enzyme activity appears, along with one of its two required substrates. ii) The remaining substrate required for type 'O' activity is molecular O_2, which is supplied during the reperfusion of the tissue; with it comes a burst of $O_2^{\bar{\bullet}}$ and H_2O_2 production. iii) Iron is decompartmentalised, allowing it to catalyse $^{\bullet}OH$ generation.

XANTHINE OXIDASE AND THE JOINT

From the previous discussion it follows that the presence of xanthine oxidase in human synovium may be central to the proposal of hypoxic reperfusion injury to the joint. We have demonstrated that both normal and rheumatoid synovia exhibit xanthine oxidase/dehydrogenase activity[23], located in the capillary endothelium and rapidly converted from a dehydrogenase to an oxidase form.

Electron-spin resonance (ESR) spectroscopy is widely used as a method of identifying and characterizing free radicals in chemical systems. We used ESR spectroscopy coupled with spin-trapping techniques to study free radical generation in rheumatoid synovium subjected to hypoxic/normoxic cycles *in vitro* and observed radical generation which was suppressed by allopurinol, thereby implicating xanthine oxidase as a source[24].

It can be seen that under appropriate conditions, the human synovium has a biochemical potential to generate oxygen-derived free radicals. Does the joint possess the pathophysiological characteristics to produce a hypoxic-reperfusion event?

HYPOXIC-REPERFUSION INJURY AND INFLAMMATORY SYNOVITIS: THE EVIDENCE.

Several physiological features present within the inflamed human joint suggest that movement will provide the potential environment for hypoxic-reperfusion injury, summarised in the diagram.

The intra-articular pressure (IAP) in the normal knee joint of both humans and animals is at or slightly below atmospheric pressure (for a review see 25)[25]. Jayson &

Dixon (1970) demonstrated that in the normal joint, quadriceps contraction produces a subatmospheric pressure. In contrast, patients with RA had significantly higher resting pressures than control subjects with a simulated effusion of the same volume. On quadriceps setting RA patients produced IAPs as high as 200mmHg, well in excess of the synovial capillary perfusion pressure of 30-60mmHg[26]. We fully support these findings, and find a dynamic inverse relationship between synovial fluid oxygen tension and IAP in inflammatory synovitis[27].

The pO_2 in inflamed joints has been measured by several groups, and it is clear that inflammatory effusions have lower oxygen tensions than non-inflammatory effusions. One determinant of synovial fluid oxygen tension is the blood supply to the synovium. This should be related to the IAP, as the synovial membrane and joint capsule form a closed environment in which the IAP is transmitted directly to the synovial membrane vasculature.

We have recently studied microvascular perfusion dynamics within the synovium of the human knee during exercise using laser doppler flowmetry. In the normal knee there was a negligible reduction of capillary perfusion during exercise. In contrast, exercise of the inflamed knee produced occlusion of the synovial capillary bed for the duration of the exercise period. Reperfusion of the synovial membrane occurred on cessation of exercise[2]. Others have since confirmed these observations.

An interesting clinical observation is that joints with acute synovitis secondary to trauma do not proceed to develop chronic synovitis. We have demonstrated that due to reflex muscle inhibition, there is a failure of pathological IAP generation during exercise of joints with acute traumatic synovitis. This provides protection against putative hypoxic-reperfusion injury thereby providing a possible explanation for this clinical conundrum.

Thus, exercise of the inflamed human knee joint provides the potential pathophysiological environment for the promotion of hypoxic-reperfusion injury. We have recently verified this by demonstrating **exercise-induced** oxidative damage to lipids and IgG within the knee joint of patients with inflammatory synovitis[2]. We employed proton Hahn spin-echo Fourier transform nuclear magnetic resonance spectroscopy (SEFT-NMR) to investigate the production of low-molecular-mass oligosaccharides derived from the oxygen radical-mediated depolymerisation of synovial fluid hyaluronan. A resonance attributable to the N-acetyl methyl protons of a molecularly mobile oligosaccharide was detectable and the signal increased in intensity subsequent to exercise.

Overall, we conclude that the peculiar persistence of chronic synovial inflammation may be due, in part, to exercise-induced radical-mediated hypoxic-reperfusion injury to critical biomolecules within the joint. How do these findings relate to some well-established clinical observations in the inflammatory arthropathies?

CLINICAL OBSERVATIONS CONSISTENT WITH HYPOXIC-REPERFUSION INJURY

Joint exercise is central to the mechanism of hypoxic-reperfusion injury and the basic principles are outlined in the accompanying diagram. Therefore resting inflamed joints would mitigate against such injury, promoting a decrease in the level of inflammation. Bed rest is a well-established tool used by rheumatologists to treat inflamed joints. Isolated joint splintage is of proven benefit, and used routinely in clinical practice.

Observations concerning unilateral neurological lesions (involving the upper or lower motor neurone) leading to unilateral paralysis, and the subsequent effect on arthritic conditions, may be pertinent to the theory of hypoxic-reperfusion injury. Thompson and Bywaters (1962)[28] documented 4 cases of classical RA which occurred in hemiplegic patients. All the joints in the completely paralysed limbs were spared, but in two ambulant cases, some joints were involved in the partially paralysed but mobile limbs. All 4 patients were sero-positive, and developed unilateral radiological changes of cartilage loss and bone erosion. The lack of erosive damage on the paralysed side is most interesting. A recent study has provided convincing evidence that oxygen-derived free radicals stimulate osteoclastic bone resorption.[29] Glick (1967)[30] documented 12 cases of RA occurring in patients previously paralysed by poliomyelitis. In this series there was almost total sparing of the joints of the paralysed limb or limbs. Sparing of paralysed joints is not confined to RA, similar observations having also been made in gout and osteoarthritis.

ANTIOXIDANT THERAPY IN INFLAMMATORY SYNOVITIS

Numerous reports have shown that free radical scavengers and antioxidants alleviate symptoms in experimental models of inflammation. Properly controlled clinical studies are, however, sparse. Superoxide dismutase administered intra-articularly has shown definite, though modest effects in osteoarthritis [31]. Studies in rheumatoid arthritis are in progress. Xanthine oxidase inhibitors have not been studied.

Several earlier observations suggest a role for iron-dependent radical reactions in promoting imflammatory joint disease. However, clinical trials with subcutaneous desferrioxamine to rheumatoid patients were curtailed due to potentially severe ocular and cerebral toxicity[32]. Novel orally active iron chelators, that lack ocular toxicity (in animal models) are being developed.

Recently, substantial evidence has accumulated suggesting that long established anti-rheumatic drugs may be exerting their therapeutic effect by acting as antioxidants. Non-steroidal anti-inflammatory drugs have been shown to act as free radical scavengers[33], whilst a multinuclear mixed oxidation state complex of D-penicillamine with copper ions ($[Cu^{I}_{8} Cu^{II}_{6} (D\text{-}Pen)_{12} Cl]^{5-}$), considered to be the active species formed *in vivo,* has been shown to exhibit a SOD-mimetic function. Additionally, it has been reported that D-penicillamine, in the presence of copper(II) ions, may synthesise hydrogen peroxide leading to inhibition of T cell function and an anti-angiogenic effect through inhibition of endothelial cell proliferation [34]. We have recently demonstrated that gold also suppresses angiogenesis via a radical mechanism involving xanthine oxidase/dehydrogenase; novel analogues are being developed. A variety of other novel radical scavenging agents are presently being developed many of which also have the capacity to influence other parts of the inflammatory cascade.

By using the human model of hypoxic-reperfusion injury to dose response antioxidant drugs and investigate the effect of combination therapies, we hope that novel therapeutic regimens may be developed, providing the rheumatologist with another string to his poorly-equipped bow.

ACKNOWLEDGEMENTS

Studies reported by the LHMC Inflammation Group have been supported by grants from the Arthritis & Rheumatism Council, the British Technology Group and Dista Products (UK).

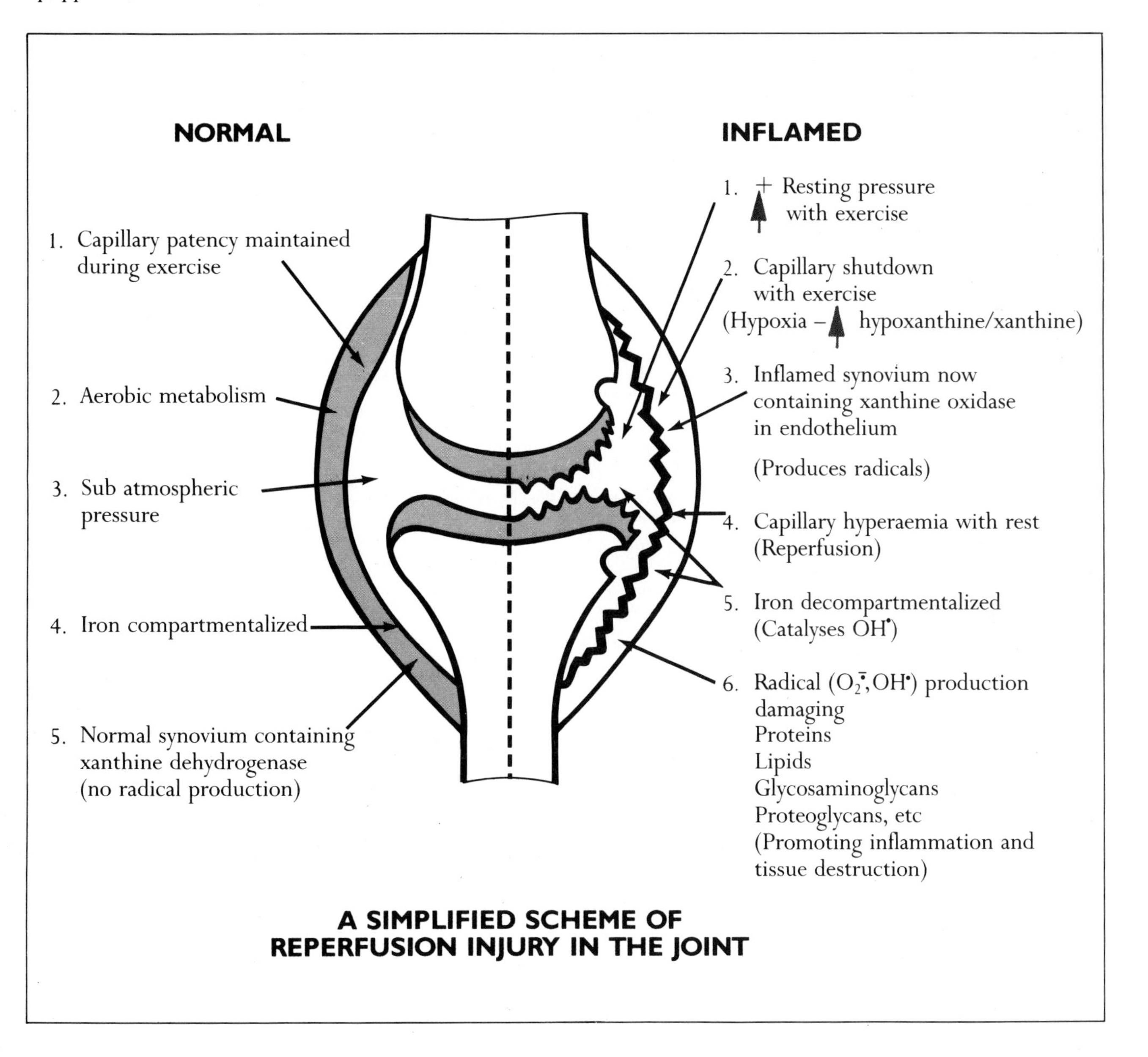

A SIMPLIFIED SCHEME OF REPERFUSION INJURY IN THE JOINT

REFERENCES

1 McCord JM. Oxygen-derived free radicals in post-ischæmic tissue injury.
New Eng J Med 1985; **312:** 159-163.

2 Blake DR, Merry P, Unsworth J, Outhwaite J, Morris CJ, Gray L, Lunec J. Hypoxic-reperfusion injury in the inflamed human joint.
Lancet 1989; **i:** 289-293.

3 Merry P, Grootveld MG, Blake DR. Physiological exercise promotes hypoxic-reperfusion injury to the inflamed human joint.
Lancet 1989; **i:** 1023.

4 Blake DR, Allen R, Lunec J. Free radicals in biological systems – a review orientated to inflammatory processes.
British Medical Bulletin 1987; **43:** 371-385.

5 Segal AW. Variations on the theme of chronic granulomatous disease.
Lancet 1985; **i:** 1378-1382.

6 Dormandy TL. Free-radical pathology and medicine. A review.
J Royal Coll Physicians of London 1989; **23:** 221-227.

7 Lunec J and Blake D R. *Oxidative damage and its relevance to inflammatory joint disease.*
Critical Reviews in Chemistry. Cellular Antioxidant Defense Mechanisms III Vol 3 **(1988) Ed.** Ching Quang Chow, 143-159

8 Lunec J, Blake DR, McCleary SJ, Brailsford S, Bacon PA. Self perpetuating mechanisms of immunoglobulin G aggregation in rheumatoid inflammation.
J Clin Invest 1985; **76:** 2084-2090.

9 Wong PS, Travis J. Isolation and properties of oxidised alpha-1-proteinase inhibitor from human rheumatoid synovial fluid.
Biochem Biophys Res Com 1980; **96:** 1449-1454.

10 Greenwald RA, Moy W W. Effect of oxygen free radicals on hyaluronic acid.
Arthritis Rheum 1980; **23:** 455-463.

11 Yoshino S, Blake DR, Hewitt S, Morris C, Bacon PA. Effect of blood on the activity and persistence of antigen induced inflammation in the rat air pouch.
Ann Rheum Dis 1985; **44:** 485-490.

12 Blake DR, Gallagher PJ, Potter AR, Bell MJ, Bacon PA. The effect of synovial iron on the progression of rheumatoid disease.
Arthritis Rheum 1984; **27:** 495-501.

13 Rowley DA, Gutteridge JMC, Blake DR, Farr M, Halliwell B. Lipid peroxidation in rheumatoid arthritis: Thiobarbituric acid reactive material and catalytic iron salts in synovial fluid from rheumatoid patients.
Clin Sci 1984; **66:** 691-695.

14 Winyard PG, Blake DR, Chirico S, Gutteridge JMC, Lunec J. Mechanism of exacerbation of rheumatoid synovitis by total-dose iron-dextran infusion: in vivo demonstration of iron-promoted oxidative stress.
Lancet 1987; **i:** 69-72.

15 Andrews FJ, Morris CJ, Lewis EJ, Blake DR. Effect of nutritional iron deficiency on acute and chronic inflammation.
Ann Rheum Dis 1987; **46:** 859-865.

16 Blake D, Hall N, Bacon P, Dieppe P, Halliwell B, Gutteridge J. The effect of a specific iron chelating agent on animal models of inflammation.
Ann Rheum Dis 1983; **42:** 89-93.

17 Lund-Oleson K. Oxygen tensions in synovial fluids.
Arthritis Rheum 1970; **13:** 769-776.

18 Edwards SW, Hallet MB, Campbell AK. Oxygen radical production may be limited by oxygen concentration.
Biochem J 1984; **217:** 851-854.

19 Woodruff T, Blake DR, Freeman J, Andrews FJ, Salt P, Lunec J. Is chronic synovitis an example of reperfusion injury?
Ann Rheum Dis 1986; **45:** 608-611.

20 Granger DN, Hollwarth ME, Parks DA. Ischæmia-reperfusion injury: role of oxygen derived free radicals.
Acta Physiol Scand 1986; **Suppl. 548:** 47-63.

21 Jarasch ED, Bruder G, Heid HW. Significance of xanthine oxidase in capillary endothelial cells.
Acta Physiol Scand 1986; **Suppl. 548:** 39-46.

22 Freidl HP, Till GO, Ryan US, Ward PA. Mediator-induced activation of xanthine oxidase in endothelial cells.
FASEB J 1989; **3:** 2512-2518.

23 Allen RE, Outhwaite J, Morris CJ, Blake DR. Xanthine oxido-reductase is present in human synovium.
Ann Rheum Dis 1987; **46:** 843-845.

24 Allen RE, Blake DR, Nazhat NB, Jones P. Superoxide radical generation by inflamed human synovium after hypoxia.
Lancet 1989; **ii:** 282-283.

25 Dixon A & Hawkins C (Eds). *Raised intra-articular pressure - Clinical consequences.*
Bath Institute for Rheumatic Diseases, Bath, **1990.**

26 Jayson MIV, Dixon A StJ. Intra-articular pressure in rheumatoid arthritis of the knee. Ill Pressure changes during joint use.
Ann Rheum Dis 1970; **29:** 401.

27 Unsworth J, Outhwaite J, Blake DR, Morris CJ, Freeman J & Lunec J. Dynamic studies of the relationship between intra-articular pressure, synovial fluid oxygen tension, and lipid peroxidation in the inflamed knee: and example of reperfusion injury.
Ann Clin Biochem. 1988; **25:** 8-11.

28 Thompson M, Bywaters EGL. Unilateral rheumatoid arthritis following hemiplegia.
Ann Rheum Dis 1962; **21:** 370-377.

29 Garrett IR, Boyce BF, Oreffo ROC, Bonewald L, Poser J, Mundy GR. Oxygen-derived free radicals stimulate osteoclastic bone resorption in rodent bone in vitro and in vivo.
J.Clin. Invest 1990; **85:** 632-639.

30 Glick EN. Asymmetrical rheumatoid arthritis after poliomyelitis.
Br Med J 1967; **3:** 26-29.

31 Goebel KM, Storck U, Neurath F. Intrasynovial orgotien therapy in RA.
Lancet 1981; **i:** 1015-1017.

32 Blake DR, Winyard P, Lunec J, Williams A, Good PA, Crewes SJ, Gutteridge JMC, Rowley D, Halliwell B, Cornish A, Hider RC. Cerebral and ocular toxicity induced by Desferrioxamine.
Quart J Med 1985; **56:** 345-355.

33 Halliwell B, Hoult JR, Blake DR. Oxidants, inflammation and anti-inflammatory drugs.
FASEB J 1988; **2:** 2867-2873.

34 Matsubara T, Saura K, Hirohata K, Ziff M. Inhibition of human endothelial cell proliferation in vitro and neovascularisation in vivo by D-penicillamine.
J Clin Invest 1989; **83:** 158-167.

July 1990

CYTOKINES IN ARTHRITIS

D J Rickard
Department of Biochemistry
University of Pennsylvania School of Dentistry
Philadelphia
PA 19104-6003
USA

M Gowen
Cellular Biochemistry
Units of Bone Biology and Immunology
SmithKline Beecham Pharmaceuticals
709 Swedeland Road
PO Box 1539
King of Prussia
PA 19406-0939
USA

INTRODUCTION

The term 'cytokine' encompasses all the soluble peptide factors that act non-enzymatically usually within a localised environment to regulate cell growth and differentiated functions. Most cytokines induce responses far beyond the cell type and activity they were originally identified to affect. Locally acting factors were first implicated in arthritis when bone resorption associated with rheumatoid arthritis (RA) could be inhibited in parallel with synovial-derived prostaglandin synthesis. Shortly afterwards cytokines released by activated leukocytes were demonstrated to stimulate bone and cartilage resorption. The involvement of cytokines in the development of osteoarthritis (OA) and RA is now indisputable. Knowledge of cytokine regulation of inflammatory and connective tissue events in these common diseases has expanded tremendously over recent years but information on general aspects of cytokine biology has been acquired at an even faster rate. The overlapping activities/redundancy in cell responses induced by different cytokines, regulation of cytokine activity by other cytokines and cytokine inhibitors, the characterisation of cytokine receptor families and receptor regulation, and the modifying influences of extracellular matrix on cytokine responses and synthesis, should all prove invaluable in furthering insight into the arthritis processes and in the search for more beneficial therapeutic approaches.

THE CYTOKINES SYNTHESIZED BY ARTHRITIC JOINT TISSUES

To address which cytokines may be important in the pathogenesis of arthritis, cytokine concentrations in synovial fluid exudates have been quantitated. However, caution must be applied when interpreting such data because: (i) samples are taken at advanced disease stages in RA and OA, and (ii) it is now appreciated that inhibitors and binding proteins that may also be present in synovial fluids interfere with cytokine assays. More reliably, expression of several cytokine proteins and messenger RNAs by many cell types has been detected in both OA and RA synovial tissue (Table 1) (1). The greater mass of synovium in RA due to hyperplasia results in a higher total cytokine output compared to the OA joint. A similar set of cytokines is prevalent in both conditions and it is therefore unlikely that one in particular is responsible for each disease; the balance between different cytokines, and between cytokines and their inhibitors, will probably be of greater significance than the concentration of individual cytokines. The actions of some cytokines implicated in arthritis are summarised in Table 2.

Table 1. CYTOKINES PRESENT IN RA AND OA SYNOVIAL FLUID AND SYNOVIUM.

Cytokine	Presence in synovium and synovial fluid	Producing cell types
IFNγ		T_{H1},MP
IL-2	+/-	T_{H1}
IL-4	-	T_{H2}
IL-1 (mostly β)	+++	MC, MP, ET, AC, OB, OC?
TNFα	++	MC, MP, OB, OC?
IL-6	++++	MC, MP, LC, FB, ET, AC, OB, OC?
IL-8	++	MC, MP, AC, FB, ET, OB
GM-CSF	++	MC, MP, FB, ET, AC, OB
TGF β	+	MC, MP, LP, FB, ET, AC, OB, OC?, PL
FGF	+	MP
PDGF	+	MP,PL

Key: Cells producing cytokines: TH1 = TH1 cells, TH2 = TH2 cells, LC = lymphocytes, MC = monocytes, MP = macrophages, FB = synovial fibroblasts, ET = endothelial cells, AC = articular chondrocytes, PL = platelets, OB = osteoblasts, OC = osteoclasts

Interleukin 1 (IL-1) and tumour necrosis factor-α (TNF α)

These cytokines are best considered together because

Table 2.
POSSIBLE CYTOKINE ACTIONS IN THE ARTHRITIC JOINT.

effect / cytokine	IL-1	TNF-alpha	IL-6	GM-CSF	IFN-gamma	TGF-beta
MC/MP activation	↑	↑	—	↑	↑	↓
mononuclear cell infiltration	↑	↑	↑	↑	↑ T-cells only	↑ chemotaxis ↓ adherence
synovial vascularization	—	—	↓?	↑	—	↓
synovial fibrosis/ hyperplasia	↑	↑	↑?	—	↓	↓
cartilage breakdown	↑	↑	↑?	↑?	↓	↓
bone resorption	↑	↑	↑↓	↑?	↓	↑↓

Key: ↑ = stimulation, ↓ = inhibition, ↑↓ = conflicting reports, **?** = weak effects only observed *in vitro* may contribute, MC = monocyte, MP = macrophage.

of overlapping activities and their production by the same cell types, often in response to identical stimuli. IL-1 and TNFα induce synthesis of each other, and in some cell types IL-1 induces its own mRNA. Consequently, IL-1 and TNFα frequently co-exist. Generally TNFα is 100-1000 times less potent than IL-1, but this may be overcome by the ability of TNFα and IL-1 to synergise. IL-1 and TNFα affect numerous cell types to elicit a network of pro-inflammatory and degradative responses (2). Major sources of these cytokines are synovial macrophages (OA and RA) and infiltrating mononuclear cells (RA). Bone cell-derived cytokines may account for the active remodelling in osteophyte tissue in OA, and subchondral bone resorption and increased incidence of osteoporosis in RA (3). Cytokine synthesis by osteoclasts has recently been reported, perhaps not surprisingly considering their monocyte/macrophage lineage, and IL-1 and TNFα are potent stimulators of osteoclast formation and resorptive activity.

IL-1β and TNFα are probably among the first cytokines generated by activated macrophages in an immune response, and stimulation of cytokine release/activation of neighbouring non-immune cells amplifies cytokine concentrations resulting in severe inflammation. Infiltration of monocytes, lymphocytes, and neutrophils into the synovium is also augmented via IL-1/TNFα-induced release of chemoattractants by vascular endothelial cells (eg IL-8, gro α, macrophage chemotactic protein [MCP]-1) and by elevated expression of cellular adhesion molecules (ICAM-1, VCAM-1) on endothelial cell surfaces (4). These adhesion proteins are specifically recognised by integrins on circulating monocytes, lymphocytes and neutrophils. IL-1/TNFα induce IL-6 and GM-CSF synthesis which also promote infiltration, haematopoiesis and angiogenesis through increased endothelial cell proliferation. In the rheumatoid synovium the endothelial cell actively participates in inflammation and the creation of an environment permissive to synovial hyperplasia. Indeed the endothelial cell is ideally situated at the blood-interstitial tissue boundary for displaying and releasing 'signals' (adhesion molecules and cytokines) that affect behaviour of cells distal to the joint.

A primary action of IL-1 and TNFα is stimulation of metalloproteinase synthesis by articular chondrocytes, synovial macrophages, fibroblasts, invading macrophages and neutrophils. Metalloproteinases such as collagenase, stromelysin, and proteoglycanase (gelatinase) are released as zymogens that require activation. Plasminogen activator, whose production is induced by IL-1/TNFα in the same cells, probably indirectly activates these enzymes by generating plasmin. The metalloproteinases systematically degrade bone and cartilage collagens and proteoglycans (5). Although chondrocytes produce metalloproteinase inhibitors (TIMP 1 and 2) their synthesis is suppressed by IL-1, and that remaining is probably degraded since in RA and OA the proteases are produced in excess. Interestingly, chondrocytes from OA cartilage exhibit elevated expression of type 1 IL-1 receptors and this may explain their apparent heightened sensitivity to IL-1: lower IL-1 concentrations induce metalloproteinase production in these cells compared to those from healthy individuals.

Lastly, IL-1/TNFα stimulation of synovial fibroblast proliferation, type I collagen, and fibronectin synthesis represents a major mechanism for the development of fibrosis and pannus formation in RA.

Granulocyte/macrophage colony-stimulating factor (GM-CSF) and interferon-γ (IFNγ)

A controversial issue surrounding the involvement of cytokines in arthritis, particularly in RA, is the relative importance of GM-CSF and IFNγ in disease progression (6). Although GM-CSF aggravates whereas IFNγ inhibits chronic disease processes such as cartilage and bone resorption, they both activate cells and stimulate major histocompatibility complex (MHC) class II antigen expression, thereby enabling these cells to activate lymphocytes via antigen presentation. GM-CSF - derived mainly from IL-1/TNFα-stimulated synovial macrophages and fibroblasts - is detectable in rheumatoid synovial fluid and tissues but IFNγ - a product of activated macrophages and T-lymphocytes - frequently is not. This has important implications; firstly, GM-CSF, not IFNγ, is probably the predominant activator of resident/infiltrating monocytes, macrophages and other cells. Secondly, it implies that T-cell derived cytokines and a T-cell generated immune response are unnecessary for the maintenance of chronic inflammation. However, it is quite possible that T-cell cytokines like IFNγ participate in early stages of joint invasion before synovial hyperplasia and matrix degradation has begun. In chronic inflammatory (late) stages of RA synovial fluid T-cells mostly comprise memory-type T_{H1} cells that are inactive and non-secretory. Thirdly, because IFNγ specifically inhibits TNFα mediated matrix degradation, lack of IFNγ and over-production of TNFα by tissue macrophages suggests that the detrimental actions of TNFα proceed virtually unopposed. The mutual antagonism between TNFα and IFNγ on synovial fibroblast, chondrocyte, osteoblast and osteoclast responses are unusual because in most other tissues IFNγ acts cooperatively with TNFα, partly through TNF receptor up-regulation. In bone and cartilage IFNγ inhibits matrix resorption probably by blocking osteoclast precursor proliferation and multinucleated osteoclast formation, and by reducing metalloproteinase synthesis, respectively. In synovial fibroblasts IFNγ antagonises TNFα but not IL-1 stimulated proliferation, collagenase and GM-CSF production (7). In clinical trials IFNγ has shown limited success in ameliorating RA and this may be because its effectiveness is dependent upon disease stage and ability to block only the actions of TNFα and not those of IL-1 as well. Therapy targeted at abolishing the activities of a single cytokine may regularly prove unsuccessful given the redundancy of action amongst many cytokines.

Besides monocyte/macrophage activation, other major functions of GM-CSF include stimulation of monocyte differentiation and neutrophil degranulation, and initiating angiogenesis of the synovial membrane through increased endothelial cell migration and proliferation.

Transforming growth factor-β (TGFβ)

Synthesized by virtually every cell type in the arthritic joint (Table 1), TGFβ may also be released from cartilage and bone undergoing resorption. Secreted latent TGFβ is probably activated proteolytically by enzymes such as plasmin. Major TGFβ activities can be categorised as either immunosuppressive or anabolic since they restrict inflammation and stimulate net extracellular matrix synthesis(8). Often described as a 'chondroprotective' agent, TGFβ inhibits metalloproteinase and stimulates protease inhibitor production by chondrocytes. Production of type I collagen, fibronectin and proteoglycans is enhanced in fibroblasts, osteoblasts, and chondrocytes. TGFβ is a potent mitogen for immature osteoblasts and simultaneously inhibits osteoclast generation resulting in net bone formation.

The presence of TGFβ may account for the low activation state of synovial fluid T_H cells: IFNγ-induced MHC II antigen expression is reduced and macrophage activation is potently inhibited. Seemingly opposing the reduced adherence of neutrophils and lymphocytes to endothelial cells (by down-regulation of endothelial cell ICAM-1) is the ability of TGFβ to act as a powerful chemoattractant for neutrophils and monocytes(9). Neutrophil diapedesis is enhanced by TGFβ via induction of TGFβ receptors on neutrophils and stimulation of chondrocyte IL-8 release. Monocyte chemotaxis is stimulated directly by TGFβ and through synoviocyte stimulation of MCP-1 production. Whether TGFβ prevents or enhances cellular infiltration *in vivo* is unclear but in 'knockout' mice possessing a non-functional $TGF\beta_1$ gene produced by homologous recombination, massive infiltration of mononuclear cells into vital organs was observed resulting in generalised inflammatory disease (10). Many TGFβ actions are regulated in a biphasic manner and whether stimulation or inhibition occurs will depend critically on the prevailing TGFβ concentration.

Interleukin 6 (IL-6)

A cytokine almost as pleiotropic as IL-1, IL-6 is produced in abundance by various cells (Table 1) in which its synthesis is strongly induced by IL-1 and TNFα (11). Despite high levels of IL-6 production in afflicted joints and correlation with disease activity the role of IL-6 is largely unclear. IL-6 concentrations in serum are also elevated, and systemic rather than local effects may be of greater significance. For example, IL-6 (i) is the only cytokine that induces hepatocytes to synthesize all the acute phase proteins, (ii) supports differentiation of haematopoietic progenitors, and (iii) IL-6 together with IL-1β may be responsible for generalised osteoporosis, a common complication of RA and IL-6 producing myelomas(12). In the latter regard, IL-6 may increase osteoclast precursor differentiation from haematopoietic GM-CFU blast cells. Within the joint IL-6 stimulated B-cell differentiation into plasma cells may account for high concentrations of rheumatoid factor and incidence of hypergammaglobulinaemia in RA.

Platelet-derived growth factor (PDGF) and fibroblast growth factors (FGFs)

These matrix-derived cytokines are also synthesized by rheumatoid and osteoarthritic synovium (13). PDGF alone and in synergy with IL-1 stimulates fibroblast proliferation and induces endothelial and synovial cell release of monocyte chemotactic factors. Basic FGF (bFGF) enhances IL-1 stimulated cartilage breakdown mediated by metalloproteinases.

NEW PERSPECTIVES AND POSSIBILITIES FOR THERAPEUTIC INTERVENTION

Cytokine inhibitors

Treatment by administration of drugs blocking cytokine secretion may induce side-effects due to their lack of specificity. The discovery of naturally occurring cytokine inhibitors makes selective cytokine control a possibility (14). Inhibitors may be of many types: (i) Soluble cytokine receptors produced either by shedding of membrane-associated receptors (eg soluble TNF receptors, TNF-R) or by the alternate splicing of the membrane-associated receptor's transcript (eg many haematopoietin receptors). Soluble receptors may inhibit cytokine action by preventing cytokine binding to the membrane receptor, and recombinant receptor ligand binding domains could be efficient inhibitors. However, soluble IL-6Rs are still functional. (ii) Distinct binding proteins (eg insulin-like growth factor binding proteins). (iii) Pure receptor antagonist proteins. The best characterised cytokine inhibitor is the IL-1R antagonist protein (IRAP or IL-1ra) originally identified in patients with monocytic leukaemia or juvenile RA. Synthesized by differentiated but not immature monocytes/macrophages and possibly in a reciprocal manner to IL-1, IRAP shares homology with IL-1α and β and binds to type I IL-1Rs with equal affinity to IL-1, without transducing a signal. IRAP inhibits prostaglandin E_2 and collagenase production by synovial cells and chondrocytes, IL-1 (but not TNFα) stimulated bone resorption and IL-1 stimulated neutrophil adherence to endothelial cells.

IRAP is produced in RA and OA synovium mostly by perivascular infiltrating monocytes and synovial macrophages, respectively (15). Paradoxically, IRAP expression in diseased synovium was elevated compared to normals suggesting imbalance in IL-1: IRAP production is not the cause of arthritis. The inability of IRAP to curtail IL-1 activity and disease progression may be the requirement for a vast excess of IRAP over IL-1 for effective inhibition because $<5\%$ IL-1R occupancy is necessary for IL-1 responses. Alternatively, as previously mentioned, redundancy in cytokine action may by-pass the effects of one cytokine inhibitor; blockage of both TNFα and IL-1 actions may prove more successful as the concerted effects of cytokines producing similar responses are targeted.

Cytokine-matrix interactions

One of the most potentially relevant advances in cytokine biology to understanding arthritis is the role of extracellular matrix (ECM) in modifying cytokine activity and responses to cytokines (16). (i) Several cytokines are functional when bound to matrix components: the activity of TGFβ bound to the proteoglycan decorin (whose synthesis TGFβ stimulates) is decreased because the complex does not bind TGFβ receptors, whereas binding to the matrix glycoprotein thrombospondin protects active TGFβ prolonging its half-life. Most bFGF in bone and cartilage is sequestered by heparan sulphates in ECM, and generation of soluble heparan sulphates is necessary for bFGF to bind cell surface FGF-Rs. FGF concentration in the vicinity of the FGF-R is increased by cell surface heparan sulphates. Elevated FGF activity in arthritis may be due to formation of soluble heparan sulphates as a consequence of excessive matrix degradation by plasmin or neutrophil-derived heparinases. (ii) Complexing with matrix constituents renders cytokines immobile thereby limiting their effects to adjacent cells. TGFβ, IGF-1 and IGF-II released from bone matrix by osteoclast activity may 'couple' bone resorption to bone formation by stimulating osteoblast precursors. A matrix-associated form of leukaemia inhibitory factor (LIF, a cytokine with similar activities to IL-6) differs from the diffusible form in an extra N-terminal peptide sequence that may be a protein sorting signal directing proteins to ECM (17). Whether matrix-bound cytokines perform different functions to their soluble counterparts is unclear. Cytokines may also be immobilised on cell surfaces, and a relevant example is the presentation to circulating leukocytes of chemotactic and adhesion-inducing cytokines (IL-8, MCP-1, MIP-1β) bound to endothelial cell surface proteoglycans (18). Bound in this manner, macrophage inflammatory protein (MIP) -1β induces T-cell chemotaxis and adhesion: T-cells transiently interacting with endothelial cells via selectin-type adhesion molecules are activated by immobilised MIP-1β, resulting in increased expression of integrin VLA-4 (α_4 β_1), stronger adhesion to endothelial cell VCAM-1, and allowing extravasation.

Integrins promote cell attachment to ECM proteins through recognition and binding of the sequence Arg-Gly-Asp (RGD). It can be speculated that the fusion of this motif or of the putative ECM-targeting sequence (above) to cytokine inhibitors/antagonists or to anti-inflammatory/anabolic cytokines may firstly increase the local antagonist concentration and simultaneously prevent cell-cell and cell-matrix interaction, and secondly improve the targeting to matrix thereby providing tissue specificity - an important consideration given the widespread function of most cytokines.

Cytokine receptors.

Redundancy between some cytokines (eg the haematopoietin superfamily; IL-3,4,5, and 6, CSFs, LIF) but not others (eg IL-1 and TNFα) is explained by the sharing of receptor subunits. Haematopoietic growth factors bind homologous heterodimeric receptors composed of low affinity, ligand specific α-subunits and signal transducing β-subunits (19). Different α-subunits share the same β-subunits implying that each ligand activates the same intracellular pathways; indeed these cytokines exhibit broadly similar responses. Therefore, cytokine specificity within the haematopoietins mainly depends upon expression of the α-chain. Heterodimeric receptors in which both subunits are required for high affinity binding but only one is capable of intracellular signalling is a common configuration also adopted by IL-2, TGFβ, prolactin, and growth hormone receptors, and suggests receptor dimerization is necessary for signal transduction. A potentially specific approach to attenuating cytokine responses is the use of antisense oligodeoxynucleotides to cytokine receptors. Antisense oligonucleotides block translation by forming hybrids with complementary mRNAs. Therefore this approach is advantageous only when receptor turnover is high. Oligonucleotides to the type I IL-1R inhibited IL-1 stimulated PGE_2 synthesis in cultured fibroblasts and neutrophil infiltration in mice (20). Again 'dual' therapy including another cytokine target would probably be necessary in OA and RA, but exceptions may include antisense oligonucleotides to the common β-subunits of haematopoietic receptors, and to proteins whose synthesis/activity marks the 'end point' of concerted cytokine effects, for example plasminogen activator, HLA-DR MHC antigen, or the osteoclast proton pump.

At the present time intervention at the level of intracellular signalling is not feasible because for most cytokine receptors the intracellular pathways involved have not yet been completely elucidated. In any event it is probable that multiple pathways will be stimulated by most receptors, and the presence or absence of consensus sequences within receptor cytoplasmic domains is unreliable for determination of signalling mechanisms since, for instance, receptors lacking intrinsic tyrosine kinase domains may still induce tyrosine phosphorylation.

REFERENCES

1. Firestein GS, Alvaro-Gracia JM, Maki R. Quantitative analysis of cytokine gene expression in rheumatoid arthritis. *J Immunol* 1990;**144:** 3347-3353

2. Kirkham B. Interleukin-1, immune activation pathways, and different mechanisms in osteoarthritis and rheumatoid arthritis. *Ann Rheum Dis* 1991; **50:** 395-400

3. Gowen M. Cytokines regulate bone cell function. *Rheumatol Review* 1991; **1:** 43-50

4. Mantovani A, Bussolini F, Dejana E. Cytokine regulation of endothelial cell function. *FASEB J* 1992; **6**: 2591-2599

5. Murphy G, Hembry RM. Proteinases in rheumatoid arthritis. *J Rheumatol* 1992; (suppl 32) **19:** 61-64

6. Firestein GS, Zvaifler NJ. How important are T cells in chronic rheumatoid synovitis? *Arthritis Rheum* 1990; **33:** 768-773

7. Alvaro-Garcia JM, Zvaifler NJ, Firestein GS. Cytokines in inflammatory arthritis. V. Mutual antagonism between interferon-gamma and tumour necrosis factor-alpha on HLA-DR expression, proliferation, collagenase production, and granulocyte/macrophage colony-stimulating factor production by rheumatoid arthritis synoviocytes. *J Clin Invest* 1990; **86:** 1790-1798

8. Wahl SM, McCartney-Francis N, Mergenhagen SE. Inflammatory and immuno-modulatory roles of TGFβ. *Immunol Today* 1989; **10:** 258-261

9. Gamble JR, Vadas MA. Endothelial cell adhesiveness for human T lymphocytes is inhibited by transforming growth factor-β. *J Immunol* 1991; **146:** 1149-1154

10. Shull MM, Ormsby I, Kier AB, et al. Targeted disruption of the mouse transforming growth factor-β_1 gene results in multifocal inflammatory disease. *Nature* 1992; **359:** 693-699

11. Hirano T, Akira S, Taga T, Kishimoto T. Biological and clinical aspects of interleukin 6. *Immunol Today* 1990; **11:** 443-449

12. Roodman GD, Interleukin-6; An osteotropic factor? *J Bone Miner Res* 1992; **7:** 475-478

13. Remmers EF, Sano H, Lafyatis R, et al. Production of platelet-derived growth factor B chain (PDGF-B/c-sis) mRNA and immunoreactive PDGF B-like polypeptide by rheumatoid synovium: Coexpression with heparin-binding acidic fibroblast growth factor-1. *J Rheumatol* 1991; **18:** 7-13

14. Arend WP, Dayer J-M. Cytokines and cytokine inhibitors or antagonists in rheumatoid arthritis. *Arthritis Rheum* 1990; **33:** 305-315

15. Firestein GS, Berger AE, Tracey DE, et al. IL-1 receptor antagonist protein production and gene expression in rheumatoid arthritis and osteoarthritis synovium. *J Immunol* 1992; **149:** 1054-1062

16. Nathan C, Sporn M. Cytokines in context. *J Cell Biol* 1991; **113:** 981-986

17. Rathjen PD, Toth S, Willis A, et al. Differentiation inhibiting activity is produced in matrix-associated and diffusible forms that are generated by alternate promoter usage. *Cell* 1990; **62:** 1105-1114

18. Tanaka Y, Adams DH, Hubscher S, et al. T-cell adhesion induced by proteoglycan-immobilised cytokine MIP-1β. *Nature* 1993; **361:** 79-82

19. Boulay J-L, Paul WE. The IL-4 related lymphokines and their binding to haematopoietin receptors. *J Biol Chem* 1992; **267:** 20525-20528

20. Burch RM, Mahan LC. Oligonucleotides antisense to the interleukin 1 receptor mRNA block the effects of interleukin 1 in cultured murine and human fibroblasts and in mice. *J Clin Invest* 1991; **88:** 1190-1196

May 1993

ADHESION MOLECULES & RHEUMATIC DISEASES

D L Mattey
Senior Scientist
Staffordshire Rheumatology Centre
The Haywood
High Lane
Burslem
Stoke-on-Trent ST6 7AG

INTRODUCTION

In recent years the role of adhesion molecules in rheumatic diseases has become the focus of considerable attention. Besides increasing our understanding of the cellular interactions involved in inflammation, studies on these molecules have prompted the search for new anti-inflammatory agents which may interfere with adhesion mediated events in the inflammatory process. Before considering the importance of adhesion molecules in this pathological context a few general points about cell adhesion are worth emphasising.

The ability of cells to adhere to each other and/or components of the extracellular matrix (ECM) is a fundamental property of all multicellular organisms. Adhesions between cells may be homotypic (ie between cells of the same type) or heterotypic (eg between leukocytes and endothelial cells). Futhermore, interactions between cells or between cells and the ECM may be transient or long lasting. Cell recognition and adhesion are essential for normal development, maintenance of tissue integrity, tissue repair, and immune functions such as antigen recognition, cell mediated cytotoxicity, and lymphocyte recirculation. This central role of adhesion in normal and pathological processes has been achieved by the evolution of a large number of so-called adhesion molecules. Modern molecular biology has enabled us to obtain considerable structural information and sequence data on these molecules, revealing unsuspected relationships between molecules from diverse cell types. This information has been used to group adhesion molecules into a number of distinct families (see Table 1).

THE ADHESION CASCADE IN INFLAMMATION

A predominant feature of inflammatory diseases is the recruitment of leukocytes from the circulation and their interaction with other cell types (eg macrophages, dendritic cells, fibroblasts) within the inflamed tissue. This depends on a stepwise series of specific adhesive events mediated by different adhesion receptor/ligand pairs. The main steps in this complex process are shown in Figure 1. The principal families of adhesion molecules involved are the selectins, the integrins, the immunoglobulin supergene family, and variants of the CD44 family.

The expression of many of these molecules is common to different inflammatory sites, as is their expression on circulating cells in different rheumatic conditions. However, tissue-specific differences in expression of certain molecules are evident. This may be related to local differences in the production of cytokines and other inflammatory mediators, and/or differences in the expression of tissue-specific vascular receptors (addressins) on the endothelium, and particular 'homing receptors' on leukocyte subpopulations. One of the major problems in developing disease-specific anti-adhesion therapies is an incomplete understanding of which molecules are most important in the pathogenesis of particular rheumatic diseases. Nevertheless considerable progress has been made, and some of the principal molecules involved and their different roles will be considered here. Extensive reviews on adhesion molecules are available for further reading (1-4).

ADHESION MOLECULE FAMILIES

1. Selectins

There are three members of the selectin family, so named because of an N-terminal lectin-like domain which binds to complex carbohydrates. The natural ligands for the selectins are mucins, which are proteins heavily glycosylated with O-linked sugars (5). All the selectins are involved in the recruitment of leukocytes to inflammatory sites, and act in the initial phases of cell adhesion by mediating the rolling of leukocytes along the endothelium of the blood vessel walls (Step 2, Figure 1). There are fundamental differences in the distribution, activation and mode of expression of the different selectins.

E-selectin is expressed only on endothelial cells after stimulation by bacterial endotoxin (LPS) or cytokines such as interleukin-1 (IL-1) and tumour necrosis factor alpha (TNFα). It binds to ligands which are constitutively expressed on neutrophils, monocytes and a specific sub-population of lymphocytes, including

Table I.
Principal adhesion molecule families involved in inflammation

Adhesion molecule	Cells on which adhesion molecule is expressed	Ligand	Cells on which ligand is expressed
a) Selectins			
E-selectin (ELAM-1)	E	sLe^x, sLe^a, CLA	N, M, T (some memory)
		MAdCAM-1	HEV
L-selectin (LAM-1)	Leu	CD34	E
		GlyCAM	HEV
P-selectin (GMP140)	E, P, Meg	PSGL-1	N, M, P, NK
b) Integrins			
β1 integrins (examples)			
α4β1 (VLA-4)	Leu	VCAM-1, Fn (LDV, CS-1)	E
α5β1 (VLA-5)	Widespread	Fibronectin (RGD)	
α6β1 (VLA-6)	Widespread	Laminin	
β2 integrins			
αLβ2 (LFA-1)	Leu	ICAMs (1, 2, 3)	Widespread
αMβ2 (Mac-1)	Myeloid cells	ICAMs (1, 3), C3bi, Fb	Widespread
αXβ2 (p150/95)	Myeloid cells	C3bi, Fb	
Others			
eg			
αvβ3 (VNR)	E, tumour cells	VN, FB, Ln, VWF, Thromb	
α4β7 (α4βp)	Lymphocytes	Fn (CS-1), VCAM-1	E
		MAdCAM-1	HEV
c) Ig Superfamily			
ICAM-1	Widespread	LFA-1	Leu
		Mac-1	M, N, NK
ICAM-2	E, M, D, L (sub)	LFA-I	Leu
ICAM-3	M, N, L, E(?)	LFA-1	Leu
		Mac-1	M, N, NK
VCAM-1	E, SF, MO, D, My	VLA-4	L, M, Th
		α4β7	L
PECAM-1	E, P, M, N, T	PECAM-1	E, P,M, N, T
d) CD44 family	Widespread	HA, Fn, Col	Widespread
		Muc Ad	HEV

KEY: CLA, cutaneous lymphocyte antigen; Col, collagen; CS-1, connecting segment 1 of fibronectin; D, dendritic cells; E, endothelial cells; Fn, fibronectin; Fb, fibrinogen; HA, hyaluronate; HEV, high endothelial venules; L, lymphocytes; Le^a, Le^x, Lewis^a, Lewis^x epitopes; Ln, laminin; M, monocytes; Meg, megakarocytes; MO, macrophages; My, myoblasts; Muc Ad, mucosal adressin; N, neutrophils; NK, natural killer cells; P, platelets; T, T lymphocytes; Th, thymocytes; Thromb, thrombospondin; SF, synovial fibroblasts; Vn, vitronectin; VWF, von Willebrand Factor.

memory T cells. *In vitro* studies have shown that *de novo* synthesis of E-selectin is required for expression at the cell surface, and that this peaks about 4-6 hours after stimulation, followed by a decline to basal levels by 24 hours. E-selectin is usually absent in normal tissues but becomes expressed on the endothelium of post capillary venules during inflammation. In spite of its typical transient expression it appears to be chronically expressed in certain inflammatory conditions. It has been detected in the synovial vascular endothelium of patients with RA (6), and to a lesser extent in patients with psoriatic arthritis and OA. Although E-selectin expression appears to be confined to post capillary venules in synovium, when isolated synovial endothelial cells (SEC) are grown in culture most of them appear to constitutively express low levels of E-selectin (7). Increased expression of E-selectin is found in the blood vessels of the skin in scleroderma patients as well as in skeletal muscle and the skin in SLE. In the latter case this expression is lost upon clinical improvement (8).

L-selectin is constitutively expressed on most leukocytes. It serves as a lymphocyte 'homing receptor' in the recirculation of lymphocytes to the peripheral lymph nodes where it mediates binding to carbohydrate ligands on the endothelial cells of high endothelial venules (HEV). L-selectin is important also in the recruitment of neutrophils to sites of inflammation.

L-selectin has been reported to be present at low levels on most of the cell types within the RA, OA and normal synovium. In synovial fluid of patients with various inflammatory joint diseases, neutrophils show a common pattern of decreased L-selectin expression compared with peripheral blood neutrophils (9). This is characteristic of activated neu-

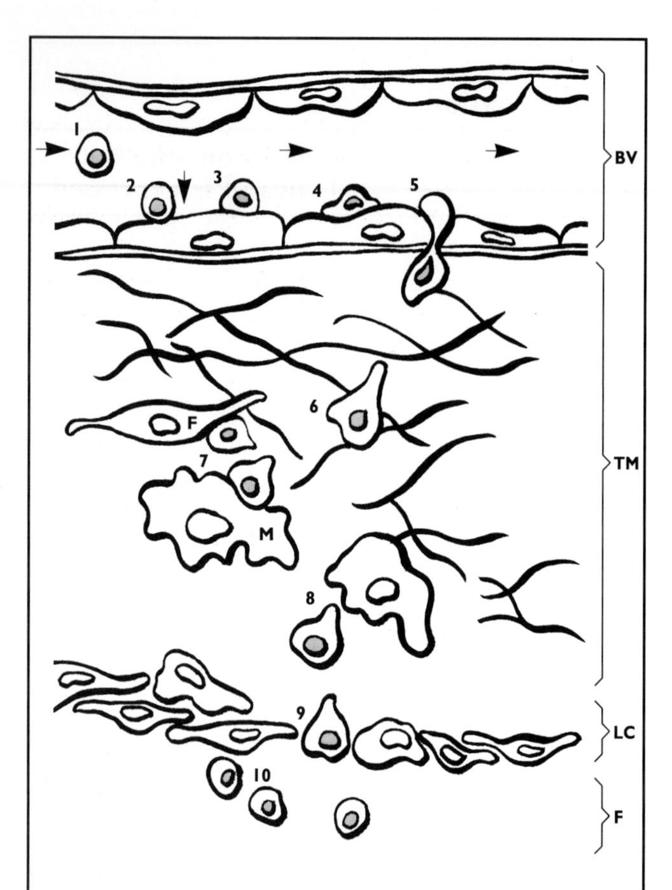

KEY: (1) circulating leukocytes, **(2)** transient rolling adhesion of unactivated leukocytes on selectins of activated endothelium, **(3)** increased adhesion of leukocytes following activation of leukocyte integrins such as LFA-1 and VLA-4, **(4)** flattening and migration of leukocytes on the endothelium, **(5)** extravasation by migration through endothelial junctions, **(6)** attachment and migration on ECM components (eg fibronectin, collagen), **(7)** interactions with resident cells such as macrophages (M) and fibroblasts (F), **(8)** de-adhesion and migration through lining cell (LC) layers, **(9)** into extracellular fluids **(10)**. Blood flow in the blood vessel (BV) is indicated by horizontal arrows. F - extracellular fluid, TM - tissue matrix.

Figure 1. *Adhesive interactions in the recruitment of leukocytes from the blood into inflamed tissue and extracellular fluids.*

trophils, and together with decreased CD44 (see below) and increased complement receptor 3 (Mac-1), suggests a similar degree of neutrophil activation in inflammatory joint diseases with different pathogenic mechanisms.

The expression of P-selectin is not dependent on new protein synthesis because it is stored in the secretory granules (Weibel-Palade bodies) of endothelial cells and platelets. P-selectin is rapidly translocated to the cell surface within minutes of stimulation of the endothelium by thrombin, histamine or reactive oxygen species such as H_20_2. P-selectin is a receptor for a mucin on neutrophils and monocytes but does not bind the majority of lymphocytes. It is strongly expressed in the endothelium of RA, OA and normal synovium. In scleroderma, P-selectin does not appear to be upregulated in the endothelium of the skin but is increased in the stratum granulosum during early stages of the disease (10).

2. Integrins

Each integrin is a heterodimer with an α and β chain that traverse the plasma membrane and provide a link between the extracellular environment and the intracellular cytoskeleton. In humans there are at least 15α and 8β chains which can be found in various but not all possible combinations. The integrins are the major receptors used by cells for attachment to extracellular matrix proteins such as fibronectin, vitronectin and collagen. They also mediate important cell-cell interactions, particularly between leukocytes and other cells.

The integrins can be divided into a number of subfamilies in which each member shares a particular type of β subunit (Table 1). Many α subunits will only associate with a single β subunit, but several α subunits (eg α4, α6, αv) can associate with more than one β unit. The most important integrins for binding of leukocytes to endothelium and transmigration into the underlying tissues are the β1 and β2 integrins.

The β1 integrins (also called the very late antigen (VLA) family) are principally involved in binding of cells to ECM components (Table 1), although VLA-4 (α4β1) is unusual in also being able to bind to cell surface VCAM-1 (vascular cell adhesion molecule-1), a member of the immunoglobulin superfamily (see below). Recently it has been found that the α4 chain can also associate with the β7 subunit to form the lymphocyte-specific α4β7 integrin which also acts as a receptor for VCAM-1. Like VLA-4, α4β7 also binds the CS-1 region of fibronectin, a 25 amino acid sequence present in the alternatively spliced IIICS region of fibronectin.

A recent report demonstrated a striking increase of α4β7 expression on T cells in the rheumatoid synovium compared with synovial fluid and peripheral blood (11). There is also enhanced expression of β1 integrins on these intrasynovial lymphocytes, the majority of which are memory cells demonstrating increased expression of α4β1 and α5β1 integrins. These molecules recognise different binding sites on fibronectin (α5β1 binds the Arg-Gly-Asp peptide sequence, a motif predominantly used in integrin binding to ECM molecules). Significantly, it has been found that the expression of CS-1 containing variants of fibronectin is markedly increased on endothelium of RA synovium (12), and that CS-1 peptides inhibit binding of peripheral blood T cells. This binding is further inhibited using combinations of CS-1 with anti-VCAM-1 or anti-VLA4α. Taken together, these findings provide some explanation for the high expresssion of α4β7 and α4β1 on T cells in the RA synovium, and implicate these particular integrins in the homing of lymphocytes to, and their persistence within the inflamed tissue. Moreover, it may be significant that α4β7 also acts as a lymphocyte homing receptor for mucosal tissues where it binds to MAdCAM-1 (mucosal addressin cell adhesion molecule-1), a glycoprotein expressed selectively on mucosal lymphoid HEV and on gut lamina propria venules (13). It has been proposed that abnormal traffic of lymphocytes between the gut and the inflamed joint may provide a clinical link between chronic inflammatory bowel disease and synovitis (14).

The β2 integrins are expressed only on leukocytes where their adhesiveness (avidity) is modulated by conformational changes in the molecule following leukocyte activation. Their adhesiveness can thus increase without altering their level of surface expression, although upregulated surface expression (but not necessarily avidity) of Mac-1 (CR3, CD11b) and p150/95 (CR4, CD11C) can occur through translocation from intracellular stores. Both Mac-1 and p150/95 mediate adhesion of myeloid cells to endothelium, and also act as receptors for the complement product C3bi. Their pattern of increased expression on macrophages in the RA synovium suggests their importance in the migration of these cells into and through inflamed tissue.

3. Immunoglobulin superfamily

Each member of this superfamily (IgSF) is characterised by one or more immunoglobulin domains. The Ig domain has been adopted widely in evolution, the IgSF of the immune system having originated from more ubiquitious cell recognition molecules common in all metazoan species. Members of the IgSF include the immunoglobulins (antibodies), the T cell receptor, and adhesion molecules such as CD2 and its ligand CD58, intercellular cell adhesion molecules (ICAMs 1, 2 and 3) and VCAM-1. Of these, ICAM-1 and VCAM-1 are particularly important in endothelial-leukocyte interactions and regulation of their expression on endothelial cells will affect the binding and transmigration of leukocytes during inflammation (Steps 3-5, Figure 1). Members of the ICAM family are ligands for the leukocyte (β2) integrins while VCAM-1 is a ligand for the β1 integrin VLA-4 (α4β1) and the lymphocyte integrin, α4β7. These ligand-receptor pairs establish the strong adhesion of leukocytes to endothelium following the initial transient selectin-mediated adhesion, and appear to be neccessary for extravasation to occur. The transmigration process is believed to involve further interactions between leukocyte ligands and PECAM-1 in endothelial cell intercellular junctions.

The expression of ICAM-1 is inducible by LPS and the cytokines IL-1 and TNFα, which both synergise with IFNγ. Low levels of ICAM-1 are seen on some synovial venules in normal synovium (15), but its expression is greatly increased and more widely distributed in RA synovium, and includes endothelial cells, macrophages, synovial fibroblasts and lymphocytes (16,17). The major difference between RA and OA synovium appears to be the much greater expression of ICAM-1 on RA macrophages. ICAM-2 is found on resting endothelial cells and is not upregulated by cytokines. It is detected on a significant proportion of endothelial cells in normal and OA synovium, although there seems to be some disagreement as to whether there is increased expression in RA. Similarly there are conflicting data on the distribution and expression of ICAM-3. Normally found at high levels on resting leukocytes it does not appear to be expressed by resting or cytokine-stimulated endothelial cells. However, one study suggests that ICAM-3 is expressed on endothelial cells, macrophages and lining cells but not on synovial lymphocytes of RA patients (16), while another shows intense expression by the majority of lymphocytes and macrophages but little or no expression by endothelial or lining cells (17). Such differences may be due to recognition of different epitopes by different antibodies, or due to differences in the degree of lymphocytic infiltration. Increased ICAM-1 expression has been reported in tissues from other rheumatic diseases such as scleroderma where ICAM-1 is increased on endothelial cells of affected skin, and SLE where there is an increased number of ICAM-1 positive interfibre dendritic processes in skeletal muscle.

VCAM-1 in normal synovium is strongly expressed in the synovial lining layer on the type B or fibroblast cells, where it may be involved in intercellular adhesion between fibroblasts and the associated lining layer macrophages. *In vitro* studies have demonstrated that both VCAM-1 and ICAM-1 are constitutively expressed on synovial fibroblasts, and that their expression is further increased by stimulation with IL-1β, TNFα, and IFNγ (18). IL-4 also induces VCAM-1 but not ICAM-1 expression. There is little or no expression of VCAM-1 on the normal synovial endothelium but it is upregulated both in OA and RA blood vessels. It has been suggested that VCAM-1 may be more important in determining the distribution of B- than T- lymphocytes in the lymphocytic aggregates of non lymphoid tissues such as RA synovium and the labial tissues from patients with Sjogren's syndrome (19). Little or no VCAM-1 expression is seen on vessels surrounded mainly by T cells, while B cells are only seen at the centre of such aggregates when VCAM-1 positive cells are present.

4. CD44 family

CD44 is the principal receptor for hyaluronate and exists as several variants. It is a multifunctional molecule involved in diverse functions such as T cell activation, lymphocyte binding to HEV, lymphocyte homing, release of cytokines from monocytes, and triggering of homotypic cell aggregation. CD44 is widely expressed on many cell types in the normal synovium and has been reported to be upregulated on synovial lining cells, macrophages and fibroblasts of RA and OA synovial tissues (20). There are conflicting data as to whether expression is increased more in RA than OA. This may be due to differences in the degree of lymphocyte infiltration in the OA samples since CD44 levels appear to be related to the degree of synovial inflammation. Enhanced expression of CD44 is particularly marked in the skin of scleroderma patients where it is found at high levels on lymphocytes, macrophages and endothelial cells. Unlike P-selectin and VCAM-1 there is no difference between early and late stage disease, suggesting that CD44 may be important both in early inflammatory leukocyte-endothelial interactions and later fibrotic processes.

SOLUBLE CELL ADHESION MOLECULES

A number of adhesion molecules can exist as soluble forms in the circulation. These soluble adhesion molecules lack transmembrane and intracellular domains and are probably shed or proteolytically cleaved from the cell membrane after their expression. Based on the premise that these circulating molecules may reflect cellular activation during inflammatory episodes, several studies have investigated whether these circulating forms are useful as markers of disease activity. Soluble forms of ICAM-1, VCAM-1, E-selectin, L-selectin and CD44 have all been found in plasma/serum/synovial fluid of patients with various rheumatic disorders. However, in some cases the data are conflicting. For example, in RA patients, soluble ICAM-1 (sICAM-1) was found at levels which are either lower or higher in the serum/plasma compared to synovial fluid. This leaves a question mark as to the origin of sICAM-1 in the circulation. With regard to disease activity, one study showed a weak but significant correlation of sICAM-1 with ESR and joint score (21), while another, in patients with a wide range of disease activity, showed no significant correlation with ESR or CRP (22). There is disagreement also on the levels of sICAM-1 in SLE, with reports showing either normal or elevated serum levels (22, 23). In all these studies it should be borne in mind that sICAM-1 can exist as different isoforms, and that different monoclonal antibodies may recognise different epitopes. Furthermore, like other soluble adhesion molecules, sICAM-1 is functionally active and a proportion of molecules may be bound to their cell surface ligand (LFA-1 or Mac-1). In contrast to sICAM-1, sVCAM-1 has been shown consistently to be raised in the plasma/sera of patients with RA, SLE and vasculitis, and in each case appears to correlate with disease activity. As with measurement of cytokines and cytokine receptors, there is clearly a need for caution in the interpretation of results on soluble adhesion molecules.

CURRENT THERAPIES AND ADHESION MOLECULES

It has become evident that many of the drugs currently used in the treatment of rheumatic diseases have effects on cell adhesion. Most non-steroidal anti-inflammatory drugs (NSAIDs) reduce the aggregation of neutrophils mediated by the β2 integrin, Mac-1. The upregulation of Mac-1 by neutrophils and monocytes has also been shown to be inhibited by sulphasalazine but not sulphapyridine (the inactive moiety), while the anti-inflammatory effects of methotrexate may result from inhibition of β2 integrin mediated adhesion of leukocytes, caused by an increased release of adenosine from injured connective tissue cells (24).

Corticosteroids alter lymphocyte trafficking, and may affect the expression of adhesive molecules on endothelial cells. In RA, clinical remission induced by corticosteroids, is associated with a decrease in E-selectin expression on synovial blood vessels. *In vitro* studies have confirmed that corticosteroids inhibit the binding of neutrophils to endothelial cells by reducing the expression of E-selectin and ICAM-1 in response to LPS and IL-1. Furthermore corticosteroids inhibit leukocyte-endothelial interactions and homotypic adhesion of lymphocytes by down-regulating LFA-1 and CD2 following activation. TNFα-induced expression of ICAM-1 on synovial fibroblasts *in vitro* is also inhibited by corticosteroids.

Gold treatment of RA patients has been shown to decrease E-selectin expression on the synovial endothelium (25). Also, E-selectin mediated endothelial-neutrophil interactions are inhibited by nanomolar concentrations of colchicine, an anti-inflammatory drug used for many years in the treatment of gout. Recently, two newly developed agents (bucillamine and tenidap) which are effective in RA, have been shown to inhibit leukocyte-endothelial cell adhesion. Bucillamine appears to inhibit the binding of T cells to EC through the production of hydrogen peroxide, while tenidap inhibits the binding and chemotaxis of neutrophils through an unknown mechanism.

Clearly, some of the anti-inflammatory effects of current drug therapies may be due to interference with the expression or activation of adhesion molecules. The extent to which the anti-adhesive properties of these drugs contribute to their efficacy is unkown, and some of their non-selective effects on cell adhesion may equally cause side effects.

NEW DEVELOPMENTS

There is a great deal of interest in developing agents which interfere specifically with leukocyte-endothelial interactions. Monoclonal antibodies (mAbs) against adhesion molecules have been shown to suppress inflammatory responses in animal models of allograft rejection, cardiac reperfusion injury, haemorrhagic shock, experimental autoimmune encephalomyelitis and antigen-induced arthritis. Most studies have used anti-CD18 or anti-ICAM-1 mAbs which interfere with β2 (leukocyte) integrin/ICAM-1 mediated interactions, although anti-VLA-4 antibodies have also been shown to prevent experimental autoimmune encephalomyelitis, and adjuvant induced arthritis in rats. To date only one study has been published on the use of anti-adhesion molecule therapy in RA (26). In an uncontrolled trial, treatment of refractory RA with a mAb to ICAM-1 resulted in a transient clinical improvement in 13 of 23 patients after receiving anti ICAM-1 mAb therapy for 5 days. Several patients developed transient cutaneous anergy, suggesting that T cell recirculation was modified by this treatment.

Some of the difficulties in using mAb therapy include the development of anti-mouse antibodies after mAb injection, a reduction in therapeutic effect after prolonged use, and risk of increased susceptibility to infections. Furthermore, widely distributed molecules such as ICAM-1 may not provide the best target, and molecules specifically involved in the homing of leukocytes to particular inflammatory sites need to be identified. Other new approaches include the use of soluble and/or genetically engineered forms of adhesion molecules which compete with cell associated molecules for binding to the appropriate ligand, or the use of carbohydrate molecules which interfere with selectin-mediated adhesion. Adhesion molecules may also be targeted indirectly by inhibiting cytokines (such as TNFα) which upregulate their expression. With regard to diagnostic potential, new developments are being made in the use of radiolabelled mAbs (eg anti-E-selectin) to image the specific localisation and quantification of adhesion molecule expresssion *in vivo*. All these new strategies will provide further insight into the role of adhesion molecules in the pathogenesis of rheumatic diseases and may provide alternatives to current therapies. It remains to be seen whether any of them can provide long term benefits.

REFERENCES

1. Springer TA. Adhesion receptors of the immune system. *Nature* 1990; **346**: 425-434.

2. Hemler ME. VLA proteins in the integrin family: Structures, functions, and their role on leukocytes. *Ann Rev Immunol* 1990, **8**; 365-400.

3. Cronstein BN, Weissmann G. The adhesion molecules of inflammation. *Arthritis Rheum* 1993, **36**; 147-157.

4. Harlan JM, Liu DY (Eds). *Adhesion. Its role in inflammatory disease.* 1992. WH Freeman & Co. New York.

5. Shimizu Y, Shaw S. Mucins in the mainstream. *Nature* 1993; **366**: 630-631

6. Koch AE, Burrows JC, Haines GK, Carlos TM, Harlan JM, Leibovich J. Immunolocalization of endothelial leukocyte adhesion molecules in human rheumatoid and osteoarthritic synovial tissues. *Lab Invest* 1991; **64**: 313-320.

7. Abbot SE, Kaul A, Stevens CR, Blake DR. Isolation and culture of synovial micro-vascular endothelial cells. Characterization and assessment of adhesion molecule expression. *Arthritis Rheum* 1992; **35**: 401-407.

8. Belmont HM, Buyon J, Giorno R, Abramson S. Up-regulation of endothelial cell adhesion molecules characterizes disease activity in systemic lupus erythematosus. The Shwartzman phenomenon revisited. *Arthritis Rheum.* 1994; **37**: 376-383.

9. Humbria A, Diaz-Gonzalez F, Campanero MR, et al. Expression of L-selectin, CD43, and CD44 in synovial fluid neutrophils from patients with inflammatory joint diseases. Evidence for a soluble form of L-selectin in synovial fluid. *Arthritis Rheum* 1994; **37**: 342-348.

10. Koch AE, Kronfeld-Harrington LB, Szekanecz Z, et al. In situ expression of cytokines and cellular adhesion molecules in the skin of patients with systemic sclerosis. Their role in early and late disease. *Pathobiology* 1993; **61**: 239-246.

11. Lazarovits AI, Karsh J. Differential expression in rheumatoid synovium and synovial fluid of α4β7 integrin. A novel receptor for fibronectin and vascular adhesion molecule-1. *J Immunol* 1993; **151**: 6482-6489.

12. Elices MJ, Tsai V, Strahl D, et al. Expression and functional significance of alternatively spliced CS1 fibronectin in rheumatoid arthritis microvasculature. *J Clin Invest* 1994; **93**: 405-416.

13. Erle DJ, Briskin MJ, Butcher EC, Garcia-Pardo A, Lazarovits AI, Tidswell M. Expression and function of the MAdCAM-1 receptor, integrin α4β7, on human leukocytes. *J Immunol.* 1994; **153**: 515-528.

14. Sheldon P. Rheumatoid arthritis and gut related lymphocytes: the iteropathy concept. *Ann Rheum Dis* 1988; **47**: 697-700.

15. Fairburn K, Kunaver M, Wilkinson LS, Cambridge G, Haskard D, Edwards JCW. Intercellular adhesion molecules in normal synovium. *Br J Rheumatol* 1993; **32**: 302-306.

16. Szekancz Z, Haines K, Lin T, et al. Differential distribution of intercellular adhesion molecules (ICAM-1, ICAM-2, and ICAM-3) and the MS-1 antigen in normal and diseased human synovia. Their possible pathogenetic and clinical significance in rheumatoid arthritis. *Arthritis Rheum* 1994; **37**: 221-231.

17. El-Gabalawy H, Gallatin M, Vazeux R, Peterman G, Wilkins J. Expression of ICAM-R (ICAM-3), a novel counter-receptor for LFA-1, in rheumatoid and non-rheumatoid synovium. Comparison with other adhesion molecules. *Arthritis Rheum* 1994; **37**: 846-854.

18. Morales-Ducret J, Wayner E, Elices MJ, Alvaro-Gracia JM, Zvaifler NJ, Firestein GS. α4β1 integrin (VLA-4) ligands in arthritis. Vascular cell adhesion molecule-1 expression in synovium and on fibroblast-like synoviocytes. *J Immunol* 1992; **149**: 1424-1431.

19. Edwards JCW, Wilkinson LS, Speight P, Isenberg DA. Vascular cell adhesion molecule 1 and α4 and β1 integrins in lymphocyte aggregates in Sjogren's syndrome and rheumatoid arthritis. *Ann Rheum Dis* 1993; **52**: 806-811.

20. Haynes BF, Hale LP, Patton KL, Martin ME, McCallum RM. Measurement of an adhesion molecule as an indicator of inflammatory disease activity. Up-regulation of the receptor for hyaluronate (CD44) in rheumatoid arthritis. *Arthritis Rheum* 1991; **34**: 1434-1443.

21. Cush JJ, Rothlein R, Lindsley HB, Mainolfi EA, Lipsky PE. Increased levels of circulating intercellular adhesion molecule 1 in the sera of patients with rheumatoid arthritis. *Arthritis Rheum* 1993; **36**: 1098-1102.

22. Mason JC, Kapahi P, Haskard DO. Detection of increased levels of circulating intercellular adhesion molecule 1 in some patients with rheumatoid arthritis but not in patients with systemic lupus erythematosus. Lack of correlation with levels of vascular cell adhesion molecule 1. *Arthritis Rheum* 1993; **36**: 519-527.

23. Sfikakis PP, Charalambopoulos D, Vayiopoulos G, Oglesby R, Sfikakis P, Tsokos GC. Increased levels of intercellular adhesion molecule-1 in the serum of patients with systemic lupus erythematosus. *Clin Exp Rheumatol* 1994; **12**: 5-9.

24. Cronstein BN, Eberle MA, Gruber HE, Levin RI. Methotrexate inhibits neutrophil function by stimulating adenosine release from connective tissue cells. *Proc Natl Acad Sci* USA. 1991; **88**: 2441-2445.

25. Corkhill MM, Kirkham BW, Haskard DO. Barbatis C, Gibson T, Panayi GS. Gold treatment of rheumatoid arthritis decreases synovial expression of the endothelial leukocyte adhesion receptor ELAM-1. *J Rheumatol* 1991; **18**: 1453-1460.

26. Kavanaugh AF, Davis LS, Nichols LA, Norris SH, Rothlein R, Scharschmidt LA, Lipsky PE. Treatment of refractory rheumatoid arthritis with a monoconal antibody to intercellular adhesion molecule 1. *Arthritis Rheum* 1994; **37**: 992-999.

January 1995

OPIOID PEPTIDES - 15 YEARS ON

J M H Rees
Senior Lecturer in Pharmacology
Department of Physiological Sciences
University Medical School
Manchester

Since the identification of two pentapeptides with morphine-like activity in 1975, the volume of literature on the opioid peptides has been extraordinary. But those who have been involved in the work since then must look back with a degree of disappointment that whatever physiological and biochemical advances may have been made, the pharmacological management of pain has not benefited to any significant extent.

Nevertheless the advances in scientific understanding are impressive, as is apparent in the annual proceedings of the International Narcotic Research Conference whose last meeting was in Albi *(1)*. It is droll to note that this most erudite group gives itself a nomenclature incompatible with its own recommendations. *Opiate* and *Opioid* remain adopted terms that are commonly misunderstood, mispelt or inappropriate. Some highlights of this conference are summarised by Haynes *(2)*. It is significant that in this short report attention is focused on opioid receptor identification at the molecular level, and the development of novel opioid antagonists, no mention is made of the control of pain.

An update of opioid biology in 1987 in Bailliere's Clinical Rheumatology *(3)* provides numerous references to the story so far – the following summary builds on this background and concentrates on some recent reports.

THE OPIOID PEPTIDES

In this context the opioid peptides have remained well defined for several years. However unusual it might be amongst neuro-peptides, there are three families of opioid peptide all of which have similar physiological properties, namely the enkephalins, the endorphins and the dynorphins. In each family there is more than one member, though it still remains difficult to distinguish between an identified peptide neurotransmitter and its metabolite.

Each family is derived from its own polypeptide precursor which have different genetic origins. The precursors are Proenkephalin, Pro-Opiocortin and Prodynorphin.

The number of amino acid residues in the neurotransmitters ranges from 5 to 31 though all commence with the sequence YGGF (which lacks biological activity). The fifth amino acid residue is either methionine or leucine. It is curious that the two pentapeptides [Met] enkephalin and [Leu] enkephalin represent the family of the enkephalins, yet the endorphins are extensions of one sequence (YGGFM....), and the dynorphins of the other (YGGFL....).

Structural manipulation of the peptide molecules since the 1970's has been as extensive as was the manipulation of morphine in the decades that preceded it. By and large the search for the ideal analgesic based on the naturally occurring peptide sequence has been less successful than anticipated. Several major industrial laboratories seeking the stable 'natural' analgesic have closed down within the last year or so.

Two goals were sought. Firstly, the small pentapeptides were too unstable for research, let alone therapeutic use. Secondly, with greater awareness of receptor subdivisions, greater selectivity of drug action may be achieved.

It is a simple matter to turn the sequence YGGPM into a stable peptide by substitution at the 2 position (eg D-Ala^2, D-Leu^5 enkephalin), and such a structure is not only more stable, but has a degree of selectivity for one of the receptor populations (see below). However peptides of interest seem to depend on a semi rigid structure in which the terminal tyrosine is stabilised. Many interesting compounds are based on rigid derivatives at the tyrosine residue, though one cannot help but remark that if the chemists try hard enough they will come up with the structure of morphine. A most authoritative survey of the pharmacological consequences of adaptation of the opioid peptide structure has been made by Shimohigashi and colleagues *(4)*.

The distribution of the opioid peptides has been reviewed by Watson and colleagues *(5)*, and can be considered alongside current thoughts as to the sub-groups of opioid receptors.

OPIOID RECEPTOR SUB-GROUPS

Although the number of receptor types approaches double figures in some reviewer's minds, only three types have convincing durability, and it is a tribute to two fine laboratories that they independently arrived at a complementary nomenclature using totally different research philosophies.

The μ and κ receptors were distinguished by Martin and his colleagues in the months preceding the identification of the first opioid peptides. The work built on research first published a decade earlier when the same authors concentrated on the relative potencies of naloxone as an opioid antagonist. Using behavioural tests they could distinguish between two profiles – morphine-like, and ketocyclazocine-like. Shortly after,

Kosterlitz and his colleagues identified the δ receptor on one of the peripheral tissues which they had used as a model for CNS receptors.

As a gross oversimplification the μ receptor is associated with high susceptibility to naloxone antagonism and high dependence potential. Naloxone is a weaker antagonist at κ receptors, and κ- agonists have lower dependence liability. Naloxone is also a weaker antagonist at δ receptors, at which the enkephalins have particularly high affinity. A constant problem in teaching and research is that some opioids are agonists at one receptor and antagonists at another. Some are also partial agonists, an esoteric concept peculiar to pharmacologists.

Further characteristics of opioid receptors may be found in recent reviews *(7, 8, 9)* which also refer to additional, less clearly-defined receptor types. Caution must be expressed when considering these proliferating receptors.

1. There is a disregard by some researchers of the differences between two unrelated characteristics of receptor pharmacology, selectivity and potency. In this way some opioid agonists have gained a reputation as being selective at one receptor, whereas it is simply more potent than others and has little selectivity *(10)*.

2. There is a false assumption that if a chemical can bind to a tissue (erroneously called a 'receptor') this indicates biochemical or pharmacodynamic activity. Whilst high binding affinity can be indicative of either agonist or antagonist activity, it can also be indicative of an absence of such activity. Some opioids bind to inanimate objects.

3. Despite the genetic and anatomical differences between the three families of opioid peptide there is a big overlap between them and their receptors. No opioid peptide has yet been identified that does not have significant affinity for all opioid receptors.

4. Though reviews cited below can provide further detail, the use of opioid antagonists to explore the neurochemistry of opioids has often been inappropriate (see 3).

OPIOID ANTAGONISTS

Prior to the isolation of naloxone in the 1960's, nalorphine was the drug of choice as an antidote to morphine poisoning. But nalorphine possessed both opiate agonist and antagonist properties (we now know at different receptors), and naloxone was preferred (despite its short duration of action).

During the 1970's naloxone became the key to the search for an endogenous opioid compound, and it was the cornerstone of all authoritative research. But time has passed by, and it has now become the wrong key. Naloxone is a poor antagonist of opioid peptides acting at δ and κ receptors, and little conclusion can be made of experiments attempting to identify biochemical roles for the peptides when naloxone is used as the tool. As this reviewer has remarked elsewhere, the intravenous injection of naloxone in a concentration far in excess of that necessary to cause a dramatic reversal of morphine coma, has virtually no subjective or objective effect, and sceptics should try it. Contrast this with the dramatic pharmacodynamic effects of other 'pure' neurotransmitter receptor antagonists such as strychnine, propranolol, tubocurarine and atropine.

Amongst the methods used to explore the neurochemical role of opioid peptides, the administration of opioid antagonists in general and naloxone in particular has been foremost. However unpalatable this may be, and whatever acreage of research may have been published, much of it must be reconsidered.

Early attempts to synthesise more selective receptor antagonists concentrated on peptide structures. One such selective antagonist at δ receptors was ICI 174864, but it was of low potency. More recently a range of more selective and potent antagonists has been synthesised in various laboratories (see 2). *Naltrindole* now becomes a candidate for a selective δ receptor antagonist, whilst the bimorphinan derivative *nor-binaltorphimine* is similarly a selective κ antagonist. Whilst naloxone has always been essentially a μ antagonist, cypridime has greater selectivity (though of less potency).

The significance of these drugs is enormous. Firstly it is noted that all of them are unrelated to a peptide structure, and this is a lesson that has taken ten years to learn. Novel, more selective, agonists and antagonists are going to originate from alkaloid related structures. Secondly, and this is a numbing thought for any reviewer, a large proportion of research which has utilised naloxone as a research tool must now be repeated with these novel antagonists and their successors, and the role of opioid peptides re-evaluated.

PHYSIOLOGICAL ROLE OF OPIOID PEPTIDES

There is an understandable tendency in the literature and in industrial research to concentrate on the analgesic role of opioid peptides. But considerations of their distributions (notably of the enkephalins and dynorphins) in the central nervous system *(6)* and elsewhere, could suggest a far more widespread role. By way of current clinical knowledge, the actions of morphine on the brain stem include interference with consciousness, respiration, vomiting, cough and vagal control centres.

The following notes concentrate on two aspects of opioid function of interest or relevance to this readership, namely pain control and the immune response. Other summaries cited below include the role of the peptides in behaviour, tolerance and dependence, memory, and psychiatric disorders *(11)*, interference with endocrine systems *(12, 13)* and the control of blood pressure *(14)* . This last reference illustrates the general points emphasised above. There is no doubt that there is an involvement of opioid peptides in the maintenance of blood pressure. However, morphine (as the erstwhile type substance opioid agonist) and naloxone (as an antagonist) essentially cause no cardiovascular change in realistic concentrations.

OPIOID PEPTIDES AND PAIN CONTROL

When considering the role of opioid peptides and alkaloidal opiates in pain control it is not misleading to draw a distinction between pain threshold and pain tolerance. The former is controlled from spinal mechanisms (linked to the brain stem), the latter (the reactive, or psychological response) being governed by the limbic system and linked structures.

Electrophysiologists have tended to concentrate on the spinal cord trying to integrate the opioid peptides into the developing theories that originated from the Gate Control *(15)*. Whilst μ, δ and κ-opioid systems are identifiable in the cord of both the experimental animal and man, analgesic control would seem to involve primarily μ and δ systems (which immediately contrasts with earlier postulates of a primary responsibility of κ-systems, and absence of δ-activity). Perhaps opinion should be reserved until full analysis has been made with more selective antagonists. It is also worth remarking that the considerable clinical advances that have been made in the management of pain using spinal application have used classical opiates, and the success has been technical and empirical rather than a consequence of understanding of spinal opioid systems.

A further thought (developed below) is that spinal opioids have a neurological function which extends far beyond the interpretation of afferent nociceptive stimuli, involving other sensory perceptions in addition to autonomic and motor control *(15)*.

By comparison, studies of the reactive component of pain perception cannot enjoy such precise methodologies. Whilst intrathecal administration of opiates can be of such clinical value, when opiates are administered orally or systemically it is commonly accepted that the major benefit is an increase in pain tolerance, rather than an elevation of pain threshold. Here the emotional response to pain is predominant and at this stage, to equate electrophysiological studies in the limbic system of rodents to the psychological response of human patients in pain is far too great a leap.

The relationship between opioid peptides and chronic pain still awaits much research – laboratory studies of peptide changes in models of arthritis have been summarised by Przewlocki *(16)*.

'PHYSIOLOGICAL' OPIOID-MEDIATED ANALGESIA

Since the early observation that some forms of analgesia not involving drug administration could be antagonised by naloxone, research has concentrated on means of harnessing this potential mechanism of providing 'natural' pain relief.

The physiological analgesia of *exercise* is a phenomenon familiar to us all, but methodology to investigate its mechanism is daunting in human volunteers, and likely irrelevant in experimental animals. Many studies are reviewed by Sforzo *(17)*, but it is very difficult to come to any conclusion. That author suggests that evidence of endorphin release into the circulation only accompanies high intensity exercise (about 75% of maximum capacity). This reviewer would remark that the high sympathetic output of exercise is a more likely target of research in view of the marked analgesic activity of sympathomimetic drugs.

The related consideration of *stress*-induced analgesia has attracted more research since laboratory study is better defined. Links between stress, catecholamines and opioid systems are reviewed by several authors (see *18*).

Following the identification of opioid peptide systems, attention rapidly turned to the analgesia of *acupuncture* and electro-acupuncture. This is a suitable point at which to conclude consideration of 'natural' analgesia. Here is a technique that has been used for 2000 years and found to produce satisfactory analgesia in a limited proportion of patients and animals (and who can claim anything better?) The technique was generally ignored in Western medicine until the identification of the opioid peptides in the 1970's. Lian Fang He *(19)* has reviewed progress to date, where emphasis is made on the range of CNS areas involved, the interaction with other neurotransmitter systems, notably catecholamines, and the limitations of traditional Western laboratory techniques in evaluating the mechanism.

There is little doubt of the range of predictable CNS areas that seem to be involved (dorsal horn, periaqueductal gray, raphe nucleus, limbic structures). Many references to the effects of naloxone on acupuncture are cited including those that show antagonism and those that do not. For reasons that are evident in this review, naloxone antagonism can no longer be regarded as a 'necessary condition to characterise an analgesic manipulation as narcotic', in just the same way as failure to demonstrate naloxone reversal eliminates an opioid mechanism.

Interference with opioid peptide synthesis (see below) has also been employed to identify opioid peptide involvement but the peptidase inhibitors commonly used lack satisfactory specificity (cycloheximide).

Most importantly Lian Fang He emphasises the clear interaction between potential opioid systems, and those neurotransmitters that have been associated with pain perception for a good deal longer than opioid peptides – the monoamines, notably 5 hydroxytryptamine.

Studies showing changes in blood and CSF opioid peptide concentrations during acupuncture are erratic and, as this reviewer has much cause to remember, one wonders of the relevance of changes in these peptides in any event. Perhaps it is unfair to be pessimistic, but the mechanism of acupuncture must remain unclear for the next decade, hopefully not for the millenium.

OPIOIDS AND THE IMMUNE SYSTEM

Opioid peptides have certainly been the neurochemical flavour of the decade and attention has inevitably turned to that most exciting unknown aspect of brain function – the control of the immune system. Optimists will see great scope here, but recent reviews emphasise the relative dearth of convincing research, or urge caution at this stage *(20, 21)*, to which I would add the problems apparent above. Can naloxone be used as the *'Sine qua non* of an opioid receptor-mediated effect' *(19)?* If opioid peptides affect the immune system, how do they get there, and what is the relevance of their getting there? At the time of writing opioid peptides have not been identified in cells from the immune system.

Satisfactory binding studies require evidence of saturation, from a range of ligands, that equilibrium dissocation constants be in the low nanomolar range (high affinity), and stereospecificity.

On these criteria there is little convincing evidence of binding, but it is clear that researchers have not designed their work with these classical criteria in mind. Yet it is clear that opioid agonists and antagonists are capable of altering immune systems acting on monocytes, macrophages, mast cells, lymphocytes and natural killer activity.

THE FUTURE

The optimism of 15 years ago must be tempered. A massive re-evaluation of research is necessary, and a large proportion of published work must be discarded (some with hindsight, some apparent on publication). The most obvious immediate advance is going to be a greater understanding of receptor activity and that linked to ion channel function. Far more is known about opioid receptors and systems than about any other neurotransmitter. The range of receptor sites and receptor ligands is unequalled in neurochemistry. This will all contribute to the understanding of the evolution of neurochemical transmission.

But reflection is necessary. Why are there so many opioid peptides with different origins but similar actions? There is only one Substance P. Why should we possess a pharmacologically important μ-receptor for which endogenous peptides have low affinity?

New, more selective clinically-useful drugs must come. Whilst the truly selective analgesic may be very far away, surely an analgesic lacking respiratory depressant activity with low dependence liability must be close. Elimination of emetic and constipative effects from an analgesic drug must remain a realistic goal. Modern methods of computer drug design will eliminate the hit and miss screening of the past.

Manipulation of endogenous opioid systems has been and remains an immediate goal. This manipulation can include agents which cause release of peptides, and those that prevent their breakdown.

Releasing agents continue to be relatively ignored despite the existence of a most potent clinical analgesic in nitrous oxide. Nitrous oxide is at present a unique drug, and uniqueness is not a common pharmacological characteristic.

Peptidase inhibitors have been a target for drug developers since the identification of the opioid peptides, but problems of specificity have continued because of accompanying interference with other peptide systems notably the kinins. Nevertheless peptidase inhibitors are being employed more often to study opioid peptide function *(22)*, and after many false starts an enkephalinase inhibitor shows promise as an analgesic of low dependence liability *(23)*.

REFERENCES

1. Cros J, Meunier J. Cl and Hamon M (eds), *Progress in Opioid Research, Adv Biosci* 1989. **75**

2. Haynes L, Opioid receptors and signal transduction. *Tr Pharmac Sci 1988*, **9:** *309-311*

3. Rees J M H, *Endogenous Opioids. Bailliere's Clinical Rheumatology 1987*, **1:** 27-56

4. Shimohigashi Y, Stammer C H and Costa T, Synthetic enkaphalin analogs: Designing new drugs of pharmacological interest. *Synthetic Peptides in Biotechnology: Adv Biotechnol Processes* 1988, **10:** 203-233

5. Watson S J, Akil H, Khatachurian H el al, Opioid systems: anatomical, physiological and clinical perspectives. In *Opioids – Past, Present and Future* (ed Hughes J, Collier H O J, Rance M J and Tyers M B) 1984 pp 147-178. London : Taylor & Francis

6. Mansour A, Khatachurian B, Lewis M E, Akil H and Watson S J, Anatomy of CNS Opioid receptors. *Tr in Neurosci* 1988, **11:** 308-314

7. Kosterlitz H W, Endogenous opioids and their receptors. *Pol J Pharmac Pharm 1987*, **39:** 571-576

8. Akil H, Bronstein D and Mansour A, Overview of the endogenous opioid systems: anatomical, biochemical and functional issues. In *Endorphins, Opiates and Behavioural Processes (ed Rodgers R J and Cooper S J) 1988, pp* 1-23, Chichester: John Wiley

9. Pasternak G W, Multiple morphine and enkephalin receptors and the relief of pain. *JAMA, 1988*, **259(9):** 1362-1367

10. Kosterlitz H W, Opioid peptides and their receptors. *Proc Roy Soc Lon, Series B* 1985, **225**, 27-40

11. Rodgers R J and Cooper S J (ed) *Endorphins, Opiates and Behavioural Processes* 1988, Chichester: John Wiley

12. Bicknell R J Endogenous opioid peptides and hypothalamic neuroendocrine neurones. *J Endocrinol* 1985, **107:** 437-446

13. Millan M J and Herz A, The endocrinology of the opioids. *Int Rev Neurobiol* 1985, **26:** 1-83

14. Szilagyi J E, Endogenous opiates and the pathogenesis of hypertension. *Clin Exp Hypertension* 1989, **All:** 1-24

15. Yaksh T L, Spinal opiates: a review of their spinal function with emphasis on pain processing. *Acta Anaesthesiol Scand 1987*, **31:** supp 85: 25-37

16. Przewlocki R, Opioid peptides in relation to antinociception. *Pol J Pharmacol Pharm* 1987, **39:** 600-621

17. Storzo G A, Opioids and exercise. *Sports Med* 1988, **7:** 109-124

18. Grossman A (ed), Neuroendocrinology of stress, *Bailliere's Clinical Endocrinology and Metabolism 1987*, **1**

19. He L F, Involvement of endogenous opioid peptides in acupuncture analgesia. *Pain* 1987, **31:** 99-121

20. Sibinga N H S and Goldstein A, Opioid peptides and opioid receptors in cells of the immune system. *Ann Rev Immunol 1988*, **6:** 219-249

21. Fischer E G, Opioid peptides modulate immune functions – a review. *Immunopharmac Immunotoxicol* 1988, **10:** 265-326.

22. Roques B P, Physiological role of endogenous peptide effectors studied with peptidase inhibitors. *Kidney International* 1988, **34 Supp 26:** 27-33

23. Chipkin R F, Latranyi M B and McHugh D, SCH34826, an enkephalinase inhibitor anlagesic, does not produce tolerance or dependence in rats. *Adv in the Biosciences* 1989, **75:** 763-766

April 1990

AUTHOR'S ADDRESSES WHICH HAVE CHANGED SINCE THE REPORTS WERE FIRST PUBLISHED

CURRENT ADDRESS	REPORT TITLE(S)
Dr D C Anderson MD FRCP 403 Pacific House 20 Queen's Road Central HONG KONG	Paget's disease of bone
Dr R A Asherson MD FACP FCP (SA) 5 Fir Tree Avenue Bantry Bay Cape Town 8001 South Africa	Antiphospholipid antibodies: their clinical significance
Dr C Barnes BSc FRCP Dept of Rheumatology The Royal London Hospital (Mile End) Bancroft Road London E1 4DG	Bechet's syndrome
Dr R M Bernstein MA MD FRCP Consultant Rheumatologist Rheumatism Research Centre Manchester Royal Infirmary Oxford Road Manchester M13 9WL	Antibodies to cells and connective tissues
Dr H A Bird MD FRCP Clinical Pharmacology Unit Chapel Allerton Hospital Chapeltown Road Leeds LS7 4SA	Work related syndromes Rheumatic complaints in the performing arts Methods available for evaluating bone mineral content
Prof D R Blake FRCP Bone & Joint Research Unit The Royal London Hospital 25-29 Ashfield Street London E1 1AD	Free radicals and hypoxic-reperfusion injury
Prof P Brooks Dept of Rheumatology St Vincent's Hospital Victoria Street Darlinghurst Sydney, New South Wales NSW 2010 Australia	Monitoring drug therapy in RA: toxicity

Prof M A Chamberlain BSc DCH FRCP
Rheumatology & Rehabilitation
Research Unit
University of Leeds
Research School of Medicine
36 Clarendon Road
Leeds
LS2 9NZ

Assessing disease activity and disability

Dr R B Clague MD MRCP
Consultant Rheumatologist & Physician
Noble's Isle of Man Hospital
Westmoreland Road
Douglas
Isle of Man

Autoimmunity to cartilage collagens

Mr R J Cooper BA MCSP DipTP
(Formerly Principal, School of
Physiotherapy at Guy's Hospital)
Malvern Cottage
Fosse Road
Oakhill
Somerset
BA3 5HX

What can physiotherapy offer?

Prof H L F Currey MMED FRCP
Emeritus Professor of Rheumatology
The London Hospital Medical School
London
E1 2AD

Acute monoarthritis - management and differential diagnosis

Dr A St J Dixon OBE MD FRCP
Tregisky
Coverack
Cornwall
TR12 6TQ

Osteoporosis and the family doctor

Dr J C W Edwards BA MD MRCP
Bloomsbury Rheumatology Unit
University College London
Arthur Stanley House
40-50 Tottenham Street
London
W1P 9PG

Synovial structure and function

Professor Paul Emery MA MD FRCP
Head of Rheumatology and
Rehabilitation Research Unit
University of Leeds
36 Clarendon Road
Leeds
LS2 9NZ

Systemic lupus erythematosus (SLE)

Dr T Gibson MD FRCP
Rheumatology Unit
Shepherd's House
Guy's Hospital
London
SE1 9RT

The treatment of gout: a personal view

Dr M Gowen PhD
Dept of Cellular Biochemistry
SmithKline Beecham Pharmaceuticals
709 Swedeland Road
PO Box 1539
King of Prussia
PA 19406-0939
USA

Cytokines and arthritis

Dr I Haslock MD
Dept of Rheumatology
South Cleveland Hospital
Marton Road
Middlesborough
Cleveland
TS4 3BW

The management of low back pain: a personal view

Prof D A Isenberg MD FRCP
Professor of Rheumatology
The Bloomsbury Rheumatology Unit/
Division of Rheumatology
Department of Medicine
University College London
Arthur Stanley House
40-50 Tottenham Street
London
W1P 9PG

Mechanisms of autoimmunity

Dr R W Jubb BSc MD FRCP
Consultant Rheumatologist
Selly Oak Hospital
Raddlebarn Road
Selly Oak
Birmingham
B29 6JD

Anti-rheumatic drugs and articular cartilage

Alison M Leak MD BSc MRCP
Consultant Rheumatologist
Thanet General Hospital
St Peters Road
Margate
Kent
CT9 4AN

Juvenile chronic arthritis

Dr J A Mathews MS MD FRCP
Dept of Rheumatology
St Thomas's Hospital
Lambeth Palace Road
London
SE1 7EH

Acute neck pain - management and differential diagnosis

Dr T F Paine
The Family Practice
Western College
Bristol
BS6 6DF

Referral guidelines for general practitioners - which patients with limb joint arthritis should be sent to a rheumatologist?

Dr D L Scott BSc MD FRCP
Dept of Rheumatology
King's College Hospital
Denmark Hill
London
SE5 9RS

Mortality of rheumatoid arthritis

Dr J T Scott MD FRCP
Winter's Lodge
Huish Champflower
Taunton
Somerset
TA4 2BZ

Baker's cyst or deep vein thrombosis?

Dr D P M Symmons MRCP MD
ARC Epidemiology Research Unit
University of Manchester
Stopford Building
Oxford Road
Manchester
M13 9PT

Mortality of rheumatoid arthritis

Dr L Turner-Stokes DM MRCP
Regional Rehabilitation Unit
Northwick Park Hospital
Watford Road
Harrow
Middlesex
HA1 3UJ

Treatment & control of chronic arthritic & back pain

Dr K I Welsh PhD
Dept of Immunology
Oxford Transplant Unit
Churchill Hospital
Oxford
OX3 7LJ

Immunogenetics of rheumatoid arthritis

Prof V Wright MD FRCP
Rheumatology & Rehabilitation
Research Unit
Research School of Medicine
University of Leeds
36 Clarendon Road
Leeds
LS2 1NZ

Methods available for evaluating bone mineral content

Psoriatic arthritis

INDEX

The index was compiled by Dr Robin Butler MD, FRCP